# MASTERPLOTS II

## WORLD FICTION
## SERIES

# MASTERPLOTS II

## WORLD FICTION SERIES

## 4

Sei-Z

*Edited by*
**FRANK N. MAGILL**

SALEM PRESS

Pasadena, California    Englewood Cliffs, New Jersey

**Library of Congress Cataloging-in-Publication Data**
Masterplots II: world fiction series.
 Bibliography: p.
 Includes index.
 Summary: Examines the themes, characters,
plots, style, and technique of 347 works by authors
from the non-English speaking countries of the
world, including Poland, France, Czechoslovakia,
Austria, Germany, and Russia.
 1. Fiction—19th century—Stories, plots, etc. 2.
Fiction—19th century—History and criticism. 3.
Fiction—20th century—Stories, plots, etc. 4. Fic-
tion—20th century—History and criticism. [1. Fic-
tion—Stories, plots, etc. 2. Fiction—History and
criticism] I. Magill, Frank Northen, 1907-    . II.
Title: Masterplots 2. III. Title: Masterplots two.
PN3326.M28   1988       809.3       87-33695
ISBN 0-89356-473-7 (set)
ISBN 0-89356-477-x (volume 4)

PRINTED IN THE UNITED STATES OF AMERICA

90-2971

# LIST OF TITLES IN VOLUME 4

# LIST OF TITLES IN VOLUME 4

# MASTERPLOTS II

## WORLD FICTION
## SERIES

# THE SEIZURE OF POWER

*Author:* Czesław Miłosz (1911-     )
*Type of plot:* Political
*Time of plot:* From 1944 to 1950
*Locale:* Warsaw and other sites in Poland
*First published: Zdobycie władzy*, 1953 (English translation, 1955)

> *Principal characters:*
>> PETER KWINTO, a young intellectual employed as a journalist by the Soviet-sponsored Polish Workers' Party
>> WOLIN, a former Polish nobleman in charge of organizing the security forces of the People's Republic of Poland on behalf of the Soviets
>> PROFESSOR GIL, a middle-aged professor of classical literature
>> MAJOR BARUGA, the Director of Publications for the Polish Workers' Party
>> STEFAN CISOVSKI (SEAL), a cadet officer in the Polish underground army
>> MICHAEL KAMIENSKI, a Fascist ideologue and anti-Semite
>> JULIAN HALPERN and
>> JOSIAH WINTER, prewar acquaintances of Kwinto who are promoting the communization of Poland

*The Novel*

The events depicted in Czesław Miłosz's two-part political novel *The Seizure of Power* take place in Poland during the final ten months of World War II and the first five years of the postwar era. Miłosz tells the story of this turbulent period though a series of interconnected sketches that involve a score of characters drawn from diverse elements of society. To some extent, *The Seizure of Power* is a *roman à clef*, and readers who are well versed in the circumstances in Poland during the Stalinist era will be able to match many of the fictive figures in the novel with their historical counterparts. Miłosz, moreover, uses a character named Peter Kwinto to reflect his own spiritual disquiet before he defected to the West in 1951 from his diplomatic post as First Secretary for Cultural Affairs at the Polish Embassy in Paris.

Part 1 opens in the summer of 1944 as the soviet army is in the midst of an offensive that has brought it to the outskirts of Warsaw. Inside the capital the branch of the Polish underground officially designated as the Home Army (Armia Krajowa) rises in revolt against the Nazis on August 1 in the belief that the entry of the Red Army is imminent. To the dismay of the Polish rebels, the Soviets decide to suspend military operations along the entire Warsaw front and thereby give the Germans a free hand to suppress the uprising inside the city. Peter Kwinto is a witness to these events, since he is serving as a political commissar in a unit known as the First Polish Division that is operating in conjunction with the Red Army. He shares his Soviet hosts' distrust of the motives of the Home Army, since its hierarchy owes its allegiance to the Polish government-in-exile based in London. Kwinto, who is steadfastly opposed to a restoration of the reactionary social order that prevailed in prewar Poland, views the Polish Committee of National Liberation that was established at Lublin under Soviet sponsorship as a preferable alternative to the government-in-exile. Nevertheless, he follows the tragic course of events unfolding inside Warsaw with mixed emotions.

Miłosz's account of the Warsaw uprising focuses on the fighting that takes place within the old city, where the Home Army withstands the Germans for a month before evacuating its forces from the district on September 2 through the sewers. The most memorable of the resistance fighters depicted by Miłosz is Stefan Cisovski, who is nicknamed "Seal" because of his manner of moving and his prowess as a swimmer. Separated from his wife by the fighting, Seal commits an act of sexual infidelity with Joanna Gil, the daughter of a professor of classical literature. Shortly thereafter she is killed by German shell fire while assisting a wounded man at Seal's behest. In the process of escaping from the old city, Seal abandons a seriously injured comrade named Gdula in the belief that his wounds are terminal. Reproaching himself for the fates of Joanna and Gdula, as well as for having violated his marriage vows, Seal is overwhelmed by guilt. Miłosz does not inform his readers of Seal's eventual fate until part 2 of the novel. Placed in an internment camp in Germany after the capitulation of the Home Army on October 2, Seal returns to Warsaw after the war to help in the reconstruction of the capital and learns that his wife had been killed during the insurrection, one day before he committed adultery with Joanna Gil. He also visits Joanna's father and assists Professor Gil in recovering Joanna's remains from the ruins of the city. Later in the year he is arrested by Polish security forces for having been a member of the Home Army during the German Occupation. After being detained for approximately four years without trial, Seal is taken to court and sentenced to an additional four years of imprisonment.

Most of part 2 deals with the process by which Communist rule is imposed on Poland. The key figure is a Soviet agent named Wolin who has been placed in charge of organizing the Polish Security Department. His mission, in addition to liquidating those who are opposed to the imposition of Soviet hegemony over Poland, is to recruit collaborators from among the opponents of Communist ideology, wherever it is expedient to do so. Wolin's greatest success occurs in the course of a dialogue with Michael Kamienski in which he persuades this former leader of a Fascist youth group to head a pro-Communist organization of Catholics. The process of rationalization through which Kamienski comes to terms with the political realities of postwar Poland is far from atypical. Kwinto himself, who at this juncture of the novel is employed in the Bureau of Publications as a propagandist for the new regime, finds that his humanistic values have been steadily eroding. Hoping to rekindle the ideals nurtured by his prewar university training, he decides to take advantage of an opportunity to serve in a diplomatic post at the Polish embassy in Paris. At the last moment, Wolin has doubts concerning Kwinto's political reliability and attempts to revoke his exit visa. Wolin's emissaries, however, are unable to reach the airport in time to detain Kwinto, who boards a plane to Paris just as the year 1945 draws to a close and the first snow of the new winter has begun to fall.

Each of the novel's parts begins with a short meditation by Professor Gil on the state of affairs in Poland after five or six years of Communist rule. There is also an epilogue of a similar nature. Gil, it turns out, was forced to retire from his professorship and is currently engaged in translating Thucydides' history of the Peloponnesian War into Polish. He is able to draw many parallels between the civil strife described by Thucydides and the postwar situation in Poland. Miłosz uses this device to validate the misgivings concerning the future course of liberty in Poland that prompted Kwinto to seek spiritual renascence in the West.

## The Characters

Prior to the outbreak of World War II, Peter Kwinto appeared destined to become a member of the bourgeois literary establishment in his native land. He had, for example, written a doctoral dissertation on French poetry and had received government grants enabling him to reside in France to pursue his research on the writings of Paul Valéry. Setting Kwinto apart from most other members of his social class, however, is a staunch commitment to the principles of social justice. Although deeply disturbed by the totalitarian character of the postwar Polish regime, he is by no means immune to the psychological gratifications derived from the exercise of power. The turning point for Kwinto comes when he tells a dream he has had to a friend and confidante. The dream, in essence, involves Kwinto's encounter with a kindly figure whom he at first mistakes for God the Father but later correctly identifies as Joseph Stalin. The dream has a twofold significance. First, it underscores the fact that Kwinto, as an apostate Catholic, is in danger of succumbing to a blind faith in a secular father figure. Second, it reflects Kwinto's ambivalent attitude toward his own father, a man of firm anti-Communist convictions who was killed during the Polish-Soviet War of 1919-1920. Teresa interprets the dream as a warning and urges Kwinto to leave Poland as soon as possible.

Wolin, like Kwinto, had been thoroughly indoctrinated with bourgeois cultural values in his youth. Despite this background as a member of the Polish gentry, Wolin became convinced that the triumph of socialism and Communism was mandated by the laws of dialectical and historical materialism. This conviction led him to fight on the Loyalist side in the Spanish Civil War. He is totally dedicated to the objective of making Poland over in the image of the Soviet Union. From his perspective, people such as Seal and Professor Gil are historical anachronisms whose ultimate fate as individuals is of no import.

Operating on a lower level of authority than Wolin are three Polish citizens of Jewish ancestry: Josiah Winter, Julian Halpern, and Major Baruga. Although never stated directly by Miłosz, it is clear that each of these individuals views the communization of Poland as the best means of exorcising the demon of anti-Semitism from its national psyche. Josiah Winter most directly affects Kwinto's destiny. In the fall of 1939, after Poland has been overrun by Nazi and Soviet forces, Kwinto finds himself residing temporarily in the Communist-occupied eastern provinces of the country. He is placed under arrest by Soviet security forces once it becomes known that he has written an article highly critical of several Russian poets whose work has official sanction. Winter, it is discovered, has divulged this information to the Soviets under interrogation. Sentenced to a slave labor camp in Siberia, Kwinto is on the verge of death when all Polish prisoners and deportees are granted political amnesty after the German invasion of the Soviet Union on June 22, 1941. Shortly thereafter, he joins the Soviet-sponsored First Polish Division and, much to his dismay, discovers that Winter is one of his comrades. By an ironic coincidence, Winter is subsequently appointed Second Secretary to the Polish embassy in Paris and leaves Poland on the same plane that carries Kwinto to his own diplomatic post in the French capital.

*Themes and Meanings*

The central themes of *The Seizure of Power* are underscored by two extensive quotations from Thucydides' *History of the Peloponnesian War*. The first quotation is taken from section 82 of the third book and pertains to the perversion of language that occurred in the course of the civil strife between the partisans of Sparta and those of Athens. In Miłosz's novel, such concepts as democracy, national sovereignty, and nonviolent revolution take on meanings, in the vocabulary of the postwar regime, that are virtual antonyms of their traditional denotations. Similarly, the police agents who rule the country designate themselves a government, and an army commanded by Russian officers is called Polish.

The second quotation from Thucydides comes from section 48 of the fourth book and deals with the cruel slaughter perpetrated by the pro-Athenian faction against their fellow citizens who supported the Spartan cause. Miłosz clearly intends to draw a parallel between the gratuitous violence described by Thucydides and the fate of those individuals serving in the Home Army during the German Occupation. Even if one concedes that the Warsaw uprising was an act of folly, resulting as it did in the deaths of more than two hundred thousand Poles and the destruction of the capital, the rank and file members of the Home Army who fought in the epic battle did not merit the persecution accorded to them by the new masters of Poland.

At the conclusion of the epilogue, Professor Gil frankly acknowledges that the primary problem faced by any citizen of the People's Republic of Poland is to "preserve himself from the taint of sadness and indifference." In Professor Gil's own case, it is evident that he derives his greatest solace from a conviction that the Polish masses will succeed in preserving their historical cultural values despite all the efforts being made to indoctrinate them with an alien ideology, and that they will reassert their commitment to these values at some future date. With the emergence of the Solidarity movement at the outset of the 1980's, such a faith in the moral stamina of the Polish people has been amply justified.

## Critical Context

Because Miłosz defected to the West in 1951, *The Seizure of Power* had to be published by the Polish émigré press in France. The same holds true for the poetry and essays which he published during the 1950's, as well as for his only other novel, *Dolina Issy* (1955; *The Issa Valley*, 1981). When a translation of *The Seizure of Power* was published in France in 1953 under the title *La Prise du pouvoir*, Miłosz received the Prix Littéraire Européen. Even more successful in terms of critical acclaim was *Zniewolony umysłosz* (1953; *The Captive Mind*, 1953), in which Miłosz recapitulates much of the critique of Soviet totalitarianism found in *The Seizure of Power*. Whereas the merits of *The Captive Mind* were appreciated throughout the free world at the time of its publication, it was not until the English translation of *The Seizure of Power* was reissued in 1982 that this work received proper critical recognition in the United States and other English-speaking countries. Renewed interest in the novel was prompted by Miłosz's receipt of the Nobel Prize for Literature in 1980. *The Seizure of Power* has withstood the test of time and retained both its political and aesthetic viability.

## Sources for Further Study

Bell, Daniel. Review in *The New Republic*. CXXXII (May 16, 1955), pp. 41-43.

Czarnecka, Ewa, and Aleksander Fiut. *Conversations with Czesław Miłosz*, 1987.

Guérard, Alfred. Review in *Books Abroad*. XXVIII (Autumn, 1954), pp. 436-437.

Harrington, Michael. Review in *Commonweal*. LXII ( July 8, 1955), p. 356.

Miller, Jim. Review in *Newsweek*. C (October 4, 1982), p. 72.

*World Literature Today*. CII (Summer, 1978). Special Miłosz issue.

*Victor Anthony Rudowski*

# A SENTIMENTAL JOURNEY
## Memoirs, 1917-1922

*Author:* Viktor Shklovsky (1893-1984)
*Type of plot:* Memoir
*Time of plot:* 1917-1922
*Locale:* Petrograd, Persia, Galicia, Ukraine, and Berlin
*First published: Sentimentalnoye putishestiye: Vospominaniye, 1918-1922,*
  1923 (English translation, 1970)

Principal character:
>THE NARRATOR, a Russian novelist, literary theorist, and
>soldier

*The Novel*

A Sentimental Journey is a novel difficult to describe or categorize. Its narrative line emerges only in discontinuous episodes, memories, character studies, and literary discussions. Yet the cumulative effect of these separate pieces communicates in very personal terms the sweep of events in the revolutions and civil war bringing the Soviet Union into being. The novel is a literary experiment growing out of the commitment of Viktor Shklovsky and other Russian Formalist literary critics to the renewal of Russian prose in the first quarter of the twentieth century. Shklovsky calls the work "memoirs," but he shapes these memories of World War I, the February and October Revolutions, and civil war as he would a novel, though no conventional novel. The title is an ironic reference to Laurence Sterne's eighteenth century English novel, *A Sentimental Journey Through France and Italy* (1768); previously, Shklovsky had published a celebrated analysis of Sterne's *Tristram Shandy* (1759-1767). The episodic structure and self-conscious narrative devices of Sterne's works had excited Shklovsky in his search for ways to make a fresh start in the Russian novel. Sterne's eccentric and leisurely commentary on his casual travels in Europe is a far cry, however, from the hair-raising history which Shklovsky offers with acute objectivity and tragic irony.

New times bring the need for new forms: Shklovsky's memoirs make of his experience "a case study for posterity," as he describes his aim. He communicates events sifted through his own consciousness just as a realistic novelist might do, but he organizes his material using radically different unifying devices.

The novel is in two parts: "Revolution and the Front" and "Writing Desk." The first part recounts in intensive detail the coming of the February Revolution among soldiers in the armored division in which Shklovsky served; the effort of the Provisional Government under Aleksandr Kerenski to continue the war; the Kornilov revolt; and the Russian army in Persia and its wasteful withdrawal. Shklovsky is an active participant in each of these military undertakings. Part 2 describes, after the seizure of power by the Bolsheviks, Shklovsky's efforts to support the constitutional government of the February Revolution, first in Petrograd and then in German-held Ukraine, and afterward his joining the Reds to fight the White General Wrangel's attempt to restore the czar. Both parts also present personalities and activities of the Futurists and the Serapion Brothers, Shklovsky's literary friends and students. The groups present themselves as creative and human in contrast to the inhumanity of the surrounding violence and death. Episodes follow depicting the deprivation of life in civil war Petrograd. Facing arrest as a member of a secret group opposing the Bolsheviks, Shklovsky flees to Berlin. He writes the second part of the novel in Berlin, and the work is published there in 1923. The book ends with an account of a humanitarian effort by an American doctor and missionary in Persia to save the children of the Aissors, who are fleeing the Turks when the Russian army withdraws.

The events described are superb as history, giving the texture and tone of the swift and shifting changes in this great hinge of Russian life. The scrupulous accuracy of the incidents recounted is that of an objective historian, but their selection and intimacy derive from their shaping by a novelist. This is indeed a literature of "fact," a term and interest the new writers defined. The work offers a meaningful, exact, and convincing image of the times.

Nevertheless, *A Sentimental Journey* is also a novel, a work of imagination arranged to develop an interpretation of this life. Shklovsky achieves this hybrid by a dazzling use of literary devices: ironic detachment; abrupt and meaningful digressions; brilliant and fresh metaphors that gradually reveal fuller richness in their meaning by repeated returns in new contexts; lyrical passages about nature or art set against descriptions of wartime brutalities merciless in their accuracy; intrusion of the narrator from the perspective of his later sensibility of exile in Berlin; transitionless shifts of subject that later show their coherence; and direct address to the reader to draw attention to the art. The full impact of Shklovsky's view of the events he represents is available only cumulatively; it is carefully built in by literary devices over the course of the novel, and the devices are part of the meaning.

Showing the way he uses metaphor can suggest the blend he achieves of history and fiction, and perhaps give a specific sense of the content. One powerful metaphor is that of the falling stone. Shklovsky first suggests the figure early in "Revolution and the Front" when he leaves for Galicia in June, 1917, while the Bolsheviks jockey for position in Kerenski's government: "I left for the front . . . and fell into another world." The fall is like that of Alice's fall down the rabbit hole, in that Shklovsky as narrator thereafter fits into a variety of military worlds organized each according to its own inner logic, worlds at first seeming wildly different from one another. As he falls from episode to episode in the chaos of an empire in revolution, the falling stone gradually takes on the meaning of the relentlessness of Russia's fate in those years, like gravity and the inability of the individual to change anything. Shklovsky adds, however, in "Writing Desk" that he is a "stone that falls and can, at the same time, light a lantern to observe its own course." Thus, Shklovsky links his historical narrative with his theme of the artist as maker.

Another richly developed metaphor is that of the motor vehicle, a figure deriving from the writer's attachment to a motor unit in the army. What happens to the trucks and automobiles in the February Revolution represents the sudden disintegration of the country. Shklovsky sees "trucks and automobiles piled high and spilling over with soldiers, not knowing where they were going or where they would get gasoline, giving the impression of sounding the tocsin throughout the whole city. . . . It was the slaughter of the innocent cars. . . . The city resounded with crashes." When Shklovsky requests transfer to Persia just before the October Revolution, he describes a general's inability to take effective action as "spinning his wheels," a metaphor that has since become common. "The motor turns over, the car roars, the chains on the wheels clank and spew lumps of mud—and the car doesn't budge." The decay of army discipline in Galicia and the disorderly withdrawal from Persia show a nation spinning its wheels. Yet the Bolsheviks eventually win. As a means of showing how the Bolsheviks are able to hang on, Shklovsky explains in highly specific detail how the Gnome engine continues to operate though army mechanics confuse the gasoline lines and the oil lines. "The Bolsheviks held out, are holding out and will hold out, thanks to the imperfections of the mechanism which they control."

### The Characters

While the novel teems with brief but vividly realized images of famous and unknown actors in the drama of the revolutions and the civil war, the only character moving through the whole novel is Shklovsky himself. Direct characterization is fugitive: He states explicitly, for example, that the soldiers under his command were friendly to him. At times he addresses the reader directly to reveal the suffering man beneath the objective reporter: "No, I shouldn't have written that. I warmed my heart. It . . . aches."

The reader by more indirect means comes to understand and appreciate this complex human being responding to a chaotic world. Shklovsky selects and reports brutal incidents in such a way as to argue for the humane treatment of human beings by one another, canceling old hatreds; he describes his mad and at first single-handed attempt to stop a pogrom in a Persian bazaar. His personal courage and enterprise in wartime crises appear again and again with the most offhand and casual reporting. He also tells about the death of two of his brothers and his sister in terms which show his acute sense of justice and compassion, again with striking understatement.

This characterization is essential to the form—his insistence on the artifice—and essential to the impact of the work. He notes at one point that his wife sees that he is absorbed into whatever milieu he enters. The ability to enter into the highly divergent scenes of war and revolution allows the full realization of the damage. His ability, nevertheless, to endure and look with hope to the future, even as he celebrates the rare examples of generous and life-caring humanity, makes him what he wishes to be, the writer with a lantern.

### Themes and Meanings

It is ironic that a major part of the meaning of this painful novel is its innovation in form. Art ordinarily pales in importance in time of war. The vitality of the young critical theorists—among them Boris Eikhenbaum, Lev Lunts, Osip Brik, Yevgeny Zamyatin, Yury Tynyanov—sets their sense of the importance of their thought and practice in verbal art against the destructive elements in all that Shklovsky encounters. Their ideas have since permeated literature in the West: the emphasis on craftsmanship, on the importance of the word, on the necessity to "estrange" reality by means of literary devices in order to let readers feel and see reality more clearly; the power of past forms to generate the nature of new ones; the pressure of changing reality to generate new forms of expression; new ways of integrating "fact" into literature. This novel is a generator for a whole way of writing in the twentieth century.

The theory, however, is not what stays with the reader. The effect of the formal innovation is to deliver awareness of a new reality. Readers can literally see the Revolution happen, see the diverse ways in which people respond to its challenge, live through the hatred of one ancient people for another in Persia in Shklovsky's appalled yet sympathetic representation of the Aissors and the Kurds. A value system emerges of patriotism, personal courage, commitment to truth, respect for life, deep distrust of war, hatred, and prejudice, respect for competence when it appears in anyone's work, revulsion at violence, honor for generosity, and an overriding compassion for human beings. Composed of bits and pieces as the novel is, a mosaic image comes into being that, like a Russian icon, combines pity and judgment. It is a work demanding deep attention, defining excellence, pinioning evil, and humanizing those who can hear what the narrator has to say.

### Critical Context

Viktor Shklovsky began his career as a Futurist in 1913, only a few years before the cataclysmic events that he chronicles in *A Sentimental Journey*. Russian Futurism was an avant-garde movement designed to overcome the then-predominant Symbolist techniques and to renew Russian literature after the sense arose that its great triumphs in realism were over. Vladimir Mayakovsky, Osip Brik, and other Futurists welcomed the Revolution and, in fact, contributed richly to its literature, though most of them came to grief when the Party took charge of literary policy. In postwar Petrograd, especially during the civil war, Maxim Gorky protected artists and literary critics; he set up the House of Arts as a place to house and feed them and to let them work. Bringing the writers and theorists together created a kind of nuclear reaction, and the articles and artistic works emerging from Opoyaz (Society for the Study of Poetic Language), an organization formed before the war but renewed in the early 1920's, generated Formalism, a major strain of twentieth century literary criticism in the West.

These groups emphasized breaking up the smooth surface of Symbolist prose, exploring linguistics for a more scientific grasp of language and the word, and responding more directly to reality (the Symbolists lived for the transcendental) while no longer striving to mirror reality.

*A Sentimental Journey* is a demonstration of the new devices and ideas about form that these groups espoused, but, because it was written in exile in Berlin after the harrowing experiences of his military life, the novel also became a magnificent documentary history of the period. The book shows the influence of Sterne, but Shklovsky also learned much from Andrey Bely, a Symbolist novelist and theorist of the preceding generation, and from Vasily Rozanov, a radical prose stylist who wrote ironic apothegms in a highly conversational diction.

Richard Sheldon, who translated this and other Shklovsky novels, gives Shklovsky credit for the device of estrangement (similar to Bertolt Brecht's alienation effect) and for "impeded form," a device using verbal intricacy designed to make "palpable" the reality it presents. Impeded form is the basis for the ornamental prose used by many writers early in the Soviet period, and *A Sentimental Journey* provides an example.

The slowness with which twentieth century Russian literature has reached the West, hindered by Soviet censorship and Western hostility to the Soviet Union, alone explains why this novel has had only a modest audience in the West. It is a humane and innovative work that allows the reader to participate in the Russian revolutionary years, from 1917 to 1922.

*Sources for Further Study*

Grits, Fyodor S. "The Work of Viktor Shklovsky: An Analysis of *Third Factory*," in *Third Factory*, 1977.

Kern, Gary, and Christopher Collins, eds. *The Serapion Brothers: A Critical Anthology of Stories and Essays*, 1975.

Monas, Sidney. "Driving Nails with a Samovar: A Historical Introduction," in *A Sentimental Journey: Memoirs, 1917-1922*, 1970.

*National Review*. Review. XXII (April 21, 1970), p. 420.

Sheldon, Richard. Introduction to *A Sentimental Journey: Memoirs, 1917-1922*, 1970.

_____ , ed. *Viktor Shklovsky: A Complete Bibliography of Works by and About Him*, 1977.

*Martha Manheim*

# THE SETTING SUN

*Author:* Osamu Dazai (Tsushima Shūji', 1909-1948)
*Type of plot:* Psychological realism
*Time of plot:* Shortly after World War II
*Locale:* Tokyo and a country house in Izu
*First published: Shayō*, 1947 (English translation, 1956)

> *Principal characters:*
> KAZUKO, the narrator, a young girl living with her mother
> NAOJI, her brother, a frustrated writer
> THE MOTHER of Kazuko and Naoji, an aristocratic lady
> UEHARA, a debauched novelist who becomes Kazuko's lover

*The Novel*

*The Setting Sun* details the difficulty of a formerly aristocratic family in coming to terms with the new morality and economic reality of postwar Japan. Each member of the family copes with the problems of integrating past and present in a different way; only Kazuko, the narrator, is able to survive. The novel presents in diary fashion her reaction to events as they occur and her reflections on the family's past: The plot consists more of impressions and flashbacks than of connected events. The narrator also includes part of her brother's journal and his long, meditative suicide note, in which he despairs over his artistic and romantic failure.

The novel opens with an evocative description of Kazuko's mother eating soup in a ladylike way; aristocratic behavior, the narrator reflects, does not mean exaggerated manners but an effortless grace—even the mother's urinating in the family garden suggests to Kazuko a genteel innocence that has been replaced by a more formal and rigid code of behavior. Shortly after the end of the war, Kazuko's Uncle Wada tells her and her mother that they can no longer afford to live in Tokyo and must move to a more rustic house in Izu. The mother and daughter attempt to reconcile themselves to the less elegant surroundings, but both are disappointed, and the mother becomes ill with a high fever. Eventually she recovers, and the pair begin to accustom themselves to the simple rural life-style.

One day Kazuko burns some snake eggs, thinking them to be from a viper. When she learns that the snakes would not have been harmful, she feels remorse for the needless destruction, and her mother, witnessing the burning, also suffers from Kazuko's action. Ten days later, Kazuko through carelessness sets fire to the woodpile, and the fire almost sets the entire village ablaze. Greatly ashamed of her carelessness, Kazuko goes from house to house begging forgiveness. Shortly afterward, the mother receives word that her son Naoji will return from military service and that he has become an opium addict. The harshness of her life makes Kazuko think of leaving and living with a man whom she had loved when she was married—Naoji's patron, the novelist Uehara. Still, the situation of the mother and daughter is calm and happy until Naoji returns.

Naoji is taciturn and bitter, and he ridicules the new family home. Upset with their fallen status, he turns to drugs and alcohol. Kazuko discovers her brother's "Moonflower Journal," written six years earlier, in which he detailed his addiction, his suicidal despair, and his difficulty in both writing and finding self-esteem. Kazuko remembers how at that time her efforts to pay for her brother's addiction had led to her divorce: One day she took money to Naoji's friend Uehara, and he kissed her; she later fell in love with him, and her secret led her husband to doubt her faithfulness.

She decides to write a declaration of her continuing love to Uehara, proposing indirectly to be his mistress. After no response, she writes a second letter telling him that she has received a proposal but that she wants to bear his child; still Uehara does not answer, and she writes a third unsuccessful letter. Finally she decides to visit Uehara, but her mother becomes ill again, and her disease is diagnosed as incurable tuberculosis. Her mother's condition worsens and she dies in the autumn twilight.

Naoji returns from Tokyo with a girl, and Kazuko uses the opportunity to visit Uehara. She meets Uehara's wife at his home and goes in search of him, eventually finding him at a disreputable bar. Uehara takes her to an inn and leaves her there, and when Kazuko wakes up, Uehara is lying beside her. That same morning Naoji commits suicide. His testament tells that he began taking drugs to be strong like other boys, to be coarse and abandon his aristocratic background; now, Naoji laments, he is still not accepted by the people, and he cannot return to his aristocratic world—even if he could return, he would not fit in. Naoji also tells of a painter (apparently Uehara) whose wife he loves. The painter is coarse and commercializes on a vulgar, modern style, while the painter's wife is a refined and traditional Japanese woman. Like his attempt to recapture his aristocratic past, Naoji's love is doomed from the beginning. To overcome his sense of failure, he turns to dissolution, but his consciousness continues to torment him.

After spending a month by herself in the country, Kazuko writes a letter to Uehara, acknowledging that he will forget her, that they are both "victims of a transitional period of morality." Still, she has been able to push back the old morality and will fight to do so with her child by Uehara, the child of the man she loves. This child and her love for it will be her moral revolution and will ensure her survival, a survival that none of the other characters manages to find.

## The Characters

The three major characters, Kazuko, Naoji, and their mother, are vividly and sympathetically drawn. To some extent each represents an aspect of the novelist's personality. Like Naoji, Osamu Dazai struggled bitterly with the problem of artistic expression and also eventually committed suicide. Like Kazuko, he managed to give his anguish a form by writing the novel—his equivalent of Kazuko's child. Like the mother, he found himself drawn to the old world but unable to live in it.

Kazuko is the most complex of the three characters. While she conceals much of her motivation and emotions with a narrative reticence, she is also forthright and honest in her portrayal of shame and suffering. She understands and admires her mother's gentility and is disappointed that she does not embody such aristocratic virtues. At the same time, Kazuko is aware that moral standards as well as class distinctions are changing, and she faces the need to adjust to the world, however painful this change may be. Throughout her crises, Kazuko never loses her essential compassion for her mother and brother. This understanding and sympathy show that her affair with Uehara is not simply expedient or self-serving.

Naoji does not lack such compassion, as his diaries and his clumsy attempt to help his sick mother reveal, but ultimately he finds no outlet for such emotions except the outpourings of his journal and the impossible love for a married woman. Uncomfortable in either the dying aristocratic world or the coarser postwar world, he represents the difficulty that any artist must face when confronting change, especially cataclysmic social revolution. His suicide, then, reflects the dead end of the artist, or any individual, who cannot break with the past.

Naoji's mother also cannot survive in the modern world. She lives, however, with a graceful accommodation to her situation and refuses to impose her own suffering on others, concentrating her love on Naoji.

The novelist Uehara represents one final alternative for the modern writer. Uehara profits from his abandonment of traditional values and his frank handling of dissolution. In this rebellion, Kazuko finds strength. Yet while Uehara is generous with his fellow drunkards, his lack of essential compassion makes his alternative less appealing than that of Kazuko; Uehara's writing, while realistic, does not seem to capture the suffering that Naoji's journal, or the novel itself, does.

### Themes and Meanings

By focusing on the members of a declining class at a time of social upheaval, *The Setting Sun* delineates the theme that change is inevitable and must be faced but is nevertheless painful. No simple solution will fit every situation, and the individual must confront reality honestly, without imposing a comfortable illusion. Along with honesty, compassion enables one to cope with painful change, but it does not by itself provide any permanent answers.

Kazuko's ultimate acceptance of change marks her awareness of the need for revolution and love. Her own social revolution—bringing up her illegitimate child—is a desire to break from the old morality so that rigid standards will not claim further victims, so that her child can grow up healthy and strong.

The novel also reveals the importance of communication. While the characters are often indirect in their speech, they manage at times to establish a channel for their suffering, particularly Kazuko and her mother—a delicate channel that allows for the sharing of grief and pain. Kazuko's letters to Uehara also prepare him to accept her love, even if he does not return that feeling equally. Most significant, Kazuko's diarylike narrative establishes a bond between herself and the reader, who can respond with sympathy and understanding. Her writing, like the novel itself, refuses to superimpose an orderly, preset form of experience, relying instead on momentary observations, flashbacks, snippets of conversation, letters, and the journals of Naoji, all loosely connected. *The Setting Sun* shows modern literature, in contrast to the realistic nineteenth century novel, reflecting the fragmentary and subjective quality of the modern world.

*Critical Context*

*The Setting Sun* is typical of Osamu Dazai's later works in both form and theme, employing a fragmentary structure and conveying a strong sense of disillusionment. His last important novel, *Ningen shikkaku* (1948; *No Longer Human*, 1958), is even bleaker than *The Setting Sun*. Most of Dazai's work is in the tradition of the Japanese "I novel," focusing on the first-person narrator's subjective perceptions and often blurring the distinction between author and narrator. More recent Japanese novels use the first-person narrator but rarely in so profound a manner. The subject matter of Dazai's novel marks it as a key postwar Japanese novel, dealing frankly with the nation's sense of loss and confusion. (Indeed, so great was the impact of Dazai's novel that the term "Setting Sun people" was widely used to refer to the dying class whose epitaph Dazai wrote.) Because of the novel's preoccupation with and sympathy for the declining aristocracy, it has been compared to Anton Chekhov's *Vishnyovy sad* (1904; *The Cherry Orchard*, 1908), but *The Setting Sun* is also a very modern work in its structural fragmentation and emphasis on the individual consciousness.

*Sources for Further Study*

Lyons, Phyllis I. "'Art *Is* Me': Dazai Osamu's Narrative Voice as a Permeable Self," in *Harvard Journal of Asiatic Studies*. XLI (June, 1981), pp. 93-110.

_____ . *The Saga of Dazai Osamu: A Critical Study with Translations*, 1985.

Miyoshi, Masao. "Till Death Do Us Part: Dazai Osamu—*The Setting Sun*," in *Accomplices of Silence: The Modern Japanese Novel*, 1974.

Rimer, J. Thomas. "Dazai Osamu: The Death of the Past—*The Setting Sun*," in *Modern Japanese Fiction and Its Traditions: An Introduction*, 1978.

*Steven L. Hale*

# THE SEVEN DAYS OF CREATION

*Author:* Vladimir Maximov (Lev Samsonov, 1930-    )
*Type of plot:* Social chronicle
*Time of plot:* From the Russian Revolution through the 1960's
*Locale:* Russia
*First published: Sem dnei tvoreniia*, 1971 (English translation, 1974)

> *Principal characters:*
> PYOTOR LASHKOV, an elderly Communist Party functionary
>     who becomes a Christian
> ANDREI LASHKOV, his brother, a warden in the Kurakin forest
> VASILII LASHKOV, his brother, a janitor in Moscow
> ANTONINA LASHKOV, his daughter, whose return home with
>     an infant son reinforces Pyotor's belief in religion
> VADIM LASHKOV, his grandson, a debauched variety artist

*The Novel*

*The Seven Days of Creation* chronicles the anguished searching of three generations of the Lashkov family for the meaning of human suffering. In six chapters, each representing a weekday preceding Sunday, the author portrays the increasing cynicism and growing alienation of this Russian family and the subsequent attempts of its members to attain a rewarding life and to rejoin the human family safely and hopefully.

In the course of the novel, the characters travel across Russia literally and spiritually, seeking more redeeming relationships. Specific incidents prompt dreams and flashbacks. The activities and interactions of family members elicit varying responses, some empathic and others accusative.

One July dawn, the intractable Pyotor Lashkov awakens to the bitter realization that he has alienated himself from his family and friends. Sensitive, however, to his middle-aged daughter's drunken despondency, he resolves to renew human ties. When he seeks to pay respects to the family of a deceased acquaintance, he mistakenly visits a home in which religious services are being held. This encounter foreshadows the eventual conversion of the elderly atheist.

When his bewildered grandson, Vadim, visits, Pyotor advises the despairing young man to find solace with Pyotor's brother Andrei, a warden in the Kurakin forest. In a flashback, Pyotor recalls his own disturbing visit with the shell-shocked Andrei, before Andrei became a warden. Yearning to revive family attachments, Pyotor seeks out his brother Vasilii in Moscow, whom he has not seen for more than forty years. The brothers are so ill at ease that when Vasilii goes out to buy more liquor, Pyotor hastens away, repulsed by the stench and premature decay in the room.

The first chapter, "Monday: A Traveler in Search of Himself," relates several other attempts to amend self-indulgences. Antonina marries Nikolai Leskov; it is an ill-fated marriage, but one which promises some redeeming fulfillment. Acknowledging responsibility for his estrangement from family and friends, Pyotor resolves to rectify his errors and to reestablish family ties, hoping by this change to ensure the preservation of both his family and the country that he loves.

The second chapter, "Tuesday: The Cattle Drive," details Andrei's first assumption of a leadership role: evacuating cattle from Uzlovsk and the surrounding district, which stretches to the distant mountains. As he has never been one to give orders, Andrei initially lacks the confidence to act with authority. Nevertheless, he succeeds in saving the life of a lame concertina player, befriending a philosophical veterinarian, herding freezing cattle into a church, and transporting a critically ill child to a doctor. Seduced by the sharp-tongued yet respected Alexandra, he refuses to flaunt their affair and becomes a target for her vituperative reproaches. In the course of time, they resolve their differences and marry.

Vasilii's interactions with the tenants in his building form the basis of the third chapter, "The Yard at the Midpoint of Heaven." These residents, a motley crew, form an extended family as they share one another's joys and sorrows. For example, they help Otto Stabel, an Austrian plumber, erect a house for himself and his beloved wife, Grusha. Everyone suffers when the authorities require portions of the walls demolished in order to conform with building specifications. Such restrictions exemplify the governmental control that negates individual creativity. A frail woman, Shokolinist, who was the original mistress of the house, adds a supernatural quality. Continuing to collect overdue books for the library, this wraith outlives Vasilii, who dies observing her in the yard where Stabel's house had been.

The fourth chapter, "Late Light," begins with Vadim's observing the snowy streets of Moscow as he rides to the hospital. The vivid description of his ward parallels scenes in other Russian works, such as Aleksandr Solzhenitsyn's *Rakovy korpus* (1968; *Cancer Ward*, 1968). Visits from Pyotor and special treatment by the hospital director, who ultimately commits suicide, do not deter Vadim from escaping with the aid of a nurse and Natasha, a young woman whom he has befriended.

"Friday: The Labyrinth," the fifth chapter, recounts the experiences of Antonina and Nikolai as they join a building work team in Central Asia. Attracted to the Jewish foreman, Osip Meckler, Antonina sleeps with him, comforting him in his despair at realizing that the team is building a prison. When he commits suicide and Nikolai is imprisoned, she writes to her Christian friends, seeking assistance.

In "The Evening and Night of the Sixth Day," Pyotor visits the friends of the deceased Vasilii, attends the wedding of Andrei and Alexandra, and welcomes home Antonina and her infant son, who bears his name. Tenderly clutching his grandson, Pyotor strides into the spring dawn.

## The Characters

Having been exposed to the harshness of orphanages and reform schools, and later to the confinement of mental hospitals, Vladimir Maximov sensitively sketches his characters, all of whom feel estranged from themselves and from society. They attempt to counteract their deplorable situation with a yearning for relationships and with loving concern for others. An Orthodox Christian, Maximov believes religion is the hope for these disillusioned Russians. His background as an itinerant bricklayer informs the peripatetic lifestyle of his characters. At the same time, his career as a poet and playwright allows him to create articulate characters who express a vivid love of nature. Pyotor, the protagonist, becomes increasingly sensitive to the wonders of creation as he seeks to renew ties with estranged relatives. At the end of the novel, when Pyotor carries his infant grandson toward the horizon of a dawning spring day, Maximov describes his response to the glorious occasion: "He went, and he knew. He knew, and he believed."

Pyotor's ability to satisfy his yearnings and his desire to begin again eventually convert the elderly Communist to Christianity. Gupak, a recurring character, expounds traditional religious values to Pyotor, as well. Gupak charitably befriends Antonina and in his relationships with others demonstrates principles which form the basis of religion.

Vadim's life experience parallels Maximov's youthful rebellion and travel throughout Russia. Both see distress in the eyes of their compatriots and empathize with their fear of alienation from society. Like Maximov, Vadim expresses skill with words and shrewdness in establishing an identity in the minds of others.

Women play a forceful role in this novel. Among them, Alexandra, Andrei's wife, exhibits feminist qualities. Although sarcastic, she works hard, gaining the respect of the men on the cattle drive. She wins Pyotor's admiration when, in later years, he attends her marriage to Andrei. Pyotor appreciates her attempt at "wresting her share of belated happiness from fate at long last." Antonina offers greater depth of characterization. Initially she appears as a middle-aged drunk who lacks purpose; after converting to Christianity and suffering in a work camp, she returns home bearing the gift of rebirth: her infant son.

## Themes and Meanings

Houses serve as an important motif in *The Seven Days of Creation*, signifying the human creative instinct. The novel opens and closes at Pyotor's house. Initially, the house signifies Pyotor's isolating of himself from society.

At the conclusion, however, he redecorates the home in anticipation of Antonina's return with her son. This creative urge reflects his openness to the world and his refusal to remain confined by selfish concerns. Throughout the novel, homes and home substitutes offer evidence of the characters' well-being and security. The residents in Vasilii's building develop into an extended family. The same rapport develops among the residents of Vadim's hospital ward.

Transportation and vehicles play a prominent role in the novel. The city of Uzlovsk grew as families settled around a railroad station "halfway from Moscow to nowhere." For those characters who lack love and concern for others, the journey remains one to nowhere. The success of a character's effort to rejoin the stream of humanity depends upon the character's traveling beyond an insulated sphere, by train, taxi, or ferry.

Using a journey motif, Maximov delineates Pyotor's transformation from Communist to Christian. The Russian travels from his home in Uzlovsk to visit his brothers, about whom he has seldom concerned himself. Each trip evokes dreams or recollections of the past, ultimately fostering Pyotor's love of family members and respect for himself. After much self-searching and more self-recrimination, Pyotor discovers that love of the created world and its inhabitants revives his love of, faith in, and charity for humankind. Pyotor changes from a disgruntled, lonely old man who bemoans the beginning of each dull day into a proud grandfather walking expectantly toward the morning horizon with enduring faith and newly found hope for the future of his infant grandson and his country. The final chapter consists of a title only: "AND THE SEVENTH DAY DAWNED—THE DAY OF HOPE AND RESURRECTION. . . ." Thus, the journey ends with a new beginning.

*Critical Context*

Publication of *The Seven Days of Creation* forced Maximov to leave the Soviet Union. Ironically, his first novel, *Zhiv chelovek* (1962; *A Man Survives*, 1963), won for him praise inside and outside his country. In that novel, as in most of his works, Maximov portrays the alienated person's redemption through compassion. *Karantin* (1973; *Quarantine*, 1981) further develops the journey motif. Quarantined because of a cholera epidemic in Odessa, train passengers relate their individual stories. *Kovcheg dlya nezvannykh* (1979; *Ark for the Uncalled*, 1985) relates the experiences of a young soldier and a government official as they journey to the Kuril Islands, ultimately confronting disillusionment and the possibility of rebirth.

*The Seven Days of Creation* is considered a powerful description of Soviet life. This example of dissident literature inspires comparisons to the works of Fyodor Dostoevski and Aleksandr Solzhenitsyn. *The Seven Days of Creation* substantiates innate human goodness and relates the struggle against the sense of alienation fostered by an authoritarian state.

*Sources for Further Study*

Brown, Deming. *Soviet Russian Literature Since Stalin*, 1978.

Gray, Paul. Review in *Time*. CV (February 3, 1975), p. 68.

Moore, Harry T., and Albert Parry. *Twentieth-century Russian Literature*, 1974.

Rubenstein, Joshua. Review in *The New York Times Book Review*. LXXX (February 23, 1975), p. 10.

*Beatrice Christiana Birchak*

# SHORT LETTER, LONG FAREWELL

*Author:* Peter Handke (1942-    )
*Type of plot:* Philosophical realism
*Time of plot:* The late 1960's or the early 1970's
*Locale:* The United States
*First published: Der kurze Brief zum langen Abschied*, 1972 (English translation, 1974)

> *Principal characters:*
> THE NARRATOR, a young Austrian writer
> JUDITH, his wife
> CLAIRE MADISON, an American with whom he has an affair
> DELTA BENEDICTINE, Claire's daughter
> JOHN FORD, the seventy-six-year-old American film director

*The Novel*

*Short Letter, Long Farewell* is one of Austrian novelist and playwright Peter Handke's typically enigmatic works, a decidedly meditative novel which defies simple summary or definitive explanation. It seems to involve at once too little plot and too much; its events follow one another in bewildering succession and fail to form any clearly meaningful pattern.

The novel is divided into two nearly equal parts, "The Short Letter" and "The Long Farewell," each preceded by a brief passage from Karl Philipp Moritz's *Anton Reiser* (1785-1790; English translation, 1926). The first passage deals with the need to attend closely to physical facts and the second deals with the way in which travel enables one to "forget what we don't like to think of as real, as though it were a dream." Dreams play an important part in Handke's novel, as do physical facts, and it is between the elusive otherness of the first and the swamping immediacy of the second that both the narrator and the reader must negotiate their way.

The novel begins in April—like Geoffrey Chaucer's *Canterbury Tales* (1380-1390) and T. S. Eliot's *The Waste Land* (1922)—on the narrator's second day in the United States, only a few days before his thirtieth birthday. The reader follows him on his cross-country travels from Providence, Rhode Island, to New York, Philadelphia, St. Louis, Tucson, and finally California. Where Walt Whitman traveled the land transcendentally, "afoot with [his] vision," Handke's narrator is adrift with his nightmare—Whitman's exuberance and faith having collapsed into the black hole of Handke's bleak aesthetic. Whether his narrator's travels comprise a quest or an escape is left in doubt, for they cannot be divorced from those of his wife, Judith, from whom he has recently separated but who has since come to the United

States. At first, it is the narrator who seems to be following his wife, but it soon becomes equally likely that she is the tracker and he the prey. He is perhaps not so much tracked as lured to his death, but it is a death that she seems more intent on dreaming about than actually causing.

The novel's ambiguous action is rendered in an equally ambiguous style that may best be described as absurdist realism. The sentence, "The bus took the Bruchner Expressway through the Bronx, turned off to the right, and crossed the Harlem River to Manhattan," is typical of this style, one in which the specific details do not contribute to any Jamesian "solidity of specification" but instead suggest that they have been arbitrarily chosen; they are not so much insignificant as nonsignifying. They hint that the narrator's larger world, and that of the reader as well, may be similarly devoid of meaning. The style is too realistic and serves only to accentuate the gap between language and physical reality on the one hand and language and understanding on the other. The narrator observes and records everything but, along with his reader, understands nothing. Realizing his own ignorance and incapacity, he pursues an art of deflection, hoping that, by describing accurately what is near at hand, he will be able to delude himself into believing it to have the "momentous" importance it clearly does not possess. It is a style marked above all by coordination rather than subordination, an art of catenation rather than comprehension: an ultimate superficial realism surprisingly like the disjunctive dream logic by which one scene leads, as if inevitably, to the next.

The narrator searches for reasons and motives but finds only his own explanations. Since he is also a random event in the world, his actions are themselves similarly absurd. "Then and there I decided to spend the money living as lazily and frivolously as possible" is a statement that is open to the reader's interpretation but not to any definitive explanation. Like the narrator, it does not *mean*; it *is*.

### The Characters

The only character who is fully drawn in this novel is the narrator. His Austrian citizenship and his work as a playwright suggest some connection to Handke, and his anonymity implies the elusiveness that will trouble both him and his reader. Turning thirty during the course of his cross-country travels, he appears at once experienced and naïve and, therefore, ill-prepared for the strangeness of American reality. He is a careful observer of his immediate surroundings, of others he meets, and of himself, yet he is fearful and suspicious as well. Highly self-critical, he finds that his criticism results only in making him more uncertain about himself; he fears that his identity may be "dissolving." As a result, he desires to detach himself from others in order to preserve his own tenuous identity, yet he alternately feels completely cut off from life and longs for engagement with others, a longing that travel both satisifies and frustrates. Chiefly, he desires to be other than he is, for his failed marriage serves as the constant reminder of his own helplessness. Fearful of making himself still more vulnerable, he withdraws into the very self he finds "superfluous."

Whether it is self-loathing or self-awareness that best characterizes him, the depth of the narrator's isolation and loneliness is evidenced by his overwhelming need to tell his story and, in this way, to authenticate or at least to certify his existence. This need appears all the more desperate as he places the words he speaks or thinks to himself within quotation marks. His narrative trick transforms monologue into dialogue but only at the cost of further alienating the narrator from himself, splitting him in two; he becomes both speaker and listener, writer and audience. A similar detachment marks his every action. His desire not "to be alone anymore" is certainly understandable, but his remedy—to write "a woman in Phoenixville, a small town west of Philadelphia, to say that I might go and see her"—sounds at best indifferent and at worst inhuman.

Claire Madison is the "woman" with whom he hopes to experience something of a phoenixlike rebirth, following the breakup of his marriage to Judith. The narrator remembers, "It was only when I met Judith, and for the first time really experienced something, that I began to see the world with something more than a malignant first glance." By the end of their marriage, however, husband and wife are *only* able to see malignantly, and the return to this same malignant point of view, coupled with his cold detachment, suggests that the narrator's rebirth in Phoenixville will come to nothing more permanent than his relationship with Judith.

It is significant that Judith's "love of whatever can be used up or exchanged" (including husbands) and her tendency "to make a magical idol out of every trifle" make her seem quite like the narrator, to whom she writes her short letter: "I am in New York. Please don't look for me. It would not be nice for you to find me." Nevertheless, she follows his every move or lures him into following her. (Their roles are in a sense interchangeable.)

Claire provides him with an alternative but a rather ambiguous one, for while she represents for him all that America promises (a fresh start, a haven for the homeless, and so on), the fact that she is a few years older and has an odd and oddly named daughter, Delta Benedictine, suggests that Claire may not be a new beginning at all but instead, in her capacity as an instructor of German at a nearby college, a reminder of the past that the narrator hopes to leave behind.

### Themes and Meanings

The problem that the narrator faces and that Handke poses for his readers involves a variation on the familiar existentialist theme of the need to know the world in all of its absurdity and, once that knowledge has been gained, to act in that same world authentically. For the narrator, the problem is compounded by the fact that he is a playwright (or at least claims to be), so the verb "to act" is invested with a dual meaning: to perform an action and to play a role. In *Short Letter, Long Farewell*, the purely existential world of Jean-Paul Sartre gives way to Handke's awareness that man does not live by existentialism alone, for his world, as well as his relationship to it, is semiotic. At every turn, the narrator finds his life ordered, or contaminated, by structures of signs drawn from both high art and pop culture. Thus, he describes, as if naturally, a certain day as having "passed as quickly for me as the days in horror films"; more disconcerting is the way in which his reading of four-frame *Peanuts* comic strips have shaped the structure of his dreams. Literature and pop culture are not presented as the means by which life can be better apprehended but instead as substitutes for that life, sign systems apprehended as if they were reality. This is especially evident in the narrator's reading of Gottfried Keller's novel *Der grüne Heinrich* (1854-1855, 1879-1880; *Green Henry*, 1960). Believing himself to be insignificant, the narrator wants to transform himself into whatever literary character he happens to be reading about at the time: Heinrich, for example, or F. Scott Fitzgerald's Great Gatsby.

At times, *Short Letter, Long Farewell* reads like a parody of Sartre's novel *La Nausée* (1938; *Nausea*, 1949); the effect is to ironize the narrator's desire to live authentically, to turn it into the oblique evidence of his inauthenticity. Something similar, though less damning, occurs if he is read as the hero of a Jamesian "international novel" in reverse (the innocent European coming to an America that is not so much culturally as semiotically rich) or as a latter-day Huck Finn making his way through a semiotic wilderness where "the artificial signs and objects of civilization [have] become nature" and where the truths that are held to be self-evident are no longer life, liberty, and the pursuit of happiness but the pursuit of signs which (the pursuer would like to believe) stand beyond interpretation, transformed into eternal verities. Not surprisingly, the narrator feels some jealousy because a mere child, Delta Benedictine, can be so at home in such a world, having the ability to look "on symbols and representations as having an existence of their own."

Aboard the riverboat *Mark Twain*, the narrator interprets the "bestial shriek" of the steam whistle as the summons to a resurrection, a uniting of all that had seemed disjoined "in a single, painful and theatrical revelation of history"—of American history, which is to say American myth—that leaves the narrator enthralled and convinced: a willing believer.

His own life in disarray, the traveler becomes a pilgrim and makes his determined way to one of the patriarchs of that myth, one of its founding fathers, the seventy-six-year-old film director John Ford, whose films about the American past—*The Iron Horse* and *Young Mr. Lincoln* in particular—have taught the narrator most of what he knows about America and about the need "to understand history by seeing people in nature." Ford's pictures, the narrator says, made him happy, for what they provide is a myth that serves as an alternative to the narrator's own loneliness and existential isolation. As Ford explains, "[W]e don't take our egos as seriously as you Europeans."

Relief from the narrator's typically European self-consciousness comes at a high price, however, one that the narrator is only half-willing to pay. Expecting that Ford is about to tell a story, the narrator leans forward only to realize "that I was imitating the gesture of a character in one of his pictures." Although the narrator never quite attains the state of authentic action, his self-awareness saves him from the inauthenticity he both craves and fears.

*Critical Context*

Instead of telling the narrator and his wife a story, Ford asks them for their story, which Judith then supplies. When the director asks if what Judith has said is true, she answers, "[I]t all happened." "It all happened" are the last three words in Handke's novel, and the "it" that she refers to did occur but only in Handke's fiction and perhaps only *as* fiction; the reality beyond her words and beyond the narrator's as well remains untellable. Pointing to the pile of manuscripts he has been sent for his consideration, Ford says, "There are some good stories in there. . . . Simple and clear. The kind of stories we need."

Handke's language and syntax are certainly simple, but his story is anything but clear. Yet the story is needed not despite its ambiguity but for it, for it is story which deals with the difficulty of distinguishing the myths on which man would like to depend from the reality that lies beneath, or perhaps beyond, the semiotic surface.

In his earlier works, Handke tended to emphasize the opacity, the arbitrariness, and the self-reflexivity of language, while in later works, he has become more and more concerned with the possibility of a nearly mystical truth lying somewhere beyond this same linguistic surface. The strength of *Short Letter, Long Farewell* derives largely from Handke's relentless depiction of the way in which the individual can delude himself in his quest for meaning and self-definition and, just as important, it deals with his pursuit of a truth less bleak—not a myth but a necessary story, an authentic fiction.

*Sources for Further Study*

Kaufman, Stanley. "It All Happened," in *The New Republic*. CLXXI (September 28, 1974), pp. 29-30.

Klinkowitz, Jerome, and James Knowlton. *Peter Handke and the Postmodern Transformation*, 1983.

Lavers, Norman. "With Peter Handke (in Spirit) in Eastern Austria," in *The American Poetry Review*. XIII (September/October, 1984), pp. 15-16.

Schlueter, June. *The Plays and Novels of Peter Handke*, 1981.
Wilkie, Brian, and James Hurt. "Peter Handke," in *Literature of the Western World*. II (1984), pp. 2241-2243.

*Robert A. Morace*

# SHOSHA

*Author:* Isaac Bashevis Singer (1904-    )
*Type of plot:* Historical realism
*Time of plot:* 1914-1952
*Locale:* Warsaw, Poland, and Tel Aviv, Israel
*First published: Neshome Ekspeditsyes*, 1974 (English translation, 1978)

*Principal characters:*
AARON GREIDINGER, the narrator, a writer
MORRIS FEITELZOHN, a writer and Greidinger's mentor
DORA STOLNITZ, an idealistic Communist, one of Aaron's
    mistresses
CELIA CHENTSHINER, another of Aaron's mistresses, an
    intellectual
HAIML CHENTSHINER, Celia's husband
BETTY SLONIM, a Russian-born Jewish actress, another of
    Aaron's mistresses
SAM DREIMAN, Betty Slonim's rich American patron and lover
TEKLA, the maid at Greidinger's apartment house, another of
    Aaron's mistresses
SHOSHA SCHULDIENER, Aaron's childhood playmate, whom
    he later marries

*The Novel*

The year is 1914. Aaron Greidinger, the seven-year-old son of a rabbi,
lives in an apartment at number ten Krochmalna Street in Warsaw. Across
the hall live Bashele and Zelig Schuldiener and their nine-year-old daughter,
Shosha. Although Aaron is a prodigy of learning and Shosha is intellectually
backward, he finds her attractive, and the Schuldieners' apartment, as lav-
ishly furnished as his own is sparse, becomes his second home.

This youthful idyll soon ends when the Schuldieners move to number
seven Krochmalna Street, two blocks away. Under constant scrutiny because
he is the rabbi's son, Aaron no longer can visit Shosha. Other difficulties follow. World War I brings poverty and hunger, so that by 1917 the Greidingers
are forced to move to Old Stykov in Galacia, where Aaron's father and then
his brother Moishe serve as rabbi.

While his family clings to traditional Judaism, Aaron does not. Impressed
with the Haskalah, the Enlightenment, that comes to Poland with the war, he
returns to Warsaw to earn his living as a writer. Here he begins an affair with
Dora Stolnitz, a member of the Communist Party who regards the Soviet
Union as the Promised Land. At the Writers' Club he encounters the eccentric philosopher Morris Feitelzohn, author of *Spiritual Hormones*. At once

lecherous, mystical, religious, and skeptical, he becomes Aaron's spiritual and intellectual guide.

Morris also helps Aaron monetarily. Though he is himself always in need of five zlotys, he introduces Aaron to Betty Slonim and Sam Dreiman, who have come to Poland in search of a play. Betty is a minor actress, but Sam wants to make her a star. To achieve this end, he is prepared to rent a theater in Warsaw and commission a play. He chooses Aaron as his dramatist when he learns that Aaron already has written the first act of a play about a nineteenth century woman who becomes a Hasidic rabbi. For his efforts, Aaron receives regular and generous advances. Aaron's dramaturgical abilities are not great, though, and he suffers further from the assistance of Betty, Sam, and other members of the proposed cast. The result is an unproducible piece that fails in rehearsal.

Aaron's association with Betty Slonim leads to more than a botched play, though. When he is not writing—which seems to be most of the time—he often serves as Betty's lover and tour guide. On one of their excursions, Aaron takes her to see his old street, which he has not visited in twenty years. There he finds Shosha; she has hardly changed, remaining essentially a child both mentally and physically. Inexplicably, he falls in love with her, and after the failure of his play he moves in with Shosha and her mother, severing his ties with his former associates and with the members of the Writers' Club.

With Sam Dreiman's blessing, Betty offers to marry Aaron and take him to the safety of America. Although he realizes that to stay in Poland is to invite death at the hands of the Nazis, he rejects her offer. Instead, he resolves to marry Shosha and remain in Warsaw.

Again war comes, and again Aaron's life changes. He flees Warsaw with Shosha, but she is too frail to survive the ordeal; two days out of the capital, she dies. Dora Stolnitz vanishes, and Betty commits suicide. Aaron reaches America through the Orient and becomes a successful writer, but he remains haunted by his past.

## The Characters

Aaron Greidinger is a portrait of Isaac Bashevis Singer as a young man. Both are red-haired vegetarians who grew up on Krochmalna Street. Both are the sons of rabbis but have abandoned traditional Judaism for the secular world. Both are writers, and both write about dybbuks, demons, and false Messiahs. Both are puzzled by the mysteries of the universe; both are irresistibly attractive to and attracted by women.

*Shosha* is not, however, absolute autobiography. Whereas Singer's first-known literary effort (in 1925) won a prize, Aaron must struggle many years before success comes to him. Aaron also remains in Poland longer than did Singer, who left in the early 1930's and thus did not face the rising tide of anti-Semitism in the country. Nor did Singer ever return to live on Kroch-malna Street once he had left. Through Aaron, then, he seems to imagine what his life might have been like had he chosen another course.

While Aaron bears certain similarities to Singer, Shosha does not at all resemble his first wife. This woman (Shosha) who remains a child does not seem likely to interest Aaron, who is involved in affairs with four other women when he meets her again after two decades. Perhaps, though, her innocence fascinates him; perhaps, too, in marrying her, he seeks to reunite himself with a past that he has rejected intellectually but emotionally has never abandoned. Throughout his adulthood, he has dreamed of Shosha, suggesting that while his rational life is rooted in modernism, his irrational side that expresses itself only in dreams remains bound to tradition.

One may thus regard Shosha as an allegorical representation of the old Jewish ways. Her very name is a variation of Shoshana, the rose, hinting at the biblical Rose of Jacob that is the Jewish people. Her death in the flight from Warsaw reflects the demise of European Judaism with its centuries of culture and tradition. Like this way of life, she cannot survive when severed from her roots on Krochmalna Street. (One must recall that in the 1930's, Warsaw, with its 300,000 Jews, was the epicenter of Jewish literature and philosophy.)

The other women in *Shosha* also represent aspects of life before World War II. Dora is the self-deluded idealist. Even after she hears of the arrests and murders of foreigners who have come to the Soviet Union, she refuses to believe the reports. She maintains that those who have been imprisoned, tortured, and killed by Joseph Stalin deserve their fate, that those who are innocent have nothing to fear.

Celia Chentshiner, an atheist, worships the intellect. Brilliant but bored, she represents European secular culture. She, too, dies in Warsaw as World War II destroys the world with which she has identified herself. Betty, meanwhile, is the artist, devoted to beauty rather than to intelligence, and Tekla is the peasant, neither brilliant nor artistic. She is, however, dependable, doing her work effectively, stolidly, tied to the ways of the country and the rhythms of nature even when she lives in the city.

*Themes and Meanings*

*Shosha* is Singer's *Paradise Lost*, an attempt to justify the ways of God to man. It is *Paradise Lost* written from the perspective of one who has seen two world wars and the Holocaust and who lives in the shadow of nuclear Armageddon. "If God is wisdom, how can there be foolishness? And if God is life, how can there be death?" asks Haiml Chentshiner. Shosha wonders why flies bite and why horses cannot live to be a hundred. "What can one do? How is one to live?" Dora asks. Singer's reply is less confident than John Milton's. In the final scene of the book, Haiml poses questions to Aaron as they sit in a small dark room. Haiml's second wife opens the door and asks these symbols of wondering humanity why they sit without light. Haiml replies, "We're waiting for an answer."

If an answer exists, it has not yet been given. Meanwhile, what remains for man to do? For one thing, he must remember. "Let us say that a fly has fallen into a spiderweb and the spider has sucked her dry. This is a fact of the universe and such a fact cannot be forgotten," Haiml states. Aaron writes about Jewish history: the false Messiahs of the seventeenth and eighteenth centuries, the Maiden of Lublin of the nineteenth century. Writing for him is an act of memory. *Shosha*, too, is such an act. By summoning the sounds, smells, tastes, and sights of a vanished Warsaw, Singer preserves that vanished world. Shosha and Celia are dead, the Warsaw ghetto is no more, but through literature one can again experience the past. As Alexander Pope wrote, "The groves of Eden, vanished now so long,/ Live in description and still are green in song." So, too, the streets and people of another era remain alive in the pages of fiction.

One cannot, must not, forget the past, but one must live in the present. On the eve of World War II, Aaron observes that in the opera houses one sees the same old comedies and tragedies, as though destruction were not imminent. In the store windows, one finds the same jewelry and furniture. The women still wear the latest fashions, and the men still ogle them approvingly. Even as Aaron contemplates the absurdity of the charade, he smells coffee and fresh rolls, and he, too, yields to his present appetite. He realizes that "every one of us will die with the same passions he lived with." For life must go on. Celia dies, but Haiml remarries. Aaron's life in Poland ends, but he creates a new one in America.

For the suffering in this life there is no explanation. From suffering, however, one does learn. Aaron becomes a vegetarian after watching the atrocities in a slaughterhouse. Haiml learns that insects and mice are also God's creatures. In Nazi-ruled Warsaw, Morris Feitelzohn finally discovers the philosophical insights that have eluded him for so long. The false Messiah Jacob Frank had urged Jews to sin, and Feitelzohn claims that in a sense Frank was correct: One should oppose the will of God to achieve salvation. "If He wanted evil, we had to aspire to the opposite. If He wanted wars, inquisitions, crucifixions, Hitlers, we must want righteousness, Hasidism, our own version of grace."

### Critical Context

A few months after *Shosha* appeared in English translation, Singer was awarded the Nobel Prize in Literature. Just as the Nobel Prize is a fitting tribute to a lifetime of letters, so *Shosha* is an epitome of that life. Like all Singer's other work, it is superficially a simple narrative. Yet it articulates all the themes that inform Singer's writing. Here is the mysticism of dybbuks and demons, which Shosha sees in her dreams. Here is the closed world of Hasidic Jewry confronting the infinite secular universe. Here are the passions of the flesh and the metaphysical yearnings of the soul. Here is the search for the meaning of suffering and life, and here is the lack of an answer.

Though Singer has left the world of Polish Hasidism behind him, he carries it with him, too. In the yeshiva, the best student is not the one with the right answers but the one with the right questions. For *Shosha*, Singer deserves to go to the head of the class.

*Sources for Further Study*
Alexander, Edward. *Isaac Bashevis Singer*, 1980.
Kresh, Paul. *Isaac Bashevis Singer: The Magician of West 86th Street*, 1979.
Miller, David Neal. *Fear of Fiction: Narrative Strategies in the Works of Isaac Bashevis Singer*, 1985.
Sinclair, Clive. *The Brothers Singer*, 1983.
Walden, Daniel, ed. *Isaac Bashevis Singer: A Reconsideration*, 1981.

*Joseph Rosenblum*

# THE SIBYL

*Author:* Pär Lagerkvist (1891-1974)
*Type of plot:* Philosophical fable
*Time of plot:* Unspecified
*Locale:* Delphi
*First published:* Sibyllan, 1956 (English translation, 1958)

*Principal characters:*
THE SIBYL, formerly the Delphic Pythia
A FOREIGNER, who, though unnamed, is unmistakably
AHASUERUS, the Wandering Jew
THE SIBYL'S SON, a graying, middle-aged idiot
A ONE-ARMED MAN, the Sibyl's lover

*The Novel*

A prefatory scene emphasizes the tale's timeless character. On the side of a wild mountain, high above the paths beaten by pilgrims on their visits to Delphi's temple, an old woman lives in isolation with her feebleminded son. Every so often, the morning light reveals a girl, fresh from her bath in a sacred spring, being led by priests to a nuptial rendezvous with the god. The old woman knows the girl's thoughts and sensations: In her youth, before being cursed by everyone and driven from the city, she had herself served as consort to Apollo.

The novel proper begins with a stranger's ascent of the stony slope to the Sibyl's hut. A pilgrim, he was turned away from the oracle because the question he brought was unanswerable. After roaming the city in despair, he was directed into the mountains by an old blind beggar to consult an ancient oracle "who can answer all that a man can ask." Now that he has found her, he explains his mission by recounting an incident in the distant past "which had scored itself so deeply into his memory that he seemed not to recall anything besides; an event which left his soul no peace."

The man (implicitly recognizable as Ahasuerus, the Wandering Jew) had been enjoying a prosperous, easy life with his wife and young son in a house which faced the road to Calvary. The sight of criminals condemned to crucifixion being led past by the soldiers was a common one. One day, one such prisoner was so exhausted by the task of carrying his cross that he leaned against the house to rest. Ahasuerus, fearing that bad luck might descend on the house through the unfortunate man's touch, chased him away, and thereby, ironically, earned the crossbearer's curse: to wander the earth for eternity, never to find rest, even in death. Ahasuerus thought this a strange pronouncement, for mankind had always looked upon immortality as the most wonderful of gifts, not as a punishment; moreover, it seemed a simple matter to ignore the curse and go on living as he had before. His wife, however, immediately saw a terrible agedness in his eyes which began to irradiate their marriage, and she eventually fled with their child. Years later, Ahasuerus learned that the boy had been taken by the plague and that his wife had died after old age had exhausted all of her beauty. In having joylessly survived his family, and all the many subsequent generations, he says, he has carried the burden of the unique destiny of meaningless existence imposed on him by the criminal some now said was a god. He has also learned of a religion based on this god's teaching of love, but the embittered man has rejected it as absurd.

After Ahasuerus has told his story, the Sibyl invites him into her hut, where, in the presence of her idiot son, she relates her own experience of encountering a god. Reared by pious parents who practiced the religion of nature in its most unsophisticated form, she had been one of the few virgins left in Delphi, a city grown corrupt from its commerce as a sacred site. Her innocence, combined with a susceptibility to suggestion, convinced the priests to select her as the temple's new oracle. As soon as she was led into the holy cave to spread her legs over a fissure in the earth's living rock and become the vessel of Apollo, her special affinity for her role was evident; at every festival thereafter, she ate laurel leaves to induce a trance and then received the god, who had taken the appearance of a goat.

The fulfillment the girl initially derived from her ecstasy began eluding her, however, when she understood that the priests were using her for their own venal purposes, and the realization that she meant nothing to the god other than as a means of spending his lust made her feel spiritually forsaken. A hag assigned to be her attendant deepened her misery by constantly speaking of human vileness; although the Sibyl tried to defend herself against this misanthropic instruction, her resistance gradually crumbled. The young woman who had accepted isolation as the price for the peace of oneness with the divine came to believe that she had been played for a fool. Thus, after being summoned to her dying mother's bedside, she stayed behind to keep house for her father.

One day, while fetching water at a spring near her home, she saw a one-armed man, a childhood friend who, because he was just returning from war, knew nothing of her service as the Pythia. Each immediately fell in love with the other, and they soon consummated their passion. Although the Sibyl feared the consequences, she abandoned herself to this new form of happiness; nevertheless, when the priests commanded her to resume her office at the temple, she obeyed. The one-armed man's curiosity caused him to follow. Later, she learned that he had violated the sanctuary and heard her screams in the intensity of her orgasmic union with the god. Her happiness with her human lover had come to an end: No mortal could bear the thought of competing with the passion of a god.

After some months had passed, she was again called to serve the god. At the very moment that her divine consort, who appeared to her in the form of a black goat, ravished her as never before, the one-armed man was drowned by the rising sacred river at precisely the spot where they had first made love. Because the man had died clutching a laurel branch that had broken off as he tried to pull himself up from the water, she was sure that his death was the god's vengeance.

When the Sibyl realized that she was pregnant, she cherished the life she believed her human lover had planted within her body. This thought sustained her after the hag who attended her learned her secret and spread word of the scandal. As the Sibyl awaited punishment for infidelity to the god, the angry citizens of Delphi threatened to rip her apart. Only the kindness of a humble man who swept the temple saved her: While she hid in the sanctuary, he beat the crowd back with his broom. Strangely, in this moment of danger she experienced a new feeling of serenity with god and suddenly walked into the mob's midst. Perhaps because they were taken aback by her audacity, her tormentors allowed her to escape into the mountains.

Throughout a long, hard winter, she foraged for food; then, in the spring, she noticed that she attracted animals, and she fed on goat's milk. The child that grew within her, however, showed no sign of being ready to be born. Finally, during a furious lightning storm at the end of summer, a herd of goats led her to the mountain's summit, where, on a carpet of goat dung that reminded her of the ritual cave at the temple, she gave birth. Only then did it occur to her that the child had been conceived by the god.

Now that she has finished her tale, the Sibyl wonders aloud over the cruel joke the god has played on her, whether the witless creature she has reared to manhood is indeed his child. Then, suddenly, she realizes that her son has disappeared, and she suspects that, despite his apparent insensibility, he has understood her lamentations. Frantically, she and Ahasuerus follow his footprints until, as though he had ascended bodily to Heaven, they vanish on the top of the mountain.

Observing her anguish, Ahasuerus speaks of her son's departure as another terrible proof of divine malevolence, similar to his own curse, but the Sibyl rejects his conclusion. Life, she declares, can only be accepted; the ways of God lie beyond human comprehension. Ahasuerus refuses to be mollified, and, reminding her of the purpose that brought him to Delphi, he asks her to describe his destiny. Yet she can supply neither an explanation nor a prophecy. God, she says, is his destiny, and the hatred he feels may be merely his experience of the divine:

"Perhaps one day he will bless you instead of cursing you. . . . Perhaps one day you will let him lean his head against your house. Perhaps you won't. I know nothing about that. But whatever you may do, your fate will be forever bound up with god, your soul forever filled with god."

As Ahasuerus treads down the mountainside to resume his unending journey, a girl clad for a nuptial ceremony with the god is seen walking the sacred path to the cave.

## The Characters

The tale's protagonists represent contrasting responses to life's mystery. Lacking charity, Ahasuerus seeks a meaning for existence that is based solely on reason and justice; since no such answer can be revealed to him, he is doomed to search forever. Not even the whole of the world can deliver satisfaction, because he is ultimately inadequate within himself. That human limitation is the basis of his suffering—a kind of crucifixion akin to the human agony of Jesus on the Cross. The Sibyl, on the other hand, is wholly giving and makes herself completely vulnerable to the divine will. Nevertheless, her love is also not a final answer. At the end, she seems to understand that love is only the means for acceptance of the mystery.

## Themes and Meanings

Pär Lagerkvist confronts paganism with theism, as well as an Old Testament concept of God with the Christian gospel of love, to produce an ironic and extremely complex vision of man's condition. The Sibyl assumes a role that obviously parallels that of the Virgin Mary. Her ecstatic surrender to God fails, however, to provide a realization of her humanity; that comes to her only through the human love she finds with the one-armed man. Then, by drowning her lover, God seems to emphasize man's insufficiency (the man has only one hand with which to grasp for safety, and the branch from the laurel that is sacred to the god snaps as if to scorn his effort) and to punish her for daring to believe in her happiness.

She continues to cling to an earthly answer to life's pain by looking upon the child in her womb as a kind of resurrection for her lover. That hope, too, seems mocked when it becomes clear that the god has fathered her son. The boy's idiocy might make sense if she could interpret it as punishment, but she is denied even that consolation—that God's son should be so horribly flawed appears to be utterly meaningless.

Yet the grief she feels when her son disappears and, in his disappearance, reveals his divinity finally discloses the lesson in life's paradox. In a curious way, it is the same lesson she presents to the stranger who has come to her seeking a solution to the riddle of the human relationship to God. Ahasuerus is a Job without faith, a Job who despairs, but even that despair is better than nothingness. God manifests Himself in man's pain and hatred as well as in his love. Even the attempt to reject Him is an acknowledgment that His mysterious power cannot be escaped.

*Critical Context*

Although he is best known outside Sweden for his parable-like novels, Lagerkvist was also a poet, dramatist, and essayist who, throughout his career, adopted radical positions. Like Fyodor Dostoevski, whose views bear some resemblance to his own, Lagerkvist demonstrated an early interest in socialism, but his deepest motivations stemmed from his striving to understand man's relationship to God, primarily as expressed symbolically through the Crucifixion.

His first novel, *Dvärgen* (1944; *The Dwarf*, 1945), which was a great popular as well as artistic success, treated intertwined themes that recur in all his mature work: the elusiveness of truth, the unfathomability of life's ends, and man's irreconcilability to the reality of his condition. *Barabbas* (1950; English translation, 1951), his second novel, focused that inquiry in a retelling of the Crucifixion from the point of view of the thief who was spared and who then spent his life trying to deny that Christ's death had transformed his life. *The Sibyl*, published several years later, returns to that obsession. Lagerkvist's most ambitious work up to that time, it confirmed his place among the giants of twentieth century literature; shortly after it appeared, he was awarded the Nobel Prize. Subsequently, he extended his narratives dealing with the Crucifixion in the Tobias trilogy, a series built around the emblematic figure of Ahasuerus.

*Sources for Further Study*

*Scandinavica*. X, no. 1 (1971). Special Lagerkvist issue.

Spector, Robert Donald. *Pär Lagerkvist*, 1973.

Swanson, Roy A. "Evil and Love in Lagerkvist's Crucifixion Cycle," in *Scandinavian Studies*. XXXVIII (November, 1966), pp. 302-317.

Vowles, Richard B. "The Fiction of Pär Lagerkvist," in *Western Humanities Review*. VIII (Spring, 1954), pp. 111-119.

Weathers, Winston. *Pär Lagerkvist: A Critical Essay*, 1968.

*Frank Gado*

# SIDDHARTHA

*Author:* Hermann Hesse (1877-1962)
*Type of plot:* Bildungsroman
*Time of plot:* The sixth century B.C., at the time of the Buddha
*Locale:* India
*First published:* 1922 (English translation, 1951)

*Principal characters:*
SIDDHARTHA, a Brahman's son
GOVINDA, his boyhood friend
KAMALA, a courtesan
KAMASWAMI, a rich merchant
VASUDEVA, a ferryman
GOTAMA, the Buddha

*The Novel*

*Siddhartha* centers on the lifelong search of Siddhartha, the young son of a Brahman, for enlightenment. As a boy, he is trained in the traditional rituals and meditations of the learned, but there is a restlessness in his soul. He cannot stop questioning and speculating, and he doubts whether any of his teachers is truly enlightened. Against his father's wishes, he decides to join a group of Samanas, wandering ascetics, and his friend Govinda accompanies him. For three years, Siddhartha lives the ascetic life of self-denial. He cultivates a dislike of the sensual world and tries to empty himself of desires in order to reach the innermost core of his being. Eventually, however, he becomes dissatisfied, and guesses that the Samanas are no closer to enlightenment than the Brahmans who had taught him in his early youth.

Leaving the Samanas, Siddhartha and Govinda travel to see Gotama the Buddha, who has the reputation of being a wise man and supreme teacher. The young men are impressed by the Buddha's quiet bearing and peaceful countenance, but Siddhartha, unlike Govinda, does not become his disciple. Siddhartha is skeptical of all teachings, convinced that enlightenment cannot be taught but can only be experienced by the individual for himself. He resolves to leave behind all doctrines and teachers. This decision is a major turning point for him, as he becomes more accepting of himself and more ready to appreciate the beauty of the sensory world. He is now alone, free of past ties, and ready to travel in whatever direction he chooses.

The second part of the novel relates Siddhartha's gradual immersion in the world of sensual and material activities. Reaching a large town, he meets Kamala, a beautiful courtesan. She teaches him the art of love and finds him employment with a rich merchant named Kamaswami. Siddhartha prospers in business, and, as the years go by, he becomes rich and acquires a taste for luxurious living. At first, he had regarded business as a game and was unable to take seriously the small pleasures and desires of ordinary people. Gradually, however, he becomes deeply entangled in the life he has chosen. He becomes ruthlessly acquisitive, gambles recklessly, turns discontented, weary, and full of self-disgust. When he realizes that he can no longer hear the inner voice which once guided him, he concludes that life is worthless and decides to leave the town, never to return.

This journey marks another turning point in his life. In despair, Siddhartha wanders into a forest and comes upon a river. As he is about to drown himself, from somewhere within the deepest recesses of his being he hears once more the sacred sound "om," the beginning and ending of all Brahman prayers. In that moment, he realizes his folly. He falls into a restorative sleep, and when he awakes he feels reborn. He meets an old ferryman, Vasudeva, who invites Siddhartha to stay and live with him. Siddhartha becomes a ferryman, and as time passes he finds peace of mind with the saintly old man.

Many years later, followers of the Buddha, on a pilgrimage to see their dying master, come to be ferried across the river. Among the pilgrims is Kamala, who has renounced her former life to become a benefactress of the monks. She is accompanied by a son she bore to Siddhartha, conceived on their final meeting. When Kamala is bitten by a snake and dies, the boy is left in Siddhartha's care. The youth is restless and bad-tempered, however, and he cannot return Siddhartha's love; eventually he runs away, and Siddhartha never sees him again. Through his possessive love for his son and its sad outcome, however, Siddhartha learns to have sympathy for the common folk; their simple passions no longer seem trivial to him. He also continues to grow in his knowledge of the unity of all things. He talks at length with Vasudeva, whose attentiveness, love, and serenity seem to Siddhartha like that of God. Together they listen to the river, in which Siddhartha discerns the whole stream of cosmic life, good and evil, joy and sorrow.

In the final episode, Siddhartha meets Govinda for the second time since they parted as young men. Govinda is still a seeker, and he asks Siddhartha to share some of his wisdom with him but finds Siddhartha's words strange and difficult to understand. Siddhartha asks him to kiss his forehead, and as he does so, Govinda experiences a transforming illumination. He sees all the forms of the cosmos—animals, humans, gods—both the good and the bad, contained in Siddhartha's smiling face, and he realizes, as Kamala in her dying moments had also nearly guessed, that there is no difference between Siddhartha and Gotama the Buddha.

## The Characters

In keeping with this novel of ideas, all the major characters in the novel, with the exception of the merchant Kamaswami, are spiritual seekers, each after his own fashion. Most important among them is the protagonist, Siddhartha. Siddhartha is a romantic in the sense that he rejects familial and institutional ties in order to discover truth through his own personal experience. He must make his own mistakes and learn from them, just as his son must do in his turn. Yet Siddhartha possesses a superior soul; his intrinsic purity inevitably reasserts itself, even though he is caught for many years in the false life of sensual pleasure. His personal qualities are less important, however, than the philosophical nature of his quest for enlightenment.

Govinda is always the loyal disciple, never the leader or trailblazer. He accepts a position subordinate to Siddhartha from the outset. Siddhartha is the one who will do great things, and Govinda wants no more than to be his servant and companion. It is Siddhartha's decision to join the Samanas, and it is also his decision to leave them. It is appropriate that Govinda remains as a disciple of the Buddha; he is happier when he can follow a set of teachings along a prescribed path. By the end of his life, he has won the respect of the younger monks, but he still remains a seeker. Following the conventional path, he has not found peace, a fact which confirms Siddhartha's earliest suspicions.

Even the courtesan Kamala has spiritual yearnings. She understands Siddhartha better than Govinda does, because, curiously, she is more like Siddhartha: She is unlike other people; like Siddhartha, she has a stillness inside her, a sanctuary to which she can retreat. Then, too, she realizes that he remains a Samana at heart. It is significant that Kamala becomes Siddhartha's only close friend, and it comes as no surprise that many years later she goes on a pilgrimage to see the Buddha and that she finds peace when she spends the last moments of her life with Siddhartha.

Vasudeva is the teacher who does not teach. Everything about his being radiates serenity and calm, but he has no doctrine, only the wisdom of experience. Uneducated in the conventional sense, and in his own mind lacking eloquence, he inspires confidence through the quality of his silence; he is an excellent listener, and he does not judge. Others seek him out for counsel. The simple ferryman claims that it is the river, Hermann Hesse's symbol of life itself, which has taught him everything. Vasudeva knows the unity of things and the perfection of the world, and Siddhartha comes to resemble him.

*Themes and Meanings*

The single theme of the novel is Siddhartha's search for unity, which is identical with his search for the true nature of the self. He cannot find either by rejecting the world, but neither can he take the opposite route and indulge the senses. He must indeed embrace the world, but only when he is able to experience it *sub specie aeternitatis*, in its essential form. He must come to know that the individual self, the Atman, is identical to the universal self, the Brahman, although by the end of the novel the terms have shifted.

He has, even while remaining an individual, become indistinguishable from the universal nature of the Buddha.

To attain this enlightenment, the most important lesson he learns is the ability to be passive, to wait and listen. If he can cease his own small willing and striving, he can learn to embrace the great contradictory harmonies of the world. He can, in his own person, reconcile all the strife of opposites; he can overcome the illusion of time and thus experience the myriad, diverse forms and events—past, present, and future—as a simultaneous present, and hold them in a quiet serenity which accepts and loves everything, seeing no fault.

Hesse's great image, in which the whole meaning of the novel is contained, is the river. Siddhartha is reborn as he sleeps by the river's edge, and he resolves to stay there and learn from it. Vasudeva has spent a lifetime ferrying travelers across the river (in Buddhist thought, enlightenment is said to be the knowledge which goes "to the other shore," and the sage is the one who steers the boat). The river symbolizes life. It is from the river that Siddhartha learns that time has no existence. The river is everywhere at the same time; it flows on forever and has neither past nor future. Siddhartha realizes that this quality is also true of human life and that suffering takes place only within that false mental construct which is called time, yet which has no reality.

Siddhartha hears all the different voices of the river and discerns all the forms it contains. He sees his own past and all the people he has known. He also sees the insatiable desire which drives all life toward its goal. Yet he also knows that every act is necessary and good; every thing and every creature contains the Buddha-nature within it, and that all goals are reached, after which life changes its form and continues. When he hears the ten thousand voices of the river together at the same time, he realizes that none is separate from any of the others, and when he does not try to attach himself to any one particular voice, the sound of the river becomes a great song, the music of life in its eternal perfection. Armed with this knowledge, he can love and respect all creatures.

## Critical Context

From his childhood, Hesse was interested in the Orient, and he visited India in 1911. His mother had been born in that country, and his father was a missionary there. Hesse went there, he said, "to see the sacred tree and snake (of Buddha) and to go back into that source of life where everything had begun and which signifies the Oneness of all phenomena." He later wrote of his "deep veneration of the spirit of the East, which in Indian or Chinese dress . . . has become my consolation and prophecy."

Hesse started *Siddhartha* in 1919 and finished it in 1922. The writing was interrupted for eighteen months while he immersed himself in the comparative study of religion. The major texts of Buddhism had been translated for the first time only twenty years previously, when Hesse was in his early twenties.

*Siddhartha* has always been one of Hesse's most popular novels, and, not surprisingly, it has appealed to the East as well as the West. It was translated into nine Indian dialects and also achieved great popularity in Japan. In the elegance of its style and in the simple yet profound philosophy of life it expresses, it is probably the Western novel which best captures the spirit of India. *Siddhartha* represents the culmination of a long fascination which the Western literary mind, particularly German Romantics such as Novalis, whom Hesse venerated, felt toward the East.

*Sources for Further Study*
Boulby, Mark. *Hermann Hesse: His Mind and Art*, 1967.
Paslick, Robert H. "Dialectic and Non-attachment: The Structure of Hermann Hesse's *Siddhartha*," in *Symposium*. XXVII (1973), pp. 64-75.
Shaw, Leroy. "Time and the Structure of Hermann Hesse's *Siddhartha*," in *Symposium*. IV (1957), pp. 204-224.
Timpe, Eugene F. "Hermann Hesse's *Siddhartha* and the *Bhagavad-Gita*," in *Comparative Literature*. XXII (1970), pp. 346-357.
Ziolkowski, Theodore. *The Novels of Hermann Hesse: A Study in Theme and Structure*, 1965.

*Bryan Aubrey*

# SIGISMUND
## From the Memories of a Baroque Polish Prince

*Author:* Lars Gustafsson (1936-    )
*Type of plot:* Magical realism
*Time of plot:* 1973
*Locale:* West Berlin; Västmanland, Sweden; Cracow, Poland; and East Berlin
*First published: Sigismund: Aus den Erinnerungen eines polnischen*
   *Barockfürsten*, 1976 (English translation, 1985)

>*Principal characters:*
>LARS, the narrator, a Swedish writer
>LAURA G., an artist and a friend of the narrator
>UNCLE STIG, the narrator's Swedish uncle
>AUNT CLARA, the narrator's Swedish aunt
>SIGISMUND III, King of Poland from 1587 to 1632

## The Novel

*Sigismund: From the Memories of a Baroque Polish Prince* explores the inner reality of man's existence through a series of loosely connected meditations, fantasies, and memories. The novel, written in the first person and often addressed directly to the reader, depicts the struggle of the narrator, a Swedish writer, to create an authentic identity despite the alienating forces of modern society. Alternately, he identifies with Sigismund III, King of Poland from 1587 to 1632 and with an alter ego, the painter Laura G., who journeys to Hell. He also plays a small role in an intergalactic war that ultimately resurrects Sigismund, and he re-creates scenes from his childhood in Sweden. Juxtaposed to his imaginative life are brief scenes that underscore the emptiness of his roles as intellectual and family man.

The main section of the novel, "Memories from Purgatory," begins with a strange anecdote that breaks down the distinction between reality and fiction. The story, told years in the past by a former professor, is "so unbelievable, so absurd, and so alien" that it jars the original audience as well as the reader. The narrator validates this world, however, by relating the story in the present tense and by identifying with its main character, "Prince W.'s flunky serf." He views the so-called ordinary world as the real absurdity and lives emotionally in his daydreams and fantasies. Meanwhile, his "stand-in" participates in this absurdity; he writes newspaper articles, discusses politics with his wife and friends, and tries to communicate with his children.

The public persona of the narrator conforms to the conditioning of a culture that rewards superficial cleverness and punishes any violation of the rules. Friends and students respect his ideas; colleagues envy his many accomplishments. As he goes through the motions, however, he secretly despises his petty bourgeois life. He is alienated from his work and emotionally detached from his wife and two children, who are unnamed. The only person who evokes any real feeling is his friend Zwatt, but he sublimates his desire for her into intellectual conversation and only obliquely hints at his feelings in a letter to her. On the surface, he is normal; his ideas are politically correct; his behavior is socially acceptable.

What he considers his real life—his philosophical speculations and fantasies—is richer and much less predictable. He regularly escapes to pastoral scenes from his childhood in Västmanland or loses himself in fantastical adventures. A comic strip, pasted on an outhouse wall, suddenly comes alive. Just as Flash Gordon breaks through the glass bubble that has imprisoned him for thirty years, so the narrator and the reader enter another level of reality. Perceiving further challenging of accepted notions of time and the material world, Sigismund begins to stir in his sarcophagus.

Perhaps the narrator is particularly obsessed with Sigismund because he too was a Swede fated to live in another country. Just as Sigismund unsuccessfully tried to unify Sweden and Poland, the narrator tries to integrate his memories of humus-filled lakes and solitary canals with the squalor of thirty-story tenements and the ugliness of the Berlin Wall. Trying to make sense of his life, he re-creates the stories of two people who played a significant part in his early development. Both his Uncle Stig and his Aunt Clara symbolize the possibility of asserting one's individuality in opposition to conventional expectations.

His Uncle Stig initially appears to have been a failure. A socialist, he is repeatedly cheated out of the profits from his inventions, because he refuses to deal with the capitalist system. He is finally defeated, not by the capitalists, but by his own loss of faith. His most spectacular invention is an aerodynamic bicycle, dedicated to the cause of socialism and world peace and designed to compete with an automobile. After he recovers from his seventy-mile-an-hour crash, he lives the rest of his long life a silent, ordinary man. Yet his attempt to create more satisfying alternatives to the status quo generates a metaphorical wind of freedom that sustains the narrator in his own moments of crisis.

The story of Aunt Clara has an opposite ending but suggests the same possibilities for freedom. Jilted by a socially prominent politician, she leaves home with a blind, slobbering beggar who is revealed to be a surreal incarnation of Homer. Clara dies of exposure after a few months of wandering through the rain, but the narrator believes that she dies "completely happy." The common denominator in both stories is the escape from self-imposed limitations and from the narrow restrictions of society.

The lessons from the past are interwoven with the narrator's vision of possibilities. A conversation with Laura G. about selling one's soul to the devil triggers an extended fantasy that divides the novel into two plots. The fictional Laura G. meets with the friendship delegation from Hell, negotiates with them on the price of her soul, and takes a sight-seeing trip to assess the living conditions of her eternal destination. Like the narrator, she is less interested in superficial enticements—enduring fame and huge sums of money—than in the possibility of understanding herself and the world. Her final demand, to be another person for a day, corresponds to the narrator's need to escape the prison of the isolated ego.

As these fantastic events are unfolding, the narrator frequently interrupts with comments on his fictional strategies in the novel, his opinion of his readers, and his interpretations of good and evil, heaven and hell, God and the devil, freedom and reality, and sanity and madness.

In the brief coda, "Sigismund Walks Again," the narrator appears to be overwhelmed by the darker side of this dichotomy. His wife and children have gone back to Sweden. Isolated in his apartment, he faces chaos and disintegration. At the point of despair, however, he once again affirms the power of the imagination to transform the sordid details of commonplace reality, and the novel ends in a double victory. Laura G. has been granted her request. Now a young man, she experiences the supreme horror and pleasure of being a completely different person. The narrator is rescued by the resurrected King Sigismund. Just before this climactic moment, the narrator repeats the idea that recurs throughout the novel and is the key to both the action and the theme: "We begin again. We never give up."

## The Characters

The similarities between the author and the narrator are deliberately emphasized in this fictionalized autobiography. Like the author, the narrator was reared in Sweden, attended the University of Uppsala, was a visiting professor in Germany, and is a writer named Lars. The novel is dedicated to Zwatt, one of the minor characters, and the narrator frequently comments on the progress or difficulties he encounters in writing *Sigismund*. Yet because Lars Gustafsson, and his protagonist, reject facile distinctions between reality and fiction, a complete identification of author and narrator is meaningless. In the same way that everyone fictionalizes his life, Gustafsson gives us a fragmented and fictionalized version of his. He is concerned with his inner, spiritual life, precisely what cannot be documented with factual accuracy.

His need to discover a meaning for his own life as well as human history leads to an unresolvable dialectic between freedom and security, belief and skepticism. He divorces himself from the mundane details of his outer life, because he sees no way to change the destructive forces of civilization. (Indeed, he seems to have little effect on his own children.) At the same time, his mind fixates on the most grotesque reminders of the sickness in Western culture. At breakfast, he engages in a carefully structured debate with his wife over an abstract political idea while mentally focusing on the image of a man who has burned himself alive. He curses the cleverness through which he has secured his position in society, yet his respectability suppresses his two greatest fears—"the fear of going crazy and the fear of being without money." Like Flash Gordon or Sigismund, he longs to break free. Only in his imagination, however, is he able to transcend the traps that he has created for himself.

Before he can achieve emotional freedom, he must come to terms with what he sees as the essential duality of the universe. His attempt to find an acceptable answer leads to an existential crisis. Close to madness, he contemplates giving up writing, implying that language is only another illusion. In the process of accepting his worst fear, he paradoxically affirms the power of the imagination. In an insane world where people are mass-bombed, he decides "it is probably not so odd that you get a desire to flee into a really elegant, deliciously balanced insanity." By surrendering to his imagination, even if it might appear to be madness, he realizes that humankind creates its own heaven or hell. Although he can find nothing to believe in beyond human existence and in spite of Auschwitz and Hiroshima, he affirms the power of human faith and love.

The other characters in the novel are primarily important as a reflection of the narrator or as a means of conveying his ideas. His interaction with his wife and children merely show his alienation from domestic life. Other characters, such as the Bulgarian poet-in-exile and his friend B., who is cheated by a theater agent, serve as examples of his social milieu or as a vehicle for him to work out his ideas. Other characters, such as his friend Zwatt, allow the narrator to reveal his emotional reactions. None of them is a fully realized character.

The most extended and fully developed of these figures is the artist Laura G., whose successful bargain with the devil parallels the narrator's quest. She is the mirror image of the narrator. She believes that it is possible to achieve perfection in her art, whereas the narrator is beset with both artistic and personal self-doubt. She actively pursues the answers to her metaphysical questions; the narrator frequently tortures himself with introspection and passively waits for Sigismund to save him. Her story adopts an independent life, and a large portion of the novel is devoted to her journey. The narrator, however, makes it clear that she is, like Sigismund, a projection of his own fantasies and desires.

### Themes and Meanings

The ability to create the meaning of one's life, to construct one's own dreams and possibilities, is the central theme of the novel. Often this means rejecting traditional concepts of reality or even walking the fine line between sanity and madness. Like the historical Sigismund, whose attempt to unify

Sweden and Poland resulted in hostility and wars that lasted twenty years after his death, and like the stories of Uncle Stig and Aunt Clara, the quest for political harmony, for freedom, for love, may appear to end in failure. Yet the belief in the possibility and the risks one must take to sustain that belief make the human condition bearable. Each attempt is a triumph as long as it is preserved in human memory. The fact that Uncle Stig's dreams are shattered in a rain-soaked field does not stop the Monteverdi wind that he has generated from blowing across time and turning the narrator in the direction of freedom.

Yet freedom itself is a problematic concept in the novel. Although the narrator is attracted to some of the promises of socialism, he finds few answers in politics of any kind. Neither capitalism nor socialism fosters creativity or individual expression. Symbolically, Gustafsson's vision of Hell, the ultimate socialist utopia, is static and boring. Secure from monetary worries, violence, even taxes, it nevertheless lacks passion or growth. Laura G. finds it tedious and is nonplussed at the absence of children or bicycles. As the narrator tells Zwatt, "We would live much worse off in a utopian society if there were no one there who loved us."

Above all, Gustafsson emphasizes the power of the individual. All the adventures, contradictions, and emotional struggles throughout the novel illustrate the courage required to think independently, to break away from conventional expectations, and, especially, to love. The concept of "I" is, in fact, cosmic in importance. "I" is God. Gustafsson rejects the idea of an omnipotent God, while he celebrates the human power to create divinity. The millions of people who have projected the finest of themselves onto the idea of Jesus or Muhammad have created a force for good that has become divine: "It is history that creates gods, and their power comes from all the love we have given them."

Gustafsson acknowledges the difficulty in portraying the power of the individual in an age dominated by cynicism and anonymity. Yet he argues that a deeper cynicism lies in the refusal to take responsibility for the heaven or hell of our own lives. To awaken his readers, Gustafsson uses stylistic techniques that reflect the theories of Walter Benjamin, the Marxist literary critic admired by the narrator and discussed briefly in the novel. Benjamin's belief in the need to shock the audience through the technique of "montage" provides the key to the structure of *Sigismund*. The discontinuity of the action, the interpolation of fantastic elements into the account of daily life, and the surrealistic images that blend together in the final section of the novel preclude a complacent reading of the work. Just as the narrator explicitly urges readers to create the meaning of their own lives, so he implicitly challenges them to create the meaning of the novel. He provides no easy answers, and he is not above using the shock value of a direct insult. As the novel moves toward its incredible denouement, the narrator forces readers to choose sides, to ally themselves with the visionary few or with the limited majority: "I suspect that most of my readers are privileged, dumb, without fantasies, and a little bit cruel." Those who do identify with the visionary world of the narrator must then expand their preconceived notions of the universe and accept the quixotic transformation at the end of the novel.

### Critical Context

*Sigismund* is the fourth in a series of five loosely connected novels. Although each of the novels in the series is complete in itself, they share a common theme: the importance of the individual and the necessity for self-definition. As Gustafsson noted in an interview conducted by one of his English translators: "More and more people are realizing that the meaning or sense of their lives is the one they have to give to themselves." All of his characters are engaged in this struggle, which provides the only possibility for freedom.

*En biodlares död* (1978; *The Death of a Beekeeper*, 1981), the only other work in Gustafsson's series that has been translated into English, asserts the significance of the individual, even over a hypothetical god. The protagonist declares, "if there is a god, then it is the task of the human being to be his negation." Like *Sigismund*, the novel expresses an optimistic belief in the human power to persevere and repeats the refrain that runs through all the novels: "We begin again. We never give up."

Most of Gustafsson's work has not been translated into English. Yet he is well-known in Sweden and Germany as a poet, dramatist, and literary critic, as well as a novelist. *Sigismund* is an excellent example, in both structure and theme, of the postmodern novel. Rooted in the tradition of Laurence Sterne and Miguel de Cervantes, as the epigraph from *Don Quixote of the Mancha* (1605, 1615) makes clear, the novel self-consciously plays with the conventional rules of fiction. The work of other, contemporary, writers, such as Vladimir Nabokov, Jorge Luis Borges, Julio Cortázar, John Barth, and John Fowles, provides a useful context for Gustafsson's achievements. He asks the timeless questions that place his novel with the best of this genre in world literature.

### Sources for Further Study

*Best Sellers*. Review. XLV (May, 1985), p. 48.
*Kirkus Reviews*. Review. LII (November 15, 1984), p. 1061.
*Library Journal*. Review. CX (February 1, 1985), p. 112.
*Publishers Weekly*. Review. CCXXVI (December 14, 1984), p. 38.
Voltz, Ruprecht, ed. *Gustafsson lesen*, 1986.

*Linnea Aycock*

# SILENCE

*Author:* Shusaku Endō (1923-        )
*Type of plot:* Historical novel
*Time of plot:* The seventeenth century
*Locale:* Nagasaki, Japan
*First published: Chimmoku*, 1966 (English translation, 1969)

> *Principal characters:*
> SEBASTIAN RODRIGUES, the seminarian who leads a mission to track down his former teacher to learn why he has renounced his faith
> CHRISTOVAO FERREIRA, a Jesuit missionary priest to Japan who apostatizes
> KICHIJIRO, Rodrigues' guide during his search for Ferreira, who defames then embraces the Christian faith
> INOUE, the Japanese magistrate who pursues and compels the Japanese Christians under torture to apostatize

## The Novel

*Silence* is a well-crafted historical novel that dramatizes Christianity's entrance into Japan and its near extinction in the early seventeenth century. During this time, the so-called hidden Christians were hunted down and forced to trample upon the *fumie*, a plaque symbolizing Christ, manufactured by their persecutors to facilitate their renunciation of their faith. Shusaku Endō tells roughly the first half of his story primarily through the correspondence of a young Portuguese seminarian, Sebastian Rodrigues, who journeys to Japan with two other students to learn why their former mentor, Father Christovao Ferreira, has renounced his faith in Christ. As the story unravels, Endō shifts to an omniscient narrator who reveals the slow and painful movement in Rodrigues, as he begins to understand the plight of Japanese Christians struggling to make this Western faith their own and eventually identifies with the outward apostasy his flock has performed.

A prologue begins the novel, explaining the circumstances of the Japanese missionaries in the early seventeenth century and the events that lead a group of Portuguese seminarians to investigate the reports about Ferreira. A renowned theologian and missionary, Ferreira had spent thirty years building the church in Japan when word arrived in Portugal that he had abandoned his faith. Three of his former students are baffled by this report and, wondering if it were not mere propaganda sent out by the Japanese or by their Dutch rivals, determine to discover why "their much admired teacher... faced with the possibility of a glorious martyrdom, has grovelled like a dog before the infidel." Two years pass before the seminarians can gain approval from their superiors to embark finally upon a year's journey to the shores of Japan.

They learn quickly the awful news of social upheaval, of the Shimabara revolt—which prohibits Portuguese ships from sailing to Japan—and they are forced to hire a Chinese vessel and the conniving, drunken Japanese guide, Kichijiro, a man Rodrigues immediately suspects is vacillating and unreliable, a shifty character not to be trusted. He later learns that Kichijiro is a "former Christian" who repudiated his faith to avoid martyrdom, and this increases Rodrigues' contempt for him. When one of the three travelers falls ill, the investigative mission falls to the young seminarians, Rodrigues and Francisco Garrpe.

Four letters from Rodrigues addressed to his superiors in Portugal now further the story. As the priests land near Nagasaki, Kichijiro has no trouble helping them locate Christians among poor inhabitants of the village of Tomogi, and they are given accommodations in a mountainside hut by the farmers and fishermen who travel secretly to them for the Mass. Impressed by their devout faith in the midst of great persecution, especially in view of what he has seen in Kichijiro, Father Rodrigues ascribes a reason for Christianity's success for which his missionary training had not prepared him:

> The reason our religion has penetrated this territory like water flowing into dry earth is that it has given to this group of people a human warmth they never previously knew. For the first time they have met men who treated them like human beings.

Christianity's prime appeal, he muses, is not to the well satisfied, but the destitute: "[I]t is easy enough," Rodrigues writes, "to die for the good and beautiful; the hard thing to do is to die for the miserable and the corrupt." Ironically, Rodrigues imagines a glorious martyrdom for himself, but his glib pontificating about the state of Japanese faith rings hollow; it is not the priest—in the place of Christ—who is called upon to "die" for anyone. Rather, he soon discovers, it is the heroic Japanese who are martyred in the place of their stubborn priests.

Emblematic of this is the dramatic martyrdom of the young Christian Yuki. To prevent her non-Christian lover from trampling the *fumie*, she lays her head on the plaque; if he steps on it to save his life, he must step on her face. In his refusal, both are condemned and executed. Amid the escalating horrors, Rodrigues himself, after having explained away the doubts of Kichijiro, challenges Heaven, "Dear God . . . why are you silent? How can you stand by and watch?" He is himself eventually captured and compelled to watch whole villages martyred, and his companion Garrpe drowns while swimming after a boat from which bound Christians will be cast into the sea.

Rodrigues' major crisis comes in the presence of Ferreira, the priest he has come to question. While the two debate the viability of Japanese Christianity in overly intellectualized terms, Rodrigues comes to the realization that Ferreira's apostasy as well as Kichijiro's—and, later, his own—can be interpreted as an act of sacrificial love, to save their flock from martyrdom. Following this confrontation, he is brought before the magistrate a final time to step on the *fumie*; urged by the face of Christ, "who came to be trampled on by men," Rodrigues chooses apostasy, no longer to be identified with Christ or the Church. The novel's final scene finds the apostate priest giving absolution to the once-despised Kichijiro, finally able to accept him as his brother. As "the last priest in the land," he understand that, indeed, God was not silent; "even if he had been silent, my life until this day would have spoken of Him." Rodrigues has found reconciliation for Kichijiro and for himself.

### The Characters

*Silence* ultimately is the spiritual odyssey of Sebastian Rodrigues, a man transformed before the reader's eyes from a naïve young priest with textbook theories about evangelism and vague aspirations toward martyrdom into a mature man who understands that conventionalized Western Christianity must be "translated" to survive and thrive in Eastern soil. As the novel moves from his letters to the omniscient narrator who explains his inner thoughts and motivations, Rodrigues learns that to renounce his faith by stepping on the *fumie* is to renounce only a "version" of institutionalized Christianity that bears little relation to the life of Christ himself. It is utterly fitting, then, that it is Christ's face on the *fumie* which compels him to apostatize. Upon hearing Kichijiro's confession, he believed that

> his fellow priests would condemn his act as sacrilege; but even if he was betraying them, he was not betraying his Lord. He loved him now in a different way than before. Everything that had taken place until now had been necessary to bring him to this love.

In his apostasy, Rodrigues learns to love the unlovely, to embrace as his brother the Kichijiro whom he once rejected as a betrayer. Here, then, he is asked to translate his faith into Eastern sensibilities.

Kichijiro's character appears to Western readers as a Judas figure, but to Endō, his devotion to the suffering martyrs which compels his betrayals of the priests makes him worthy of a real but painful salvation. Kichijiro represents what one critic calls a more "maternal, forgiving" Christ figure, who will "accept human beings in their weakened, sinful state so long as their shortcomings are compensated by a willingness to love others and share in their private burdens." By confessing his weakness, Kichijiro emerges as a more noble figure than Father Ferreira, a shadowy presence in the story until he confronts Rodrigues. Ferreira emerges as a pragmatist who apostatizes not so much to save the Japanese from martyrdom, but because he came to believe that Christianity is inappropriate for the East, and, if inappropriate, not worth dying for.

It is left to Inoue, the Japanese magistrate, however, to raise this most crucial issue authentically, namely, whether Christianity is not simply too alien to Japanese culture to survive. Cool and calm, like Fyodor Dostoesvki's Grand Inqusitor, Inoue gives voice to the doubts of hundreds of Japanese intellectuals among Endō's contemporaries: "Japan is not suited to the teaching of Christianity. . . . You were defeated by the swamp of Japan," Inoue challenges. Rodrigues' answer is also Endō's: "My struggle was with Christianity in my own heart."

*Themes and Meanings*

*Silence* is a dark, epistolary novel of apostasy and betrayal, a tale of great faith and faithlessness among both Western and Eastern men, men whose integrity as believers and as human beings is under constant attack. While Father Ferreira believes that Christianity cannot survive in Japan—"The sapling I brought quickly decayed to its roots in this swamp"—it is clear that Endō believes that it is Western Christianity that has trouble taking root, and that a Gospel more responsive to the Eastern perspective must be brought to the people of Japan.

It is this more Eastern view that Father Rodrigues comes to understand and embrace, an "apostate faith" that sees devotion to the individual superseding allegiance to institutionalized religion. The "silence" of the title is God's silence, His apparent willingness to allow the acute suffering of his people without explanation. It is this silence, however, which Rodrigues eventually recognizes as the voice of Christ.

Rodrigues' capture by the authorities, seemingly inevitable from the start, is nevertheless brought off with drama and suspense as the reader wonders whether Rodrigues' faith will survive. In contrast with Ferreira's confrontation with Inoue, the Japanese magistrate who embodies a very contemporary marriage of intellect linked to a detached humanity, Rodrigues emerges as a stalwart believer, affirming the presence of God even in his apparent absence. *Silence* is based on the historical fact that at the beginning of the seventeenth century, the Edo emperors came to the conclusion that Christianity did not "fit" Japan, banishing Christian missionaries and persecuting their flocks of converts. Endō turns that conclusion on its head, establishing that, in fact, Christianity and Christ fit nowhere, even in the West, yet they also fit every place where men and women strive for dignity and hope. Endō's Christ responds faithfully to man's homelessness in the world, his loneliness, offering compensation for the pain of this brief life in eternity.

## Critical Context

Because so few of his lighter, more comic novels and his numerous historical and theological essays—works no less interesting and provoking than his
other works—are available to Western readers, it is possible to form a view
of Endō as a rather somber, overly moralistic writer. Certainly, if one knew
only Endō's interpretive biography, *Iesu no shōgai* (1973; *A Life of Jesus*,
1973), and his historical novels, *Silence* and *Samurai* (1980; *The Samurai*,
1982), one would gain a distorted picture of both his range of concerns and
his innovation as a writer. Endō has proved himself to be a master of light
comedy as well as serious contemporary drama.

Certainly, however, *Silence* is rightly regarded as Endō's major work and
clearly has drawn the most critical attention and applause in the West.
*Silence* dramatizes and authenticates the dismal record of Christianity in
Japan, bitterly chronicling both the heroism and shallow ambitions of the
missionaries who dared to invade the Japanese shores in the seventeenth century and the moral malaise of the Japanese themselves, who first welcomed
the visitors and then condemned them to brutal martyrdom. Endō's *Silence*
has proved popular enough to be produced as a film, and it has also been
adapted for the stage in a version titled *Ogon no kuni* (1966; *The Golden
Country*, 1970).

Endō's keen insights into the failure of Christianity to take root in Japanese soil emanate from his own childhood conversion to Catholicism, a
Catholicism tempered by an education in France, where he was exposed
to such Catholic writers as François Mauriac, Paul Claudel, and Georges
Bernanos. Endō recognizes that as a Japanese Christian he is a walking
oxymoron. His own faith, he candidly admits, has been a struggle against
tradition and cultural identity. This clear sense of his novelistic task—and the
problematic nature of writing religious fiction in irreligious Japan—has produced in *Silence* the most remarkable and unlikely fiction in the postwar era,
and has rightfully earned for him his reputation as one of Japan's foremost
novelists alongside Yukio Mishima and Yasunari Kawabata.

Ultimately, Endō shares the vision of Saint Cyril of Jerusalem, his ancient
brother in the Catholic faith who once wrote, "The dragon sits by the side of
the road, watching those who pass. Beware lest he devour you. We go to the
Father of Souls, but it is necessary to pass by the dragon." In commenting on
this passing, the American Catholic writer, Flannery O'Connor, once remarked that "No matter what form the dragon may take, it is of this mysterious passage past him, or into his jaws, that stories of any depth will be concerned to tell, and this being the case, it requires considerable courage at any
time, in any country, not to turn away from the storyteller." Shusaku Endō
refuses to turn away from the dragon or the storyteller and asks of his twentieth century audience—East or West—the same courage.

*Sources for Further Study*

Elliot, William. "Shusaku Endō: A Christian Voice in Japanese Literature," in *The Christian Century*. LXXXIII (September 21, 1966), pp. 1147-1148.

Gallagher, Michael. "A Japanese Catholic Novel," in *Commonweal*. LXXXV (November 4, 1966), pp. 136-137.

Mathy, Francis. "Shusaku Endō: Japanese Catholic Novelist," in *Thought*. XLII (Winter, 1967), pp. 585-614.

Rimer, J. Thomas. *Modern Japanese Fiction and Its Traditions*, 1978.

Startzman, Eugene. "Can There Be Faith in Betrayal: A Review of *Silence*," in *Christianity Today*. XXVIII (October 19, 1984), pp. 62-63.

*Bruce L. Edwards*

# THE SILENT CRY

*Author:* Kenzaburō Ōe (1935-     )
*Type of plot:* Psychological realism
*Time of plot:* The early 1960's
*Locale:* The Okubo village in Shikoku, Japan, and Tokyo
*First published: Man'en san'nen no futtoboru*, 1967 (English translation, 1974)

> *Principal characters:*
> MITSUSABURO (MITSU) NEDOKORO, the narrator, who is
>      withdrawn and world-weary
> TAKASHI NEDOKORO, a reformed student-activist
> NATSUMI NEDOKORO, Mitsu's wife, who is prone to alcohol
>      abuse
> THE EMPEROR, a Korean, a former laborer and now owner of
>      a supermarket chain

## The Novel

*The Silent Cry* tells of two brothers, Mitsusaburo ("Mitsu") and Takashi Nedokoro, who return to their native village in Southeast Japan in order to find out about their family's involvement in a peasant riot in 1860, and perhaps to begin a new life. The course of the events is related by Mitsu; far from being linear and objective, his deliberately stylized account is characterized by subjective similes and frequent excursions into the past.

The novel opens at predawn with the narrator's descent into a septic-tank pit at his Tokyo home. While Mitsu is alone on the wet ground, his thoughts introduce all the events and topics, which like gigantic leitmotifs manifest the novel's underlying symbolic structure. Suffering from the loss "of some ardent sense of expectation," Mitsu remembers the bizarre suicide of his best friend, with whom he shared a successful career translating books about animals: The friend painted his head red, "stripped, thrust a cucumber up his anus, and hanged himself." The narrator is convinced that this act was a silent cry to tell some important truth. With clues too equivocal, however, Mitsu cannot grasp what it might be and must go on with life quite literally half blind from a childhood accident which has rendered his right eye useless.

Upon his return from America, Takashi challenges Mitsu, whose wife has taken solace in cheap whiskey since their mentally retarded baby was given away to an institution. Takashi, who calls his brother a rat, confronts him with the idea of starting anew in their native village. There, "the Emperor," a local upstart, plans to buy the family's hundred-year-old storehouse in order to use it as a fancy restaurant in Tokyo. Furthermore, Takashi wants to learn the truth about their great-grandfather, who built the storehouse, and his younger brother, who led the peasant youths during the 1860 uprising. Supported by some historical evidence, Mitsu insists that the younger brother had sold out and died a member of the establishment; this is a vision which Takashi refuses to accept.

Upon their arrival in Okubo, Mitsu soon sets up solitary residence in the storehouse and refuses to become involved in the life of the village. Takashi, who brought with him a young mechanic, Hoshio, and a teenage girl, Momoko, takes a liking to Mitsu's wife Natsumi and begins to get active on behalf of the village's young men's association, whose chicken farm has been wiped out as a result of food scarcity and an early cold. His commitment brings Takashi into conflict with the Emperor, the financial backer of the farm whose supermarket (one of a huge chain) has ruined the other stores in the village.

After the chicken disaster, Takashi sets up a football team to train the village youths. In his conversations with Mitsu, Takashi relishes his self-fashioned role of "effective evildoer," and his inspirational addresses to his young followers on New Year's Eve exploit tales from the 1860 uprising.

Cleverly, Takashi transforms an official "giveaway" at the supermarket into an episode of looting and encourages the villagers to participate in this lawless act. The fire of enthusiasm for the plundering is fanned by the well-known fact that the Emperor was once one of the Korean forced laborers who were brought to the village during World War II. Takashi has an additional emotional investment in the riot, since his elder brother S, upon his return from the war, was slain under controversial circumstances in the Korean settlement. Throughout the second day of what Takashi self-consciously terms a riot of the imagination, the leader rallies support by establishing a link to 1860. His men perform a topical version of the old ritualistic Nembutsu dance and coerce every household into "disgracing" itself by participating in the organized looting.

The following morning brings to Mitsu Hoshio's eyewitness account of Takashi's sexual intercourse with Natsumi; Takashi also confesses to her that he is torn between a desire for intense self-punishment and an impulse to be "a man of violence." Confronting Mitsu, his brother is defiant and hints at his possession of a truth of such import that the teller—like Mitsu's friend who killed himself—will not be able to live.

Just as Mitsu has returned to a translation which keeps him detached and occupied, Natsumi brings news that Takashi has tried to rape and has killed a village girl and, deserted by his followers, is awaiting collective revenge. In the main house, Mitsu fiercely challenges his brother and insists that the deed was an accident and the murder Takashi's invention. Takashi, however, insists that he is guilty and retires with Mitsu to the storehouse.

In the aged building, Takashi confides his final truth to his brother. After the war, while living with faraway relatives, he initiated sexual relations with his mildly retarded sister. His sister followed his instructions for secrecy to the point of inventing a rape when she got pregnant; after her abortion and sterilization, she came to him searching for closeness. Horrified at her request immediately after the operation, Takashi rejected and slapped her. The next morning, his sister killed herself. Mitsu reacts coldly and accuses his brother that he, despite his need for self-punishment, will always find a "way out." He even rejects Takashi's offer of his retinas after his death and leaves him. Later that night, Takashi shoots himself, and his brother is left with a dream about a "retrial."

When the Emperor finally comes into Okubo and orders the dismantling of the storehouse, a cellar is discovered where their great-grandfather's younger brother lived in hiding after 1860, mysteriously reappearing above ground only once in 1871 to lead a nonviolent, successful upheaval. Shaken, Mitsu decides that he has misjudged his great-uncle and his brother and at night climbs into the dank cellar, thus entering his second pit at the novel's close. There Mitsu realizes that it is he who cannot confront his "agonizing fear of death" and rise "above his private hell," as the other two Nedokoros have done. Instead, he relies on a newly found notion of tenderness, which he discovered in a picture of the Buddhist Hell that his great-grandfather commissioned after the 1860 rising.

Greeted by his wife, the narrator leaves the pit and decides to bring back his son from the institution and to launch himself into a new job. Once, Takashi insisted that the touchstone for humanity after a possible nuclear war would be the decision regarding reconstruction of zoos; now, Mitsu will go as translator on an African expedition which aims to capture elephants for Japan.

## The Characters

Mitsusaburo Nedokoro might strike the reader as being the most negative character of *The Silent Cry*; after all, he voluntarily isolates himself from life and cherishes a "profound insensitivity" toward others. Still, it is essential to remember that "the rat" is set on his "downhill journey" by the double impact of traumatizing blows; the loss of his retarded son and the suicide of his best friend have anesthetized him to the point where Mitsu stubbornly insists that even a rat has an identity.

His apparent intellectual delight in destroying his brother's comfortable fantasies of the past are the end result of his merciless use of his analytical capabilities and his refusal to live a life built on lies. There is a silent heroism in Mitsu's decision that all the "roots" linking him to his native village are ultimately as fictional as the old story that their family name means "the soul's roots" in an Okinawan dialect. The protagonist-narrator's indifference also serves as a means of surviving the insults of his brother, who clandestinely sells all of their estate and seduces his wife. In the end, Mitsu is saved by Natsumi, whose tenderness fills his inner abyss. Her drinking helped to drive her husband into isolation, but her final appearance at the pit offers the chance of redemption.

Takashi's restless attempts at healing through action the inner wound his sister's suicide inflicted stands in radical opposition to the detachment of his older brother. Takashi is violent both in his self-punishment (as in his masochistic encounter with a black prostitute whom he asks to "rape" him) and in his rebellion. His grandest action, the instigation of communal looting, earns for him the admiration of the local priest, who greets the upheaval as a sign that the young men have finally embarked on a farsighted course of action and gained freedom by having "created of their own free will a situation that can't be cleared up by their own free will, and have taken responsibility for it." This, too, describes what Takashi would like to achieve for himself by proclaiming himself a murderer; in the cruelest moment of *The Silent Cry*, however, his brother's denial of Takashi's capacity to carry out such an act of existential courage triggers his suicide.

Yet despite the riot's collapse, Takashi's imagination brings a desperately needed cultural revival. Most important, the village takes up his resurrection of the Nembutsu dance, a tradition which had been lost.

## Themes and Meanings

At the heart of *The Silent Cry* is a conflict centered on man's response to the chaotic and abysmal in his life. Both Mitsu and Takashi must cope with the unspeakable horror of life; whereas the older brother cannot decipher the silent messages of suffering sent to him, Takashi is torn by his inability to reveal his painful truth. In these brothers, Kenzaburō Ōe's novel presents two alternatives for coming to terms with an uncaring universe; each of the brother's solutions has its shortcomings and is far from being a simple guide.

Furthermore, *The Silent Cry* is concerned with the influence of the past and the possibility of a present reenactment of a bygone power struggle. The strange doubling of the novel, which inevitably places Mitsu and Takashi in the roles of their ancestral antagonists, also raises the question of social responsibility versus individual care of the self.

Again, Ōe refuses easy answers. As in the past, when the young brother sacrificed his life (in his voluntary self-incarceration in the cellar) and thus let the conservative element continue the family line, there is again a gentle fusion of the two elements. Thus, in the final battle between historical fact and fictional truth, it is Takashi's vision of the world as a collective story that triumphs. Takashi enriches this story with his own contribution when he, like his favorite ancestor, enters the village's cultural history as one of the "spirits" of the Nembutsu dance. It is Mitsu, however, whom the author leads out of the village to continue life and care for Natsumi and Takashi's illegitimate child, in whom the Nedokoro family will survive.

## Critical Context

*The Silent Cry* bears the traits of Ōe's fascination with existentialism, with which his study of French literature has thoroughly acquainted him, and whose influence has made Ōe the foremost postmodern author of Japan. Mitsu's hints at the "nausea" with which he regards his brother's activities are a direct allusion to Jean-Paul Sartre's novel of the same name, *La Nausée* (1938; *Nausea*, 1949). With his insistence on a freely conceived murder as an act of existential liberation, Takashi finds himself on the same level as the protagonist of Albert Camus' *L'Étranger* (1942; *The Stranger*, 1946).

*The Silent Cry* achieves a vision which enables Ōe to close on a note of tenderness for the weak and the promise of a final defeat of futility for the adventurous. As with the protagonist of his earlier novel, *Kojinteki na taiken* (1964; *A Personal Matter*, 1968), Mitsu's ultimate decision to bring his retarded son into his family constitutes a liberating moment in its submission to primal human values in the face of inexplicable truths and too many silent cries. As for the heroic, Takashi's death shows the achievement of meaning on a mythic or fictional plane; like Mitsu's friend, he will be remembered.

## Sources for Further Study

Kimball, Arthur G. *Crisis in Identity and Contemporary Japanese Novels*, 1973.

Ōe, Kenzaburō. "A Game of Football," in *Japan Quarterly*. October-December, 1973, pp. 428-429.

Sakurai, Emiko. "Kenzaburō Ōe: The Early Years," in *World Literature Today*. LVIII (Summer, 1984), pp. 370-373.

Wilson, Michiko N. "A Narrative of Simultaneity: *The Football Game of the First Year of Manen*," in *The Marginal World of Ōe Kenzaburō*, 1986.

Yamanouchi, Hisaaki. *The Search of Authenticity in Modern Japanese Literature*, 1978.

*Reinhart Lutz*

# THE SILESIAN TETRALOGY

*Author:* Horst Bienek (1930-      )
*Type of plot:* Poetic realism
*Time of plot:* 1939-1945
*Locale:* Gleiwitz, Upper Silesia (then a border area between Germany and Poland)
*First published:* 1975-1982: *Die erste Polka*, 1975 (*The First Polka*, 1978); *Septemberlicht*, 1977 (*September Light*, 1987); *Zeit ohne Glocken*, 1979; *Erde und Feuer*, 1982

*Principal characters:*

VALESKA PIONTEK, a piano teacher, the mother of Irma and Josel

LEO MARIA PIONTEK, her ailing husband, a former photographer

JOSEL, her son, who is fifteen years old in the first novel and later becomes a soldier

IRMA, her daughter, who marries a German soldier in the first novel and later becomes widowed

ULLA OSSADNIK, Valeska's most promising piano student, later a famous pianist, the childhood sweetheart of Josel

WILLI WONDRAK, Valeska's brother, a lawyer and her closest business associate

GEORG MONTAG, a magistrate with Jewish ancestry who is working on a biography of the Polish politician Wojciech Korfanty

## The Novels

The first three books of the Silesian tetralogy narrate the fate of the border city of Gleiwitz (Gliwice) and its inhabitants on three single days before and during World War II: August 31, 1939, the night before the outbreak of the war in *The First Polka*; September 4, 1939, in *September Light*; and Good Friday, 1943, in *Zeit ohne Glocken*. The last novel, *Erde und Feuer*, concludes the tetralogy with events surrounding the end of the war and the westward flight of many of the city's inhabitants. The omniscient narrator chronologically recounts the events of the family of the matriarch Valeska Piontek and her family—and to a lesser extent their acquaintances.

*The First Polka* revolves around the wedding of Irma Piontek and a soldier in the Third Reich, whom she met just days before. While the couple is married by the judge and not by the archpriest Pattas (a fact that troubles the devout Catholic Valeska immensely), the guests gather for the wedding celebration in the most exclusive hotel in town. On their way to the hotel, the two teenagers Ulla Ossadnik and Andreas, Valeska's nephew, witness a strange civilian attack on the radio station in Gleiwitz. Several men get out of limousines and carry what looks like a body into the station. As it turns out, this incident, staged by the Nazis themselves, was then interpreted as an attack on the radio transmitter by Polish Nationalists and was used as grounds for the invasion of Poland by Nazi Germany.

Uneasy about the events they have just witnessed but unaware of the immense political ramifications, the youngsters resume their trip to the hotel, where the wedding celebration has reached its climax. The dancing of the polka is taken as an expression of the ethnic qualities of the people in this border region. For the teenagers, this dance signifies a rite of passage in more than one sense. It is a culmination of their budding erotic feelings, and it opens the door to adulthood for them. (It is the first time they have danced the polka.) On a more somber note, it is also the last day of peace, the last day of innocence for them. In a few hours, the war will prematurely turn them into adults.

After much drinking and dancing, the fateful night ends with the bride's brother, Josel Piontek, having to leave town. He is under the impression that he killed a German soldier who tried to rape Ulla, his childhood sweetheart, on their way home. The novel closes with Valeska's return from the hotel to her bedridden husband, Leo Maria Piontek. Outwardly, he is suffering from asthma, but inwardly he is ailing from a general lack of will to live with a domineering wife who smothers her family with her love. As Valeska is describing the private events of the wedding, Leo Maria tells her about the public aspects of the night, the strange interruption of the radio program, followed by agitated Polish voices and then by silence.

The second novel, *September Light*, begins with the funeral of Leo Maria attended by the whole town. After the conclusion of this festive and spectacular event (the music of Frédéric Chopin is played on a gramophone, a fact so unusual that Valeska had to obtain permission for it from Pattas) and the departure of the more or less sincere mourners from the cemetery, another very quiet funeral takes place. It is that of Georg Montag, a "retired" magistrate who, as the Nazi ideology became stronger, rediscovered his Jewish ancestry. His father had attempted to erase their religious and cultural heritage by rearing Georg as a Catholic and by hiding Georg's grandfather in the house because he looked too Jewish. Georg Montag committed suicide after completing his life's work, a biography of Wojciech Korfanty, a Polish politician who fought for the independence of Silesia and against corruption in his own government.

As the war claims its first victim in Georg Montag, Ulla's parents, Franz and Anna Ossadnik, hope to profit from the war, which will attach more importance to Franz's job as a railroad engineer. Anna, despite her six children, manages to read romantic adventure novels and looks forward to her husband's promotion in hopes of improving their limited income.

In the next novel, *Zeit ohne Glocken*, the Ossadniks indeed profit from the new regime. The improvement in their living standard, however, is accompanied by pangs of conscience on Franz's part, because he knows that he is transporting Jews to the concentration camp. When he is on the brink of volunteering for the army to escape his complicity, however, his wife convinces him to continue, because their standard of living had never been as high as it is during the latter stages of the war. The winners—Valeska had also profited from the war with real estate speculation—are outnumbered by the victims and the sacrifices: Arthur Silbergleit, a Jewish writer who returned to his hometown, is transported to a concentration camp and put to death in a gas chamber.

The war has entered a new stage in which all personal and material resources are mobilized. With Good Friday, 1943, the bells, customarily silent on this church holiday, will be silent forever. They are confiscated and turned into war matériel. Old men and boys are recruited for the national defense. The widowed Irma has since remarried and is about to give birth to her second child. Folk myth and religious symbolism surrounding Good Friday cast their dark shadows on the impending birth.

The ominous events on Good Friday anticipate the content of the last book, *Erde und Feuer*: the approach of Russian soldiers in January/ February, 1945. The Reich is losing the war, and all signs point to capitulation: A feverish rush to the railroad stations begins as people hurry to obtain a place on westbound trains. Work camp inmates regain their freedom because their watchmen disappeared during the night. All but the lowest party officials have deserted the town for the West. The remaining population prepares for the Russians' advance by burning the portraits of Adolf Hitler with which they decorated their homes, schools, businesses, and offices to endear themselves to prying Nazi Party officials. Incriminating documents are destroyed, and the white flags of surrender are prepared. Abandoned houses and stores are looted by ordinary citizens. The inhabitants of Gleiwitz perform these tasks with the quiet and efficient routine of a border people which is accustomed to changing political regimes.

Valeska and her daughters and granddaughters, along with her brother and his wife, flee to Ulla in Dresden, the only common address in the West that they and her son, Josel, have. As they arrive, Josel, who is a soldier by now, has been wounded and is hospitalized in Dresden. As he contacts Ulla, Valeska attempts to look for Ulla but is surprised by a fierce bombing raid which sets Dresden aflame for five days and nights. With its members scattered over the burning city, the story of the Piontek family ends.

In Gleiwitz, Ulla's father, Franz Ossadnik, is arrested by the Russians, and the remaining family members are forced to dismantle the factories. The Silesian tetralogy thus concludes with the displacement of its central character, Valeska, and her family. The remaining inhabitants of Gleiwitz will presumably adjust to the new political system as they had to the previous ones.

## The Characters

The events and characters in these novels are to some extent autobiographical. The main character, Valeska Piontek, is named and modeled after Horst Bienek's own mother. Both are piano teachers, and both are married to sickly men who are in early retirement. In the novel, Valeska is portrayed as a strong, domineering mother figure who, on the one hand, teaches Chopin even though it is officially forbidden, and on the other hand is a shrewd businesswoman profiting from real estate speculation. With her own brand of Catholicism, rich with colorful elements of a border region, and her possessive love for her children, Valeska symbolizes Silesia with its unique qualities of a land between two cultures.

Her husband, Leo Maria, appears to be her complete opposite. He is not commercially successful in his photography studio; instead, he takes excursions into the Silesian countryside to photograph old towers and other landmarks. As his wife meddles in the studio, his last refuge of privacy, he takes to his bed and dies a few years later. Leo Maria's love for Silesia, as exemplified in his secret production of political leaflets against the war propaganda, is devoid of the economic opportunism characteristic of his efficient wife.

His son, Josel, combines character traits of both parents: He is a member of the Hitler Youth and simultaneously a participant in the Bosco Bund, a religious organization. He stands up for his beliefs (his love of Dostoevski) but at the same time takes advantage of the soldiers whom the war has brought into town. He rents them an empty shed where they can be alone with their women.

## Themes and Meanings

Remembering the time, place, and atmosphere of childhood is a central theme in the Silesian tetralogy. The author is able to recapture the sensual qualities, the sounds and smells, as well as the myths, religious qualities, language mixture, and history of a region no longer accessible for the people who fled it after the war. The motifs of Leo Maria's photography, Montag's life's work (the Korfanty biography), and the almost filmic quality of the remembered image of a bygone milieu underscore one purpose of the novel: to give permanence to a fleeting moment in history. The task of the writer is summarized in the magistrate Montag's allegorical story about the three bridges over the Klodnitz River: All are destroyed, and only one bridge, made of paper, leads the people who trust it across the water. Bienek thus builds such a bridge made of paper into the past by writing against the inevitable floods of forgetfulness. The most predominant theme, however, is the analysis of the everyday Fascism which slowly eroded the already well-worn moral fiber of average citizens in the days preceding World War II.

Another major concern in the tetralogy is to show the unheroic side of wartime existence, with its quiet, unspectacular catastrophes. Gunfire can be heard only in the background, and death reaches the town only in the form of letters informing the families about the deaths of husbands, fathers, sons, and brothers killed in action.

Focusing on the individual consciences of his characters, the narrator creates history on a personal level which incorporates events from the public domain as they affect the private lives of his characters. At the same time Bienek shows how the average citizen participated in Fascism without necessarily being aware of doing so. The fate of the train engineer, Franz Ossadnik, who transports Jews to Birkenau illustrates this blindness for the political consequences of the characters' actions: Franz's wife is quite surprised when the Russians arrest him and label him a Fascist. Her perplexed comment that Franz had never even been to Italy indicates that, for her, politics are made by others, and Franz was merely doing his duty.

The narrative thus oscillates between the private and the public, between autobiography and historical account, and culminates in the interweaving of both narrative levels in the symbolic events such as the simultaneity of the wedding celebration and the radio transmitter incident. The theme of frontiers, between childhood and youth, between two historical eras, between two peoples, two cultures, and two languages, unites both narrative levels, the realistic and the symbolic.

The narrative moves slowly in chronological order, almost in the old-fashioned manner of nineteenth century realists such as Theodor Fontane. One can also detect traces of Russian realism as the individuals are shown among their family and their circle of friends against the backdrop of their historical situation.

In particular, Bienek acknowledges his debt to the narrative tradition of the American South, specifically to William Faulkner, Thomas Wolfe, Truman Capote, and Carson McCullers. Bienek labels his style "poetic" realism, because he sees the writer as one who travels the frontiers between consciousness and reality. The motif of the frontier is thus both a thematic and stylistic device to give the novels a metaphysical dimension beyond the autobiographical and historical levels of meaning.

*Critical Context*

The Silesian tetralogy is Bienek's most substantial work. Previously, he had produced only smaller volumes of prose and poetry. His earlier works include *Traumbuch eines Gefangenen* (1957; a prisoner's dream book), *Die Zelle* (1968; *The Cell*, 1972), *Bakunin, eine Invention* (1970; *Bakunin, an Invention*, 1977), and several small volumes of poetry. The time span being re-created by these volumes is the more recent past of Bienek himself, the time and experience of his physical and psychological suffering during early adulthood. Bienek was arrested in the German Democratic Republic by the Russians when he was only twenty-one years old and was sentenced to twenty-five years of forced labor in the notorious camp of Varkuta in the Gulag Archipelago. He was released in 1955, after four years of incarceration. His writing in these earlier volumes centered on the traumatic experience of imprisonment and suffering. It is during this time that he aesthetically relates to Jean Cayrol's "lazarene literature," of which traces can still be found in the Silesian tetralogy, especially in the fate of the Jews Montag and Silbergleit.

After aesthetically coming to terms with his more recent past, Bienek found it necessary to take another step back in time, back into his childhood. His autobiographical past coincides with the historical period of Germany's darkest hours. As such, it forms a complex poetic analysis of Fascism as it manifests itself in the lives of average people in everyday situations. Bienek shows how normal human beings are forced to produce the ideology of a system in themselves, how a general sense of dissatisfaction can be turned against an artificially created image of an enemy, and how people learn to take advantage of the opportunities a system provides—even though they realize that it is not morally proper to do so. The author also shows how these changes create a general sense of uncertainty and thus moral ambiguity.

Motifs in Bienek's poetry thematically centering on his childhood in Gleiwitz recur in the Silesian tetralogy. These four volumes represent his coming-of-age as a full-fledged novelist in the tradition of Günter Grass, a contemporary who recovers the ethnic qualities of Danzig during a similar time span.

*Sources for Further Study*

Frühwald, Wolfgang. "Sprache als Heimat: Zu Horst Bieneks Gleiwitzer Tetralogie," in *Arbitrium: Zeitschrift für Rezensionen zur germanistischen Literaturwissenschaft*, 1984.

Hamburger, Michael. "Dance to the Sound of Gunfire," in *The Times Literary Supplement*. March 25, 1977, p. 378.

Kott, Jan. "*The First Polka*: Coming of War, Coming of Age," in *The New York Times Book Review*. LXXXIX (April 8, 1984), p. 26.

Krüger, Michael, ed. *Bienek lesen*, 1980.

Piontek, Heinz. "Oberschlesische Polka," in *Das Handwerk des Lesens*, 1979.

Snead, James A. "Sun Rise, Sunset, *Septemberlight*," in *The New York Times Book Review*. XCII (February 22, 1987), p. 35.

*Karin A. Wurst*

# THE SILVER DOVE and PETERSBURG

*Author:* Andrey Bely (Boris Bugayev, 1880-1934)
*Type of plot:* Symbolic allegory
*Time of plot: The Silver Dove,* c. 1900; *Petersburg,* 1905
*Locale: The Silver Dove,* the village of Tselebeyevo and the town of Likhov,
  Russia; *Petersburg,* St. Petersburg
*First published: Serebryagolub,* 1909 (English translation, 1974); *Peterburg,*
  1913, revised 1916 and 1922 (truncated English translation, 1959; complete
  translation, 1978)

> *Principal characters:*
> *The Silver Dove*
> PYOTR DARYALSKY, an educated young poet summering near
>   Tselebeyevo
> KATYA GUGOLEVO, the young woman to whom Daryalsky
>   becomes engaged and whom he abandons
> MATRYONA, the peasant woman with whom Daryalsky is
>   paired by Kudeyarov
> KUDEYAROV, a carpenter who lives with Matryona and the
>   leader of the revolutionary "Doves"
>
> *Petersburg*
> NIKOLAI APOLLONOVICH ABLEUKHOV, a romantic nihilist who
>   has carelessly promised a revolutionary cell that he will
>   assassinate his father
> APOLLON APOLLONOVICH ABLEUKHOV, Nikolai's father, a
>   prominent government official
> SOFYA PETROVNA LIKHUTINA, the wife of an army officer and
>   the object of Nikolai's infatuation
> ALEXANDER IVANOVICH DUDKIN, a terrorist who is Nikolai's
>   contact with the revolutionaries

## The Novels

In an introduction to *The Silver Dove,* Andrey Bely explained that it
would be the first volume of a trilogy under the general title "East or West"
and that many characters would be continued throughout the three novels.
The second work, *Petersburg,* however, carries over none of the characters
from *The Silver Dove*; the two novels are connected by their mutual concern
with revolutionary politics and by their dense poetic style. The projected
third volume was tentatively entitled "The Invisible City," but there is no evidence of its ever having existed. A third novel of the period, *Kotik Letayev*
(1917-1918, serial; 1922, book), is an autobiographical work completely

unrelated to either of the earlier novels.

In *The Silver Dove*, the young poet Pyotr Daryalsky makes a summer visit to a friend near the small village of Tselebeyevo and falls in love with Katya Gugolevo, who lives at the nearby Gugolevo estate with her grandmother, the Baroness Todrabe-Graaben. Daryalsky is quickly identified by a carpenter named Kudeyarov as the right person to father a messiah for the revolutionary group, the "Doves," which Kudeyarov leads. The chosen mother is Matryona, the peasant woman who lives with Kudeyarov and whose mysterious, hypnotic earthiness lures Daryalsky away from Katya. Kudeyarov's plan comes to nothing, however, as Daryalsky and Matryona produce no messiah. When Daryalsky eventually realizes his difficult situation, he rebels and decides to leave for Moscow. The Doves, however, feel compromised by his knowledge of them, and they murder him.

The historical conflict between the East and the West is worked out allegorically in the physical geography of the setting. The village of Tselebeyevo is located between the old Gugolevo estate to the west and the town of Likhov to the east. It is in Likhov that the Doves meet to plan their Asiatic, revolutionary, destructive schemes against the Western aspects of Russian culture as represented by the aristocratic Gugolevo estate. The novel ends inconclusively with Daryalsky's death, and *Petersburg*, its intended continuation, develops new characters in a different setting.

The theme of East and West has a more precise historical context in *Petersburg*. The novel is set in October, 1905, and the Revolution of 1905 and the Russo-Japanese War loom ominously in the background. The theme is worked out in the conflict between an elderly government bureaucrat, Apollon Apollonovich Ableukhov, and his emotionally and philosophically confused son, Nikolai Apollonovich. They have both been left somewhat bereft by Nikolai's mother's scandalous elopement to Spain with her Italian lover.

Nikolai lives at home with his father, and their relationship is tense and difficult. Moreover, he is abjectly in love with Sofya Petrovna Likhutina, the wife of an army officer who is Nikolai's friend. Nikolai has somehow become involved with a revolutionary group identified only as "the party," and in a weak moment has agreed to assassinate his father. The novel begins when a terrorist named Alexander Ivanovich Dudkin brings Nikolai a bomb concealed in a sardine tin. Dudkin asks Nikolai to store the package, and the unwitting Nikolai does so without comprehending what he is hiding.

In his misery over Sofya, Nikolai resorts to going around in a mask and red cape, badly frightening Sofya. She inadvertently comes into possession of a letter to Nikolai that explains what he is to do with the bomb, and when Nikolai receives the letter at a masquerade ball and realizes the implications of the package, he tears off his mask and leaves in a panic. His father, at the same ball, does not know the identity of the man in the red domino, but the color offends him as a symbol of the revolutionary menace that threatens the state. He also is told that his son is one of the plotters.

Father and son meet the next day but before anything can happen they learn that Anna Petrovna, the wife and mother, has returned to St. Petersburg. Nikolai, confused and distraught, absentmindedly winds up the clockwork apparatus attached to the bomb, setting it to go off in twenty-four hours. Nikolai then seeks out Dudkin to clarify the party's demands, and he is reassured that the conspirators would not demand an act of parricide. Nikolai leaves to go home and destroy the bomb. Dudkin goes to his boss, Lippanchenko, and learns that, indeed, Nikolai is ordered to kill his father and will die if he refuses. Finding himself consequently under suspicion, Dudkin returns to Lippanchenko's home that night and murders him.

Meanwhile, Apollon Apollonovich has resigned his position as a result of Nikolai's conduct. When he discovers the apparently innocuous sardine tin, he removes it to his quarters to look at later. Thus upon his return Nikolai cannot find the bomb and is miserable until it explodes harmlessly with no one in the room. Events conclude with Apollon Apollonovich reunited with Anna Petrovna in rural retirement, while Nikolai lives in Europe and studies philosophy and archaeology.

## The Characters

Pyotr Daryalsky, the central character of *The Silver Dove*, embodies the allegory of a Russia caught between the East and the West. He is a young man, vaguely poetic, of no special talent or notable background, who insinuates himself into the Gugolevo estate. He is not a designing manipulator, but instead a romantic weakling who is glad of an occasion to abandon Katya Gugolevo when he feels the occult attraction of Matryona's mysterious peasant sexuality.

Daryalsky perhaps represents the Russian intelligentsia, caught in history between the exhausted Western tradition personified in Katya and Gugolevo, and the chaotic but vital movement from the East represented by the Doves with their roots in the life of the common people. His death and the inconclusive ending of the story leave the allegory rather unsatisfactorily suspended.

Neither of the two women, Katya and Matryona, is developed realistically. Katya has no remarkable qualities other than her beauty and serves in the novel primarily as the embodiment of a vague spirituality that contrasts with Matryona's earthiness. Matryona is not physically attractive, and her appeal lies in her powerful projection of a mysterious life force that seems to be sensed more by Daryalsky than by anyone else.

Kudeyarov is an oddly divided figure, who sets up the relationship with Daryalsky and Matryona but at the same time suffers jealousy when he is successful. The ambivalence of his nature is reflected in his features, for his face appears split into two opposed halves. In his carpenter's occupation, his hopes for a messiah, and the sharing of bread and wine that introduces the Doves' rituals there are analogues to the New Testament; these details remain allusions that resist any coherent assimilation into the allegory.

Apollon Apollonovich Ableukhov, the protagonist of *Petersburg*, feels painfully the loss of his wife to her Italian lover. Anna Petrovna's betrayal has left him alone in his old age, sharing a home with a son from whom he becomes increasingly estranged. Personal relationships are exhausting for him, and he feels much more comfortable when appreciating the satisfactions afforded by St. Petersburg's geometric street alignments. His disappointment with Nikolai culminates in the discovery that Nikolai has been appointed to assassinate him, and although there is ultimately no real commitment to murder by Nikolai, the realization of his son's perfidy and weakness shocks Apollon Apollonovich into resigning his government post. When his wife returns, he quickly forgives her. He is an aging man whose life has been devoted to his work and who finds himself slightly superannuated and adrift in his personal life. Anna Petrovna's return restores meaning to his last years.

Nikolai is also disturbed by Anna Petrovna's betrayal. Before her elopement he had been an attentive, if perhaps dreamy, student of Kantian philosophy, always up in the morning and neatly dressed in his student's uniform. After his mother leaves he becomes slothful, unable to enjoy morning coffee with his father, and addicted to pacing the floor of his study in a Bokhara dressing gown and a Tartar skullcap—sartorial emblems of his attraction to the vital but destructive forces of the East. He also takes up company with the party of terrorists, seeking something to fill the void in his philosophy. His relationship with the party seems never to be more than an immature flirtation brought on by personal crisis. The woman he loves, Sofya Petrovna Likhutina, soon loses interest in her husband and is apparently ready for a serious affair with Nikolai, but he is too naïve to realize this and probably emotionally incapable of consummating an illicit love affair. His grotesque behavior in the red cape and mask reveals the extent of his removal from reality. After his absurd escapades as a red-caped mystery man and a fledgling terrorist, he is lucky to get out of his situation with no more disastrous result than a bomb that blows up harmlessly. He is then glad to take up a life as a scholar in Europe, and he does not return to Russia until his father dies.

The other characters need little comment. Sofya is a flirt married to an ineffectual husband. The revolutionary Dudkin does not seem to be made of the stuff of real terrorists, for he flinches when he learns that the package he delivered to Nikolai is a bomb intended for the murder of Apollon Apollonovich. The terrorist leader Lippanchenko, however, exudes genuine menace and was probably suggested to Bely by the double agent Azev, who during the Revolution of 1905 was in the employ of both the czar's secret police and the revolutionaries.

*Themes and Meanings*

*The Silver Dove* and *Petersburg* share the theme of East and West in a context of revolutionary politics. Both dramatize the plight of czarist Russia looking backward to a Western cultural heritage at the same time that it is faced by the potential energy of an age of masses in revolution. There is, in truth, little about the revolutionary movement that could accurately be described as Eastern, but the specter of an Asiatic East, thronging with swelling populations of people untutored in European refinements, makes a convenient symbol for an age nervous about the collapse of its class structure under pressure for liberal democratic reforms. Pushed no further than this, Bely's dichotomy of East and West works well enough in his allegorical approach to fiction, but most readers will probably find it difficult to be much more precise in explication of his themes. Nikolai and Daryalsky are alike in that they are both more comfortable with poetry and philosophy than with revolutionary politics, and each finds himself accidentally swept into patterns of action for which he has no heart and from which he feels impelled to extricate himself. In that they are both members of the Russian intelligentsia they can be seen as representative of the impotence felt by that intelligentsia when confronted by historical forces dimly sensed but not rationally comprehended. Bely's nervous, impressionistic style well suits the depiction of such characters and their bewilderment.

*Critical Context*

Bely's real name was Boris Bugayev. His father was a professor of mathematics at the University of Moscow, and it was partly through acquaintance with his father's friends that he gained knowledge of and access to the Russian Symbolist movement in literature. His own university education was in mathematics and philosophy, and he quickly became identified with Symbolist aesthetics and was branded as "decadent" by conservative critics. He had a long-lasting interest in mystical doctrines, and in 1912 devoted himself to a study of the anthroposophy of Rudolf Steiner.

Many of these concerns are put into practice in his heavily symbolic and allegorical novels. Both *The Silver Dove* and *Petersburg* are written in prose that relies heavily on poetic devices such as kaleidoscopic images, passages of fantasy, and evocative symbols. In *The Silver Dove*, for example, Bely introduces in an early chapter a "ragged bush" that stands beside the highway from Tselebeyevo to Likhov and from the village appears to be a "dark wayfarer." This bush appears several times and, since it is on the road to Likhov, seems to lead mysteriously to the East and all that region's attendant menace. Similarly, in *Petersburg* there are hallucinatory appearances of Peter the Great, in the apparition of the Flying Dutchman. The bush and the Flying Dutchman both contribute to the impression of a transcendental dimension to Bely's fictional realm that can be expressed only figuratively.

Bely's status with Soviet critics, equivocal at best, and the comparatively late translation of his works into English have hampered the development of his reputation as a major twentieth century artist. His devotion to Symbolist theory and his undeniable gift for its application make him a significant figure in the history of modernism. His sensitivity to the great changes impending in Russia led to these two novels of East and West in which so much of twentieth century history is enigmatically prefigured.

*Sources for Further Study*
Cioran, S. *The Apocalyptic Symbolism of Andrey Bely*, 1973.
Elsworth, J. D. *Andrey Bely: A Critical Study of the Novels*, 1983.
Janecek, Gerald, ed. *Andrey Bely: A Critical Review*, 1978.
Mochul'sky, K. V. *Andrei Bely: His Life and Works*, 1977.

*Frank Day*

# A SIMPLE STORY

*Author:* Shmuel Yosef Agnon (Shmuel Yosef Czaczkes, 1888-1970)
*Type of plot:* Psychological parable
*Time of plot:* The late nineteenth and early twentieth centuries
*Locale:* Szybusz (Poland) and Galicia
*First published: Sipur pashut,* 1935 (English translation, 1985)

> *Principal characters:*
> THE NARRATOR
> HIRSHL HURVITZ, a young storekeeper's son, at first too timid
>     to declare his passion for Blume Nacht
> BLUME NACHT, the daughter of Mirl and Hayyim Nacht
> MINA ZIEMLICH, the daughter of a wealthy merchant from
>     Malikrowik, later to be Hirshl's wife
> BARUCH MEIR HURVITZ, Hirshl's father
> TSIRL HURVITZ, Hirshl's mother
> GEDALIA ZIEMLICH, Mina's father
> BERTHA ZIEMLICH, Mina's mother
> DR. LANGSAM, a neurologist
> YONA TOYBER, a matchmaker from Szybusz
> AKAVIA and TIRZA MAZAL, a young couple

*The Novel*

Using an obtrusive narrator, a native of Galicia wise and tolerant concerning the foibles of men and women in love, Shmuel Yosef Agnon narrates a "simple" tale that grows ever more complex and meaningful. He begins with the fortunes of Blume Nacht, an attractive, clever, and industrious young woman who, as a penniless orphan, arrives at her cousin's home at Szybusz, a Jewish shtetl (village) in southern Poland. Baruch Meir Hurvitz and his wife, Tsirl, decide that she might well serve as a maid in the household to earn her modest keep, and they agree to shelter her. Their only son, Hirshl, looks at the girl with deeper appreciation. Though he soon falls in love with her, he is too inexperienced in the ways of the world to approach Blume and instead allows fate to take control of his romance. While he vacillates, the shtetl matchmaker, Yona Toyber, works out for the young man a much more promising match—with Mina Ziemlich, from the nearby village of Malikrowik.

Passively, Hirshl allows his parents to prepare for this marriage; passively, he courts the equally inexperienced Mina; passively, he weds her. Always he had thought (or perhaps had hoped) that Blume might intercede for him and that they might run off together. Such things do not generally occur in the village of Szybusz, however, where people follow Jewish traditions, and Hirshl is, if anything, obedient.

Only after his marriage does he show signs of agitation that swell into re-volt against the conventions of married life and finally turn into depression and near-madness. Desperate with his unrequited love for Blume, Hirshl strays from his home, suffers an emotional breakdown in the forest, and—with the assistance of his worried family—is placed in the care of the wise Dr. Langsam, a neurologist, and committed to a sanatorium. There, allowed time for sleep and the renovation of his frayed nerves, Hirshl regains his san-ity. Indeed, he recovers more than his wits: He returns home to his wife and to his vocation as a shopkeeper with a new vigor. His rebellion is finished. Restored to his wife and children, content with his lot as an ordinary person in an imperfect world, he resumes a life of complacency. What of Blume? The narrator chooses not to discuss her fate; hers is another "simple story."

### The Characters

On the surface, many of the villagers in Agnon's novella resemble stock figures of Jewish folk tradition. Tsirl, the typical manipulative mother, con-trols both her unassertive son and her genial husband. Yona Toyber is the shtetl matchmaker, whose wisdom derives as much from the conventions gov-erning his vocation as from his own subtlety and the sense of tact which he acquired by observing human nature. The youthful protagonist, Hirshl, resembles in certain comic ways the classic schlemiel, the feckless victim of other people's caprices.

Yet upon closer inspection, these characters appear to be less stereo-typical, more complicated than a reader might suppose. After Hirshl suffers a nervous collapse, his parents act with unexpected sense to assist their son with proper help. Instead of reproving him, Tsirl supports him with motherly constancy. Yona Toyber is by no means the typical gossipy factotum of Jewish folklore; he is a man of religious erudition and not a gossip at all. A gentle, dignified, self-trained psychologist in his own right, he is one of the two authority figures who represent the internal harmony and continuity of a God-fearing community. The other is the university-trained neurologist, Dr. Langsam. Although a secular Jew with a wider range of intellectual and cul-tural interests than those held in common by the shtetl, he is nevertheless a religious man. Dr. Langsam's professional "treatment" for Hirshl is, when judged according to the test of efficacy, just as appropriate as Yona Toyber's professional choice of Hirshl's mate. Dr. Langsam's regimen of rest and quiet introspection works to heal Hirshl's mental agitation; Toyber's selection of Mina is, after all, appropriate. Hirshl's soul is too small (or too conventional) to have pleased the nobler Blume.

A mysterious "night flower," as her name may be translated from the Yiddish/German, Blume is by no means a stock character of Jewish folk lit-erature. Her potential is great—as great in powers of self-sacrifice as it is in moral strength. Because she stands apart from the petty people of the shtetl, she must continue her story in the imagination of the reader, beyond the confines of the pages of Agnon's book.

Within the small village of Szybusz are diverse souls, none as unique as Blume is, all comprising a community united by tradition and by the mysterious force of a destiny shaped by Divine Will. From Yona Toyber and Dr. Langsam through a range of the most humble persons—including the conventional lovers Akavia and Tirza Mazal (whose full story Agnon tells in a work of 1923, "Bidmi yameha")—all members of the community are linked, frozen in time and commemorated as a lost portion of Jewry.

### Themes and Meanings

How simple, indeed, is Agnon's novella? His narrative pattern, seemingly straightforward, is full of strange twists. The reader at first supposes that Hirshl's love for Blume will, after overcoming the impediments of his parents' opposition, eventually triumph. Instead, Hirshl marries Mina, a lesser-spirited but otherwise suitable mate. At this point, Blume's role in the story as the romantic focus diminishes, although it never entirely fades; she persists in Hirshl's imagination as the unattainable fair one. The reader now expects that Hirshl will persist in his quest for Blume, and that, somehow (perhaps with tragic consequences), his desperate ardor will win her heart. Again, however, Agnon surprises: Hirshl, to be sure, is driven nearly mad with vexation over his unrequited passion, but Blume remains chaste and is indifferent to his clumsy advances. What therefore will become of the pining lover deprived of his amorous goal? The reader expects that Hirshl will decline as a result of his erotic madness into a deeper pit of depression. Not so. He recovers and, against expectations, returns home as a solid, respectable Szybusz merchant. Instead of changing his temperament, he reverts to his former condition, now more mature as a husband and a father, more responsible as a businessman, more conventional as a Jew.

What, then, is the moral of this folk parable? That the old ways, the ways of traditional obligations and traditional constraints upon freedom, are the best (as Hirshl finally comes to his senses and abandons his foolish dreams of pursuing his romantic dream)? Or does Agnon mean to say that Hirshl, a decent enough fellow but not truly extraordinary, does not deserve the finely tempered Blume? Does Agnon side with the winds of change in complaisant Szybusz or with the solid verities of the past? More to the point, how is the reader to interpret this bittersweet story which lacks villains but also lacks heroes? The most nearly heroic figure is Dr. Langsam, who represents the emerging educated Jewish professional class but who still maintains tenuous links to his Orthodox religious heritage. A victim of existential doubt, he is torn between two worlds, able to heal the neuroses of others but not his own psychological wounds.

What of Blume? Agnon's treatment of this sharply defined character is very curious. The story begins with an account of her struggles to survive and approaches the end enigmatically with these words: "Hirshl and Mina's story is over, but Blume's is not. Everything that happened to Blume Nacht would fill another book." The reader is left to imagine the incidents of such a book. In spite of Agnon's reticence in disclosing information about Blume's future (she has rejected another lover), her image remains fixed. Will she emigrate from Szybusz to seek a more spacious, freer life abroad? Will she ever find a lover worthy of her? From what the reader already knows about her, he can not only imagine a different fate for her but also a better one than that of the historically doomed Galician Jews. As the dark (or nocturnal) flower that her name symbolically suggests, Blume's mystery remains fragrantly external to the central parable of the novella.

### Critical Context

Like the other fiction by the 1966 Nobel Prize winner, *A Simple Story* recreates the lost world of early twentieth century Jewish life. In general, Agnon's work is—at least superficially—nostalgic, conservatively religious, often moralistic. On a deeper level, however, his fiction treats a quest for values in a once-static society slowly disintegrating because of modern pressures. As such, *A Simple Story*, like *Oreach nata lalun* (1939, 1950; *A Guest for the Night*, 1968) and *Hakhnasat kala* (1931; *The Bridal Canopy*, 1937), should be read not merely as an old-fashioned narrative depicting a bygone age but also as an ambiguous moral parable that concerns the human soul in turmoil.

In *A Simple Story*, Agnon's parable lacks a distinct moral focus because his vision is comic. From the vantage point of retrospection, he examines his characters with amused tolerance for their follies, with compassion for their suffering. His tale ends, as most great comedies end, with an impulse toward reconciliation; with the ceremony of marriage for many of the minor characters; with the promise of integration and unity for the entire community. As is also true of great comedies, Agnon's miniature world is touched by the sadness of life. No one who reads the account of Hirshl's early discontent in a loveless marriage can dismiss the book merely as a folk romance. More in the pattern of Ivan Olbracht's neglected masterpiece *Golet v údolí* (1937; *The Bitter and the Sweet*, 1964) than of Sholom Aleichem's popular stories, Agnon's comic vision rarely sentimentalizes or trivializes the past. As both a realist and a man of deep religious faith, Agnon treats his characters no better than they are—but also no worse.

### Sources for Further Study

Aberbach, David. *At the Handles of the Lock: Themes in the Fiction of S. J. Agnon*, 1984.
Alter, Robert. "Shmuel Yosef Agnon: The Alphabet of Holiness" and "The

Israeli Novel," in *After the Tradition*, 1969.
Band, Arnold J. *Nostalgia and Nightmare: A Study of the Fiction of S. Y. Agnon*, 1968.
Fisch, Harold. *S. Y. Agnon*, 1975.
Hochman, Baruch. *The Fiction of S. Y. Agnon*, 1970.

*Leslie Mittleman*

# THE SLAVE

*Author:* Isaac Bashevis Singer (1904-     )
*Type of plot:* Historical fiction
*Time of plot:* The middle and late 1600's
*Locale:* Poland and Palestine
*First published: Der Knekht,* 1961 (English translation, 1962)

    *Principal characters:*
        JACOB, the protagonist, a devout and scholarly Jew
        WANDA BZIK, Jacob's non-Jewish mistress, later his wife
        JAN BZIK, Wanda's peasant father and Jacob's master
        DZIOBAK, the village's Catholic priest
        ADAM PILITZKY, a pessimistic Polish nobleman who owns the
           village of Pilitz
        THERESA PILITZKY, his wife
        GERSHON, Pilitzky's Jewish overseer, Jacob's rival

*The Novel*

In the Chmielnicki massacres (1648-1649), the Cossacks kill Jacob's wife and children. He survives by fleeing his native Josefov, but his fate is little better than his family's: Captured by brigands, he is sold as a slave to Jan Bzik.

Wanda, Jan Bzik's daughter, falls in love with Jacob. When he tends the cattle in the mountains during the summer, she brings him special foods from the village. When he is sick, she cares for him; when he is bitten by a snake, she saves his life. Because he remains an orthodox Jew, Jacob will not work on the Sabbath—thus, Wanda performs his chores for him. She wants Jacob to marry her or, if he will not marry, to live with her.

For a long time Jacob resists. Wanda is not Jewish, so he cannot marry her, and without marriage he refuses to sleep with her. Finally, though, his love and lust overcome his scruples. Further, despite Polish law, which makes the conversion of a Gentile a capital offense for both the convert and the Jew who has caused the conversion, Wanda embraces Judaism.

Jacob's life with Wanda ends abruptly when Jews from Josefov ransom Jacob from slavery. Back in his native village he teaches Hebrew, serves as beadle in the study house, and restores damaged sacred texts. The Jewish community wants him to remarry and finds a rich widow for him. One night, shortly before the marriage is to occur, he dreams that Wanda is pregnant with his child; the next morning he sets off to find her.

Reunited, Jacob and Wanda go to a new village, Pilitz. Wanda assumes the name of Sarah, the first Jewish convert. To prevent the community from discovering her lack of Yiddish and her peasant accent, she feigns dumbness. When Adam Pilitzky, in a drunken fit, threatens her husband, though, Wanda/Sarah breaks her silence to plead for his life. Instead of destroying their scheme, her action benefits them. Pilitzky believes that he has witnessed the miracle he has longed for; convinced that Jacob and Wanda are holy people, he appoints Jacob as his overseer in place of the dishonest Gershon.

In labor, Wanda speaks again, revealing her entire history. The Jewish community, which had never accepted Sarah, rejoices at the exposure of the "miracle" and excommunicates Jacob for seeking to convert her. They reject the conversion and her marriage, declaring her son, Benjamin, to be illegitimate. After her death in childbirth, the Jews refuse her burial in holy ground. Jacob's son is taken from him, and he is arrested by Pilitzky.

On his way to certain death, Jacob escapes once more. He returns to Pilitz for his son, and together they flee to Palestine. Twenty years later, he comes back to Pilitz to reclaim the bones of his wife, so that he may bury them in Palestine, but no one can find her unmarked grave. Jacob suddenly sickens and dies; preparing to bury him, the gravedigger finds Wanda's corpse, still preserved. Taking this discovery as an omen, the elders agree to bury Jacob next to her and finally accept her not only as a Jew but also as a saint.

*The Characters*

Although *The Slave* is filled with villagers and peasants, only two characters, Jacob and Wanda, are fully developed. Physically, Jacob does not look quite Jewish: He is tall and blue-eyed. He speaks a better Polish than his Jewish compatriots in Pilitz, and while they cringe before their Gentile overlord, Jacob stands up to him. Jacob is ashamed of his coreligionists' failure to resist the Cossacks; when soldiers attempt to carry him off, he fights and defeats them.

Jacob is different, not because he is less Jewish but rather because he is more. Jacob, whose biblical namesake was a successful wrestler, admires the ancient Jewish heroes, whom he takes as his model. His beliefs, too, are firmly rooted in the Bible. Alone in the mountains, he begins to engrave the commandments on a large rock, just as Moses had. He keeps a calendar and, like the Jews in the days of the Temple, watches the phases of the moon so that he may observe all the holidays at their proper time. To avoid violating the Sabbath, he gathers extra food for himself and his cattle during the week, just as the Jews in the desert collected extra manna on Friday because none fell on the Sabbath.

Observing the rituals is important to Jacob, but even more important is respect for his fellowman. Following Amos, he is just, merciful, humble. Unlike his predecessor, also supposedly a religious Jew, he does not abuse Pilitzky's trust, nor does he foment factionalism in the community. During his last visit to Pilitz, he chooses to sleep in the poorhouse rather than in more comfortable lodgings.

It is in the spirit of biblical Judaism that Jacob converts Wanda, for he knows that before Christian law forbade the practice, Judaism was a proselytizing religion. Yet Wanda is no ordinary Christian any more than Jacob is a typical Jew—she senses that she has a Jewish soul that has mistakenly been born into a Gentile body. She rejects numerous eligible Christian husbands, and her behavior differs so markedly from that of her mother, sister, and the other villagers that they dub her "the Lady." Her love for Jacob is equaled by her passion for learning and decency in a world of ignorance and nastiness.

Like Leah, Rachel, and Ruth, she leaves her family to follow the God of Jacob. Her devotion allows her the right to rebuke the Jews who have rejected her and earns for her a saintly reputation after her death.

The other characters in the book are not as well developed; they are types rather than individuals. Adam Pilitzky is a decadent, despondent nobleman, autocratic yet weak, domineering yet henpecked. He is too hesitant even to carry out evil intentions, such as killing Gershon or banishing the Jews from his village. In his despair and dissolute nature, he represents the decaying aristocracy that left Poland a prey to her neighbors.

Dziobak is an anti-Semitic, ineffectual priest. If he were to spend as much time and energy teaching his parishioners the Gospel of Christ as he does inciting them to hate the one Jew in their midst, he might overcome some of the paganism that is the real religion of the peasants.

Gershon, a Jewish leader in Pilitz, differs little from Dziobak—there are hypocrites in all religions. He observes the minutest of rituals but cheats his employer. Like Dziobak, too, he plots against Jacob, even after Jacob saves his life.

### Themes and Meanings

For Isaac Bashevis Singer, history is not linear but cyclical; the past is never lost. Toward the end of the novel, as Jacob, impoverished, flees with his son across the Vistula, he thinks about his patriarchal namesake:

> His name was Jacob also; he too had lost a beloved wife, the daughter of an idolater, among strangers; Sarah too was buried by the way and had left him a son. Like the Biblical Jacob, he was crossing the river, bearing only a staff, pursued by another Esau. . . . Perhaps four thousand years would again pass; somewhere, at another river, another Jacob would walk mourning another Rachel. Or who knew, perhaps it was always the same Jacob and the same Rachel.

The forests have not changed since Creation. The peasants seem to predate that event, vestiges of worlds that God made and destroyed before He created Earth. Even the Chmielnicki massacre, though a discrete historical episode, is part of a recurring cycle of persecution. The line of history curves back on itself.

Nothing changes, not even the Jews. Jacob thinks of the first chapter of Isaiah, in which the prophet rejects prayer and sacrifice unaccompanied by human kindness. Like those Jews in Isaiah's time, the Jews of Pilitz observe the easy commandments; they eat kosher food and go to the synagogue. While they discharge their duties to God, however, they ignore their responsibilities to their fellowman. The poor are not cared for properly. Beile Peshe will not assist Wanda in childbirth. The burial society steals Jacob's money.

If the Jews have wandered from the biblical ideal, the Christians have strayed even farther. Jacob notes the distance between Jew and Christian when he visits Pilitzky's castle, where "the very air... smelled of violence, idolatry, and concupiscence." The Jews of Pilitz are not vegetarians (Jacob is), but they do not wantonly destroy animals, either. Though they gossip, they do not murder or launch pogroms. Given the choice between victim and victimizer, Singer chooses the former.

Singer also offers another sort of choice, that between types of slavery. On one level, the novel's title refers to Jacob as Jan Bzik's slave. Jacob realizes, though, that "man cannot be entirely free. . . . Man goes in harness, every desire is a strand of the rope that yokes him." Pilitzky owns a village, but he is a slave to his wife, who in turn is such a slave to lust that she hangs herself when one of her lovers abandons her. Waclaw the ferryman believes that he is free, for he lives alone and owns nothing. He has paid a high price for that liberty, though: He refuses to marry and cuts himself off from all ties of family and friendship. If life, if society, is to continue, "somebody must plow and reap. Children must be raised."

Everyone, then, is a slave. Jacob chooses to be God's slave. His master, Bzik, the peasants, Pilitzky, Gershon are slaves, too, slaves to their greed, passions, or fears. Jacob frees himself by surrendering himself to God, while the others, casting off God's yoke, only make tighter chains for themselves.

Singer thus offers choices, for he believes in free will. The world is a motley web: "Next to the poorhouse, in garbage and excrement, grew grass and wildflowers—white blooms, yellow blooms, feathery seed puffs, hairlike green fringes." One may focus on ugliness or on beauty. Jacob tells the well-meaning Reb Leibush Mayer, "One should look for the good in people, not the bad." Like the Bible it so often echoes, *The Slave* offers its readers a choice between spiritual life and death and urges them to choose the former.

*Critical Context*

Singer has said that writing can rely on words or action; he has always sought to portray deeds. *The Slave* is faithful to this intention, for it is full of adventure and suspense. Will the peasants kill Jacob? Will he and Wanda be reunited? Will the Jews of Pilitz learn Wanda's secret identity? Singer never forgets that one reads a novel first of all for the story.

*The Slave* also offers many passages of great lyricism: Singer is a master of words as well as of action. When Jacob looks at the night sky, he sees that "the stars looked like letters of the alphabet, vowel points, notes of music." He likens the snow to "fleece and the dust of diamonds." Singer evokes the life of the peasantry and the benighted spirit of seventeenth century Poland.

Beneath this brilliant surface lies a profound metaphysic. Here is the eternal battle between good and evil, the sacred and the diabolical, fate, foreknowledge, and free will. Though he writes from a modernist perspective, Singer nevertheless worries about the salvation of his characters' souls, for he believes in souls, salvation, and damnation. Perhaps even more significant, he makes his reader worry about this issue also. For Singer, God is alive, ruling the world wisely if not mercifully. In later works, Singer steps back a bit from such optimism, but in *The Slave* he expresses a belief in the triumph of virtue and of man's capacity for redemption. Like the biblical story that the novel retells, narrative serves philosophical and religious ends.

*Sources for Further Study*
Alexander, Edward. *Isaac Bashevis Singer*, 1980.
Allentuck, Marcia, ed. *The Achievement of Isaac Bashevis Singer*, 1969.
Buchen, Irving. *Isaac Bashevis Singer and the Eternal Past*, 1968.
Malin, Irving, ed. *Critical Views of Isaac Bashevis Singer*, 1969.

*Joseph Rosenblum*

# SLEEPLESS DAYS

*Author:* Jurek Becker (1937-     )
*Type of plot:* Social criticism
*Time of plot:* The 1970's
*Locale:* East Berlin and a small resort in Hungary
*First published: Schlaflose Tage*, 1978 (English translation, 1979)

> *Principal characters:*
> KARL SIMROCK, an East Berlin high-school teacher who later
>     works as a bakery truck driver
> RUTH, his first wife and the mother of his daughter, Leonie
> ANTONIA, a former physics student who becomes his lover

*The Novel*

    *Sleepless Days* narrates the story of an identity crisis precipitated by what may have been a heart attack. Karl Simrock, a high-school teacher in East Berlin, suddenly realizes that he is mortal and that, without ever being dissatisfied with a routine life, he spent thirty-six years waiting for some unspecified event that never came. It is time to take inventory. The apparent satisfaction with his life was an illusion born of powerlessness and a fear of commitment. In actuality, he is deeply disturbed by the fact that he has never dared to form an opinion and to make his voice count. His marriage is lackluster, held together by a tiresome bedroom routine. He cares little for either his daughter or his mother. In school, he is required to advocate a spurious moral code that is determined by the administration and not at all his own. Even though he has accepted Marxist principles as valid, he has never made an effort to examine their efficacy. Simrock realizes that he must either take his life in hand or live to regret a wasted existence. He decides to act. This decision takes courage, and its implementation drains him of energy. Yet in the end, his heart—which he had thought was in bad shape—is bearing up nicely, and anxiety becomes an energizing force.

    The process of changing his life is often painful and, at times, deeply disappointing. It is a process of gain and loss. After divorcing his wife, Ruth, he falls in love with Antonia, a former physics student, and comes to trust her, only to learn that she never fully trusted him. Eventually, she attempts to escape to the West without him. East Berlin, with a housing shortage typical for a Communist state, has no apartments for divorced people, and Simrock is forced into an uncomfortable living arrangement with his mother until he moves into Antonia's two-room, makeshift home.

    He loses his teaching position because of insubordination and ends up driving a bakery truck to make a living. Even though he tries to retain his Marxist worldview and to have it confirmed by working as a laborer, he is soon forced to admit to himself that his fellow workers are motivated not by Marxist ideals of the proletariat working enthusiastically for the common good but by a spiritless attitude: "What do I care as long as I get by?" When Antonia ends up in prison, Simrock briefly cherishes visions of fighting the state bureaucracy, only to recognize that a common citizen in a Communist state cannot penetrate even the outermost walls of the power structure, which rules without considerations of an individual's needs and rights. Simrock suffers, but he never regrets his decision to participate actively in life.

## The Characters

Even though the novel is told by a third-person narrator, the protagonist has some rather obvious autobiographic traits. Like Karl Simrock, Jurek Becker lived in East Berlin when he wrote this novel, and Simrock's concerns are those of contemporary intellectuals who believe that, in a closed Communist society, they are merely existing rather than living. Simrock is trapped not only by his environment but also by his own inertia. For years, practically throughout his adult life, he has successfully suppressed any urge to think independently or to act as an individual. A fear of the consequences of leaving his comfortable niche has slowly forced him into a vegetative state in which time passes unnoticed. Nothing but an occasional outburst of rage indicates that beneath Simrock's calm outer appearance there exists a human soul. Simrock is a sensitive man who is not ashamed to weep. He is filled with self-doubt and often fearful. He is essentially a loner who does not easily relate to others. He blames his mother for his father's early death and dislikes her matter-of-fact manner, yet he married Ruth, who seems to have a similar approach to life. He is without close friends and remains aloof from his colleagues in school.

Once Simrock embarks on his journey into a new existence based on self-determination, the complexity of his character allows him to develop new habits such as asking an acquaintance for help when he needs an apartment (his request is denied) or trusting Antonia enough to tell her that, in applying to the state for a summer job, he had reasons other than those stated in his application. (This kind of deception is an act of defiance, a rebellion for personal gain against the authorities.) Defiance marks his relationship with the representatives of the state. His courage slowly increases until, in the end, he is able to refuse an offer to be reinstated as a teacher, because the school administration's demands would have violated his personal integrity. Simrock is finally able to sustain relationships, but all of his newfound friends, such as Boris, the other bakery truck driver, and Antonia, the woman he loves, are outsiders in a society which they no longer respect.

The novel is written entirely from the protagonist's point of view. All other characters remain secondary and one-dimensional. Their significance derives from their involvement with Simrock. The women in the novel, Ruth,

Simrock's mother, and Antonia (Simrock's daughter, Leonie, remains in the background), have traditional nurturing qualities. Ruth, in her brusque manner, reassures Simrock when he believes that he has suffered a heart attack. Later, she is deeply angered by his decision to divorce her but is well able to take care of herself and their child. The protagonist's mother offers him her spare room, even though his presence in her apartment is inconvenient and she must sense that her son has no genuine love for her.

Antonia truly shares with Simrock his newfound life. She understands his concerns, because her own experience in a state whose leaders believe that they must quash any signs of individual development has been devastating. She was dismissed from the university because she voiced doubts about the usefulness of the study of "scientific socialism." Her three-year marriage ended in divorce. Having asserted her independence, she is without friends or family. Her outlook on life has become somewhat cynical. The fact that she lives in a two-room storefront with a homey smell of vanilla underscores her nurturing character. The temporariness of this living arrangement reflects the insecurity which marks her life.

### Themes and Meanings

In *Sleepless Days*, the author has adapted to his needs two familiar themes of German literature. He fuses an artist's sympathy with an individual's struggle against the demands of an unrelenting society, and he recalls the legend of Sleeping Beauty, which equates reaching maturity with awakening from a long sleep. The protagonist has spent exactly half of a lifetime in oblivion when he finally awakes to "sleepless days" and to a new awareness. Like Sleeping Beauty, he also awakes to a new love in his life, but, instead of living happily ever after as in a fairy tale, he must cope with the oppressive society around him.

Society in this novel is represented by the educational system. It can easily deal with cynics such as Simrock's colleague and vice principal Kabitzke, who accommodates the irrationality of the totalitarian state by putting on a front that will further his career. From Kabitzke's point of view, honesty, as Simrock practices it, is nothing but a method of self-destruction. Yet the protagonist is no longer willing to conform to a schizophrenic system in which basic human rights, such as thinking independently or even honestly abiding by the law of the land, are called acts of defiance and punished by denying Simrock his teaching position and Antonia a place as a university student.

Just as sleep is a metaphor for self-induced passivity and stupor, physical ailments symbolize the state of Simrock's mental health. Twice in the course of the novel the protagonist feels ill. The crisis that will change his life is initiated by sudden sharp chest pains, signifying an illness gnawing at the core of his existence, at his heart and soul. Once Simrock changes, his heart never bothers him again. At the conclusion of the story, he is overcome by nausea when he feels powerless against the Kabitzkes of this world, who cheerfully yield to every whim of their oppressive superiors. "Ingesting" this atmosphere of deception, selfishness, and cynicism makes Simrock sick, literally and figuratively.

Antonia, who had cherished secret hopes to beat the system by using Simrock in her escape from the confining sphere of the German Democratic Republic while on vacation in Hungary, learns to love the protagonist truly when she experiences the terror of being sentenced to a seventeen-month prison term for having committed a crime against the state (escaping from the country). She realizes that she is considered utterly worthless and expendable by everybody except Simrock, who loves her unconditionally.

## Critical Context

As the personal account of the identity crisis of a man in his thirties and as a political novel of social criticism, *Sleepless Days* joins the mainstream of the contemporary German novel, from Franz Kafka's *Der Prozess* (1925; *The Trial*, 1937) to Günter Grass's *Die Blechtrommel* (1959; *The Tin Drum*, 1961) and Heinrich Böll's *Ansichten eines Clowns* (1963; *The Clown*, 1965). Neither of these aspects renders the novel publishable in the German Democratic Republic. It appeared in the Federal Republic of Germany while the author was living, temporarily, as he says, in West Berlin. The fact that Becker writes as a dissident accounts for the novel's more frequent classification as a political novel, while it is less often placed in the category of a psychological *Bildungsroman*. The novel is by no means a political tract. It simply develops the universal theme of an existential crisis against the backdrop of an oppressive society well familiar to the author. Similar to Becker's other novels, *Sleepless Days* avoids moral outrage or frantic preaching. Its effect on the reader grows out of convincing arguments presented with clarity in a quiet and judicious manner. Becker disregards absolutely the prescriptive norms of Socialist Realism, a prerequisite for a successful writing career in a Communist state.

## Sources for Further Study

Binding, Paul. Review in *New Statesman*. XCVIII (November 30, 1979), p. 895.

Bremer, T. "Roman eines Störenfriedens: Über Jurek Beckers *Schlaflose Tage*," in *Neue Rundschau*. LXXXIX (1978), pp. 470-476.

Demetz, Peter. *Postwar German Literature*, 1986.

Howe, Irving. Review in *The New York Times Book Review*. LXXXIV (September 16, 1979), p. 7.

Wickenden, Dorothy. Review in *The New Republic*. CLXXXI (November 3, 1979), p. 38.

*Rita Terras*

# SLOW HOMECOMING

*Author:* Peter Handke (1942-    )
*Type of plot:* Philosophical realism
*Time of plot:* The late 1970's and the early 1980's
*Locale:* The United States and France
*First published:* 1979-1981 (English translation, 1985): *Langsame Heimkehr*,
    1979 (*The Long Way Around*, 1985); *Die Lehre der Sainte-Victoire*, 1980
    (*The Lesson of Mont-Sainte-Victoire*, 1985); *Kindergeschichte*, 1981 (*Child
    Story*, 1985)

> *Principal characters:*
> *The Long Way Around*
> VALENTIN SORGER, a geologist
>
> *The Lesson of Mont-Sainte-Victoire*
> THE NARRATOR, a writer
>
> *Child Story*
> THE ADULT
> THE CHILD

*The Novels*

    *Slow Homecoming* consists of three, very loosely connected texts—*The Long Way Around*, *The Lesson of Mont-Sainte-Victoire*, and *Child Story*—which are veiled in fiction but remain strongly autobiographical. The various characters in the stories are stylized variations of the author's persona. The three texts document a spiritual and artistic quest. The first work is a third-person narrative that treats the character of Valentin Sorger, a European geologist who is working above the Arctic Circle in Alaska. It consists largely of reflections on art and existence. Sorger lives in a small, primitive Indian village and makes "sketches" of the wild and half-formed landscapes. He feels estranged from the reality of his past. One day, he decides that he must return to his home in Europe.

    Sorger first goes to San Francisco, where he has a home. He enters a state of extreme alienation and can barely speak. He is deeply interested in the forms and colors of nature and meditates on landscapes. What he seeks is a vision of some eternal law, a salvation. His sketching becomes a way of orienting himself, of locating himself in reality.

    Sorger then flies to Denver to visit a former schoolmate who is a skiing instructor. He learns, however, that the man has just died. After staying a few days, he flies on to New York. He continues to meditate on the eternal law or "Form" that he seeks. There he meets a man named Esch, with whom he has a long and intense conversation. The text ends as he flies back to Europe.

*The Lesson of Mont-Sainte-Victoire*, the second text in the series, is a first-person narrative that concerns a writer who has returned to Europe. He wants to travel to Mont-Sainte-Victoire in the south of France, because he is deeply involved in the art of Paul Cézanne, who often used the mountain landscape as the subject of his painting. The text consists of the narrator's aesthetic reflections as he wanders the countryside observing the landscape and the forms of nature. Cézanne was for him the great creator who could transform nature and the experience of life into the eternal forms of art.

The narrator has a bizarre experience on the mountain when he comes by a Foreign Legion camp and confronts a half-crazed guard dog behind the barbed-wire fence. The violent and insane dog brings him a revelation concerning all the hate, violence, and negative energy that surrounds each individual. He longs for the salvation of the aesthetic realm, for the *nunc stans*, literally the "static now," the eternal moment captured in works of art. He also reflects on his past and on other writers and mystics. The work ends with his thoughts about a forest painting by a Dutch artist and with a description of a similar forest near Salzburg.

*Child Story*, the third text, is a third-person narrative concerning a single parent, a writer, taking care of his young child. The text chronicles the every-day interactions between the adult and the child and consists of reflections on the adult's own childhood, art, love, loneliness, and the strains and joys of living with another person.

The narrative begins with the birth of the child—a girl—and the eventual breakdown of the parents' marriage. The adult and child move to Paris and rent a house. The child must adjust to a new environment and a new language. She attends a sectarian school and must make new friends. The dramatic point of their relationship occurs when the adult loses his temper one night and strikes the child. He feels great remorse over his action.

The adult speaks against the modern world, its hypocrisy and false values, yet he tends, on the other hand, to idolize the child, with her innocence and spontaneity. The adult longs for a sense of transcendence, for a "law," a "myth" that will transform his life, and he seems to see that in his child.

### The Characters

The figures in Peter Handke's texts are not traditional novelistic characters with well-defined personalities and emotional structures. Instead, they are philosophical schemata which serve as the starting point for the author's reflections on art, existence, and his own past. To be sure, they are grounded in Handke's autobiography but to a very distanced degree. In *The Long Way Around*, Valentin Sorger, for example, is a somewhat vague and abstract figure struggling with an existential crisis. In interviews, Handke has said that these are his own personal concerns. Sorger's thoughts, however, reveal little of a personality in the typical realistic sense of the word. This holds true for the figures in the other two texts of the series as well.

The narrator of *The Lesson of Mont-Sainte-Victoire* is also somewhat of an intellectual construction; he is concerned with reflecting upon literature, art, and aesthetics. There is some discussion of his emotions and his past life but only in an abstracted sense. He needs to justify or establish his right to be a writer; his experiences require formulation in literary texts.

*Child Story* proceeds at an even more abstract level. Since the story is so clearly autobiographical—Handke reared his daughter as a single parent in Paris—this level of abstraction is a distancing device. The adult and child figures are never given names; thus, they have a kind of universal status. Although there is a definite emotional interaction between the two, it is depicted in a rather reflective manner.

*Themes and Meanings*

*Slow Homecoming* is a fictionalized vision of an artist's personal odyssey that closely reflects the concerns and preoccupations of its author. It is a fanciful account of Handke's coming to terms with both his aesthetic program as an author and his own past life. Although, in terms of surface plot, *Slow Homecoming* does not seem to comprise a connected series of short novels, it is clear that, on a thematic level, the three texts are intimately joined as a whole. Indeed, Handke has expressly indicated that they should be considered as a unit.

To understand what is meant by "homecoming," it is necessary to discuss briefly Handke's biography. He had received international recognition as a novelist and a playwright at the young age of twenty-four in 1966. Almost immediately thereafter, he left Austria and lived—as a single parent with his young daughter—in a number of cities in Germany and finally settled in Paris in 1969. He stayed there for almost ten years. In 1979, he did return to his homeland and has since resided in Salzburg.

The reasons for his self-imposed "exile" are several. He was reared in a provincial area of Austria (the province of Carinthia) and wanted to experience the outside world. The international and cosmopolitan city of Paris is the exact opposite of the small and culturally stifling towns in which he had lived as a child. More important, Handke needed to distance himself from all that his homeland represented to him; on a political level, he vehemently rejects Austria's connection with the Nazis and its often prejudiced and narrow-minded provincial life. The alienated state of his characters reflects to a large degree the author's own existential dislocation.

In the diary *Das Gewicht der Welt* (1977; *The Weight of the World*, 1984), Handke called Austria "the fat on which I have been choking." His childhood had been a painful one. His real father, a soldier in the German army, had never married his mother and his adoptive father was a drunken and rather abusive man. Considering the depressing account he gives of his mother's life in *Wunschloses Unglück* (1972; *A Sorrow Beyond Dreams*, 1974), he must have grown up in a cold and disturbing environment. Handke's early teenage years were spent in a very strict and guilt-ridden Catholic seminary, and it was there that he became aware of the deep feelings of alienation that plagued him. He found that reading (and writing) fiction offered him a temporary escape from the oppressive atmosphere around him, and it was at this early age that he made the decision to become a writer.

The notion that art affords the alienated individual a momentary experience of transcendence from the suffering of life has been the central factor in Handke's work since the beginning of his career and has informed all of his writings. It is primarily an existential view of art. If there is no absolute meaning in the universe but only the significance that the individual human being posits, then the creative faculty is the mode by which mankind ultimately defines itself. In so far as one projects sense onto the senselessness of existence, one is able to transcend, if even for a moment, the pain that being entails. Each text of the *Slow Homecoming* series attempts to work out this idea about the nature of aesthetic creation.

Handke's project as author is intimately connected to his estranged past, and it is no wonder that with artistic success, he fled the source of his pain. With time and age, however, comes healing and a longing to establish a connection to one's roots, to the origins of one's being. The slow "coming home" that is described in these books is an abstracted yet personal record of the author's attempted reconciliation with his inner self and of his efforts to define his task as an artist.

In *The Long Way Around*, Sorger's activity as a geologist serves as a chiffer for Handke's work as a creative artist. Sorger makes sketches of the primitive Alaskan landscape in which the geological story of a millennium is clearly visible. He searches for the eternal forms of nature—not the transitory forms of civilization—that point out the unchanging nature of being. These forms are to be found in the transformations of nature through art. Sorger seeks (almost literally) to be "grounded" in nature just as, at the end of the novel, he longs to return home to the ground of his birthplace. Sorger is an estranged individual and suffers from prolonged feelings of being unconnected, unrelated to the world around him. His sketchings of nature are an attempt to find that sense of connection and totality between his consciousness and the world.

At the midpoint of the text, for example, he draws a geological formation that evidences severe earthquake activity and finds within his sketch the shape of an ancient Indian mask that symbolically depicts the earthquake spirit. Here, reality (the geological formation) and consciousness (the artistic representation of this formation in ritual art) are joined. This provides him with an experience of connectedness to the universe and humanity. He realizes that every moment of his life does fit together in a totality but that he must himself create or imagine the connection. In other words, his art, his imagination, provides the meaning to his life. This same thought is repeated verbatim toward the end of *The Lesson of Mont-Sainte-Victoire*. The presence of this idea in both works points to the centrality of art as the mode of existential transcendence in the *Slow Homecoming* series. The journey home that Sorger begins in the first work is a major part of that search for meaning.

*The Lesson of Mont-Sainte-Victoire*, with its extended reflections on the painter Cézanne, continues the idea of art as transformation and transcendence. Like Sorger, the narrator of this second text is also estranged from civilization, especially the violence and cruelty that it seems to breed. This is made clear in his confrontation with the half-crazed guard dog. The Foreign Legion installation to which the dog belongs represents nationalistic militarism and war, the worst that twentieth century civilization has produced. It is not the production of anxiety and hate or separation and alienation that he seeks but that same sense of totality and connectedness that motivates Valentin Sorger.

This sense of totality—the linking of the inner and outer worlds, of consciousness and reality—the narrator finds expressed in the paintings of Cézanne. The French artist's work captured the *nunc stans*, the almost mystical moment of transcendence when the painful rift between self and world, the cause of all suffering, is momentarily relieved.

The concept is a philosophical notion that finds pertinent expression in the ideas of the nineteenth century German philosopher Arthur Schopenhauer. To exist, Schopenhauer thought, entailed only suffering and pain because of the individual's separation from the "Will," the life force that is the ultimate ground of all being. All living things desire, and desire brings only grief. The only respite from this cycle of desire and suffering is to be found in the contemplation of art, because art halts the activity of the Will in an eternal moment of transcendence; for that moment, the individual can feel a sense of union with the Will.

This kind of aesthetic transcendence is what the narrator finds in the paintings of Cézanne and in the works of other writers and artists. Here, there is a distinct quasi-mystical, quasi-religious dimension to Handke's vision of the aesthetic. The secret of the transformation exists in the imagination, in the creation of forms, colors, words, and fictions. This is the teaching that the narrator discovers in the artist's renderings of the Mont-Sainte-Victoire.

*Child Story*, despite its distanced narration, is a very intimate document of the relations between parent and child, of what each learns and suffers from the other. As with the characters of the first two texts, the adult is seeking some kind of transcendent relationship to reality, and as is also the case with many real-life parents, he finds that connection in his child. He feels that his child somehow incorporates a "law" that can guide his life. There is a degree of romantic idealization of children—their innocence, vulnerability, and emotional spontaneity—yet, as with every cliché, there is an element of truth. Adults have always had a nostalgia for the seemingly unspoiled nature of childhood. This touches upon the rejection of civilization and its corrupting effects that appears as a theme in this and the other texts. The modern age produces alienation in the individual, and the child has not yet become as estranged as the adult.

Like the narrator of *The Lesson of Mont-Sainte-Victoire* and Sorger in *The Long Way Around*, the adult in *Child Story* experiences mystical moments of transcendence when he perceives a harmony or simultaneity between his consciousness and the outside world. For example, near the beginning of the book, he is watching his daughter playing in a park at sundown. For a moment, he observes the bushes on the riverbank swaying in unison with her hair. Again, one finds objective reality (the bushes) in harmony with subjective consciousness (his love for his child). For that second, he is at one with the universe and relieved of his painful feelings of separation. Again, this is an experience of the *nunc stans*, a sense of totality and harmony with the world. He realizes that his task as a writer, as difficult as it may be, is to give form or expression to such moments of transcendence, to such eternal "laws" or "myths" that shape human experience.

## Critical Context

The *Slow Homecoming* series is an ambitious and bold project that is unlike any other work in contemporary German literature. The works do, however, continue the main themes established in earlier Handke texts. The alienation of the individual's consciousness and the subsequent longing for some kind of connection to existence have been major issues in the author's writings since the beginning of his career. Earlier expressions of the longing for a mystical moment of harmony can be found in texts such as *Der kurze Brief zum langen Abschied* (1972; *Short Letter, Long Farewell*, 1974) and even in *Die Angst des Tormanns beim Elfmeter* (1970; *The Goalie's Anxiety at the Penalty Kick*, 1972). In his works of the 1980's, this desire to establish a relationship to the world has attained an almost religious intensity. Handke develops a kind of aesthetic mysticism which sees art as mankind's salvation, as that which preserves and gives meaning to the otherwise random events of life. This is a romantic notion the roots of which go back to the late eighteenth century, in works by writers such as Friedrich Hölderlin, and which has been carried on in the early twentieth century by such German poets as Stefan George and Rainer Maria Rilke.

A number of critics have termed Handke a representative postmodernist author, and the *Slow Homecoming* series serves as a good example of this type of literature. Usually, one associates postmodernism with a deconstruction of cultural myths or signs, an uncovering of the hidden origins of cultural and literary institutions. This is indeed true, but there is also a "constructionist" dimension to the movement, a celebration of the human capacity to generate symbols and signs. If all one's systems of truth or values are arbitrary constructs of language, then one does exist as an aesthetic being who fashions a reality out of the significations that he creates. Man is the only creature who defines himself out of "fictions," who generates his possibilities out of the capacity to imagine other "realities." Handke's works address this theme directly. He writes about the human need to generate myths, because such stories link mankind together. Humanity is defined by its myths.

*Sources for Further Study*

Barańczak, Stanisław. Review in *The New Republic*. CXCII (June 17, 1985), p. 31.

Bradbury, Malcolm. "*Slow Homecoming* by Peter Handke," in *The New York Times Book Review*. XC (August 4, 1985), pp. 10-11.

Dyer, Geoff. Review in *New Statesman*. CX (August 2, 1985), p. 28.

Fellinger, Raimund, ed. *Peter Handke*, 1985.

Melzer, Gerhard, and Jale Tükel, eds. *Peter Handke: Die Arbeit am Glück*, 1985.

Renner, Rolf Günter. *Peter Handke*, 1985.

Schlueter, June. *The Plays and Novels of Peter Handke*, 1981.

Voris, Renate. Review in *Library Journal*. CX (June 15, 1985), p. 72.

*Thomas F. Barry*

# THE SNAIL ON THE SLOPE

*Authors:* Arkady Strugatsky (1925-    ) and Boris Strugatsky (1933-    )
*Type of plot:* Science-fiction satire
*Time of plot:* The near future
*Locale:* A great forest on a foreign planet
*First published: Ulitka na sklone*, 1966-1968 (English translation, 1980)

> *Principal characters:*
> PEPPER, a linguist, once fascinated by the forest, who now
> tries to leave the Directorate
> KANDID, a scientist, marooned in the forest among primitive
> villagers, who sets out to find a way home
> NAVA, Kandid's child-wife
> CLAUDIUS-OCTAVIAN HAUSBOTCHER, the worst bureaucrat of
> them all
> ACEY, a driver at the Directorate and a dedicated sex maniac
> ALEVTINA, a woman who tries to become Pepper's mistress

*The Novel*

*The Snail on the Slope* actually consists of the two largely independent stories of Pepper and Kandid, which are nevertheless brought together by the forest, their continentwide silent antagonist. Whereas Pepper tries to understand this primal mass of foliage from the outside and is entrapped by the Kafkaesque superbureaucracy of the Directorate, Kandid is trapped inside the forest and tries to find a way back to his civilization. On a political level, both protagonists stand for the struggle of the intellectual to find his place in a bureaucratic mass society bent on progress and knowledge; in the end, each arrives at a different solution.

Pepper's story begins with his unsuccessful attempts to leave the Directorate, an institution which has been set up to explore and exploit a gigantic forest. Pepper persuades driver Acey to smuggle him out of the compound after he is caught by the obnoxious, ever-snooping Claudius-Octavian Hausbotcher while sitting on a precipice and lobbing pebbles down into the green mass. Back at work, Pepper is again confronted with the hilarious meddling and inefficiency of a monstrous, self-sufficient bureaucracy, the work of which, like Pepper's multiplications on a faulty machine, produces utterly meaningless results.

At night, Pepper is thrown out of his hostel because his visa has expired. He finds refuge in the compound's library, where he is discovered by Acey and Alevtina, who unsuccessfully tries to entice him to come home with her. Spending a night in Acey's parked truck, Pepper is awakened by the cheerful manager of the garage, who tells him of Acey's punitive relocation to a biostation and keeps him busy with games of chess, until an address by the Director to all personnel distracts the manager. Because his office has been moved, Pepper is the only man without a telephone to hear the address; he is desperate to leave when he meets his superior, Kim, from Science Security, who promises to organize a meeting with the Director for the forlorn linguist.

In a scene reminiscent of Franz Kafka's work, Pepper is ushered through a door labeled NO EXIT, but instead of meeting the mysterious Director he is sent on his way in a truck leaving for the biostation, where the office workers receive their paychecks. Entering the forest for the first time, Pepper finds everything nauseating. Together with Stoyan Stoyanov, the head scientist, and reunited with Acey, Pepper sets out for a brief exploration of some of the forest's wonders. Returning too late, Pepper is picked up only to find himself in the middle of a nighttime alarm: Back at the Directorate, a machine has escaped and everyone is sent searching for it.

After an exhausting night, Pepper finally succumbs to the charms of Alevtina. The next day, he is shooed off the precipice again by Hausbotcher, who chases him all the way to the Director's empty, palatial office. Suddenly, Pepper realizes that he is the next inhabitant of the office. Settling down, he dreams of instituting radical change by means of drastic reorganization and the encouragement of constructive criticism. These dreams are shattered when Alevtina enters and demands his daily directive. Jokingly, Pepper orders the members of the Eradication Group to eradicate themselves and watches in horrified disbelief as his secretary translates this into the serious order to the eradicators to "commit suicide with the aid of firearms today before twenty-four hundred hours. In charge—Hausbotcher."

Kandid's story begins in the forest, where he crashed in his helicopter and is now trapped in the timeless, mildly absurd world of the primitive villagers. He finally rallies his energies for an effort to leave for "the City," village folklore's term for the outside world. Accompanied by his child-wife, Nava, Kandid stands up to the fantastic dangers of the forest and narrowly escapes robbers who are waiting in ambush to abduct Nava. Led by Nava, Kandid arrives at a strangely desolate village. At night, he is awakened by the zombie-like figure of Karl Etinghof, a supposedly dead surgeon from the biostation, who warns off Kandid and Nava, as the villagers suddenly emerge from the forest.

The next morning, Etinghof's village, like others before it, is destroyed by a flood, called "the Accession" by the forest people. Pocketing the surgeon's scalpel, Kandid continues with Nava on their search for "the City." They arrive at a mystical spring shrouded in lilac fog, the place of an otherworldly metamorphosis of the forest's creatures into "deadlings," masses of protoplasm shaped in human form. To his surprise, the "deadlings" are the products of a band of female Amazon-bioengineers who have been responsible for the flooding of the villages in the name of a progressive transformation of the forest. Nava's mother appears and takes back her child; like her two female companions, she hardly takes notice of Kandid, whom they all regard with the arrogant indifference they deem appropriate for dealings with a dumb "lamb," as they call all males.

Killing a "deadling" with Karl's scalpel, Kandid flees and returns to his village alone, where he accepts his fate as a prisoner of the forest—a status he prefers to the company of the female harbingers of a merciless progress.

## The Characters

When Acey and Alevtina find Pepper in the library, Alevtina calls him "pathetic," which is not an inappropriate characterization of the protagonist of *The Snail on the Slope*. It is not that Pepper lacks insight—quite to the contrary. In the beginning, lobbing pebbles into the "living and silent, . . . all-enveloping indifference" beneath, Pepper is not only frustrated by his personal failure to come to terms with the mysterious collective entity of the forest, which has evaded all of his attempts at understanding, but he is also upset with the Directorate, the other collective life-form. Although he came expressly to study the forest, he has never been able to obtain a permit until he rather accidentally stumbles into the biostation; his talents are wasted by the bureaucracy.

Pepper is exhausted because he sees so clearly the futility, even maliciousness, of the efforts of scientists and engineers, who fail to accomplish even their foolish directives to "eradicate" in the name of progress that which evades their intellectual grasp. He accuses the library books of not helping humankind to make any real intellectual progress because they are either stuffed with comfortable lies or lack any use in the alien reality of the forest, which calls for intuitive idealism instead of bureaucratic fumbling and bone-dry scholarly instructions. Describing his ideology as "emotional materialism," Pepper has the intellectual capacities to become a scientist-hero. Like no other character, he shows compassion when he sympathizes with the escaped machine; he equates it with himself and believes that the robot "probably couldn't stand it. . . . They made it do stupid things, . . . and in the evenings they left it, tortured, drained of strength in a hot dry cubicle."

What does make Pepper "pathetic" is his final sell-out and the novel's merciless demonstration of his limitations. In the bitterest moment of *The Snail on the Slope*, the tormented Pepper longs for "people"—"clean, shaved, considerate, hospitable. No high-flown ideas necessary, no blazing talents . . . somebody [who] can run and fill the bath . . . and put the kettle on." Alevtina's luring offer—a hot bath and a warm bed—is the trap through which Pepper falls right into the Director's chair. In Boris and Arkady Strugatsky's novel, plain human goodness is obviously not good enough: It is a trap for those willing to lower their standards in a moment of human weakness.

Kandid, on the other hand, makes the conscious choice to stay with the primitive villagers rather than succumb to the dubious promise of comfort and progress. What triggers this decision is his detection of the total lack of compassion in the female bioengineers, as he witnesses it in their destruction of villages and forest wildlife in order to create their strange protoplasmic homunculi. Nauseated at their "clouds of controlled viruses, columns of robots," Kandid is willing to put his abilities—his skill with Karl's scalpel—to use to defend his village from the engineers' living machines of destruction, the "deadlings," who abduct the villagers' women in order for them to be educated by the Amazons.

Among the minor characters at the Directorate, there are the bureaucrats such as Hausbotcher and Proconsul, who impede everybody, and the specialists, who could do better if they had better directives. The workers do not care and try to cope by avoiding all stress and having as much crude fun as possible; characters such as Acey and driver Voldemar provide for the most humorous moments of *The Snail on the Slope*. In the forest, too, the villagers are drawn with a heartfelt touch of the absurd, thus complementing their civilized counterparts with great irony.

## Themes and Meanings

The responsibilities of the intellectual are a central topic of *The Snail on the Slope*, and the final picture the novel paints is a bitter one. The alternative to compromise is quite literally the barbarous jungle of self-isolation, and Kandid's scientific training is as wasted there as Pepper's linguistic ability is in the chair of the Directorate. In response to the primal forest, human efforts are sorry indeed.

*The Snail on the Slope* contains elements of the fantastic (at the core of Kandid's adventure) and of straightforward science fiction; these elements are linked by political satire, which extends even to the forest scenes. As a science-fiction novel, *The Snail on the Slope* contains a marvelous discussion of the relationship between man and machine. With a touch reminiscent of Thomas Pynchon's postmodern masterpiece *V.* (1963), the Strugatskys' machines have gained uncanny independence. If a worker's account is credible, one of them once left its crate, stretched its metal legs, crawled in again, and nailed shut the lid from the inside, with the spikes of the nails remaining as protruding witnesses. More than this, either because of Pepper's own conviction that the Directorate has turned people into machines or because the machines, like their human counterparts, have developed a growing disaffection for their stupefying work, Pepper even "overhears" their conversation while he is huddled in a depot hoping to outsit the hunt for the renegade robot.

Women and sexuality are put in a rather ambiguous light in *The Snail on the Slope*. The portrayal of the female forest engineers in Kandid's story is balanced by treatment of the equally obnoxious male bureaucracy of the Directorate; instead of misogyny—hatred of women—Soviet critics have charged the Strugatskys with misanthropy—hatred of mankind. It is, nevertheless, Alevtina's femininity which ultimately allows her to entice Pepper. Nava remains a positive figure primarily because of her youth and innocence (she has no children with Kandid), and, as a final touch, Acey's monomaniacal desire for sexual relations seems to fit so well into the Directorate that it is Pepper's first reforming dream to have him castrated, and thus start change in earnest.

## Critical Context

*The Snail on the Slope* was published at the end of the mid-1960's "thaw" in Soviet intellectual life and was made possible by the Strugatskys' successful careers as writers of such science-fiction stories as are collected in *Putna Amalteiu* (1960; *Destination Amalthea*, 1962). Set in the near future on a planet that resembles their home country more than anything else, *The Snail on the Slope* falls into the science-fiction category of the thinly disguised cautionary tale and thus continues the tradition founded in Russia by Yevgeny Zamyatin, whose novel *My* (1952, written 1920-1921; *We*, 1924) was never published in the U.S.S.R., although it is well-known there. Similarly, Kandid's and Pepper's stories first were published separately, and the only complete Russian edition of *The Snail on the Slope* was published in the Estonian Republic in 1972.

*The Snail on the Slope* combines caustic satire, wonderful humor, and fascination with the alien landscape around a carefully eked-out gray bloc of bureaucratic "normalcy." The Strugatskys' novel is powerful because it mercilessly points out human error and arrogance, while, on the other hand, it never loses touch with its unfortunate, obstinate subjects. There is some small hope left that people such as Acey and the villagers will survive despite all attempts to eradicate them, yet bitterness is not diluted in *The Snail on the Slope*'s survey of human scientific achievement. Bureaucrats and technocrats will continue to fail when their work is not coupled with idealistic heroism, but instead gives in to the human predilection for pettiness and the desire to overregulate and suffocate genuine understanding.

## Sources for Further Study

Greene, Diana. "Male and Female in *The Snail on the Slope* by the Strugatsky Brothers," in *Modern Fiction Studies*. XXXII (Spring, 1986), pp. 97-108.

Griffiths, John. "Retreat from Reality," in *Three Tomorrows: American, British, and Soviet Science Fiction*, 1980.

McGuire, Patrick. "Forbidden Themes and Devices (II): The Cautionary Tale," in *Red Stars: Political Aspects of Soviet Science Fiction*, 1985.

Pike, C. R. "Kandid Thoughts," in *The Times Literary Supplement*. November 7, 1980, p. 1264.

Suvin, Darko. "The Literary Opus of the Strugatskii Brothers," in *Canadian-American Slavic Studies*. VIII (Fall, 1974), pp. 454-463.

*Reinhart Lutz*

# SNOW COUNTRY

*Author:* Yasunari Kawabata (1899-1972)
*Type of plot:* Psychological realism
*Time of plot:* The mid-1930's
*Locale:* An unnamed hot-spring resort in Niigata Prefecture, Japan
*First published: Yukiguni,* 1935-1937, serial; 1947, book (English translation,
  1956)

> *Principal characters:*
> SHIMAMURA, a Tokyo literary man whose chief interest is
>   Western ballet
> KOMAKO, a geisha whom Shimamura meets at a hot-spring
>   resort; she reportedly was once engaged to Yukio
> YUKIO, the tubercular son of Komako's music teacher
> YOKO, a girl nursing the dying Yukio; she is Komako's
>   supposed rival for his affection

*The Novel*

In Japan's hot-spring resorts, the distinction between the geisha and the
prostitute is blurred; it depends solely upon the conduct of the particular
woman involved. Yasunari Kawabata's *Snow Country* details the love affair
between one such hot-spring geisha, a young woman named Komako, and a
sophisticated literary man from Tokyo named Shimamura. The novel begins
with Shimamura's early December journey by train from Tokyo to the mountain resort at which he first met Komako the previous spring. It is bitterly
cold once the train passes through the tunnel under the Japan Alps connect-
ing the Tokyo side of Honshu with the "snow country" in Niigata Prefecture
on the other side. Shimamura amuses himself by watching two of his fellow
passengers, a young man obviously suffering some kind of illness and the
younger woman who fusses over him during the journey. The girl has the
fresh beauty that Shimamura finds attractive. He watches the reflection of
her face in the darkened window of the train. "Particularly when a light out
in the mountains shone in the center of the girl's face, Shimamura felt his
chest rise at the inexpressible beauty of it." By contrast, his memory of
Komako is not stirred by this kind of visual stimulus. His hand, "and in particular the forefinger, even now seemed damp from her touch, seemed to be
pulling him back to her from afar."

This detail recalls the fact that Shimamura and Komako became lovers
toward the end of his initial visit to the resort, and it suggests his motive for
returning to the same place in December. In conjunction to his attraction to
the girl on the train, a young woman named Yoko who is nursing the dying
Yukio, Shimamura's sexual attraction to Komako suggests a fundamental

split in his attitude toward women. It also foreshadows the hopelessness of his continuing his relationship with her. Shimamura was attracted to Komako in May because she possessed the innocent freshness he attributes to Yoko. She was not officially a geisha but a music student, and she worked at parties when the inns in the small resort had too many guests. Shimamura tests Komako by asking her to call a real geisha for him—by implication a woman willing to have sexual intercourse with him—and is satisfied by the shy modesty she displays at the request. "With her skin like white porcelain coated over a faint pink, and her throat still girlish, not yet filled out, the impression she gave was above all one of cleanliness, not quite one of real beauty."

Shimamura's attraction to Komako's girlish innocence does not prevent him from taking sexual advantage of her during that May visit. One of Komako's jobs is to drink with the parties of sightseers visiting one or another of the inns in the village. She often slips away from a party to visit Shimamura's room, and in time they become lovers. When he returns to the resort in December, Shimamura finds that Komako has become a professional geisha. She seems to have taken this step to earn the money needed to nurse Yukio, who may or may not have once been her fiancé. Shimamura is disconcerted by this "so ordinary a bit of melodrama" and nearly refuses to believe it. He finds the facts of Komako's situation at variance with the romantic image of her that he cherishes, and as she forces the facts on him, Shimamura is less attracted to her. She confides, for example, that between Shimamura's May and December visits, she considered marrying a man from Hamamatsu. She had thought she was pregnant and needed a father for the child—either Yukio's or Shimamura's, but not that of the man she considered marrying.

When Shimamura leaves the resort at the end of his December visit, he is both convinced that Komako is in love with him and certain that she has not resolved her feelings for Yukio. She accompanies him to the station to catch his train, and Shimamura observes an argument, almost a scuffle, between Komako and Yoko, who appears at the station to call the geisha to the dying Yukio's bedside. When Shimamura emerges on the Tokyo side of the tunnel under the Japan Alps, he feels that he has left Komako behind. He returns to the hot spring the following autumn, however, to find that Yukio has died, that Yoko haunts the cemetery where he is buried, and that Komako still works as a geisha.

Shimamura's third visit to the resort destroys the illusions he has cherished about Komako. She tells him, for example, the story of Kikuyu, another geisha, who lost the restaurant purchased for her by a wealthy patron when she fell in love with an unreliable man who jilted her. Komako is suggesting that Shimamura is just the same sort and that economic necessity requires that she follow her head and not her heart. She says that Shimamura cannot know how it feels to work as a geisha under contract to others, and she recounts details of her routine, including the fact that she must undergo periodic medical examinations for venereal disease. At this point, Shimamura distances himself from Komako and begins to dream of Yoko, seeing her as the embodiment of the purity that he once attributed to Komako. A conversation with Yoko at the inn, where she now works in the kitchen, dispels this illusion. Yoko asks Shimamura to take her into his home in Tokyo as a maid, and the implication exists that she might be willing to grant him sexual favors in return. Strangely enough, Komako is not opposed to the idea that Shimamura might take Yoko away. "Whenever I look at her," Komako says, "I feel as though I have a heavy load and can't get rid of it." She reveals the latent hostility she feels for Shimamura, accusing him of exploiting her emotional vulnerability, and he concedes to himself that she may be right. He believes that the time has come for him to leave.

## The Characters

The ending of Kawabata's *Snow Country* confirms Shimamura's judgment of the situation and makes clear the fact that Komako and Yoko are more than rivals for the attention of Yukio. Shimamura has lingered in the resort, and the first snow of the season falls. It is cold, although not as bitterly so as during his December visit the previous year. Toward the end of day, he meets Komako and goes for a walk, so they are together when the alarm signals a fire at a silk-cocoon warehouse used as a film theater. As the two rush to the scene, Komako speaks frankly about their relationship. "I'm afraid to leave you," she says. "But please go away. I won't forget that you made me cry." She adds, "If you leave, I'll live an honest life." When Komako forces herself past the firemen and into the burning building to seize the body of Yoko, unconscious from smoke inhalation, the juxtaposition of the two women, their essential identity as victims, causes Shimamura to recognize the anguish in his long relationship with Komako. He tries to go to the two women but loses his footing and falls; "his head fell back, and the Milky Way flowed down inside him with a roar."

The attainment of self-awareness implied by this image develops slowly in Shimamura's consciousness, for he has not wanted to recognize the essential hollowness of his own approach to life. Part of his initial attraction to Komako was to the fact that she is interested in the books and plays that her provincial life makes unattainable. Shimamura himself takes pleasure in that which he cannot attain. Initially a student of traditional forms of Japanese dance, he shifts his interest to the Western ballet and its performers precisely because the imaginative pleasure he takes in them cannot be affected by the reality of actual performances. "Nothing could be more comfortable than writing about the ballet from books. A ballet he had never seen was an art in another world. . . . He called his work research, but it was actually free, uncontrolled fantasy." Shimamura's interest in Komako and then in Yoko also reveals this reluctance to accept reality and the desire to pursue an image of beauty from another world. Initially, he is annoyed by the reality of Komako's life. He finds the facts linking her to Yukio and Yoko a barrier to seeing her as a lovely object, and he finds her own emotional attachment to him equally destructive of the fantasy he has about her.

Kawabata brings Shimamura face-to-face with this tendency to romanticize by causing him, just before the fire in the cocoon warehouse, to visit the outlying villages in which a kind of cloth called *chijimi* was once manufactured. The fabric is a kind of linen, particularly expensive because of the conditions under which it was made. "The thread was spun in the snow, and the cloth woven in the snow, washed in the snow, and bleached in the snow." Shimamura is a collector of this linen, a folk product no longer made, and has several summer *kimono* of the old cloth. He subscribes to the superstition that the fabric's coolness in summer results from its manufacture in snowy weather. Having visited the villages in which the cloth was made, he recognizes that production of *chijimi* depended upon exploitation of the young women considered most skillful as weavers. Yoko, he recalls, is from just this sort of village, and in an earlier time she might have been one of the exploited workers. The economic constraints of the present, therefore, are hardly different from those of the past. The reasons that Yoko and Komako must sell themselves to men visiting the hot-spring area are hardly different from those compelling the girls of a hundred years before to prostitute themselves to the production of linen.

*Themes and Meanings*

In *Snow Country*, as in so much of the fiction produced during his career, Kawabata deals with a man preoccupied with the preternatural beauty of one or more young women. Here he presents a typical protagonist in Shimamura, a dilettante from Tokyo, a man in retreat from ordinary life and susceptible to female beauty in its most innocent, virginal form. Kawabata uses a series of reflections, images of mirrors, to demonstrate both the strength of that attraction for Shimamura and its ambiguous nature. The first of these is the sight of Yoko reflected in the window of the train bringing Shimamura to the resort in December. Komako is also observed in her mirror. "The white in the depths of the mirror was the snow, and floating in the middle of it were the woman's bright red cheeks. There was an indescribably fresh beauty in the contrast." The red and white in the mirror link these motifs to others in *Snow Country*, even to the title of the novel itself. The alternation of passion and restraint which the colors suggest marks Shimamura's observation of Komako herself and Kawabata's characterization of her as well. She lives in December in a room lined in white paper that once housed feeding silkworms, the color contrasting with Komako's "vermilion sewing-box" and the "brilliant red under-*kimono*" that she wears as a geisha. The flush that alcohol and passion bring to her cheeks foreshadows the conflagration with which *Snow Country* ends. The fire in the cocoon warehouse, its red flames against the snow, with Komako carrying the unconscious Yoko while the Milky Way shines above Shimamura's head, embodies the indictment of his lack of passion with which the novel ends.

When Shimamura sees Yoko in Komako's arms, the term "metamorphosis" comes to his mind. She wears a patterned *kimono*, a design of arrows on a red background, that links her to her double. Many of the images in the novel recall the resort's previous economic dependence upon textile production, and both Yoko and Komako are like the silkworms in that the economy of the region depends upon their transformation from one condition to another. Equally important is Kawabata's treatment of Komako as a genuine artist. In contrast to his preoccupation with a Western ballet that he has never seen performed, Shimamura acknowledges that Komako's performance on the *samisen* is masterful. The effect is to transform him into a mirror, an instrument reflecting the metaphysical gulf in the universe that is a hallmark of Kawabata's fiction: "A chill swept over Shimamura. . . . The first notes opened a transparent emptiness deep in his entrails, and in the emptiness the sound of the *samisen* reverberated." The sound Shimamura hears is the sound of his own mortality, of life's essential insignificance, of his own unimportance in the larger scheme of things.

*Critical Context*

The male protagonists of many of Kawabata's other novels come to perceive the nothingness at the core of creation; like Shimamura, many of them come to this recognition through the agency of one or another woman. Such characters are found in Kawabata's *Meijin* (1954; *The Master of Go*, 1972), *Yama no oto* (1954; *The Sound of the Mountain*, 1970), and *Nemureru bijo* (1961; *The House of the Sleeping Beauties*, 1969). While *Snow Country* is not the first of his novels to deal with the subject, it is perhaps his most famous treatment of the essential emptiness to be found in the pursuit of beauty. It is the novel for which Kawabata is best known.

*Snow Country* is not, however, the easiest of Kawabata's novels. It lacks the economy of construction of *The House of the Sleeping Beauties*, for example, or the explicitness of the characterizations in *Utsukushisa to kanashimi to* (1965; *Beauty and Sadness*, 1975). The novel also lacks the allusions to Buddhist doctrine that make both these books more coherent statements about the human condition. Because *Snow Country* is an early work, Kawabata is feeling his way toward philosophical positions that come clear in his later fiction. Because the book was written serially over a long period, the novel appears to shift its focus from Shimamura to Komako. If the novel had stopped at the end of the first half of *Snow Country*, the part dealing with

Shimamura's visits to Komako in May and December, it would have been the story of a cynical man's affair with a hot-spring geisha. The second half of the novel, however, the material dealing with Shimamura's autumn visit in the following year, clarifies the factors inducing the irrational behavior that Shimamura observes in both Yoko and Komako. This part of the book makes sense of their suffering, indicates its psychological and economic foundations, and gives it cosmic significance.

*Sources for Further Study*

Keene, Donald. *Dawn to the West: Japanese Literature in the Modern Era*, 1984.

Lippit, Noriko Mizuta. *Reality and Fiction in Modern Japanese Literature*, 1980.

Petersen, Gwenn Boardman. *The Moon in the Water: Understanding Tanizaki, Kawabata, and Mishima*, 1979.

Ueda, Makoto. *Modern Japanese Writers and the Nature of Literature*, 1976.

Yamanouchi, Hisaaki. *The Search for Authenticity in Modern Japanese Literature*, 1978.

*Robert C. Petersen*

# THE SNOW WAS BLACK

*Author:* Georges Simenon (1903-     )
*Type of plot:* Psychological realism
*Time of plot:* The decade of the 1940's
*Locale:* An unnamed city in a Central European country
*First published: La Neige était sale*, 1948 (English translation, 1950)

> *Principal characters:*
> FRANK FRIEDMAIER, a profligate, robber, and murderer
> LOTTE, his mother, a former prostitute and owner of a brothel
> FRED KROMER, his partner in crime and contact with members
>    of the occupying army
> GERHARDT HOLST, his neighbor, a former intellectual and
>    currently a streetcar conductor
> SISSY, Gerhardt's daughter, the object of Frank's debasement
> THE "OLD GENTLEMAN," the foreign officer-interrogator who
>    prods Frank into confession

## The Novel

*The Snow Was Black* begins in a café during winter, in a city occupied by unidentified troops, probably Nazis. Frank Friedmaier, nineteen years old, having borrowed a knife from a friend, Fred Kromer, decides to kill a non-commissioned police officer sitting at a nearby table with two women. Frank does not know the officer's name; he has no apparent reason to kill, as he is not a member of the Resistance. Frank waits outside in an alley, his back against the wall of an unoccupied building, in the darkness, for his unwary prey to pass. He hears footsteps; he sees his neighbor, Gerhardt Holst. He realizes that Holst has recognized him and will know that he is responsible for the murder, but Frank is not deterred.

At home in his mother's apartment, where she keeps a small brothel for the use of the officers of the occupying army, there is the warmth of four working fireplaces and a cornucopia of food donated by the patrons. In a city of scarcity, in a building where their neighbors, including Holst and his sixteen-year-old daughter, Sissy, have little heat and food, Frank and Lotte, his mother, live in relative luxury served by two "employees," Bertha and Minna, who live with them. Frank occupies Bertha and Minna's beds, but he has no feeling for the women who satisfy his sexual appetites. He has no pity for the young violinist upstairs who is arrested for the murder of the police officer, or for the mother who mourns her only son and who will sicken and die from heartbreak. Frank is a pimp, a procurer for his mother; he deals in the black market; he associates with louts and miscreants. Even Sissy, who is infatuated with him, cannot long retain his interest. Frank takes Sissy to the cinema and to the café, where Fred Kromer sees her for the first time. Later, in the café, Frank tells Kromer about Sissy, tantalizing his lecherous business partner, whom he despises, with the prospect of an introduction. In turn, Kromer talks about a general of the occupying army who is a collector with a lust for old watches and who will pay a good price for any that the dealer can obtain. Fifty-fifty, says Frank; fifty-fifty, responds Kromer.

Provided with a car and two accomplices by Kromer, Frank goes to a nearby village, where he had lived as a child, to the home of the old watch-maker, Vilmos, who years before had wound a set of antique watches in the ear of the young Frank. Vilmos is dead, but his sister is forced to divulge the hiding place of the watches, and, because she identifies "little Frank," without mercy, without hesitation, without a scintilla of humanity, he murders the elderly woman.

Frank is capable of any enormity. He plots with Kromer to lure Sissy into a darkened bedroom in his mother's apartment. Frank and Kromer will switch places so that the latter may possess the virginal Sissy. The conspiracy is thwarted; Sissy turns on a light, screams Frank's name, and escapes into the street, leaving behind a purse with the key to her apartment. It is still winter. It is dark and it is cold, and Sissy wanders aimlessly outside in an area of vacant lots, without stockings, over banks of snow. Fearful that she will die of exposure, Frank attempts to find her to return the apartment key, but she mistakes his motives and eludes him. Later, she is brought home and nursed by her father.

Inexplicably, Holst says nothing to Frank and does nothing. Frank is drinking more heavily, flashing a large roll of bills, the proceeds of the robbery-murder. He is restless and reckless; he starts arguments; he has vague premonitions of torture and incarceration. Then, before Christmas, when he least expects it, he is taken into custody by the authorities, ironically for a crime for which he is suspected but which he did not commit.

In a former school building, in a classroom converted into a cell, Frank lives in solitary confinement. He hears other prisoners, sees them thrust into a courtyard to be shot, listens to their moans and to their feeble attempts to communicate with one another. He is taken to an office and questioned by an army officer, who, losing patience, hits Frank with a brass ruler, knocking out three of his teeth and bloodying his mouth. Returned to his cell, Frank sees a woman at a distant window hanging out her wash and fantasizes about her life and that of her child and husband—an ordinary life, a happy one offering a contentment for which he seems to yearn, and that he will not know. Frank is then questioned by another officer, the "Old Gentleman," more skillfully, persistently, and without violence. The interrogations go on for long periods of time, Frank seated on a stool without a back or standing, worn down because his sleep is constantly interrupted; the "Old Gentle-man" with infinite patience, seemingly omniscient, chain-smoking, the butts overflowing a small ashtray. Frank is visited by his mother, who is allowed to bring him food and clothing; she tries to persuade him to cooperate with the authorities. Nevertheless, Frank is still recalcitrant, until he is promised a visit from Holst and Sissy. Frank wants that; he becomes more malleable, more willing to provide information. Holst and Sissy come; Holst forgives Frank, and Sissy declares her love for him. Frank has received absolution; he confesses to the two murders and goes contentedly, almost exultantly, before the firing squad.

## The Characters

To Georges Simenon, the character of Frank Friedmaier is not representative of an ultimately guilty man, bent on self-destruction, but of a victim. Deprived during his childhood, never having known his father, farmed out to strangers, Frank appears at the beginning of the novel to be completely amoral, contemptuous of everyone; he hates both the world and himself. He kills without remorse. Yet even before his arrest, incarceration, and interrogation, there are signs of better emotions. He displays some semblance of compassion: He is concerned about Sissy's physical well-being after her escape from the clutches of Kromer; he gives money to an acquaintance to pay for his sister's eye operation; and he genuinely craves understanding from Holst, whom he regards as a father substitute.

The other characters in *The Snow Was Black* are not as well drawn. They are shadowy figures in a bleak landscape. Until the end, Holst is inscrutable. He lives next door, taking care of his daughter, keeping his own counsel; although he witnessed the murder of the German officer and knows that the young man who is taken into custody is innocent, and although Sissy has been attacked through Frank's connivance, Holst does not inform the authorities. In the novel, he plays the role of the father who absolves Frank of his sins. By visiting him in prison, by placing his hand on Frank's shoulder, "exactly as Frank always thought a father would do," Holst brings Frank peace of mind and solicitude. Holst also tells Frank the sad story of his own son, who stole in order to finance his medical school education, and upon discovery, committed suicide. "He was," says Holst, "twenty-one years old."

Simenon gives the reader few clues to the backgrounds and personalities of the novel's other main characters. Almost nothing is known about Frank's mother except for her profession and that she dotes on her wayward son. Almost nothing is known about Sissy except that she makes a pathetic living by painting flowers on teacups and that she inexplicably worships Frank and is willing to sacrifice herself for him. Nothing is known about the "Old Gentleman" except that he chain-smokes. Like the unknown city in an anonymous country, occupied by an unidentified enemy nation, in the pall of a winter season during an unspecified year, *The Snow Was Black* is largely peopled by phantoms who lurk in the background and who have no voices.

## Themes and Meanings

It is impossible to generalize about the great body of Simenon's work or to place any one novel in a proper perspective. The statistics of Simenon's production are staggering; the frequency of publication is almost incredible. From 1929 to 1973, when he decided to stop writing fiction, renowned for his detective stories and for his character Inspector Maigret, he published under his own name more than two hundred novels. More than fifty films have been made from the novels; it is estimated that there are fifty million copies of his books in print. By any measure, he is certainly one of the most popular and the most prolific of twentieth century writers.

There are, however, certain themes that critics have discerned throughout Simenon's most significant works of fiction which make him one of the great writers of the post-World War II period in French literature. *The Snow Was Black* is regarded as one of Simenon's most powerful evocations of life's disappointments. Frank reflects an effort by man to affirm himself, to give himself an identity; he does it by the only method commonly available, according to Simenon: by violence and crime. In his novels, time and again, the protagonists are violence-prone, and the narratives end in a murder; there is often a rape or a suicide as well. In *The Snow Was Black*, there are murders, an attempted rape, a suicide; torture and executions are perpetrated by the invaders. The novel also portrays the solitude and the alienation of modern life, the inability to communicate, and the escape through sensuality and drunkenness.

The theme of salvation by paternity is also exemplified. To Simenon, the father is often the friend, the teacher, the protector, the exorcist of evil. The strength of paternal love may save Simenon's male characters from debauchery and vice or finally exculpate them from their sins. In *Pedigree* (1948; English translation, 1963), one of Simenon's more autobiographical novels, it is the father's illness that saves Roger Mamelin from moral ruination; in *The Snow Was Black*, it is the father figure who puts Frank at peace.

Finally, in *The Snow Was Black*, as in many other novels by Simenon, there is a jaundiced portrait of women. All the female characters, except Sissy and Vilmos' sister, are prostitutes. Yet even Sissy is like all other women, willing to give up her virginity too easily in return for Frank's attentiveness. Women are enemies and sex objects, to be used, debased, and humiliated. Craving love and affection, they are often servile, treated with indifference, scorned, and rejected. The more soiled they become, the more attractive they appear; Frank, who is bored by Sissy, is more interested in her after the seduction scene with Kromer than he was before it.

## Critical Context

*The Snow Was Black* is an expression of all these themes and of something more. It gives the reader an unremittingly somber portrayal of the loss of pride and value in a society caught in the vise of a totalitarian regime. At the same time, it is only one small piece—though an important one—in the mosaic of Simenon's phenomenal fictional productivity. When *The Snow Was Black* was first published in 1948, it was one of four novels that Simenon had completed during that year, and it was one of nineteen that were written since the end of the German Occupation in 1944. By that time, the French author was being compared to Honoré de Balzac and proclaimed by his compatriot, André Gide, as one of the greatest novelists in the contemporary world.

*Sources for Further Study*

Becker, Lucille F. *Georges Simenon*, 1977.
Bresler, Fenton S. *The Mystery of Georges Simenon: A Biography*, 1983.
Raymond, John. *Simenon in Court*, 1968.
Rolo, Charles J. "Simenon and Spillane: The Metaphysics of Murder for the Millions," in *New World Writing*, 1952.
Simenon, Georges. *Intimate Memoirs: Including Marie-Joe's Book*, 1984.

*David L. Sterling*

# SOLARIS

*Author:* Stanisław Lem (1921-      )
*Type of plot:* Science fiction
*Time of plot:* The distant future
*Locale:* A laboratory station hovering over the ocean which covers Solaris, a
   planet orbiting a double star somewhere in the Milky Way
*First published:* 1961 (English translation, 1970)

>    *Principal characters:*
>        KRIS KELVIN, the narrator, a scientist newly arrived at the
>            Solaris station
>        SNOW, his colleague
>        SARTORIUS, another colleague, who never leaves his
>            quarters
>        RHEYA, a "Phi-creature" formed out of Kelvin's thoughts

## The Novel

Solaris, a planet which orbits a double star, is covered with an "ocean." The ocean is a colloidal substance which, by altering its shape, somehow maintains the orbit of the planet, which otherwise would plunge eventually into one of its suns. Solaris was found by space travelers from Earth in the century previous to the setting of the novel. Its remarkable single inhabitant, the ocean, has caused an entire field of Solarian studies to arise and has produced an enormous library of scientific publications.

Kris Kelvin, a young researcher in "Solaristics," arrives from Earth, descending from an orbiting rocket ship to a laboratory station which hovers above the Solarian ocean. He expects to join three researchers who have been there for some time. He finds the laboratory in great disorder and one of the scientists, Gibarian, dead from a recent suicide. Another, Sartorius, refuses to leave his room, and the third, Snow, reacts in terror to Kelvin's arrival. He has to be convinced that Kelvin is who he claims to be.

Kelvin has an eerie feeling that he is being observed even when he is alone, and *Solaris* is thus, in part, a detective story, in which Kelvin, through a series of deductions, discovers what has caused the disruption in the work of the laboratory.

The Solarian ocean, in fact, is found to be a sentient being, capable of reading the human mind and creating, apparently out of its own substance, exact copies of persons from one's erotic past. Gibarian has been driven to suicide by the presence of his "visitor," a giant African woman whom Kelvin finds sleeping next to Gibarian's corpse. Sartorius remains locked in his room, and Kelvin hears the wild laughter of a child through the locked door.

Snow never permits Kelvin to see his visitor, who nevertheless always seems to be hovering nearby.

Kelvin's first response to these apparitions is to assume that he has lost his mind, but when he checks what he has observed against the laboratory computer's data he finds, somewhat to his dismay, that he is completely sane. At this point Rheya, Kelvin's wife, who killed herself ten years before when he abandoned her, appears in his room—or so it seems. In fact, the visitor is not Rheya, though she obviously believes that she is. Kelvin's response is to trick her into boarding a space shuttle, which he launches into orbit. This is only a temporary solution; a second "Rheya" appears. When she is shut in a room, she claws her way out because these "Phi-creatures" must constantly accompany their hosts. The wounds she suffers in this ordeal heal almost immediately, and when Kelvin tests her blood, he discovers that the ocean has created her body not out of atoms but from subatomic particles.

Kelvin has no illusion that this Rheya is the actual woman he once knew, but her devotion to him is so great that he is determined to save her, even though he suspects that the Phi-creatures cannot survive anywhere but on Solaris. Snow and Sartorius, however, develop a plan for destroying the visitors. Since they emanate from a human's unconscious thoughts during sleep, they might disappear if an encephalogram of the person's mind—his conscious thoughts—were beamed into the ocean. Kelvin agrees to let them use his encephalogram for this purpose.

Rheya listens to a tape in which Gibarian, before he died, explained his theories about the visitors. In despair, she attempts to kill herself by drinking liquid oxygen, but she recovers immediately. She and Kelvin both know that she is not Rheya, but Kelvin tells a lover's lie: that she actually is human. He is determined to remain with her at the station for the rest of his life.

When Rheya asks Snow to confirm the truth of what Kelvin has told her and he does not, she convinces him to destroy her by means of the "destabilizer" which he and Sartorius have perfected. In his sorrow over the loss of Rheya, Kelvin asks Snow to join him in a recommendation to the four-power council on Earth for the total destruction of the ocean. Snow refuses; he still wants to achieve the great goal of human exploration of space—contact with an alien intelligence, a process understood in the novel as something resembling divine revelation.

Finally, Kelvin leaves the station to set foot on a kind of beach, a scrap of "land" created by the ocean, because he wants to make contact with the single creature of Solaris. When he holds out his hand to a wave, the "water" enfolds his hand but does not touch it. It is a despairing moment for Kelvin because he can see now that contact with the mind of the ocean is impossible and because he is sure that Rheya will not return. In spite of his disillusionment, he intends to stay on Solaris, hoping for nothing but persisting in "the faith that the time of cruel miracles was not past."

## The Characters

At the beginning of the novel Kris Kelvin is a confident and capable scientist who comes to Solaris convinced that he knows everything about the planet that can be known through existing knowledge and technology. In the chaos which he encounters in the station, he stands in contrast to Snow and Sartorius, who clearly have become unhinged by their experience. Kelvin's devotion to the rational ideals of science is so great that when he proves that the visitors exist, he almost wishes that, instead, he had found that he was merely insane.

By the end of the novel Kelvin has achieved an essentially tragic wisdom. For too long, he had managed to conceal his responsibility for Rheya's suicide even from himself, repressing his own emotions, which she embodied. Ironically, one of his specialties is psychology, but his knowledge of the human mind does not equip him for what he encounters on Solaris. He has lived since Rheya's death with a deep sense of guilt which he has submerged along with his own emotions. The ocean brings this out and gives it shape in the form of the Phi-creature "Rheya." Kelvin's relationship to this creature is, in this sense, that of the conscious, rational mind to the unconscious mind. Just as Kelvin, in a sense, killed his wife, Rheya, so he kills the first Rheya sent to him by the ocean, and the suicide of his wife is repeated in the suicide of the second Rheya. The effect of this confrontation is his realization of the value of the emotional side of human existence.

Sartorius is essentially invisible in the novel because he remains in his quarters, apparently unwilling to permit his colleagues to see his "visitor." Snow keeps his visitor in a locker when Kelvin visits his quarters, and it seems even more ominous because it is never seen. Snow himself is a proponent of the idea of "Contact," that is, of human encounter with an alien intelligence, but he also seems to recognize that no such contact is possible.

In a sense, the most important character in the novel is the "ocean" itself, although it cannot be characterized. Indeed, that it cannot be known is the point of the novel. From one point of view it is a malign being playing tricks on its human visitors. Snow suggests that it may only be a courteous host, who gives the Phi-creatures to its guests as "presents." From another view it is almost divine, an omnipotent god who can give or take from humans as it wishes. In any case, the ocean can only be defined in terms of human knowledge, and this dilemma of the essentially anthropomorphic limitations of all definitions of alien reality is the heart of Stanisław Lem's theme.

## Themes and Meanings

Lem's story is dual: It deals with the relationship between Kelvin and his visitor at the same time that it unfolds the many philosophical implications of the attempt to make contact with the mind of the ocean. Lem's thesis is that all attempts to define reality, on earth or in space, are inevitably anthropocentric. An author of one of the books in Solarian studies maintains that all scientific achievements reveal the projection of anthropomorphic definitions on all reality. As a result, genuine contact between humans and a nonhuman intelligence or civilization is, by definition, impossible. Snow tells Kelvin that all space travel is nothing more than the attempt to define the entire cosmos in the terms of Earth: "We are only seeking Man. . . . We don't know what to do with other worlds. A single world, our own, suffices us; but we can't accept it for what it is."

This idea is repeated in a passage which relates the cosmic implications of Lem's thesis to the relationship between Kelvin and "Rheya": "Man has gone out to explore other worlds and other civilizations without having explored his own labyrinth of dark passages and secret chambers, and without finding what lies behind doorways that he himself has sealed." In other words, at the same time that human beings impose human definitions on the rest of the universe, they neglect to take account of their own human nature. They thus fail to understand both the universe without and the universe within.

Lem's theme, therefore, in spite of his condemnation of this double human failure, is emphatically humanist. That human knowledge is burdened with limitations does not mean that humans should not use that knowledge to explore to the fullest the human condition here on earth, both the inner world of the mind and emotions and the external moral world of social and personal relations.

Finally, the novel suggests a theological implication of the human encounter with Solaris. Kelvin defines for Snow an imperfect and even sick god, a god whose power and knowledge are limited and who thus creates horror: a god, like the ocean, who simply exists. For Kelvin, this would explain the inability to make contact with the ocean. If it is like the god he has hypothesized, its creation of the visitors has been to no purpose, neither benign nor evil. This notion also supports Lem's thesis that the acquisition of human knowledge is hopelessly flawed and leads inevitably to tragedy. If the god of the cosmos is like the ocean, then the attempt to make contact with it is doomed and subject to the experience of its "cruel miracles." The only appropriate effort is the exploration of human psychology, the improvement of relations between individuals and societies, and the maintenance of sane and healthy life on earth.

*Critical Context*

*Solaris* may be understood, in part, as an expression of Lem's basic criticism of the science-fiction genre. Lem is convinced that if alien worlds truly are alien they cannot be known or understood in terms of human preconceptions. The predicament of the Solarian scientists, in other words, is that of science-fiction writers, whom Lem accuses of denying the existence of the predicament and thus falsifying the reality they seek to present.

In this connection, it is ironic that Lem's own account of a human encounter with an alien intelligence is presented through the traditional methods of the "realistic" novel. He gives titles to his chapters, he employs conventional methods of characterization, and his plot bears considerable resemblance to that of a detective story. Lem seems deliberately to have chosen these traditional methods in order to demonstrate his basic premise: One can comprehend a new reality only in the terms one already knows.

If *Solaris* is itself a critique of science fiction as a genre, it also offers an extraordinary example of a complete planetary environment, with its own nonterrestrial phenomena and its own science for explaining those phenomena. *Solaris* is a paramount example of science fiction. The circumstances it describes are based upon Lem's virtually total scientific understanding of the novel's scene.

*Sources for Further Study*

Ketterer, David. "*Solaris* and the Illegitimate Suns of Science Fiction," in *Extrapolation*. XIV (1972), pp. 73-89.

Rose, Mark. "Filling the Void: Verne, Wells, and Lem," in *Science Fiction Studies*. VIII (1981), pp. 121-142.

Solotaroff, Theodore. "A Master of Science Fiction—and More," in *The New York Times Book Review*. LXXXI (August 29, 1976), pp. 1, 14.

Suvin, Darko. "Afterword: The Open-ended Parables of Stanisław Lem and *Solaris*," in *Solaris*, 1971.

Ziegfeld, Richard E. *Stanisław Lem*, 1985.

*Robert L. Berner*

# SOME PREFER NETTLES

*Author:* Jun'ichirō Tanizaki (1886-1965)
*Type of plot:* Psychological realism
*Time of plot:* March through June, 1929
*Locale:* Osaka, Awaji, Kobe, and Kyoto
*First published: Tade kuu mushi,* 1928-1929, serial; 1936, book (English
   translation, 1955)

*Principal characters:*

> KANAME, the protagonist, in his mid-forties, a sinecurist in his
>    father's company, who for eight years has sexually
>    withdrawn from his wife
> MISAKO, Kaname's wife, who for the last two years has been
>    having an affair
> HIROSHI, the ten-year-old son of Kaname and Misako, a
>    sensitive boy who is trying to conceal his anxiety about
>    his parents
> MISAKO'S FATHER
> O-HISA, the longtime mistress of Misako's father
> HIDEO TAKANATSU, Kaname's divorced cousin, a businessman

## The Novel

In the first of what may be regarded as the novel's four main parts (chapters 1-3), the unhappy and taciturn couple dress in traditional kimono, take train and taxi to downtown Osaka, and then join Misako's father and O-hisa at the Benten Theater to view the puppet play *The Love Suicides at Amijima.* While Kaname has accepted the invitation in order to ensure one filial act before his father-in-law is informed of the couple's marital discord, he becomes intrigued by the play and the puppets, especially that of the heroine— a kind of prototype of the ideal woman for his father-in-law and himself. In contrast, Misako has unwillingly attended, seeking the earliest excuse for the couple's departure so that she may "go to Suma," the euphemism she and Kaname out of reciprocal consideration use for her trysts with a Mr. Aso. (Kaname has given his consent to the affair.)

In the second part (chapters 4-8), arriving from a regular business trip to China, Takanatsu delivers gifts to Hiroshi (a greyhound named "Lindy," after the famous Charles Lindbergh), Kaname (an unexpurgated set of *The Arabian Nights' Entertainments*), and Misako (her choice of scarves), although his main purpose at Kaname's behest is spurring the indecisive and delaying couple to act: either to reconcile, or more probably to separate.

In the third part (chapters 9-12), the theater motif is resumed when, at the invitation of his father-in-law, Kaname joins him and O-hisa in Awaji to see performances of the puppet theater at its rural birthplace and possibly accompany the couple on a pilgrimage to shrines on the island. Staying a few days to see the plays and puppets, Kaname declines the pilgrimage and departs for Osaka, stopping at Kobe to visit an Englishwoman's foreign brothel in the narrative's surprise revelation of Kaname's two-year relationship with the Eurasian courtesan Louise (of Russian and Korean extraction).

As the second part opens with a letter (Takanatsu's to Hiroshi), so does the fourth section (chapters 13-14), with Misako's father responding to Kaname's detailed written report of the reasons for divorce and for Misako to marry Aso. Courteously but firmly summoned, Kaname and Misako travel to the aging parent's house in Kyoto, where Kaname is importuned to reconsider and then left to dine with O-hisa while Misako's father takes his daughter to dinner and attempts to dissuade her from the couple's announced plan. The novel closes with Kaname in the guestroom bed at night, awaiting the return of Misako and her father, wondering if Misako has been dissuaded from divorce (a decision which Kaname would accept), listening to the rain that has been imminent for some time, and through the bed's mosquito netting observing first the female puppet his father-in-law purchased in Awaji and then the doll-like O-hisa, who brings some old Japanese woodblock books for him to leaf through as he waits.

## The Characters

Both this novel and Jun'ichirō Tanizaki's *Fūten rōjin nikki* (1961-1962; *Diary of a Mad Old Man*, 1965) open with the protagonist attending the theater (art is a pervasive motif in the majority of Tanizaki's novels) and relating to the drama by sexual attraction to the heroine. Whereas Tokusuke Utsugi in *Diary of a Mad Old Man* is enticed by a male actor playing a female role, emblematic of Utsugi's masochism in the full sense, Kaname is allured by the puppet Koharu's appearance of classical beauty that is "withdrawn, restrained, careful not to show too much individuality"—in short, the submissive "eternal woman" of Japanese tradition. The failure of Kaname's complete attachment to Misako in part results from her being neither the courtesan type (Koharu's role in the play) nor, as a modern woman, a puppet deprived of human individuality.

Nearly all the novel's characters, caught in a variety of conflicting circumstances and forces, are described with the imagery and vocabulary of theater, reflecting their adoption of or coercion into roles. Obliged to conceal their unorthodox arrangement from Misako's father and Aso's relatives, Kaname and Misako have "to put on their disguises and act their parts"; Misako has to "play the part of the wife" before her father; irritated by her restlessness at the Benten Theater, Kaname thinks Misako "ought to restrain herself and play the part of the wife"; and the couple are relieved that "there was no need to act in front of" Takanatsu and that they are momentarily "free not to play at being husband and wife." From dread of their separation as well as solicitude for his parents' burdens, Hiroshi is "perhaps acting a part as carefully as they were, hiding his troubles from them."

Devoted to tradition, Misako's father at the Benten Theater wears clothing "like the costumes of the puppets," at Awaji is "appointed like a doll on the stage," and at his house in Kyoto looks "ready for the role of a poet on the stage." O-hisa, from her upbringing and temperament accepting her pupillary role, is recurrently compared to a beautiful, docile puppet or doll; Misako's father ultimately acquires a real doll as well (significantly, Misako relegates the dolls her father bought her for the Doll Festival). Indeed, even Kaname's acquaintances in the demimonde are caught up in role-playing. The ostentatious brothel owner Madame Brent, even when mourning her brother, is "striking too many poses," while the pretentious Louise has "the manner of a melodramatic actress of the new school" and a "dramatic bill of complaints" with "straining and storming."

Only the admirable Takanatsu, cigar-smoking and garlic-chewing (the latter habit prophylactic, derived from his contact with Chinese culture), remains outside the role-playing and in his concluding letter (chapter 13) discloses the novel's most trenchant actions (his telling Hiroshi the truth, to spare the boy further uncertainty and inure him to the ways of the real world) and analyzes (Misako's absolute necessity to leave Kaname; Kaname's self-pampering that needs a serious blow).

## Themes and Meanings

An overarching theme is the threading of life, particularly Japanese life, with dualities that produce tension, discomfort, or obstacles. These dualities, often interrelated, include East versus West, Osaka or Kyoto culture (crude, old-fashioned, tranquil) versus Tokyo culture (sophisticated, modern, busy), past versus present, the courtesan versus the mother or goddess (the male's perception of women), active versus passive, and art or artifice versus life. The first of these subsumes the continual contrast between kimono versus Western dress, the music of the puppet theater versus jazz, the Joruri puppet versus the Occidental marionette, the Japanese versus foreign wing of an affluent home, the Oriental degradation of women in drama versus Hollywood deification.

While Misako's father and O-hisa choose East, Osaka and Kyoto, the past and tradition, and the roles of dominant male and submissive female, Kaname and Misako are torn and waver. Added to this paralyzing irresolution is the passivity inherent in Tokyo values. Early in the novel Kaname dimly realizes that "the son of Tokyo," in contrast to the Osakan, is prone "to an excessive concern with appearances and a timid unwillingness to act"; in the middle of the novel he recollects thinking:

the ancients would perhaps have called it girlish sentimentality, this inability to face up squarely to the sorrow of a farewell. Nowadays, however, one is counted clever if one can reach a goal without tasting the sorrow, however slight it may be, that seems to lie along the way.

Appropriate to their watery vacillation, among the most prevalent imagery in the novel is that of liquid, often associated with Kaname or Misako or both. Despite the Tanizakian irresolution of the novel's end, the rain (which culminates the recurrent liquid imagery) suggests that, like the heavy, static, irresolute climate, Kaname's and Misako's lives have languidly drifted to precipitating conclusion.

## Critical Context

Among Tanizaki's twenty-five or so original novels, *Some Prefer Nettles* falls among those that are short—the majority, with the notable exception of *Sasame-yuki* (1943-1948; *The Makioka Sisters*, 1957); set in the twentieth century (the other novels being set in the past, anytime from the Fujiwara to Tokugawa periods); and written after Tanizaki's transforming experience of the great Tokyo-Yokohama earthquake of 1923 (referred to three times in *Some Prefer Nettles*) and his subsequent resettlement in the Kyoto-Osaka region (as several of the characters have also done in the novel). The novels of this period are generally considered to be his best, with *Some Prefer Nettles* often nominated as the leader; indeed, up to his death, Tanizaki was regarded as a leading candidate for the first Nobel Prize for Literature to be awarded to a Japanese writer. Tanizaki is reported to have written in 1948 that the novels he liked best were *Some Prefer Nettles* and *Yoshino kuzu* (1931; *Arrowroot*, 1982).

Some of the longest discussions of aesthetics occur in *Some Prefer Nettles*, in which art (drama, music, ceramics) is so often a part of the plot and the characters' interests. On this point, the novel is closest to "Shisei" ("The Tatooer"), "Mōmoku monogatari" ("The Blind Man's Tale"), and "Shunkin shō" ("A Portrait of Shunkin"). In fact, the blind samisen player from whom Misako's father and O-hisa take lessons foreshadows the centrality of an analogous character in "The Blind Man's Tale" and "A Portrait of Shunkin." In the former short work, the narrator (who is the title character) receives and transmits clandestine coded messages through variations of samisen music, which leads to the climactic downfalls of himself and the noble samurai household he serves and loves; in the latter, the blind mistress Shunkin and her self-blinded servant (and lover) Sasuke devote their lives to their musical art, to the exclusion of the surrounding world. In *Some Prefer Nettles*, art and life are often shown interacting—comically when audience noise and public juvenile urination drown out the puppet play performance in Awaji, and when the puppeteers (possibly in retaliation) enact in one of their plays a character stepping outside to urinate before going to bed.

*Sources for Further Study*

Keene, Donald. *Dawn to the West: Japanese Literature of the Modern Era*, 1984.

Lippit, Noriko Mizuta. *Reality and Fiction in Modern Japanese Literature*, 1980.

Petersen, Gwenn Boardman. *The Moon in the Water: Understanding Tanizaki, Kawabata, and Mishima*, 1979.

Seidensticker, Edward G. Introduction to *Some Prefer Nettles*, 1955.

Ueda, Makoto. *Modern Japanese Writers and the Nature of Literature*, 1976.

*Norman Prinsky*

# A SORROW BEYOND DREAMS

*Author:* Peter Handke (1942-    )
*Type of plot:* Philosophical realism
*Time of plot:* The early 1920's to the early 1970's
*Locale:* A small Austrian village, Berlin, and Frankfurt
*First published: Wunschloses Unglück*, 1972 (English translation, 1974)

> *Principal characters:*
> THE NARRATOR, a writer who tries to tell his mother's life story
> HIS MOTHER, a housewife who has committed suicide

## The Novel

*A Sorrow Beyond Dreams*, the story of the life and death of Peter Handke's mother, can be considered a novel in the sense that all biography and autobiography verge upon fiction when the writer imposes a pattern of meaning upon the facts. Handke recognizes a conflict when he tells the reader that "in looking for formulations I was moving away from the facts," and he fears reducing his mother's story to a mere "literary ritual." At the same time, he sees that readers other than himself will want to move beyond his mother's specific case to "generalizations" about the human condition; for them, the formulations are more interesting than the unvarnished facts.

*A Sorrow Beyond Dreams*, then, is not only the story of Handke's mother but also the story of Handke composing the story about his mother. The novel opens with a quotation from a small-town Austrian newspaper: "In the village of A. (G. township), a housewife, aged 51, committed suicide on Friday night by taking an overdose of sleeping pills." The sparse, objective report is followed by the narrator's subjective reaction to the death, a mixture of horror and apathy, and his rationale for writing about the death: He wants to explain it, to bring himself "back to life," and "to represent this VOLUNTARY DEATH as an exemplary case." More important even than these reasons, he senses a need to transcend "moments of extreme speechlessness" and seek control over experience, or at least control over its impact on him.

The writer's mother (who is never more specifically named—indeed, the narrator never names himself) was born in the early 1920's of peasant stock in a small Austrian village. Education was barely imaginable for boys, and it was "unthinkable" for girls; "a girl's future was a joke." Desiring to study something and, in so doing, create a life for herself, she left home as a girl to learn cooking at a resort hotel. For a short time, she was happy. She embraced Adolf Hitler and the communal pride he promoted, went out on dates, enjoyed herself, and fell in love with a married man—a German party member by whom she conceived her first child, the narrator himself.

Pregnancy brought an end to the incipient struggle for freedom and personhood; instead, it allowed the triumph of duty when the mother married a man she detested, an army sergeant from Berlin, "to give the child a father." From this point forward, the narrative is a descent into hopelessness, an account of a joyless marriage punctuated by three more births and three secret abortions and a story of a dreary routine, which offered little reward.

When, after the war, the alcoholic husband lost job after job in Berlin, the couple returned to the Austrian village of the wife's birth. It was a time when the woman "could laugh anyone to silence," and she seemed to use laughter as a defense against powerlessness. She certainly used it to destroy her husband's dreams. Laughter was the only thing that was hers. If, in the city, she had allowed herself to become a "type," in the village no personal life at all remained possible, and "individual" was a dirty word. Her energy went into "scrimping" when there was barely enough income to support existence; it went into "imitating the *pattern* of middle-class life." She sensed that there was something more to be had from living but had no one to help her find it.

Eventually, the acquisition of household appliances changed her life. She had time to read books, to form political opinions, and to become a person rather than function merely as a machine. Yet heightened awareness brought heightened misery: headaches, a nervous breakdown, and a feeling of futility. In quest of a reason to go on living, the woman wanted to adopt a child but was denied one because of her husband's tuberculosis. Methodical, tidy, and compulsively clean to the last, "she wrote letters of farewell to everyone in her family" and lined her underpants with diapers before she lay down to die.

The mother's death does not conclude the story. Her son leaves his home in Frankfurt to attend the funeral, feels a need to write about his mother, does write about her, and decides, "It is not true that writing has helped me." He feels "like a decaying animal . . . attacked by. . . horror." In one last desperate effort to make meaning of his mother's life and of his feelings about it, Handke records a series of brief observations in the last few pages of his narrative, concluding with the line: "Someday I shall write about all this in greater detail."

## The Characters

What the narrator chooses not to say about his mother is almost as revealing as what he does say. He does not record her name because, among family members, she was nearly always called "Mother." He does describe the "swollen scar on her index finger," to which he "held on" as a child. It is as if the woman did not exist for herself as an individual; she existed only in the prescribed roles she played: wife, mother, and caretaker. According to the critic Jerry Varsava, the power of language to keep women in their traditional roles is a major theme in the novel. Indeed, Handke's mother was no different from all the other women in the village, women whose progress through life could be reduced to the formula: "Tired/Exhausted/Sick/ Dying/Dead." Formulas seemed to exist to describe every occasion, encouraging little deviation into individuality: Husbands "got FRESH" and wives "had to be SEVERE," and so on.

If Handke's mother never fully emerged into individuality, it was not for the lack of desire to do so. As a child, she sought knowledge in order to feel "something of herself." Later, in adulthood, when labor-saving appliances gave her a respite from housework, she read "books with stories she could compare with her own life." Literature, however, merely showed her "everything she had missed" rather than what she still might do. It is no coincidence that the days in which "she was gradually becoming an individual" were quickly followed by blinding headaches, debilitating guilt about her duty toward family members, and a nervous breakdown.

Woman's role, as it was conceived in her village, did not permit individuality. (One might add that the men seemed scarcely more fortunate.) Recovery from the breakdown could only bring a return to a meaningless existence. The suicide was an act of individual assertion by a woman who could not imagine any release from her suffering much less a positive course of action that would allow her to create a motive for continuing to live.

In searching for the significance of his mother's story and in creating that significance, the narrator pursues his own quest for meaning. Just as "*telling* about it was a need with her," telling about it is a compulsion with her son. Whether the writing helps him in the sense of soothing him or allowing him to believe he has explained the tragedy is beside the point. He claims it does not help. Nevertheless, writing is his characteristic activity; he worries over it, writes about it, and discusses the composing process with the reader. The narrator fears losing control of the process and finds in it no salvation. He is his mother's son in thinking that there should be something more, something he has not yet discovered. Yet unlike her, he has not given up the attempt to make meaning out of recalcitrant materials. The promise, or threat, to "write about all this in greater detail" sounds like a joke, following, as it does, the detailed account the reader has just perused. It may also be a recognition that writing—like life—is an unfinished process until death ends it, and the narrator is still engaged in both those processes, busily creating a world of words even if it does not allow him to escape the feeling that he is "rotting away from second to second." "He not busy being born is busy dying," reads an epigraph, quoted from a Bob Dylan song, to the novel. Critics Jerome Klinkowitz and James Knowlton would argue that Handke, in creating this "Life Story," re-creates himself. He is busy being born.

*Themes and Meanings*

*A Sorrow Beyond Dreams* can be classified as "metaliterature," literature which explores the process of making literature and which, self-reflectively, asks the reader to think about what literature is and does. The fact that the novel begins not with the mother's life story but with the narrator's discussion of his reasons for writing that story makes the reader acutely aware that the narrator's account is his version of events. There is no pretense of mere disinterested objectivity; from the beginning, the narrator hopes for some sort of personal salvation through telling the story.

Nevertheless, he worries that the very conventions of storytelling will discredit his story: " 'it began with . . .'; if I started like this, it would all seem to be made up." When, in the following sentence, the narrator writes, "Well then, it began with . . . ," he seems to suggest that all stories are made up, even true ones. Throughout the novel, the reader sees the narrator's process of making up the story, which he presents as a series of fragments separated by asterisks (or other marks) and interrupted by explanations of his method.

The themes the narrator explores in his mother's story appear simple enough: the oppression of women, the deprivation produced by lack of education, and the need for individual self-fulfillment. The narrator presents his mother as a bright but uneducated woman who never had a chance to make something more of herself than a slave to duty and who killed herself as a result.

This neat, tidy analysis of the mother's suicide is undercut by the narrator's recurring horror and sense of futility. He, after all, has gone to a university, has read the right books, and has become a sophisticated writer. He has had opportunities his mother never had, opportunities for achievement, self-fulfillment, and individual expression. Yet he, too, is tortured by existence. Pity and fear for his mother become pity and fear for himself, as he struggles both to interpret her life and to understand his own. Finally, the horror that haunts him is not merely the consequence of a particular set of circumstances—those of his mother's life; it is an inescapable part of self-conscious human existence. Artistic activity can neither explain away the horror nor allow the narrator to forget about it for long; if anything, writing about the fear keeps it constantly before him. Still, the writing appears to be a defense against the horror in that it keeps the writer alive and gives him readers, with whom he can share his fear. He is less isolated than his mother even if he is just as afraid. The life story is his rather than hers.

*Critical Context*

*A Sorrow Beyond Dreams* may be the most accessible and the most moving of Handke's works, all of which deal with the (often tenuous) connections between art and life and with the process of making literature. Handke seeks to discredit the old mimetic conception of art; art is not necessarily a mirror of life that allows its audience to see life more clearly. The world created by the work of art is different from the real world; there may be parallels between the two worlds, but the patterns of meaning in the work of art are created by the artist and, as such, may not correspond to anything discoverable in the real world.

What the "real world" consists of is another question, one which the artist may not be able to answer, according to Handke. On the other hand, it may be that the artist knows as much as anyone can, for facts by themselves are empty; only interpretations of the facts are meaningful. One fictionalizes the facts (creates one's own version of events) before one can deal with them.

Since Handke wishes to challenge traditional assumptions of what art is and can do, his work is, at times, deliberately unsettling, as in the play *Publikumsbeschimpfung* (1966; *Offending the Audience*, 1969), which methodically thwarts the audience's expectations. While such works are clever, the audience or reader is offended. In *A Sorrow Beyond Dreams*, it is the narrator who is thwarted and frustrated by the limitations that artistic conventions necessarily impose, and the reader watches and sympathizes. The novel engages the emotions as well as the intellect. After all, what reader has not sought to make meaning out of a tragedy that has befallen him? *A Sorrow Beyond Dreams* is not only a provocative piece of meta-literature but also an enduring work of art that speaks to every reader.

*Sources for Further Study*

Klinkowitz, Jerome, and James Knowlton. *Peter Handke and the Postmodern Transformation*, 1983.

Mixner, Manfred. *Peter Handke*, 1977.

Schlueter, June. *The Plays and Novels of Peter Handke*, 1981.

Varsava, Jerry A. "Auto-Bio-Graphy as Metafiction: Peter Handke's *A Sorrow Beyond Dreams*," in *CLIO*. XXIV (1985), pp. 119-135.

Wilkie, Brian, and James Hurt. "Peter Handke," in *Literature of the Western World*. II (1984), pp. 2241-2243.

*Linda Seidel Costic*

# THE SOUND OF THE MOUNTAIN

*Author:* Yasunari Kawabata (1899-1972)
*Type of plot:* Psychological realism
*Time of plot:* The early 1950's
*Locale:* Kamakura, Tokyo, and Shinshu
*First published: Yama no oto*, 1949-1954, serial; 1954, book (English translation, 1970)

> *Principal characters:*
> SHINGO, an elderly businessman
> YASUKO, his wife
> SHUICHI, their son
> FUSAKO, their daughter
> KIKUKO, Shuichi's wife

## The Novel

*The Sound of the Mountain* narrates the events in the life of a certain elderly Japanese businessman, Shingo, and demonstrates the way these events impinge on and help shape his psychological states. Shingo, whose creeping senility is counterpoised by an ever more vivid memory of the past, seems to desire nothing more than to recede from the hubbub of daily life. Unfortunately, just as he might begin to indulge himself in idle philosophical contemplation, a pastime perhaps suited to one awaiting death, he finds himself embroiled in the most mundane of problems: the difficult and troubled marriages of his son and daughter.

Shuichi, Shingo's son, is having an affair with a war widow and thus begins to neglect his wife, Kikuko. Since the young couple live in Kamakura with Shingo and his wife, Yasuko, the difficulties with the marriage are manifest and all the more disturbing to Shingo. He is distraught at what he regards as his son's dissolute and immoral behavior, but of even greater concern to him is the health and well-being of his beautiful but delicate daughter-in-law. Meanwhile, Shingo's daughter, Fusako, is also known to have marital problems; she may even have been beaten by her husband. After a period of some vacillation, she decides to move back to Kamakura to be with her parents, bringing her two young children with her. There, Fusako relinquishes her children to the care and supervision of Kikuko and appears to resign herself to a long and unhappy life. Shingo, troubled by his daughter's bitterness and apathy, tries to embolden her with a sense of purpose and direction, but to no avail.

Shingo clings tenaciously to the hope that his children's marriages will weather the storms that are besetting them and survive. Regardless of his children's prospects for happiness, Shingo seems to uphold the institution of marriage: Although it cannot guarantee a happy life, he believes that marriage can at least provide the basis for a meaningful and moral one. This attitude, implicit in all that Shingo does or says, is clearly endorsed by Yasunari Kawabata. No doubt it reflects, in general, the difference between Japanese and Western attitudes with regard to the proper balance between social responsibility and self-realization. Shingo's own marriage to Yasuko is really no less unhappy than the ones he tries to nurse back to health, but this is as much a fact to him as the reality and finality of death.

Kikuko, without the family's knowledge, becomes pregnant and, for reasons of her own, has an abortion. When Shingo learns of the matter, he is shocked at Kikuko's actions, but forgives her nevertheless. After all, it was Shuichi's cruelty, he argues, which led to this tragedy. Still worse, because he had not intervened in time, Shingo cannot help but sense that he himself must carry some of the responsibility for the ill-conceived deed. Later, Shingo learns that Shuichi's mistress also is expecting a baby. Motivated by a kind of poetic justice, he entreats her to have an abortion but is eventually haunted by the thought that, should the woman in fact accede to his request, he would be implicated in yet another murder.

Shuichi and his mistress become estranged. She leaves Tokyo for the provinces, apparently to have her baby. Meanwhile, Shuichi and Kikuko seem to be reestablishing a bond, making Shingo hopeful that their marriage will indeed survive. Fusako, on the other hand, remains unreconciled with her husband, who has barely survived a suicide attempt. The novel closes on a quiet note, with a dinner scene at which the family of seven must share three pieces of trout. Shingo, ignoring for the moment the signs of inharmonious cohabitation, proposes that the family go to the country soon to look at the maples.

*The Characters*

The protagonist, Shingo, is a man in his early sixties who is preoccupied with growing old. Incessantly, he reflects upon his encroaching ailments, shooting pains, and the deaths of old acquaintances. He is an aesthete and takes great pleasure in beauty. Whether it be the alluring charms of a woman, the finely sculpted features of a Nō mask, the bright colors of cherry blossoms, or the hue, aroma, and flavor of gyokuro tea, beauty, in all its manifestations, consoles and sustains Shingo. His aesthetic sense might be deemed peculiarly Oriental, for he shows little sign of discriminating between the aesthetic pleasures of art and those of nature. To Shingo, a devoted student of Japanese art and literature, a rock formation, butterfly, flower, or even pampas grass will, more often than not, suggest one or another of his favorite artistic works. There is, however, a dark underside of beauty of which Shingo is equally aware: its transient and evanescent nature, beyond which lurk dissolution, death, and decay.

Shingo strives to live a morally decent life as he sees it, but the effort he expends in doing so only seems to contribute to his feelings of guilt and inadequacy. His genuine and fatherly love for his daughter-in-law seems, to him, sullied and degraded by his finding in her a sexually appealing woman. Although he tries to assist Fusako through her periods of crisis, he is haunted by the plausible notion that at the heart of his daughter's problem is a dearth of paternal care and affection. He married Yasuko—or so he remembers—to rescue her from the clutches of her cruel brother-in-law, yet he has withheld from her the very tenderness and affection which his marrying her had intended to restore. Shingo's love of beauty and Yasuko's lack thereof seem to be at the core of the problem. Shingo habitually recalls Yasuko's beautiful sister, who is now long dead and with whom he was secretly infatuated. This woman is Shingo's ideal, whose flesh-and-blood counterpart he restlessly and compulsively seeks. On learning that Kikuko has had an abortion, for example, he entertains the depressing thought that the baby might finally have turned out to be Yasuko's sister incarnate.

The other characters are all subordinate to the protagonist, their roles essentially limited to fragments of Shingo's consciousness. The character of Fusako, very sketchily drawn, serves mainly to remind Shingo of the colder side of his nature. Shuichi's womanizing, although it excites Shingo's sense of moral revulsion, also makes Shingo rueful of his own inexperience with women. Yasuko, an unremarkable and unattractive woman, is the reality of Shingo's everyday existence, in marked contrast to her sister, who is now only the stuff of dreams. The beautiful Kikuko incessantly evokes the memory of Yasuko's sister but is at the same time Shingo's last link to the here and the now.

*Themes and Meanings*

Together, dissolution, death, and decay constitute an important theme of *The Sound of the Mountain*. Edging toward the precipice, Shingo continually ponders the series of deaths of old acquaintances. For Shingo, a student of nature, images of budding, blossoming, wilting, death, and decay abound. They symbolize the passing of the seasons and keep him in touch with the rhythmic cycle of life and death. The utter predictability and regularity of this cycle lend a static dimension as well, which is rendered sensible by the novel's static, painterly prose.

As Shingo's circumstances increasingly require him to face the fact of his own mortality, he is comforted by evidence of immortality, wherever he may find it. After learning of the discovery of two-thousand-year-old lotus seeds and their subsequent sprouting, he seizes upon this fact as if it were his own personal victory. Too tired to live but too afraid to die, Shingo often expresses the desire to be put in a kind of suspended animation. Yet he knows that all such attempts are doomed. Once, a friend who was obsessed with the idea of getting rid of his gray hair pulled out every such strand as it appeared. When his head of dark brown hair was fully restored, he died suddenly; the act of rejuvenation was revealed to be a sham.

The evanescent but self-renewing beauty of nature is the other important theme of the novel. Shingo, who has witnessed many comings and goings in his life, perceives in even the most perfect flower the telltale signs of death and decay. The mountain which towers over his garden is an inexhaustible source of beauty, but also emits eerie sounds from the underworld and is the harbinger of death.

A subsidiary theme of the novel might be the encroaching influence of the West and the clash of things Oriental and Occidental. There are several references to changes in Japanese society which can be attributed to Western influence, from the new basic family unit (formed now by husband and wife, not by parent and child, as before) to the new way of measuring time in the long term. Even the small differences between Oriental and Occidental methods are significant to Shingo, who obsessively mulls over matters such as relative age. He always carries two timepieces, a pocket watch and a wristwatch, and neither one ever agrees with the other.

*Critical Context*

*The Sound of the Mountain* may be regarded as Kawabata's most important work. The pared-down yet highly evocative prose of the novel as well as its focus on the subjective reality of the protagonist was anticipated as early as the mid-1920's by *Izu no odoriko* (1926; *The Izu Dancer*, 1955), which established Kawabata's reputation. That novel is not, however, characteristic of the writer's early period, which is noted instead for its reliance upon imported Western forms. Kawabata was a leader of the so-called Neo-Perceptionists, a group of young writers who endeavored to modernize Japanese literature by exposing it to as many "isms" from the West as it could absorb.

Kawabata's best works, however, shed all obvious Western influences and are noted for their very Oriental sensibility. In *Yukiguni* (1947; *Snow Country*, 1956), for example, a story of a country geisha is simply told with a structure and imagery that recall *haiku* and *renga* verse. *Sembazura* (1952; *Thousand Cranes*, 1958) is built around the tea ceremony of Zen Buddhist origin, yet it is also Kawabata's most experimental postwar novel. *Meijin* (1954; *The Master of Go*, 1972) recounts the defeat of an aging go master once regarded as invincible, taking up as a main theme the dichotomy between the glorious but stuffy world of art and the perhaps more wholesome beauty of nature.

Though by no means single-handedly, *The Sound of the Mountain* has certainly called attention to the subtle and masterful craft at work in modern Japanese fiction. It treats such familiar themes as beauty, death, and traditional values with sensitivity and depth. The multitudinous aspects of nature, described with both passion and detachment, are the correlatives of Shingo's shifting moods and states of mind. Thus Kawabata's prose, bearing the characteristics of both naturalism and impressionism, resonates with symbolic meaning.

*Sources for Further Study*

Backstead, Richard C. *Kawabata and the Divided Self*, 1972.

Miyoshi, Masao. *Accomplices of Silence: The Modern Japanese Novel*, 1974.

Petersen, Gwenn Boardman. *The Moon in the Water: Understanding Tanizaki, Kawabata, and Mishima*, 1979.

Tsuruta, K. "Two Journeys in *The Sound of the Mountain*," in *Approaches to the Modern Japanese Novel*, 1976.

Ueda, Makoto. *Modern Japanese Writers and the Nature of Literature*, 1976.

*Greg Nehler*

# THE SPELL

*Author:* Hermann Broch (1886-1951)
*Type of plot:* Allegory
*Time of plot:* The twentieth century
*Locale:* The Austrian Alps
*First published: Die Verzauberung*, 1976 (English translation, 1987)

Principal characters:

THE NARRATOR, a country doctor, formerly a staff doctor in a
    city hospital
MARIUS RATTI, a spellbinding dictator
WENZEL, a dwarf, Ratti's henchman
WETCHY, an insurance agent, the victim of Ratti's hatred
MOTHER GISSON, an aging guardian of the earth spirit
IRMGARD MILAND, the Mountain Bride, who is murdered in a
    ritual fertility sacrifice

*The Novel*

The Spell chronicles events in a remote mountain village. The sleepy, almost atavistic goings-on of the town are gradually disrupted when Marius
Ratti suddenly appears, looking for work. He draws more and more people
under his hypnotic spell, causing dissension, suspicion, and violent outbursts
in a previously harmonious environment. Told from the perspective of many
years' distance, the village doctor's tale seems to be a search for answers as
he describes what took place in his town.

Most of the people in the village have lived there their entire lives, with
the exception of the narrator, a doctor who at one time worked as an ob-
stetrician in a large urban hospital, and Wetchy, an insurance agent. The lives
that these people lead are simple, and the rituals by which they mark the
passing of the seasons blend pagan and Christian practices, as if this isolated
town were somehow fixed out of time. Ratti arrives in March and immediately begins agitating for changes, criticizing the villagers' activities and trying to disrupt their routines. His anger is directed chiefly toward another outsider, Wetchy. Ratti despises him both because Wetchy and his family look
different from the other villagers and because Wetchy sells wireless radios on
the side.

Ratti focuses on the impropriety of the radio as an example of the town's
tainted values and urges people to give up these devilish devices and return
to a purer way of life. Gradually, the villagers begin to see the "wisdom" of
his teachings and not only stop using their radios but also look upon Wetchy
and his family as undesirables, scapegoats for the village's problems.

As spring advances into summer, the town crowns Irmgard Miland as its new Mountain Bride, a throwback to the pagan custom of choosing a May Queen, a goddess of fertility and the harvest. Like others in the town, Irmgard has fallen under Ratti's spell to the point of wishing to become his bride and bear his children. Ratti, however, is impotent, but he promises that they can be physically and spiritually united once her blood is returned to the nurturing earth. Ironically, during this time the true guardian of the earth spirit, Mother Gisson, has been teaching Irmgard the old ways—where to gather healing herbs, when to plant, when to brew concoctions, and so on— grooming her to become the village's new matriarch when Mother Gisson dies. The summer and fall bring a contest of wills between the destructive Ratti and the ancient Mother Gisson.

Irmgard is murdered at a summer festival which develops into a ritual sac- rifice, held at the Cold Stones, an area whose significance to the village's wel- fare dates back to the rites of shadowy pagan times. In the meantime, Ratti has won the villagers to his point of view, and Wenzel, his dwarf henchman, has persuaded the men of the village to reopen a dangerous mine in search of gold. The villagers seem unable to escape these two men's mesmerism; they willingly do whatever is asked of them, to the point of committing several murders and beating the outsider, Wetchy—all in the name of returning their village to Ratti's promised state of purity by restoring the old ways.

By fall, a semblance of order has been restored to the small village, even though Ratti by that time is a member of the town council. The mines that the townspeople hoped contained the gold of their salvation have been closed by the state. Wetchy and his family are moving to a city where he believes that he can overcome the traumas associated with his mistreatment in the vil- lage. Agatha, the young woman trained in Irmgard's stead, is soon to have a child, and Mother Gisson dies, somehow mystically reunited with her hus- band and Irmgard. As the narrator seems to suggest, the cycle of the seasons continues despite the feeble attempts of dictators such as Ratti to use ancient rituals to their own ends.

*The Characters*

Many of the characters in *The Spell* seem to be modeled on figures from classical myths and fairy tales, particularly Mother Gisson, who represents Demeter, the spirit of the earth. She stands against Ratti's bullying insistence on change and sacrifice. In fact, it is she who has been responsible for train- ing the next mother figure, Irmgard, taking her to look for herbs and teach- ing her the ancient healing ways. She is also one of the people whom Ratti cannot abide, as he knows that she represents a true union with the powers of nature. It is no coincidence that Mother Gisson dies shortly after the fall harvest, since in the Greek myth, Demeter must return to the underworld for the six months of winter.

Ratti is a classic outsider who corrupts the village. His ideas of right and wrong contradict the established norms of the poor townspeople, who, until he appeared just after spring planting, had lived together in relative harmony. Ratti operates under the mistaken assumption that technology is evil and that only by returning to the old ways of doing things can the villagers prosper and find happiness. Ironically, Ratti is impotent, unable to consummate any physical relationship and thus unable to participate in the very natural cycle to which he insists that the villagers atune themselves. Despite the fact that he himself is an outsider, he also fosters in the villagers an irrational fear of difference in his insistent persecution of the homely Wetchy.

The narrator, a healer himself, observes this behavior, but he seems powerless to stop the events that unfold during those six months. The doctor provides some insight into his character when he recounts, in the form of a long aside, an early love relationship that he had with a young Communist revolutionary, Dr. Barbara. Yet he too becomes swept up in the hysteria of the ritual of the Cold Stones during which Irmgard is murdered. Almost against his will, he finds himself joining in the derision of Wetchy, in the chanting and in the madness of the evening. As a representative of educated reason, his seduction by Ratti's ranting is dismaying.

Finally, Wenzel, Ratti's grotesque dwarf sidekick, seems to be the exaggerated alter ego of the impotent village dictator. He is the one responsible for goading the village men into reopening one of the condemned mines, with disastrous results: the death of a man. He is also the one who makes lewd suggestions to the women, perhaps acting in Ratti's stead. Unlike Ratti, however, Wenzel is punished; his back is crushed when a mine called the Pit of the Dwarfs collapses.

## Themes and Meanings

In a brief commentary on this novel written in 1941, Hermann Broch makes it clear that he intended the book to be an allegory reflecting the early years of Nazi Germany. Set in a traditional German fairy-tale mode and removed from the real here and now, *The Spell* was Broch's way of condemning what he viewed as the frightening events of the 1930's. The parallels are simple: Ratti is driven by the same insane impulses as Adolf Hitler; he insists that he alone knows how to restore the village to its rightful place of power. His formula involves renouncing the modern world and returning to the more pure pagan practices of the past. Yet he wants these things for the wrong reason, for power rather than to bring the villagers into closer harmony with the forces of nature. His selfishness is made clear during the riot which he starts at the Cold Stones ritual. He also incessantly persecutes the mousy Wetchy, simply because he is homely and has ugly children. These actions are meant to parallel Hitler's persecution of the Jews and his insistence on Aryan supremacy. Like Hitler, Ratti began by bewitching the young people of the town, yet by the time of the ritual at the Cold Stones, even the narrator finds himself saluting Ratti.

Mother Gisson, the real spirit of the earth, the nurturing mother, is in direct opposition to Ratti. She, not Ratti, is a true practitioner of the old ways. Living in harmony with her world, she gathers healing plants and tends to and understands the needs of the people of the town in ways that neither Ratti nor the narrator can appreciate or duplicate. As a Mountain Bride herself, Mother Gisson makes certain that the old ways will continue after she is dead by teaching first Irmgard and then the pregnant Agatha all that she knows. In Agatha and her new child lie the real hope for the village, the healthy connection with the never-ending natural cycle. It is significant that Ratti is unable to kill Mother Gisson and that the doctor is unable to talk her out of dying. Instead, she knows when it is appropriate for her to go to the next realm, to join the murdered Irmgard. She accepts this transition willingly, as she has accepted everything that the natural world has given her in life.

## Critical Context

Although Broch died in 1951, *The Spell* was not published until 1976. He had completed the original draft in 1934 but had not been pleased with the manuscript and, subsequently, revised it two more times, changing and adding material in order to make it more nearly conform to his vision. He was in the process of making a third extensive revision of the manuscript when he died with only about half of the work done. Thus, what exists today as the published work is actually a reconstructed draft of a novel-in-progress.

Broch has sometimes been referred to as the Austrian James Joyce, and *The Spell* is vaguely reminiscent of Thomas Mann's *Der Zauberberg* (1924; *The Magic Mountain*, 1927). It was written after Broch's best-known trilogy, *Die Schlafwandler* (1931-1932; *The Sleepwalkers*, 1932), and before *Der Tod des Vergil* (1945; *The Death of Virgil*, 1945). *The Spell* is particularly important to those wishing to understand the reaction to the rise of Nazism as well as those interested in the study of contemporary allegory and myth.

## Sources for Further Study

Arendt, Hannah. "The Achievement of Hermann Broch," in *The Kenyon Review*. XI (1949), pp. 476-483.

Herd, Eric. "Hermann Broch and the Legitimacy of the Novel," in *German Life and Letters*. XIII (1960), pp. 262-270.

Schlant, Ernestine. *Hermann Broch*, 1978.

Sparks, Kimberly. *A Geometry of Time: A Study of Hermann Broch's Prose Imagery*, 1964.

Ziolkowski, Theodore. *Hermann Broch*, 1964.

*Melissa E. Barth*

# SPERANZA

*Author:* Sven Delblanc (1931-     )
*Type of plot:* Philosophical historical fiction
*Time of plot:* 1794
*Locale:* A slave ship crossing the Atlantic
*First published:* 1980 (English translation, 1983)

Principal characters:
>    COUNT MALTE MORITZ VON PUTBUS (MIGNON), a young
>        Swedish aristocrat
>    HOFFMANN, Mignon's German tutor
>    ROUSTAM, Mignon's black servant
>    ROUET, the ship's doctor
>    ABBE MARCELLO, the ship's chaplain

*The Novel*

Presented as the diary of Count Malte Moritz von Putbus (or Mignon, as he is familiarly known), *Speranza* consists of this young Swedish aristocrat's memories and thoughts, combined with his notations of the sometimes puzzling events aboard a slave ship bound for the New World. The narrator's attempt to understand the truth about his external circumstances becomes the impulse for an inward journey; both processes lead from the comfort of illusion to the dreadful awareness of a new, devastating truth.

Through repeated exclamations of bliss in the novel's first pages, Mignon creates the impression that the sea voyage is the fulfillment of his heart's desire; in fact, as the reader quickly learns, the enthusiast is being sent into exile. Inspired by the writings of the philosophes and the bold ideals of the French Revolution, he had founded the Brothers of Liberty, a clandestine group of liberal thinkers dedicated to the spread of an egalitarian creed through social upheaval. Upon learning of this sedition against their class, his father threatened him with a year's banishment to the Virgin Islands. The son did not take the threat seriously at first, but the intertwining of politics with sex aggravated his danger. Grethel, the daughter of a parish clerk, caught Mignon's fancy, and he eventually convinced her to cast off the "bigotry" of the old, repressive social order so that she might experience the erotic ecstasy available "under Liberty's banner." Alas, she became pregnant. When the young revolutionary allowed Grethel's tears to wash away his "principled" objections to marriage, his mother, who had entertained loftier ambitions for him than this girl from a lower caste could accommodate, angrily supported her husband's plan for correcting their son.

The night prior to the diary's opening entry, the *Clotho*, on which Mignon had first embarked, began taking on water, and its passengers were forced to abandon it for another ship, the *Speranza*. Since, as Sven Delblanc reminds the reader, Clotho is the Fate who holds the distaff on which the thread of life is wound, and since the name of the second ship is the Italian word for "hope," the start of the voyage symbolically implies a shift from the fatalism embedded in the old order of society to the optimistic, revolutionary belief in man's freedom to invent his life's course and meaning. Mignon may complain about having to pull off his own boots his first night on the new ship—an adumbration of his class's loss of privilege—but he also finds the novelty of living as a democrat exhilarating, and (in what is obviously the novelist's extension of the boot metaphor) he delights in the sensation of sliding over the deck in his bare feet. The *Speranza* seems to him "a cloudy cathedral of white sails" being carried into the future by faith in human possibility.

The sight on the poop deck of a solitary black woman, beautiful beyond compare in her nakedness, excites Mignon's imagination to still more rhapsodic flights. Even though he supposes her to be some wealthy passenger's servant, he describes her as an Aphrodite of the Night—the classical idea of eroticism expressed through the physical perfection of the noble savage. While his mind is given over to aesthetic conceits, however, a terrible stench rising from belowdecks assaults his nose, and he wonders what cargo could be so foul. At last, Mignon realizes that his black Aphrodite and the malodorous distraction are connected: The *Speranza*, which he has poetically construed into an elegant symbol of the new age of liberty, is actually a slave ship.

With his awareness of this fact, the diarist's perception of the two men closest to him undergoes startling changes. Hoffmann, Mignon's tutor and the man who introduced him to the gospels of the Enlightenment, now advises him to stow his lofty ideas about natural rights in his travel bag: Survival dictates discretion, even to the point of cowardice. In contrast to the scholar's craven behavior, Roustam, the Count's black valet, begins to show insolence. Treated as a fashionably dressed pet monkey back in the court at Putbus, Roustam was a figure of amusement, but here the remnants of his European affectations seem to mock his master, and there is menace in the realization that, stripped of his clothes, he cannot be distinguished from the savages in the hold.

New acquaintances among the Caucasians on board further undermine Mignon's previous assumptions. The ship's doctor, Rouet, represents the humanism and scientific rationalism on which Europe has based its civilization since the Renaissance; confronted with the horror of slavery which that same civilization promotes, however, Rouet takes refuge in bitter cynicism. If Mignon persists in his delusion that there is an essential dignity in human existence, the physician says, observing the forced feeding of the slaves to keep their valuable bodies alive should prove a sovereign cure. Disclosure that the Church participates in this cruel trade produces an even worse shock. The Jesuits have a standing requisition for slaves to operate the order's Caribbean rum distillery, and their emissary, Abbe Marcello, is charged with guarding the Sacred Society's financial investment in the *Speranza*'s miserable cargo against cheating by its secular partners.

Mignon's response to his discovery of evil is to offer to buy the blacks out of slavery. The idea is patently naïve: Even if his fortune were sufficient for the purpose, the profit from the sale of this particular oppressed lot would only drive another expedition into Africa to mine her "black gold." Yet the flaw in Mignon's proposal lies deeper than the slavery he condemns. Earlier, the lusty young idealist had caught himself thinking of raping his black Aphrodite—a notion abhorrent to his Enlightenment creed; now it transpires that the real motive behind the plan to exchange his fortune for the slaves' freedom is to earn the Aphrodite's gratitude and thus place her under an obligation that she would presumably acquit by granting him sexual favors.

By the time the *Speranza* has reached the equator, a drastic deterioration in living conditions has virtually erased distinctions between the Europeans and the Africans: The heat has forced removal of the clothes that indicate differences in rank; both groups are eating the same diet of worm-infested pork and yams; a shortage of water for washing produces the same overpowering odor among the whites that had previously emanated from the quarters of the confined blacks. The greatest leveling force is sex. With no moral code to inhibit them, the whites act out their wildest libidinous fantasies with their captives. Even Mignon finally succumbs to the temptation by snatching the carnal pleasures promised by the black Aphrodite he now calls Eve.

Prompted as much by their despair as by the breakdown of order, the blacks plan a revolt, and Roustam, now their leader, calls on the man who once supplied his livery to side with the oppressed. Mignon's recognition of the corruption within himself, however, has extinguished the former firebrand's ardor for Liberty: When fighting erupts, he runs his rapier through one of the rebels. This instinctive choice seems a fatal error, given that the whites are far outnumbered, but then the captain shrewdly seizes the black women as hostages and announces that he will kill one after another until the rebels surrender. Eve is the first; after the third is slain, the uprising collapses.

Mignon's last entries in his diary are dreamlike fragments reflecting a mind tortured by guilt that stems partly from his lascivious conduct with Eve, partly from a homosexual experience he now acknowledges he had with Roustam the night he was asked to join the rebellion. As if to escape his conscience, he resigns his will—first to the Christianity of Abbe Marcello, then to absolute dictatorship of the ship's captain—but he becomes convinced that he will never have peace of mind as long as Roustam, who knows his terrible secret, remains alive. The eventual execution of Roustam, however, fails to deliver Mignon from his misery. If *speranza*, the last word he writes in the diary, represents the hope he says he must never give up, that hope is also mocked by the horrific vision of humanity which the *Speranza* has revealed.

## The Characters

The nondramatic presentation dictated by the diary form virtually prevents an evolution of characters in the conventional sense. Every element of the story reflects Mignon's mind—a very restricted consciousness in which to operate, not only because of the young man's impercipience but also because the events unfolded through him are intended to promote an examination of ideas rather than to exercise sensibilities.

Within these limits, however, the reader can infer the narrator's personality. As his nickname suggests, Mignon is a mama's boy. Once he is expelled from his protected childhood because he has gratified a sexual itch, the weight of evidence indicating human depravity steadily crushes his naïve confidence in humans as rational beings. The worst moment in this process of discovery comes with the recognition that evil is not an aberration but a fundamental part of human nature—indeed, that Mignon himself surpasses the vileness of those he once contemned.

Except in the respect that the doctor is never guilty of fatuous self-deception, Rouet's course in the story parallels Mignon's. Although he cannot rescue the slaves from their circumstances, he visits them in the hold to try to alleviate their suffering; although he believes every man's psychosexual being conceals a "penchant for cruelty" which is expressed in a "magical desire to see a woman begging for mercy," he chooses to act as though a "sense of innate decency" might ultimately prevail. Yet even Rouet finally yields to the futility of his humanistic efforts to temper hell. After abandoning his medical efforts, he dies of gangrene at the novel's close. The materialist thus succumbs to the rottenness of his human matter.

The antithesis to Rouet is Abbe Marcello, the supreme bureaucrat who is the incarnation of evil. Passed through the mill of his casuistry, any vice, any predation, any horror practiced on earth becomes justified as an instrument leading to the soul's fulfillment in heaven. Marcello is intellect divorced from human lenity. Although he knows and exploits the base desires of others, he himself seems utterly devoid of emotion.

Hoffmann calls Pangloss to mind (one of several respects in which Putbus resembles Voltaire's Westphalian court). At the start, the tutor's use of scholarship as a shield for his lechery has a certain roguish charm, but once he boards the *Speranza*, his shameless pandering to those in authority discloses his true character. Hoffmann is a coward who aspires to being a bully. When he reveals that, along with every other adult male in Putbus, he has rogered the Countess, his only motive is to destroy Mignon's belief in his mother's goodness and thereby convince him that everything human is swinish.

Roustam, though the most remote of the major characters, is psychologically the most complex; if the novel were a film, the questions evoked by his physical presence would almost certainly become the commanding interest. Virtually the court jester in Putbus because of his incongruity with the setting, on the *Speranza* he is doubly a menacing, nightmarish force—at once the avenging instrument of the oppressed and the embodiment of the id, bursting through the layers of hypocrisy imposed by civilization. (It is worth noting that the first three letters in the names of this black rebel and the ship's doctor are the same, and, further, that *stam* is the Swedish word for tribe, while *et* is simply the definite article.)

### Themes and Meanings

In addition to being a novelist, Sven Delblanc teaches comparative literature at the University of Uppsala. *Speranza* reflects that academic career. As in Voltaire's *Candide* (1759), Joseph Conrad's *Heart of Darkness* (1902), and Herman Melville's "Benito Cereno" (1855), the tale's protagonist is deluded by assumptions about human goodness and the ideals of civilization that subsequently collapse under the weight of grim experience. A second, not entirely unrelated motif, presented through Abbe Marcello, derives from Fyodor Dostoevski: As in the Grand Inquisitor section of *The Brothers Karamazov* (1912), a cleric's argument that humankind will gladly surrender its freedom to the absolutism of the Church in exchange for bread and order strikes at a fundamental philosophical issue.

These allusions indicate something beyond a literary collage drawn from the tradition of Western fiction, however. Arguably to a greater extent than that of any other Western European country, Sweden's recent history has been shaped by a philosophical materialism that preaches the inevitability of social progress as the result of rational analysis. If that creed has helped produce a paragon of social and economic democracy, it has also fostered what the Swedes themselves call a "blue-eyed" intellectual naïveté. As a child of the Renaissance who believes in human perfectibility, Delblanc's diarist reflects modern Europe's secular faith, but the more particular image indicated by this metaphoric figure is the radical young Swede who, ever since the Vietnam War, has self-righteously condemned his elders and all political views based on perceptions of human nature that are less romantic than his own. In addition to reminding his countrymen of their pride in their nation's imperialistic past, Delblanc exposes the racial and class prejudice on the underside of Sweden's liberal dogma. The author's harshest attack on his audience's self-deception, however, strikes at the foundations of human behavior. Beneath noble Mignon's lofty assertions is a psychosexual bog where sadism and incestuous desires writhe.

### Critical Context

Since his novelistic debut in 1962 with *Eremitkräftan* (the hermit crab),

Sven Delblanc has averaged close to a book a year in the course of establishing himself as arguably the foremost Swedish writer of his generation. His importance as a literary figure extends beyond the reputation he has created with his novels. Delblanc is also a respected critic and literary historian. In 1987, in partnership with another academic coeditor, he launched a projected six-volume recapitulation of Swedish literature, from ancient times to the present day.

Although Delblanc has not joined the rush to the avant-garde which has drafted most of his compatriots who profess to be serious writers, a survey of his bibliography reveals that he is versatile as well as prolific. *Speranza* falls between *Kastrater* (1975; *The Castrati*, 1979) and *Jerusalems natt* (1983; the night of Jerusalem) in a sequence that the author rather loosely calls a trilogy; along with its associated volumes, it belongs to a small group of philosophical fictions that are rather different from a variety of more conventional novels. He first won fame with the Hedeby series, a tetralogy begun in 1970 and completed in 1976, about the change in a rural community as Stockholm's urban expansion digested it during the decades bracing World War II. On the heels of that popular success, he started another, even more highly regarded novel sequence that is a fictionalized version of his own family's history. (Delblanc was born in a Swedish immigrant family in western Canada; his family returned to Sweden while he was still a boy.)

*Sources for Further Study*
*Booklist*. Review. LXXXIX (August, 1983), p. 1447.
*Books Abroad*. Review. XLVIII (1974).
*Germanic Review*. Review. XLIX (1974).
*Kirkus Review*. Review. LI (July 1, 1983), p. 712.
*Library Journal*. Review. CVIII (August, 1983), p. 1501.
*Publishers Weekly*. Review. CCXXIV (July 15, 1983), p. 42.
*Sweden Now*. Review. II (1983).

*Frank Gado*

# THE SPLENDORS AND MISERIES OF COURTESANS

*Author:* Honoré de Balzac (1799-1850)
*Type of plot:* Melodrama
*Time of plot:* 1824-1830
*Locale:* Paris
*First published: Splendeurs et misères des courtisanes*, 1838-1847 (English translation, 1895): *Comment aiment les filles*, 1838, 1844 (*The Way That Girls Love*, 1895); *À combien l'amour revient aux vieillards*, 1844 (*How Much Love Costs Old Men*, 1895); *Où mènent les mauvais chemins*, 1846 (*The End of Bad Roads*, 1895); *La Dernière Incarnation de Vautrin*, 1847 (*The Last Incarnation of Vautrin*, 1895)

> *Principal characters:*
> JACQUES COLLIN (alias VAUTRIN), a brilliant professional criminal posing as a Spanish priest, the ABBÉ CARLOS HERRERA
> LUCIEN DE RUBEMPRÉ, a charming but weak young man whom Collin loves and schemes to place in a high social position
> ESTHER COBSECK (LA TORPILLE), a prostitute who becomes the main instrument of Collin's machinations
> JACQUELINE (ASIA) COLLIN, Collin's aunt and primary coconspirator

*The Novels*

*The Splendors and Miseries of Courtesans* is a long narrative in four volumes. The main character is not a courtesan, despite the novel's title, but a brilliant criminal who manipulates other people's lives to his own satisfaction. Only the first two volumes actually treat the vicissitudes of a prostitute's life, the last two books being given over to the villain's incarceration in prison and the conditions there.

The first part, *The Way That Girls Love*, opens at a fashionable masquerade ball in Paris in 1824. The attention of the gossiping masquers is arrested by the appearance of three figures: a handsome young man named Lucien de Rubempré; a mysterious caped man who follows the young gentleman intently; and the beautiful prostitute, Esther Cobseck, known as La Torpille (the torpedo), who accompanies Lucien and is in love with him. Esther, thinking that she is not recognized in her costume, is humiliated when she is identified by a group of rakes who gossip about her pruriently, and she leaves the ball in consternation.

Esther is then discovered by the sinister caped personage from the ball in her dreary quarters, where she has made a clumsy attempt at suicide. Her rescuer passes himself off as a Spanish priest, Carlos Herrera, and convinces her that she must enter a convent. Esther soon wastes away melodramatically in the convent, however, stricken by her passion for Lucien, who does not know where she is. The priest, whose interest in and ambitions for Lucien include marrying him to one of the daughters of the wealthy Duc de Grandlieu, placates Lucien by setting Esther up secretly in an apartment where the young man may visit her. After four years of this life, Herrera runs low on money. When a wealthy banker, Baron Nucingen, spies Esther and falls desperately in love with her, Herrera devises a scheme to swindle the Baron and use the proceeds to finance the purchase of property that will give Lucien the credibility he needs to win the Duc's daughter.

The comic story of the bilking of Baron Nucingen makes up the second volume, *How Much Love Costs Old Men*. Many of its events revolve around the ludicrous efforts of three rogue policemen—Contenson, Corentin, and Peyrade—to execute the orders of the Baron in his efforts to track down and seduce Esther. Their counterparts are the three scamps in the employ of Herrera—his factotum, Paccard; Esther's maid, Prudence Servien, best known as Europe; and Herrera's indefatigably wily lieutenant, Asia, who is actually his aunt, Jacqueline Collin. Herrera himself, it is revealed, is an incorrigible criminal named Jacques Collin, alias Vautrin, who murdered the real Abbé.

The farcical twists and turns conclude with Esther's committing suicide out of depression over the prospect of losing Lucien and having to give herself to the absurd but ardent Baron. She leaves 750,000 francs for Lucien, money she had coaxed out of the Baron, but Europe and Paccard find the bank notes and immediately abscond with them. Just before Esther dies, it is discovered that she is the niece and heir of the wealthy discount broker, Gobseck, and that he has died and left her seven million francs. Unfortunately, when Europe goes to give Esther the happy news, the maid finds her mistress already dead. The result of these confusing developments is that both Lucien and Collin are arrested for complicity in theft and murder.

In *How Much Love Costs Old Men*, Honoré de Balzac writes at length about the history and customs of the French penal system before settling down to the subject of Lucien and Collin in prison. The authorities immediately suspect the true identity of the bogus priest but cannot prove it. The examining magistrate, Monsieur Camusot, cannot break Collin's story, but the much weaker Lucien is quickly tricked into admitting everything. Just as Camusot learns the truth, however, he finds himself in difficulties with various prominent society ladies with whom Lucien has had affairs. Some harbor grudges from old slights and are eager to see Lucien suffer, but two of them—the Duchesse de Maufrigneuse and the Countess Sérisy—still love Lucien and are tormented at the thought of their private love letters becoming known. These two influential ladies want Lucien released, and their interest in the case makes Camusot regret his success in the interrogation of the hopeless dandy. Lucien's distress at his plight leads him, however, to commit suicide in his cell, setting up the denouement of the fourth book, in which the scheming priest is pitted against the authorities.

The opening sections of volume 3, *The End of Bad Roads*, reveal Balzac's interest in the penal system. He describes at great length the procedures by which accused persons are processed and interrogated, and even includes a brief essay on criminal law under the French Code, with an account of the history, structure, and uses of the Palais de Justice. As part of his preoccupation with prisons and prison life, Balzac later writes a fascinating essay on prison slang, a discussion that leads to philosophizing about the social role of thieves and prostitutes. In this same context, he remarks that the criminal population and the police population both number sixty to eighty thousand individuals, and he explains much of his purpose when he adds, "The antagonism between all these people who reciprocally seek and evade each other constitutes an immense duel, eminently dramatic, sketched in these pages."

Balzac also explains something of the politics and sociology of the underworld in his brief disquisition on the society called the Grand Fanandels, an elite society of gang chiefs with private fortunes which served the everyday felon as "the court of appeal, the academy, the house of peers." The Grand Fanandels created the order of the Ten Thou', so called because none of them would take on an operation promising less than ten thousand francs. These discussions of the criminal milieu contribute greatly to developing an ambience and often satisfy the reader who is surfeited with melodrama.

The title of volume 4, *The Last Incarnation of Vautrin*, alludes to the name by which Collin, alias the Abbé Herrera, had been known in a previous novel, *Le Père Goriot* (1835; *Daddy Goriot*, 1860; better known as *Père Goriot*). When Collin learns of Lucien's suicide and reads his friend's farewell letter, he is prostrated. He soon regains his interest in life, however, because of a conversation with the hardened rogues in the prison yard. (This section, incidentally, becomes the occasion for an absorbing essay by Balzac on the language and behavior of prisoners.) Meeting a group of old lags, many of whom know him from the past and acknowledge him as Dodgedeath, their informal leader, he is stunned to find out that his long-lost companion and the object of his pederastic love, Théodore Calvi, is in the prison and about to be hanged. Collin recovers his bravado, contrives a furtive meeting with Calvi, and begins to scheme to save Calvi's life. While the master criminal is playing a cat-and-mouse game with Bibi-Lupin, a former convict made police chief, his confederate, Asia, is also working on his behalf. In a complicated finale, Collin creates a strategy based on the power he has by virtue of having the ladies' love letters to Lucien and on the money he collects from a complicated scam worked on one of his fellow prisoners. With all of his designs successful, Collin—alias Dodgedeath, alias the Abbé Herrera, alias Vautrin—assumes the respectable role of Bibi-Lupin's deputy.

## The Characters

Collin says at one point, "If I were not a materialist, I shouldn't be what I am!" This admission says much about the speaker. He is a cold-blooded manipulator of human lives, a brilliant but absolutely cynical rogue who is without scruple or transcendental conviction. Only in his love for the two young men, Théodore Calvi and Lucien de Rubempré, does he reveal any compassion for the fate of another human being; even that love is tainted by its perverse sexual motive and the Mephistophelian urge to control the lives of the two young men.

Collin had first met Calvi in 1819, when the youth, then eighteen, had been sentenced to life imprisonment for murder and became Collin's chainmate. When Collin engineered their clever escape in 1820, they accidentally became separated near Rochefort, and it was during Collin's search for his mate that he met the feckless dandy Lucien. Transferring his affections immediately to his new friend, Collin promptly began scheming to establish Lucien in society, for, as Balzac says, "in Lucien he had seen a Jacques Collin, handsome, youthful, ennobled, in the position of an ambassador."

Ultimately, it is difficult to make of Collin any kind of Satanic hero. He is that familiar Romantic figure, the man of great intelligence who uses his powers in the wrong cause, and it is easy to be moved by the sense of such a great waste in his deployment of these powers. Nowhere, however, does Balzac indicate that Collin is motivated by a conviction of having been wronged. He belongs in literature with such figures as William Shakespeare's Iago and Herman Melville's Claggart in *Billy Budd, Foretopman* (1924), villains whose behavior often seems prompted by no motive more obscure than the simple pleasure of manipulating and wrecking others' lives. His psychology can perhaps best be explained by a deep alienation from society derived from his homosexuality and his resentment at not having been born to a station in life commensurate with his great abilities.

Collin is such a dominating figure in several of Balzac's works that his past warrants close attention. Besides appearing prominently in two other novels, *Père Goriot* and *Illusions perdues* (1837-1843; *Lost Illusions*, 1913), he was also the subject of the unsuccessful play *Vautrin* (1840; English translation, 1901). When he first appears as Vautrin in *Père Goriot* (set in 1819-1820), he is forty years old. He is a short man, broad and powerful, of impressive appearance. He lives on a fund of money entrusted to him by his criminal friends, money they have to put in safekeeping while in prison. Eventually, he is apprehended and put in chains, and it is then that he meets Calvi. Collin reappears in *Lost Illusions*, in which he escapes from jail, murders the Abbé and takes the priest's credentials, and then scars his face with vitriol to create a disguise. Collin turns up next in *The Splendors and Miseries of Courtesans* with Lucien at the masquerade ball, where the criminal is recognized by Rastignac, one of the former boarders at the Pension Vauquer in *Père*

*Goriot*. Rastignac is shaken by the encounter but too frightened to reveal the priest's true identity.

Something of Collin was probably suggested to Balzac by the careers of two real men: Vidocq, a notorious criminal who eventually became a police chief, and Pierre Cogniard, a thief who stole the papers of a French nobleman, made a career under this identity in the military, and finally reverted to the life of a master burglar.

Lucien was born Lucien Chardon and takes his mother's maiden name, de Rubempré, only when, under the influence of Collin, he attempts to make a grand career. The young man has little to recommend him, when he first appears in *Lost Illusions*, other than his good looks and a faint skill at writing verses. These assets suffice to introduce him to society women of literary pretensions. Lucien soon flees from Angoulême to Paris with one of his admirers, Mme de Bargeton. He is about twenty years old; she is almost twice that age. The affair quickly collapses, and Lucien struggles to survive as a journalist and is swept into the role of kept lover of an actress named Coralie. The vicissitudes of their relationship culminate in Coralie's death and Lucien's misery at having forged some letters of credit that have ruined his brother-in-law. It is at this point that he decides to kill himself and is saved by the false Abbé, who is in search of his beloved Théodore. This much knowledge of Lucien's past is necessary to clarify for readers of *The Splendors and Miseries of Courtesans* the many allusions to his previous escapades.

Collin is attracted to Lucien by the younger man's good looks, and the homosexual is apparently not long in discovering in Lucien a bisexual of such extremely plastic character that he can shape him as he wishes. Thus, for Collin, Lucien is exactly what he wants in order to give his perverse life meaning: a lover over whom he can exert complete control and a passive personality through whom he can indulge his will to power, all the while remaining the gray eminence in the background.

Lucien is happy to comply with Collin's plans. Although he does seem to love Esther genuinely, he enjoys her company only secretly while working to marry the daughter of the Duc de Grandlieu. Lucien has no compunction about being Collin's pawn, none about using Esther, and none about scheming to deceive the Duc and his daughter. Meanwhile, he has accepted the favors of two prominent women of society, Mme de Maufrigneuse and Mme de Sérisy. Lucien, who could himself be called a prostitute, nevertheless finds his greatest gratification with Esther, the woman of the streets.

Esther undergoes a moral regeneration when she meets and falls in love with Lucien. She becomes pious, and after her abortive suicide attempt allows Collin to establish her in a convent. Yet the pining away that she suffers, ostensibly because of her love of Lucien, is perhaps also partly a yearning for the dissolution of her old life. At least, that is Collin's cynical summation when he sneers, "You're a whore, and you always will be a whore. Because despite all the attractive theories of the cattle breeders, one can never become anything in this world except what one is."

Collin's aunt, Jacqueline Collin, better known as Asia (she was born in Java in 1774), is a sinister creature who executes some of Collin's most important errands. It is she who threatens Mme de Maufrigneuse and Mme de Sérisy with exposure of their letters to Lucien if they do not help get him released. Jacqueline also appears in other novels.

The Baron Frédéric de Nucingen, the wealthy banker whom Collin is able to gull repeatedly because of his helpless infatuation with Esther, is a splendid buffoon. A ruthless financier who has accumulated his fortune unscrupulously, the Baron is a truly comic figure with his ridiculous accent and his inability to comprehend the way he is being used by Esther.

Among the other characters, the trio of contemptible policemen stand out for their shabby behavior and absurd disguises. Corentin, Peyrade, and Contenson are indistinguishable in their behavior from the felons and scoundrels whom they pursue. Corentin is nothing but a spy, paid by the police; he is cold-blooded, without loyalties, and suited by temperament to his occupation. Peyrade is a good-natured sensualist, no more scrupulous than his employer, Corentin. Nevertheless, Peyrade is humanized by his genuine love for his daughter, and his devotion to her leads to his death at the hands of Collin. The third in the triumvirate, Contenson, is even worse than Peyrade and Corentin, despite his really being Bernard-Polydor Bryond, Baron des Tours-Minières. Corentin is depraved enough to do anybody's dirty work for a few francs. Altogether, the three present a pessimistic picture of their profession.

## Themes and Meanings

One dominating theme of *The Splendors and Miseries of Courtesans* is the terrifying power that love can exert over human lives. It is primarily his love for Lucien that drives Collin to his machinations, and it is his love for Calvi that rejuvenates Collin in prison after Lucien's death. For Lucien, his love for Esther creates a focus for his life that goes beyond his hopes for social advancement. Esther's love for Lucien is her only satisfaction in life. The melodramatic posturings of these two lovers provide some of the novel's more preposterous scenes. Most driven and possessed of all in their apparently incessant sexual hunger are Mme de Maufrigneuse and Mme Sérisy. Their love letters to Lucien are not revealed, but the accounts of them hint at their extreme salaciousness. Finally, it is the sexual desire of the ludicrous Baron, over sixty and past, so he thought, the age of such dangerous yearnings, that generates the whole swindle around which the plot of the first two books gathers. None of these loves could long survive without the strong erotic elements that foster them in the first place.

The corruption of the characters by lust is part of the generally pessimistic view of human nature that colors the whole novel; nowhere does there appear an admirable character. The higher levels of society are represented by the several women who at one time or another pursue Lucien, and by the extremely wealthy banker, Baron Nucingen, whose faults are obvious and extreme. Among the representatives of law and order, the self-serving trio of Corentin, Peyrade, and Contenson is on the legal side more by convenience than by conviction. Even the magistrate, Camusot, who begins his interrogations of Collin and Lucien with good intentions, is seen to be easily swayed by political expediency. The picture of human society in *The Splendors and Miseries of Courtesans* is grim.

The subject of homosexuality was an extremely sensitive one in the nineteenth century, and Balzac must have known how carefully he had to tread in writing about it. The only explicit statement of Collin's sexual preference comes in one of the prison scenes, when an experienced convict says of Collin that "he wants to see his queen who's due to be executed." This epithet is clarified a few lines later, when queens are said to belong to "the third sex." In his treatment of this topic, Balzac was bold for his day.

*Critical Context*

Balzac was an indefatigable writer who produced close to one hundred novels and short stories, which he collectively titled *La Comédie humaine* (1829-1848; *The Human Comedy*, 1895-1896). They constitute one of the most impressive attempts to portray the complete spectrum of the human passions. Among these works, he referred to some as "Scenes of Provincial Life," and to others as "Scenes of Parisian Life"; it is in the latter group that *The Splendors and Miseries of Courtesans* falls. Seen from another perspective, the novel can also be understood as forming the third in a trilogy of novels focusing on Jacques Collin in his many incarnations, *Père Goriot* and *Lost Illusions* being the first two.

One feature of Balzac's work that demands comment is the frequency with which characters are repeated in his works. The practice seems justified in the light of his attempt to create one unified vision of human affairs, and most of the stories and novels are generally intelligible enough without reference to the previous related works, although that is not universally the case. The opening of *The Splendors and Miseries of Courtesans* is puzzling to the reader who does not know from the two previous books about Collin and the escapades of Lucien. References to Coralie, for example, as well as the mysterious recognition of the bogus priest by Rastignac, can leave the reader wondering about what he has missed.

The haste with which Balzac wrote left him with little time to devote to style. He was clearly the kind of writer who wants to get it all down while time is short and was ready to pay the consequences. Balzac's devotion to his lessons on human nature often produced miniature essays and didactic commentaries in the midst of his narratives. Some of these (such as the passages on the language of criminals) can be rewarding, but the moralizing passages are seen by many readers as damaging to his artistic responsibilities. An even more pronounced fault—especially in *The Splendors and Miseries of Courtesans*—is the constant melodrama, such as Esther swooning with love for Lucien, the unbelievable ability of Collin to talk his way out of prison, the disguises of the absurd police trio.

Despite these flaws, Balzac's originality and imagination appear strongly in *The Splendors and Miseries of Courtesans*, as he creates an unforgettable cast of mostly despicable people. Most impressive of all of his virtues, however, is the sharp gaze which he turns on the actions of his puppets. Over and over, the reader pauses to appreciate a particularly acute comment on man's foibles. It is surely this quality which accounts for his enduring appeal.

*Sources for Further Study*
Brooks, Peter. *The Melodramatic Imagination*, 1976.
Curtius, Ernst Robert. *Balzac*, 1933.
Festa-McCormick, Diana. *Honoré de Balzac*, 1979.
Marceau, Felicien. *Balzac and His World*, 1966.
Rogers, Samuel. *Balzac and the Novel*, 1969.

*Frank Day*

# SPOKOINOI NOCHI

*Author:* Andrei Sinyavsky (as Abram Tertz, 1925-    )
*Type of plot:* Phantasmagoric memoir-novel
*Time of plot:* The 1940's through 1971
*Locale:* Moscow
*First published:* 1984

> *Principal characters:*
> ANDREI DONATEVICH SINYAVSKY, a Soviet literary scholar who
> becomes a dissident writer under the pseudonym ABRAM
> TERTZ
> MARIA, his wife
> DONAT EVGENIEVICH SINYAVSKY, his father
> SERYOZHA (also known as "S."), Sinyavsky's childhood friend
> and mentor who betrays him to the KGB
> HÉLÈNE, a French diplomat's daughter who becomes
> Sinyavsky's secret courier

## The Novel

*Spokoinoi nochi* is a highly fragmented, phantasmagoric memoir-novel about Andrei Sinyavsky's life as a Soviet intellectual and secret dissident writer (under the name Abram Tertz), his betrayal, trial, and years in a labor camp. Written after his emigration to France, it is an attempt to understand his life and to trace the development of his worldview as man and artist. Reared an orthodox Communist, Sinyavsky evolved into a sophisticated, paradoxical artist and thinker who came to believe that "reality" is phantasmagoric and understandable only in such terms. *Spokoinoi nochi* uses the phantasmagoric aesthetic to probe the harrowing story of Sinyavsky's life as Abram Tertz. Although this technique is aesthetically effective, it yields a chaotic, impressionistic narrative that is fully accessible only if the reader is already familiar with the historical context and the basic outlines of Sinyavsky's life.

The last years before the death of Soviet tyrant Joseph Stalin in 1953 were a nightmare of paranoiac despotism. Millions were in labor camps. The arts were reduced to primitive propaganda under the rubric "Socialist Realism." Andrei Sinyavsky was a young scholar specializing in twentieth century Russian literature at the prestigious Gorky Institute of World Literature in Moscow. Like many of his friends, he was deeply disturbed by the official revelation in 1956 of the crimes of Stalin, which resonated with certain of his own unpleasant experiences. The fear of a possible return of Stalinism led the young critic, under the pseudonym Abram Tertz, to write two works which were smuggled to the West, where they were published to great acclaim. One of these, the essay *Chto takoe sotsialisticheskii realizm* (1959; *On Socialist Realism*, 1960), attacked the state-imposed literary doctrine and argued for a freer, speculative, "phantasmagoric" fiction. The essay's principles were exemplified in a short novel, *Sud idyot* (1959; *The Trial Begins*, 1960), which painted a surreal picture of Soviet life in the last months of Stalin's life. Sinyavsky continued his double life until 1965, when he was betrayed to the KGB, receiving the maximum sentence of seven years at hard labor for "anti-Soviet propaganda." Released in 1971, he and his wife were permitted to emigrate two years later.

The ironically titled *Spokoinoi nochi* (the Russian for wishing someone a sound night's sleep—usually rendered in English as "good night" but more precisely rendered as "[have] a good night") is loosely structured around five widely separated "nights," both real and metaphorical, which stand as nightmarish nuclei in the author's life. Each "night" is a chapter. The first, "Turncoat," recounts his arrest. Whisked to the KGB's dreaded Lubyanka prison, he meets his interrogator, Lieutenant Colonel Pakhomov, who will be almost his sole human contact for several months. The trial itself is a travesty in which the audience applauds his conviction and which the author compares to an imperial Roman gladiatorial fest. Here, as throughout the narrative, the biographical facts serve as points of departure for meditations often only remotely and metaphorically related to actual events. In addition to these "digressions," Sinyavsky incorporates grotesque set pieces, fictional vignettes, which further illuminate the absurdity of events.

Soviet camps allow brief annual conjugal visits in special quarters set aside within the camp. The second "night" centers on a visit by Sinyavsky's wife, Maria. Much of the night in the bugged room is taken up with an exchange of written (and promptly destroyed) notes speculating how the narrator came to be detected. The prisoner relives in memory his secret life: the first word that his work had appeared in the West; the speculation about the identity of "Abram Tertz"; the sense of a net tightening around him.

The third "night" revolves around Sinyavsky's father and his own childhood. A former member of the privileged classes, Sinyavsky's father was a non-Bolshevik radical who ardently embraced the Revolution only to find himself a suspect outsider. In the darkest night of Stalinism in 1951, he is arrested for supposed espionage for the Americans during famine relief work thirty years earlier. Released from interrogation before his exile, he takes a last walk with Andrei and talks, quite rationally, of the tiny radio transmitter implanted in his brain.

March 5, 1953, the date of Stalin's death, is the fourth "night" of *Spokoinoi nochi*, and the dictator's ghost is the focal point of a wide-ranging conceptual montage. Sinyavsky spends much of the day reading an old account of Russia's Time of Troubles, a bloody interregnum during the seventeenth century. Seizing upon parallels between present and past, Sinyavsky weaves a strange verbal tapestry incorporating ghostly images of Stalin.

Sinyavsky's final nightmare, "In the Belly of the Whale," is a portrait of two friends who played crucial roles in his life. The first, Seryozha, a friend from Sinyavsky's childhood until his arrest, betrays him (and others) to the KGB. The second is Hélène, the French naval attaché's daughter, who meets Sinyavsky while the two were fellow students at Moscow University in 1947 and introduces him to Western culture. Learning of the friendship, the KGB unsuccessfully pressures Sinyavsky to entrap her. It is Hélène who later serves as the courier who takes the works of "Abram Tertz" to the West. In their opposing ways, Seryozha and Hélène lead to the creation of Abram Tertz and the events chronicled in *Spokoinoi nochi.*

## The Characters

Reality, in the traditional sense of events and people, plays a very secondary role in Sinyavsky's autobiographical tale. Characters are not, for the most part, realistically developed, nor, apart from the narrator, do they have continuing roles throughout the narrative. Each major figure serves as the focal point of one of the "nights," but their images are sometimes very diffuse. In "The House of Meetings," in which Sinyavsky's beloved wife visits him in the camp, she remains shadowy and remote for the reader. Hélène, who plays an enormous role in Sinyavsky's personal and moral development, is equally abstract: a symbol of purity, a damsel in distress, but not a living person.

Sinyavsky-Tertz, whose consciousness holds the whole together, is the only fully developed character. The narrative takes Sinyavsky's life as the illegal Abram Tertz as its subject: how Sinyavsky became Tertz, who, incidentally, is listed as the sole author of the original Russian edition. Tertz is Sinyavsky's *Doppelgänger*, his fantasy double. Sinyavsky, physically unimpressive, wall-eyed, describes himself as "an honest intellectual, given to compromise and the solitary contemplation of life." In contrast, Abram Tertz is the legendary hero of an underworld ballad about the thieves' quarter in the Jewish section of Odessa, a criminal world with its own incorruptible code of honor. Tertz is everything Sinyavsky is not: thief, gambler, a cool, calculating figure only too willing to slip a knife into someone's side. Sinyavsky's use of the Tertz figure as his double has thematic resonance: the inherently dissident (criminal) nature of real art. Even more to the point is that the Sinyavsky/Tertz relationship mirrors the theme of the interpenetration of reality and fantasy that is central to the book.

Two other characters stand out: Sinyavsky's father and Seryozha. As the aging narrator sits in his Paris apartment, he reflects on various episodes from his father's unhappy life and his growing sense of identity with his father. First arrested for political activities in czarist times, Donat Evgenievich felt betrayed by the duplicity of the Communist government. An impractical idealist, he moved from wretched job to job, but nevertheless strove to instill his sense of ideals and honor in his son. It is his arrest that sows doubt in the mind of his orthodox son, and his madness that prompts the narrator's seminal reflections on the murky relationship between delusion and reality.

The most enigmatic character is Seryozha. A brilliantly gifted aesthete, Seryozha started Sinyavsky on the intellectual odyssey that led to the speculative artist-thinker and modernist. Other aspects of their relationship had equally important but more dire consequences. Episodes from Seryozha's life reflect a curious, disinterested viciousness. Eventually he denounces two young and innocent historians, and, perhaps, even Sinyavsky, to the KGB. These acts are not politically motivated, for Seryozha is as apolitical as he is amoral. Sinyavsky is fascinated by the personality of his longtime friend, who plays such a double-edged role in his life. In some sense, Sinyavsky sees elements of himself in Seryozha.

*Themes and Meanings*

The central theme of Sinyavsky's memoir-novel is the evolution of the young Sinyavsky, a decent but thoroughly conformist member of Soviet society, into a dissident artist-thinker who holds "reality" to be so tenuous, so bizarre, that it can be understood only through a phantasmagoric art which is the writer's salvation. A second major theme is Stalinism, that peculiar form of twentieth century despotism, which shaped Sinyavsky's life. The central metaphor expressing this theme and the one underlying the entire narrative is "night." Sinyavsky sees his epoch as part of an ages-long, disastrous meteor shower during a pitch black August night. This bombardment proceeds from the constellation "Stalin-Kirov-Zhdanov-Hitler-Stalin," the Zodiac sign under which Sinyavsky was born. Stalinism is, however, but one episode in the long dark night called History, a nightmare that is transcended only by art.

Sinyavsky writes for a small, sophisticated audience. The language is ornate, drawn from a diverse range of stylistic levels. The frequent cultural allusions are often arcane. The style is elliptic, jumping from one topic or set of images to another. Only upon reflection will the reader find the secret link that makes one passage, seemingly unrelated, illuminate another. Repeated reading reveals that the theme of each chapter is rendered by a mosaic of extended metaphors and parables. Only by viewing the mosaic as a whole is the exquisite thematic pattern visible. The final chapter, "In the Belly of the Whale," offers a splendid example. The opening meditations on Assyrian relief carvings, then the reflections on the French "Cave of Mutilated Hands" from which the author emerges into a nocturnal meteor shower, obscure in themselves, set the scene for the Nightmare of History theme that concludes Sinyavsky's chilling novel-memoir. The formidable demands on the reader are well repaid by the artistry and insight of Sinyavsky's chef d'oeuvre.

*Critical Context*

Andrei Sinyavsky is the godfather of the post-Stalin renaissance in Russian literature. Although the arid, official policy of Socialist Realism has been relaxed in the Soviet Union, almost all intellectually provocative and stylistically innovative Russian literature has come from underground or émigré artists. This new writing has picked up and continued the two major strands of the Russian literary tradition that were broken off around 1930 with the introduction of Socialist Realism: the "critical realism" tradition represented by such figures as Leo Tolstoy, and the more aesthetically oriented modernist, antirealist tradition represented by figures such as Andrey Bely. Aleksandr Solzhenitsyn and his followers have resurrected the older tradition. Sinyavsky has continued and developed the techniques of the earlier avant-garde and pointed the way for younger Russian writers. Both Vassily Aksyonov, the most important younger writer to emerge in the 1960's, and Sasha Sokolov, the leading stylist of the 1970's and 1980's, follow the path of "phantasmagoric art" advocated by Sinyavsky in his seminal 1956 essay, *On Socialist Realism*.

Sinyavsky has continued to contribute to his artistic vision since his emigration. In addition to teaching at the Sorbonne, he has established his own publishing house and journal under the name *Sintaksis*. His irreverent and idiosyncratic critical studies of such icons of Russian literature as Alexander Pushkin and Nikolai Gogol have been extremely controversial among Russian readers. Noteworthy among his nonscholarly works is *Golos iz khora* (1973; *A Voice from the Chorus*, 1976), a collection of meditations, quotations, and aphorisms culled from his labor-camp letters to his wife. His many stories are stylistically akin to what will probably remain Sinyavsky's major contribution to Russian literature, *Spokoinoi nochi*.

*Sources for Further Study*

Fanger, Donald. "A Change of Venue: Russian Journals of the Emigration," in *The Times Literary Supplement*. November 21, 1986, p. 1321.

_____. "Conflicting Imperatives in the Model of the Russian Writer: The Case of Tertz/Sinyavsky," in *Literature and History: Theoretical Problems and Russian Case Studies*, 1986. Edited by Gary S. Morson.

Hayward, Max. "Sinyavsky's *A Voice from the Chorus*," in *Writers in Russia: 1917-1978*, 1983.

Hingley, Ronald. "Arresting Episodes," in *The Times Literary Supplement*. February 15, 1985, p. 178.

Labedz, Leopald, and Max Hayward. *On Trial: The Case of Sinyavsky (Tertz) and Daniel (Arzhak): Documents*, 1967.

Lourie, Richard. *Letters to the Future: An Approach to Sinyavsky-Tertz*, 1975.

*D. Barton Johnson*

# STRAIT IS THE GATE

*Author:* André Gide (1869-1951)
*Type of plot:* Psychological realism
*Time of plot:* The late nineteenth century
*Locale:* The French province of Normandy
*First published: La Porte étroite*, 1909 (English translation, 1924)

> *Principal characters:*
> JÉRÔME PALISSIER, the narrator, a scholar
> ALISSA BUCOLIN, his first cousin, whom he loves
> JULIETTE BUCOLIN, Alissa's younger sister
> FÉLICIE PLANTIER, the cousins' aunt

## The Novel

Drawing its title from Luke 13:24 ("Strait is the gate and narrow is the way. . ."), André Gide's second *récit*, or short novel, tells the tale of a totally earnest yet ultimately futile quest for sainthood, or at least for salvation.

Appalled in early adolescence by the discovery of her mother's blatant infidelities, Alissa Bucolin seeks to elevate her awakening feelings for her slightly younger cousin Jérôme Palissier to a truly spiritual love worthy of divine approval. Aware, as Jérôme is not, of her younger sister Juliette's unrequited feelings for him, Alissa at first seeks to divert Jérôme's attentions in Juliette's direction; when that strategy fails, owing as much to her own feelings as to his, Alissa embarks deliberately on a search for a mystical, nonphysical love in which she and Jérôme will be joined for all eternity. To that end, she dresses plainly and even neglects her physical appearance, rejecting Jérôme's clumsy advances as she retreats increasingly from "the world," willfully denying her intelligence, education, and culture by forsaking literature in favor of religious tracts.

Jérôme, limited by literal-mindedness and a rather plodding nature, believes his own love to be unrequited when Alissa dies, in seclusion, from "no known cause." After Alissa's death, however, her diary is discovered. Although a number of pages are missing, those which remain are a stunning revelation to Jérôme. Alissa's diary, excerpts of which are given in the novel, makes clear to Jérôme what the reader has already guessed: that her love for him was strongly sensual. The diary also reveals to Jérôme her scheme to match him with Juliette. Finally—the most ironic note in a darkly ironic conclusion—the diary suggests that, for all her single-minded pursuit of sainthood, Alissa died without the consolation of faith.

## The Characters

Evidently inspired by Gide's recollections of his courtship with his future wife Madeleine Rondeaux (like Alissa, a slightly older first cousin), *Strait Is the Gate* departs from autobiography in the author's skillful presentation of characters both major and minor. Jérôme Palissier is an unreliable narrator, a literal-minded pedant who ignores clues in Alissa's behavior that are readily perceived by the reader. Alissa herself, her sensuality seeping out despite— or perhaps even because of—her willful quest for sainthood, is a truly masterful creation, delicately balanced just on the credible side of caricature. Although doubtless aware of Sigmund Freud's early studies of repressed sexuality, Gide in *Strait Is the Gate* manages to establish the link between Alissa's mother's nymphomania and her own outraged reaction without resorting to obvious stereotype. Alissa's bizarre quest, although solicitously portrayed throughout by Jérôme, is undermined from the start by her evident stubbornness, a manifestation of self-centeredness that argues against any true vocation. Throughout the novel, Alissa's renunciations and "sacrifices" are simply too deliberate and willful to sustain the reader's complicity, even as he or she might feel tempted to share the same ideal. Like Michel, the protagonist of Gide's earlier *récit*, *L'Immoraliste* (1902; *The Immoralist*, 1930), who sacrifices his marriage and other relationships for the goal of self-realization, Alissa will fail to reach her chosen goal.

Set among the rich bourgeois and landed gentry of late nineteenth century Normandy, *Strait Is the Gate* nearly qualifies as a novel of manners, thanks to Gide's perceptive delineation of the minor characters involved. Juliette Bucolin, Alissa's younger sister, is earthy and spontaneous; despite her early infatuation with Jérôme, Juliette's successful and prolific marriage to the prosperous Tessières, many years her senior, surprises the reader less than it does the other characters. Mme Félicie Plantier, the cousins' aunt, emerges delightfully as a busybody who supposes that her meddling is unobtrusive. Abel Vautier, son of the Protestant pastor whose sermon on Luke is credited with launching Alissa on her quest, flees the family hearth for a career in journalism and sudden notoriety as the author of a sensational novel which Alissa, by then, will refuse to read. Jérôme's widowed mother (a reflection of Gide's own) and his British governess Miss Ashburton (modeled on Anna Shackleton) help to fill out the picture of comfortable, well-educated French aristocracy sufficiently idle to be especially vulnerable to such aberrations as Alissa's initially thoughtful, ultimately thoughtless striving toward a sainthood envisioned after listening to Pastor Vautier's sermons.

*Themes and Meanings*

Throughout his literary career, Gide was especially concerned with the nature, consequences, and limits of potential human freedom. His short novels or *récits*, in particular, explore the limits of human identity and freedom in a frequently cautionary manner, rather like extended parables. *The Immoralist*, Gide's first experiment in the genre of the short novel, describes the sensual and psychological awakening of an archaeologist recovering from tuberculosis. Never fully aware of life until his close brush with death, the bookish Michel thereafter pursues vitality with a vengeance, even refusing his wife's prayers on the grounds that he does not wish to owe his recovery to God or to anyone else. In search of new adventures and sensations, Michel twice conspires with those who are out to steal his own property, then recklessly endangers the health of his wife, Marceline; as Marceline sickens and dies, Michel remains all but unmoved, secure in his proven "superiority." In many ways, as Gide himself noted, *Strait Is the Gate* should be seen as a companion piece to *The Immoralist*, showing willful self-abnegation to be just as dangerous and ill-advised as willful self-indulgence. Regardless of whether sainthood can be attained, a question Gide leaves open, it surely cannot be striven for in the manner that Alissa chooses. Reminiscent, as is Michel, of Honoré de Balzac's notorious monomaniacs, Alissa is blinded by her *idée fixe* to such a degree that she displays few, if any, of the traditional Christian virtues, such as charity. Arguably, her quest is little more than a defense against her own sexuality; pushed to an extreme, however, that defense becomes in a sense a crime against humanity, especially her own, and her final lack of faith rings true with an ironic justice.

Born and reared as a Protestant, a distinct minority in France, André Gide would soon lose his faith, but never the theological patterns of his thought. *Strait Is the Gate*, like *The Immoralist* before it and *La Symphonie pastorale* (1919; *The Pastoral Symphony*, 1931) after it, is in essence a morality tale, although with a non-Christian or at least anticlerical moral. For Gide, even agnosticism was an intensely theological issue, carefully worked out after weighing the qualities and defects of both Roman Catholicism and his native Protestantism. Like Voltaire—among the earliest and most vocal of French anticlericals—Gide focuses primarily upon the human injustices perpetrated in the name of faith or the Church; unlike Voltaire, who cared most about social injustice, Gide in the *récits* and elsewhere concentrates upon perceived psychological injustice, the warping of human minds by biblical commands often misread or misinterpreted. Like the hypocritical, morally blind pastor of *The Pastoral Symphony*, Alissa is ultimately portrayed as a victim of Christian teachings and practice, although a most willing one. Nevertheless, a number of turn-of-the-century readers tended to see in Alissa a sympathetic character somehow undeserving of her fate even as she seems to have invited it; Gide himself admitted that he had initially planned a more bitingly satirical work, gradually changing his project as the character of Alissa asserted itself in his mind.

### Critical Context

Winner of the Nobel Prize in 1947, three years and several months before his death at age eighty-one, André Gide lived his last years as a celebrity, often photographed and quoted, generally considered among the major writers and prose stylists of his time. In the decades after his death, however, Gide's reputation diminished considerably; his work is no longer considered nearly equal in stature to that of Marcel Proust, a close contemporary whom he outlived by nearly thirty years. Nevertheless, Gide remains a significant figure in Western literary history, a major practitioner (along with Hermann Hesse) of what Ralph Freedman has termed the "lyrical novel."

*Strait Is the Gate* was the first of Gide's works to attract both popular and critical notice, calling attention also to his earlier, Symbolist-influenced prose works and to *The Immoralist*, published seven years previously, to a minimum of comment. Gide, responding to the reception of his second *récit*, claimed that he would never have written *The Immoralist* had he not also planned to write *Strait Is the Gate*. Taken together, the two works in fact constitute a coherent, thought-provoking fictional treatise on the nature and limits of human freedom, illustrated by truly credible and memorable characters. Only once more, with the somewhat shorter *The Pastoral Symphony*, would Gide return to the *récit* (tale), as opposed to the longer, more fully developed *roman* (novel). Only once, in fact, would Gide apply the designation "novel" to a work of long fiction, in the case of *Les Faux-monnayeurs* (1925; *The Counterfeiters*, 1927), a massive, thickly populated volume that deals in depth with a number of the same issues already raised in his shorter fictional pieces. Thanks in part to the credible if disheartening portrayal of Alissa, and in part also to the social background evoked, *Strait Is the Gate* remains among Gide's more memorable and frequently reprinted efforts, together with *The Immoralist*.

*Sources for Further Study*
Brée, Germaine. *Gide*, 1963.
Cordle, Thomas. *André Gide*, 1969.
Fowlie, Wallace. *André Gide: His Life and Art*, 1965.
Freedman, Ralph. *The Lyrical Novel*, 1963.
Hytier, Jean. *André Gide*, 1962.
Ireland, George William. *André Gide: A Study of His Creative Writings*, 1970.
Starkie, Enid. *André Gide*, 1954.

*David B. Parsell*

# THE SUNDAY OF LIFE

*Author:* Raymond Queneau (1903-1976)
*Type of plot:* Domestic comedy
*Time of plot:* The late 1930's and early 1940's
*Locale:* Paris
*First published: Le Dimanche de la vie*, 1952 (English translation, 1976)

> *Principal characters:*
> VALENTIN BRÛ, an army private
> JULIA, his wife, a shopkeeper
> CHANTAL, her sister
> PAUL BATRAGRA, Chantal's husband

*The Novel*

Raymond Queneau's *The Sunday of Life* is a bright, cheery work that looks with an ironic distance on the small foibles of ordinary people. The title is taken from a celebrated phrase in Georg Wilhelm Friedrich Hegel's discussion of Dutch painting, in which the philosopher speculates that because of their innocence and cheerful spirit, the peasants in Pieter Brueghel the Elder's painting must be close to the Ideal. Queneau seems to share this belief, which keeps the often-mordant humor of the work from becoming a negative judgment on his simple characters.

The novel opens in a popular quarter of Paris, where "popular" signals a working-class orientation and lack of sophistication. Two sisters, Julia and Chantal, are viewing the street scene from the window of their mother's haberdashery. Chantal is happily married to Paul Batragra, but Julia's sharp tongue and shrewish nature have kept her from finding a suitable match, and she is now in her mid-to-late thirties. When they see a handsome soldier walking down the street, Chantal teases her sister that she should marry him. Unknown to Private Valentin Brû, the machinations are already set in motion that will lead to his marriage with Julia.

First, Chantal makes the necessary inquiries at Valentin's regimental headquarters. Having learned his name and where he is stationed, her husband, Paul, begins the next round of inquiries by tracking Valentin to his favorite café where he is always to be seen drinking *vin blanc gommé*. After a long conversation, his head spinning with repeated drinks offered by Paul, Valentin agrees to marry Julia. Valentin's commanding officer agrees to his temporary discharge, and, together with Julia, he helps to run the haberdashery after their marriage. The couple runs into a problem immediately as to whether they can neglect the family business long enough to take a honeymoon. Together they deliberate:

No, of course, not, said Valentin. You see, then, said Julia. And yet, said
Valentin, and yet it's obligatory, a honeymoon. . . . Maybe we could put the
honeymoon off until our next vacation, suggested Valentin. And when will we
take the vacation, then? Julia objected. And he had no answer to that.

They ended up by adopting the only possible solution, the one and only, to
wit that Valentin would go on the honeymoon alone.

Julia makes elaborate plans and packs his suitcase for him, but Valentin, in
his timid simplicity, makes a mess of the itinerary. In fact, he never leaves
Paris, loses his suitcase, and has various amusing encounters with taxi driv-
ers, barmen, and prostitutes.

Luckily, the next thing he knows, Valentin comes upon a funeral, which
happens to be that of his mother-in-law, so he is reunited with his wife and
family. This surprise reunion gives a happy cast to the otherwise sad proceed-
ings, so the two couples decide to have a postfuneral dinner celebration. At
the dinner, however, Valentin has to face one of his worst fears—raw
shellfish—because the others insist on having champagne and oysters. They
notice that he is not participating in the feast, and Valentin defends himself
by saying that the oysters are still alive:

> "They're only just alive," said Paul.
> "They're just as alive as you and me," said Valentin.
> "Funny comparisons you make," said Julia.
> "It's true, though," said Valentin. "An oyster, it's a living creature. Just as
> much as I am. Zno difference. Zonly one difference: between the living and the
> dead."
> "You aren't very tactful," said Chantal.

Here the reader cannot help but be struck by Queneau's characteristic humor, which often succeeds in bringing up obliquely other, weightier, matters.

When they return to their conjugal life, Julia takes up a side profession as
a fortune-teller, under the name of Madame Saphir. Her income helps to offset the drop in business which they experience in the haberdashery. Valentin
takes advantage of the lull in business to take a trip to Germany to explore
his ancestral heritage. He returns disappointed, however, since the tour,
organized in Paris, has as its primary goal visiting the sites of Napoleon
Bonaparte's battles. When he returns to work in the shop, Valentin uses
his sharp ear for gossip in order to collect information for Madame Saphir.
With this aid, the fortune-telling business more than makes up for the shop's
lack of trade.

When Julia suffers a stroke and is confined to bed, it appears that the
fortune-telling business will come to an end. Valentin, however, steps in and
assumes the role of Madame Saphir. With his strange brand of simple wisdom, Valentin is actually more successful than his wife, and Madame

Saphir's fame spreads. With the growing climate of war that presages the outbreak of World War II, however, Madame Saphir's prophecies grow increasingly bleak. Her business is closed for good when Valentin is remobilized at the outbreak of the war. Captured and made a prisoner of war, Valentin is released when the hostilities end, and through her usual resourcefulness, Julia is able to locate his regiment once again. When she sees him at last, he is helping some women refugees to climb into the window of a crowded train: "Julia choked with laughter: it was so as to get his hand on their behinds." Whatever befalls these characters, in Queneau's world of humorous distance and irony, one can always be sure that somewhere, someone is having a good time just the same.

## The Characters

Valentin is a classic Queneau character. His simplicity of spirit is such that he agrees to marry a woman fifteen years his senior, whom he has never seen. Because of practical considerations, he takes the subsequent "honeymoon" by himself and yet never reaches his destination because of a series of adventures. Valentin thinks that when a prostitute invites him to her room, she is merely being friendly, and he gets into more trouble as a result. He is the perfect comic character, cheerfully oblivious to the confusion that he sows around him.

On the other hand, Valentin's simplicity is a sort of wisdom. His fear of eating oysters leads him to reflect on the nature of life and death. His total lack of jingoistic patriotism keeps him from falling into the war hysteria that surrounds him, and his insight into a variety of human situations makes him a very successful fortune-teller when he takes over for his wife. Valentin spreads mirth around him wherever he goes, but it is always humor with a kernel of profound truth.

Julia is sharp-tongued and extremely quick in her witty repartee. She spends most of the book making puns and verbal allusions with her sister Chantal that comment in an incisive way on the petty faults of her fellow humans. Luckily for Valentin, most of her humor is over his head. Together, the two of them, when they discuss a question or problem, almost invariably arrive at the most outrageous conclusions or solutions. Although Julia's quick thinking resolves many tricky situations, her schemes always seem to create more.

Chantal and Paul are essentially foils for Valentin and Julia, a more or less normal complement to the other couple's quirky unpredictability. They aid Julia in her original design on Valentin but end up resenting the fact that Chantal's mother leaves the haberdashery to Valentin. All through the story, they are too dull to comprehend the deeper sympathy that Valentin evokes in others. Chantal is a good match for Julia's quick wit, and Paul is a good partner for Valentin, though only a touch less simple than his brother-in-law is.

*Themes and Meanings*

*The Sunday of Life* is an important example of Queneau's belief in the deep wisdom of simple people. Viewed with a detached irony, his characters confront age-old problems, such as marriage, death, and war, with a simplicity of spirit that may result in some pratfalls but always eventuates in a kind of peaceful resignation and understanding. For Queneau, humor is a way of life, a way of commenting and thus overcoming some of its bleaker or more tragic aspects.

Situational humor abounds in Queneau's writings. A woman teases her sister about an attractive soldier walking down the street and ends up arranging their match. The happy couple cannot agree on when to take a honeymoon, so the groom sets off on the trip by himself. At the funeral of their mother, the two couples end up arguing over the existential status of raw oysters. These situations, as well as many others, become a sort of repertoire for Queneau and allow him to represent in miniature, through the intimacy of a few people together, larger issues of life and death. That philosophers treat these same issues in terms of metaphysics worries Queneau not at all. He would rather explore the understanding of simple people, an understanding which by implication is always more real and thus more profound than any abstract theorizing.

Besides the humor of situations, Queneau's main vehicle for humor—and understanding—is language itself, especially spoken language and slang. Yet he is also capable of using an extremely erudite vocabulary for the same purpose. In the scene at the restaurant, the oysters are referred to as "ostreicultivated animals," "goblike mollusk," "lamellibranchia," and "raw mollusks." Though this display of erudition may send German philologists scurrying to their learned editions, the effect in the scene is one of highly effective counterpointing to the simple truth of the thoughts expressed. One is left wondering, at the end, whether the knowledge of the erudite person is any more profound than the implicit wisdom of the vulgar person.

It is in language, finally, that Queneau's characters and situations have their being. The characters may be ludicrously simpleminded and the situations filled with incongruities, but the total effect of the novel is to make one realize the incredible richness and diversity in the most mundane setting, sparked by the endless creativity of language itself.

*Critical Context*

*The Sunday of Life* is Raymond Queneau's thirteenth novel, but it was the first of his works to enjoy an overwhelming public acceptance. Along with *Zazie dans le métro* (1959; *Zazie in the Metro*, 1960), it marked a change in Queneau's novelistic career away from the somber and often-pessimistic atmosphere of his early work and toward a more sunny and cheerful approach. Queneau also wrote the script for the screen adaptation by Claude

Chabrol, which enjoyed wide popular success.

Queneau was a leading figure in the French literary world for more than forty years. From his early works, which owe their existence in part to his collaboration with the Surrealist movement, and the works in his middle career such as *The Sunday of Life*, which were more popular in orientation, to his meditative and philosophical later works, Queneau remained a writer fascinated with the materiality of language. More than any other writer of his century perhaps, he was responsible for the acceptance in France of word-play and slang into the realm of serious literature. In many ways, his work anticipated the experimentalism of the New Novel movement of the 1960's.

*The Sunday of Life* is arguably Queneau's most cheerful work. Essentially a domestic comedy, the novel shows that a work with a light tone that treats simple characters can nevertheless raise important questions about language and show how the language people use reveals their implicit metaphysical thinking. As with all Queneau's work, *The Sunday of Life* is an important example of how ordinary life, through the scrutiny of language, can be made to yield an extraordinary richness.

*Sources for Further Study*

Brée, Germaine, and Margaret Guiton. *An Age of Fiction: The French Novel from Gide to Camus*, 1957.

Cobb, Richard. *Raymond Queneau*, 1976.

Guicharnaud, Jacques. *Raymond Queneau*, 1965.

Shorley, Christopher. *Queneau's Fiction*, 1985.

Thiher, Allen. *Raymond Queneau*, 1985.

*Peter Baker*

# SUTTER'S GOLD

*Author:* Blaise Cendrars (Frédéric Louis Sauser, 1887-1961)
*Type of plot:* Historical chronicle
*Time of plot:* 1834-1880
*Locale:* Switzerland, New York, Missouri, Hawaii, Oregon, Canada, Alaska, California, Pennsylvania, and Washington, D.C.
*First published: L'Or: La Merveilleuse Histoire du général Johann August Suter,* 1925 (English translation, 1926)

> *Principal characters:*
> JOHANN AUGUST SUTTER, a Swiss adventurer, ruined by the discovery of gold on his California land
> ANNA SUTTER, Sutter's wife, who journeys with their children to rejoin him in California
> JUDGE THOMPSON, the chief magistrate of California, who rules on Sutter's case and later befriends him
> JAMES W. MARSHALL, the carpenter who discovers gold on Sutter's land
> JOHANNES CHRISTITSCH, the leader of a Christian sect in Pennsylvania who takes control of Sutter's spiritual and legal affairs

*The Novel*

For his first, and still most popular, novel, Blaise Cendrars reshaped the life of an actual historical personage, the ill-fated grandfather of his friend, the Swiss sculptor August Sutter. Following his solitary emigration to the Western Hemisphere, Johann Sutter (in the French text, Cendrars persists in giving the name its original spelling, Suter) had managed to become virtual emperor of California, until the discovery of gold on his property in the Sacramento Valley precipitated an uncontrollable rush of prospectors, who ruined him. Ironically, vast deposits of the precious metal reduced the wealthiest man in North America to destitution and madness.

*Sutter's Gold* begins with the appearance of a lone stranger in a remote Swiss village. Johann Sutter has come to apply for a passport, but, when the authorities refuse to provide one to the unknown thirty-one-year-old, he crosses the French border anyway, leaving behind his wife and four children. The vagabond lives by his wits, not always by the law, and manages to book passage on a ship to New York. He vows to himself to conquer the New World.

Sutter spends two years in New York before moving on to St. Louis. He becomes haunted by alluring tales of the Western frontier and is determined, despite the many hazards, to travel to California. En route, the flip of a coin assures him that he will succeed. From Vancouver, he sails to Hawaii, and, after some time in the islands, he arranges passage with Russian sailors to Alaska. From Sitka, Sutter sails down the coast, to find himself at last alone on the deserted beach of San Francisco.

Excited by the luxuriant land he sees in the Sacramento Valley, Sutter proposes to build his New Helvetia there and is told by the Mexican governor to do as he pleases. Overcoming the natural and human dangers and the vagaries of politics, he succeeds in creating a magnificent empire. Yet, at the moment of his greatest triumph, as the forty-five-year-old Sutter prepares to send for his family in Europe, James W. Marshall, a carpenter in New Helvetia, accidentally digs into a lode of gold. By precipitating a frenetic rush onto the Sutter lands, the discovery of the valuable metal ends the sovereignty and the prosperity of the wealthiest man on the continent. Sutter loses control of his property to thousands of avaricious prospectors, and, when Anna Sutter and his four children finally arrive, they encounter a broken pauper. On seeing her husband, Anna collapses and dies.

Sutter sets to work again, and, for a time, his affairs once more flourish. He is honored as a hero by the mayor of San Francisco, and Judge Thompson rules that Sutter possesses full ownership of all the property in New Helvetia. The legal decision provokes a riot, a rampaging mob burns and ransacks the estate, and Sutter is again reduced to poverty, while his eldest son, Emile, is driven to suicide.

A shattered man, Sutter wanders about quoting the book of Revelation. He joins a religious sect in Pennsylvania and comes under the sway of its leader, Johannes Christitsch, who takes charge of his legal appeals. Sutter then becomes a familiar, pathetic figure in Washington, D.C., futilely petitioning Congress for the restoration of his property. Abandoned even by Christitsch, Sutter dies on the steps of the Capitol, at the age of seventy-three, unable to withstand the excitement caused by a cruel lie told to him by a seven-year-old child, that Congress has voted Sutter one hundred million dollars.

*The Characters*

Although it features a cast of thousands, *Sutter's Gold* is the story of one monumentally obsessive man. Other figures, including his wife, his employees, and his advisers, put in flitting, fleeting appearances, but Sutter is the one character who dominates every sentence of the narrative.

Cendrars' Sutter is an adventurer and a visionary, a fundamentally solitary man possessed of almost indomitable will. Once he determines to establish his empire in California, he refuses to allow any obstacle, human or natural, to stand in his way. Sutter is a European's image of the American self-made man, the penniless immigrant who, by dint of sheer raw ambition, manages to re-create himself as lord of a vast enterprise. He is a grandiose figure, beyond good and evil, who is destroyed by the cupidity of a society that rejects his pastoral dream and by his own stubborn insistence on waging a holy war against the soldiers of gold.

Cendrars neglects and refashions complicating details from the actual life of Sutter in order to transform him into a myth rather than a fully rounded character. The fact that Sutter's wife survived him by a year did not deter Cendrars from describing her melodramatic death at the moment of their reunion in California. In addition, though the historical Sutter died in a hotel room two days after learning that Congress had adjourned without taking action on his petition, *Sutter's Gold* presents him as a Greek hero tragically collapsing at false news relayed by a juvenile messenger.

Cendrars' Sutter is the last rugged individualist in a world tyrannized by a faceless, soulless mob. He is an adventurer at a moment when adventure ceases to be highly regarded. He is the flamboyant personality who gives *Sutter's Gold* its only character.

*Themes and Meanings*

The novel's first four brief sections, which portray Sutter in Europe, are narrated in the past tense. Once he crosses the Atlantic, however, his veritable life begins (what the French subtitle calls "the marvelous history of General Johann August Sutter"), and the remainder of the novel is in the present tense. The effect is to simulate the immediacy of cinema, a young art form that held great appeal for Cendrars. Much of *Sutter's Gold* seems not so much narrated as filmed, using visual techniques similar to the flashbacks, closeups, and dissolves common to the films that Cendrars admired and on which he collaborated.

*Sutter's Gold* is constructed of seventeen chapters, each subdivided into one or more sections. In all, there are seventy-four sections in the entire novel. The sentences, paragraphs, and chapters of the book are strikingly brief. Chapter 7, for example, consists of only one section, and section 65 consists of only one paragraph. Many of Cendrars' paragraphs contain only one sentence and some sentences only one, monosyllabic word. In its terse style and structure, *Sutter's Gold* seems less akin to the traditional novel than to the screenplays that Cendrars was also writing.

Designed to show more than to tell, it is a text fraught with spectacular scenic effects reminiscent of director Abel Gance, under whom Cendrars worked as an assistant. Sutter's arrival at the frenetic docks of New York, his trek across the American wilderness, his stepping ashore, alone, from an Alaskan schooner onto the deserted California coast, the sudden death of Anna at the very moment of reunion with her famous husband, the torching of the Sutter mansion by a crazed mob, his collapse on the vast steps of the Capitol in Washington, D.C.—all are such stuff as that of which the epics of the silent screen were made or the novels that would emulate these visual effects. The novel's severe verbal economy intensifies the sense of an implacable fate, the inevitability of defeat for its overreaching hero.

*Critical Context*

The first and shortest of Cendrars' novels, *Sutter's Gold* anticipates the individualist adventurers of *Moravagine* (1926; English translation, 1968), *Les Confessions de Dan Yack* (1929), and *Rhum: L'Aventure de Jean Galmot* (1930). While much of the Swiss author's diverse output in poetry, fiction, and nonfiction remains untranslated or otherwise unavailable, the brevity, immediacy, and simplicity of *Sutter's Gold* have made the novel his most accessible and popular, though not most representative, work.

*Sutter's Gold* embodies some aspects of the personality of Cendrars, himself an elusive traveler and adventurer. Its techniques reflect his intense interest in the nascent art of cinema, even as they anticipate the further development throughout the twentieth century of the cinematic novel, of narratives that have adapted the strategies of film. Flawed as a document of American history, the novel is nevertheless a vivid, if melancholy, embodiment of enduring American myths of frontier opportunity and individual assertion.

*Sources for Further Study*

Birkerts, Sven. "Blaise Cendrars," in *New Boston Review*. V (June/July, 1980), pp. 5-8.

Bochner, Jay. *Blaise Cendrars: Discovery and Re-creation*, 1978.

Chefdor, Monique. *Blaise Cendrars*, 1980.

Kellman, Steven G. "Blaise Cendrars's *L'Or* as Cinematic Novel," in *POST SCRIPT: Essays in Film and the Humanities*. IV (1985), pp. 16-28.

*Studies in Twentieth Century Literature*. III, no. 2 (1979). Special Cendrars issue.

*Steven G. Kellman*

# THE SWAN VILLA

*Author:* Martin Walser (1927-    )
*Type of plot:* Social realism
*Time of plot:* Late summer, the late 1970's
*Locale:* Southwestern Germany, near Lake Constance
*First published: Das Schwanenhaus*, 1980 (English translation, 1982)

> *Principal characters:*
> GOTTLIEB ZÜRN, a real estate agent
> ANNA, his wife
> ROSA,
> MAGDA,
> JULIA, and
> REGINA, his daughters
> PAUL SCHATZ and J. F. KALTAMMER, his competitors

## The Novel

*The Swan Villa* is yet another of Martin Walser's novels dealing with the mid-life crisis of an unexceptional male character. For Gottlieb Zürn, a real estate agent, the crisis is exacerbated not by ill fortune—this he is able to ignore—but by an exceptional opportunity that forces him to realize his hidden hopes and fears. Such a bourgeois conformist and opportunist would be the perfect object of satire and scorn, as evidenced in the works of Heinrich Mann (and even the young Walser), for example. Yet here the reader is given a sympathetic portrait of the everyday concerns of a relatively successful citizen in modern West Germany. His problems and fears are trivial on a global scale, yet they are representative of so many and are presented so intimately and credibly that the reader can understand, and even sympathize with, the hapless "hero."

From the outset, Gottlieb's family seems to be collapsing around him. His daughters are troubled: Rosa is pregnant by an irresponsible filmmaker, Magda is apathetic, Julia is rebelling, and Regina is suffering from a protracted, and increasingly serious, undiagnosable illness. Moreover, the dog is failing obedience school. Gottlieb's wife, Anna, is so preoccupied with these domestic problems that she cannot muster any enthusiasm for her conjugal duties.

Amid the rising chaos of his domestic life, Gottlieb Zürn suddenly has the professional opportunity of his lifetime: to gain the exclusive listing to a splendid art-nouveau property, the Swan Villa, on the shores of Lake Constance. This would mean not only a tremendous boost to his sagging real estate business (and to his income), but also a triumph over his professional rivals and social superiors, Paul Schatz and J. F. Kaltammer.

For Gottlieb, the Swan Villa also represents his unspoken ambitions and desires. As a child, he envied the inhabitants of the villa. Now, it epitomizes his dreams of social acceptance and an untroubled, idyllic life. He is so consumed by this project that he does not take notice of the situation in the family. Fortunately, his wife is able to deal with each separate problem and resolve it satisfactorily. In fact, she is the one who has been closing all Gottlieb's real estate sales of late, and it is only because of her capabilities that the business remains solvent. Gottlieb, to soothe his troubled mind, went on a spending spree and then had a costly automobile accident; since any recent financial successes are a direct result of his wife's strength and subtle skills, Gottlieb's ability to provide adequately for his family's future appears questionable.

Nevertheless, he perseveres in his own halting way. Intimidated by the finesse of his rivals, Schatz and Kaltammer, and by the social grace and stature of the villa's owner, he can only scheme and hope. His attempt to acquire the listing for himself meets with failure, as does his appearance at a prestigious social event. At every turn, his incompetence and lack of social presence are exposed. Yet despite continuing embarrassment, he remains obsessed with the Swan Villa.

By the end of the novel, life has progressed, though with an ambiguous conclusion for Gottlieb Zürn. The myriad problems within the family have been resolved for the better, largely because of the calm and steady supervision of his wife: Rosa will continue her studies and have her baby; Magda has gained new self-assurance and interest in life; Julia has acquired some measure of self-discipline; and Regina's health is gradually improving. Gottlieb, however, has lost the listing of his beloved Swan Villa; indeed, he has lost the villa itself and all that it represents to him. His unlikely rival, Kaltammer, acquires the exclusive listing and proceeds to demolish the exquisite structure, with the intent of building unsightly but profitable concrete condominiums on the site.

### The Characters

Gottlieb Zürn is not a business genius. He is a modestly talented man with a lower-middle-class background, that is, with lingering dreams and aspirations that can never be realized. He hopes for social advancement and monetary success, yet he does not deserve them and does not know how to achieve them. His present domestic problems (his eldest daughter's pregnancy and unfinished education and the other daughters' lack of ambition, success, and vitality) are indeed troublesome. Still, with the image of the Swan Villa before him, its acquisition as a listing becomes an obsession, representing simultaneously his secret goals of success and a positive self-image. Gottlieb would be happiest in a childish existence, free from responsibility and the accompanying social pressures; he is insecure and would prefer to spend his days listing old farmhouses rather than competing with his sophisticated rivals, Schatz and Kaltammer. Yet his deserved inferiority complex is suppressed by his hopes and dreams.

One trenchant example of Gottlieb's hidden desires is his recurring erotic fantasies. During one of his shopping sprees, he buys a Polaroid camera in the hope of introducing it to his wife to spice up their sex life; needless to say, he does not have the courage to broach the subject with her, and the right moment does not occur naturally. In social situations, he cannot help but secretly admire the physical attributes of attractive females, though, again, he is powerless to act; because of his bourgeois insecurities (and his sincere devotion to his wife), he is completely incapable of an adulterous affair. In fact, in a weak moment, he admits that he is completely satisfied with his wife's companionship, indeed, that she is too good for him. For these reasons, he is most attracted to the painted nude nymphs on the murals in the Swan Villa. He secretly admires the nymphs' graceful freedom and can fantasize harmlessly to his heart's content. With the destruction of the villa, however, he must find a different, yet acceptable, outlet for his fantasies or forsake them entirely.

*The Swan Villa* is exclusively the story of Gottlieb Zürn's mid-life crisis. The other figures, though deftly drawn in a few strokes with unforgettable personality traits, play supporting roles. Their appearance or absence creates situations that are designed to reveal Gottlieb's character. For example, he is surrounded by females, primarily his wife and four daughters (like Martin Walser himself). These female characters represent yet another dimension of Gottlieb's life that he does not understand and cannot control.

Like most of Walser's protagonists, Gottlieb Zürn has no close male friends. Despite frequent contact with two local figures of questionable reputation (who seem to embarrass Gottlieb with their bizarre, friendly gestures), Gottlieb is attracted more to his two idols, the more successful and charismatic realtors J. F. Kaltammer and Paul Schatz. Although he revels at any hint of their possible failure, he also secretly admires their flair, their individuality, and their social status. Gottlieb's only regular contact is with the caretaker of the Swan Villa; Gottlieb always remembers to bring him some wine and to inquire about his dog. Nevertheless, the reader may be suspicious of Gottlieb's sincerity, since the caretaker is also a major source of information regarding the coveted Swan Villa.

To judge from Walser's works, it appears that modern men are condemned to a lonely existence without sympathetic male companionship. Precisely for this reason, the female figures in his prose, the wives of these mediocre men, gain importance. It is the women who hold the families together, promote their husbands' business successes, and provide the only understanding and companionship in the men's lonely lives. For the men, this friendship is often confused by their own sexual urges. Though the women function quietly and effectively in these various roles, the men have difficulty realizing and separating the multiple positive aspects of their wives.

## Themes and Meanings

Gottlieb Zürn is scarcely a traditional hero, either in the ordeals that he suffers or in his personal stature. With consummate skill, Walser brings the reader into this modest life, communicating the innermost thoughts and fears so that the reader shares intimately in Gottlieb's mundane existence. From the first sentence of the novel, the reader experiences daily events simultaneously with the main character—as seen through Gottlieb's eyes and reflected in his mind—and learns the significance of each event for him. With the exception of sporadically scattered dialogue, the bulk of the novel consists of Gottlieb's unspoken thoughts and reactions in the form of interior monologues. Through this narrative perspective, the reader develops an understanding of the hero's existence, suffers with him through various trials and tribulations, and ultimately sympathizes with his fate, no matter how trivial. Walser treats his main character with sympathy and good humor so that Gottlieb's embarrassments evoke empathy rather than scorn.

Gottlieb represents that great number of outwardly successful businessmen in industrial societies. He is forced to compete—not for survival, but for much higher stakes: for social acceptance and thus prestige. Constantly measuring himself against superior competitors, Gottlieb is basically insecure, secretly preferring to quit in order to avoid the inevitable humiliation when he is exposed for exactly who and what he is: a child of little consequence or value. Since he is playing a game by someone else's rules and therefore cannot win, he would prefer not to play at all.

To divert himself from this realization, he periodically escapes into reveries or manic shopping binges; a camera, a Persian rug, and ornate fixtures from the villa all distract his attention but threaten to bankrupt him as well. Perhaps he flirts with penury so that he will no longer be required to compete, to strive for unattainable goals, and can simply settle down to an unpretentious existence in a modest farmhouse. This may be where he belongs, and it would be a tremendous relief for him to accept such a fate. Unfortunately, Walser will not permit him this easy escape. Like his many colleagues around the globe, Gottlieb must struggle within his present circumstances and find accommodation as best he can.

The Swan Villa is the predominant symbol within the novel. For Gottlieb, it represents an idyllic refuge far from the constant concerns of everyday life. By its very existence, it provides him the means with which to escape reality. He is not interested in purchasing the villa himself, for he knows that he could not afford it and that he does not belong on such an estate. Yet it must exist, so that he can dream of it. With the destruction of the villa and its loss as a permanent symbol of Gottlieb's secret desires, he must relinquish some of his long-hidden and unrealistic fantasies. Throughout this intense obsession with the villa, he has been forced to confront, if ever so briefly, his actual existence, his accumulated hopes and desires, his limitations. He realizes that he must attempt to live in the present and not in a fantasized future that was only compensation for his inferiority complex. In so doing, Gottlieb has taken at least one halting step toward learning to live with himself as he is.

*Critical Context*

All Martin Walser's works are centered on his native region (approximately the triangle between Stuttgart, Zurich, and Munich). Several prose cycles are especially noteworthy: for example, the trilogy featuring Anselm Kristlein as the main character or the two works depicting Helmut Halm. Yet another cycle traces several male members of an extended family as they embark on their respective mid-life crises: Gottlieb Zürn in *The Swan Villa*, Xavier Zürn in *Seelenarbeit* (1979; *The Inner Man*, 1984), and Franz Horn in *Jenseits der Liebe* (1976; *Beyond All Love*, 1982) and *Brief an Lord Liszt* (1982; *Letter to Lord Liszt*, 1985). In this cycle, Walser portrays the saga of three men: by outward appearances, the male representatives of a successful, extended family in a modern, industrial nation.

All the main characters listed above must be considered passive "heroes"; they are too insecure to be men of action. Often, an external stimulus creates a seemingly insurmountable obstacle for the main character, or an unexpected opportunity encourages him to fulfill a lifelong dream. Regardless of the situation, a typical reaction is one of faltering indecision or even paralysis, rather than a confident, aggressive approach to resolve a problem or to attain a goal.

Walser's fiction has grown increasingly popular and has gained critical acclaim as well. Together with Günter Grass, he is perhaps one of the two most widely known contemporary German writers, especially for his accurate depictions of modern life and its attendant problems. His subtle craftsmanship and seemingly informal narrative style have created an enviable reputation since the mid-1970's.

*Sources for Further Study*

Doane, Heike A. "Martin Walsers Ironiebegriff," in *Monatshefte*. LXXVII (1985), pp. 195-212.

Kaes, Anton. "Porträt Martin Walser," in *The German Quarterly*. LVII (1984), pp. 432-449.

Parkes, K.S. "Crisis and New Ways: The Recent Development of Martin Walser," in *New German Studies*. I (1973), pp. 85-98.

Parkes, Stuart. "Martin Walser: Social Critic or *Heimatkünstler*," in *New German Studies*. X (1982), pp. 67-82.

Pickar, Gertrud B. "Narrative Perspective in the Novels of Martin Walser," in *The German Quarterly*. XLIV (1971), pp. 48-57.

Thomas, R. Hinton. "Martin Walser: The Nietzsche Connection," in *German Life and Letters*. XXXV (1982), pp. 319-328.

*Todd C. Hanlin*

# THE TARTAR STEPPE

*Author:* Dino Buzzati (Dino Buzzati Traverso, 1906-1972)
*Type of plot:* Metaphysical allegory
*Time of plot:* The late nineteenth or early twentieth century
*Locale:* A military fort in the mountains and an unnamed city, two or three
    days' ride away
*First published: Il deserto dei Tartari*, 1940 (English translation, 1952)

> *Principal characters:*
> GIOVANNI DROGO, an officer, assigned at the beginning of his
>     career to the Bastiani Fortress
> ORTIZ, a captain at the fortress when Drogo arrives
> ANGOSTINA, a lieutenant, with whom Drogo becomes friends

## The Novel

*The Tartar Steppe* is generally considered to be Dino Buzzati's major
work. It is also the one which, more than any other, has contributed to the
linking of his name with that of Franz Kafka—an association often reiterated
by critics, but denied by Buzzati himself, who claimed not to have read
Kafka at the time.

The novel opens with the hero, Giovanni Drogo, a young lieutenant newly
commissioned from the Royal Military Academy, preparing to leave for his
first posting to the Bastiani Fortress. The major themes of anticipation and
the passage of time are present from the first page: Drogo's sense of disappointment now that the long-awaited moment has actually arrived, and his
feeling that those months and years of slogging study and preparation at the
academy are already in the past, a lost youth, never to be repeated.

Riding into the mountains, he can find no one to tell him the way to the
fortress. Those he asks know nothing about it; they even deny the possibility
of its existence. Thus, in the style of Kafka, the fortress gradually acquires an
aura of mystery and unreality, augmented by the scenery which becomes
more forbidding as he climbs even higher, as the shadows descend and
evening falls. On the following day, he meets another officer, Captain Ortiz,
returning to the fortress where he has served for eighteen years, who
explains to young Drogo that this is a second-rate fort on a "dead" tract of
frontier. Beyond it is nothing but wild desert terrain stretching away in a vast
plain, bordered by rocky peaks. This is known as the "Tartar Steppe": No
one knows of any Tartars having been there; it is probably no more than a
legend. For more than a century no enemy has come this way. The Bastiani
Fortress has never been of any use.

Drogo is repelled by the fortress and wants to arrange for an immediate
transfer but is persuaded to remain for four months. Gradually, as the days
pass, Drogo becomes friends with other officers: Morel, Angostina, Grotta.

He becomes imbued with the attitude of others, for example of Colonel Filimore, commander of the fortress for eighteen years, who live in constant expectation of a war during which the neighboring country will attack from the north and the officers of the fortress will cover themselves with glory. Haunted by a sense of exile and by an indefinable anxiety, Drogo goes to the doctor when the four months have passed for a certificate which will enable him to obtain a transfer to the city. The winter sun, however, illumines the white fortress in the snow, rendering it beautiful with a fascination of mystery; the trumpet rings clear in its martial call, the bayonets of the changing guard gleam silver in precise rows: Drogo decides that he cannot leave. The very monotony of his existence has become a habit, a part of him that, already, he cannot shake off.

Two years pass. Drogo finds himself in command of the guard at the New Redoubt, a minor outpost some three-quarters of an hour's march from the fortress. During the watch, something can be seen moving far out on the steppe. What Drogo feels, however, is merely irritation that it should happen to him, and fear. In the morning light, the mysterious movements are seen to be those of a stray horse, possibly one belonging to a recruit in Drogo's own watch. Instead of glory, the event ends in futile tragedy, as the miserable recruit, having forgotten the password, is shot and killed by a sentry from his own camp.

Anticipation and anticlimax: The following morning there is again movement out on the steppe—a thin black line stirring on the horizon. Again, and at last the chance of military glory—and then a dispatch arrives from the chief of staff to say that these are peaceable units from the Northern Kingdom, tracing the frontier, who will not come near the fortress. After the wild moment of excitement, "in the fortress everything stagnates once more in the rhythm of customary days."

A detachment, commanded by Captain Monti, by the elegant and aristocratic Lieutenant Angostina, and by a sergeant major, goes into the mountains to ensure that the antagonists from the north mark the frontier correctly. Monti is irritated by Angostina's elegance and needles him. In fact, Angostina, already ill, is unprepared for such an expedition. A snowstorm descends suddenly. The units from the north occupy the summit. To save face, under their ironic eye, Angostina and Monti, exposed to the cold, play cards. Proud and isolated in his mantle, Angostina refuses to follow Monti when the latter finally seeks shelter, and dies in the snow, echoing a dream Drogo had earlier. Presentiment of death is also a form of anticipation.

Drogo has now been at the fortress four years. Ortiz advises him to leave before it is too late. In the spring he takes two months' leave and returns home, but he finds himself wholly estranged from everyone he has known, including his mother and his friend Maria. Meanwhile, orders are received to reduce the personnel of the fortress; all of those who so desire are to apply for a transfer. Among those who fail to hear of this order are Drogo and his friend Ortiz, and when they do hear of it, it is too late. All the transfers have been made. Drogo still hopes; he is still young, only twenty-five.

Shortly after the departure of half the troops, one of those left behind, Lieutenant Simeoni, spots further activity out on the steppe. The Northern Kingdom is building a road. There is the usual fever-of-war talk, excitement, and anticipation, followed by the inevitable disillusionment.

Fifteen years later, the road, which had been built to within a kilometer of the fortress, has been seemingly abandoned, forgotten. Drogo applies for a month's leave in town, but his mother is dead, his brothers are gone. He is forty years old and a stranger in his own city. On his way back to the fortress, he meets a young lieutenant, Moro, who has just been assigned there. The meeting repeats Drogo's meeting with Ortiz at the beginning of Drogo's career. In Moro's arrival, Drogo recognizes the repetition of his own youth, his own career. He would like to warn Moro away but cannot bring himself to do it, and anyway, he senses that it would most probably be useless.

Time flows on. Drogo is fifty-four, a major and second in command of the now-thin detachment in the fortress. He is ill but steadfastly refuses leave, conspiring with the doctor, his friend, to remain at the fortress. He carries out his duties from his bed.

At last, joy pervades the fortress. Word flies that battalions are coming from the north along the neglected road and will probably arrive in two days' time. The message has come that reinforcements are being sent to the fortress. Drogo leaves his bed to look for the Commandant, Simeoni, but he faints, and Simeoni orders him to leave: His room will accommodate three of the new arriving officers.

Coming down at last from the mountains, away from the fortress, Drogo meets one of the new battalions on the way up. The officers salute him, but he overhears a voice commenting ironically on the comfort in which he is traveling. He stops for the night at an inn. From the window of his room, seated in an armchair, he cannot see the fortress, or even the mountains. He faces the ultimate enemy, realizing that this is the most difficult death, alone, in a strange inn. "In the open air, in the midst of the fray, in his own body still young and healthy, amid triumphal trumpet echoes," death would have been glorious, but this requires far more courage. He thinks of Angostina who, after all, died a hero's death. Drogo gathers his courage, straightens himself in the chair, readjusts his collar, and smiles at death in the dark.

*The Characters*

Critics have tried to identify Giovanni Drogo, the principal character of *The Tartar Steppe*, with the writer himself. Drogo, however, is far from being an autobiographical portrait of Dino Buzzati. What Drogo does reflect, as Buzzati has explained, is the author's sense of the ineluctable passage of time, as day followed day, while he worked the night shift as editor of the *Corriere della sera*. Swamped in monotony, Buzzati wondered if all of his youth, all of his life, would waste away, as had those of other, older men, whom he watched working on to oblivion. This experience is transposed, in *The Tartar Steppe*, into a military setting because it seemed to him that in such a setting the story would "acquire the force of allegory referring to all mankind." Moreover, military life corresponded to his nature, insofar as it provided security to the individual, even of weak character, as opposed to the feeling of anxious waiting and anticipating the worst.

Although Buzzati himself admitted that he lacked the ability to create characters, Giovanni Drogo and some of the other officers closely associated with him achieve a real presence. Nothing is known about Drogo's appearance, only that he is not handsome, and that, old and ill, he is even thinner than he was formerly. Giovanni Drogo is not a completely individualized psychological entity—his preoccupations with the passage of time and wasted youth, the endless wait for the enemy and longing for military glory, are shared by, and reflected in, other characters—but he is recognizably human, not merely a type. He is not strictly speaking a hero, nor is he the conventional antihero, but he is the one on whom the author's spotlight is focused. The reader can understand and share his anxieties, his solitude, his fears and disappointments, without feeling the lack of other qualities which might have given him greater depth of character. While his history merges into that of the general life of the fortress, it is not effaced by it, and he still remains the center of the reader's interest.

Several of the characters are not described at all and some are sketched in very lightly in one or two details. Angostina, aristocratic, with a casual elegance, is pale, has a small mustache, is delicate of constitution, with a habitual air of detachment as though he were there by accident and took no interest in his surroundings. After two years of service, when he has a choice, he refuses to leave the fortress and Drogo interprets this as a gesture of proper pride. By contrast, Drogo's permanence at the fortress will not be a positive gesture, but a series of negative gestures, of succeeding refusals, of "not yet," until it is too late and he is unable to tear himself away. Angostina's death, also, is opposed to Drogo's in its overtly heroic quality in the face of the "enemy" above him on the mountain ledge. Angostina provides, above all in the novel, a series of positive, correct gestures in contrast to the torpor, and the refusal or inability to act, of some of the other characters.

As well as the characters who are caught up in the endlessness of life at the fortress and who move along in predestined stages—lieutenant, captain, commander, retirement—in endless cycles, there are those who can and do choose to break away: Lagorio, Morel, and others. They are minor characters, whose departure merely serves to emphasize the weight of the chains which hold those who remain.

More vague still are the characters in the city: Drogo's mother, his friend Maria, Francesco Vescovi, and other friends who are left unnamed. They pinpoint the passage of time in the city, with the changes this passage brings, against the curious immutability, or at least apparent immutability, of the fortress. In the fortress, individuals grow old and disappear, but the pattern remains. Young Lieutenant Drogo's meeting with the older Captain Ortiz exactly mirrors the older Drogo's meeting with the newly appointed Lieutenant Moro: In fact, nothing has changed.

## Themes and Meanings

Like Kafka's *Das Schloss* (1926; *The Castle*, 1930), Buzzati's novel functions above all on a symbolic plane. Giovanni Drogo's life, which is nothing but an endless wait for an event which will not materialize, or at least, not for him, is the symbol of human existence which wastes away in the futile anticipation of a significance which will bring brightness into its dull monotony.

Within the solid, geometric lines of the fortress, Drogo is cocooned in the illusion that he can escape the inexorable passage of time which shapes men's destiny. "There was no one to say: Beware, Giovanni Drogo! Life appeared to him inexhaustible, obstinate illusion, although the bloom of youth had already begun to fade." The passage of time is the dominant theme of this novel, but there are two dimensions of time. There is the time which flows scarcely at all, as represented by the mountains and the desert, and by the fortress in its cycle: an important outpost lauded by His Majesty, then neglected with its personnel heavily cut back, then catapulted into importance again with several battalions being rushed to it to face the enemy threat. Like the steppe and the mountains, the fortress achieves a feeling of timeless permanence. Opposed to this is the time of the human individual, measured by the course of a brief life span. The life of the fortress renews itself constantly, as young men replace those who have grown old in its service; for the individual, however, there is no renewal. From the very beginning, the novel insists on this terminal quality in a human life with the reiterated emphasis on Drogo's youth being over and behind him.

Connected with this theme of time and decay is that of loneliness. The physically isolated position of the fortress symbolizes the moral isolation of the individual, an isolation which is masked by the presence of others, although there are piercing moments of awareness. On sentinel duty, on the dark ramparts, Drogo thinks, "perhaps it's all like this, we think all around there are creatures like us but instead there is only ice, stones which speak a foreign language; we are about to greet a friend but our arm falls back, inert, our smile dies away, because we realize we are completely alone." From the feeling of angst which this realization brings, escape can be sought and found in form: in the geometric lines of the fortress, in the routine of military life with its timed round of duties.

In the repetition of meaningless gestures, in time which has slowed down to a barely perceptible crawl, in the anxious wait for a coming which does not materialize, Buzzati does more than reflect Kafka: He also foreshadows Samuel Beckett and *En attendant Godot* (1952; *Waiting for Godot*, 1954), in particular. It is perhaps this aspect of his thought which, whether consciously apprehended or not, accounts for the esteem in which *The Tartar Steppe* continues to be held.

## Critical Context

Published in 1940, in the wake of two short novels which had attracted little attention, *The Tartar Steppe* was the book which brought Buzzati fame. It is the one which springs most immediately to the lips of critics and, in 1972, it was mentioned in Buzzati's obituaries almost to the exclusion of his other works. The novel brought together, perfectly fused, all of his main themes: the passage of time, a human life wasted away in futile monotony, decay, isolation, and metaphysical angst. Of this book Buzzati himself said: "While I was writing it I understood that I should have gone on writing it for the duration of my existence and finished it only on the eve of my death." He lacked that courage, however, and when his publisher asked him for a novel in March, 1939, Buzzati gave him the complete manuscript of *The Tartar Steppe*. Released as it was in 1940, it was seen by many as a premonition of war.

*The Tartar Steppe* is not only important in Buzzati's career. One enthusiastic critic, in 1972, called it "one of the few great Italian chefs d'oeuvre . . . of this century": an opinion not generally contested.

## Sources for Further Study

Atchity, Kenneth John. "Time in Two Novels of Dino Buzzati," in *Italica*. LV, no. 1 (1978), pp. 3-19.

Barberi Squarotti, Giorgio. "La fortezza e la forma: *Il deserto dei Tartari*," in *Dino Buzzati*, 1982. Edited by Alvise Fontanella.

Geerts, Walter. "Forma, spazio, visione: alcune osservazioni sul *Deserto dei Tartari*," in *Dino Buzzati*, 1982. Edited by Alvise Fontanella.

Livi, François. *Le Désert des Tartares: Dino Buzzati*, 1973.

Mignone, Mario B. *Anormalità e angoscia nella narrativa di Dino Buzzati*, 1981.

Rawson, J. "Dino Buzzati," in *Writers and Society in Contemporary Italy*, 1984. Edited by Michael Caesar and Peter Hainsworth.

Schettino, F. "The Dream-like Technique in *Il deserto dei Tartari*: The Reader's Digest and the Critic's Nightmare," in *The Anxious Subject*, 1983. Edited by Moshe Lazar.

Veronese-Arslan, Antonia. *Invito alla lettura di Buzzati*, 1974.

*Ada Coe*

# THE TEMPLE OF THE GOLDEN PAVILION

*Author:* Yukio Mishima (Kimitake Hiraoka, 1925-1970)
*Type of plot:* Psychological realism
*Time of plot:* The early 1940's through July 2, 1950
*Locale:* Japan, most notably Cape Nariu and Kyoto
*First published: Kinkakuji*, 1956 (English translation, 1959)

*Principal characters:*
MIZOGUCHI, the protagonist and narrator, a young Zen
    acolyte
TSURUKAWA, a young acolyte at the Golden Temple with
    Mizoguchi
KASHIWAGI, a clubfooted student at Otani University with
    Mizoguchi and Tsurukawa
FATHER TAYAMA DOSEN, the Superior of the Golden Temple

*The Novel*

In *The Temple of the Golden Pavilion*, Mizoguchi narrates the story of his troubled life from his middle school years until age twenty-one, when he commits what he considers to be an inevitable deed. From the beginning of his narration, Mizoguchi stresses his isolation and feelings of alienation: Born on a remote cape to impoverished parents, a physically frail only child, he recognizes early that he is ugly and that his speech impediment—a stutter— locks him away from easy communication with the rest of the world. He lives virtually in an inner world, scorning the reality of the world around him. Throughout his narrative Mizoguchi stresses that "not being understood by other people had become my only real source of pride."

Mizoguchi comes to believe that his troubled life leads him inevitably to the destruction of the Golden Temple. To explain this deed, Mizoguchi alerts the reader "that the first real problem I faced in my life was that of beauty." Mizoguchi's father, a tubercular country priest, taught his young son that nothing was more beautiful than the Golden Temple in Kyoto. When he feels death approaching, Mizoguchi's father takes his young son to see the Zen temple and to meet Father Tayama Dosen, an old friend and the Superior of the Golden Temple. Having nurtured the idea of the temple's beauty for years in his inner world, Mizoguchi is initially disappointed with the temple. The reality does not satisfy his ideal vision. Yet once away from Kyoto, he again visualizes the temple as beautiful. After his father's death in the summer of 1944, Mizoguchi goes to Kyoto to finish his education under the care of Father Dosen. The young acolyte continues his lonely and alienated life: At his father's cremation, he sheds no tears; a flashback describing an incident when Mizoguchi is thirteen explains his hatred for his mother; and even after a year with Father Dosen, Mizoguchi feels no personal connection to him. Only the temple holds fascination for the young Zen acolyte.

While studying at the temple, Mizoguchi is befriended by another young acolyte, Tsurukawa. The two students seem quite different: Tsurukawa comes from a prosperous Tokyo family, has a promising future as a priest, and in Mizoguchi's eyes has a cheerful and carefree disposition. During these years, only Tsurukawa is aware of Mizoguchi's special feeling toward the Golden Temple.

Mizoguchi's feelings about the temple are always strong, but they vary with time. Initially, he is troubled to learn that the temple embodies so much beauty because this makes him realize the lack of beauty in his own life on the remote cape. During the late war years when Mizoguchi lives near the temple, he feels the strongest affinity with it. He feels akin to the temple rather than estranged from it because he believes that both the temple (through air raids) and he (once he reaches conscription age) will be destroyed by the war. Strangely, this belief that they would perish together comforts him. After the defeat of Japan, however, he again feels estranged from the temple and unable to see any beauty in his own life. With the defeat of Japan, his renewed estrangement from beauty, and his continued isolation from reality, Mizoguchi decides, "I shall plunge as deep as I can into an inner world of evil." He enjoys lying to Tsurukawa and refuses to confess his part in a prostitute's miscarriage.

After Tsurukawa and Mizoguchi enter Otani University, they drift apart. Tsurukawa easily makes new friends, but Mizoguchi finds it more difficult to do so. He eventually begins a relationship with Kashiwagi, a clubfooted student who quickly asserts that he has faced the same problems as Mizoguchi but with more intensity and with better results. Both students believe that because of their handicaps they have been placed in an antagonistic relationship to the rest of the world. While Mizoguchi struggles to attain a normal life, Kashiwagi seems content with his misanthropic attitude and his willingness to use people to provide himself with as much comfort as possible.

Kashiwagi urges Mizoguchi to experience life, although to experience it selfishly, nihilistically. Yet the influence of the Golden Temple continues to draw him away from reality. Mizoguchi wavers: At times, he tries to participate more in life, but at other times he prays that the beauty of the temple will protect him from the ugly realities of life. Trying to reconcile these two positions has always been Mizoguchi's problem, the problem of beauty. Mizoguchi cannot simultaneously function in the real world and fully appreciate beauty; he senses that a choice between the two must be made.

Prompted by the knowledge that Father Dosen will no longer consider Mizoguchi his successor as priest of the Golden Temple, Mizoguchi flees from the temple and travels to his birthplace. Here, by the rough sea, Mizoguchi realizes that he must set fire to the Golden Temple in order to free himself to enter the world of reality. Although Mizoguchi returns to the temple and spends almost eight more months as a university student, he never wavers from his decision to destroy the temple. He merely awaits the right moment. His confused logic leads him to action when he senses that the Superior will no longer tolerate his shirking of his studies and his disrespectful behavior. The outbreak of the Korean War also precipitates his action. Mizoguchi is pressured into believing that if he does not act quickly, he will miss his opportunity.

In the early morning hours of July 2, 1950, Mizoguchi sets fire to the Golden Temple, the beautiful Zen structure more than five hundred years old. He watches the burning with the feelings of "a man who settles down for a smoke after finishing a job of work. I wanted to live."

## The Characters

The narrator-protagonist of *The Temple of the Golden Pavilion* is based on a historical figure, a young Zen acolyte who burned an ancient Zen temple in Kyoto in 1950. Mizoguchi and the historical arsonist share certain traits—ugliness, a stutter, a preoccupation with the beauty of a Zen temple. Yet Mizoguchi's story is not simply a transference of an actual event into literary form. The historical incident of the burning of the temple serves as the impetus for the novel, but Yukio Mishima creates his own fictional world and characters to serve his artistic purposes.

All the other characters in *The Temple of the Golden Pavilion* are secondary to the narrator-protagonist. He dominates the novel, and it is from his stance that the other characters are viewed. Despite the dominance of the narrator-protagonist, the reader never gets close to Mizoguchi. In part, this fact may be the result of his characterization: He holds himself aloof; he lives mainly in his internal world and scorns close association with others. Furthermore, the narrative method seems to promote distance rather than involvement with Mizoguchi. Although the novel is narrated in the first person, Mizoguchi is quite stolid in detailing the events of his problematic young life.

It is important to recognize Mizoguchi as a dual character in the novel: The narrator Mizoguchi tells the story of the protagonist Mizoguchi in retrospect; some differences between the narrator and protagonist are apparent. The desire for death that the protagonist occasionally expresses is missing in the narrator, who accepts his status. The protagonist is proud of not being understood by others, while the narrator repeatedly makes comments such as "I hope that people will recognize how carefully I went about everything" and "I hope that I am making myself understood." It is only near the conclusion of the novel that the protagonist, like the narrator, yearns to be understood: "The desire to be understood by others had so far never occurred to me, but now I wished that Father Zenkai alone would understand me." In a first-person-retrospective narrative, when the character catches up to the narrator, the story is finished. The two major differences between the protagonist and narrator are bridged at the end of this novel, and the implication is that the burning of the temple brings about the character change in the protagonist, causing him to want to live and to be understood.

Tsurukawa and Kashiwagi play similar, yet opposing, roles in the novel. Each portrays a character in contrast with Mizoguchi. Tsurukawa is the light figure to Kashiwagi's dark. Each has some influence over Mizoguchi for brief periods. Neither Kashiwagi nor Tsurukawa is a fully realized figure, yet each has a facet of complexity that makes him more than a mere stereotype. Kashiwagi, perhaps, is the clearer figure, because, except for the narrator, he is the character who speaks most in the text. (The protagonist— as differentiated from the narrator—seldom speaks in the text, and his stutter is never reproduced, although occasionally it is mocked.) Tsurukawa's apparently lighthearted existence is called into question late in the novel when the narrator reveals that Tsurukawa's death, reported as an accident, was probably a suicide.

Father Tayama Dosen is a stock character: He is the Superior of the Zen temple, whose free time is devoted to various satisfactions of the flesh. The remaining minor characters serve to elucidate Mizoguchi's psychological state or simply to further the action.

## Themes and Meanings

It would be easy to dismiss Mizoguchi and his actions by merely labeling him a madman; indeed, the protagonist justifiably realizes that only a madman would destroy the temple. Yet the conflicts that are experienced by Mizoguchi not only are conflicts of madmen but also point to themes that are the proper concern of sane, humane men. Mizoguchi's feelings of alienation reveal more modernity than madness. His desire to discover the role imagination plays in determining reality links him intellectually with the artist. Further, his main concern—trying to reconcile beauty and reality—springs from his environment. The action of *The Temple of the Golden Pavilion* is couched between the beginning of World War II and the beginning of the Korean conflict. Air raids, the black market, food shortages, death—all play a central role in the adolescent life of Mizoguchi. How beauty survives in the same world as his ugly life is the koan this Zen acolyte tries to master. This is not to say that Mizoguchi is a sane, stable character; quite the contrary. Reaching a stage of enlightenment through contemplation and intuition is the Zen Buddhist's goal; solving paradoxes through violence is not. Yet eventually arson is the only means Mizoguchi finds for continuing his life. This failure of Mizoguchi to unravel his concerns logically, peacefully, and eternally is expected. Providing easy answers to his three conflicts would produce a fairy tale, not a modern novel.

The other characters appearing in the novel also mitigate the importance of Mizoguchi's mental state. Except for Father Zenkai, who makes a brief appearance in the novel, no character is happy and stable. Mizoguchi's parents, his Superior, and his peers all reflect problems in their personal or social worlds.

A technical aspect that could affect the meaning of the novel remains ambiguous. The narrator, who speaks after the burning of the temple, is more contented and more stable than the troubled protagonist before the arson. It would be interesting to know from what stance he speaks. Is he free physically as well as psychologically? Is his physical freedom unimportant once he has acted to liberate himself psychologically? Is his act of arson effective for him beyond the immediate moments of exhilaration?

*Critical Context*

Yukio Mishima—an essayist, poet, dramatist, and novelist—was a prolific writer. Although at times he purposely geared his writing for popular rather than critical success, his serious novels reflect such a range and expertise that he is generally considered the best Japanese novelist of his generation. Throughout his career, strong and original works indicate his importance: *Kamen no kokuhaku* (1949; *Confessions of a Mask*, 1958) brought critical attention to the young writer; *The Temple of the Golden Pavilion* secured his reputation abroad as well as in Japan; *Hōjō no umi* (1969-1971; *The Sea of Fertility: A Cycle of Four Novels*, 1972-1974) demonstrated that Mishima died with his artistic abilities strong.

*The Temple of the Golden Pavilion* was both a popular and a critical success: Enormously popular, it was later adapted to film; critics often cite this work as Mishima's best single novel. Although his novels vary greatly in style, a number of themes found in *The Temple of the Golden Pavilion* surface repeatedly in Mishima's fiction. Several of his works are based on historic incidents. For example, both this novel and Mishima's "Yūkoku" ("Patriotism") present an imaginative re-creation of an event prominent in the minds of his Japanese contemporaries. Whether dealing with the burning of a temple or an attempted coup in the military, both the novel and the short story reflect the impact Japan's military situation had on Mishima and his preoccupation with, and association of, beauty and death. A romantic, spiritual, or fiercely loyal attachment to the old order is found in both the young lieutenant in "Patriotism" and Mizoguchi in *The Temple of the Golden Pavilion*. Mizoguchi's feeling of alienation, his sexual difficulties, his preoccupation with beauty, and his struggle with the idea of suicide are all ideas prominent in other works by Mishima. The divided individual and the vision of the world as ultimately meaningless are recurrent themes in Mishima's fiction.

Although Mishima was adamant about keeping separate his art and his life, it is inevitable that after his public disemboweling hints will be sought about the artist in his art. Personal, artistic, and political reasons have all been alleged for Mishima's *seppuku*, and all these concerns are embodied in *The Temple of the Golden Pavilion*.

Yet the importance of this novel goes far beyond any possible autobiographical elements. One of Mishima's most successful novels, both popularly and critically, *The Temple of the Golden Pavilion* embodies the modern spirit. Although a Buddhist temple is the backdrop for the action, the concerns of the novel are not limited to the East but are familiar in the Western novel and the Western psyche as well.

*Sources for Further Study*

Arlow, Jacob A. "Pyromania and the Primal Scene: A Psychoanalytic Comment on the Work of Yukio Mishima," in *Psychoanalytic Quarterly*. XLVII (1978), pp. 24-51.

Dana, Robert. "The Stutter of Eternity: A Study on the Themes of Isolation and Meaninglessness in Three Novels by Yukio Mishima," in *Critique: Studies in Modern Fiction*. XII (1970), pp. 87-102.

Duus, Louise. "The Novel as Koan: Mishima Yukio's *The Temple of the Golden Pavilion*," in *Critique: Studies in Modern Fiction*. X, no. 2 (1967/1968), pp. 120-129.

Miyoshi, Masao. "Mute's Rage," in *Accomplices of Silence: The Modern Japanese Novel*, 1974.

Pollack, David. "Action as Fitting Match to Knowledge: Language and Symbol in Mishima's *Kinkakuji*," in *Monumenta Nipponica*. XL (Winter, 1985), pp. 387-398.

*Marion Boyle*

# THE TENNIS PLAYERS

*Author:* Lars Gustafsson (1936-     )
*Type of plot:* Philosophical satire
*Time of plot:* 1974
*Locale:* The University of Texas in Austin
*First published: Tennisspelarna,* 1977 (English translation, 1983)

> *Principal characters:*
> LARS GUSTAFSSON, a visiting professor of Swedish literature at
>     the University of Texas
> DOOBIE SMITH, Gustafsson's favorite student
> BILL, a graduate student who questions the accepted literary
>     criticism on August Strindberg
> CHRIS, a tennis player and computer genius

*The Novel*

Although the novel is entitled *The Tennis Players*, it is less about tennis than it is about academe. The story is told from the point of view of the main character, Lars Gustafsson, who happens to share the name of the author. Gustafsson, a Scandinavian professor of literature, reminisces about one year in his life which he spent teaching a seminar in nineteenth century European thought at the University of Texas. At first, he is able to take advantage of his year in the Texas sunshine to bicycle and to perfect his tennis serve, but he is reluctantly drawn into a series of events concerning university matters that drag him away from his beloved tennis courts.

The novel has many picaresque elements, in that it is somewhat unstructured. While the details are specific and concrete, the separate events are generally unrelated, and the various characters interact only with the central character. For example, Doobie and Bill are students of Professor Gustafsson and are presumably in the same seminar, but they do not seem to know each other. Also, the fact that the author and the central character share the same name and occupation suggests that the novel is, at least to some extent, autobiographical. While the main character is not a picaro because he hardly qualifies as a rascal, he does, as a visitor from Sweden, stand outside the social order of south central Texas and find that many of its traditions and mores are incomprehensible to him.

The title of the first chapter is "Siegfried's Rhine Journey," which the narrator explains is an aria from Richard Wagner's opera *Götterdämmerung.* It is this tune that Professor Gustafsson tries to whistle as he bikes to his favorite tennis court, across from Fred's vegetable stand. The hero of the opera, Siegfried, is a respected warrior who goes about slaying dragons and other evil creatures and rescuing damsels in distress. Although the narrator is quick to point out that he is not the legendary, daring Siegfried, nor is he biking his way "down a dark, foggy river toward strange Germanic adventures in gathering gloom," the juxtaposition suggests that the professor from Sweden is clearly on his way to some peculiarly American adventures.

One adventure involves a student with the unlikely name of Doobie Smith. Doobie, a brilliant student who has learned Norwegian in order to read Henrik Ibsen in the original, is enamored of Berlin as it was in the late nineteenth century. What intrigues the professor about Doobie is her commitment to Nietzschean philosophy and her uncanny resemblance to the photographs of Lou Salomé, the young woman whom Friedrich Nietzsche hoped would become his intellectual and personal companion. The world of reality intrudes upon the world of ideas when Doobie tries to supplement her meager income by appearing in the campus production of another Wagner opera, *Das Rheingold*. She is cast as Flosshilde, one of the Rhine Maidens, but the Italian conductor is more interested in Doobie's body than her voice.

Learning of Doobie's plight, the narrator offers to intervene on her behalf. Before he has a chance to rescue the fair maiden, however, another campus adventure intrudes. The Board of Trustees is threatening to fire the president of the university, John R. Perturber, Jr., a former professor of forestry. This time the issue is the spring concert. The trustees want to scrap *Das Rheingold* in favor of Giuseppe Verdi's *Aïda*, complete with live elephants. The trustees have charged that the president's decision to go along with the German opera, which was the choice of the orchestra and the chorus, actually constitutes a political statement because of the large German-speaking population in the area, which usually votes Democratic. The members of the Board are Republicans. The students and faculty, led by the English Department, are outraged and a full-fledged riot is in the making. Fortunately, the crisis is averted when Chairman of the Board Hugh Frisco is discovered having sex with a hotel waitress on hallowed ground, namely the batter's box of the university baseball stadium. The batter's box, it seems, is reserved for the best university batter and his girl on the night before an important game. The resulting scandal means that the president gets to keep his job, the students get to keep their opera, and the narrator, unlike Siegfried, avoids a confrontation with both the Texas National Guard and the Italian conductor.

A third crisis involves Professor Gustafsson more directly because it challenges some widely accepted assumptions about the Swedish novelist and dramatist August Strindberg. It seems that Bill, one of the narrator's graduate students, has unearthed an obscure book by a Polish exile with the unpronounceable name of Zygmunt I. Pietziewzskoczsky. The book, entitled *Memoires d'une chimiste*, which translates as *Memoirs of a Chemist*, details the efforts of Pietziewzskoczsky and other Polish exiles to spy on Strindberg, who was at the time writing his novel *Inferno* (1897; English translation,

1912) and experimenting with making gold. According to the memoirs, the Polish exiles were watching Strindberg in order to learn his secrets of alchemy. This new information challenges the assumption that Strindberg's paranoia about being watched was simply the ravings of an insane mind. If *Memoirs* is to be believed, Strindberg criticism will have to be reevaluated, at considerable inconvenience to scholars who have built their reputations on the current theory. This rather thorny problem embroils the narrator in his next escapade.

On the tennis court, the narrator meets Chris, a computer whiz who just happens to have access to one of the largest computers in Texas. In spite of the fact that Chris is on the Central Intelligence Agency's blacklist, he has a part-time job at the Strategic Air Command, where he monitors the airspace in the Southern Air Defense District. Chris offers to use the Command's computer to determine whether Strindberg's *Inferno* and Pietziewzskoczsky's *Memoirs* do, in fact, correspond. The procedure overloads the Early Warning System and causes it to black out for two hours. Unfortunately, before Chris can get an answer to the Strindberg question, he is fired from his job for taking part in the campus demonstrations to save the Wagner opera.

The novel ends when Lars Gustafsson boards the plane for Santa Barbara on his way back to Sweden. Bill, the Strindberg enthusiast, has dropped the whole pursuit in favor of attending Harvard Business School. As far as the professor and Chris know, a computer somewhere out in the Texas desert is still trying to solve the problem of whether Strindberg was truly insane or was the victim of real persecution.

### The Characters

Since the narrator-protagonist of *The Tennis Players* has the same name as the author, and a photograph of the author (playing tennis) appears on the front cover of the book, the novel must be considered to be to some extent autobiographical. Yet the events are at once so bizarre and so amusing that it is clear that the characters are fictional. In his lecture on "The Wagner Case," the professor asks his students the meaning of Nietzsche's complaint against Wagner when Nietzsche makes the following comment: "Now the musician becomes an actor; his art develops more and more into a talent for lying." In *The Tennis Players*, the writer becomes an actor and gives himself the starring role in his own novel. Gustafsson has said: "My writing is mainly an inventory of the different layers of lies and truth in the society where I live." It seems, therefore, that Gustafsson would add to Nietzsche's phrase that as the actor delves into his psyche he also develops a talent for discovering the truth.

None of the other characters is well developed and each is seen only in relation to Professor Gustafsson. Their interior lives are never probed. For example, Bill, the graduate student whose discovery of the memoirs of an unknown chemist threatens to disrupt the entire body of criticism of August Strindberg, is never given a last name. Of his physical description, the reader is told only that Bill is black, tall, skinny, and excitable. While Bill's theory may be brilliant, he is described as being "quite mad." Bill's decision to give up the humanities in favor of more practical pursuits when he is accepted into Harvard seems implausible, if amusing.

Except for the fact that Chris is a better-than-average tennis player, he is a fairly typical computer hacker. He is nearsighted, recovering from a nervous breakdown, emotionally immature, and a mathematical wizard. His room, on the third floor of the large antebellum-style home of his psychiatrist, is a clutter of notebooks, a minicomputer, cushions, and a telescope, but no furniture.

Doobie Smith is the most fully developed character after Professor Gustafsson, but explanations of what motivates her seem philosophical rather than personal. The professor's interest in Doobie seems to stem more from her remarkable resemblance to Lou Salomé than from her own personality. Although a product of a Baptist college in San Antonio, Doobie accepts the Nietzschean philosophy that truth is that which serves life; therefore, morals can be invented. Belief, however, is not action, and Doobie, who is actually a good little Southern girl, ends up calling on the good professor to save her from the amorous clutches of the Italian conductor.

## Themes and Meanings

While tennis and the tennis players whom the narrator meets have very little to do with plot or characterization, they do have something to do with Gustafsson's themes. The narrator comments that there are only two things that a superior being from outer space would find to admire on earth: One is the opera *Don Giovanni* by Wolfgang Mozart; the other, he insists, is the tennis serve. The tennis serve is difficult, erratic, and embarrassingly public. Like the queen in chess, no other move has so many options, but nothing is as disastrous as a bad serve/move or as effective as a good serve/move.

The game of tennis, then, becomes a metaphor for the game of life. Perhaps this relationship explains why the professor is content to drift along until some other character forces him to act. Yet this reluctance to involve himself in events allows him, not unlike his theoretical visitor from outer space, to stand back and observe the natives. The natives do come in for a bit of gentle ribbing. The impressive University of Texas tower that looks like an erect phallus, the dignified chairman of the Board of Trustees committing an indecent act in an open field, the engineering students packing SR-51 minicomputers in holsters just as cowboys of the American West used to carry their guns, and the fragility of America's sophisticated defense weaponry all seem a bit silly when viewed through the eyes of an objective observer.

*Critical Context*

Lars Gustafsson, philosopher, novelist, dramatist, and critic, is a highly respected Swedish writer. He is best known for his poetry and his cycle of five novels which he wrote from 1971 through 1978. The novels have many elements of a *Künstlerroman*, a type of novel in which the writer/protagonist struggles toward an understanding of his purpose as a creative artist. James Joyce's *A Portrait of the Artist as a Young Man* (1916) is the most famous example. Gustafsson's novels of piercing self-examination have influenced other Swedish writers to develop more liberated expressions of values and morals.

*The Tennis Players*, begun in 1974 when Gustafsson was Thord Gray Professor at the University of Texas, and completed in 1977, interrupts the more somber novel cycle. In this case, Gustafsson is not looking inward as much as he is looking outward at American and especially Texan mores. The result is both amusing and thought-provoking. The delightful translation by Yvonne L. Sandstroem preserves the spirit of the original. One suspects that Gustafsson would dismiss *The Tennis Players* as simply a potboiler. Henry James said the same thing about *The Turn of the Screw* (1898), the novel which has perhaps received more critical attention than any other of his works. Unfortunately, Gustafsson's novel has received very little critical attention by writers in English.

*Sources for Further Study*

*Booklist*. Review. LXXIX (March 15, 1983), p. 945.

*Kirkus Reviews*. Review. LI (January 15, 1983), p. 75.

McKnight, Christina Soderhjelm. "Two Contrasting Images of America in the 1970's: P. O. Enquist and Lars Gustafsson," in *Scandinavian Studies*. LVI (Spring, 1984), p. 196.

*Publishers Weekly*. CCXXIII (February 11, 1983), p. 64.

Sandstroem, Yvonne L. Review in *World Literature Today*. LII (Summer, 1978), pp. 479-480.

Updike, John. "As Others See Us," in *The New Yorker*. LIX (January 2, 1984), pp. 87-88.

Voltz, Ruprecht, ed. *Gustafsson lesen*, 1986.

*Sandra Hanby Harris*

# THAT AWFUL MESS ON VIA MERULANA

*Author:* Carlo Emilio Gadda (1893-1973)
*Type of plot:* Impressionistic realism/antinovel
*Time of plot:* February and March, 1927
*Locale:* Rome
*First published: Quer pasticciaccio brutto de via Merulana*, 1957 (English
translation, 1965)

> *Principal characters:*
> FRANCESCO INGRAVALLO (DON CICCIO), a Roman police
> inspector
> CORPORAL PESTALOZZI, a carabiniere (a member of the
> national police)
> TERESINA MENEGAZZI, the robbery victim
> LILIANA BALDUCCI, the murder victim
> GIULIANO VALDARENA, the murdered woman's cousin
> ZAMIRA PÀCORI, an old woman who runs an unsavory shop

## The Novel

Set against the backdrop of Benito Mussolini's new Fascist order in Italy,
*That Awful Mess on Via Merulana* recounts the police investigation of two
apparently related crimes. As the novel begins, Inspector Francesco Ingravallo, a friend of Liliana Balducci and her husband, is summoned to their
apartment building on Via Merulana, where one of their neighbors, a wealthy widow, has been robbed. The robbery victim, Teresina Menegazzi, reports hysterically that the thief was an attractive young man who, posing as
an electrician, entered her apartment, terrorized her with a knife, and fled
with her jewelry. Hardly has Ingravallo's investigation of this crime begun,
however, when Liliana Balducci herself is discovered with her throat cut and
some of her jewelry stolen.

Dismayed by the murder of Liliana, for whom he has felt perhaps more
than friendship, Ingravallo proceeds with an intensive, methodical investigation. Suspicion temporarily rests on a cousin of Liliana, Giuliano Valdarena,
but this lead proves false and the young man is cleared. Other possible
suspects include a retired government official in the same building, Commen-
datore Angeloni, and Liliana's husband, Remo Balducci. Both men, however, also prove to be innocent.

A more promising lead is discovered when the investigation focuses on
some young women formerly employed as maids by Liliana. Suspecting that
one of them may have been involved as an accomplice, Ingravallo now begins
to track down the girls and their male associates. His search leads him into
the seamy underside of Roman street life, a world he already knows in-

timately. In this chaotic realm of petty thieves and prostitutes, hustlers, beggars, street vendors, off-duty soldiers, and drifters, the shop of Zamira
Pàcori is a kind of epicenter. Ostensibly a seamstress who employs several
girls as helpers, Pàcori, in all likelihood, operates an informal brothel, as well
as dispensing wine, love potions, and quack remedies to her clientele. Two of
her "seamstresses," Ines Cionini and Lavinia Mattonari, have also served as
household servants for Liliana; each of the girls, moreover, is connected with
a suspicious male friend, Diomede Lanciani and Enea Ratalli, respectively,
either of whom could fit Teresina Menegazzi's description of the thief.

By this point, the investigation has brought in the Italian national police,
or carabinieri, since the search for the young women and their suspected
accomplices goes beyond the territorial jurisdiction of the Roman police. The
seedy, brutal Corporal Pestalozzi and his associates crack the case wide
open. Pursuing their network of leads to a village outside Rome, they find
the jewelry stolen from Teresina Menegazzi in a cottage occupied by Camilla
Mattonari, a cousin of Lavinia.

It would seem, following this startling discovery, that the solution to both
crimes is at hand. A few pages later, however, the novel simply comes to an
end, with the "awful mess" of the title still unresolved. Carlo Emilio Gadda
has chosen to leave the story in a deliberately unfinished form.

*The Characters*

The nearest character to a protagonist in the kaleidoscopic world of the
novel is Inspector Ingravallo. A tough, cynical policeman, his world-weary
view of human nature expresses Gadda's own cynicism. His affection for the
murdered woman involves him emotionally in the investigation, while his
plodding approach seems the only rational way to pick apart the tangled, sordid threads that make up the convoluted action of the novel.

The novel, however, is not really about the perceptions and destinies of
significant individuals. Although Ingravallo does serve as an organizing intelligence within the world of the novel, he is nevertheless merely part of the
action. Indeed, there is little practical difference between the major and
minor characters, whether in terms of the descriptive space allocated to them
or their worth as human beings. None of them is a figure against a background so much as a piece of a mosaic.

All of them, though perhaps to a lesser degree in Ingravallo's case, are
presented satirically. Gadda's Romans represent humanity at its most fallible
and least attractive. They are motivated by greedy, hormonal drives; they
speak and think in clichés; they are mutually suspicious and self-serving yet
compulsively gregarious. Even the murder victim herself generates little
sympathy. A pathetic, sexually attractive but childless woman approaching
middle age, she takes in young women as maids to fill the place of the children she desires, while possibly harboring homosexual longings for them.

The thematic counterpoint between her and the witchlike hag Zamira Pàcori, who also surrounds herself with young women, contributes to the sordid implications of Liliana's actions. The other crime victim, Teresina Menegazzi, is hysterical and silly, while Liliana's cousin, Giuliano Valdarena, is a smug, ambitious young man apparently more concerned about his own welfare than Liliana's death.

At the other end of the social spectrum, the carabinieri led by the arrogant Corporal Pestalozzi represent the petty, sadistic kind of temperament given new legitimacy under Mussolini's Fascist regime. Though their brutalization of their suspects is reprehensible, it must be admitted that such treatment is no worse than that to which these young women are accustomed or expect. The women too are cynical and tough and, like the other characters, look no further than their own immediate self-interest. Their speech may be marked by pious exclamations, but this is no more than a cultural verbal style, a linguistic heritage signifying the durability of ethnic and geographic bonds. It may be said that the city of Rome itself is the real protagonist of the novel, as a complex social organism whose members are less important as individuals than as component parts of the structure.

Gadda's Romans define themselves through myriad social interconnections in which place is the most consistent reference point: street names, shops, churches, neighborhoods, and hometowns. The image of an anthill or beehive comes to mind; everyone in the novel is constantly going to or coming from somewhere not very far away, and their lives are interconnected quite simply by proximity. Even though the interconnections are often circumstantial or apparently insignificant, in the aggregate they make up a powerful, if invisible, bond out of which individual destiny is generated.

*Themes and Meanings*

That the plot of the novel remains unresolved is in itself thematically significant. A manuscript version of the story discovered posthumously (and evidently intended as a possible film treatment) shows Enea Ratalli to be the thief and murderer. In the published novel, Gadda deliberately suppressed the expected plot resolution in favor of an open-ended, ambiguous conclusion. Despite the obvious affinities with conventional detective fiction, this novel is not a whodunit. Rather than the solving of a mystery, Gadda's concern is with the convoluted mysteries of life itself. A tidy ending might gratify the reader's expectations, but it would be false to Gadda's fictional purposes.

The lives of Gadda's characters are interlocked in complex, often obscure ways. In Gadda's view, what is called "destiny" or "fate" is also the product of unseen correspondences, of overlapping fields of psychic force generated by proximity, or intention, or merely blind circumstance. It is the ironic interconnection between ostensibly unrelated lives that forms the real thematic core of the novel: a web of significance not amenable to a simple unraveling, even by the most skilled detective.

Gadda's convoluted, digressive style not only mirrors the substance of his philosophical vision; it actually constitutes that vision. Self-conscious and elaborate to an extraordinary degree, Gadda's prose is an amalgamation of various contrasting elements: pedantries of all sorts (literary allusions, Latin quotations, scientific and medical terminology); puns and neologisms; topical references, often obscure, to his contemporary Italian society; and the dialect and slang of Roman vernacular speech. All these elements are embedded in highly nuanced, complicated sentence structures. The tone of Gadda's writing covers a similarly wide arc of possibilities, from artificially elegant to deliberately crude, witty to sardonic. Far from being a transparent medium, Gadda's style approximates the mosaic quality of the substance of the novel.

The organic continuity of Rome in terms of its culture, myth, and history is also a central thematic element. Past impinges upon present in complex, minute, and ironic ways. Thus, for example, the names of numerous characters (Pompeo, Diomede, Ascanio, Lavinia) recall the mythical and heroic heritage of Rome; the streets they traverse and the churches and public buildings that serve as landmarks are constant reminders of Renaissance and Baroque magnificence. Against such a backdrop, the shabby, brutal realities of Mussolini's dictatorship take on a particular loathsomeness. This contrast is the basis of much of Gadda's satire. Gadda also conveys the strong impression, however, that his Romans act, think, and feel much as they have for centuries, and that the story of this novel is part of a continuum composed, as Ingravallo puts it, of "that system of forces and probabilities which surrounds every human creature."

*Critical Context*

Gadda's work is often compared to that of James Joyce, and, in several ways, *That Awful Mess on Via Merulana* bears a family likeness to *Ulysses* (1922): its complex, revolutionary use of language; its interwoven elements of lyricism and satire, mythic significance, and pedestrian reality. Gadda's impact on Italian literature may also be compared to that of Joyce on English-language literature in the early twentieth century. Like the earlier novelist, Gadda has moved from the status of a cult figure venerated by a small band of devotees to widespread critical acknowledgment and admiration.

Gadda's work earned for him the Prix Internationale de Littérature in 1963 and established him among Italian literary critics as that country's most important prose master of the period. Within the context of postwar Italian neorealism, Gadda's nonconventional writing, and especially this novel, made a powerful impact. Rather than following the canons of his time—objectivity, psychological concern, and verisimilitude—he demonstrated new possibilities for Italian fiction in the realms of satire, stylistic experiment, and the nonobjective representation of reality.

In the latter regard, Gadda belongs in the first ranks of the postwar European literary avant-garde. In particular, *That Awful Mess on Via Merulana* helps to define that species of novel which, appearing first in the mid-1950's, is known as the New Novel and has assumed such significance in the spectrum of twentieth century literature. Published in 1957, the novel demonstrates the same kind of kaleidoscopic focus, skeptical, disenchanted vision, and rejection of conventional narrative form that marks the work of Gadda's better-known contemporaries in France, such as Michel Butor, Nathalie Sarraute, and Alain Robbe-Grillet.

*Sources for Further Study*

Caesar, Michael, and Peter Hainsworth, eds. *Writers and Society in Contemporary Italy*, 1984.

McConnell, Joan. *A Vocabulary Analysis of Gadda's "Pasticciaccio,"* 1973.

Pacifici, Sergio. *The Modern Italian Novel from Pea to Moravia*, 1979.

Ragusa, Olga. "Gadda, Pasolini, and Experimentalism," in *From Verismo to Experimentalism: Essays on the Modern Italian Novel*, 1969. Edited by Sergio Pacifici.

*Charles Duncan*

# THAT VOICE

*Author:* Robert Pinget (1919-    )
*Type of plot:* Impressionistic realism
*Time of plot:* Unspecified
*Locale:* The fictional French villages of Fantoine and Agapa
*First published:* Cette Voix, 1975 (English translation, 1982)

*Principal characters:*
ALEXANDRE MORTIN, the village chronicler, deceased
ALFRED MORTIN, Alexandre's dead brother
THÉODORE, the nephew of Alexandre
MADEMOISELLE MOINE, Théodore's niece, the president of the
    Dieudonné Foundation
MADEMOISELLE FRANCINE DE BONNE-MÉSURE, another of
    Théodore's nieces, a bookbinder
MARIE, the Mortins' housekeeper
LOUIS, Marie's nephew

*The Novel*

On All Saints' Day, Théodore takes chrysanthemums to place on the grave
of his uncle, Alexandre Mortin, with whom he lived as a child and whose heir
he has become. At the cemetery, he meets someone who introduces himself
as Dieudonné, or Dodo for short, the pet name that Théodore used for his
uncle. Théodore takes up residence in the Mortin crypt, where he works at
sorting his uncle's papers.

Alexandre himself never succeeded in organizing his many notes relating
to the life of the village; he merely gathered all the gossip and history he
could find in his wanderings around the town. Much of the material that he
assembled concerned the misdeeds of his neighbors. For example, Magnin's
wife cuckolded him, but rumor also claims that he had an affair with the
Cruchet girl. Alexandre's own sister-in-law also proved to be unfaithful, running off with a Spanish juggler.

Stories also circulate about Alexandre, particularly regarding his relationship with Théodore. According to one version, Alexandre compelled the boy
to live with him instead of with the boy's own mother because they were having a homosexual affair. Another version maintains that Théodore took
advantage of his uncle's debilitated condition to forge a will that left him the
sole heir. Other accounts are more sinister still, claiming that Théodore
stabbed or strangled his uncle and then robbed him. Still others say that the
old man was killed by his housekeeper, Marie, or by her nephew, Louis.

Whatever the truth about the relationship between Alexandre and Théodore, the latter does accept the responsibility of trying to organize his uncle's
papers, just as Alexandre tried to make sense of all the notes that his brother

Alfred bequeathed him. Yet when Théodore dies, he has made no more progress than either of his relatives had. He leaves the Mortin house to the parish, which decides to convert the attic into the public library. Théodore's niece, Mademoiselle Moine, the town librarian and president of the Dieudonné Foundation, inherits the task of classifying the Mortin papers, which will reside in what is now both the local archive and the Mortin ancestral home.

Together with the older members of the Dieudonné Foundation, Mademoiselle Moine at length produces a three-hundred-page manuscript volume, which Mademoiselle Francine de Bonne-Mésure agrees to bind. The book is then chained to a desk, where one may consult it but not take notes. Yet some who visit the library claim that no manuscript volume is there.

As the novel ends, the narrator returns to his grave to await, he says, "the resurrection of the dead." Meanwhile, the village routines continue as always. Madame Buvard dies, the corn grows tall, and Marie "methodically grows leeks, parsley, and tomatoes."

*The Characters*

Like all Robert Pinget's other works, *That Voice* challenges the reader to sort out the characters' identities, a task that ultimately proves as impossible as organizing Alexandre Mortin's papers. In the preface to the French edition, Pinget highlights this problem: "Someone is speaking, someone is lying, someone is playing at dying by degrees and at killing his family circle. Who is the uncle? Who is the nephew? Who is the maid?"

Alexandre Mortin is Théodore's uncle, or great-great-uncle, but Alexandre also bears the name Dieudonné, which is the French version of the Greek Theodore—the gift of God. Théodore further fuses his identity with his uncle's by going to live in Alexandre's house or grave, or both, and by assuming the lifelong task that his uncle had set for himself. As Pinget writes, Théodore works on his uncle's papers "until the day when he realizes that he himself has become this juggler at the end of his tether, and that the story of this contorted, concocted, controversial manuscript is now well and truly his own, Mortin reincarnated in his nephew." Théodore even wears his uncle's glasses. Moreover, Théodore is also an uncle, and just as his uncle bequeathed him the dubious legacy of the papers, so he leaves the manuscript to his niece, who in turn assumes her dead uncle's task of codification.

Just as Alexandre and Théodore meld into each other, so both fuse into Alfred Mortin, another would-be historian of the village. At times, it is not clear which of the Mortins was supposedly stabbed; characters seem to be "confusing one funeral with another." Just as Alexandre is Alfred's heir, so Théodore's is Alexandre's; just as Théodore may have lived with Alexandre, so Alexandre may have lived with Alfred. The stories repeat, changing only the names of the actors.

Among the lesser characters, the confusion is even greater. One cannot be sure of the names of the women who gather at the grocery store. Is it Madame Thiéroux or Piéroux, Madame Dubard or Buvard? Madame Thiéroux-Piéroux is being driven by her husband, but is he her first or her second? Is Marie the Mortins' only maid, or is there a second? Is Louis Marie's nephew or her lover? Who is telling this entire story—the dead Alexandre, the dead Théodore, or an unnamed observer?

Stories about the characters contradict one another. Marie is an alcoholic; Marie hates drink. Alexandre is rich; Alexandre is so poor that he cannot pay the housekeeper. He snoops around the maid's room; she spies on him. He dies of a heart attack; he is stabbed; he is strangled; he commits suicide. As the narrator observes toward the end of the book, "In short, it's all as clear as mud."

Like so many other Pinget characters, Alexandre and Théodore attempt to find their identities, in their cases by sorting through papers that they hope will disclose the secret of their personalities. Their inability to make sense of those papers reflects the impossibility of their quest. Personalities change; people fuse into one another; uncles are reincarnated as their nephews and nieces. Pinget's characters discover the truth of Henry Adams' observation that order is the dream of man, but chaos is the law of nature.

*Themes and Meanings*

In the preface to his first book, *Entre Fantoine et Agapa* (1951; *Between Fantoine and Agapa*, 1983), Pinget declared that he sought "to abolish all the constraints of classical writing" because such literature relies on reason. Pinget, on the other hand, claims, "I don't give a damn for logic!" Hence the narrative unfolds through a series of seemingly unrelated, contradictory, or redundant episodes. A phrase recurring throughout the short novel is "Impossible anamnesis," and indeed Pinget had considered calling the book *Anamnase* (anamnesis), referring to the surfacing of memories from the distant past.

According to the preface to the American edition of *That Voice*,

> The structure of this novel is precise, although not immediately apparent. The different themes are intermingled. One cuts into another point blank, then the other resumes and cuts into the first, and so on until the end. The first example of this procedure, at the beginning of the book, is the theme of the cemetery, cut into that of the gossip at the grocery, then resumed shortly afterwards.

This stream of consciousness, or, more precisely, stream of unconsciousness (since that is the source of the random memories), forces the reader to become like Alexandre Mortin, Théodore, and Mademoiselle Moine in piecing together random bits of conversation, rumors, and recollections to create a coherent story.

Again like the characters within the novel, though, the reader is doomed to fail. At the center of the novel, Pinget places a brief conversation illustrative of the problem:

"Do you understand what you're reading?"
"No M'sieur."
"Go on."

Immediately afterward, someone recalls "Master saying to me, what do we know of the truth, where do you think it hangs out, down the well stark naked, poppycock, in the heads that their owners call cool, certainly not there either, the truth requires secret places to hide."

Suggestive of the elusiveness of the truth is the story about the discovery of a coffin with a rabbit bone inside it. Did the deceased choke on that bone? Did a rabbit tunnel its way into the coffin and then die? Did the man ask to be buried with his pet rabbit? Did the deceased share a pagan belief in the power of such a relic and so had it buried with him? The mystery remains, as does the question of Alexandre Mortin's death. One cannot decide who killed him, how he was killed, or even that he was killed. Always there are doubts as one story, one memory, contradicts or comments on another.

Even the eccentric punctuation contributes to this sense of uncertainty. In the French version, the only punctuation used is a period at the end of each paragraph. The English edition adds occasional commas, but the effect is the same. The reader must choose among various possible ways of combining words and phrases to make sense, if sense is even possible, for language conceals as well as reveals. What is the correct reading: "A candle was burning at the deceased's bedside" or "A handle was churning up his diseased backside"? Does a leaflet advertize copper or copiers? Nothing in the text, including the text itself, is fixed. Instead, flux and doubt reign. Pinget's fiction thus reflects a world in which light is both wave and particle, in which mass and energy are interchangeable, in which a primary principle of physics is uncertainty.

*Critical Context*

Although Pinget shuns labeling, his work reveals the influence of the New Novel and its advocates. In 1959, the French critic Maurice Blanchot observed that henceforth the novel "ought not to bring itself to a conclusion or be able to begin; a work which is, as it were, in default in terms of itself, at a distance from what it expresses and for what it expresses, it flourishes in that distance, deposits itself in it, preserves itself in it, and finally disappears in it." Alain Robbe-Grillet, another important practitioner and theorist of contemporary literature, makes a similar point: "The modern novel . . . is an exploration, but an exploration which itself creates its own significations as it proceeds. . . . We no longer believe in the fixed significations, the ready-made meanings which afforded man the old divine order and subsequently the rationalist order of the nineteenth century." In all Pinget's writings, the world of Fantoine and Agapa is constantly changing, as characters seek to discover their identities and readers try to sort out the truth from among the incomplete and conflicting details.

At the same time that this novel typically presents an impressionistic view of reality, it is firmly rooted in the cycles of country life—the placing of chrysanthemums on the graves on All Saints' Day, the late summer harvest, the delivery day at the bistro, the Sunday celebration of Mass. For all its talk of death, *That Voice* is filled with life: "cornflower, poppy, pheasant's eye, betony, . . . meadow sage, butter-and-eggs, marjoram, delphinium, a fearful avalanche . . . that causes the resurgence of the old myths." The book begins with the resurrection that the voice of the narrator seeks at its end. Alexandre is reincarnated in Théodore, who is reincarnated in Mademoiselle Moine, even if the gravediggers do jumble all the bones together. Recurrent metamorphosis creates confusion but also generates life. From chaos comes a voice that creates a world.

*Sources for Further Study*

Henkels, Robert M., Jr. *Robert Pinget: The Novel as Quest*, 1979.
Livington, Beverly. "From A to F and Back: Pinget's Fictive Arena," in *Yale French Studies*. LVII (1979), pp. 72-85.
Marantz, Enid G. "The Conflict of Words and Voices in Pinget's *Cette Voix*," in *The Review of Contemporary Fiction*. III (Summer, 1983), pp. 134-140.
Updike, John. "Between Pinget's Ears," in *The New Yorker*. LIX (July 11, 1983), pp. 96-99.

*Joseph Rosenblum*

# THE THAW

*Author:* Ilya Ehrenburg (1891-1967)
*Type of plot:* Social criticism
*Time of plot:* The early 1950's
*Locale:* A small town in the Soviet Union
*First published: Ottepel*, 1954 (English translation, 1955)

> *Principal characters:*
> DMITRI KOROTEYEV, an engineer
> IVAN ZHURAVLIOV, a factory director
> LENA ZHURAVLIOV, Ivan's wife
> VOLODYA PUKHOV and
> SABUROV, artists

## The Novel

*The Thaw* is not a novel in the usual sense but rather a series of character portraits united by the fact that all the people involved in the story live in a small town and lead intertwined lives. Dmitri Koroteyev is an engineer in the local factory and known for his honesty, hard work, and intelligence. The successes of the factory are attributed to him, although the director, Ivan Zhuravliov, officially receives the credit. The town librarian even considers Dmitri an expert on literary matters. The local Party committee values him highly. Dmitri, however, is not happy; the great love of his life died during World War II, and he has now fallen in love with Lena, Ivan's wife.

Lena is unhappy at home. Her husband thinks only of his factory and its successes, although it is clear that he loves his wife and child. This love, however, is not manifested very often; Lena is more like an article of household furniture than a partner in a marriage sustained by intense feelings of love. Lena has fallen in love with Dmitri, but the two do not declare their love to each other.

Ivan is a typical Soviet factory manager; within his realm he rules despotically, ruining the careers of those who do not agree with him. At the same time he cultivates talented people such as Dmitri, who can bring him praise and perhaps a promotion to a higher position in a location closer to Moscow or Leningrad.

Volodya Pukhov is the son of a retired schoolteacher. Unlike his father, who is idealistic and was devoted to his students, Volodya is cynical. He paints according to the tenets of Socialist Realism, the prescribed genre for artists, even though he realizes that his productions are trash and that the official theory concerning art is nonsense. This cynicism carries over to his life in general. He values nothing except his own success and is willing to do whatever the authorities ask, ridiculing them and himself as he does so.

Saburov is also an artist living in the small town. Unlike Volodya, Saburov is unwilling to paint in a style which he believes is alien not only to him but also to true art. He lives off the meager earnings of his wife, a cripple, who adores him. Saburov is content to paint masterpieces which will probably never be shown to appreciative audiences; he is willing to sacrifice fame and fortune in order to paint what he considers to be good art.

The reader views this menagerie of characters, which Ilya Ehrenburg portrays as typical for a small Soviet industrial town, with sympathy. Their lives are complicated by personal crises, but by the end of the novel it is clear that all the characters, with the exception of Ivan Zhuravliov, are weathering their crises and looking forward to a better life. They overcome the worst aspects of their crises: Family feuds are settled or, at least, reduced to a manageable level, Lena leaves her husband and the hope of a relationship with Dmitri emerges, and Volodya finds his true love, which enables him to temper his cynicism. Saburov shows his paintings to Volodya, whom he has considered a hack and hostile to real art. Volodya praises the work, and Saburov breaks through the official taboos and has two works accepted for an official exhibition.

The title, *The Thaw*, is an imperfect rendition of the original Russian, which means a "warming up," and this is what occurs in the lives of the characters. They warm up to one another and to life against the backdrop of the end of winter and the very beginning of the thaw in nature.

*The Characters*

The development of characters is more important to Ehrenburg than the continuation of a coherent story line. In fact, the personal dramas of the characters are, for the most part, separate from one another.

What is most important in the novel, however, is not the development of any individual character but the author's attitude toward these people in general. Ehrenburg has taken stock characters of Soviet life and literature—the energetic worker, the factory manager, the idealistic teacher, the bored housewife, and the artists—and concentrated on their personal crises rather than on their public personae. Socialist Realism, the official method for literature and art in the Soviet Union, discouraged such forays into the personal domain and preferred that writers employ more public-spirited themes, such as heroic workers at construction projects, soldiers at the front fighting for their country, and Party intellectuals performing great feats in the battle to construct a classless society. Ehrenburg ignores these themes and concentrates on the personal problems of the characters. The result may seem commonplace to the Western reader, but this method was considered revolutionary in the Soviet Union of the 1950's, so much so that the title, *The Thaw*, is commonly applied to the loosening of restrictions in the Soviet Union following the death of Joseph Stalin in 1953.

## Themes and Meanings

The central theme of this novel is that Soviet life has grown cold and needs to warm up. During the period of Stalin's leadership in the Soviet Union, a rigidly totalitarian police state was constructed which was kept in place through the liberal application of terror and a highly developed system of spying on one's neighbor. Promotions were often based upon Party loyalty rather than on meritorious service, and an unwieldly bureaucracy, overloaded with people interested mainly in retaining privileges, stifled creativity in all sectors of life, industrial as well as artistic. The effects of this system on personal relationships were devastating: Neighbors informed on one another, children informed on their parents, and a type of subterranean guerrilla warfare replaced neighborly relations.

Ehrenburg portrays such a situation in *The Thaw*. The system, as perceived by the author, needs to be loosened up, and the people within the system must shed their rigidity and warm up to one another. Individuals within the system, especially the leaders, must realize that each person is important in his or her own right, not merely as a cog in a system or as a stepping-stone to a perfect future society. The personal crises endured by the characters in the novel are as important as the grandiose plans of the Party and the State, perhaps even more important.

An obvious secondary theme in the novel is the stifling of creativity. Saburov, by far the better artist, is reduced to living in poverty and being supported by the low wages of his crippled wife, while Volodya paints bad pictures in the approved style and receives the material advantages of the system, at least until he rashly criticizes his superiors in a rare moment of candor. Ehrenburg leaves no doubt as to where his sympathies reside— with Saburov and the abandonment of an officially controlled artistic establishment.

Another example of the stifling of creativity is in the industrial sector. Ivan jealously guards his prerogatives and makes sure that all the credit for any achievements falls to himself. Since Dmitri cares nothing for glory and is more interested in the prosperity of the factory, Ivan can tolerate his superior talent. Other individuals, not quite so selfless, are demoted or transferred.

A third theme is the almost despotic control which factory managers have over their enterprises and workers. Ivan subverts funds meant for improved worker housing into the general factory fund so that even more credit might accrue to him. An unforeseen storm arises and destroys much of the existing substandard housing; at this point Moscow finally acts and Ivan is replaced by a new manager, much to the joy of the local populace. Once again Ehrenburg leaves no doubt as to his opinion of the issue: Managers such as Ivan, who have no concern for their workers, must be replaced.

The common denominator among these themes is the emphasis upon the individual rather than the collective. Individuals have emotional needs and feelings, and this aspect of the social situation is just as important as the concerns of the collective, whether it be the local Party cell or the entire government bureaucracy.

## Critical Context

The publication of *The Thaw* in 1954, so soon after Stalin's death, had social as well as literary significance. The appearance of the book was a signal to the public that some loosening of the system was indeed in progress and that some constructive criticism would be tolerated in the Soviet Union. As such, it achieved immediate fame and popularity in the Soviet Union, which had suffered twenty-five years of Stalinist regimentation.

In the literary arena, the novel achieved the same fame. It was viewed by other writers and readers as an announcement of the loosening of control over the artistic realm. The themes presented in *The Thaw* were also developed by younger writers, such as Vladimir Dudintzev, in his novel *Ne khlebom edinym* (1956; *Not by Bread Alone*, 1957). The fact that the entire de-Stalinization process has been called "the thaw" indicates the importance which was attached to this work.

## Sources for Further Study

Alexandrova, Vera. *A History of Soviet Literature*, 1963.
Brown, Edward J. *Russian Literature Since the Revolution*, 1982.
Goldberg, Anatol. *Ilya Ehrenburg*, 1984.
Rogers, Thomas. *Superfluous Men and the Post-Stalin Thaw*, 1972.
Slonim, Marc. *Soviet Russian Literature*, 1964.

*Philip Maloney*

# THÉRÈSE RAQUIN

*Author:* Émile Zola (1840-1902)
*Type of plot:* Naturalism
*Time of plot:* The Second Empire (1852-1870)
*Locale:* A dismal, damp arcade on the Left Bank in Paris
*First published: Un Mariage d'amour*, 1867, serial; *Thérèse Raquin*, 1867, book (English translation, 1881)

*Principal characters:*

MADAME RAQUIN, the widowed owner of a small dry-goods shop

THÉRÈSE RAQUIN, her illegitimate niece and frustrated daughter-in-law

CAMILLE RAQUIN, Madame's frail, dull son and Thérèse's husband

LAURENT, a sensual friend from Camille's school days

POLICE COMMISSIONER MICHAUD,

OLIVER,

SUZANNE, and

GRIVET, the members of a regular Thursday-night domino game

*The Novel*

*Thérèse Raquin* is a tale of lust, murder, and suicide set amid the poverty of mid-nineteenth century Left Bank Paris. It involves a classically limited cast of characters such as that used by French dramatists Pierre Corneille and Jean Racine. At the center of the drama lies the triangle of Thérèse, Camille, and Laurent. The novel's action is observed and recounted objectively by an omniscient narrator, who nevertheless occasionally slips in a moral judgment.

As the novel opens, the reader is introduced to the miserable Pont Neuf locale—the tiny dry-goods shop and the three rooms above it—where the three Raquins, Madame, her son Camille, and his wife Thérèse, are installed. The three barely survive on the money made from the shop's sales and on Camille's wages as a clerk at the Orléans railroad. Thus Émile Zola establishes the mixture with which he begins his "experiment": a dull, listless husband and a sensual wife watched over by an old woman and her fat cat, François.

Into this milieu one evening Camille introduces Laurent, a school friend whom he has encountered by accident at the railroad. Laurent, a former law student and a dabbler in oils on canvas, seems to Thérèse to have all the glamour and virility her husband lacks. While Camille is out buying wine to celebrate Laurent's finishing of a portrait and Madame is downstairs in the shop, Laurent and Thérèse come together on the floor. Soon a full-blown affair is under way.

Difficulties in continuing their rendezvous in Thérèse's bedroom eventually force the lovers to murder Camille in a boating "accident." Laurent wrestles him into the Seine, suffering a bite on the neck in the process. Two weeks later, the corpse shows up in the morgue, which Laurent has visited each day, and Camille is declared officially dead. Under the eyes of Madame Raquin, the cat, and the regular Thursday-evening domino party, Thérèse and Laurent hide their guilt and for fifteen months resume their routines, without ever being alone together. Increasingly, however, they are unable to sleep at night because of nightmare visits from Camille. The two arrange matters so that their marriage, which they believe will bring them ease, is proposed by Madame and Police Commissioner Michaud, a member of the "Thursday Club." The ceremony accomplished, Thérèse and Laurent's wedding night is ruined by the ghost of the murdered Camille, who comes between them; the killing of Camille has killed their passion for each other. The pain of Laurent's neck wound increases after he forces the reluctant Thérèse to kiss it.

The couple is trapped under the eyes of Laurent's portrait of Camille, the cat, and the increasingly paralyzed and speechless Madame. Terrified, hating and distrusting each other, and sleepless by night, they continue to keep up the appearance of "turtle-doves" for the Thursday group. Laurent rents a studio, but, no matter what he attempts, he can paint only portraits of Camille. Thérèse goes her promiscuous way among the students in the local bars. Nevertheless, the pair is bound together by hatred, distrust, and a growing fear that the other one will report the crime to the authorities. Their life together has become a hell of recrimination and blows under the eyes of Madame, who accidentally learns everything but can tell no one. The pregnant Thérèse deliberately exposes her belly to Laurent's kicks; she miscarries. Each decides to kill the other: She has a sharpened kitchen knife, he has prussic acid. Detecting each other's intentions, under the brooding, hate-filled eyes of Madame, they share the prussic acid and fall dead, Thérèse's mouth on the scar left by Camille on Laurent's neck.

*The Characters*

At the center of this novel is the smoldering, frustrated Thérèse. Her arranged marriage to her cousin, Camille, teams her with a sickly, dull husband, and the stage is set for the entry of the third member of the "love" triangle. Laurent allows his appetite for the easy life and sexual gratification to lead him into Thérèse's embraces. Like a surgeon working on a corpse, as he comments in his preface to the second edition of *Thérèse Raquin*, Zola traces with his "analytical method" the actions and reactions of the "human animals" in his experimental scene. Adultery leads to murder, and murder to what passes for remorse, or at least to a breakdown of the overburdened nervous systems of the participants. Zola then dispassionately records in their interior monologues the detailed workings of their passions, instincts, and mental processes, culminating in their double suicide.

Watching this breakdown is the speechless figure of Madame, who contributes greatly to the tension between Thérèse and Laurent. She sets the cycle in motion and presides horrified over what it becomes. Brooding also over the couple are the gothic elements of Laurent's portrait of Camille and the tiger cat, François, which Laurent hurls out of the upstairs window and flattens on the opposite wall of the alley.

The damp, dismal, penny-pinching setting also plays an important role in the drama. Rendered almost exclusively in pervasive shades of gray or black or depressing greens, the oppressive environment functions like another character, ever present in the minute, carefully labeled details of the realistic artist. Thérèse's name is written ominously in red across one of the panes of the shop door. Each character works exquisitely on the sensibilities of the others in a manner not far removed from that of Jean-Paul Sartre's protagonists in *Huis-clos* (1944; *No Exit*, 1946).

## Themes and Meanings

*Thérèse Raquin*, despite the young Zola's theories on scientific objectivity, is a cautionary tale on the text of the biblical commandments against adultery and murder. Once Thérèse and Laurent surrender to their adulterous sexual urges, they are launched on a path to murder. Those who engage in sexual indulgence often, in Zola's work, deteriorate into bestiality. The sensitive, even puritanical young author is obsessed with this theme. When murder is added to the list of sins, all concerned head further toward despair, madness, revenge, and retribution—none of which is "scientific" but instead is clearly called for by the author. The first lover who comes back, alive or dead, to trouble the second is also a common theme in Zola's fiction.

The very real tension in the unfolding of these events, however Zola tips the scale of objectivity, is helped enormously by the oppressive environment and gloomy atmosphere which he creates to accompany it. The drama, which is almost palpable and which makes *Thérèse Raquin* Zola's most successful theatrical piece, is created in no small part by its gothic setting. The squalid shop; the play of light and dark; the greenish portrait of Camille; the long description of the corpses in the morgue; the bite-scar; the baleful presence of the cat; the brooding, speechless figure of Madame—all play their nightmarish parts. The comic relief and the bathetic contrast—supplied by the dull banality of the Thursday-evening domino group—also play their necessary roles. Zola very expertly, both in his structuring of events and in his selection of macabre details, creates his impressive moral world. It is perhaps amusing to contemplate the furor that would have arisen had he done otherwise—had he, for example, permitted Thérèse and Laurent to live happily ever after. As it was, Zola was accused of dealing in the putrid and the pornographic when he was actually painting his own highly moral view of reality, with all of its "wallowing," "brutality," and "blood"—to cite but three words very often repeated in *Thérèse Raquin*.

*Critical Context*

At the center of the naturalistic literary school, which Zola was instrumental in forming, is the idea of character and temperament. According to this theory, the people chosen make the events happen: The author is merely the objective reporter, watching, like everyone else, the characters he sets in motion. This at least was the conscious theory, which nevertheless postdated the early *Thérèse Raquin*, though it increasingly dominated the subsequent novels of Zola's famous series, *Les Rougon-Macquart* (1871-1893; *The Rougon-Macquart Novels*, 1885-1907), including *Le Ventre de Paris* (1873; *The Markets of Paris*, 1879, better known as *Savage Paris*), *L'Assommoir* (1877; English translation, 1879), *Germinal* (1885; English translation, 1885), and *La Terre* (1887; *The Soil*, 1888, better known as *Earth*).

*Thérèse Raquin* is the earliest of Zola's novels to have maintained a position of merit in his canon. He was at some pains subsequently to fit it into the naturalistic scheme that he developed during his extensive chronicling of the Rougon-Macquarts in the decades which followed. This ultrarealistic approach to writing sprang from the sociopolitical world which Zola inhabited in the second half of the nineteenth century. The middle class was in the process of increasing in numbers and power, and in replacing the nobility as a potential audience for books. Aristocratic characters were thus no longer the primary interest. In a movement which was international (including Charles Dickens in Great Britain and Frank Norris and William Dean Howells in the United States) and also involved painters such as Édouard Manet and Paul Cézanne, who were Zola's personal friends, the realist spirit was an outgrowth of the scientific determinism of the age. The writings of Charles Darwin, Herbert Spencer, and Claude Bernard, as understood by many creative writers, suggested to novelists that they too might employ the "scientific method" in their creation of human characters and milieus. The characters acted upon are, in this view, almost always lower class; the milieu is invariably (perhaps inevitably) constraining, if not actually depressing.

In this context, then, Zola set about, in the manner of his friend Gustave Flaubert, who had created the character of Emma Bovary (with whom Thérèse shares many important traits), to describe the world as objectively as possible, and to portray that world and its denizens as realistically as possible. The novelist had no overt thesis, no moral point of view, in theory anyhow, that he had to communicate. His task, as Zola saw it, was simply to record faithfully what takes place when a repressed female encounters a libertine and both surrender to their physical appetites.

There is little doubt about the graphic success of Zola's writing in the novel form. In *Thérèse Raquin*, he displayed the nervous sensitivity and atmospheric tension which raised his subsequent series of novels beyond social commentary to a level of impressionistic realism very rare in literature. Zola saw people and places in the fashion of the Impressionist painters who were his friends. That the world of the Second Empire was a corrupt one he was not at pains to demonstrate in his fiction beyond the interaction of his carefully chosen subjects. In this novel, his naturalistic treatment was neither as broad nor as rich as it would become subsequently, but the critical storm produced by the novel gave him both the money and the attention he needed to continue writing. In his life beyond literature he did indeed take stands on issues, most noticeably in the celebrated case against Captain Alfred Dreyfus, in which Zola accused the establishment as a whole of wrongdoing, at no small inconvenience to himself. His literary achievement is that he created an organic world despite the constraints of the current naturalistic determinism to which he, in theory, subscribed. From viewing sexual intercourse as a manifestation of society's weakness, he moved over a lifetime of writing to something approaching hope for a world in which fecundity and a gradual socialism would have a future.

*Sources for Further Study*
Grant, Elliott M. *Émile Zola*, 1966.
Hemmings, F. W. J. *The Life and Times of Émile Zola*, 1953, 1966.
Levin, Harry. *The Gates of Horn*, 1963.
Walker, Philip. *Zola*, 1985.
Wilson, Angus. *Émile Zola: An Introductory Study of His Novels*, 1952.

*Archibald E. Irwin*

# THIRD FACTORY

*Author:* Viktor Shklovsky (1893-1984)
*Type of plot:* Documentary novel
*Time of plot:* The 1920's
*Locale:* The Soviet Union
*First published: Tretya fabrika*, 1926 (English translation, 1977)

Principal character:
VIKTOR SHKLOVSKY, the narrator, a Formalist literary critic
and novelist

## The Novel

*Third Factory* is a short, plotless novel made of autobiographical fragments representing discontinuous memories, unsent letters to friends, anecdotes, dreams, and theoretical discussions. These fragments create an artistic
work with a contradictory but unified theme, like fiction. The narrator is the
author himself; the memories and apostrophes and stories are composed
around the theme of the life of a Formalist literary critic in the Soviet Union
in the 1920's. The result is a critique of the literary experience and responses
of this unique individual. This critique is not the only point of the book; the
implicit critique of former novels, in the form of innovations in this one,
opens lines of development for new work. At a deeper level yet, the
narrator's interest is to understand the time in which he lives and to explore
the correct role of the writer and the nature of verbal art. These latter issues
have special significance for the Soviet state and Soviet writers, as the state
begins to define the artist's task.

The novel is arranged chronologically in three parts, one for each "factory." A factory is the life experience that turns the narrator into the "product" that he has become. The first factory is his home and school life (this
part takes place before the Revolution). The second is the intense experience
of his professional life as a literary theorist in Petrograd in the early 1920's,
the period of the emergence of Formalism as a literary school and of the
group of writers known as the Serapion Brothers as its innovative practi-
tioners. This second factory includes apostrophes to Osip Brik, encouraging
him to continue his theoretical work, and to Roman Jakobson, who Viktor
Shklovsky believes has deserted his comrades and their work.

The third factory, and the longest section of the novel, is set in the Soviet
film industry, where Shklovsky's work is to revise films. He brings the values
of the second factory to bear on this new work, while a variety of pressures
on the film compete in its shaping. The focus, however, is on the defense and
further definition of Formalism; literary theory is the hero of this section and
of the novel. Shklovsky includes a story-within-a-story in the third factory,

"Envy Bay"; the tale is full of implications for the time even as it practices a major Formalist device, the self-conscious baring of the technique, as well as shifts in point of view and special attention to the role of the narrator. Several of Shklovsky's innovations have been adopted by later twentieth century writers in the U.S.S.R. and the West.

He also addresses letters to several of the early Formalists: to Boris Eikhenbaum about *skaz*, a specifically Russian narrative technique; to Lev Yakubinsky about Marxism and about puns and language. He tells Yury Tynyanov about the way literature changes by expanding into nonliterature: "Art converts the particularity of things into perceptible form." A preoccupation in all these letters is Shklovsky's effort to explore the connection between objective reality, the consciousness of the writer, and the artistic work. He is attempting to apply his Formalist principles in the new and unfriendly context of proletarian literature—and the coming Socialist Realism—as the Party begins to assert its control of literature.

The poignancy of the narrator's experience is expressed in continuing metaphors. One of the most compelling and complex is the image of flax, which has been explained by Fyodor S. Grits, a Soviet critic. The narrator introduces the metaphor, with no primary explanation of its meaning, then plays with its range of meanings, developing the figure before making a clear explication. Shklovsky had a job treating flax at one time, and this firsthand knowledge moves into art, coming to mean the suffering and "unfreedom" of the artist necessary to the artist's work: "Terror and oppression are necessary." What the oppression is remains muted: Is it Party pressure on literature or is it the writer's necessary submission to his material? Writers were being beaten, like flax, into conformity in the Soviet Union in the late 1920's, but Shklovsky seems to suggest that the necessary suffering is the artist's compulsion to respond to his material freely: as the material, not the government, demands. The difficulty of keeping alive the achievements of his own theoretical work, of staying in touch with his fellow theoreticians, and of letting the work go forward accounts for the deep sadness of the novel. Yet it ends in a reference from Vergil, about the call to Aeneas to leave Troy—to rebuild, to continue to hope.

### The Characters

Only the character of the narrator receives sustained development. The images of those friends whom he addresses are suggested, but as characters they are all significantly absent. Nevertheless, each emerges as a unique individual, with moral views, style, and professional gifts.

Shklovsky emerges as an able, witty, melancholy man deeply devoted to his profession, his country, and his family. He is sensitive to his time, imaginative and fresh in his ability to express his experience, and full of integrity and honesty. He has a range of abilities and interests that make his sympathy wide. He thinks deeply, feels deeply, and does not say everything he thinks and feels. The reader cannot help but identify with him, although he is contradictory and elliptical. The intimate details of living through the period of the great shift from czarist Russia to Socialist U.S.S.R. make the reader see the complexity of making judgments in that ambiguous and painful context.

*Themes and Meanings*

The themes in the novel are the nature and function of literature, the freedom of the artist, and the relation of literature to reality. The nature of the artist is a theme often considered, but this book is new in its making literary theory and its fate in the new Soviet society the center of concern. One expects such material in a scholarly discussion, not in a novel. Shklovsky treats the themes with such freshness, demonstrating convincingly the importance of literary theory to human life in general, that the reader takes the issues as seriously as he does. These themes are in all of his novels, but the challenge by the Party to the artistic positions Shklovsky and his friends had formulated makes this treatment of his favorite themes moving and melancholy. The excitement with which the writer discusses literary ideas in earlier novels, *Sentimentalnoye putishestiye: Vospominaniye, 1918-1922* (1923; *A Sentimental Journey: Memoirs, 1917-1922*, 1970) and *Zoo: Ili, Pisma ne o lyubvi* (1923; *Zoo: Or, Letters Not About Love*, 1971), gives way here to deep reconsideration and reassertion of the humane values that underlay the early Formalist discussions.

What appears here, then, is a brilliant display of new techniques, the dazzling form itself asserting the value of the ideas. Metaphors emerge from areas of life and language new to literature: the writer as flax in a field to be processed into a product; the new literary critics as vegetable soup; the writer as oyster, the bivalve's behavior described in technical terms but ending in a poignant image of a writer who cannot write what he wishes. Plot as such disappears, replaced by interest in the gradual elaboration of the metaphors, a pattern of meaning slowly emerging. Sudden shifts of subject and seemingly arbitrary digressions are finally seen to be part of the unified fabric. It is a fabric the reader may never have seen before. A new view of reality is suggested, too, by the shifts in point of view, suggesting the complexity of reality in very modern times. The book is full of intellectual interest to anyone who cares about this creative art.

The meaning of *Third Factory* goes beyond the purely intellectual. In the end, the understated emotional life of the narrator in the Soviet Union in the twentieth century makes the novel powerful. How can a thinking person, devoted to homeland, language, and fellow citizens, come to terms with political shifts which obliterate the work which gives his or her life meaning? The cumulative effect of the metaphors is to dramatize the loss of creative freedom in the Soviet Union, and the loss to that country of the intellectual achievements it might otherwise have enjoyed. The image of a person of feeling searching his way through the challenges and maintaining a commitment to truth in a miasma of contradictions lifts the novel into a rank beyond what is suggested by its brevity and the fact that it has received little recognition.

## Critical Context

The year 1925 brought the first explicit Party resolution, "On Party Policy in the Field of Imaginative Literature"; it was the beginning of political control over writers. The comparative freedom of the early 1920's began to die, and the Formalists, Futurists, and other experimental groups felt the shock. Shklovsky, as a member of LEF, an organization of Futurists and Formalists attempting to define in their own terms the way to respond to the new life after the Revolution, recognized the implications of the resolution. They saw that it paved the way for an essentially reactionary literary theory. (The policy would emerge as Socialist Realism in the early 1930's.) LEF died out in 1925, and Shklovsky says that *Third Factory* began as an attempt to accommodate to his times. Having returned from exile in Germany only in 1923, certain that he had to share the life of his country whatever fate that might bring, he apparently meant to try to follow Party guidance. Nevertheless, the book wrote itself differently. The habit of his mind was contradiction, according to Richard Sheldon, who translated the book into English, and the Formalist views Shklovsky had had so large a part in developing could not so easily be deserted. As a result, his persisting (though developing) view of literature not as a mirror of reality but as a complex verbal construct kept undermining his attempts to conform to Party thinking. Instead, the most he could do was to begin to consider that the rationalist approach of Marxism might well have something to add to the Formalists' rationalist approach to literature. He seemed prepared to learn about it; later twentieth century neo-Marxist criticism in the West would have been extremely interesting to Shklovsky.

At the same time, however, his literary foes rejected *Third Factory* for its tone of depression and its rejection of the emerging Party views on literature. Soviet critics recognized the persisting influence of Formalist ideas, and the book was not well received.

The book was unavailable to Western critics for half a century. As a result, Shklovsky's techniques deserve exploration: the brilliant experimentation with point of view, estrangement, the elaborated metaphor instead of plot to establish unity, ironic devices such as illogical deduction, surprising semantic parallels, parody, oblique comparison, personification of contemporary abstractions, and anthropomorphism for common and unexpected objects. The book is brief but filled with surprise and innovation.

*Third Factory*, like much of the literature written in the Soviet Union in the second quarter of the twentieth century, has not had the wide and receptive world audience it would have had without the advent of Stalinism and Party control of literature. Shklovsky's realization of the coming decline of all that he held important to the art accounts for the deep sadness of the book, but it does not prevent the delivery of a book of dazzling virtuosity and deep humanity.

*Sources for Further Study*
*Choice*. Review. XIV (January, 1978), p. 1506.
Erlich, Victor. *Twentieth Century Russian Literary Criticism*, 1975.
Grits, Fyodor S. "The Work of Viktor Shklovsky: An Analysis of *Third Factory*," in *Third Factory*, 1977.
Sheldon, Richard. "Viktor Shklovsky and the Device of Ostensible Surrender," introduction to *Third Factory*, 1977.

*Martha Manheim*

# THOUSAND CRANES

*Author:* Yasunari Kawabata (1899-1972)
*Type of plot:* Psychological realism
*Time of plot:* The late 1940's
*Locale:* Kamakura and Tokyo, both cities in Japan
*First published: Sembazuru,* 1949-1951, serial; 1952, book (English
   translation, 1958)

>    *Principal characters:*
>        KIKUJI MITANI, roughly twenty-eight years old, a bachelor
>            and the protagonist
>        CHIKAKO KURIMOTO, an instructor in the tea ceremony,
>            formerly the mistress of Mitani's father
>        YUKIKO INAMURA, a girl Mitani meets through Chikako
>        MRS. OTA, the widow of an associate of the elder Mitani, his
>            mistress during the last years of his life
>        FUMIKO OTA, the widow's daughter

*The Novel*

Yasunari Kawabata begins *Thousand Cranes* with a formal tea ceremony on the grounds of the Engakuji Temple in Kamakura. Kikuji Mitani, a bachelor in his late twenties, attends the ceremony at the invitation of Chikako Kurimoto, an instructor in the art of tea who, when Mitani was eight or ten years old, was his father's mistress. Mitani is not a student of the tea ceremony, but he cannot refuse Chikako's invitation. She is hosting the gathering to introduce him to Yukiko Inamura, one of her students and a prospective bride. Chikako's relationship with Mitani's father had not lasted more than a few years. When it had ended, she appeared on the days the family entertained guests to help in the kitchen. In time, she became Mitani's mother's confidante, complaining noisily of the behavior of Mrs. Ota, the widow who was the elder Mitani's mistress during the last years of his life. With the deaths of both Mitani's parents, Chikako has become a surrogate mother.

Mitani finds Yukiko as graceful and charming as Chikako had promised: "She carried a bundle wrapped in a kerchief, the thousand-crane pattern in white on a pink crape background." The colors of the cloth and the auspicious cranes, signifying a long and happy life, suggest that Yukiko is indeed the right bride for Mitani. The situation is complicated, however, by the uninvited presence of Mrs. Ota and her daughter Fumiko. Tea is served Mitani, and then Mrs. Ota, in a black *Oribe* bowl originally belonging to Mrs. Ota's husband, then to Mitani's father, and now to Chikako. The bowl itself is a valuable utensil, dating from the sixteenth century when the rituals of the tea ceremony were codified. The effect of sharing this relic is to prompt Mitani and Mrs. Ota into bed together on their way home from the gathering. While Mrs. Ota is at least twenty years older than he, Mitani "felt as if he had for the first time known woman, and as if for the first time he had known himself as a man." Two weeks later, however, Fumiko visits Mitani at his home and says that she has taken steps to prevent her mother from seeing Mitani. It is inappropriate, Fumiko adds, in the light of the fact that he is clearly going to marry Yukiko Inamura.

On the anniversary of the day of Mitani's late father's annual tea ceremony, held in a cottage in the garden of their home, Chikako arrives unannounced to arrange a memorial ceremony. She calls Mitani at his downtown Tokyo office and tells him to come home. She has invited Yukiko. The evening is a pleasant one, and Mitani can imagine himself marrying Yukiko. The next day, however, Mrs. Ota arrives at the house, tears in her eyes, having been telephoned by Chikako with the news that a marriage has been arranged between Yukiko and Mitani. He denies this but accuses Mrs. Ota of confusing him with his father. She seems to live in "another world, in which there was no distinction between his father and himself. So strong was the sense of the other world that afterwards this disquietude came over him." Early the following morning Mitani receives a telephone call from Fumiko, who tells him that Mrs. Ota has died from an overdose of sleeping pills.

Eight days after Mrs. Ota's death, Mitani calls on Fumiko at her home. The flowers he had sent for the seventh day memorial service are in a *Shino* water jar, a utensil for the tea ceremony. Fighting the emotion prompted by his memories of his last meeting with Mrs. Ota, Mitani admires the water jar, and Fumiko gives it to him as a momento of her mother. The conversation between the two is brutally direct. Each expresses guilt for Mrs. Ota's death, and this frankness draws them together. Mitani sees the mother in the daughter. "In Fumiko's round, soft face he saw her mother." Several days later, Chikako arrives at Mitani's door, ostensibly to clean the tea cottage in the garden but in fact to assess Mitani's feelings about Mrs. Ota's death. "You're too young to understand such people," Chikako tells him. "For your sake, it was good of her to die. That's the truth." On the surface, she is referring to the possibility of Mitani's marriage to Yukiko. She also expresses her own hostility to Mrs. Ota.

Chikako opposes the relationship that she senses is growing between Fumiko and Mitani, who seems to find the guilt he feels over the death of Mrs. Ota easing when he spends time with her daughter. "When a person is too much of a man or too much of a woman," Chikako claims, "the common sense generally isn't there." The older woman stages another informal tea ceremony, this one seemingly a memorial to Fumiko's mother, but the thrust of her conversation is to drive a wedge between Mitani and the younger woman. Fumiko brings Mitani a *Shino* tea bowl that Mrs. Ota had used on a daily basis. "The woman in Fumiko's mother came to him again, warm and naked." Chikako uses Mrs. Ota's *Shino* water jar as one of the utensils for serving tea, and she presses Mitani so strongly about an engagement to Yukiko that he tells her plainly, in front of Fumiko, that he does not intend to marry the girl.

It still comes as a shock, however, when Chikako comes to Mitani several weeks later with the news that both Yukiko and Fumiko are married. The story is a lie, and realization of the fact leads to a revealing conversation between Mitani and Fumiko. She tells Mitani that she regrets having given him her mother's *Shino* tea bowl. "There is much better *Shino*," she says. "The bowl reminds you of another, and the other is better." The surface discussion of the merits of various pieces of pottery barely disguises Fumiko's real subject, a distinction she perceives between her mother and herself and her own growing love for Mitani. The two of them go to the tea cottage to look at the *Karatsu*-ware bowl Mitani's father habitually used, and they place Mrs. Ota's *Shino* next to it: "Kikuji could not bring himself to say that the *Shino* bowl was like her mother. But the two bowls before them were like the souls of his father and her mother." As if sensing what is in Mitani's mind, Fumiko breaks her mother's bowl. The action frees Mitani, in his own eyes, and he allows himself to love her. "She had become absolute, beyond comparison. She had become decision and fate." Fumiko herself, however, seems overwhelmed by guilt, and she disappears, perhaps to commit suicide.

### The Characters

Kikuji Mitani is typical of the protagonists of Kawabata's fiction in being a man drawn, without being too conscious of the fact, into a complex triangular relationship involving a fair, virginal girl such as Yukiko Inamura and a dark, guilt-ridden girl such as Fumiko Ota. Kawabata's Yoko and Komako in *Yukiguni* (1947; *Snow Country*, 1956) are the most famous examples of this typical female pair, as Shimamura, the protagonist of the same novel, is of the male type. Kawabata sketches the same three-sided relationship in *Thousand Cranes* in the story of the elder Mitani's affairs with Chikako Kurimoto and Mrs. Ota. The history of the older generation affects the behavior of Fumiko Ota and young Mitani himself. Kawabata filters the action of *Thousand Cranes* through Mitani's mind, but he is like Shimamura in his passivity. He does not so much seek out Yukiko and Fumiko as exploit the potential for emotional involvement presented him by the actions of others. Mitani is not so much a victim of the tangled life of his father as he is of a moral corruption of his own that Mrs. Ota and Fumiko exploit.

Yukiko Inamura is a shadowy figure. She is not really involved in the action of *Thousand Cranes* but serves to suggest the ordinary happiness Mitani might have if he could break through the sexual infatuation with Mrs. Ota that ties him to the past. Part of Mitani's motivation is a barely recognized Oedipal impulse. His earliest memory of Chikako Kurimoto is the sight of a birthmark disfiguring one of her breasts, and his attraction to Mrs. Ota is characterized by attraction to her maternal nature. Aware of it or not, Mitani wishes to supplant his father in the affections of his father's mistresses, surrogate mothers who attract him emotionally and sexually. In this context, his attraction to Fumiko is doubly wrong. She is Mitani's sister, if Mrs. Ota is his metaphorical mother, as well as a substitute in his mind for her dead mother. He believes that when Fumiko breaks her late mother's *Shino* tea bowl, she has broken the hold of the past. "That fact, one might think, told how deep he had sunk into the meshes of the curse, how complete the paralysis was; but Kikuji felt the reverse, that he had escaped the curse and the paralysis." Fumiko's disappearance, perhaps to commit suicide as her mother had done, terminates the relationship with Mitani. Her actions reveal superior insight, for she knows that Mitani and she are fated to repeat the obsessive, ultimately destructive affair of their parents.

In a sense, a similar recognition prompts Mrs. Ota's own suicide. Mitani is right to accuse her of being unable to distinguish between father and son, and Chikako may be correct in claiming that Mrs. Ota intends, by her death, to throw Mitani and Fumiko together. While Mrs. Ota is a victim of her continuing emotional bond with the elder Mitani, Chikako's actions spring from a malevolent dislike of Mrs. Ota and resentment of the fact that Mitani's father terminated his affair with her. Chikako repeatedly describes Mrs. Ota as a witch and cautions the younger Mitani to be cautious, but she herself is the dark enchantress of *Thousand Cranes*. While consciously motivated by the desire to save the young man from being entrapped by the Ota women, Chikako repeatedly acts in ways that throw Mitani and both Fumiko and her mother together. It is as if, like Otoko Ueno in *Utskushisa to kanashimi to* (1965; *Beauty and Sadness*, 1975), Chikako manipulates the situation without being aware of it to gain the deepest revenge upon her former lover by incapacitating the younger Mitani for normal sexual and emotional relationships.

*Themes and Meanings*

The major thematic point of *Thousand Cranes* is a statement about the degree to which men and women are mastered by a fate beyond their control. Nothing in Mitani's own character ought to keep the cool and innocent Yukiko at a distance, but the dark secrets shared by his father, Mrs. Ota, and Chikako predetermine the direction his life will take. Pursuit of ideal beauty, as so much of Yasunari Kawabata's fiction suggests, almost always results in revelation of the passion and egotism beneath the surface attractiveness. The character relationships in *Thousand Cranes*, both the mirroring sets of love triangles and the implicit parallels between characters that these relationships establish, objectify Kawabata's sense of the fate that controls human destiny.

So much in the lives of the characters in *Thousand Cranes* is subject to chance. Kawabata uses the tea ceremony to suggest this. Mitani's father, for example, met Chikako Kurimoto because of a mutual interest in the tea ceremony and the utensils used to practice it. Mrs. Ota is the widow of a man the elder Mitani knew because of this shared interest; many of the most valuable objects in the Mitani collection of utensils were purchased from Mrs. Ota. Others come into the younger Mitani's hands as gifts from Fumiko. Kawabata brings the characters of *Thousand Cranes* together at least once in each major section of the novel to practice the tea ceremony. Mitani meets Yukiko at a formal ceremony arranged by Chikako for just this purpose, and he meets Mrs. Ota and Fumiko again on the same occasion. Chikako stages tea ceremonies to encourage the relationship between Yukiko and Mitani, to memorialize the death of Mrs. Ota, and to recognize the date on which the elder Mitani had an annual party in the tea house. The climax of Fumiko and young Mitani's relationship occurs in that tea house in the Mitani garden. There Fumiko breaks her mother's *Shino* cup and submits for the only time to Mitani's sexual advances.

In marked contrast to the impurity of human motives and actions is the perspective provided by the utensils for the tea ceremony itself. Looking at the *Shino* bowl belonging to Mrs. Ota and at his father's *Karatsu* bowl, Mitani thinks, "The tea bowls, three or four hundred years old, were sound and healthy, and they called up no morbid thoughts. Life seemed to stretch taut over them, however, in a way that was almost sensual." Kawabata stresses the perspective on human passions that these objects provide. They have passed through many hands and bear witness to the lives of owners now virtually forgotten. Awareness of this fact puts human feelings into a perspective suggesting the relative unimportance of the love and suffering of any single man or woman.

*Critical Context*

In balancing the claims of individual passion against the perspective of time, *Thousand Cranes* is typical of Yasunari Kawabata's novels. Awareness of mortality is hardly consolation for human suffering, but in books such as *Meijin* (1954; *The Master of Go*, 1972) and *Yama no oto* (1954; *The Sound of the Mountain*, 1970), Kawabata focuses on the necessity of attaining such a stoicism. Pursuit of the pleasures of this world, he demonstrates in novel after novel, results in confrontation with the cosmic emptiness of all of time itself. *Thousand Cranes* is not as stark and uncompromising a depiction of this confrontation as is Kawabata's *Mizuumi* (1955; *The Lake*, 1974), but its conclusions are uncompromising. It depicts a Japan in which all forms of traditional discipline, including that of the tea ceremony, have been subverted. The characters in the novel lack the moral perspective that any form of discipline would provide.

Knowledge of the tea ceremony and familiarity with the various ceramics from which its utensils have been made would enrich the reading of *Thousand Cranes*, but such information is not essential to an understanding of the novel. Like *Beauty and Sadness*, the book deals with a woman's attempt to extract revenge from a lover, even to the extent of inflicting suffering on his son. Chikako Kurimoto misuses her knowledge of the art of tea by making use of the tea ceremony as an occasion for manipulating the feelings of young Mitani. *Thousand Cranes* testifies, in addition, to the degree to which the way of tea represents the influence of the elder Mitani on the life of his son. In this case, the influence does not lead to the traditional purification of mind and spirit associated with the discipline of the tea ceremony. It leads to the very opposite.

*Sources for Further Study*

Keene, Donald. *Dawn to the West: Japanese Literature in the Modern Era*, 1984.

Lippit, Noriko Mizuta. *Reality and Fiction in Modern Japanese Literature*, 1980.

Petersen, Gwenn Boardman. *The Moon in the Water: Understanding Tanizaki, Kawabata, and Mishima*, 1979.

Ueda, Makoto. *Modern Japanese Writers and the Nature of Literature*, 1976.

Yamanouchi, Hisaaki. *The Search for Authenticity in Modern Japanese Literature*, 1978.

                                                                    *Robert C. Petersen*

# THE THREE-CORNERED WORLD

*Author:* Sōseki Natsume (Kinnosuke Natsume, 1867-1916)
*Type of plot:* Philosophical realism
*Time of plot:* Around 1906
*Locale:* The Japanese resort village of Nakoi
*First published: Kusamakura*, 1906 (*Unhuman Tour*, 1927; better known as
   *The Three-Cornered World*)

   *Principal characters:*
      THE NARRATOR, an artist; unable to paint or write in the city,
         he travels the countryside
      O-NAMI SHIODA, the divorced daughter of the resort-keeper,
         who flirts with the narrator
      KYUICHI SHIODA, her cousin, a painter and draftee
      DAITETSU, the abbot of a nearby Zen monastery

*The Novel*
   In *The Three-Cornered World*, an artist, the novel's first-person narrator,
tells about his journey into the Japanese countryside, where he hopes to find
the natural environment necessary for his artistic powers to unfold. Sōseki
Natsume's novel is unconventional in its minimalist approach to its characters, but its silence here is counterbalanced by presentation of philosophical ideas, haiku, and graphic description of natural scenery, all of which are
integrated into the overall structure of the narrator's excursion.
   The novel begins a few miles from the hot springs of Nakoi, where the
springtime countryside invites the narrator "to rise above emotions, to view
things dispassionately." Ironically, however, a heavy spring rain modifies his
abstract ideas and brings home to him the "vulgar" in human existence:
Completely drenched, the young artist finds refuge in a roadside teahouse.
   There, an old woman waits on him until Gembei, a packhorse driver from
Nakoi, stops over. In conversation with him, the old woman casually brings
up the story of Shioda's unfortunate daughter. After her studies at Kyoto,
where she fell in love, O-Nami Shioda was married to another man to suit
her father's finances; what arouses the narrator's interest is that O-Nami
divorced her husband upon his sudden bankruptcy and returned to Shioda's
hotel.
   Arriving late at night and resting in his room, the artist observes a female
figure singing under an aronia tree in the moonlit garden. The young woman
vanishes at his approach, only to reappear shortly afterward, searching the
room's cupboard while the narrator feigns sleep. In the morning, the artist
meets his night visitor—Shioda's daughter, in whose room he is lodging—

and finds "absolutely no consistency in her expression": Beneath a snooty surface is real need. Discovering that the haiku poems about the sad singer he composed that night have been jokingly amended by their subject, the narrator begins to feel "a thin thread" being spun between them by fate. Nevertheless, O-Nami rejects his sketch of an ideal landscape for her as being too "cramped and uncomfortable" and representing a two-dimensional world.

The local barber insists to the narrator that O-Nami is mad and dangerous; as he returns to his room, he observes the young woman dancing on the opposite veranda, clad in her bridal gown and oblivious of the onset of a spring rain. Soaking in a hot tub, the artist dreams of painting William Shakespeare's Ophelia drowning herself with an expression of gentle relaxation; suddenly, half shrouded in the mist of the bathhouse, O-Nami stands naked before him and disappears before her visionlike quality is lost by a further advance.

After tea with Abbot Daitetsu, O-Nami's confessor at the local Kankaiji temple, and old Shioda, the artist tries to explain to O-Nami how a Western romance novel can be subject to a "non-human, objective approach" when it is read in portions picked at random. In a delicate maneuver, the narrator relates this method to the possibility of his falling in love with O-Nami without their ever marrying. His female counterpart, however, shocks him with her sudden request to be painted while drowning herself.

Visiting Kagami pond, the artist decides that he cannot successfully paint such a picture because of the absence of compassion in O-Nami's countenance. Joined at the pond by Gembei, he learns from the horse driver that an earlier Shioda girl really drowned herself here; soon after, O-Nami briefly appears on a rock above the lake, again startling the narrator.

On the morning after a nighttime discussion with Daitetsu, the artist climbs a gentle hill, convinced that O-Nami would be the perfect actress since she naturally behaves as if she were onstage, thus conveying an unselfconscious beauty and aesthetic purity which he finds absent in contemporary players. Accidentally, he witnesses the appearance of a rugged fellow, possibly a mercenary, and O-Nami. After she hands him a purse in a moment of sheer beauty of poise and composition, the man disappears. Discovering the peeping narrator, the young woman shocks him a third time by confiding that the ruffian was her ex-husband, who has decided to make money by serving in the ongoing Russo-Japanese War in Manchuria. Together, O-Nami and the narrator visit Shioda's nephew Kyuichi, a painter and draftee who is also ready to go to the war.

The journey of *The Three-Cornered World* ends with the Shiodas and the narrator accompanying Kyuichi to a railway station whence he will join his unit. During their final boat ride, the narrator argues with O-Nami, to whom nothing but a heroic death seems appropriate for her cousin, and who insists again on the narrator's painting her; he still cannot do it, since there is "something missing" in her expression.

A final change comes when the train pulls out of the station and O-Nami detects her ex-husband on it. Now, she looks after his disappearing figure "with that 'compassion' which had hitherto been lacking." Hence O-Nami is redeemed, and the narrator concludes the novel with his whisper to her: "That's it! That's it! Now that you can express that feeling, you are worth painting."

### The Characters

The narrator of *The Three-Cornered World* occupies the triple position of protagonist, philosopher, and poet-artist. Through his poems, which demonstrate mastery of the haiku form, he longs to arrive at an aesthetically satisfying understanding of his life. It is always at crucial moments during his journey that the narrator becomes most poetically active; after his first, nighttime discovery of O-Nami, he puts his tempestuous mind at rest by composing the seventeen-syllable poems until he finds sleep. As a complete artist, however, he is still in a state of development. His dependence on nature as "a land which is completely detached from feelings and emotions" is not uncriticized. "A man cannot be said to have completed his education until he can stand at Nihonbashi in the center of Tokyo, and lay bare his soul to the world without embarrassment," advises Daitetsu. Furthermore, the narrator has not yet painted a single picture—and thus worked in his prime artistic profession—when he leaves Nakoi on the final boat ride.

O-Nami functions as a catalyst for the narrator, who becomes intellectually fascinated by the prospect of a love relationship between them. Yet she is driven by a dynamic force of her own and refuses to comply with outside expectations or restrictions. Her self-asserted independence is labeled as "madness" by the villagers, who place her in a long row of similarly dangerous female ancestors; these have their Western counterparts in the "madwomen" of such nineteenth century novels as Charlotte Brontë's *Jane Eyre* (1847).

In their subtle relationship, the narrator believes that O-Nami is "definitely ahead in the game." It is she who startles the protagonist with her direct ideas and unconventional frankness; at times, Shioda's daughter shames him by her implicit demonstration of his shortcomings as aesthete and romancer. Thus, the narrator finds himself first blaming the moonlight singer for indecency before succumbing to the beauty of her act. Similarly, he is inclined to dismiss her dance in the rain as madness. O-Nami reminds him that it was he who casually mentioned to the old women of the teahouse how he would like to see her dancing in her old bridal gown, and who now failed to recognize her act as being a special performance for him.

O-Nami's closeness to the narrator's feelings and visions is uncanny; this quality gives her an impact far beyond the other characters', who all remain somewhat distant. Although their traits and problems are multilayered, their conflicts stay static. Old Shioda's obsession with knickknacks is demonstrated, but there never emerges a consistent criticism of his collection, which transfers such artifacts as a precious inkstone from their intended functional contexts to the sterility of a museum. Similarly, Kyuichi can be viewed as the artist's younger double, who has to decide between artistic vocation and patriotic duty; again, he leaves the novel in tranquillity before his conflict has really erupted.

### Themes and Meanings

The central topic of *The Three-Cornered World* is the role of the artist in turn-of-the-century Japan. Sōseki explores this topic in the philosophical essays with which the narrator's account of his journey and fragile would-be romance is interspersed. In these thoughtful excursions, the novel becomes less conventional and plot-centered, to the point of completely abandoning fiction and allowing the emergence of serious, contemporary demands at a crucial point in the cultural history of Japan.

*The Three-Cornered World* is structured around the great dichotomy between the Oriental and Western civilizations, a fact of life for Japan after her forced opening to the West after 1868. Sōseki insists on artistic independence and defends the idea that one must paint Japan in her own colors, without reference to the now-fashionable Western techniques and styles. At the same time, however, the narrator does paint in the Western style and indirectly defends this method by refusing to submit it to a hopeless test by Daitetsu, who wants to adorn Japanese sliding doors with "a Western style picture."

In the struggle for objective detachment versus (Western) overindulgence in subjectivism and human interest, the narrator finds himself opposed to Western novels with their prosaic worldliness and undue concern with a passion-filled plot. Against this, the protagonist sets the experience of the classical Japanese Nō drama; indeed, *The Three-Cornered World* can be seen as Sōseki's literal application of the principle of Nō—to have "three-tenths real emotion, and seven-tenths technique."

Finally, modern technology is seen as destroying nature's most powerful quality, that of inducing in the observer an absolute feeling of assimilation and loss of human concern. Whereas the narrator is able happily to reconcile himself with the existence of a vulgar barber because the latter is too insignificant to disturb the grand serenity of spring, the railway train which is to carry Kyuichi and "hundreds of people crammed together in one box" is seen as an "unsympathetic and heartless contraption . . . typical of twentieth century civilization." It not only destroys individuality but also marks its presence with such stench and noise that its impact can no longer be absorbed by nature.

## Critical Context

Sōseki's own experience informs *The Three-Cornered World*, which ultimately is about the Japanese intellectual's place in a modernized and Westernized society. In that experience, early studies of Chinese literature (which has traditionally influenced Japanese culture) were balanced by a life-long interest in and study of English and a two-year stay in London at the turn of the century. In *The Three-Cornered World*, Sōseki delivers at times caustic criticism of the West; this is not done out of mere conservatism or xenophobia but represents a necessary corrective to immature and faddish imitation of Western culture in post-1868 Japan. The artistic independence of Sōseki, as of Mori Ōgai, distinguished him among his Japanese contemporaries. Sōseki's insistence on intrinsically Oriental values in a world in which changes are clearly seen has earned for him a place among Japan's most respected modern writers.

*The Three-Cornered World* is a powerful novel about artistic integrity and achievement. Sōseki has been criticized for being elitist; after all, he describes the artist's ideal habitat as "the triangle which remains after the angle which we may call common sense has been removed from this four-cornered world." Yet his radical vision of an aesthetic life that requires objectivity and personal distance convinces because of its ironic tenderness and ultimate humanism. Thus, it is fitting that the artist-protagonist goes beyond perceiving change for the better in O-Nami; it is her transformation into a compassionate human being that finally liberates his pent-up artistic energy and sets him free to paint the picture which has glimmered unrealized in his head throughout his journey in his three-cornered world.

## Sources for Further Study

McClellan, Edwin. "An Introduction to Sōseki," in *Harvard Journal of Asiatic Studies*. XX (1959), pp. 150-208.

Miyoshi, Masao. "Through the Glass Darkly," in *Accomplices of Silence: The Modern Japanese Novel*, 1974.

Okazaki, Yoshie. "The Romanticism and Idealism Around Sōseki," in *Japanese Literature in the Meiji Era*, 1955.

Yu, Beongcheon. "The Frustrated Years, 1903-1907," in *Natsume Sōseki*, 1969.

*Reinhart Lutz*

# A TICKET TO THE STARS

*Author:* Vassily Aksyonov (1932-        )
*Type of plot:* Social criticism
*Time of plot:* The summer of 1960
*Locale:* Moscow and the Baltic coast
*First published: Zvezdnyi bilet*, 1961 (*A Starry Ticket*, 1962; better known as
   *A Ticket to the Stars*)

> *Principal characters:*
>    DIMKA, a seventeen-year-old who has recently been
>       graduated from high school
>    YURKA and
>    ALIK, Dimka's classmates
>    GALYA, Dimka's girlfriend and classmate
>    VICTOR, Dimka's older brother, a space scientist

*The Novel*

*A Ticket to the Stars* is the story of four young Russians who, after gradu-
ation from high school, find themselves at a crossroads, undecided about
their future. Dimka, Yurka, Alik, and the only girl among them, Galya, all
seventeen years old, are tired of school and so are not interested in attending
college, at least for the present. Yurka is a good athlete, Alik writes poetry,
Galya has acting ambitions, and Dimka is a well-rounded young man without
any special aspirations. Dimka's older brother, Victor, is a space scientist
who would like to help him decide about his future. Victor would like to see
Dimka go to college because he firmly believes in Dimka's abilities.

The young people spend their days wandering around, doing nothing constructive, and discussing the possibility of going away from Moscow; it does
not matter where, as long as it is away from home. The apartment house
where they live, their parents, older relatives, and the authorities all fill them
with boredom and a desire to rebel. Dimka does not want to follow in his
successful brother's steps. His words speak for the group as a whole:

> Victor, it was Pa and Ma who planned your life for you while you were still
> kicking in your cradle. . . . In your whole life you've never even once taken an
> important decision, never accepted a serious risk. To hell with that! Before
> we're even born, everything is worked out for us, our whole future is all
> mapped out. . . . I'd rather be a tramp and suffer all sorts of setbacks than go
> through my whole life being a nice little boy doing what others tell me.

The group finally decides to go west, toward the Baltic coast, leaving
everything to chance and to their lucky star. Victor realizes that he cannot
change their minds and reluctantly resigns himself to their decision. They be-

come "kilometer eaters" and in a few days on a train reach a small Estonian town on the Baltic Sea. Enjoying full freedom for the first time in their lives, they feel exalted and intoxicated by the fresh sea air; the provisions from home are still plentiful. Nevertheless, pangs of homesickness and anxiety begin to gnaw at them. They meet all types of people: some dubious characters, some honest workers. They take on menial jobs, more out of boredom than out of necessity, although their money is slowly running out. In addition, Galya and Dimka admit for the first time that they are emotionally involved, which complicates matters because they are living as a group. The three boys eventually find jobs with a fishing trawler and go out to sea every morning, coming back late in the afternoon. In the meantime, Galya has made the acquaintance of a middle-aged actor who promises to help her start her acting career. Dimka is visibly unhappy about this change, yet he is unable to prevent her from becoming involved with the actor.

Back in Moscow, Victor is debating whether to defend his dissertation in nuclear physics even though he has discovered new material that would render his dissertation subject obsolete. His advising professor urges him on, in order to get the diploma, but Victor, for the first time in his life and undoubtedly under the influence of his younger brother's independent spirit, decides to forgo the official title and pursue his independent research instead.

Dimka is also pleased with his freedom despite his setback with Galya, the hard work in the fishing co-op, and being too busy to enjoy the company of his friends. He is aware that this is not exactly what he and his friends had hoped for, yet he realizes that this is real life and that he has finally experienced it. He does not want to go back to his life in Moscow. Galya soon decides to come back to him, having been disappointed by her actor friend, who was apparently a fraud. Just as life begins to seem settled, Dimka receives a telegram informing him that his brother has been killed in an air crash while pursuing his duties as a space engineer.

Dimka returns home alone, having said good-bye to his boyhood and his adolescent dreams of freedom and independence. His brother's death has forced him to grow up overnight. He realizes now that his brother has left him a legacy that he cannot ignore. There are ways one can be both independent and dutiful without obeying others' commands. As he looks at the evening sky from the window of their home, he sees the same stars that his brother must have seen for the last time. He knows that Victor has left him a ticket to the stars, which he must pursue even though he does not know yet where that ticket will take him.

## The Characters

Dimka, the hero of the novel, is a representative of the generation of Russian youth born during World War II, who have little firsthand knowledge of the hardships which their parents experienced. He shows a healthy mixture of boldness and independence of mind, willing to buck the trend and to follow his own path no matter where it might lead him. Dimka is basically honest, though rebellious. He does not mind telling his parents and his older brother that he will not settle for being a hypocrite. At the same time, he is not sure of himself and does not know what he really wants in life. He wonders:

> Was it possible that the answer was—nothing? Was it possible that I could wish for nothing beyond standing at a bar and admiring the gleam of artificial stars on the ceiling? Wasn't I capable of anything more daring than rock 'n' roll, the Charleston, calypso, the smell of coffee and brandy. . . . No, hell, I know what I want. Or rather, I feel that knowledge is hiding inside me. But I'll get to it.

Even though his first attempts at independent life are not an unmitigated success, he has moved toward that unknown goal, and the reader is convinced that eventually he will reach it.

In this respect, Dimka and Victor are similar. Victor seems to follow obediently the path mapped out for him by his elders, as Dimka protests, yet Vassily Aksyonov suggests that there is nothing wrong in becoming a space engineer and working for a meaningful goal. Victor, too, displays integrity of character when he refuses to play the game of official titles and privileges, convinced that what he is doing is much more important than professional benefits. Victor and Dimka are reaching for the same stars but trying to get there by different paths. Aksyonov suggests that both the official and unofficial paths are honorable as long as they are followed without selling one's soul.

Other characters are somewhat less developed, though they too play a role in the author's vision of reality in the Soviet Union. All three young people who leave home with Dimka are woven of the same fabric. They all have their dreams—Yurka as a success in the world of sports, Alik as a budding young writer, and Galya as an actress—and they are all willing to sacrifice the comfort and security of their sheltered lives in order to achieve their goals. Alik is more withdrawn and art-oriented; Yurka has his feet placed more firmly on the ground; and Galya is much more naïve in her belief in success, but it is symptomatic of their common bond that they understand one another and seek one another's company. They have rejected the herd morality of their peers, who have allowed themselves to be led without questioning.

One cannot help but be impressed with these young people. Their aspirations do not seem any different from those of the youth in other parts of the world. Their existence vouches for the simple truth that the human desire for freedom and self-fulfillment cannot be eradicated by the intense pressure of a politicized education and environment.

## Themes and Meanings

*A Ticket to the Stars* contains several themes that are particularly relevant to Russian society and, at the same time, universal. The theme of the independence of mind and spirit is played out in a society that has fought against such independence from the very beginning of its existence. Mindful of the significance of educating the young according to the Party blueprint, Soviet society has always worked to inculcate in its youth the spirit of obedience and single-mindedness. Until the 1950's, there were very few literary works available depicting any deviation from that path. Writers have been compelled, or have agreed, to present Soviet youth in one light only: as totally obedient members of a society that does not tolerate difference of opinion. Only since the death of Joseph Stalin have Soviet writers been able, with greater or lesser success, to depict themes and characters that deviate from the norm as dictated by the tenets of Socialist Realism. In this respect, the four characters in Aksyonov's novel present a refreshing change. More important, they are believable characters of flesh and blood, rather than the cardboard imitations of human beings found in most Soviet literature prior to the 1950's. In this respect, the theme of the independence of mind and spirit among young people is not only novel in Soviet literature but also indicative of the indestructibility of the human spirit.

*A Ticket to the Stars* also depicts normal, vibrant life going on within Soviet society despite the oppressiveness of its regime. Young people want, to a degree, to say "no" to the authorities. Some people can still choose a profession other than driving a tractor on a collective farm or being a simple laborer in a factory. People enjoy themselves as they can and express themselves rather freely on matters other than politics or ideology. Human beings seem able to adjust to any situation and maintain a zest for life and an idealism aside from, and in spite of, Party dictates. It is encouraging to know that people have been able to preserve their idealism amid all the cynicism that accompanies a life in which so much is decreed and decided by others.

Finally, it is heartening to see that the youth of Russia are moved to imitate the ways of their peers in other parts of the world. Right or wrong, tasteful or tasteless, such imitation shows that the world is indivisible, despite the artificial barriers erected to prevent the exchange of ideas and modes of life.

## Critical Context

When Aksyonov published *A Ticket to the Stars* in 1961, he was one of many young writers dedicated to blazing new paths in Soviet literature, introducing themes and styles which until then were considered taboo. To be sure, the freedom emerging in the late 1950's and early 1960's was a relative one—writers could still not express themselves as freely as they wished—but the change was noticeable. Aksyonov played a significant part in this process with several short stories and novels, *A Ticket to the Stars* being perhaps the most important among them. His contribution included the use of a livelier and freer style. The dialogue is much more true to life and full of previously impermissible slang, although it is toned down considerably in translation. The author did not feel compelled to pattern his plot or characters after the prescriptions of Socialist Realism. Most important, the novel is not a period piece; it has lost little of its charm and pertinence with time.

Aksyonov eventually paid the price for his efforts to free Soviet literature from its confines. Forced to emigrate in 1980, he settled in the United States. Although Aksyonov's later works are bolder, more experimental, than *A Ticket to the Stars*, this novel retains its significance as the first successful work of an unmistakable talent.

## Sources for Further Study

Clark, Katerina. *The Soviet Novel: History as Ritual*, 1981.

Gaev, A. "The Decade Since Stalin," in *Soviet Literature in the Sixties*, 1964. Edited by Max Hayward and Edward L. Crowley.

Meyer, Priscilla. "Aksyonov and Stalinism: Political, Moral, and Literary Power," in *Slavic and East European Journal*. XXX (Winter, 1986), pp. 509-525.

Mozejko, Edward, Boris Briker, and Per Dalgard, eds. *Vasiliy Pavlovich Aksenov: A Writer in Quest of Himself*, 1986.

Richardson, Maurice. "Dragooned," in *New Statesman*. LXIII (1962), pp. 804-805.

*Vasa D. Mihailovich*

# THE TIME OF INDIFFERENCE

*Author:* Alberto Moravia (1907-    )
*Type of plot:* Psychological realism
*Time of plot:* 1929
*Locale:* Rome
*First published: Gli indifferenti,* 1929 (English translation, 1953)

*Principal characters:*
MARIAGRAZIA ARDENGO, a middle-aged widow
CARLA ARDENGO, Mariagrazia's twenty-four-year-old
    daughter
MICHELE ARDENGO, Mariagrazia's son, a first-year law
    student
LEO MERUMECI, a forty-two-year-old businessman and the
    lover of Mariagrazia and Carla
LISA, Leo's former mistress

*The Novel*

On the eve of her twenty-fourth birthday, Carla Ardengo longs to escape her dreary existence, to find a new life. Visiting the Ardengos this evening is Leo Merumeci. He is a frequent guest because he is the lover of Carla's widowed mother, Mariagrazia, and the holder of the mortgage on the Ardengos' fashionable villa. Leo has become tired of Mariagrazia, who has been his mistress for fifteen years; he propositions Carla, and she agrees to come to his apartment the next day.

Lisa, who had been Leo's lover and fiancée before he met Mariagrazia, is also at the villa. Mariagrazia suspects that Lisa and Leo want to renew their affair and that Lisa has come to her house to arrange a rendezvous. The object of her quest, however, is not Leo but Michele, Mariagrazia's son. Just as Carla consents to give herself to Leo, Michele agrees to see Lisa.

Leo's attempted seduction suffers a setback at Carla's birthday party the next day. To make her more pliable, he fills her glass again and again with champagne, so that by the end of the meal she is drunk. They go for a walk on the villa's grounds, where they happen upon an old shed conveniently equipped with a bed. Just as Leo prepares to have sex with Carla, she becomes ill from the wine, and he must wait until night to consummate the affair.

Lisa's hopes, too, are temporarily dashed. She has lured Michele to her apartment with the promise of interesting a rich relative in him and so securing a good position for the youth. When Michele arrives the next morning, no relative is waiting. Lisa goes into the hallway, pretending to call him, but Michele sees that she does not even pick up the phone, and he leaves.

When Michele returns later that day, he finds Leo alone with Lisa; again Michele leaves. By the time he makes his third visit, Lisa knows all about Leo's relationship with Carla. Michele accuses Lisa of chasing after Leo, but she replies that Leo would not have her; he already has Michele's sister.

Although Michele does not feel anger on learning about his sister's affair, he senses that he should act. He buys a cheap pistol, goes to Leo's apartment, and tries to kill him. Michele has forgotten to load the gun, so his attempted murder fails. Carla, who has been sleeping with Leo, emerges from the bedroom to learn the cause of the confusion. Michele seizes the opportunity to urge her to abandon Leo, arguing that the family can sell the villa and pay Leo what they owe him.

Leo knows that if the Ardengos put the villa on the market they will get far more than the eight hundred thousand lira that they owe him. He will thus lose the house, his new mistress, and perhaps his old mistress as well. Consequently, he offers to marry Carla, allow the Ardengos to continue to live in the villa, and find Michele a job. Michele still opposes the marriage, but Carla consents because, even though she does not love Leo, she is eager for the money, fine clothes, and parties that the marriage will bring her.

Following the confrontation at Leo's apartment, the two Ardengo children return home. Carla and her mother prepare to attend a masked ball, a fitting emblem of the life of concealment that they lead. Michele and Lisa, meanwhile, plan yet another tryst, and he promises that this time he will not rebuff her advances.

*The Characters*

Michele is the first of a number of effete intellectuals appearing in Alberto Moravia's fiction. He would like to feel passion, to love Lisa and despise Leo, but he cannot. His only response to life is indifference, because he lacks any moral sense. Although he pretends to be angry when he learns that his sister has become Leo's mistress, he had in fact considered "selling" Carla to him in exchange for an allowance. If Leo had preferred Lisa, Michele was prepared to give her up for the same terms.

Whereas Michele feels nothing, Carla suffers deeply. Seeing her present life as barren, she longs for change and will do anything to effect it. She even agrees to Leo's proposition and then his proposal, only to realize, too late, that nothing has been altered; she is merely taking her mother's place.

Lisa, too, hopes for redemption. She thinks that Michele will bring "sunshine, blue sky, freshness, enthusiasm" into her gray world. Given Michele's character, Lisa is doomed to disappointment: Enthusiasm is hardly one of his attributes. The gap between her imagination and reality is evident when her would-be lover first comes to her apartment. She has been fantasizing about an elaborate seduction, but all that she can say when Michele arrives is, "Well, how goes it?" At the end of the novel her affair with Michele is still inchoate despite Michele's promise to accept her advances. Even if they do sleep together, her life will change no more than Carla's, since neither Leo nor Michele can offer any realistic hope of salvation.

Michele, Carla, and Lisa would like to change their situation but cannot. Mariagrazia and Leo, on the other hand, want everything to stay the same. The former dreads poverty and the loss of social position so much that she consents to her daughter's marriage to her own former lover, a man who claims to regard Carla as his "almost daughter." Leo, too, wants to retain his comforts, including the pleasant Ardengo villa and sex with Carla. If he must sacrifice nominal bachelorhood to keep these, he will, but he tells himself at the end of the novel, "Even when you're married, you'll be the same old Leo." He will still chase any woman he desires and will remain a frequent guest of Mariagrazia.

## Themes and Meanings

As Michele ponders his condition, he observes, "Once upon a time, it appeared, men used to know their paths in life from the first to the last step, but now it was not so; now one's head was in a bag, one was in the dark, one was blind. And yet one still had to go somewhere; but where?" All the characters are groping blindly in a world that has lost what Moravia calls "the traditional scale of values" in the aftermath of World War I. This blindness is perhaps best symbolized by the scene at the beginning of the novel when the electricity fails in Mariagrazia's house. In the ensuing blackness, Mariagrazia seeks vainly for Leo, who is hiding behind the curtains and flirting with Carla, and Lisa arranges an assignation with Michele.

The entire novel is suffused with gloom and blackness. Much of the action occurs at night, and the rest unfolds under the rainy, gray skies of winter, the season of death. This bleakness also invades the characters' houses. Mariagrazia's drawing room is cold and bleak. An arch divides it into two unequal parts, emblematic of the present and the future. Little light shines in the present, where the characters sit, and the other section, the future, offers no change: It "remained plunged in a shadowy blackness in which reflections from mirrors and the long shape of the piano could barely be distinguished." The dark future merely reflects and repeats the grim present.

Just as the Ardengos' gloomy drawing room embodies that family's life, so Lisa's apartment exposes her sad experience. Inside she looks at the "mute, dead shapes of old pieces of furniture" and a gray, chilly bathroom with "dull, painted pipes"; outside all she can see is an equally dull piece of red roof. From a distance, her drawing room seems an exception to this pervasive gloom, and it is here that she plans to seduce Michele, who, like the room, appears to hold out hope for change. Upon closer examination, though, one finds the same desolation here as everywhere else: "the upholstery was discolored and in places threadbare, . . . the sofa was torn and the cushions shabby." Neither this drawing room nor Michele will offer relief from the general dreariness.

To escape this oppressive reality, Moravia's characters construct dream-worlds. Carla imagines a new life. Michele seeks "a pure woman, neither false nor stupid nor corrupt," and wants a "world governed by instinct and sincerity." Mariagrazia harbors visions of wealth and a beauty that will retain Leo's love for her. They are not above lying to themselves and others to support these fantasies. Thus, Lisa conjures up a rich relative to induce Michele to visit her, even though she could just as easily have invited him without the pretense. Michele tries repeatedly and unsuccessfully to assume emotions that he does not feel; Mariagrazia pretends to a superiority over Lisa which she lacks. Even though the characters often look at their reflections in mirrors, they fail to see themselves and their world as it is, for they have lost touch with reality.

*Critical Context*

Moravia's depiction of middle-class life as dull, gloomy, and false shocked and stimulated Italian audiences when the novel first appeared. The product of a bourgeois upbringing, Moravia revealed his own boredom with that existence. His critique went beyond a personal aversion to middle-class values: It anticipated the existential view that people have become so self-absorbed that they cannot relate to any world outside themselves. Moravia's characters are as much strangers as Albert Camus', and like Jean-Paul Sartre's, they can find no exit from their self-enclosed worlds.

Moravia's work thus provided a powerful and early exploration of the modern condition. Equally significant for Italian literature, it did so in the novel form. Italy was known as the land of poets: Dante, Petrarch, Ludovico Ariosto, and Torquato Tasso. In 1929, the Italian novel was barely one hundred years old. Moravia had attempted to write this novel as a tragedy rather than as prose fiction, and many of these dramatic elements remained in the final version. For example, it relied heavily on dialogue and monologue, and it adhered closely to Aristotle's unities of time and place, with the locale confined to three houses in Rome and the action unfolding over a period of forty-eight hours. By choosing to use the novel rather than a more classical genre, however, Moravia encouraged others to adopt that mode as well and so impelled Italian fiction toward its important place in world literature.

*Sources for Further Study*

Kibler, Louis. "Imagery as Expression: Moravia's *Gli indifferenti*," in *Italica*. XLIX (1972), pp. 315-334.

Pedroni, Peter N. "Playing at Living: Form and Content in Moravia's *Gli indifferenti*," in *Perspectives on Contemporary Literature*. VI (1980), pp. 104-109.

Radcliff-Umstead, Douglas. "Moravia's Indifferent Puppets," in *Symposium*. XXIV (1970), pp. 44-54.
Ross, Joan, and Donald Freed. *The Existentialism of Alberto Moravia*, 1972.

*Joseph Rosenblum*

# TITAN
## A Romance

*Author:* Jean Paul (Johann Paul Friedrich Richter, 1763-1825)
*Type of plot:* Romance
*Time of plot:* Unspecified
*Locale:* Italy and the mythical principalities of Hohenfliess and Haarhaar in Germany
*First published: Titan*, 1800-1803, 4 volumes; (English translation, 1862)

Principal characters:

>ALBANO, the young Prince of Hohenfliess, who is approaching manhood ignorant of his parentage but following the dictates of his assumed father
>JULIENNE, his twin sister, who is reared apart from him and is unknown to him
>SCHOPPE, his resident tutor, companion, and friend
>DON GASPARD, a knight, Albano's assumed father, who is intent on joining his family to the royal line
>LINDA, Gaspard's daughter, who is reared with Albano and later falls in love with him
>LUIGI, Albano's older brother, the crown prince, a degenerate
>WEHRFRITZ, a landscape architect who rears Albano
>ALBINE AND RABETTE, Wehrfritz's wife and daughter
>LIANE VON FROULAY, the daughter of the prime minister of Hohenfliess, Albano's beloved
>ROQUAIROL, her brother, Albano's sworn friend, who is in love with Linda
>IDOINE, the Princess of Haarhaar, a double of Liane

## The Novel

*Titan* recounts, in four volumes, and with numerous shifts backward and forward in time, the rearing of Albano, the Prince of Hohenfliess, from childhood to his coming into his rightful inheritance as a man. The recounting, however, is far from clear or plausible, even in summary. The reader first meets him when, following his education *in absentia*, during which he has been forbidden to return to his native city of Pestitz, he has just been summoned to join his supposed father, Don Gaspard, whom he has never seen. He has been reared by Wehrfritz, an elderly landscape architect, who has given him free rein to pursue his own interests; this has been encouraged by Schoppe, an Italian vagabond, who has been appointed Albano's tutor by Don Gaspard. Schoppe's zany and somewhat cynical preference for small, concrete satisfactions over grandiose ideals has helped to temper Albano's tendency toward dreamy extravagance. Nevertheless, Albano has become an extremely romantic, oversensitive, intensely passionate young man.

An episode early in the novel discloses both this condition and Jean Paul's thematic strategy. Albano and his friends travel by boat to Isola Bella in Lago Maggiore, a site of incredible natural beauty. Albano lies in the boat with his eyes closed while his friends describe the splendor that he is missing. A gradual approach is not for him. He suspends the experience until he can open his eyes at the moment of peak intensity, so that he can be flooded with total ecstasy. At this point, he is a magnet of passionate longing for union with being, in part because he has been deprived of a father.

Albano's long-awaited reunion with his father takes place under mysterious circumstances. Don Gaspard is remote and aloof; he has come to escort Albano back to Pestitz, but he sheds no light on the motives behind his exile or of his reasons for ending it so abruptly. (Albano later learns that the old Prince of Hohenfliess and his wife—Albano's real father and mother—have just died.) Moreover, a series of apparitions, illusions, and disembodied voices begin to surround Albano's life, all apparently directing him to prepare for a fateful encounter with the lover he has long sought in his dreams. These culminate in the apparition of her head (a wax bust, in reality) emerging from the waters of Lago Maggiore, during which an invisible voice intones, "Love the ever fair one; I will help you find her." Albano suspects that someone is staging these illusions to manipulate him, but he has no idea why.

At any rate, the apparent hallucinations remind him of his dream love, a girl on whom he has never set eyes, Liane von Froulay, the daughter of the prime minister of Hohenfliess. He is similarly infatuated with Roquairol, Liane's brother, with whom at an early age he shared a fencing and dancing master. This master praised the brother and sister so extravagantly that Albano feels that they are engraved in his heart. One story about Roquairol particularly impresses him. That young gallant had attended a costume ball in the character of Johann Wolfgang von Goethe's Werther; there he had met and fallen violently in love with Linda, the daughter of Don Gaspard, who was dressed as Lotte, Werther's beloved. She rejected his love, so he seized a pistol and shot himself in the head, just as Werther did, succeeding, however, only in wounding himself in the ear. Nevertheless, his spectacular daring impresses Albano.

The two do not meet until several years later. Still, Albano has remained so impressed that he resigns all claim to Linda in deference to his sworn friend. They become inseparable; Roquairol joins Albano at Blumenbuhl, where Liane has also taken up residence. This is the happiest period of Albano's life, for Liane proves to be everything that he has dreamed, and Roquairol pursues Rabette, the innocent daughter of Wehrfritz. The two couples spend an idyllic summer; Liane's formerly fragile health—her vision is particularly delicate—improves. This happy scene, however, soon shatters, since it does not fit in with Gaspard's machinations. He has Liane informed of Albano's true identity, whereupon she realizes that she cannot aspire to royalty. Without giving Albano a reason, she breaks off relations. His response is, understandably, one of anger. Brokenhearted, she begins to suffer physically: Her eyesight fails, and she dies.

At this, Albano, feeling somehow responsible, suffers a breakdown. To relieve him, his tutor brings Idoine, the Princess of Haarhaar, to his sickbed. An almost exact double of Liane, Idoine impersonates her and is able to persuade Albano that he is forgiven. He revives, only to be struck down again by Roquairol's confession that he has seduced and then abandoned Rabette.

At this point, Gaspard summons him to the reunion, and Albano's mysterious apparitions begin again. Still, Gaspard does not bring Albano back to Pestitz; instead, he sends him to Rome, where Albano becomes intoxicated with the past grandeur of the empire and dedicates himself to recovering that glory and bringing the ideal of individual freedom to fruition. As part of this, he plans to join France's Great Revolution. In the meantime, he encounters his older brother, Luigi, the crown prince, in Rome. To his disappointment, Luigi has degenerated, in the hands of an agent of the Prince of Haarhaar, into a rake and a sot, unfit for leadership of a state. Finally, in Ischia, Albano rejoins his twin sister Julienne, from whom he had been separated since birth. Linda is with her, and he realizes that Linda is the incarnation of the love apparitions that he had previously experienced. She possesses all the qualities of body, intellect, and spirit that he has longed for in a woman. Gaspard's plot seems to be working: He is on the verge of uniting his house with that of the royal family.

Now Gaspard finally brings Albano, Linda, and Roquairol to Pestitz, where the stage seems set for Albano's accession. Gaspard, however, has not taken full account of the human factors in his plan. Linda proves intractable; her passions demand a romantic liaison with Albano, not a conventional marriage. These passions make her fair game for Roquairol's lust. Seizing on her night blindness and the similarity of his voice to Albano's, he sets up an assignation with her in the very same park in which Albano and he had earlier sworn eternal friendship. She spends the night with him, thinking he is Albano. The following night, Roquairol stages a play in the park, in which he takes the lead; in the final act, he actually commits suicide. Linda, considering herself Roquairol's widow, leaves with her father, whose plots have come to nothing. Disconsolate, Albano visits the tomb of Liane, where he once again meets Idoine. He recognizes now that she is the woman of whom he has dreamed. Like him, she is an heiress; like him, she is intelligent and dedicated to the welfare of her subjects. Further, she has created a model Edenic estate for them to nurture and enjoy. Since Luigi has died, Albano finally comes into his own, marries Idoine, and unites their thrones.

## The Characters

Jean Paul's characters have been controversial ever since the first publication of *Titan*. Some viewed the characters as the most sublime embodiments of idealized human nature; others found them incredible, strained, and implausible, both too grotesque and too abstract to be believable. That division has persisted: Modern critics either praise Jean Paul for the nobility and intensity of his creations or damn him for his distortions and exaggerations. Even his admirers note the inexplicable gap between his high critical celebrity and his lack of readership. Some of this can be attributed to the difficulty of his style; yet that has not proved to be a handicap to even the greatest writers, including William Shakespeare.

The dilemma can be resolved in part by recognizing certain qualities of Jean Paul's period and certain consequences of his central themes. First, his era. Jean Paul was an almost exact contemporary of Sir Walter Scott and Lord Byron. Like them, he seized on the larger-than-life possibilities that seemed implicit in the critical and political theories of the revolutionary phase of Romanticism. He, too, suffered from the waning of those ideals in later, more cynical periods. Like these other authors, Jean Paul ceased to appeal to the common reader, for whom extravagance of any kind became increasingly out of fashion.

Second, his themes require a unique manner of characterization. Jean Paul's aim was to use words and images in order to set the imagination free, to release it from material bonds and enter the sphere of eternity, where it naturally belonged. To achieve that, he set everything in his novels into tumultuous motion and emotion, as if images and characters could then shake themselves free. Thus, all the characters exhibit "Titanic" energy. One result of this technique is that characters who seem very different at the outset appear fundamentally alike in the end.

Thus all the characters are intentionally overstated. Albano's insistence on intense experience requires him to be drenched with feeling. In fact, all the main characters are "Titans": Liane is the idealist of feeling; Linda requires the passion of defying convention; Roquairol is the consummate dramatist of the self; Gaspard is the manipulator, using others as puppets to his ends; and Schoppe is both a cynical opportunist and a philosopher abstracted from life. Each has to learn to temper this Titanism; failure to do so brings loss, death, or both.

## Themes and Meanings

Characterization leads directly to theme in *Titan*, for Jean Paul saw both as means to the same aesthetic end. In part, this fusion of theme and characterization results from his appropriation and oversimplification of Johann Gottlieb Fichte's theory of the absolute ego. As he rephrased these ideas, Jean Paul began to visualize existence as an arena in which voracious egos collided; unless some means of reconciling them evolved, he saw them as either inevitably destroying one another and themselves or withdrawing into the total isolation of the self.

*Titan* is an attempt to reveal the consequences of this fusion; the novel determines both the maturation of Albano and the fates of the other characters. Albano learns the necessity of curbing his passions before they threaten the freedom of others. Similarly, all the others suffer from their failures to learn and practice such restraints; even Schoppe, who understands the situation as well as anyone in the novel, finds himself finally overwhelmed by the recognition that no one else can share his suffering, that in the end he is alone. Only Idoine seems to escape this black hole of egoism, and she is the least individualized character in the novel.

At the conclusion, the novel itself seems to contradict this vision, for it presents little hope of individual escape from this welter of conflicting egos. Few survive the inevitable collisions. That Albano and Idoine do not collide similarly results from her apparent sacrifice of her personality in order to rescue and rehabilitate his. Further, although the other characters seem to exhibit profound differences in the beginning, by the end all have become projections of the same personality. Each is mired at the center of a self-directed and self-contained universe, with no chance of communicating with or entering anyone else's. Thus Albano and Roquairol start out at opposite extremes: one a believer, the other an atheist; one an introvert, the other an extrovert; and one private, the other public. Yet in the end, neither seems capable of believing anything beyond what is created by the self. Albano reflects at the very conclusion that he is finally left alone with himself, just as everyone else is.

*Critical Context*

Jean Paul has perhaps suffered more from the vicissitudes of literary fame than any other author, and *Titan* reflects that more than any of his other works. It was widely celebrated in his lifetime as a masterwork, a monument of genius; yet it has since suffered the ignominy of silence. Even among the Germans, *Titan* seems more notorious than beloved; everyone knows about it, but very few read it.

In many respects, this is unfortunate, for the novel is enormous, rich in wit, wordplay, puns, poetic imagery, subtle prose rhythms, and brilliantly phrased descriptions. Further, it catches and reflects the imagination of the time in depth and with fascinating insights. Jean Paul himself more than once referred to it as a kind of opera, and it certainly has the grandeur, splendor, multiple-phased action, and overlayered texture of opera. It has also been strikingly influential: The great Victorian Thomas Carlyle modeled much of his style on Jean Paul and borrowed many images and ideas from him. In turn, Carlyle directly influenced the styles and views of Robert Browning,

Charles Dickens, Ralph Waldo Emerson, and Henry David Thoreau. These authors will remain a lasting tribute to the influence of Jean Paul and his *Titan*.

*Sources for Further Study*
Benham, G. F. "Jean Paul on the Education of a Prince," in *Neophilologus*. LX (1976), pp. 551-559.
Carlyle, Thomas. *Jean Paul Friedrich Richter*, 1827.
Davies, M. L. "Some Aspects of the Theme of Representation and Reality in the Works of Jean Paul," in *German Life and Letters*. XXX (1976), pp. 1-15.
Smeed, John W. *Jean Paul's "Dreams,"* 1966.
_____ . "Surrealist Features in Jean Paul's Art," in *German Life and Letters*. XVIV (1965), pp. 26-33.

*James Livingston*

# TO THE LAND OF THE CATTAILS

*Author:* Aharon Appelfeld (1932-    )
*Type of plot:* Allegory
*Time of plot:* 1938-1940
*Locale:* En route between Austria and Bukovina, a region in the border area
  between Romania and the Ukraine, now Russia
*First published:* 1986

> *Principal characters:*
> TONI STRAUSS, née Rosenfeld, a Jewish woman returning to
>   her birthplace after a seventeen-year absence
> RUDI STRAUSS, her son by August Strauss, a Gentile
> ARNA, a thirteen-year-old Jewish girl who saves Rudi's life

*The Novel*

*To the Land of the Cattails* describes the two-year journey of Toni Strauss
and her son Rudi Strauss from Austria to Dratscincz in Bukovina, a region in
the border area between Romania and the Ukraine, now Russia. Related by
a narrator who reveals Toni's thoughts, the story of the protagonists' meta-
morphoses is told by means of episodic events that occur both before and
during the allegorical journey from nationalistic assimilation to strong Jewish
self-identification.

Made possible by a legacy willed to Toni by her final lover, an old man, the
journey is prompted by Toni's desire to see her parents, whom she has not
seen since she eloped with August Strauss seventeen years earlier, and by her
desire to prevent her son from becoming like his callously brutal and abusive
father, who divorced Toni after three years of marriage and saw his son only
once.

Although Toni has not been an attentive mother because her extraordinary beauty brought her many lovers with whom she has spent her time,
Rudi loves her deeply. His education in the Austrian *Gymnasium*, however,
leads Rudi to disparage his mother's lack of knowledge and encourages him
to think like his Austrian peers, whom he resembles in appearance and behavior. Not until his last years at the *Gymnasium* does Rudi learn that to be a
Jew is to be despised. The journey, then, affords mother and son the opportunity to learn more about each other as they discuss Judaism and values,
and Rudi discovers that although Toni is a "non-believer," ironically, she is
"ready to die" for her faith.

Each encounter with other travelers, innkeepers, and guests expands
Rudi's perceptions of being Jewish, especially as he notes how differently the
common people react to him because of his handsome, tall, Aryan appearance as compared to the way they react toward his mother's beautiful but

stereotypically Jewish appearance. Toni is both pleased and frightened by her son's Austrian bearing and behavior. When he is strongly self-confident and physically aggressive against those who insult Toni's Jewishness and when he shows none of the Jewish restraint bred by centuries of anti-Semitism, she is pleased. Yet when he displays other similarly non-Jewish characteristics such as a fascination with horses, gambling, womanizing, drinking, and carousing, she is frightened that she will lose him. Nevertheless, Toni wants her son to be Jewish. As she tells Jews in one inn along their way, "I brought my son here to learn Jewishness—he needs it very badly."

The journey lasts much longer than the distance warrants and as the pair near Toni's birthplace, the land of the cattails bordering the river Prut, Toni becomes critically ill with typhus in the town of Buszwyn. In the three months it takes for Toni to recover and for the weather to become suitable for travel, Rudi's Jewish veneer begins to rub off. He forgets his mother's condition and makes love to a peasant girl who leaves him after being given an expensive gift: a very valuable bracelet belonging to Toni. Yet the illness appears to have wrought positive changes in Toni. She becomes happy and enjoys being the center of attention and gaiety until spring allows their departure. Whereas Rudi was accustomed to setting tests of values for Toni, Toni begins to set tests for Rudi and "a quiet joy dwelt in her face." Her composure, self-assurance, and resolve to return are strengthened by her illness. She gains new insight into her purpose and finalizes her determination to return home. All the while, evidence of escalating hatred and violence against Jews surrounds them.

Unexpectedly, as Rudi nears the land of the cattails, physically and mentally he becomes less and less Jewish. Toni fears that bringing her son home with her was a poor idea—that he is not ready for the epiphany:

> Deep inside herself she knew he wouldn't understand. Perhaps it was good that he didn't understand. The suffering of the Jews was far from glorious. That night the word *goy* rose up from within her. . . . Her father would sometimes, though only occasionally, use that word to indicate hopeless obtuseness.

Toni is right. When they are only two hours away from her parents' home, they stop at an unpleasant inn and remain there for weeks as Rudi drinks himself into stupor daily and finally proclaims: "The Jews are the root of all evil. . . . I hate the Jews. They are merchants and thieves."

Finally, Toni leaves her son sleeping, hires a wagon, and goes to her home. After two days, Rudi leaves to find his mother, and as he travels he thinks about the even more militaristic Austrian education he wished he had had, and he longs for the company of a woman. The two-hour journey takes him a full day, and at Dratscincz he learns that all Jews were deported earlier that day to the railroad station. Instead of starting immediately, he goes to sleep and reaches the station the next morning—only to find that the train has already left and that the next station is two hours away. He eats, smokes, and goes to sleep for an hour before leaving, arriving at the next station to see masses of Jews herded together by police. Making only a desultory attempt to find his mother, Rudi watches the train fill with Jews, sure that his mother "could not be among those wretches." Rudi continues to wander from station to station, getting drunk, hitting and being hit, seeing Jews running away from the stations and furtively dissolving into the forests, but the police and peasants accept him as one of their own.

Finally, one evening Rudi meets thirteen-year-old Arna, a hungry, frightened girl who has been in hiding ever since her family was taken away from the station as she sought water for her mother. They begin to travel together, and Arna tells Rudi about the Jewish way of life, one his mother had not lived. They wander across the countryside, seeing plundered, abandoned Jewish homes. With the onset of winter, Rudi becomes mortally ill and feverish, and they take shelter in an abandoned home. Arna's innocent, persevering determination to save Rudi is joined by her belief in God, and as the arrival of spring coincides with the end of their meager food supply, Rudi recovers enough for them to leave the cold house and ask for shelter in a common inn.

Demanding to see Rudi's papers, the innkeeper cannot believe that Rudi is Austrian, and the peasants are suspicious of him and roar with laughter at the pair, in sharp contrast to the former unquestioning acceptance of Rudi's heritage. Arna's innocent belief and the cleansing fire of prolonged illness as Rudi "wrestled with the angel of death" have led to Rudi's physical and spiritual conversion to Judaism. Rudi "lost his former essence. Astonishment filled his soul." Lengthy travel leads them to a train station where Arna and Rudi eagerly await being picked up and brought together with their people. At last they see it:

> It was an old locomotive, drawing two old cars—the local, apparently. It went from station to station, scrupulously gathering up the remainder.

*The Characters*

There are only three major characters in *To the Land of the Cattails*, and in most of the book only two are present, Toni and Rudi Strauss. Their characters can best be revealed by relating their changes as the book progresses.

Toni Rosenfeld Strauss represents a character type who, before the pre-Holocaust years, envisioned herself as an Austrian first and a Jew only by a coincidence of birth, which she fully acknowledges but from which she dissociates herself. Although reared by traditionally Jewish parents, she eloped at seventeen with August, a handsome, intelligent, kind-seeming Austrian engineer who "remove[d] his mask" as soon as they reached the city, where he beat her, even though she was pregnant. Divorced by August when she was twenty and had a child, she was too guilty to return to her parents' home, but because she is beautiful and could attract a series of lovers who gave her money, she was able to survive, even without an education. She has been tormented by memories of her parents for seventeen years and is torn between what she knows she should do for her son and what she does do. Despite her avowals of being a "non-believer," she sees marked differences between Jews and non-Jews and determines that she must do what is best for her son—make him a Jew by going on a pilgrimage to her family and place of birth.

The allegorical pilgrimage is very dangerous and the goal is elusive, because Toni is not a dedicated pilgrim, as a result of her internal ambivalence about Jews. She sees her people as compassionate, kind, and intelligent, a contrast to the brutality, drunkenness, gaming, and coarseness of the "goyim." Yet she also sees her people as physically small, weak, and timid, unwilling to stand up for their rights or even their lives, and she magnifies the flaws of a few and applies them to the whole. Therefore, she is proud that her son has Aryan features and can be physically and vocally strong in standing up for his rights while, at the same time, she deplores his father's heritage of drinking, gambling, womanizing, and disliking Jews. Before Toni can witness her son's change, she must first change—one purpose of her pilgrimage, although she does not know it.

With each group of people and each instance of increasingly violent anti-Semitism that the travelers encounter, they are tested for commitment, and the narrator records their reactions, almost as if they were being kept on a scoreboard. Toni's initial delight with her easy acceptance by non-Jews is progressively tempered by her increasing awareness of their deep hostility toward Jews.

When Toni falls ill with typhus and barely recovers, her self-imposed veil of intentional disregard for the seriousness of this hostility appears to be lifted, and she views her position among non-Jews more realistically. She has been tested and has passed; Rudi, however, does not pass the test, because of his coarse behavior during his mother's illness. With this episode, the role of mother and son are reversed: Instead of Rudi testing his mother, Toni tests her son, as she watches carefully to see how he handles the obstacles that they meet during the pilgrimage.

The next major episode, their experiences at an inn run by a fine Jewish woman—Rosemarie—who had just been killed for no reason other than her Jewishness, is an even more difficult test for Toni. Toni reaches out to help others and feels herself as close to the "lost people" grieving for Rosemarie as if they were her brothers, and she reveals that she has regained the belief she once lacked as she prophetically states that she believes in miracles. Because his mother is praised and respected by others, Rudi gains a new respect for Toni and regrets his "many past years of contempt" for her. Yet he himself does not change; his last thoughts before they leave the inn are a "murky hatred" for a man whom Rudi senses had "lusted for his mother grossly."

As their trip continues, Toni becomes more fearful of non-Jews. Yet even as she continuously tests Rudi and notes his continuing failures, Toni remains dependent upon her non-Jewish son who, instead of becoming more Jewish as a result of his pilgrimage, looks, acts, smells, and takes his pleasure more in the way of the peasants.

With Toni's extended stay at an inn two hours from her home, her unrealized pilgrimage for commitment culminates, although she loses the battle for her son. She watches Rudi take on the musculature, eating habits, and the alien peasant redness on the nape of his neck, and she even experiences his brutality as he hits her for asking him to leave the inn. Realizing that Rudi is beyond her help, she uses the strength gained from her pilgrimage, sets out alone for her parents' home, and disappears into the freight cars of the Holocaust.

Toni's history and wavering ambiguity up until the very end of her pilgrimage are neither strong nor worthy enough to overcome the heritage that she gave her son when she married August Strauss. She could enable only herself to be reborn into commitment. It falls to the lot of the third major character, Arna, an innocent, naïve girl who believes in the God of Israel because of her mother's teachings and in spite of her father's denials, to lead Rudi to the Jewishness that Toni believed he so needed.

Ultimately, it is the religious pilgrimage interrupted by her serious illness that restores Toni's self-worth and Jewish identification. Yet it is the same religious pilgrimage, also interrupted by Rudi's serious illness, that allows the miracle of the girl, Arna, to effect Rudi's conversion. Both mother and son are reborn into Judaism, but ironically, it is just this rebirth that leads them, as well as the miracle-giver, Arna, into the Holocaust.

*Themes and Meanings*

The overriding theme of *To the Land of the Cattails* is a self-identification and return to Judaism that ultimately leads to the Holocaust. Through the process of a literal and allegorical pilgrimage through bitter tests of commitment and back to the roots of faith and childhood innocence, rebirth and introspection enable the characters to discover their noblest essence—their Judaism. Recurrent are the themes of an almost elemental and omnipresent anti-Semitism among non-Jews and a recognition of equally elemental differences between Jewish and non-Jewish attitudes and behaviors.

As in many of Aharon Appelfeld's works, forests symbolize freedom, as evidenced by Toni's ability to converse more easily with her son as they travel through wooded terrain and also by the lack of inhibitions that allows Rudi to display his peasantlike characteristics that continue into his later actions.

Additionally, forests allow hidden routes to Jews escaping the train stations and deportation. Also, what people eat affords insight into their characters; thus, as Rudi loses his Jewish veneer, his attraction to heavy food and drink renders him insensitive to the danger his mother is enduring, as he gluts himself with food and then falls asleep.

Stylistically, the language is simple and direct and suits the story well. Although the reader is not required to untangle difficult allusions or unravel complex interwoven subplots, the language and descriptive imagery of simile encourage reflection and expansion.

*Critical Context*

*To the Land of the Cattails* is representative of Appelfeld's "hopeful" work, which began with *Tor-ha-pela'ot* (1978; *The Age of Wonders*, 1981) and includes *Kutonet veha-pasim* (1983; *Tzili: The Story of a Life*, 1983). The hopeful work is characterized by the presence of youth and by the indication that the return to home and to tradition and the finding of the true secrets of Jewishness permit the survival of youth into the post-Holocaust period. An interesting difference between *To the Land of the Cattails* and the other two noted above is the absence of a post-Holocaust epilogue. Yet Appelfeld leaves the reader with the unmistakable hope that Rudi and Arna, young, vigorous, and secure in their Jewishness, will somehow survive the ensuing Holocaust years and share what they have learned with a future generation. It is almost as if the author, emulating the films of the 1980's, has left an opening for a sequel.

*To the Land of the Cattails* also is noteworthy in its stronger echoes of the images and motifs of the earlier novels. Travel, used effectively, but as an incidental motif in earlier novels, becomes a major theme here, pervading the entire novel and leading almost hypnotically to the other grotesque travel image, the Holocaust train. The forest is used not only as a symbol of refuge but also as a signal of the coming of peace and as an interlude of safe haven. Rudi and Arna are epitomes of the abandoned child, and Toni is the lost mother of Appelfeld's earlier works. The theme of intermarriage, for the first time, is tied to the protagonist in an Appelfeld novel, and the ugly father image is attached to the Gentile male spouse. Although the author is slightly kinder in his portrayal of prewar Jewish society than he is in other works, a somewhat negative portrayal persists. In this novel, Appelfeld upholds his reputation as a chronicler of the Holocaust who studiously avoids its mention while brilliantly forcing the reader to think his own haunted thoughts about that period.

*Sources for Further Study*

Alter, Robert. "Mother and Son, Lost in a Continent," in *The New York Times Book Review*. XCI (November 2, 1986), p. 1.

Coffin, Edna Amir. "Appelfeld's Exceptional Universe: Harmony out of Chaos," in *Hebrew Studies*. XXIV (1983), pp. 85-98.
Lewis, Stephen. "Aharon Appelfeld," in *Art out of Agony*, 1984.
*Library Journal*. Review. CXII (January, 1987), p. 54.
Yudkin, Leon I. "Appelfeld's Vision of the Past," in *Escape into Siege*, 1974.

*June H. Schlessinger*

# THE TOBIAS TRILOGY

*Author:* Pär Lagerkvist (1891-1974)
*Type of plot:* Allegory
*Time of plot:* The Middle Ages
*Locale:* Mediterranean Europe and the Near East
*First published: Pilgrimen,* 1966: *Ahasverus död,* 1960 (*The Death of Ahasuerus,* 1962); *Pilgrim på havet,* 1962 (*Pilgrim at Sea,* 1964); *Det heliga landet,* 1964 (*The Holy Land,* 1966)

> *Principal characters:*
> TOBIAS, the pilgrim
> AHASUERUS, the Wandering Jew
> DIANA, Tobias' consort
> GIOVANNI, a defrocked priest who becomes Tobias' companion

*The Novels*

The Tobias trilogy, to which Pär Lagerkvist gave the title *Pilgrimen* (the pilgrim), is a continuation of two earlier novels, *Barabbas* (1950; English translation, 1951) and *Sibyllan* (1956; *The Sibyl,* 1958). In those two novels, Barabbas and Ahasuerus, the Wandering Jew in *The Sibyl,* both wander away from the scene of Jesus' crucifixion in quest of spiritual peace. Each, in his own way, is seeking death; more precisely, each is seeking to have truly lived, so that he can truly die. Their quest is continued in the persons of Giovanni and Tobias in the Tobias trilogy. Variously and at different personal levels, Barabbas, Ahasuerus, and Giovanni succeed in the quest. Tobias alone succeeds transcendently and seemingly in full. Together, the five novels constitute a pentalogy or, since the pentalogy begins and ends in the context of the three crosses on Calvary, a crucifixion cycle.

Ahasuerus in both *The Sibyl* and *The Death of Ahasuerus* is, apart from the second title, not named; he is called simply "the stranger" or is referred to only as a man. Like Barabbas, he has been caught in an association with Christ, which has propelled him into a lifeless existence of wandering. For each man, the wandering ends in a death implicit with having lived, a death that proves to have been the object of a troubled quest.

In *The Sibyl,* Ahasuerus moves westward from Palestine to Greece. At Delphi, he meets the Sibyl, a priestess whose parents committed her life to the service of the temple god, a composite of Dionysus, whose spirit is manifest in goats, and Apollo, whose spirit is manifest in snakes. She relates to Ahasuerus her infidelity to the god in her attempt to love a mortal man. The man was consequently destroyed after the Sibyl was impregnated not by her human lover, as she had at first thought, but by the god. The child to which she gave birth, in isolation and attended only by goats, is an idiot (in the original Greek sense, a private person), a solipsistic son of God. This son, changelessly smiling and still having the face of a child, although now gray-haired, sits in the presence of his mother and Ahasuerus but disappears unnoticed by them while his mother tells her story and, like the Palestinian Son of God, ascends to his Father. Ahasuerus then continues his wandering.

The Tobias trilogy begins with Ahasuerus' meeting Tobias in an inn that accommodates pilgrims who travel to the Holy Land. Ahasuerus appears to have moved physically farther west from Greece to, presumably, Italy and temporally further from the age of primitive Christianity to the era of cathedrals and conventional pilgrimages to the Holy Land (that is, from the latter half of the first century to no earlier than the fourth century).

Tobias is an unusual and very individualistic pilgrim. His individualism is stressed in *Pilgrim at Sea*, the second novel of the trilogy, as Giovanni tells him, "You are making a pilgrimage to suit yourself and in your own way" and as he himself decides that it is best "to choose oneself, just as one is, to dare to be just as one is without disapproving of oneself." Tobias was once a scholar, soldier, and criminal. His determination to become a pilgrim was forged by his chancing upon a recently deceased pilgrim, an old woman who bore the stigmata. When Ahasuerus meets him, Tobias is accompanied by the old woman's dog. Also in Tobias' company is a young woman whom he has raped and made his consort and to whom he has given the name "Diana" because of her hunting prowess and her affinity with nature. Diana, herself proficient with a bow and arrow, steps in the path of an arrow that is aimed at Tobias and saves his life at the cost of her own. The arrow was shot by unseen hands, possibly those of bandits. Ahasuerus, a witness to Diana's sacrifice, suggests to Tobias that the arrow was actually intended for Diana and was aimed at Tobias so that Diana could find a happy death in sacrifice.

Ahasuerus, having spent two days and two nights with Tobias and Diana (during which Tobias, in a moment of great anger, kicked his dog to death, and Diana later took the arrow into her heart) continues to accompany Tobias for an indefinite number of days until they reach the sea. At the port, Tobias learns that the pilgrim ship has already sailed, and he gives all of his criminally acquired money to the captain of a pirate ship, who falsely promises him passage to the Holy Land.

After the departure of Tobias and another indefinite period of time, Ahasuerus dies in the presence of an angelic lay brother. His last moments are marked by his realization that the crucified Jesus was his brother and not his god. He realizes this through an understanding that God is an obstacle to the divine truth for which every human being longs and by a symbolic blaze of radiant light. *The Death of Ahasuerus* begins with Ahasuerus' entering the pilgrims' inn in retreat from shafts of lightning and ends with his finding the peace of death in an embrace of sunlight. His thought toward the close of the second day with Tobias was: "How great a happiness it must be to be able to die. That is the land for which one must really long . . . the land of Death, the holy land. . . ."

Tobias becomes the "pilgrim at sea" on board the pirate ship, whose Italian crew includes Giovanni. *Pilgrim at Sea* is chiefly the story of Giovanni, to whom Tobias listens as Ahasuerus listened to the Sibyl. Like the Sibyl, Giovanni was committed to God by his parents, or at least by his mother, who named him after the disciple whom Jesus loved and who directed him unalterably toward priesthood.

As a priest, Giovanni fell in love with a woman whose confession of her extramarital love inflamed him with desire for her. His efforts to consummate his love physically were successful, and during their adulterous liaison, he learned that she kept the image of her true beloved in a locket. Giovanni stole the locket shortly before the public exposure of their affair and his consequent defrocking and excommunication. The locket proved to be empty. Giovanni kept it and wore it about his neck as his most prized possession. He is still wearing it as he recounts his history to Tobias, and Tobias views it as a symbol of the human longing which can never be satisfied but without which humans cannot live. Tobias concludes that the highest and holiest in life is perhaps only a dream that cannot endure reality but that exists nevertheless: that "true love exists and the Holy Land exists, only we cannot get to it; that we are perhaps only on our way to it, only pilgrims at sea."

The journeying in *Pilgrim at Sea* is generally eastward. At one point, the pirate ship docks alongside the pilgrim ship that Tobias missed and that is continuing en route from its western Mediterranean port to Palestine. Tobias, the individualist, rejects the opportunity to transfer to the pilgrim ship. He chooses not to part from Giovanni, not to reach the Holy Land "in their way." He will continue his pilgrimage to the Holy Land not on the pilgrim ship, but on a pirate ship headed elsewhere.

In the last novel of the trilogy, *The Holy Land*, many years appear to have passed. Giovanni, now blind and useless aboard the pirate ship, has been marooned on a bleak coast and Tobias has chosen to stay with him. The two men make a habitation out of an ancient temple that has fallen into ruins. The coastland is probably a geographical abstraction. Lagerkvist makes no specific geographical references, apart from "the Holy Land," in the entire trilogy, and "the Holy Land" is treated both literally and figuratively. Wherever or whatever it is, the coast lies below a range of hills and is inhabited only by ageless herders of sheep and goats. They are gentle and kind and help the castoffs. They know nothing about the Holy Land or about any former use of the ruined temple.

The episodes that constitute the novel are intimations of religious mystery. Tobias witnesses the herdsmen's adoration of an infant in a hut. The baby boy, whose mother died shortly after giving birth, has been brought down from the mountains by his father. Tobias excavates the icon of an archaic god, presumably the god whose priestess the Sibyl was. Vultures swarm over the coastland as sheep and goats die off in a plague. A bald, bird-faced man takes augury from the opened breast of a young vulture while its heart still beats; later, he sacrifices a lamb on the altar of the archaic god. A woman carrying a poisonous snake in a willow basket visits Tobias and Giovanni. She removes Giovanni's locket and, as he then finds peace in death, she places it about the neck of Tobias. The infant is discovered to have died, and Tobias recognizes the cause of death as a snakebite. The plague ends, and the vultures depart.

In the concluding episode, Tobias ascends the mountains and finds himself in an "eveningland" of perpetual twilight. He comes to the three crosses upon which Barabbas once gazed; they are now empty, and he ponders the inseparability of the two crosses for the evil men and the one for the good man. Later, he sees an old man staring into a dark river and, as he reaches the river, discovers that the old man is himself. Still later, he drinks from a pure wellspring and knows that he will never thirst again. Finally, he rests by a wooden image of the Virgin Mary, its carved garment painted blue. He has a visionary conversation with her, during which he revives the long-suppressed memory of his childhood sweetheart, whom he impregnated and who drowned herself, wearing the blue dress she had made. Her suicide followed the abortion imposed upon her by Tobias' wealthy parents. The Virgin Mary is transformed into this blue-dressed sweetheart; she discloses her undying love for Tobias and removes the locket from his neck. As she places it on her own neck, she becomes radiant, and Tobias dies in great peace, having found in his own heart and in death the holy land for which he has longed and to which he has been a pilgrim.

### The Characters

Each of Lagerkvist's principal characters is given a symbolic dimension in the evocation of Judaeo-Christian tradition or Greco-Roman myth. Tobias evokes the son of Tobit and Anna in the Book of Tobit. The biblical Tobias is a pilgrim to Ecbatana who is accompanied by a dog and the angel Raphael. His father has become blind. The mission to Ecbatana is successful: The divine Raphael not only ensures the success but also provides the cure for Tobit's blindness. Inversely, Lagerkvist's Tobias kills his dog, is accompanied by Ahasuerus, who is cursed instead of blessed by God, and has an incurably blind father figure in Giovanni. Like certain existentialist writers, Lagerkvist takes God out of the picture and places the responsibility for human existence with humans themselves.

Ahasuerus evokes the myth of the Wandering Jew, which derives dualistically from the evil Malchus, who flouted Jesus, and the good John, Jesus' beloved disciple, who was considered by many to be immune to death until the Second Coming of his Lord. Lagerkvist sustains this dualism from the perspectives of Ahasuerus (as Malchus) and Giovanni (as John).

Diana is the Italian equivalent of the Greek goddess Artemis, whose cult in Asia Minor, particularly at Ephesus, was overcome by early Christians. In *The Death of Ahasuerus*, Diana is victimized by a man who becomes part of the growing Christian world, and in an act evocative of Jesus, she sacrifices her life to save her victimizer, whom she loves.

Giovanni is both an extension of the Wandering Jew, as noted, and a humanistic inversion of the beloved disciple John. Jesus gave his mother to John in the Gospel of John, but Giovanni's mother gave Giovanni to Jesus, from whose godhood the defrocked priest seeks to separate himself.

### Themes and Meanings

Each of the principal characters is a personification of the human longing that becomes its own satisfaction to the extent that it resists or eliminates any expectation of its being satisfied by a divine agent. Diana longs for the hunt and the wilderness life that Tobias has denied her. She dies happily in the context of the hunt as sacrificial prey to the powers that would deny Tobias the full experience of his longing. Her death is like the demise of the Greco-Roman pantheon in the advance of the Christian deity, who came to be worshipped as the end of human longing and the savior of human souls; in Lagerkvist's view, however, Jesus is the savior of human longing. Ahasuerus and Giovanni long to elude deity and to do so ultimately through death, which Ahasuerus identifies as the holy land. Tobias longs for this same holy land, but for him it is also love. Tobias' death is representative of what Martin Heidegger termed the individual's *eigenst* (literally, "ownmost") possibility. The holy land that Tobias finds is a convergence of longing and death, a convergence informed by *fullkomlig* (true or perfect) love, not the love of Christ or of any deity, but the love that Jesus exemplified.

### Critical Context

Lagerkvist was a part of the expressionist scene in Europe. He followed his compatriot August Strindberg in expressionistic drama, and he introduced the principles of cubist literature into his native Sweden. His earliest fiction and drama is expressionist. In his late work, including the Tobias trilogy, he fully developed his cubist stylistics of planar simplicity and simultaneity of multiple perspectives. His simple prose is the equivalent of the cubist painting which emphasizes its canvas as two-dimensional and makes it, as such, an instrument of linear abstraction rather than of counterfeit three-dimensional perspective. His cubist perspectives are discernible in, for example, his superimposition of the metaphysical upon the psychological and the timeless upon the temporal, his simultaneous presentations of conflicting modes of religious mystery, or his oxymora and endoxa. An example of his oxymora is Ahasuerus' mortal immortality, the herdsmen's ageless age, or Tobias' religious atheism. Lagerkvist identified himself as a "religious atheist" in *Den knutna näven* (1934; *The Clenched Fist*, 1982). An example of his endoxa, or ambiguous probability, is his frequent use of *som om* (literally "as if," the *als ob* of the philosopher Hans Vaihinger) and of questions that admit of no answer or of more than one answer, such as, "Why were there three [crosses]? Why not just one?"

The cubist simultaneity of perspectives is especially evident in Lagerkvist's superimposition of Dionysus, the goat-god, upon Apollo, the snake-god, and his juxtaposition of Dionysus-Apollo with Christ, the lamb-god. This abstract complexity is presented on a simple prose canvas and is underscored by images of goats and snakes (in *The Sibyl*) and of goats, sheep, and the snake-woman in *The Holy Land*. In *The Holy Land* again, the vultures that descend upon the dead sheep and thereby cleanse the land, the bald man's sacrifice of a lamb, and Tobias' ascent into the hills emblematically constitute humanistic and inverse abstractions from the Descent of the Dove, the Agnus Dei, and the Ascension.

*The Tobias Trilogy* may also be viewed as existentialist in its reflection of authentic individualism, its recognition of human responsibility for the meaning or essence of human life, and its preoccupation with existence and nonexistence as opposed to preoccupation with supraexistence and a heaven that is external to humankind and the human heart.

The crucifixion cycle, initiated by *Barabbas* and concluded by the Tobias trilogy, along with Lagerkvist's last novel, *Mariamne* (1967; *Herod and Mariamne*, 1968), constitutes a crystallization of Lagerkvist's literary principles and religious symbolism: The profoundly simple narratives based on classical and biblical traditions encapsulate and project an apotheosis of human longing.

*Sources for Further Study*

Cienkowska-Schmidt, Agnieszka. *Sehnsucht nach dem Heiligen Land: Eine Studie zu Pär Lagerkvists später Prosa*, 1985.
Sjöberg, Leif. *Pär Lagerkvist*, 1976.
Spector, Robert Donald. *Pär Lagerkvist*, 1973.
Swanson, Roy Arthur. "Evil and Love in Lagerkvist's Crucifixion Cycle," in *Scandinavian Studies*. XXXVIII, no. 4 (November, 1966), pp. 302-317.
Weathers, Winston. *Pär Lagerkvist: A Critical Essay*, 1968.

*Roy Arthur Swanson*

# A TOMB FOR BORIS DAVIDOVICH

*Author:* Danilo Kiš (1935-    )
*Type of plot:* Social criticism
*Time of plot:* From the 1920's to the 1970's
*Locale:* The Soviet Union and Central Europe
*First published: Grobnica za Borisa Davidoviča,* 1976 (English translation, 1978)

> *Principal characters:*
> BORIS DAVIDOVICH, a Russian revolutionary
> ÉDOUARD HERRIOT, the leader of the French Radical Socialists
> A. L. CHELYUSTNIKOV, a Russian revolutionary
> KARL TAUBE, a Hungarian revolutionary
> FEDUKIN, a secret police investigator
> BARUCH DAVID NEUMANN, a refugee from Germany and a former Jew

*The Novel*

   *A Tomb for Boris Davidovich* consists of seven loosely related stories, which could be read separately. They all share one element, however, that gives them an organic unity. The first story, "The Knife with the Rosewood Handle," takes place, for the most part, in Bukovina, a part of Romania (now part of the Soviet Union) in the 1920's and 1930's. Miksha, a handyman who "could sew on a button in ten seconds," works for a Jewish shopkeeper until he is fired for skinning a skunk in his master's yard. Afterward, Miksha becomes acquainted with a revolutionary, Aimicke, who introduces him to the underground. In their secret activity, they suspect that a police informer is in their midst. Miksha takes it upon himself to uncover and punish the traitor; he decides that the traitor is a young girl named Hanna Krzyzewska and murders her. Later, it turns out that it was Aimicke who was informing the police about the group's activities. Miksha, who has fled to the Soviet Union, is arrested and induced to confess that he worked for the Gestapo, in the process implicating twelve Russian officials, who, with Miksha, receive sentences of twenty years of hard labor.

   In the second story, "The Sow That Eats Her Farrow," a disenchanted Irishman, Gould Vershoyle, leaves his homeland in search of a better place to live. He winds up fighting for the Republicans in the Spanish Civil War. When he informs his commander of his suspicion that Moscow is masterminding the war (not knowing that his superior is a Soviet agent), Vershoyle is sent to the Soviet Union, where he perishes in the gulag in 1945.

   In "The Mechanical Lions," Édouard Herriot, the leader of the French

Radical Socialists, is intrigued by the Soviet system of government and makes a visit to the Soviet Union in order to see whether religion is suppressed there. Everything during the visit is staged, and Herriot goes home convinced that there is indeed religious freedom in the Soviet Union. The man in charge of his visit, A. L. Chelyustnikov, is later arrested and makes a false confession implicating others. After serving his sentence, he visits Lyons and signs his name in a guest book as "an admirer of the work of Édouard Herriot."

"The Magic Card Dealing" shows another European revolutionary, a Hungarian doctor named Karl Taube, who follows his political sympathies to the Soviet Union, where he is arrested and spends years in various labor camps. As a doctor, he saves the fingers of a man who cut them in order to gain his release. When this same prisoner wins a card game with another inmate, he arranges for the revenge murder of Taube by the loser.

The main story, "A Tomb for Boris Davidovich," also deals with a revolutionary who has fought against the czarist regime from his early youth. He becomes an important official during the 1920's, only to fall out of grace and land in prison, where he is mercilessly interrogated by Fedukin, a master at his trade. Davidovich is asked to sign a confession of treason and to implicate others, which he refuses to do. After attempting to commit suicide several times, he finally agrees to be shot as a traitor rather than be hanged as a common thief. He is not shot after all but is sent instead to a labor camp, where he dies in 1937 during an escape attempt.

In "Dogs and Books," Danilo Kiš goes back in time to fourteenth century France during the pogroms against the Jews. Baruch David Neumann, a refugee from Germany and a former Jew, agrees to be converted to Christianity to save his life. Later, he recants, claiming that he agreed to conversion only under duress. After changing his mind several times, finding it impossible to renounce Judaism, he perishes under mysterious circumstances.

"The Short Biography of A. A. Darmolatov" (an obscure contemporary Soviet writer) is the most incongruous story in the novel. It is not quite clear why this man is depicted—whether because he was at one time connected with Davidovich, or because he has developed mental problems trying to be a successful writer under oppressive conditions, or because he has become a medical phenomenon by developing elephantiasis. It is also the only story in which there are no victims, Jews or others, and in which no one is arrested or forced to sign an involuntary confession.

## The Characters

The main character of the novel is Boris Davidovich, a Jew and a revolutionary from the days of his early manhood. He presents a picture of the classical revolutionary: brave, resolute, bold, cool, resourceful, loyal to the cause, and blind to questioning of his ideology. It is not quite clear whether he joins the revolutionary struggle out of a sense of justice or in quest of action or adventure, but it does not matter; once he decides to participate he does so with resolution. This steadfastness may explain why Davidovich persistently resists the efforts of Fedukin to break him during the endless hours of interrogation and torture. It is symptomatic of Davidovich's character that, once it is clear that he will die, he wants to die as an honorable man who has fought tenaciously for his cause rather than as a common thief. In this sense, he epitomizes the countless revolutionaries throughout the world who are convinced they are fighting for the right cause but are stymied in their efforts. Be that as it may, Davidovich is a classic example of a fighter who pays the ultimate price unjustly.

Karl Taube is another example of a revolutionary who pays this price, but in a somewhat different way. An intellectual who joins the struggle out of a clear, rational decision to help better the world, he becomes a victim of the whims of blind fate. He too is senselessly sacrificed by the leadership, for if they had not sent him to prison for no apparent reason, he would not be in the position to be murdered by common criminals there. Taube dies as a well-meaning but somewhat naïve intellectual who tries to use reason in solving problems in a situation that is governed by passion and blind hatred.

This situation is not the same with two other characters who stand out in the novel—Chelyustnikov and Fedukin. Both serve the Revolution faithfully but with a different attitude. Chelyustnikov is a typical *aparatchik* (an organization man), who is not only unquestioningly loyal to the cause but also without any compelling intellectual reason. He does everything that the Revolution asks him to do, even when it requires of him to play the role of a fall guy. Nevertheless, one cannot escape the conclusion that he is doing it for purely opportunistic reasons or simply out of inertia. Otherwise, he would express his doubt in the righteousness of the cause, for which he has ample opportunities.

Fedukin, on the other hand, is in the revolutionary struggle for reasons that stem from the dark recesses of his character, out of his need to do evil and hurt people to satisfy his atavistic impulses. That is the only explanation for his zeal in torturing his victims, be they guilty or innocent, especially his former comrades. He is therefore a villain incarnate, without any alleviating circumstance or rational explanation.

One other character, Baruch David Neumann, deserves to be mentioned. Having lived in the fourteenth century, he has no apparent relation to the happenings of the twentieth century. Nevertheless, he suffers the same indignities and, eventually, death for a related reason—man's intolerance for people of different mind and belief.

These and the other characters, however, are only sketchily developed because the author's intention was not to create well-rounded characters but rather to show what they stand for as types.

*Themes and Meanings*

The main focus in *A Tomb for Boris Davidovich* is on revolution and the revolutionaries whose fate is a direct and inevitable outcome of the revolution. Every story in the novel is connected with this theme in one way or another. Five stories bear directly on the theme; one has a tenuous connection, while the story of Baruch David Neumann is used as a prototype for the later revolutionary zeal. It was clear that Kiš had the Bolshevik Revolution in mind when he wrote *A Tomb for Boris Davidovich*, specifically its excesses and deviations.

Kiš goes further than merely lamenting the failures of this revolution. He does not say that, if there were no excesses and deviations, everything would have been all right; he says that by its nature a revolution is "the sow that eats her farrow" and that Stalinism was the direct result of a fundamental disregard for human values. The aftermath of the Bolshevik Revolution is "darkness at noon" and the "God that failed," to use the phrases of Arthur Koestler. In developing a dogma, the Revolution has created a new religion and a new morality, to which, as to every religion, ritual sacrifices must be made. The priests of this new religion are convinced of the righteousness of their dogma and are even surprised by "this sentimental egocentricity of the accused, their pathological need to prove their own *innocence*, their own little *truths*." Instead, as Fedukin believes, "it was better that the so-called truth of a single man, one tiny organism, be destroyed than that higher interests and principles be questioned" and that "to sign a confession *for the sake of duty* was not only a logical but also a moral act, and therefore worthy of respect."

The fanatical zeal of "true believers" is not confined to this isolated historical event. In the story "Dogs and Books," the fourteenth century victim is persecuted because it is better "to slaughter one mangy sheep than to allow the whole flock to become tainted." In fact, Kiš himself has said that he was struck by many similarities between the experiences of the two Jews, Neumann and Davidovich. The inevitable conclusion, which Kiš has expressed in several works, is that if basic human rights are ignored, the result is tyranny and death. Other themes, such as the inherent sadism of many revolutionaries, the workings of the system spawned by the revolution, and the excursions into history, are minor and are used primarily to illuminate the main theme or are deliberately left undeveloped.

*Critical Context*

*A Tomb for Boris Davidovich* is a typical thesis novel and thus represents the frequent phenomenon in contemporary literature of the heavily politicized novel. It is important for the reader to know that Danilo Kiš comes from an East European country, one where occurrences similar to those in the novel have taken place. In this manner, Kiš joins several writers, such as

Aleksandr Solzhenitsyn, Vladimir Voinovich, Milan Kundera, and Josef Škvorecký, who have voiced similar concerns in their works. Kiš is less openly political than Solzhenitsyn and Voinovich, however, and more akin to Kundera. Kiš prefers to refer directly to historical and political events and to personalities and to deal with literature of facts, rather than to couch his works in tones of allegory and irony. He is direct and uncompromising when it comes to his main theses.

The novel provoked a great controversy and quickly became a literary *cause célèbre* when it appeared, not only in Yugoslavia but also abroad. Kiš was accused of plagiarism, of lifting entire passages from archives and other sources, an accusation that he was able to refute easily by pointing out that he had used the collage technique deliberately and had quoted the sources used. The controversy lasted several years and divided the literary community, involving aesthetic judgments, political considerations, and emotional reactions. In the last analysis, it was more of a political argument than anything else, for it was clear that Kiš's frontal attack on the remnants of Stalinism in Yugoslavia, adroitly couched in the depiction of a Soviet milieu, had struck sensitive nerves. The relatively free literary conditions in Yugoslavia, along with Kiš's polemic verve, carried the day for him and for his novel.

Aside from this affair, *A Tomb for Boris Davidovich* can be considered a landmark in Kiš's literary opus. It confirms his belief in literature based on fact and in the artistic treatment of nonliterary subject matter. It also marks a turning away from the personal concerns in his earlier works toward more universal themes. Much more than a political dispute, it is a testimonial to man's yearning for freedom and dignity, which, together with Kiš's artistic skill, has made this novel an important work in world literature.

*Sources for Further Study*
Czarny, Norbert. "Imaginary-Real Lives: On Danilo Kiš," in *Cross Currents*. III (1984), pp. 279-284.
Shishkoff, Serge. "Košava in a Coffee Pot," in *Cross Currents*. VI (1987), pp. 341-371.
Vitanović, Slobodan. "Thematic Unity in Danilo Kiš's Literary Works," in *Relations*. Nos. 9/10 (1979), pp. 66-69.
White, Edmund. "Danilo Kiš: The Obligations of Form," in *Southwest Review*. LXXI (Summer, 1986), pp. 363-377.
Zimmerman, Zora Devrnja. Review in *World Literature Today*. LIII (Autumn, 1979), p. 713.

*Vasa D. Mihailovich*

# THE TORRENTS OF SPRING

*Author:* Ivan Turgenev (1818-1883)
*Type of plot:* Psychological realism
*Time of plot:* 1840
*Locale:* Frankfurt and Wiesbaden
*First published: Veshniye vody*, 1872 (*Spring Floods*, 1874; better known as
  *The Torrents of Spring*)

*Principal characters:*
  DIMITRY PAVLOVICH SANIN, a young Russian nobleman
  GEMMA ROSELLI, a beautiful Italian girl who is living in
    Frankfurt
  KARL KLÜBER, a German businessman, Gemma's fiancé
  MARIA NIKOLAYEVNA POLOZOV, a wealthy, half-Gypsy Russian
    who seduces Sanin
  IPPOLIT SIDORYCH POLOZOV, Maria Nikolayevna's phlegmatic
    husband
  VON DÖNHOF, the German officer with whom Sanin fights a
    duel for Gemma's honor

*The Novel*

  *The Torrents of Spring* is cast as a remembrance of the past. Its brief introduction, which functions as a frame for the narrative, introduces the reader
to Dimitry Pavlovich Sanin at age fifty-two. The middle-aged Sanin, who has
just returned to his rooms after an evening spent with "attractive women and
cultured men," is tormented by "the thought of the vanity, the uselessness,
the vulgar falsity of all things human" and beset by a growing fear of age,
sickness, and death. He imagines himself sitting in a small boat as horrifying
monsters rise slowly toward him. While searching aimlessly through old papers in an effort "to rid himself by some kind of external occupation of the
thoughts that troubled him," Sanin discovers a small garnet cross. This
chance discovery starts a process of remembrance through which Sanin re-
constructs a romantic incident that occurred when he was a twenty-one-year-
old, an occurrence that soured the remainder of his life.
  The youthful Sanin, as recalled by himself in middle age, is a weak-willed
Russian nobleman who is traveling about Germany before returning home to
take a civil service position. As he walks along a street in Frankfurt, he is ac-
costed by Gemma Roselli, a beautiful young woman who runs from a pastry
shop, seeking assistance for her brother, Emilio. She is convinced that he has
stopped breathing and is dying. Sanin helps restore Emilio and is applauded
by Gemma and her family as the boy's savior. Sanin is easily convinced by the
Rosellis to stay longer in Frankfurt, and he soon discovers that he is infatuated with Gemma.

Gemma, however, is engaged to Karl Klüber, a repulsively businesslike German, and this engagement is encouraged by Gemma's mother. Leonora Roselli is the widow of an Italian confectioner who has continued the family business after her husband's death, but she believes that Gemma's successful marriage to the wealthy Klüber is the only guarantee of the family's financial future. This awkward situation continues until a climactic outing at a country inn near Frankfurt, during which Gemma is insulted by an intoxicated German officer named von Dönhof. Klüber attempts to ignore the incident, but Sanin reprimands Dönhof and accepts his challenge to a duel. Although neither Sanin nor Dönhof is eager for blood and the duel ends harmlessly, Sanin's romantic action gives Gemma the courage to break her engagement with Klüber and openly express her love for Sanin.

In an effort to assure Leonora that his intentions are honorable and that the financial future of the family is secured, Sanin impetuously decides to sell his Russian estate and use the proceeds to establish a home in Frankfurt. A chance encounter with Ippolit Sidorych Polozov, an old schoolmate, provides Sanin with the opportunity to sell his estate to Polozov's wife, Maria Nikolayevna Polozov, if he will immediately travel to Wiesbaden.

With some misgivings, Gemma agrees to the arrangement, and Sanin accompanies the gluttonous Polozov to Wiesbaden. Maria proves to be a carnivorous creature, a beautiful devourer of men who has an arrangement with her impotent husband that allows her to lead an independent romantic life. To his horror, Sanin finds himself irresistibly attracted to this temptress, who slowly transforms his wholesome love for Gemma into lust for her. Finally, after a vigorous horseback ride, Maria leads Sanin to a secluded gamekeeper's hut, where he succumbs to her seductive charms. From that point on, he is completely in Maria's power, and as she gloats in her victory, he despairingly pledges his intention to follow her "till you drive me away."

Confused by guilt and passion, Sanin cannot bring himself to confront Gemma with his infidelity, so he ends their relationship with a "wretched, tearful, lying, shabby letter" that is never answered. He is so ashamed of his behavior and fearful of a confrontation that he sends the Polozovs' footman to retrieve secretly his possessions from Frankfurt. He then follows the Polozovs to Paris. For a time, he serves as an obsequious member of Maria's retinue of admirers, enduring an escalating series of humiliations until he is eventually "cast aside like a worn-out garment."

The concluding chapters of *The Torrents of Spring* return the reader to the present, in which the middle-aged Sanin decides to track down Gemma. He travels to Frankfurt and, with the help of Dönhof, discovers that Gemma is married and living with her husband in New York City. He writes to her, begging her "not to let him carry to the grave the bitter sense of his guilt." Gemma's polite and sympathetic response, in which she details the happiness and fulfillment of her married life, releases Sanin's lifelong burden of guilt

o

and fills him with a sense of new life. In the novella's final sentence, Ivan Turgenev tells his readers that "it is rumoured that he is selling his estates and is about to leave for America."

## The Characters

Throughout his career, Turgenev protested that his lack of imagination forced him to model his characters after people he had met, and *The Torrents of Spring* is, in part, based on an autobiographical incident. As a young man traveling in Germany, Turgenev, like the protagonist in the novella, was approached by a beautiful young confectioner who thought her brother was dying. This historical beauty, however, was Jewish rather than Italian, and Turgenev, unlike Sanin, returned to Russia after the incident. It is also possible that through his story of the weak-willed Sanin's obsession with the self-centered Maria Nikolayevna Polozov, Turgenev was expressing dissatisfaction with his own compulsive attraction for Pauline Viardot.

Because the novella is cast as a reminiscence, the story portrays two distinct versions of Dimitry Pavlovich Sanin: the youthful idealist who is willing to sell his inheritance for the love of Gemma and the aging man overwhelmed with *taedium vitae*, a disgust with life. Although the novella focuses on the middle-aged Sanin in only the opening and closing chapters, the image of the soul-sickened man who discovers Gemma's garnet cross at the start of the book, darkens the remainder of the narrative by providing the reader with a grim vision of the state toward which the youthful protagonist is progressing. Young Sanin is well-intentioned but shallow. The thoughtlessness of his infatuation prepares the reader for his inability to resist the sexual advances of Maria, his cowardly letter to Gemma, and his humiliating life with the Polozovs.

Like most of Turgenev's beautiful virgins, Gemma is two-dimensional, an idealized portrait of youthful energy and innocence. Yet she is also an example of Turgenev's belief in the inherent emotional strength of women, and her emotional courage and endurance effectively contrast with Sanin's weakness. Her chief flaw is her mistaken vision of Sanin as a man of independent strength and honor, an illusion that is engendered by her unhappiness with the philistine Klüber and her misinterpretation of Sanin's duel with Dönhof. Her greatest asset, besides her unshakable sense of honor, is the resilience that allows her to overcome her grief over Sanin's duplicity and build a productive life for herself.

Maria is a frightening villainess whose carnal appetite is predatory. After her sexual victory over Sanin, Maria relishes his defeat, watching him groveling at her feet with eyes that express "the ruthless insensitivity and the satiety of conquest." Turgenev compares her to a "hawk, holding a captured bird in its claws." Like Gemma, Maria personifies Turgenev's belief in women's strength, but in contrast to Gemma, Maria represents evil. Her power over Sanin seems magical, making her a kind of sexual sorceress, but she is also a portrait of the emancipated woman of the late nineteenth century in Russia, part peasant, part aristocrat. For Maria, sexual license is a form of apolitical nihilism.

Turgenev, who lived much of his adult life as an exile, was an early supporter of Westernization, but his characterization of Germans in *The Torrents of Spring* shows his growing disenchantment with Germany in the wake of the Franco-Prussian War. Karl Klüber, Gemma's fiancé, is a complete materialist, a man without character or sensitivity who treats love as a business. Dönhof, the German officer who insults Gemma, is seen as an insensitive drunkard who displays little enthusiasm for the risks of dueling.

Two other members of the Roselli household are significant, though minor, characters in *The Torrents of Spring*, because their dignity and heroism provide a striking contrast to Sanin's weakness. Panteleone, an aged, retired opera singer, lives with the Rosellis as a combination grandfather and servant. His exaggerated reminiscences of the heroic roles that he sang in his youth and his nervous participation in the duel as Sanin's second make him a comic figure. His anachronistic ideas of honor, however, become less humorous after Sanin betrays Gemma, and he is the only member of the family to have an opportunity to confront Sanin with his perfidy. Gemma's brother, Emilio, who worships the heroism that he mistakenly sees in Sanin, eventually dies fighting under Giuseppe Garibaldi. His development from an uncertain boy into a martyr for the cause of national unification contrasts with Sanin's slide into corruption.

### Themes and Meanings

In *The Torrents of Spring*, Turgenev carefully distinguishes between the concepts of love and passion. Love is associated with the innocent idealism of Gemma and Sanin. It is portrayed as an essentially asexual mutual admiration based on the virtuous, selfless characteristics they see in each other. The novella, however, demonstrates that these young lovers' perceptions are limited and immature. Their love is built on dreams, and they actually dehumanize each other by projecting their idealistic longings. In contrast, passion is portrayed as a selfish battle for emotional control, and the novella implies that sex destroys the possibility for love. Maria is a sexual predator, and her greatest enjoyment seems to derive from the conquest of men. Her seduction of Sanin is a triumph of appetite over idealism. Like the mythological Circe, she transforms her victims into spiritual swine.

In the novel *Dym* (1867; *Smoke*, 1868), Turgenev maintains that "man is weak, woman is strong, Chance is all-powerful," and *The Torrents of Spring* demonstrates this idea. Both Maria and Gemma exhibit strengths that distinguish them from the male characters. Maria's total self-possession and amorality make her powerful; Gemma's unbreakable virtue gives her the strength to survive. In contrast, Sanin, Klüber, and Dönhof display various signs of weakness, becoming secondary figures who revolve about the feminine centers of influence.

Although Turgenev rewrote the novella three times over eighteen months, he professed retrospective dismay over its message: "So immoral, I have never been." This is a reference to the shocking manner in which Sanin betrays Gemma, but the novella does not, in the end, communicate an immoral lesson. Indeed, *The Torrents of Spring* argues that the cost of sin is spiritual death. Moreover, it shows the redemptive power of forgiveness and vigorously advocates the life of honor.

*Critical Context*

Turgenev regarded his fiction as being of two distinct types, differing in length and purpose. The longer major novels—*Rudin* (1856; English translation, 1873), *Dvoryanskoye gnezdo* (1859; *A House of Gentlefolk*, 1869), *Nakanune* (1860; *On the Eve*, 1871), *Ottsy i deti* (1862; *Fathers and Sons*, 1867), *Smoke*, and *Nov* (1877; *Virgin Soil*, 1877)—are set in carefully defined social contexts. Because they focus on specific social issues, Turgenev's novels chronicle the social history of Russia in the middle of the nineteenth century. Turgenev's novellas, however, are more personal, focusing on the universal themes of love and maturation. Of these novellas, *Pervaya lyubov* (1860; *First Love*, 1884) and *The Torrents of Spring* are the most enduring.

*The Torrents of Spring* was not received well by contemporary critics, and Turgenev himself seemed to want to disown the novella after its publication. He expressed regret that he had not rewritten the second half of the novella and made Sanin resist Maria's seduction. Many commentators suggested that the novella's apolitical story proved that the expatriate author was losing touch with his homeland. Nevertheless, *The Torrents of Spring* was very popular, particularly with women readers, and *The Herald of Europe*, the magazine in which the novella was originally published, took the unprecedented step of issuing a second printing.

*Sources for Further Study*

Mirsky, Dmitry S. *A History of Russian Literature*, 1949.
Pritchett, V. S. *The Gentle Barbarian: The Life and Work of Turgenev*, 1977.
Schapiro, Leonard. *Turgenev: His Life and Times*, 1979.
Schefski, Harold K. "*Novelle* Structure in Turgenev's *Spring Torrents*," in *Studies in Short Fiction*. XXII (Fall, 1985), pp. 431-435.
Yarmolinsky, A. *Turgenev: The Man, His Art, and His Age*, 1926, 1959 (revised edition).

*Carl Brucker*

# THE TRANSPOSED HEADS
## A Legend of India

*Author:* Thomas Mann (1875-1955)
*Type of plot:* Fable
*Time of plot:* The eleventh century
*Locale:* Kurukshetra, India, and environs
*First published: Die vertauschten Köpfe: Eine indische Legende*, 1940 (English translation, 1941)

> *Principal characters:*
> SHRIDAMAN, a merchant who is well-versed in classical Indian learning
> NANDA, his friend, a shepherd and smith who is three years younger than Shridaman
> SITA, a young woman who becomes Shridaman's wife
> KALI, a Hindu goddess who is associated with motherhood but who also represents bloodshed, sacrifice, and destruction
> KAMADAMANA, a pious hermit
> SAMADHI, also called ANDHAKA, the son of Sita and Shridaman

*The Novel*

This slender, supple work achieves its ends through forms of imagery and symbolism that are revealed at each turn. The story itself, which rests upon relatively slight narrative foundations, suggests that basic antinomies in human character may yield results that are entirely unexpected; the exotic, indeed seemingly mythic setting seems to heighten the moral tension felt in this work even as it diminishes the impact of what otherwise would be some rather shocking events. Moreover, while enough details of the specific time and place are supplied to convey a distinctive and extraordinary atmosphere, these effects do not impose limitations on the more nearly universal issues that are also called forth. All the while, there is enough wry wit in the author's tone to suggest that such matters need not be taken too seriously.

At the outset, two young men become friends possibly because their seemingly dissimilar qualities are actually complementary. Shridaman, the older, has been educated in grammar and philosophy and is a merchant, and Nanda, who is more given to physical labor, tends livestock and is a smith. In quiet, secluded places, they discuss ultimate questions of truth and understanding, although they reach no particular conclusions. Their musings are pleasantly interrupted one day when a young woman, not knowing that they are about, comes to bathe in the river nearby. Without any improper overtones, they regard her lithe, delicately curved form; in particular, they admire her delicate, golden brown skin. Her graceful, unaffected movements seem admirably suited to her splendidly proportioned figure. Shridaman is inspired by her appearance to launch into a disquisition about relations between the image and the beholder in aesthetic theory; yet both he and his interlocutor seem bemused and distracted in a way that is far from intellectual. Some time later, Shridaman confesses to his friend that his philosophical cast of mind has been dulled by yearnings of a more worldly sort; Nanda maintains lightheartedly that, though Shridaman is seemingly given to cerebral pursuits, he actually cannot find means to contain the urges of his lovesickness.

It does not take very long for courtship to blossom into marriage. Although he and Sita initially are quite happy together, some misgivings begin to trouble Shridaman. His religious precepts offer him no guidance; when he enters a shrine of the goddess Kali, he becomes possessed instead with dark thoughts of propitiation. Shridaman fears that his very essence has been divided hopelessly by the conflicting claims of the mental and physical facets of his existence. The goddess is intent on exacting her due in blood and sacrifice. Accordingly, and in a stroke that admittedly seems improbably difficult to carry out, Shridaman takes up a sword and in one movement severs his head from his body. Nanda, who has been disquieted by his friend's air of gloomy preoccupation, comes upon Shridaman's corpse when he visits the temple; after only a moment's reflection, he takes up the fatal sword and decapitates himself.

When Sita comes upon this gruesome spectacle, she is, at first, inclined to join the others in death; at this juncture, however, the goddess reproaches her for any thoughts of self-sacrifice. Instead, Sita succeeds somehow in affixing the heads back on the bodies of the men. When they come back to life, however, there is an unusual twist: For each of them, the head of the one has been set upon the other's body. This turn of events leads to some oddly comic discussions between the new Shridaman and the new Nanda. At issue is whether each should construe his personal identity on the basis of his physical or his mental qualities. Both are actually a bit amused at the situation but recognize that the confusion cannot continue indefinitely. In particular, Sita would need to determine which one actually is her husband; thus, the three of them go off to a forest sanctuary some distance away, where they consult the eccentric old hermit Kamadamana. He advises them that it is the head, not the body, that confers the unique personal status identified with each individual.

The new Shridaman continues to live in a wedded state with Sita. For a time it seems that all is well; eventually, however, it appears that something is awry. Sita initially is rather pleased with the more powerful and fully developed physical state of her husband. Yet, the body is soon dominated by

Shridaman's head, the limbs and chest becoming so thin and weak that they cannot be distinguished from those of the original Shridaman. Meanwhile, the child who was conceived early in their marriage is born and is found to bear some resemblance to all three of them. Sita wearies of Shridaman and develops a pronounced penchant for Nanda; indeed, her interest has been aroused by her past experience with him as a transposed body. When she comes upon him again, she finds that, true to his calling, his body has come to resemble that possessed by the Nanda of old. Their blissful liaison lasts a day and a night; then Shridaman discovers them together and becomes distraught.

At last, Shridaman and Nanda agree to a trial by combat, with the added stipulation that neither will allow his body to betray his head. The outcome is as precise and symmetrical as their earlier decapitations; each pierces the other's heart with his sword, and both fall dead simultaneously. It remains for Sita, who has contemplated this final act all along, to commit ritual suttee by placing herself upon the funeral pyre which consumes the two men. As an afterthought, the narrator adds that young Samadhi, the son of Sita and Shridaman, is obliged by his nearsightedness to take up contemplative pursuits. He soon becomes known as Andhaka (little blind one) and acquires wide renown for his precocious mastery of learned subjects. By the age of twenty, he has become a reader to the King of Benares.

## The Characters

The participants in this metaphysical work may be considered archetypal; in no sense does any of them possess those peculiarly individual qualities that require characterization in great detail. The characters are meant to represent the incarnation of much broader attributes. The dialogue, especially that between Shridaman and Nanda, also repeatedly reaches a rarefied philosophical plane where abstract values and categories are discussed in relation to observations and experiences.

In a sense, there is a sort of philosophical dualism that is exemplified in the qualities assigned to the two men, and the physical descriptions of each of them seem further to establish this relationship between character and appearance. Shridaman has the outward bearing of a scholar; his sharp nose and soft, gentle eyes are set above thin lips and a gentle spreading beard, and his head seems disproportionately large in relation to his body. The cogitation in which he is often immersed may at times have led him to underestimate the imperatives of his bodily urges; thus, his relations with Sita involve an abrupt awakening for him. Unlike the others, Shridaman is also prone to fits of melancholy. His tendency to elicit ultimate questions from the experiences of his life foreshadows the dark brooding that leads him first to suicide and then to a fatal duel with his opposite, Nanda.

Nanda is typified by other, simpler virtues, which are set off as well by the more obvious physical contrasts between him and his friend. Readily distinguishable from Shridaman by his darker complexion, thick lips, and goatlike nose, Nanda has acquired characteristics which also seem evocative of his nature: His work as a smith has strengthened his arms and upper body to produce a harmonious effect of rugged masculine power. If he seems physically more imposing, he is not given so much to complex, troubled responses to the everyday issues of his existence. His manner of speaking is simpler and more direct than that of Shridaman; his merry laughter and forthright, unaffected manner contrast markedly with the moody, unsettled qualities evident in his friend. Nevertheless, his sense of honor and responsibility seems equal to that of Shridaman. He does not in the least recoil from the challenges to self-sacrifice and combat that are laid down by the other man.

Other vital principles are represented in Sita, although otherwise she seems less fully realized as a character than her two male counterparts. In her, there is a fusion of erotic and aesthetic elements to the extent that her being may be considered on both ideal and material levels. She appears first as an object admired and pursued by the men, but in due course, her own desires and aspirations are revealed. Another duality of sorts, which is grounded in Indian religious imagery, exists within her: the idea that divergent drives toward sexual fulfillment and motherhood are necessarily united in woman's nature. Sita's awakening joy in matters of the flesh is offset by a sense of self-sacrifice that differs from but is equally strong as that felt by the men. It would seem, however, that her thoughts and feelings arise in response to problems posed as Shridaman and Nanda grapple with moral concerns that must affect her also.

The antinomies of head and body, or intellect and substance, are resolved with mutual destruction, and the same fate is reserved for the opposition of male and female qualities. It is unclear whether the honor and status that are ultimately accorded Samadhi represent the reassertion of principles by which the inward-looking mind could again claim a place for itself in the world at large.

*Themes and Meanings*

The moral and philosophical implications of this work are numerous enough that it is best to consider, in turn, those that are overtly argued and others that are suggested more subtly. Whether a person's intellectual faculties take precedence over the physical being is a question that is clearly posed by the divergent qualities of the two leading men; this issue is raised more acutely when the head of one must inhabit the body of another. Similarly, problems of personal identity are posed by the transpositions depicted here; this matter must be resolved when Shridaman begins to assert his will over Nanda's body while the head of his friend must come to terms with a different body. Whether the body has a will and characteristics of its own is a question raised in a peculiarly sensitive manner when Sita feels drawn to the transposed versions of men she knew intimately. Human relationships and, more specifically, the competing foci of Sita's affections are recast in an oddly bifurcated form when she cannot easily choose between the cerebral and the physical manifestations of a given man once they are shared with another. Furthermore, the aesthetic issue which Shridaman discusses rather early in the novel—whether human forms are to be admired in their own right or as they are judged by the beholder—points to other problems in the mind's apprehension of those attributes that are deemed beautiful or elegantly formed. These sundry problems of idealism and dualism are enveloped in other concerns which, when dealing with problems of the corporeal being, suggest other themes.

The extinction of one's existence as a resolution of the dilemmas posed here is an expedient first suggested by Shridaman's religious learning. His deliberations on this concern, as guided by Kali, take a deeply morbid turn; it is significant, however, that Nanda, the man of direct physical action, also comes to a similar conclusion. Moreover, the same goddess expressly advises Sita not to kill herself when she comes upon the bodies and heads. It is only later, when another fatal confrontation has taken place, that Sita feels obliged finally to follow the others in death. The seemingly fatalistic outlook shared by the major characters is handled with some reticence; the gruesome sequence of two decapitations is described gently, without dwelling upon the sanguinary details. At other junctures, particularly during the final duel between Shridaman and Nanda, death is invoked as a philosophical principle which must be weighed against other efforts in order to achieve life's mental or physical ends. There is a grim finality to the calculations involved here; although there is some suggestion of miraculous agencies at work in the reconstruction of the decapitated corpses, the religious faith invoked does not allude to an afterlife or the possibility of subsequent reincarnations. On the contrary, it would seem that death is conceived as the means by which the claims of the mind and the body are rejected equally. Whether this is accurate from the standpoint of the Indian legend is a question that is left open.

Erotic inclinations are suggested, sometimes in ways that are more explicit than others. Promptings of this sort are not embraced within the dichotomy that Shridaman originally proposes; he alludes to such urges obliquely when the matter first arises, during the bathing scene where Sita first comes before them. Even for Shridaman, aesthetic appreciation cannot readily be distinguished from the inchoate erotic drives that begin to affect him. Sita has a firmer intuition of the extent to which sexual yearnings affect them in murky and sometimes unexpected ways. There are some points at which deeper patterns of antithetical symbolism, male and female principles, for example, are at work and are revealed to her by the goddess. It is also significant that for each character erotic impulses are important in establishing a sense of personal identity. In this respect, Sita has some difficulty determining which man she prefers after the transposition.

Out of this conflicting configuration of mental and bodily principles in which neither rational imperatives nor physical urges can be brought into strict harmony, it would seem that ultimately death gains dominion over all. Yet there are some expectations that elsewhere life will continue. In this sense, the identification of Sita with a universal mother figure is important.

*Critical Context*

During Thomas Mann's later literary career, much of his work was drawn from themes and settings that ranged across more distant historical periods and rather far-flung lands; in this case, he borrowed from various cultural traditions while rendering his own interpretations of the material he selected. The original source for *The Transposed Heads* is a Sanskrit legend translated by the Indologist Heinrich Robert Zimmer, to whom Mann dedicated the American edition of this work. Although he took some care to study those aspects of classical Indian culture that were important for his work, Mann acknowledged that Western thinkers had also provided inspiration for this effort. Among the more significant influences Mann mentioned are Johann Wolfgang von Goethe, who had made use of a somewhat similar theme, and the philosopher Arthur Schopenhauer, whose work inspired some of the brooding, pessimistic elements of this novel. Mann also found literary uses for the psychoanalytic doctrine of Sigmund Freud and the work of Carl Gustav Jung, whose theories of a collective unconscious stemmed in part from the study of Indian and other Asian patterns of thought.

Among the full-length works composed entirely during Mann's later life, *The Transposed Heads* could be considered rather distant from his other efforts in time, space, and cultural outlook. Mann referred to it later as a metaphysical jest which was composed while he was also at work on other novels. Although during this period of his career Mann was also reworking traditional German themes—as in *Lotte in Weimar* ( 1939; *The Beloved Returns*, 1940) and *Doktor Faustus* (1947; *Doctor Faustus*, 1948)—the closest counterpart in spirit and setting to Mann's Indian novel is the tetralogy *Joseph und seine Brüder* (1933-1943; *Joseph and His Brothers*, 1934-1944, 1948), which pursues biblical themes in pharaonic Egypt as part of Mann's quest for the elucidation of basic moral values in human relationships. Yet *The Transposed Heads* stands apart from Mann's other works by virtue of its odd choice of subject matter; while it has not been considered a major effort (indeed Mann himself did not regard it as such), *The Transposed Heads* does indicate the great range of his interests and the extent of his ability to utilize diverse materials for his own literary purposes.

*Sources for Further Study*

Fleissner, Else M. "Stylistic Confusion in Thomas Mann's Indian Legend, *The Transposed Heads,*" in *The Germanic Review*. XVIII, no. 3 (1943), pp. 209-212.

Ganeshan, Vridhagiri. "*The Transposed Heads* by Thomas Mann: An Indian Legend or a Metaphysical Jest?" in *Journal of the School of Languages*. V, nos. 1/2 (1977/1978), pp. 1-13.

Hollingdale, R. J. *Thomas Mann: A Critical Study*, 1971.

Lawson, Marjorie. "The Transposed Heads of Goethe and of Thomas Mann," in *Monatshefte*. XXXIV, no. 2 (1942), pp. 87-92.

McWilliams, James R. *Brother Artist: A Psychological Study of Thomas Mann's Fiction*, 1983.

Schultz, Siegfried A. "Form and Style in Thomas Mann's Indian Legend," in *Linguistic and Literary Studies in Honor of Helmut A. Hatzfeld*, 1964. Edited by Alessandro S. Crisafulli.

_____. "Hindu Mythology in Mann's Indian Legend," in *Comparative Literature Studies*. XIV, no. 2 (1962), pp. 129-142.

Willson, Amos Leslie. "*Die vertauschten Köpfe*: The Catalyst of Creation," in *Monatshefte*. XLIX, no. 6 (1957), pp. 313-321.

*J. R. Broadus*

# THE TRAVELS OF LAO TS'AN

*Author:* Liu E (Liu T'ieh-yun, 1857-1909)
*Type of plot:* Allegory
*Time of plot:* The late nineteenth century
*Locale:* The countryside of southern China
*First published: Lao Ts'an youji*, 1904-1907 (English translation, 1952)

Principal characters:
 LAO TS'AN, a man of good birth who travels humbly about the
  countryside
 JEN-JUI, one of Lao Ts'an's friends, a government official
 HUAN-TS'UI, a former prostitute who becomes Lao Ts'an's
  wife once he buys her freedom
 PREFECT YU, an official noted for his cruelty
 MRS. CHIA WEI, a woman falsely accused of murder but saved
  by Lao Ts'an's influence

*The Novel*
   To describe *The Travels of Lao Ts'an* as a picaresque novel would be altogether accurate except for the nature of its hero. The true picaro is a rascal
of low birth, and this characterization does not fit the aristocratic Lao Ts'an.
Also, Lao Ts'an does not perform menial tasks or engage in near-criminal
acts, as might the picaro. Instead, Lao Ts'an, who is eminently respectable,
only pretends to be something of a rascal in his role as itinerant healer.
Otherwise, this classic Chinese work adheres to the dictates of the picaresque
form long popular in Western literature.
   Following the central character's life so closely that he rarely disappears
from the action, most picaresque novels unfold through the first person. *The
Travels of Lao Ts'an* takes an informal third-person voice, whose great
charm survives even in translation. The narrator conveys such a personal
tone that he appears to be speaking directly to his reader, using techniques
such as the one with which he closes chapters: "If you don't know what happened afterwards, then hear the next chapter tell." When Lao Ts'an marries,
the narrator ends the wedding account with a coy comment: "Then of course
the newlyweds were escorted to their bedchamber, and we don't need to say
anything further."
   The novel presents a series of episodes that find their unity for the most
part in the central figure's presence. Lao Ts'an, for reasons not altogether
clear, leaves his home and wanders about the countryside, where he visits
places of interest, meets and makes friends with all classes of people, entan-
gles himself in local problems, and often proves to be the savior of those
falsely accused or mistreated. Ostensibly, he earns his way by healing the

sick, a skill he always practices successfully whenever anyone calls on him to use the knowledge he has learned from folk medicine.

Typical of the picaresque work, this novel is realistic in its depiction of setting and character. The countryside comes to life vividly, the characters' appearances and clothing are described in minute detail, and the actualities of daily life abound. For example, the narrator even gives the measurements of the rooms in the inns where Lao Ts'an stays. Food, too, plays an important part, and full menus accompany the feasts that the traveler and his friends enjoy. When Lao Ts'an attends a special musical event, he observes both the singers' renditions and the audience's reactions so closely that the account captures the joy that he experiences.

Although Lao Ts'an's travels always provide interest in themselves, they often take a satiric turn to point out the absurd acts of government officials, the pretensions of the aristocratic class, and the oddities of his own people, the Chinese. Although Lao Ts'an frequents government circles and associates with officials, he refuses to take their self-importance seriously; instead, he seizes every opportunity to criticize them and ridicule their inflated opinions of themselves, just as he does with the aristocrats. The blind adherence to tradition and the consequent refusal to make changes, no matter how advantageous, Lao Ts'an observes with a wry smile. Many of his adventures, while appearing ordinary, disguise explorations of particular unjust acts rampant in China during the late nineteenth century.

The typical picaresque hero engages in one peccadillo after another, always emerging unscathed. So does Lao Ts'an. He almost suffers the wrath of a notably cruel ruler, but escapes; rescues a prostitute from bondage, then marries her; and defies an official prosecuting a lady of good family for a multiple murder, then solves the crime. Lao Ts'an also enjoys life and people, meeting old friends and making new ones along the way. He receives the hospitality of the great and the humble, who provide him with wine, food, and sometimes lodging. Lao Ts'an extends gracious hospitality as well. At first, several of the episodes seem to depict nothing more than social occasions, but the conversation, which often takes a philosophical turn, makes them substantial.

Published first under a pseudonym as a serial in the newspaper, *The Travels of Lao Ts'an* may have included sixty chapters instead of the twenty now forming the central text. Although a forty-chapter version appeared in Shanghai in 1919, the second half was proved to be spurious. Other segments have been discovered, authenticated, and published in China—first in 1935, then in 1972. The English translation of 1952 presented the twenty original chapters which are now considered a unified account of Lao Ts'an's travels.

## The Characters
The picaresque novel does not focus on character development or such

subtleties as motivation and alteration of character. In this respect, *The Travels of Lao Ts'an* follows the tradition faithfully.

Lao Ts'an is a wanderer throughout this chronicle of his travels. Although he has encountered all kinds of people, some good and some evil, they have not changed him—nor have his experiences. Throughout the narrative, he lives by exercising a code based on nobility, kindness, and consideration; this idealized personality is rounded out with intelligence, sensitivity, and artistic appreciation.

Those he meets during his travels develop only as characters with whom he shares a meal, a lodging, a conversation, or an adventure. With nothing happening to change them during the encounters, they pass out of the picture and others take their place. For example, one of the people with whom Lao Ts'an spends the most time is Jen-jui, a government official with a sense of humor and a taste for opium. It is he who arranges the marriage, almost as a practical joke, between Lao Ts'an and Huan-ts'ui, the prostitute they had agreed to rescue. Huan-ts'ui plays the helpless girl in distress, often in tears, but once married, she fades into the background. Mrs. Chia Wei, falsely accused of murder, provides the focus for one of the fuller adventures, but as a character she does not surpass her original status as a wronged woman. Villains such as Prefect Yu also do not reform.

### Themes and Meanings

Author Liu E was a farsighted man who attempted to promote commercial, industrial, and transportational projects. Although he met with little success in his own life, he did inspire those who followed him. Lamenting his failures and dying in political exile, Liu E remained forgotten until 1925, when his identity as the author of *The Travels of Lao Ts'an* was established.

To an extent, then, Lao Ts'an represents his creator's idealized persona: a balanced man of action and meditation who brings about change. Through his character, Liu E reveals his own philosophy, which combines the precepts of Confucianism, Buddhism, and Taoism. Lao Ts'an's dedication to doing good, his hatred of tyrannical authority, his unquestioning trust of others, his honesty, and the spontaneity of his actions are all derived from these philosophies. The adventures that he enjoys during his travels might, in this light, be considered allegorical, for they illustrate how such virtues could bring about change in a stagnant and often corrupt society. Uncontaminated, selfless, and solitary, this idealized figure represents not only outward progress but also beauty of the soul, a progress far more important.

### Critical Context

The southern Chinese school of writing at the turn of the century made extensive use of satire, in particular ridiculing officialdom and indicting its representatives for their ignorance, greed, and philandering. Yet some of these works rely too heavily on censure, and their characters lack the good-natured temper that Lao Ts'an exercises.

While many of these books remain important social documents, few have found the honored place in world literature attributed to *The Travels of Lao Ts'an*. Admired in China today for its masterful use of language and its descriptive power, it speaks to the universality of both human fallibility and the concept of the ideal man, whom Lao Ts'an represents with such fullness.

*Sources for Further Study*

Doleželová-Velingerová, Milena, ed. *The Chinese Novel at the Turn of the Century*, 1980.

Link, Perry. *Mandarin Ducks and Butterflies: Popular Fiction in Early Twentieth-century Chinese Cities*, 1981.

Shadick, Harold. Introduction to *The Travels of Lao Ts'an*, 1952.

*The United States Quarterly Book Review*. Review. IX (June, 1953), p. 163.

*Robert Ross*

# THE TREE OF KNOWLEDGE

*Author:* Pío Baroja (1872-1956)
*Type of plot:* Impressionistic realism
*Time of plot:* The final decades of the nineteenth century
*Locale:* Madrid and some provinces of Spain
*First published: El árbol de la ciencia,* 1911 (English translation, 1928)

> *Principal characters:*
> ANDRÉS HURTADO, a medical doctor
> LULÚ, his wife
> DR. ITURRIOZ, Andrés' uncle and mentor

## The Novel

As Andrés waits for classes to begin on his first day as a medical student at the Institute of San Isidro, he runs into an old friend, Julio Aracil. They soon realize that they are enrolled in the same course of study, and they attend a lecture together. To Andrés' dismay, the class resembles a sideshow and the professor is like a clown, a situation representative of Andrés' overall experience at San Isidro. His enthusiasm for his studies is soon dampened. Consequently, he fails an important chemistry exam and becomes altogether indifferent toward medicine. In his second year, he attends a dissection class where the students take much pleasure in cutting bodies to pieces or in putting small bows and paper hats on corpses. He looks forward to a third-year physiology class but is disappointed by a stupid text and an inadequate instructor. In his next year, Andrés studies under the famous Dr. Letamendi and is momentarily impressed and excited by Letamendi's application of mathematics to biology. He is, at least, until a friend tells him that the entire concept is a joke, the vulgar rhetorical games of a prestidigitator. Nevertheless, as a result, Andrés becomes curious about philosophy, particularly the writings of Immanuel Kant and Arthur Schopenhauer. He finds the latter especially convincing during his internship in the hospitals of Madrid the following year, where he witnesses unimaginable abuse and misery.

Aracil takes a liking to Andrés and decides to introduce him to the sister of the girl he has been seeing (until such time as he is ready to start looking for a wife). Lulú is unattractive and has an almost caustic disposition, but she is intelligent, noble, and progressive in her thinking. Her humor is irreverent, and, like Andrés, she sees things for what they are and speaks in a forthright manner. They also share a tendency toward cynicism. Through Aracil and Lulú, Andrés comes into contact with a curious assortment of individuals, such as Doña Virginia, a procuress who takes economic advantage of girls in trouble; Rafael Villasús, a mediocre dramatist who lives and dies for the sake of romanticism; Manolo, a coward and parasite; Venancia, a former domestic of the aristocracy who defends them as inherently good and charitable; and Don Cleto, a very clean but very poor man who starves to death. When Andrés tries to sort out the disturbing impressions with which they leave him, his uncle offers a biological explanation: By design of Nature, life is a constant battle, a cruel slaughter in which all devour one another, and justice is no more than a human illusion. Man has the same instincts as the tiniest organism that feeds off other organisms in order to survive.

One day, in his final year of training, Andrés' youngest brother, Luisito, spits up blood. Startled, Andrés decides that it would be best for the boy to be in the country. He moves Luisito and their sister, Margarita, to a house in Valencia. At the end of the academic year, Andrés joins them, and all three grow happy and healthy in their new surroundings. When the father insists that they move in with some elderly, unmarried relatives to save money, Andrés loses his positive influence over his brother, and his recommendations go unheeded. Feeling out of place and bored, Andrés returns to Madrid, accepts a medical assignment in Burgos, and enjoys several serene weeks until a letter arrives informing him of Luisito's death. A few weeks earlier Luisito had contracted tubercular meningitis and died a gruesome death. Unaware of Andrés' whereabouts, the family was unable to communicate to him that Luisito, feverish and delirious, had been asking to see his older brother. The funeral took place one week before Andrés received the news.

At the end of his assignment, Andrés again returns to Madrid. In the afternoons, he visits his uncle, who takes an active interest in the professional and spiritual progress of the younger man. Andrés is in search of an explanation of the physical and moral universe.

According to Andrés, until the nineteenth century, the Greco-Semitic lie (a complex mythology based on the principle of one all-powerful God) had dominated the world, permitting the manipulation of humanity through its deluding, confusing fictions. Then the ideas of Kant broke through that lie by defining the world as knowledge of the world; that is, the mind and the object perceived are one. Therefore, things in themselves, including time, space, and reality, cease to exist. There is only cause and effect without any initial cause (God). The chain of cause and effect can also be referred to as science, the only strong construction of humankind, according to Andrés. Kant thus opens the way for science and Schopenhauer completes the philosophical system of his predecessor where world still equals mind but mind minus responsibility, freedom, and law—in other words, minus the human element. From time to time, this will, as Schopenhauer calls it, does produce a cerebral glimmering: intelligence. Existence is the balance between these two forces (will and intelligence, or truth and life) which fluctuate constantly in inverse proportions. Truth, which is arrived at through the application of science, becomes the measure of all things. Yet because science is only at its very inception, Andrés' utopia, as he envisions it, is still thousands of years away.

Dr. Iturrioz suggests usefulness as an interim standard. Moreover, he says, such intellectualism is dangerously sterile, and the analytical dissection of society would be pointless anyway since its wickedness comes from an innate human feature: self-interest. Historically, it has been through appealing to the ego of the individual, with promises of paradise, that mountains have been moved. Furthermore, to eliminate the lies, truths, and madness from life would be to eliminate life itself.

Andrés is named to a position in a town in Andalucia. The atmosphere there is stifling and the people barbaric. They manifest the characteristics associated with the biblical Tree of Life: selfishness, cruelty, envy, pride, and backwardness. Andrés feels bored and ill in Alcolea del Campo; ultimately the hostility of its people forces him to leave. The death of a local woman polarizes the town: with Andrés and the judge on one side and a lynch mob headed by Dr. Sánchez, Andrés' medical rival, on the other. Andrés and the judge prove the innocence of the woman's husband, much to the resentment of the townspeople, who feel cheated by his release. Before he leaves, Andrés makes love to the wife of his brutish landlord, but, contrary to his expectations, the episode affects him in a negative way, both physically and mentally.

Back in Madrid, Andrés renews some old acquaintances. Montaner is down on his luck, while Aracil prospers but at the expense of his wife and friends, who subsidize his luxurious life-style. Another friend, Fermín Ibarra, who had been a weakling, has grown strong since living abroad. In Belgium, he has found an environment propitious to his abilities as an inventor and intends to reside there permanently. Andrés also runs into Lulú, a happy meeting for both, and they start seeing each other regularly. A strong bond develops between the two as they share their lives. Andrés confides in Lulú the mounting bitterness and depression he feels from his experiences as a public-health doctor. Lulú, on the other hand, brings Andrés into her aura of happiness, the result of her love for Andrés (a fact to which he remains oblivious until he proposes marriage and she confesses). Against the advice of his uncle—Andrés and Lulú are both unhealthy types—they marry and live blissfully for a time. Andrés finds a new job which he enjoys, and he feels contented at home with his wife. Lulú, however, becomes pregnant and, as Andrés has suspected all along, their happiness ends abruptly when the baby is born dead and Lulú dies soon thereafter. Before her funeral takes place, Andrés commits suicide by taking a lethal dose of aconitine.

## The Characters

In *The Tree of Knowledge*, there is actually only one character who is the axis of the book. All others revolve around Andrés. Dr. Iturrioz and Lulú are two channels through which Andrés finds a mentor, someone capable of understanding and directing him. Although Andrés does not always follow the advice of his uncle, he acknowledges the soundness of his opinions and ideas and is able to test his own on him. Thus, he proceeds on his quest, his vision of existence being constantly refined, modified, and reformulated in an active exchange of ideas with Dr. Iturrioz.

Lulú, on the other hand, represents love. While Andrés benefits indirectly from Dr. Iturrioz's years of life experience, Lulú presents him with the opportunity to taste the fruit of the tree of life (which, the reverse of the biblical admonition, will produce his death) and put his theory of love into practice. Together they undergo a positive transformation through the power of love, a transformation which momentarily stops the growth of his pessimism and almost rescues him from the extreme discomfort of living. It is through his feelings for Lulú, rather than his intellectualizing about life, that he at last finds the way to happiness, only to lose it again.

There are also numerous stereotypes which function as a group to achieve the same end in the text: to portray Spanish society of the period. Most of them are not likable; none is profound or developed. Using the deformation and exaggeration characteristic of satire, the author instantly conveys the multiplicity of negative aspects present in that reality which contribute to its sorry state. From the quixotic to the repulsive, the pathetic to the tyrannical, the human material which is the real identity of a nation does not seem to offer much hope for the future or even consolation for the present.

*Themes and Meanings*

Andrés is on a quest that will end in self-destruction because his intellectuality makes him unable to survive in an environment ordered by the baser instincts. From his philosophical readings, he concludes that existence consists of the inverse relationship between will and knowledge. Like the Tree of Life and the Tree of Knowledge, there are two modes or levels of being, completely different from each other. The significance of the Tree of Life is depicted in the novel through Spanish society in the late nineteenth century. In both urban and rural settings, Andrés observes an array of behaviors and personalities motivated by self-interest. An intrinsic component of the human species and unlikely to disappear altogether, self-interest can be transcended through development of the intellect. With truth as the ultimate, indisputable measure of all things, unnecessary and counterproductive emotions can be controlled, the veil of illusion is lifted, and civilization can progress. Thus oriented, Andrés finds himself incapable of regressing to a more primitive condition. He is a seeker of knowledge, a "scientist" and therefore unfit to deal with the sordid circumstances of his time and place. Unlike Montaner, who resigns himself to failure, or Aracil, who is distracted by the accumulation of material possessions, Andrés must find a genuine, permanent means to resolve his dilemma. His suffering intensifies continually; he grows increasingly cynical, depressed, and bitter. When he least expects it, however, he experiences love and happiness with Lulú, only to lose it again. His only alternative is to abandon a life which had long since abandoned him.

## Critical Context

As the nineteenth century was drawing to a close, the loss of Spain's remaining colonies to the United States in the war of 1898 definitively marked the end of a once-mighty empire. A mood of despair prevailed among intellectuals. Two principal groups emerged, each with its particular attitude toward and theories regarding this crisis concerning the fate of Spain. The conservative faction advocated a return to God, country, and king, the foundations of Spain's former glory and her hope for the future. Liberals, however, sought an alternative solution in the ideas of European rationalism and humanism, a complete break with the past.

In his role as cynic, Pío Baroja's mission was to attack any institution or system. Therefore he identified with neither the conservatives nor the liberals. Although the destructive element of liberalism appealed to him, its constructive element did not. He abhorred traditional values and conventions, even making fun of such unusual *castizo* (Spanish traditionalist) practices as writing in the twentieth century using Golden Age (seventeenth century) language.

*The Tree of Knowledge* is Baroja's attempt to comprehend and explain Spain's destiny. In the novel, Baroja tells a pessimistic tale with a harsh message. Spain is living in the past, according to an outdated pragmatism which keeps it out of touch with the rest of twentieth century Europe. A provincial mentality is nurtured, while any attempts toward progress are suffocated in a stifling atmosphere of unreality, ignorance, and intolerance. Both society and individual operate on primitive levels to no good whatsoever. Rather than look to the future (the attitude that built Spain into a world power in the fifteenth century), the country busies itself re-creating its past through the reenactment of myths and legends which belong to former times (Don Quixote, Don Juan, and the aristocracy, among others). There are those who starve to death so as not to lose face, those who self-induce blindness and insanity in order to protect a past ideal, and those who serve as the hosts of society's parasites.

More than any other novel of its generation, *The Tree of Knowledge* conveys the climate of hopelessness in late nineteenth century Spain. It is an honest appraisal of that society, one that logically points to bleak prospects for the future. The severe tone and message make it an appropriate literary response to a time of crisis.

*Sources for Further Study*

Baeza, Fernando. *Baroja y su mundo*, 1961 (two volumes).

Baroja, Pío. *Youth and Egolatry*, 1920.

Shaw, D. L. "Two Novels of Baroja: An Illustration of His Technique," in *Bulletin of Hispanic Studies*. XL (1963), pp. 151-159.

*Krista Ratkowski Carmona*

# THE TRIAL BEGINS

*Author:* Andrei Sinyavsky (as Abram Tertz, 1925-    )
*Type of plot:* Phantasmagoric fiction
*Time of plot:* September, 1952, to March, 1953; epilogue in 1956
*Locale:* Moscow, with an epilogue in a Siberian prison camp
*First published: Sad idzie*, 1959 (English translation, 1960)

> *Principal characters:*
> THE NARRATOR, a young Russian writer
> VLADIMIR PETROVICH GLOBOV, the hero, a public prosecutor
>     and true believer in Stalinism
> SERYOZHA, age seventeen, Globov's idealistic son by a
>     previous marriage
> MARINA, Globov's beautiful second wife
> YURY KARLINSKY, a brilliant, cynical defense attorney and
>     Marina's lover
> KATYA, Seryozha's schoolgirl coconspirator
> EKATERINA PETROVNA, Globov's former mother-in-law, a
>     principled Communist
> DR. S. Y. RABINOVICH, the gynecologist who aborts Marina's
>     baby

*The Novel*

   *The Trial Begins* is a tale of Soviet life in the last few months before the death of Soviet tyrant Joseph Stalin. The novella's historical backdrop is the paranoid dictator's last purge, the "doctors' plot," of an alleged cabal of physicians (mostly Jewish) who planned to assassinate high Party officials. The plot, hatched by Stalin's security services and exposed as fraudulent after his death, was in fact a campaign against Soviet Jews, euphemistically labeled "rootless cosmopolitans."

   As the novella opens, the writer-narrator sits in his room reflecting upon the recent visit of two plainclothesmen who searched his room. They presage the supernatural visitation of the Master (Stalin), a huge phantasmagoric figure who looms over the Moscow dawn and points out to the narrator the figure of his "beloved and faithful servant," Prosecutor Vladimir Petrovich Globov: "Follow him, . . . defend him with your life. Exalt him!" The story that follows is the narrator's unsuccessful attempt to celebrate Globov.

   Globov is preparing his case against Dr. Rabinovich, an abortionist. Meanwhile, Globov's wife, Marina, is meeting her suitor, Yury Karlinsky. Condemned to spend the day alone, Globov talks with his son by an earlier marriage, Seryozha, who has attracted undesirable attention at school with questions about "just" and "unjust" wars and other moral issues. Globov brushes aside the boy's concerns, saying "The aim sanctifies the means, it justifies every sort of sacrifice."

A few days later, a nude Marina does her morning exercises before the mirror and narcissistically admires her beauty, which is unspoiled by child-bearing. That evening at her birthday party, a guest offers a toast to Marina's future daughter, a thought that elates Globov. The party ends badly when Globov, incensed by Karlinsky's intimacy with Marina as they dance, "accidentally" knocks over the record player. The couple has a bitter fight, in which Marina gloatingly tells Globov that she has just had an abortion.

Embittered by his wife and troubled by his son's dangerous unorthodoxy, Globov prepares for the Rabinovich trial by making an imaginary speech in the empty nocturnal courtroom. Rabinovich is guilty not merely of abortion; he is undermining the Soviet state. Wandering the empty court building Globov finds graffiti in the women's cloakroom. Unlike his hero, the narrator is enchanted with the beauty of these simple human words. As he muses, the ethereal voice of his Master sternly corrects him: "A word can only be an accusation." All humanity is on trial, and the trial is called "history."

Seryozha has decided that only world revolution can bring about universal justice, and he attempts to rally his school friends to form a secret society. Only Katya turns up at the meeting at the Moscow Zoo, however, where they are observed by two plainclothesmen. Meanwhile, Karlinsky continues his seduction while visiting an art museum with Marina. Globov simultaneously dreams of their assignation, but his dream segues into a guided tour of the museum led by Rabinovich, who shows him a great pulsing brain which produces "only great ideas and supreme purposes." These, Rabinovich says, give rise to the dialects of history. The doctor-guide then shows how "supreme purposes" (ends) have invariably been perverted by the ill means used to attain them: Christianity was subverted by the Inquisition; the Renaissance's creative individualism ended in cutthroat capitalism; and Communism was corrupted by what? The answer, Stalinism, is only implied.

Seryozha is soon arrested. During questioning, his interrogator shows him the masses of ordinary people on the street below. They are on trial, but Seryozha is already condemned. Globov, over the protests of Ekaterina Petrovna, Seryozha's maternal grandmother, has abandoned the boy to his fate. In a drunken rage, the teetotaler Globov smashes up his apartment with a sword, stopping only at a bust of Stalin, to whom he makes his speech of summation: "Master, the enemies are in flight. They have killed my [unborn] daughter and seized my son. My wife has betrayed me. . . . But I stand before you, wounded and forsaken as I am, and say: Our goal is reached."

It is the day of Stalin's funeral. Globov finds himself caught in the huge crowd gathered to view Stalin's body. A giant hand siezes Globov and uses him to cudgel the crowd, and Katya falls under a truck. The crowd turns on

Globov, crying out; "Where's the Public Prosecutor? They ought to be tried, people like that."

In the epilogue, some three years later, the narrator, Seryozha, and Rabinovich find themselves in the same prison camp. The narrator has been imprisoned for maliciously presenting his "positive heroes" (the Globovs and Karlinsky) "in their least typical aspects" and for giving away state secrets. He has failed to carry out his late Master's charge. While digging a ditch, Rabinovich finds a rusted dagger with a crucifix-like handle. He muses that God, formerly the point, the purpose, has become the handle, the means. Ends and means have once again been reversed. Holding the dagger to the sky, the half-mad doctor rants: "In the name of God! With the help of God! In the place of God! Against God. . . . And now there is no God, only dialectics. Forge a new dagger for the new Purpose at once!"

## The Characters

The nameless, faceless narrator charged with exalting Prosecutor Globov foreshadows the fate of his creator, Andrei Sinyavsky: Both are authors who are arrested, tried, and sentenced to a labor camp. The differences between them, however, are crucial. The narrator tries to carry out his divinely imposed mission but fails, in part because of his inadvertent awareness of the conflict between ends and means that he sees in his assigned characters. He believes in the end (Communism) but, against his own will, is distressed by the subversion and displacement of that goal by corrupting means (Stalinism). He is not a dissident. Andrei Sinyavsky, on the other hand, by virtue of writing *The Trial Begins* and smuggling it out for publication in the West, is condemning the Soviet system.

Globov, Marina, and Karlinsky constitute a triangle in more than a romantic sense. Globov is a typical Soviet bureaucrat of peasant background. Superficially cultured, he is devoid of moral insight. He is a true believer, and the Master's dictates are not to be questioned. Karlinsky is a much more interesting (and despicable) character. Cultivated, urbane, witty, he sees the primitive nature of the Stalinist state and society and finds solace in mockery, seduction, and careerism. Marina is completely absorbed in her own beauty and the amusements and comforts it can bring her. The three represent different responses to the moral abyss of Stalinism.

Seryozha and the doomed Katya are the only positive characters. Seryozha naïvely sets out to right the world's wrongs (although he too would not be above shooting the recalcitrant in his perfected society). Katya, also troubled by injustice, is even more interested in Seryozha, who is too committed (or naïve) to recognize this aspect of their relationship. Ironically, it is Katya's attempt to save Seryozha that leads to his arrest and, indirectly, to her accidental death at the hands of his father. Seryozha's grandmother, Ekaterina Petrovna, is an "Old Bolshevik," one of the idealists who made the Revolution. Although retaining their humanity, these idealists are too blinded by the radiant future to realize what has happened to their dream. Ekaterina's idealism is one of the elements that motivates Seryozha.

Dr. Rabinovich, part pathos and part joke, is, with his theory of history and argument about means and ends, the primary spokesman for Sinyavsky: part pathos, because of the historic plight of Russian Jews—of which the "doctors' plot" was a manifestation; part joke, because one Rabinovich (a common Russian Jewish name) is the hero (or butt) of endless Soviet anecdotes. The slightly unsavory depiction of Rabinovich has led to unjustified charges of anti-Semitism. Sinyavsky, an ethnic Russian, chose his Jewish pseudonym, Abram Tertz, partially as a sign of his identification with a persecuted minority, perpetual outsiders.

## Themes and Meanings

The theme of *The Trial Begins* is easily stated. The ideal of Communism has been hopelessly corrupted by Stalinism, the means used to implement that goal. This theme is woven throughout the text. Globov justifies the czarist subjugation of free mountain tribes in the Caucasus (as opposed to the British subjugation of nearby India) on the grounds that the land is necessary for the Soviet state. At a soccer game, Globov defends an unethical act by his favorite player since it was necessary for victory. Even Karlinsky finds that his goal of seducing Marina has been subverted by his means; he proves impotent. The major statement is, however, reserved for Rabinovich.

The central vehicle for expression of the theme is the trial of the novella's title, which is more accurately translated as "the court is in session." Humankind is on trial; to be accused is to be guilty. The purpose of the trial is not to establish guilt or innocence but to serve the Goal, supposedly Communism but in fact the convenience of the Master and his prosecutors, whose personal interests soon supplant the Goal. All issues are decided not on the basis of any reality, but on an a priori view of what best serves the Cause, leading to the perversion of the Revolution and an entire society. No reader will fail to note that in the end, Globov, Karlinsky, and Marina all thrive, while the idealist Seryozha, the narrator, and Rabinovich all rot in a camp.

The novella is beautifully crafted. Framed by a first-person prologue and epilogue, its seven chapters are divided into scenes that are almost dialectically juxtaposed by the omnipresent narrator. In chapter 4, the meeting at the zoo of the two young "lovers," Seryozha and Katya, with their earnest talk of reforming the world, is counterpointed with the art museum where Karlinsky seeks to dazzle Marina into bed with his witty, philosophical sexual commentary on the history of mankind.

The style of the novella is described by its author as phantasmagoric. In the opening scene, one of the plainclothesmen scoops the letters off a manuscript page, watches them writhe, and puts them in his pocket. Globov has telepathic dreams in which he eavesdrops on Karlinsky and Marina in the museum. The mythic vision of Stalin flickers in and out of the story, often symbolized by his mighty right hand. The fantastic elements in the narrative reflect Sinyavsky's reaction against the stultifying dogma of Socialist Realism and his view that only the phantasmagoric is capable of rendering the paranoic grotesquerie of Stalinist society.

*Critical Context*

The last years of Stalin were a nightmare of paranoid despotism. Millions were in labor camps, and the arts had been degraded to the level of primitive propaganda under the banner of "Socialist Realism." With Stalin's death, the first of a series of "thaws" began. A moribund literature began to revive but was impeded by recurrent "freezes." Socialist Realism continued to be the only approved form of literature. Many feared a return of Stalinism. A young literary scholar and friend of Boris Pasternak (whose publication in the West of *Doctor Zhivago* in 1957, with its English translation in 1958, had brought him both a Nobel Prize for Literature and government vilification), Andrei Sinyavsky decided to risk sending his work abroad. Using the pseudonym Abram Tertz, Sinyavsky smuggled out two works: a theoretical essay, *On Socialist Realism* (1960), decrying the sterility of Socialist Realism and calling for a new "phantasmagoric" literature; and a novella, *The Trial Begins*, which illustrated his literary argument and was a powerful indictment of Stalinism. Sinyavsky's works created a sensation and endless speculation about the identify of their author. The author's double life continued until he was betrayed and sentenced to a labor camp. After serving his sentence, Sinyavsky was permitted to emigrate to France, where he has lived since 1973. The story of his life as Abram Tertz and of his prison camp years is told in involute, ornate form in his stunning 1984 novel-memoir *Spokoinoi nochi* (good night). Sinyavsky's *The Trial Begins* is one of the foundation works in the post-Stalin rebirth of Russian literature.

*Sources for Further Study*

Browning, Deming. *Soviet Russian Literature Since Stalin*, 1978.

Dalton, Margaret. *Andrei Siniavskii and Julii Daniel': Two Soviet "Heretical" Writers*, 1973.

Labedz, Leopold, and Max Hayward, eds. *On Trial: The Case of Sinyavsky (Tertz) and Daniel (Arzhak), Documents*, 1967.

Lourie, Richard. *Letters to the Future: An Approach to Sinyavsky-Tertz*, 1975.

Mihajlov, Mihajlo. "Flight from the Test Tube," in *Russian Themes*, 1968.

*D. Barton Johnson*

# THE TRILOGY

*Author:* Samuel Beckett (1906-    )
*Type of plot:* Absurdist narrative
*Time of plot:* The indeterminate present
*Locale:* A landscape, a room, and a void
*First published: Molloy*, 1951 (English translation, 1955); *Malone meurt*, 1951
    (*Malone Dies*, 1956); *L'Innommable*, 1953 (*The Unnamable*, 1958)

> *Principal characters:*
> MOLLOY, an author of sorts
> JACQUES MORAN, possibly the "author" of Molloy
> MALONE, a man dying in a room
> THE UNNAMABLE, referring to himself as "I"

*The Novels*

In order to describe and discuss these three novels, collectively referred to
as The Trilogy, the reader must set aside all previous conceptions and expectations regarding the novel form, for, like no literature since James
Joyce's *Finnegans Wake* (1939), Samuel Beckett's awesome postwar work
expands the definition of epic literature beyond all recognizable boundaries.
While the first-person narrator (whose name and "habits of mind" may
change but who represents the author in ever-contracting modes of existence) may on the surface seem cogent and communicative, the convolutions
of his train of thought are so complex and reflexive that the "story" of his
journey must be pieced together from the shards of his shattered narrative.
Taken separately, each novel is its own perplexing narrative through landscapes and womblike environments and journeys in space and time, from the
narrator's search for his mother, through a dying man's categorization of
what is left of his physical world, to an abstract mind-state in which the narrator has become pure voice without substance. Taken together, they offer
the rawest, most philosophically honest portrait of the artist ever undertaken
by a modern writer.

The narrator of *Molloy* opens his story with the words, "I am in my mother's room." Thus, the narrator begins the cryptic description of the agonizing
journey that brought him there, to "finish dying." Molloy writes a few pages
now and then; a man named Jacques Moran (who becomes the first-person
narrator of the second part of the novel) gives him money and takes the
pages away. To satisfy them ("there is more than one, apparently," says
Molloy), he begins his story: "It was on a road remarkably bare." Molloy,
having slept in a ditch, now progresses by crutches, by bicycle, by long rests
and longer digressions, vaguely toward his mother's hometown. His mis-

adventures along the way constitute a chronicle of all that can go wrong with any journey, geographical or otherwise: missteps, falls, bruises, beatings by strangers, loss of direction, uncertainty regarding the duration of the journey to date, encounters near and distant with other travelers, interruptions caused by sexual urges toward persons of questionable gender, and a pervading sense of the absurdity and meaninglessness of any journey, any effort, whatsoever.

In part 2, Moran receives instructions from Gaber, some sort of supervisor, to "see about Molloy." If Molloy is introspective and circular, Moran is external, matter-of-fact, and direct, "so patiently turned to the outer world as toward the lesser evil." Moran's tracking down of Molloy can also be seen as an inventing of Molloy, so that the best interpretation of the relationship is that Moran actually invented Molloy, who then disobeyed orders by leaving his desk (where Gaber daily expected pages to appear) and by wandering vaguely toward his mother's home. This device, the character who grows past the author's expectations into a life of his own, is often seen in postmodern writing—for example, in the work of Italian playwright Luigi Pirandello, Spanish philosopher and novelist Miguel de Unamuno y Jugo, and Argentinian short-story writer Jorge Luis Borges. Here, the genius of Beckett adds yet another twist: Molloy and Moran may be the same person, two sides of the author himself, internal and external, the private and the public, and the celebrity and the anguished soul in the celebrity's body.

In the second novel of The Trilogy, *Malone Dies*, things are, on the surface, much less complicated. Malone, possibly the same character as in the earlier novel (and still trying to "finish dying"), is now bedridden, immobilized by the insistent, recurring leg problems so ubiquitous among Beckett's characters. Within his grasp and eyesight is a strictly limited number of objects, which he inventories in his mind as he contemplates his last moments: a cupboard, a window, a long stick, the bed, and his possessions in the corner in a little heap. A table with castors, which he moves with his long stick, serves as a vehicle for food and chamber pot ("Dish and pot, dish and pot, these are the poles"). The apparent simplicity of his situation, however, does not take into account the teeming mind, cluttered with memories called up willingly and unwillingly as Malone lies on his back, cheek to pillow. The remainder of the novel consists of Malone's attempts at conjuring, cataloging, admitting, and dismissing those memories as they come, disjointed, confused, separated by periods of sleep (signified in the text by blank lines), like stories he is telling himself. It is once again the author, this time, as always, trying to stop speaking, stop writing, stop creating. As the periods of sleep increase, the narrative tapers off, until Malone imagines "never... anything... there... any more...."

"Where now? Who now? When now?" With this, the startling opening inquiry of *The Unnamable*, the persona of Molloy/Moran/Malone awakens yet again to the universal Beckettian axiom: "Keep going, going on, call that go-ing, call that on." This time disembodied, the narrative mind questions again the perceptions as received through the senses, including memory. Here, the narrator is situated at the center of a gray landscape without features, past which the characters from the previous novels march: "Malone is there. Of his mortal liveliness little trace remains. . . . Perhaps it is Molloy, wearing Malone's hat." What follows is page after page of indescribable anguish in the present tense, as the conscious "I" seeks to imagine and describe the mo-ment of finality; the last nine pages of the novel are all one sentence, in which the narrator attempts the impossible task of perceiving the last mo-ment of perception. Echoing the opening sentences, the last phrase—"you must go on, I can't go on, I'll go on"—are the most famous and most des-perate words of all postmodern Absurdist literature.

## The Characters

Beckett's works cannot be approached from the tradition of psychological characterization. He is not interested in building from the details of personal actions and reactions a recognizable portrait of an individual human being. Beckett's reason for writing is singular: All of his efforts to stop doing so have failed. In this lies the essence of all "characterization" in Beckett. The protagonist, invariably the first-person narrator, is telling a story, his story, and it is coming out of him without order or deliberation, but inevitably, in-exorably, inexhaustibly. Molloy, sitting at his desk, turning out page after page, is the author himself. Moran, hired to gather the pages, is the author as well, looking at himself writing. Malone, dying in his bed, is the author again, this time sorting out his "possessions" in his head, discovering once again that memories are as tangible and accountable as physical objects per-ceived through the senses. Even Malone's apparent body death does not si-lence the eternal "I" of the author in *The Unnamable*, parading those char-acters as additions to the memories of the author who created them. The only psychological characteristics the reader can assign to the characters are an obsessive tendency toward self-examination, a compulsion to catalog, and an inability to stop "going on."

As part of the incessant remembrances of the narrator, bits and pieces of other characters come to light in the "catalog": Gaber's businesslike indiffer-ence to Moran's day off, Molloy's girlfriend (whose name escapes him) in the garbage dump, Mrs. Lambert calling her chickens in. These fading "frescoes of the skull," however, have no more substance than the narrator's inventions ("I have often amused myself with trying to invent them, those same lost events"). Any effort to construct whole characters out of these bare clues will not come to fruition. More valuable is the observation that all Beckett's characters share the same unromantic view of life, the same fascination with remembering, the same physical ailments of the legs and feet, the same gray landscape through which they wander, and the same attention to the possibility (never realized) of ending for good and all the scratchings of conscious thought on the skull of their unenviable existence.

## Themes and Meanings

The four sections of The Trilogy (Molloy is in two parts) are in fact four monologues by the same person, the author/creator. Beckett's themes are the themes of the existentialist: One is born, one suffers, one dies. Life is a very brief journey through an unremarkable landscape that provides painful encounters despite one's best efforts at avoiding them. Sleep is a trick, because one must awaken to oneself once again. Notions of some supernatural Maker with a Master Plan are nothing more than devices to pass the time, to divert one momentarily from the realization of one's ontological loneliness. Yet amid all the evidence that life is meaningless, hopeless, full of despair, anguish, and forlornness, one must go on. Beckett stated his obsessive theme in a dialogue with Georges Duthuit: "that there is nothing to express, nothing with which to express, nothing from which to express, no power to express, no desire to express, together with the *obligation* to express" (emphasis added). That "obligation to express" is what moves The Trilogy forward, despite fatigue, anxiety, and an overpowering desire to become "still."

The most startling observation regarding The Trilogy is the humor to be found in it. Not only does Beckett manage to express the inexpressibility of his universe but he also does so with wit and compassion. His wry observations demonstrate a remarkable attention to detail and an Irish infatuation with the pun. The fortitude of the characters, moving what might be called forward despite all impediments, causes the reader to cheer them on in their pointless marathon. Without reference to Beckett's personal past, the novels convey a sense of abandonment, of childhood neglect, of parental indifference, that gives the entire narrative a mood of infinite sadness. Beckett's style is unique: a combination of terse, telegraphic shortcuts, vague antecedents, and sudden elaborations of simple statements, daunting to the careless reader but a source of delight to those who puzzle it out.

## Critical Context

Along with William Faulkner's "unreliable narrator" fiction, the seemingly unstructured narratives of Marcel Proust and Jack Kerouac, and the microscopically detailed and unemotional "new novels" of Alain Robbe-Grillet, Beckett's trilogy signaled the advent of the postmodern novel, in which the subject of the author's examination is the act of writing itself. Rather than the carefully structured narrative that dominated the history of the novel since Homer, the postmodern novel looks inward at itself, at the writing process, at the configurations of the human intellect that create literary expression. With such contemporary writers as William Gass and Raymond

Federman, Beckett's self-creating narrators are expanded into subjective consciousnesses capable of saying anything at any time, freeing themselves from their authors in the very act of being written down.

What is lost, however, in these free-form experiments is the passion and bleakness of Beckett's vision, the philosophical irony of flinging words at the ontological void. The intellectual world discovered Beckett primarily through the amazing dramatic works *En attendant Godot* (1952; *Waiting for Godot*, 1954) and *Fin de partie* (1957; *Endgame*, 1958), but The Trilogy stands next to Jean-Paul Sartre's *L'Être et le néant* (1943; *Being and Nothingness*, 1956) as the most important treatise on existentialism ever written.

*Sources for Further Study*
Abbott, H. Porter. *The Fiction of Samuel Beckett: Form and Effect*, 1973.
Fletcher, John. *The Novels of Samuel Beckett*, 1964.
O'Hara, James Donald, ed. *Twentieth Century Interpretations of "Molloy," "Malone Dies," "The Unnamable": A Collection of Essays*, 1970.
Pilling, John. *Samuel Beckett*, 1976.
Robinson, Michael. *The Long Sonata of the Dead: A Study of Samuel Beckett*, 1969.

*Thomas J. Taylor*

# TRIPTYCH

*Author:* Claude Simon (1913-    )
*Type of plot:* Antistory
*Time of plot:* The 1970's
*Locale:* A farm valley, a Riviera beach resort, and a northern city in France
*First published: Triptyque*, 1973 (English translation, 1976)

> *Principal characters:*
> CORINNE, a middle-aged baroness
> LILY, a twenty-year-old barmaid
> THE GROOM, a young man on his wedding day
> THE BOYS, two young farmboys
> LAMBERT, an Englishman, Corinne's friend

*The Novel*

   *Triptych* is one of Claude Simon's most difficult novels to read, yet it is also a fascinating creation. The only true means of organizing *Triptych* comes from its three place settings: the farm, the beach, and the city. These locales interlock intriguingly. For example, Simon has a city theater showing a film that is the story of Corinne at the beach. While the actress playing Corinne takes a break from the filming, she reads a book that is about the young groom in the city. Similarly, the two young farmboys find discarded pieces of film from the motion picture about Corinne at the beach. Toward the end of the novel, Lambert completes a jigsaw puzzle that depicts the farm valley, and the two boys are in that bucolic scene. These are merely a few examples of how Simon encloses one story within the mechanisms of another. The effect of this constant shifting is a mild shock to the reader, who is being shown constantly that what he mistook for the real story of *Triptych* is but a section contained in another story that itself may be the true one. These shifts of focus, while perhaps annoying to some readers, do support Simon's theory that all fictions are false and unreliable, and that the reader should never take them to be accurate depictions of reality.

   Simon reiterates the theme of the falseness of art in other ways. As the novel begins, Simon describes a postcard of the beach scene lying on a table in a farmhouse. He explains to the reader about how poorly reproduced the colors are on that postcard. Similarly, during the showing of films (which occurs often), the projector breaks down more than once. At one point, after showing a very sensual love scene, the projector actually burns a hole in the film, one example of Simon's infrequent humor.

   Although it is scattered in jigsawlike pieces throughout *Triptych*, a semblance of a plot or plots does gradually emerge. In the farm sequences, two young boys go fishing, swim at a waterfall, spy on a couple making passionate love in a barn, try to reconstruct a story from small pieces of discarded motion-picture film, and let a little girl who had been left in their care drown. Also appearing in the farm scenes is an old dog-faced woman who has killed and skinned a rabbit for her supper. In this setting, too, there is a schoolboy at his desk at home gazing out of the window. He is bored and a bit frustrated with a difficult geometry problem. The reader sees his repeated but futile efforts to solve this problem, mixed in with his daydreams, interruptions from his family, and the changing view from window. This nameless boy's inability to finish his homework is analogous to the reader trying to fit together the various elements of *Triptych*.

A second set of scenes woven throughout the novel tells Corinne's story. She is a wealthy widow staying at an exclusive beach resort. Her friend Lambert is called to her aid when she learns that her teenage son has been arrested for drug dealing. Lambert pays a bribe to a Mr. Brown, who sees to it that the youngster is released from jail. In order to accomplish this act successfully, Corinne has had to give sexual favors to Lambert, but the reader is never actually shown the sexual encounters of these two.

The third sequence of scenes found within *Triptych* depicts the groom on his wedding day. His friends bring him to a city tavern to celebrate. There he makes sexual advances to the barmaid Lily, who accepts him; the two awkwardly make love standing in the rain in an alley behind the bar. Later, a man on a motorcycle follows the groom and attacks him, supposedly because of jealousy over Lily.

One constantly interrupting subplot comments on the action in these three settings. A clown in a circus ring performs his antics, sometimes with a partner or a monkey; he mimics the actions of the characters in the main scenes. For example, when the groom has trouble making love to Lily because of his drunken state, the clown stumbles around the ring as if drunk. This clown is usually introduced into the action of the novel by the same device; in this example, his face is on a poster on the barn wall where the two farm boys watch through a crack as a couple make love.

The reader of *Triptych* can only discern these elements of a plot by a close reading of each scene; as in a puzzle or game, clues are given each time that a piece of plot is repeated. Simon does not introduce these sets of scenes in any chronological order; instead, he purposely mixes events into random sequences. By the end of the novel, however, an alert reader will know a fair amount about each of the three settings and their characters.

*The Characters*

Simon only sketchily depicts the few characters in this novel. The reader finds that Corinne is actually an actress who plays a wealthy widow in the resort scenes. The young actor who portrays her son also appears in a film in which he is the groom at the bar. Lily the barmaid seems to have had a previous relationship with the man on the motorcycle who later assaults the groom. Meanwhile, a sad young bride awaits the drunken groom in a nearby hotel room.

Some of the characters that Simon creates do appear to have symbolic roles. The dog-faced, elderly farm wife may represent Cerebus, who guarded the gates of Hell in mythology. This old woman is an eerie figure, dressed mostly in black, and she reappears often in the farm scenes. She usually pushes an old baby carriage that is filled with grass to feed her caged rabbits. Similarly, Lambert at the beach resort may represent an author. When the novel closes, he is finishing a jigsaw puzzle, much as Simon creates and completes the puzzle of scenes in *Triptych*. The two young boys in the farm village remain unnamed and seem to represent all youth. They are healthy and exuberant and have an early adolescent interest in learning about sex; they not only spy repeatedly on the couple in the barn but also watch a young girl disrobe to swim, and the bits of film that they treasure mainly show the actress Corinne nude on a bed.

Simon's primary depiction of women in *Triptych* is as sexual objects available for men's enjoyment. Yet the author often has women gain the advantage over men in personal and sexual matters. Lily is unscathed after her liaison with the groom, but he is beaten severely for his interest in her. Corinne uses a sexual encounter with her friend Lambert to get him to help free her son from jail. The female farm servant in the barn sequences appears to enjoy thoroughly her sexual acts with her virile partner.

Simon does not provide the reader with characters that are at all as psychologically complex or minutely documented as those created by authors of traditional novels. The figures that the reader finds in *Triptych* represent all ages and classes of people. In this way, Simon shows the diversity of humanity, but he does so while he comments on the uniformity of experience. Sexual interests are common to almost all these characters, as are the pleasures of eating, drinking, and seeking amusement in films, books, puzzles, and drugs.

*Themes and Meanings*

Simon's purpose in *Triptych* is to shake the reader's very faith in the reality of the novel. Simon shows his reader that all fictions are merely fictional and do not represent any reality; they represent only themselves. In this manner, the author displays to his reader the truth of the novel.

By creating a distrust of fictional reality in the reader, Simon demonstrates also the overbearing role that a narrator (or even a zealous reader) may play in the traditional novel. A narrator often makes plot links for the reader and provides all types of information that the images in the novel do not actually show. Thus a narrator, especially an omniscient one, takes some of the joy of discovery away from the reader. In *Triptych*, the typical reader will strain to find details that further explain the scenes and the characters. When such information is forthcoming from the book, it is welcomed, and when it is not, the reader may feel disappointed. Through all of this process, Simon has impressed on his audience the precise function of a good reader: to see clearly what is given and no more than that.

Simon also provides more traditional themes. He emphasizes the interrelationships of sex, violence, and death. The most passionate lovemaking in *Triptych* has violent overtones. In the barn scenes at the farm, the couple finds frantic pleasure, yet Simon places the old woman carrying home her dead and bleeding rabbit just outside the barn. In the city scenes, where Lily and the groom make love in the alley, their encounter ends with the fierce beating of the groom. The groom had also struggled with Lily and shoved her away when she refused to give him his car keys. Only the sex acts of Corinne and Lambert produce a positive result—her son's freedom. Corinne's lovemaking is not that which arises out of passion (as was the case with Lily and the farm girl), however, but is sex used merely as a part of a business transaction.

In *Triptych*, Simon also is interested in contrasting the types of lives people lead in the various sections of France. In the village scenes, there is a natural spontaneity (especially among the children) and a closeness to nature. The two young boys like to fish and swim, and they hide in the cornstalks when they get in trouble with adults. Conversely, in the city, the atmosphere is dreary and desolate; it rains almost constantly, and a damp chill pervades everything. The pretty, harmonious scenery of the farm is replaced by the mechanism of flashy cars and noisy trolleys in the city. Simon's third locale, the beach resort, is a place for the rich only. He has a narrator describe the plushness and elegance of the resort buildings in a film being shown in the village.

Thus, Simon creates themes in *Triptych* that reflect his experimentation with new forms of the novel as well as his interest in more traditional ideas as presented in European novels of earlier eras.

*Critical Context*

*Triptych* is one example of the New Novel in France. Simon and other avant-garde writers, such as Michel Butor and Alain Robbe-Grillet, have been attempting to stretch the boundaries of the traditional novel since the 1950's. While Simon's *Triptych* is one of the boldest and most innovative of the new novels, it has not found favor with all literary critics; critical reaction ranges from rather positive to fairly negative. While finding it to be a unique creation by a highly talented author, critics also question whether such an avant-garde book plays a positive role in the development of the novel. In his efforts to introduce a new direction for fiction, Simon has actually done away with many of the fundamental elements of the novel, especially plot and characterization. Whether what he provides is enough to compensate the reader for the struggle to interpret this novel correctly is a question left unanswered by most critics. As Simon wishes, each reader must judge the value and importance of *Triptych* for himself.

*Sources for Further Study*
Gould, Karen L. *Claude Simon's Mythic Muse*, 1979.
Jiménez-Fajardo, Salvador. *Claude Simon*, 1975.
Loubère, J. A. E. *The Novels of Claude Simon*, 1975.
Roudiez, Leon S. *French Fiction Today: A New Direction*, 1972.
Sturrock, John. *The French New Novel: Claude Simon, Michel Butor, Alain Robbe-Grillet*, 1969.

*Patricia E. Sweeney*

# THE TRUE STORY OF AH Q

*Author:* Lu Hsün (Chou Shu-jên, 1881-1936)
*Type of plot:* Satire
*Time of plot:* 1910-1911
*Locale:* The fictional village of Weichuang in China
*First published: Ah Q cheng-chuan*, 1921, serial (English translation, 1927)

> *Principal characters:*
> AH Q, a village loafer and occasional performer of odd jobs
> MR. CHAO, one of the influential local gentry
> THE IMITATION FOREIGN DEVIL, a student just returned from
> Japan

*The Novel*

This book relates events in the last year of the life of Ah Q, a village idler and odd-jobber in the Chinese village of Weichuang. The unnamed narrator gives the reader a satirical first-person perspective on the shortcomings of the Chinese national character as mirrored in Ah Q and his fellow villagers. The story also provides a commentary on the state of the revolution which had occurred in 1911 and had supposedly done away with the feudal elements of society.

After confessing himself to be unable to ascertain Ah Q's surname, personal name (thus he is called Ah Q in lieu of a correct name), or place of origin, the narrator gives a series of vignettes showing Ah Q and his relations with his fellow villagers. It is immediately apparent that Ah Q lives in a world of self-deception. He frequently gets into quarrels with village idlers and is invariably bested by them, the disputes ending with Ah Q having his head knocked against a wall five or six times. He additionally obliges his enemies by calling himself an insect and a beast. Ah Q nevertheless manages to rationalize these defeats into victories by claiming moral or psychological superiority over his opponents.

His relations with the more influential villagers are no more amicable. Mr. Chao, whose son has just taken his bachelor's degree, despises Ah Q as a no-good and slaps his face upon learning that Ah Q has been bragging that he is related to the Chao clan. Ah Q himself hates the "Imitation Foreign Devil," a student who has just returned from Japan and wears foreign dress. Apparently, Ah Q is even more disturbed by the fact that this person is wearing a false pigtail than he is about the young man's selling out to foreign ways.

One day, Ah Q encounters a young Buddhist nun in the street and proceeds to tease her unmercifully, pinching her cheek and taunting her about monk-nun relationships. This draws laughs from onlookers but also precipitates feelings in Ah Q about sex which eventually impel him to make an indecent proposal to Amah Wu, the servant of Mr. Chao. Amah Wu, a chaste widow, is completely flustered, and Mr. Chao severely punishes Ah Q and has him pay damages. The consequence is that women now avoid him, the wine shop refuses him credit, and no one will hire him. Hungry, he wanders out of the village and eventually arrives at the Buddhist convent, where he steals turnips from the garden. He is chased away by an old nun and a ferocious black dog. At this point, Ah Q decides to leave the village and go to the city.

Several months later, Ah Q returns to the village, now with adequate money, boasting of having seen revolutionaries executed in the city. His status rises in the eyes of the villagers, and he starts selling the numerous items that he has brought back with him. Even his relationship with the more affluent villagers is changed for the better. Mr. Chao, lusting after bargains, sets aside his dislike for Ah Q and proposes to buy the goods that Ah Q has. Mr. Chao does this even though he suspects that they are stolen items and cautions his wife to keep the doors and windows locked. Later, when it is learned that Ah Q did indeed gain his money and possessions through thievery, his status is lowered again in the eyes of the villagers, especially since he is merely a petty thief and receiver of stolen goods and not a daring robber.

As word reaches the Weichuang villagers that revolutionaries have indeed entered the city, the narrative picks up its pace. Mr. Chao and his son become fearful and start currying favor with the Imitation Foreign Devil, who has joined the revolutionary party. Ah Q decides that the revolution must be a good thing, since Mr. Chao is afraid of it; indeed, Ah Q wants to become a revolutionary himself, but he is not asked to join the "revolutionary activities," such as robbing Mr. Chao's house and ransacking the convent.

At this point, Ah Q is suddenly arrested by the revolutionaries as a suspected accomplice of the splinter group which robbed Mr. Chao. Ah Q is as uncomprehending as ever and continues his self-deception and rationalization by assuming that it is the fate of everyone to be arrested at some time. Finally, as he is brought to the execution ground, he becomes dimly aware of what is happening and perceives the nature of the crowd, which is unfeeling and clamoring for a good show.

*The Characters*

Lu Hsün has placed his protagonist, Ah Q, in a fictional village modeled on his own hometown of Shaohsing. Ah Q certainly represents the outcasts of society that Lu Hsün saw there. Yet the author also intends that his character be more broadly based. In not giving him a surname, personal name, or place of origin, and in not giving a concrete description of his facial features, Lu Hsün has universalized Ah Q into the Chinese Everyman.

Ah Q does not think about the significance of what he sees or the consequences of what he does. When he causes Amah Wu to run screaming from him after his indecent proposal, he does not see how this is connected with Mr. Chao's ensuing anger. When he teases the Buddhist nun, he is only aware that it is causing the village idlers to laugh and approve. He is totally in the dark as to the meaning of the revolution, and understands only that it is a means of redressing old grievances and settling the score with his various enemies.

Ah Q also embodies other traits which Lu Hsün believed were injurious to the welfare of a nation struggling to enter the twentieth century. Ah Q adheres to old-fashioned prejudices, such as the feeling that women are inferior creatures, which have been the downfall of men throughout Chinese history. Especially damaging is Ah Q's habit of accepting defeat and rationalizing it as moral victory. At one point, the narrator satirically refers to Ah Q's "victories" as proof of China's moral supremacy over the rest of the world. The rationalizations become fatalism when Ah Q assumes that everyone is bound to be arrested. These rationalizations border on withdrawal from reality, illustrated perfectly by Ah Q slapping himself, then separating himself into slapper and slappee, and identifying himself with the slapper, who by definition is victorious. In Lu Hsün's view, the Chinese were dangerously deluding themselves.

Some attention is paid to the educated class of society in the figures of Mr. Chao and the Imitation Foreign Devil. Mr. Chao is full of Confucian precepts and adages (and high-class profanity), but he is still greedy for any advantage he can get, including bargain prices on stolen goods. For him, the revolution simply means that he will have to be careful to preserve the status quo as far as that is possible. The Imitation Foreign Devil has studied abroad in Japan and knows something about the revolution, yet he is unable to think in terms of reforming feudal evils and is more concerned with displaying his new influence and connections. His idea of revolutionary activity is to ally himself with Mr. Chao's son (whom he actually dislikes) and go to the Buddhist convent to despoil it and slap the old nun.

Of the minor characters, Amah Wu serves as a target for Ah Q's briefly awakened sexual feelings, while the younger Buddhist nun is the convenient recipient of his prejudiced feelings about women. Mr. Chao's son is ready to follow faithfully in his father's footsteps and seems to have no new ideas. The villagers themselves, in Lu Hsün's symbolism, function as another character, having some of the same qualities as Ah Q. They are especially seen as gullible and unthinking, believing, for example, that Ah Q must be guilty of the robbery (he was not) or else he would not have been executed, or that Ah Q might indeed be of the Chao clan, simply because he had once claimed it.

*Themes and Meanings*
    *The True Story of Ah Q* is concerned with the shortcomings of the Chinese national character and the deplorable state of the 1911 revolution, which toppled the old dynasty and introduced the Republic. Lu Hsün believed that the

people in general were unaware, uncritical, and tied to an outmoded past. Their fatalism, backwardness, and rationalization of defeat all hampered China's ability to compete with the West. Ah Q's last thought, marking his growing awareness, is that the crowd is like a wolf, its eyes boring into him and hungering for his death. It is an ambiguous symbol, for this same unthinking and lethal crowd (the masses), if awakened, could accomplish great work.

By December, 1921, when *The True Story of Ah Q* was completed, Lu Hsün had noted the failure of the revolution. In the novel, when the revolutionaries arrive, evidently nothing has changed. Indeed, the revolutionaries ally themselves with the local gentry. Some titles have changed, but the same people are still officials. A revolution has occurred, but the people have been barred from it—even dim-witted Ah Q notices this, and thinks that since a revolution has occurred, it should have involved something more. The uneducated masses did not understand what was taking place, and their awakening was apparently yet to come. Meanwhile, the educated were managing to accommodate themselves and the revolutionaries were engaged in nonrevolutionary activity. For Lu Hsün, the revolution effected no real change.

The author was attracted to nineteenth century Russian Romantic concepts of literature, especially those of Nikolai Gogol, which involved devices such as nature symbolism, the cult of heroism, and a preference for extreme exaggeration and irony. The Symbolist writings of Leonid Andreyev also influenced his style. Lu Hsün, unlike many of his fellow Chinese writers, did not follow the realist concepts then current, for a literal and objective representation of social reality was not the technique that he desired to use. The novel, employing exaggeration and poking fun at many of the characters, is written in a completely satiric mode, in which even the chapter titles are ironic and offer tongue-in-cheek comments, such as "The Grand Finale" (the last chapter, in which Ah Q is executed).

Although Lu Hsün was a leftist writer and was virtually deified by the Communists after his death, his criticism of society is actually classless. In his first short story, "K'uang-jên jih-chi" ("The Diary of a Madman") the madman-narrator cries out that all the children must be saved, not only the working-class children. It is notable that in *The True Story of Ah Q*, the lower classes are just as much a target of the satirist's ire as are the affluent and the revolutionaries. Lu Hsün follows the Romantic convention that the truth is spoken by the underdog or outcast. It is Ah Q, the outcast, who dimly perceives the nature of his surrounding circumstances. The truth evidently cannot be perceived by people who are members of any class or group, so it is indeed a harsh criticism of society when the truth is spoken only by madmen or outcasts.

*Critical Context*

Soon after the 1911 revolution, intellectuals called for another revolution to create a more modern literature that would educate and promote regeneration of the Chinese nation. Literature (like society) was looked upon as being bound to the past, using the outmoded classical language and rhetorical devices and containing old-fashioned themes and ideas. Taking Western literature as a general model, a call was issued for writing couched in contemporary language which addressed itself to twentieth century ideas and problems.

A member of this new group of intellectuals, Lu Hsün is credited with writing the first modern (Western-style) short story in China, "The Diary of a Madman." Of the rapidly evolving groups, it was the radical intellectuals who became the most influential and who used Russian writers as their models. Lu Hsün quickly became the most famous of these writers, and after his death, he was upheld by the Communists as the leader of the cultural revolution. *The True Story of Ah Q* was his most famous work. It is interesting, however, that he never joined the Communist Party. As a satirist, he was too independent and critical, apparently, to belong to any particular group.

*Sources for Further Study*

Fokkema, Douwe. "Lu Xun: The Impact of Russian Literature," in *Modern Chinese Literature in the May Fourth Era*, 1977.

Hanan, Patrick. "The Technique of Lu Hsün's Fiction," in *Harvard Journal of Asiatic Studies*. XXXIV (1974), pp. 53-96.

Hsia, T. A. "Aspects of the Power of Darkness in Lu Hsün," in *The Gate of Darkness: Studies in the Leftist Literary Movement in China*, 1968.

Lee, Leo Ou-fan, ed. *Lu Xun and His Legacy*, 1985.

Lyell, William A., Jr. *Lu Hsün's Vision of Reality*, 1976.

*James Muhleman*

# TUBBY SCHAUMANN
## A Tale of Murder and the High Seas

*Author:* Wilhelm Raabe (1831-1910)
*Type of plot:* Social realism
*Time of plot:* Probably the 1880's
*Locale:* A town in Germany and a farm overlooking the town, on the site of an old fortress
*First published: Stopfkuchen: Eine See- und Mordgeschichte*, 1891 (English translation, 1983)

> *Principal characters:*
> EDWARD, the narrator, who made his fortune and settled in South Africa
> HEINRICH (TUBBY) SCHAUMANN, the main character of the story, one of Edward's boyhood friends
> ANDREAS QUAKATZ, owner of Red Bank Farm
> VALENTINA, his daughter
> STÖRZER, a country postman

*The Novel*

Wilhelm Raabe's novel *Tubby Schaumann: A Tale of Murder and the High Seas* focuses on the life story of Heinrich (Tubby) Schaumann, called "Stopfkuchen" in German. The translator used the nickname "Tubby" to capture the feeling of the German nickname, which can be rendered as "cake eater," although *stopfen* (to stuff) conveys more vividly than "to eat" the grotesque image of the young Heinrich stuffing himself with desserts to the point of obesity. The subtitle includes the word "murder" because a murder influences the lives of all the major characters, and it includes "the high seas" to refer to the narrator's location on board ship as he tells his story.

As the novel opens, Edward, the narrator, is writing about his encounter with Tubby Schaumann during a short visit to his hometown in Germany. While there, he had intended to visit his old mentor, Störzer, a country postman who told him stories as a young boy about exotic places based on François Le Vaillant's *Voyage de M. Le Vaillant dans l'Intérieur de l'Afrique* (two volumes, 1790; *Travels into the Interior Parts of Africa*, 1790). Störzer's excitement about these places fired Edward's imagination and inspired him to seek his fortune in South Africa, where he now has property and a family. Learning of Störzer's death, Edward decided to visit his boyhood friend Tubby Schaumann, who had dreamed of owning Red Bank Farm, situated on the site of some fortress ruins overlooking the city, just as Edward had dreamed of travel to more exciting places.

During his visit with Schaumann and his wife, Edward is told the whole story of how Schaumann's dream was realized. When the two were boys, the farm was owned by a man named Andreas Quakatz, who lived as an outcast because the villagers suspected him of having murdered the livestock dealer Kienbaum. There was no proof of Quakatz's guilt, but that did not convince the community, who self-righteously isolated the man and his daughter. Schaumann, an outcast himself because, as Edward remembers, "in those days [he was] the fattest, laziest, and greediest of us all," had immediate sympathy for the two outsiders. He struck up an acquaintance with the daughter, Valentina, and finally one day won her friendship when he came to her defense during an attack by some village boys who used to mock her and throw stones. Being allowed to visit, he soon won the father's friendship as well. Red Bank Farm became his sanctuary, and with the passing of time, he married Valentina and settled there permanently.

In his long, slowly rambling narration, Schaumann reveals that he knows who killed Kienbaum and then does not give the final account until he and Edward go into town that evening. At an inn where there is a waitress who overhears and later spreads the information, he tells the story of Störzer's confession that he killed Kienbaum by accident. Kienbaum provoked the incident by hitting him with a whip, and poor Störzer, trying to defend himself, threw the stone which resulted in Kienbaum's death. When Störzer discovered that he had actually killed Kienbaum, he delayed reporting it, even after Quakatz was unjustly accused. Until the end of his life, he was unable to make the admission that would have cleared Quakatz's name. When Schaumann discovered the truth, Quakatz had already died, and he saw no purpose in revealing the facts as long as Störzer was alive.

Störzer's recent death and Edward's visit give Schaumann the perfect opportunity to end that chapter of his story. In the end, Edward realizes that he has no advantage over those who remained at home in Germany: "Yes, at bottom it all amounts to the same thing, whether you stay lying under the hedge and let adventure find you out or whether you let your good friend Fritz Störzer and his old Le Vaillant and Johann Reinhold Forster [a German naturalist] send you abroad to find it on the high seas or in the desert."

*The Characters*

The life stories of all five of the principal characters are interrelated in this carefully constructed narrative. Edward interprets this construction explicitly for the reader when he quotes the German philosopher Christian Wolff's principle of sufficient reason: "Nothing *is* without a reason for its being so." Störzer has influenced Edward's life through his tales of faraway places, just as his accidental killing of Kienbaum made outcasts of Quakatz and his daughter and attracted Schaumann to them, eventually making Schaumann the new master of Red Bank Farm.

The two principal characters, Schaumann and Edward, provide a double perspective to the story. On one level, there is the contrast between the traveler and the one who stays at home, and on another level, there is the conflict between the conventional man (Edward) and the individual (Schaumann), who stands outside and against society. The double perspective allows the reader to understand the feeling of the outcast through Schaumann's personal telling of his story and at the same time to see events from a certain distance through the eyes of Edward, the visitor who has since made a life for himself outside this community.

The reader gets to know the narrator mostly as a representative of society. Edward, although called an old friend of Schaumann, is actually involved in society's guilt as well. He was perhaps not an active tormentor, but he went along with the group rather than defending young Schaumann. He, too, thought (and still thinks) of Schaumann as "Tubby."

Schaumann lives up to his nickname. His corpulent, slow-moving body caused a cruel schoolmaster to use him as a scientific example of the sloth: "Look at him, all of you, Schaumann, the sloth. There he sits again on the dullard's bench, like the bradypus, the sloth." The other boys at school did their best to make him miserable, and Schaumann himself admits that he would have rather been "a jellyfish in the bitter salt sea" than "that fat, stupid Heinrich Schaumann." Unfortunately, he had no control over his physical endowments or his inability to do well in school. Eventually, he managed to come to terms with his life, a slow process which is reflected in the slow-moving narrative style that he uses to tell his story. Just as he always wanted to consume large quantities of food, he also wants to absorb the whole of life. He literally digs beneath the surface in his fossil hunting and tries to look at history in all of its depth, from prehistoric times to the present. The depth of his knowledge and his position as an outsider allow him a perspective on his own experiences and life in general, which makes him a humane person who is not quick to judge.

In the opinion of the world, Schaumann was a fat, lazy, stupid child, and it was easy enough to sneer at him. Schaumann himself affirms the description—he insists that Edward call him by his nickname, Tubby—and recognizes in it his destiny. As he says, "I've always been a little weak in the head and weak on my feet. . . . This was my weakness or, if you like, my strength. This was where destiny took hold of me. I resisted, but I had to surrender, reluctantly." Because of his weaknesses, he remained where he was and found a haven at Quakatz's farm from which to battle the world's inhumanity. Schaumann does not integrate himself into society. Instead, he separates himself from it, fleeing into his private fortress. The view from his retreat allows him a wider perspective, as do his studies of the Seven Years' War and his digging for fossils. The result is an individual perspective, not a solution to be followed by society. Unlike Green Henry, a character in Gottfried Keller's novel *Der grüne Heinrich* (1854-1855, 1879-1880; *Green Henry,*

1960), Schaumann does not experience a reintegration with the common values of society.

### Themes and Meanings

The novel is structured as a reminiscence narrative by Edward about his visit to his hometown and his boyhood friend. The narrative technique is clearly designed to diffuse any suspense. Schaumann's story is told with digressions and various interruptions which slow the plot and give the reader a chance to absorb Schaumann's way of looking at life. Although Edward is the narrator, the reader actually hears the story mainly in Schaumann's words as he tells it to Edward. Other points of view, such as Edward's and Valentina's, and comments from Edward's fellow passengers (not related to the main story), are included in the text. All the central action takes place in the consciousness of the characters.

The theme of disillusionment is an integral part of the story. Edward's view of his hometown and the world that it represents is significantly altered by the time the day has ended. His idealization of Störzer ends with the man's death and the realization of the burden of Kienbaum's murder that Störzer carried with him. The interconnected story lines of individuals— Störzer, Edward, Quakatz, and Valentina—overlap and become part of one larger picture, which Schaumann has experienced and now relates to Edward. The full picture gives him a view of the world, which is the focus of the novel, rather than the story of any specific event, such as the murder.

Time in its various levels underlines this complete view of the world. The time of the narrative is the thirty-day period on board ship during which Edward writes the story. The story itself encompasses an approximate time of thirty-two hours, the length of Edward's visit, but it describes events of his and Schaumann's boyhood, some twenty-five years before. In addition, the historical references to the Seven Years' War, when the town was attacked from the fortress on the present site of Red Bank Farm, and Schaumann's paleontological research, which takes him into the prehistoric period, broaden the time frame. These are interrelated in the narrative, just as the people are, giving it an all-encompassing perspective.

Criticism of society is embodied in the theme of loneliness and isolation. The community, in its cruelty, made an outcast of Schaumann, who became an object of scorn, and of Quakatz and Valentina, who suffered under unjust accusations. Abandoned by the others, they made Red Bank Farm into a haven for themselves, banding together in their own community against outside cruelty to give themselves strength and to overcome their individual isolation. Schaumann, a passive but tenacious man, rescues Valentina from isolation and even makes her father's life bearable through his friendship. His development as a human being leads to a type of "inner self-content" which he was able to help Valentina discover in herself as well.

The cruelty of the community is reflected on the individual level in Kienbaum and his tormenting treatment of Störzer while he was alive (and, ironically, the dead Kienbaum remained a source of torment for Störzer's conscience every day of his life). Schaumann understood well the desire to strike back against cruelty and therefore would not betray the information he had as long as Störzer was alive and could be hurt by it.

Wilhelm Raabe's criticism of society encompasses the educational system specifically. The real education of a person takes place outside school, as Schaumann's development shows. The formal educational system with its cruel teachers is shown to be a system which produces philistines with no historical perspective and no understanding of someone such as Schaumann, who slowly and methodically takes in the whole of experience. He is the one who is condemned as stupid and forced into the outsider position, which made real development possible. Schaumann's best human qualities come from converting his weaknesses, slowness and gluttony, into strengths.

*Critical Context*

*Tubby Schaumann* has been called Raabe's masterpiece and is placed among the important German novels of the nineteenth century. Raabe himself referred to it as his best work. Given the lack of translations, however, Raabe is not well-known in English-speaking countries.

The use of narration in the first person is a technique anticipated by his early work, *Die Chronik der Sperlingsgasse* (1856; the chronicle of Sperling Street), in which the narrator also reminisces about past experiences. This technique was further developed in Raabe's mature work *Braunschweig* (1870-1902; Brunswick), which is the basis of his reputation as a nineteenth century German novelist. This is Raabe's so-called Brunswick trilogy of which *Tubby Schaumann* is a part, along with *Alte Nester* (1879; old nests) and *Die Akten des Vogelsangs* (1896; the Vogelsang documents). The same first-person narrative technique connects all three novels, although *Tubby Schaumann* is considered the best of them, with its complexity of narrative form through interrelated perspectives.

Raabe's work was written during the period of German Realism (1850-1890), and *Tubby Schaumann* clearly focuses on the everyday reality experienced by the individual. His realism includes criticism of the society in which he lives. When Schaumann reveals the truth about the murder, the community judgment is revealed as false, and the persecution of Quakatz is shown as a baseless cruelty which cannot be undone. As in *Horacker* (1876; English translation, 1983), Raabe is concerned with the meanness in human beings who attack by gossip and rumor. The outward appearance of good, upstanding citizens is shown to cover a selfish and cruel core. In addition, *Tubby Schaumann* is an attack on the idealization of the past, shown in part through Edward's facing of reality after Störzer's death. Although a realist, Raabe's work is regional only in the sense that a specific region can be recognized; the novel does not contain long and detailed descriptions. His concern is human reaction to the forces of society and how those forces influence the individual.

*Tubby Schaumann* is a masterpiece which exposes the modern theme of isolation. Each character sees his hopes limited by society and is forced to seek some meaning in human existence. The central story is Schaumann's search for a way to live in harmony with his own character and physical being, but others, too, are forced into that search: Quakatz seeks to understand justice (both divine and human) as he sees himself unjustly accused, and Störzer needs to understand the purpose of life as his own life is spent in fear, first of Kienbaum, then of his conscience.

Raabe's trademark is an ironic, humorous attitude. He keeps his distance by remaining skeptical about a person's ability to control or understand the forces which determine human destiny. His protagonist tries to see the world in its full perspective but cannot change it. All Raabe's mature works reflect the suffering of individuals in a society in transition, where greed and selfishness outweigh humane values. In this context, *Tubby Schaumann* clearly shows Raabe's attitude of resignation in that the only solution is the individual's creation of a humane circle outside the cruelty of the community.

*Sources for Further Study*
Daemmrich, Horst S. *Wilhelm Raabe*, 1981.
Fairley, Barker. *Wilhelm Raabe: An Introduction to His Novels*, 1961.
Field, G. Wallis. "Poetic Realists in Prose: Raabe," in *A Literary History of Germany: The Nineteenth Century, 1830-1890*, 1975.
Pascal, Roy. "Wilhelm Raabe (1831-1910)," in *The German Novel: Studies*, 1956.
Stern, J. P. "Wilhelm Raabe: Home and Abroad," in *Idylls and Realities: Studies in Nineteenth-century Literature*, 1971.

*Susan Piepke*

# TZILI
## The Story of a Life

*Author:* Aharon Appelfeld (1932-     )
*Type of plot:* Allegory
*Time of plot:* During the Holocaust, starting c. 1939
*Locale:* Eastern Europe, from Poland or Russia to Yugoslavia
*First published: Kutonet veha-Pasim*, 1983 (English translation, 1983)

> *Principal characters:*
> TZILI KRAUS, a Jewish child abandoned by her parents when
>     they flee to escape murdering soldiers
> MARK, a forty-year-old man who lives with Tzili for a time
> KATERINA, a woman for whom Tzili works
> LINDA, the woman who saves Tzili's life

### The Novel

*Tzili: The Story of a Life* is an allegorical history of the faith and fate of the Jewish people during the Holocaust. The novel first traces the efforts of a poor family to ignore its Jewish heritage and assimilate into the Austrian culture. They demand secular academic excellence of their children while abandoning their cultural and religious Jewish heritage, including its emphasis on Jewish education and values. The focus then shifts to Tzili Kraus, the youngest child, whose anomalously innate ties to Judaism symbolize the strength of the archetypal pull to faith and the enduring nature of Judaism, traceable to its strong advancement by a selected few.

The novel opens with the narrator's observation to the reader:

> Perhaps it would be better to leave the story of Tzili Kraus's life untold. . . . Her fate was a cruel and inglorious one, and but for the fact that it actually happened, we would never have been able to tell her story.

Tzili, symbolic of the quiet, abandoned Jewish faith, spends her first seven summers and falls on the dry, dusty soil in the small plot of earth behind the family's shop. Ignored because she is peaceful and undemanding, Tzili spends her days alone and at dusk is brought inside the house, where she is also ignored, as conversation focuses on the academic achievements of her intellectually gifted older siblings. When Tzili is seven, she proves herself to be a poor student and is berated by her family and ridiculed by her peers, especially since her dullness is considered an unusual trait among Jews.

Failing to goad Tzili into academic superiority, her parents hire an old, unsympathetic man to tutor their "feeble-minded" child in Judaism. Even in this, the child does not excel, leading the old man to despair "why it had fallen to the lot of this dull child to keep the spark [of Sabbath and prayer] alive." Nevertheless, just as Tzili keeps the spark of Judaism alive, Judaism keeps Tzili alive:

[The old man's visits] filled her with a kind of serenity which remained with her and protected her for many hours afterward. At night she would recite, "Hear, O Israel" aloud, as he had instructed her, covering her face.

Upon hearing news of an imminent siege, the Kraus family flees the village, leaving Tzili behind to "take care of their property for them." Lying among barrels in the shed and covered with sacking, the child sleeps undiscovered throughout the night of slaughter and wakes to find herself alone. Guided by intuition, Tzili leaves town and wanders to a riverbank where she meets an old, blind lecher who mistakes her for one of the many daughters of Maria, the Gentile town whore, who is popular with Jew and Gentile alike. Tzili assumes this fortuitous identity which, along with her quiet stoic strength, allows her entry into the safe but brutal peasant community and enables her to survive the ensuing Holocaust years without being put into a camp. She learns what has happened to her town from a conversation between the blind man and his daughter:

"They chased the Jews away and they killed them too."
"All of them?"
"Yes."
"And their houses?"
"The peasants are looting them."
"What do you say? Maybe you can find me a winter coat?"

After wandering for many days, Tzili works first for Katerina, a prostitute, who walked the streets with Maria and shared the same men with her. Now Katerina is sick and demanding, and when she throws a knife at Tzili because the girl is unwilling to support the two of them by prostitution, Tzili leaves the warmth and femininity of the house to wander alone in the cold and without regular food for many weeks. She then begins working for an aged peasant couple whom she finally leaves because the old man tries to compromise her, and as a result, his wife beats Tzili continuously.

The young girl then joins a Jewish camp escapee, Mark, who abandoned his wife and two children to their unknown fate because they were afraid to climb through a narrow aperture and escape the camp with him. Because of Tzili's Aryan features, she is able to procure food by bartering Mark's family's clothing, which he took with him when he escaped. Almost two years elapse, and Mark becomes increasingly morbid and guilty about his past. At fifteen, Tzili becomes pregnant, and Mark, discontent with only food, demands that Tzili procure cigarettes and liquor for him with the clothing. One day, he tells Tzili that he is going to town by himself; he leaves and never returns. Tzili once again is abandoned.

Tzili resumes her wandering, bartering Mark's clothing for food. When the clothes are gone, she works for another peasant family, who beat her until she is bruised and swollen and as if they want "to tear the fetus from her body." Tzili leaves to wander alone again.

She is amazed to discover that her aimless path has led her in a circle, and she is again near Katerina's house and the place where she and Mark stayed. When the war ends and dazed survivors of camps can be seen walking across the land, Tzili joins a group of liberated Jews who have hopes of reaching Italy. Ill and weak because of her pregnancy, Tzili has difficulty keeping up with the petty, quarreling people who spend their nontravel time playing cards and gambling with one another. In their despair over the past, about which no one can talk, and because they appear to have no future, several survivors commit suicide. Another man, who exhorts the group to repent and return to their Father in Heaven, is tricked into leaving the group. Yet Tzili fears, even more than her nights in the forest, the survivors—thin, speechless, and withdrawn persons upon whom a "kind of secret veiled their faces."

Although Tzili is quiet and almost unnoticed, when she becomes too sick to continue, surprising help comes from Linda, a former cabaret dancer, who demands that the group stop for Tzili, and from a merchant, who constructs a stretcher upon which Tzili is carried the rest of the way. As if ensuring her survival has been the sole purpose of their journey, Tzili is carried aloft in triumph and with the roar "We are the torch bearers." Finally, the small band of survivors reaches Zagreb. Yet as soon as the "torch bearers" reach the town of security, food, and provisions supplied by American agencies, they refuse to shoulder their burden any longer and lay the stretcher in the shade. The merchant finally succeeds in summoning an ambulance to carry Tzili away, but he runs after the vehicle, begging in vain to be taken too because "the child is alone in the world."

The fetus, a product of guilt and a reminder of years of horror, is dead, and in a makeshift barracks hospital, Tzili undergoes surgery, now totally alone. Tzili's parents and siblings, reminders of assimilation and prewar secular and materialistic aspirations, are never seen again after they abandon Tzili, and the reader assumes that they have been victims of the slaughter.

Yet Tzili, symbol of the spark of the Sabbath and Judaism that her family had abandoned, survives the Holocaust, the dreadful years, and surgery and its excruciating aftermath. Again with the help of Linda, who complains to Tzili that the survivors now ignore her because they have "shiksas" (non-Jewish girls) to entertain them, Tzili and Linda board a ship that appears to be bound for Palestine to begin a new life.

## The Characters

Tzili, the protagonist of this novel, stands alone in her story, both literally and symbolically. Her youth is shaped by a major conflict within the Jewish culture of the time, which pits the strong attempt of many Jews to escape persecution by means of attaining intellectual superiority and with it, assimilation into the Gentile majority, against the emotional pull of the legacy of Judaism, which they have rejected. In contrast to these assimilated Jews, there is the true-to-life Tzili, who symbolizes the innocence, simplicity, and goodness of the Torah and of the Jewish faith. Because she is considered feeble-minded and therefore incapable of intellectual superiority and assimilation, only she is taught the basic tenets of Judaism. When her family faces its most fearsome challenge, the murdering soldiers, they leave Tzili and her symbolic Torah and faith behind. Saved as if by a miracle when she sleeps through the slaughter, given a safe identity, and receiving help when she most needs it, Tzili, the person and the symbol, survives to build a new life in Palestine. Tzili realizes, however, that "she would remain alone, alone forever," and if anyone would ever ask her where she was and what happened to her during the years of horror, she would not reply.

All the other characters, representations of both Jewish and non-Jewish character types, serve as vehicles to describe Tzili as a person and as a symbol. Katerina, the prostitute with pretensions to culture and femininity, gives Tzili shelter in exchange for hard work and ever more demanding tasks. Like Maria, who is only mentioned in the text, she states that she prefers the Jews to all other lovers because they are kind, generous, and always take a woman to a fine hotel. Yet the picture of the Jew who is valued for his generosity and kindness but is despised for the legacy that has given him those attributes is as ironic as Tzili, symbol of the Torah and faith that are abandoned except for times when there is nowhere else to turn.

Mark, the gray-faced, forty-year-old man who helps and is helped by Tzili, is also a character type, consumed with guilt after having left his wife and child behind when they refused to take the chance to escape camp. He, too, is the product of an assimilation-seeking family whose father put inordinate pressure on his family to be able to speak flawless German and who corrected Mark's mother in front of people when she made errors. The Torah is not part of Mark's life, but Tzili gives him comfort and companionship in the darkest period between his escape from the camp and his return to almost certain death. When he deserts Tzili, she is devastated, and like his mother, child, and wife, she searches for him and sees him in her dreams for months until she realizes that he is lost to her forever.

Linda, the fat cabaret dancer, is a mixture of the common, low-class woman exhibiting uncommon, high-principled action. She left her Gentile landowner-lover when one year of the war still remained. Although he hid her from the Germans, she regarded his brutality as worse than life in a camp, where she entertained her fellow prisoners with song and dance. In spite of her common occupation and appearance, she respects Tzili enough to stop the band of survivors and insist that Tzili be cared for and taken with them. Although the unnamed merchant performs the last favors for Tzili by caring for her during the last leg of the journey to Zagreb and by obtaining medical help for her when it appears that she may die, it is Linda who meets Tzili after she leaves the hospital and accompanies her to Palestine. Ironically, when they find more interesting diversions with the women of Zagreb, the "torch bearers" among the survivors who carried Tzili aloft abandon her in spite of the merchant's pleas. Presumably, many of them never get the opportunity for rebirth that is accorded Tzili and Linda.

*Themes and Meanings*

The irony of pursuing assimilation is the central theme of *Tzili*, as Aharon Appelfeld explores the loss of faith among Jews and their fate during the Holocaust years. Although the characters are people who surely existed, they assume even larger dimensions as character types during the Holocaust and symbols of Jewish life. As in many of his other novels, themes of the abandoned child, the cruel and insensitive father-man, travel, and the freedom afforded by forests are important elements.

The theme of dedication to the Torah and the natural simplicity of the good Jewish life are embedded in the symbolic Tzili. Her lost baby, a mere fetus to the doctor but joy and hope to Tzili, symbolizes the death of the innocent, conceived during chaos of the soul and the world and destroyed by deprivation and neglect. The destruction of Jewish life, even from the womb, begins with the old peasant woman, who, although not aware that Tzili is Jewish, beats the girl as if to destroy the life within her. Even the liberated Jews, unable to plan for the future because of past experience, cling only to the diversions of the minute, such as card playing and gambling, and do not heed the necessity for rededication and preservation of new life. Literally and symbolically, they wander through deserted areas, like the tribes of Israel wandered with Moses, in an attempt to cleanse themselves in preparation for entry to the Promised Land.

Until Linda forces the survivors to aid Tzili and what she represents, the band stumbles forward in fear but not in hope. Only when they carry Tzili aloft on a stretcher, like the Jews carrying the Torah from the destruction of Solomon's Temple, do they regain strength and purpose. Still, they remain blind to the regenerative power of faith and dedication to others when they abandon the stretcher at the first possible moment and again pursue empty worship of the Golden Calf.

The allegory reveals that life is empty and meaningless without the direction that the Torah provides. The pursuit of temporal goals such as secular academic superiority (for example, the case of Tzili's siblings and also that of a former student who kills himself after liberation) or the pursuit of petty successes such as wealth or beauty is not lasting and does not help when trouble comes. Underscoring this important theme is the camp survivors' obsession with their former diversion of playing cards and gambling; life is an empty series of card games—each played, ended, and forgotten.

Although, upon a superficial reading, the novel concerns the suffering of a young girl as she matures during the Holocaust, it is actually an allegory of the meaning of life, even a parable about how life should be lived.

Appelfeld's style in this novel is straightforward, but its poetry of description and imagery reach the reader and evoke objective correlatives with great emotional appeal. For example, Appelfeld describes the day after Tzili meets the small band of camp survivors:

> The sun opened out. The people unbuttoned their damp clothes and sprawled on the river bank and slept. The long, damp years of the war steamed out of their moldy bodies. Even at night the smell did not disappear. Only Tzili did not sleep. The way the people slept filled her with wonder. Are they happy? Tzili asked herself. They slept in a heap, defenseless bodies suddenly abandoned by danger.

Appelfeld's choice of words and sentence structure expand this brief novel into an epic because of the multitude of images and meanings the reader is impelled to envision and pursue.

## Critical Context

*Tzili*, Appelfeld's third novel to appear in English translation, shares some characteristics with his first two novels, *Badenheim, hamzah ir nofesh* (1975; *Badenheim 1939*, 1980) and *Tor-ha-pela'ot* (1978; *The Age of Wonders*, 1981), but adds a dimension that makes it possibly the most rewarding of any of Appelfeld's novels. Like *Badenheim 1939*, *Tzili* focuses on a description of Jewish society in prewar Europe and the immersion of that society into a Holocaust for which it was not prepared and which it failed to acknowledge, even in the face of reality. Like *The Age of Wonders*, *Tzili* introduces a strong autobiographical element, a pre- and post-Holocaust segment, and the tempering of pessimism by the survival of youth. Appelfeld's use of dreamlike hallucinatory allegory in *Tzili*, however, sets it apart from his other novels, and the minimalist approach places an even greater responsibility upon the reader to interpret meaning while multiple levels of interpretation are added to each word and scene.

*Tzili* includes some of the images that Appelfeld established in his earlier novels and which he later carried into his other novels, but some images are conspicuously absent. The prewar assimilated Jewish society remains a major focus, as does the abandoned child and the ugly father. Yet Tzili finds refuge in homes and among non-Jews as well as in the forest, and although travel is omnipresent, there are no trains to remind the reader of the approach of the Holocaust. Further differentiating this novel from Appelfeld's other work is his use of words ("Germans," "murdering soldiers," "screams and shots," "camp survivors") that evoke the images of the Holocaust without its mention. In previous works, such words are avoided and are instead implied in various other ways.

*Tzili* belongs to the category of Appelfeld's work that includes pre- and post-Holocaust segments and indicates that youth returning to Judaism can survive. Yet where the focus on youth has been secondary in other novels, here it is the major focus in a symbolic mode that links that youth (Tzili) with the spirit of Judaism itself. Appelfeld has said that *Tzili* is a form of autobiographical memory. Perhaps that would best explain its haunting effect, for the author is recounting a personal experience rather than an observed one.

*Sources for Further Study*

Blake, Patricia. Review in *Time*. CXXI (April 11, 1983), p. 97.

Coffin, Edna Amir. "Appelfeld's Exceptional Universe: Harmony out of Chaos," in *Hebrew Studies*. XXIV (1983), pp. 85-89.

Lewis, Stephen. "Aharon Appelfeld," in *Art out of Agony*, 1984.

Oates, Joyce Carol. Review in *The New York Times Book Review*. LXXXVIII (April 16, 1983), p. 9.

Strouse, Jean. Review in *Newsweek*. CI (March 28, 1983), p. 70.

Wisse, Ruth R. "Aharon Appelfeld, Survivor," in *Commentary*. LXXVI (August, 1983), pp. 73-76.

Yudkin, Leon I. "Appelfeld's Vision of the Past," in *Escape into Siege*, 1974.

*June H. Schlessinger*

# THE UNBEARABLE LIGHTNESS OF BEING

*Author:* Milan Kundera (1929-      )
*Type of plot:* Postmodernist
*Time of plot:* The 1960's-1970's
*Locale:* Prague, Geneva, Zurich, Paris, Cambodia, and a Czech farming
   commune
*First published: Nesnesitelná lehkost bytí*, 1984 (English translation, 1984)

> *Principal characters:*
> THE NARRATOR
> TOMAS, a respected Czech surgeon and incorrigible
>    womanizer
> TEREZA, Tomas' wife, a barmaid and photographer
> SABINA, a Czech painter, Tomas' mistress
> FRANZ, a Swiss professor, Sabina's lover

*The Novel*

   *The Unbearable Lightness of Being* is a complex postmodernist novel, at
once political, philosophical, and erotic. Milan Kundera's characters live in a
world of irrevocable choices and fortuitous events, where the public and private spheres overlap and impinge upon each other. In this novel of ideas, the
characters' actions are viewed through the narrator's erudite perspective and
in terms of a number of cultural allusions, including Parmenides, Sophocles,
Ludwig van Beethoven, and Leo Tolstoy.

   The allusions to Tolstoy's *Anna Karenina* (1875-1877) are of particular
importance in *The Unbearable Lightness of Being*. The connection is apparent from the moment Kundera introduces his heroine, Tereza, with a copy of
Tolstoy's novel under her arm. Tomas and Tereza even name their female dog
Karenin, with comical results. Like Tolstoy, Kundera employs a comparison
between two couples, Tomas and Tereza, and Franz and Sabina, but the contrast is not simply that of adultery and fidelity.

   A number of philosophical and musical motifs are woven throughout the
novel, including the notion of eternal return, Parmenides' dualism of weight
and lightness, the Platonic dualism of body and soul, Beethoven's "Es muss
sein," the German proverb "Einmal ist keinmal," a revulsion against kitsch,
Kundera's sense of the fortuitous coincidence of love and beauty, and the
paradoxical relationship of fidelity and betrayal. How do people meet and
fall in love? What is love but chance and fortuity?

   Tomas and Tereza seem destined to fall in love, though their meeting rests
on an improbable set of coincidences. Tomas, a noted Prague surgeon, was
married to his first wife for only two years before they were divorced. Spite-
ful, she refused him visiting rights to his son unless he brought her expensive

gifts. The experience leaves him fearful of women and determined to remain uninvolved. He devises a strategy of "erotic friendships" with his mistresses, based on a rule of threes: to see them either three times in brief succession and never again, or else once every three weeks. This stratagem works well until Tomas meets Tereza.

Tomas has been sent to a provincial Czech hospital to investigate a rare neurological case, and he meets Tereza, who is waiting on tables at the hotel where he stays. She admires him because he is reading a book. He orders a cognac and at that moment the radio happens to be playing a Beethoven string quartet. They meet in the park. Tomas gives her his card and invites her to look him up if she is ever in Prague. Is it chance or coincidence that brings them together? They accidentally meet in a hotel and the lives of both are forever changed. What gives Tereza the courage to change her life, to leave her job and take the train to Prague to find a man she has met only once? Tomas thinks of Tereza metaphorically as a gift, a child put in a basket and sent downstream for him to retrieve, but metaphors can be dangerous, for "a single metaphor can give birth to love."

From the beginning of their relationship, Tereza lays claim to Tomas and insists on her right to spend the entire night with him and not be put out of his apartment like his other mistresses. The intensity of her love for him is magnified by her painful awareness of his many infidelities. Tereza was rejected by her mother and made to feel guilty about her body. To be certain of Tomas' love, Tereza holds on to him compulsively in her sleep, clinging so tightly that Tomas has to pry apart her sleeping grip. Tomas eventually marries Tereza to alleviate her anxieties about his other mistresses, and they spend seven years in Prague. Tereza becomes a photographer and develops a career of her own, with the assistance of the painter Sabina, Tomas' mistress.

When the Soviets invade Czechoslovakia in August, 1968, Tomas is offered a position abroad by the director of a hospital in Zurich, so they emigrate. Sabina leaves for Switzerland also. Tereza cannot adjust to life in Zurich, away from her career, friends, language, and country, so she decides to return to Prague, even though Czechoslovakia has become a repressive police state. Tereza takes their dog, Karenin, and leaves Tomas only a note. In her weakness, she betrays him. Tomas cannot adjust to life without her, so he decides to return also, although he realizes that he will not get back his hospital position because he left the country illegally.

Finding himself without work, Tomas is forced to wash windows. For a time he is treated as a celebrity, a former surgeon now a window-washer. The freedom from his hospital routine leaves him more time for his amorous adventures, which makes Tereza all the more unhappy. Tomas is also pressured from both sides to make political statements, which he tries to avoid.

With Tomas' medical career finished, he and Tereza accept a position at a small dairy cooperative in the Czech countryside, where he will be free of political pressures. They find a measure of happiness there, but Tomas ages considerably. Both are killed when the brakes fail on their pickup truck and it careens off a steep road. Franz, Sabina's former lover, dies in Bangkok after participating in a peace march to the Cambodian border. In the meantime, Sabina has become a famous artist in America, though she has abandoned all of her responsibilities in the process. Her success serves as an ironic counterpoint to Tomas, whose responsibility to Tereza brings him back to Prague and results in the loss of his medical career. Lightness and heaviness, freedom and responsibility are the twin poles of this complex novel. The relationship of Tomas and Tereza begins and ends with dependency and personal sacrifice, although by the end of the novel the terms of the sacrifice have been reversed. Tereza finally wins complete possession of Tomas and compels his fidelity, though in terms unforeseen by either.

## The Characters

Kundera's characters play upon the polarities of masculine/feminine, strength/weakness, mind/body, intellectual/emotive, and fidelity/betrayal. They are simultaneously individuals and types. The reader's knowledge and understanding of their motives, however, are mediated by Kundera's narrator, who seems more sympathetic to Tereza and her concerns than to those of Tomas. The narrator says that Tomas is a compulsive womanizer, obsessed with discovering that millionth part of each woman that makes her unique. This explanation seems unconvincing, though, for the reader is never allowed inside Tomas' consciousness to share his perceptions. Franz is little better as a character: the brilliant professor forever seeking vicarious excitement in some political cause.

Kundera's women are more interesting as characters. Tereza is drawn sympathetically and in depth. Kundera reveals enough about her parents and her childhood through flashbacks to make her behavior quite credible. Her mother is a monster of egotism: selfish, manipulative, and utterly incapable of love. It is not surprising that Tereza is so insecure. Sabina, as well, is a victim of parental abuse. Her father, a puritanical, small-town dignitary, instills in her a distrust of men and an instinct for betrayal as a means of self-preservation. His rigidity, later reinforced by the Czech Communist Party, gives Sabina a lifelong distaste for "The Great March" of artistic or political conformity. Determined to become her own person, she marries unwisely, but her alcoholic actor-husband leaves her, and she is free to develop her talents as an artist. Sabina's craving for novelty leaves her dissatisfied with Franz, whose bourgeois decency bores her, and she leaves him after he has left his wife, Marie-Claude, for her. Their incompatibility is dramatized by a "Dictionary of Misunderstood Words," a glossary of the same words with different meanings for each.

Aside from Tereza's mother, who is unnamed but described in some detail, the other minor characters—Franz's wife Marie-Claude, Tomas' first wife, his son Simon, Franz's daughter Marie-Anne, and his student mistress—remain indistinct. There are also major historical figures in the novel, including Czech prime minister Alexander Dubček, who provide an important historical counterpoint to the fictional plot.

### Themes and Meanings

Fidelity and betrayal operate on both the personal and political levels in *The Unbearable Lightness of Being*. Kundera examines not only the metaphysics of two couples' personal relationships but also the complex political scene in Czechoslovakia before and after the Soviet invasion of 1968. The Communist coup of 1948 is seen as a betrayal of Czechoslovakia's right to self-determination, as an exercise in criminal futility by enthusiasts who thought they were on the road to paradise. Unfortunately, paradise never arrived, and the enthusiasts had to account for their murders and betrayals. President Antonín Novotný and the other Czech Stalinists who protested that they were innocent because they "didn't know" were at least as guilty as Oedipus, who, Tomas argues, was punished for his crimes even though he was unaware at first of his real identity. The final betrayal comes in August, 1968, when Leonid Brezhnev directs the Warsaw Pact armies to invade Czechoslovakia to put an end to the reforms of Dubček's "socialism with a human face" because those reforms threaten neighboring regimes. The "Es muss sein" of Beethoven becomes the Marxist-Leninist alibi of historical inevitability for the numerous crimes of repression against unwilling client states.

After Tereza returns to Prague, she no longer blames Dubček for his weakness in capitulating to Soviet pressure. She realizes that she belongs among the weak, among her people, suffering from humiliation and forced military occupation. She feels attracted to weakness, like love, as to a vertigo. Her falling in love is likened to a fear of vertigo, a weakness that asserts its superior strength over Tomas' casual promiscuity. For Kundera's characters, there are no easy choices, and each choice bears painful consequences.

The texture of this novel is as rich and complex as its multiple themes. Kundera blends the political and personal lives of his characters, using a fragmented narrative that forces the reader to reconstruct the plot. His narrative technique is circular rather than linear. Two of the seven sections repeat themselves almost as theme and variation. Dreams also serve as an important source of insight about the characters' personalities and motives. Sabina's comment about her paintings—"On the surface, an intelligible lie; underneath, the unintelligible truth"—expresses Kundera's novelistic style as well. The novel, his narrator remarks, "is an investigation of human life in the trap the world has become." Literature and politics coalesce in a world where every private act and gesture is political.

*Critical Context*

The most profound and far-reaching of Kundera's novels, *The Unbearable Lightness of Being* demonstrates his mastery of the postmodernist form. His earlier works have blended political satire with a sense of life's absurdity and a distinctive combination of eros and humor. As in *Žert* (1967; *The Joke*, 1969, revised 1982), *Směšné lásky* (1969; *Laughable Loves*, 1974), *La Vie est ailleurs* (1973; *Life Is Elsewhere*, 1974), and *Kniha smíchu a zapomnění* (1978; *The Book of Laughter and Forgetting*, 1980), the private, erotic realm becomes for Kundera's characters a means of personal expression in a world where public expression of individuality is impossible. It is a mistake, however, to read Kundera merely as a political, satirical, or erotic writer. He is all of these and more: a passionate defender of Western culture—philosophy, music, and literature—against the artistic repression of totalitarian kitsch, the fraudulent sentimentality of politics.

*Sources for Further Study*

Doctorow, E. L. "Four Characters Under Two Tyrannies," in *The New York Times Book Review*. LXXXIX (April 29, 1984), pp. 1, 45-46.

Malcolm, Janet. "The Game of Lights," in *The New York Review of Books*. XXXI (May 10, 1984), pp. 3-4, 6.

"Milan Kundera," in *Contemporary Literary Criticism*. Vol. 32, 1985. Edited by Jean Stine.

Podhoretz, Norman. "An Open Letter to Milan Kundera," in *Commentary*. LXXVIII (October, 1984), pp. 34-39.

*Andrew J. Angyal*

# UNDER THE SUN OF SATAN

*Author:* Georges Bernanos (1888-1948)
*Type of plot:* Religious drama
*Time of plot:* The beginning of the twentieth century
*Locale:* The rural northwest area of France
*First published: Sous le soleil de Satan,* 1926 (*The Star of Satan,* 1927; better
known as *Under the Sun of Satan*)

> *Principal characters:*
> GERMAINE "MOUCHETTE" MALORTHY, a sixteen-year-old
> murderess and suicide
> ANTOINE MALORTHY, her father, a brewer
> JACQUES DE CADIGNAN, Germaine's lover, an impoverished
> marquess
> FATHER MENOU-SEGRAIS, the canon of the church in
> Campagne
> FATHER DONISSAN, his assistant, later the curé of Lumbres
> SATAN (also known as LUCIFER), disguised as a provincial
> horse trader

## The Novel

*Under the Sun of Satan* is divided into three quasi-independent sections.
Part 1, a sort of prologue entitled "The Story of Mouchette," is an account
of a teenage victim of child abuse. Germaine Malorthy, nicknamed "Mouchette," is sixteen and pregnant. The father of the unborn child is a forty-
five-year-old nobleman, the Marquess of Cadignan. Germaine will not reveal his name to her parents, but her father, Antoine, correctly suspects his
identity and goes to confront the philanderer at his château. Cadignan denies
everything, and Germaine, when quizzed again by her parents, remains silent. That night, she sneaks out of the house, hoping never to return.

She goes to see Cadignan, who recognizes a certain obligation for causing
her predicament and agrees to sell some property and give her part of the
proceeds. Germaine, however, wants him to marry her. He refuses, and she
tries to get back at him by denying that she is pregnant and by claiming that
she is the mistress of the local physician, Dr. Gallet. This admission puts
Cadignan into such a rage that he rapes her. Afterward, when she tries to
leave, he makes an effort to stop her, but in the scuffle, she grabs a loaded
hunting rifle from the wall and shoots him at close range, under his chin. She
then returns home before her parents are awake. The authorities rule that
the death of Cadignan is a suicide.

Germaine now takes a new lover, Dr. Gallet. During one of their regular
trysts, she tells him the truth about Cadignan's death, although Gallet does

not believe her. She wants her lover to give her an abortion, but he refuses. Germaine is by now so upset that, after her confession of murder, she goes into a hysterical fit and has to be hospitalized. A month later, following the stillbirth of her child, she is released as cured.

Part 2, entitled "The Temptation of Despair," is the section that Georges Bernanos wrote last, after he wrote part 3. "The Temptation of Despair" deals with the struggle of the young, naïve curate of Campagne, Father Donissan, to discover his proper relationship to God and to his fellowman. His search will be long and difficult, compounded as it is by his own lack of education and by the obstinacy of his nature. He "has neither education nor manners, and there is more zeal than wisdom in his extreme piety," his superior, Father Menou-Segrais, observes.

One night, as Donissan is on his way to a nearby village to help with confession during a local retreat, he becomes lost and stumbles across the fields in the darkness. Yet he is not alone. Satan appears in the guise of an itinerant horse trader and offers to help him find his way back to the road. At first, Donissan does not realize to whom he is speaking. He regards the stranger as a friendly presence upon whom he can rely for support. When the truth is known, however, Donissan meets it without flinching: "Get thee behind me, Satan!"

The confrontation continues. Satan is up to his old tricks and even changes his appearance to that of Donissan himself, a resemblance so subtle that it is "like the unique and profound idea which every human being has of himself." Finally, Satan leaves, realizing that he has met his match, but before he goes, he issues a warning that he will continue to work his evil on Donissan. "There isn't a lout we can't make use of," he says tauntingly.

Donissan, alone once again, decides to return to his village. On the way, he meets Germaine. His encounter with the Devil has led him to discover that he has been given the gift of reading people's souls, and thus he is able to reveal to Germaine details about her shooting of Cadignan. Donissan hopes for her salvation, but the encounter only convinces Germaine of the meaninglessness of her life. When she returns home, she desperately calls on the Devil for succor. Then, she takes her father's straight razor and "fiercely and coldly" slashes her throat in front of a mirror.

Meanwhile, Donissan tells Menou-Segrais about the previous night's experiences, including his ability to "see into another soul, with my own eyes, through the wall of flesh . . . by a special and miraculous grace." Menou-Segrais suggests that, if Donissan really believes that this talent is a miracle, he should report it to the bishop.

While the two men are conversing, the housekeeper rushes in with the news that Germaine has killed herself. Donissan immediately goes to the stricken girl's house but finds her still alive. She begs him to take her to the church to die; he does so, despite the protests of her father and Gallet.

Donissan's act is condemned by the church authorities: "Such excesses belong to a different age, there are no words fit to describe them." There is no lasting scandal, but Donissan is forced to pay for his imprudence by doing penance in a Trappist monastery. Five years later, he is appointed priest of the tiny parish of Lumbres.

In the final section of the book, "The Saint of Lumbres," Donissan is old, sick, and near the end of his life. Despite a weak heart, he nevertheless maintains a full schedule of parish duties, staggering "under the weight of his glorious burden."

Knowing of his reputation for saintliness and good works, a woman from a nearby village sends for him to cure her son, who is suffering from meningitis. Unfortunately, Donissan arrives too late, but the local priest, Father Sabrioux, encourages him to perform a miracle and bring the boy back to life. Donissan returns to the death chamber and, lifting up the dead boy's body as he would raise the Communion host, manages to get the corpse to open its eyes. Overcome with the thought that this act is an act of despair, stemming from a lack of faith in God's mercy, Donissan leaves with remorse, despite his success.

The effort at resurrection has taken its toll: Donissan has a heart attack. Near death, he fears that in playing God he has committed a great sin and endangered his soul. He returns to his parish and writes an account of what has happened, addressing it to his superiors. He then goes to the confessional to continue to serve his flock and the hundreds of pilgrims who come to him to receive absolution.

A member of the French Academy, the distinguished writer Antoine Saint-Martin, arrives in the village to see him. He waits for Donissan in the rectory. When the priest does not return, however, Saint-Martin goes to look for him, searching first upstairs in the priest's private quarters, where he is shocked to see that the walls are covered with dried blood from the beatings Donissan has given himself. Saint-Martin next goes to the church and finally discovers Donissan in the confessional, dead "like a sentinel picked off by a bullet in his sentry box"; the body retains, "in its grotesque immobility, the look and attitude of a man whom surprise has brought suddenly to his feet."

*The Characters*

Bernanos continually refers to Father Donissan as a saint and is obviously eager that the reader agree with him. He even provides a lone footnote crediting the priest with the miraculous restoration of sanity to the mother of the dead boy. The real proof of Donissan's sanctity, however, lies in the priest's extreme piety, his heroic struggle with evil, and his lifetime of good works.

Donissan is a man of disquieting extremes, the most important of these being his insuppressible masochism. The first time he is introduced, he is wearing a bloodstained hair shirt so tightly fastened that in places the skin has either been rubbed away or is in blisters "as broad as a hand-stretch." Then there are his autoflagellations. On one horrible occasion, graphically described by Bernanos, he beats himself so mercilessly with a brass chain that he opens his back in one "burning wound, cut into strips, wet with steaming blood," tearing off a chunk of flesh "like a chip of wood under a plane."

Donissan walks a fine line between rationality and hallucination, between what is lived and what is imagined, between consciousness and sleep, between religious fervor and outright perversion. In certain quarters, such behavior might pass for evidence of true devotion to God, but too much is known about psychosexual pathology for the reader not to be skeptical about the motivation of such faith. Donissan's purity does not suspend the reader's disbelief; it tests his credulity. That such self-hatred allows him to love others better is not convincing.

Bernanos would seem content to explain away any contradictions with the ubiquitous presence of Satan: "He taints holy water, he burns in the consecrated wax, his breath is the breath of virgins, he is in the hair shirt and the scourge, he corrupts every path." When good and evil inevitably meet, Donissan asks Satan what he wants. Satan answers that he is there to tempt the priest for the rest of his life. Even if one believes that such encounters with the Prince of Darkness are literally possible, it would be difficult to see how Bernanos' Devil could possibly have much success in stealing the souls of grown men.

A lackluster priest is possible, but a boring Devil is inexcusable. Presumably, Satan has had many years in which to hone his wit and charm, yet Bernanos' creation is silly, sometimes talking in a sort of childish patter: "You go bye-bye on me, my little chick-a-biddy!" The dialogue is as absurd in the original French. Part of the problem lies in Bernanos' habit of presenting his characters as stooges for his own formalistic arguments about good and evil. The dialogue also loses strength in repetition. In addition, Donissan's discovery about what evil lurks in the hearts of men does not much advance the reader's knowledge of the characters.

A different sort of adversary appears in Bernanos' tormented teenager, Germaine. Like Donissan, she has a fairly low self-esteem, and, in different ways, she is just as disturbed. Germaine has abused her gift of free will by leading a sinful life; she therefore becomes less of a victim of society than the circumstances seem to warrant. In her suicide, she willfully separates herself from God's mercy. Unfortunately, the character of Germaine is not well integrated with the rest of the story—the whole first section has a tacked-on quality—not really justifying the amount of space allocated to it.

*Themes and Meanings*

In this first novel, Bernanos had a special purpose. Donissan waged war against Satan on a lonely country road, while the author fought a more public war of his own against the democratic, republican, materialistic Third Republic, whose wicked system he hoped to replace with a restored Catholic monarchy. Action Française, to which Bernanos belonged, wanted to restore order, piety, and authority to France, and the organization adopted as its patron and symbol the recently canonized Joan of Arc to epitomize divine intercession in national affairs. Bernanos would have found this association with Joan particularly fortuitous, since he was married to a descendant of the saint's brother.

Yet the author's battle against Satan transcended the political arena. Bernanos was also fighting an incarnation of evil, demonstrated in the way French society had changed from one of faith to one of secularism and indifference to the nature of God. The dilemma of the novel's main character, Father Donissan, a man of religion out of step with a changing world, was also that of the author. Bernanos' sense of alienation became particularly strong because of his service in World War I, whose horrendous devastation produced "a new world in which even death had lost its sacred meaning." To come to terms with the personal trauma suffered in that great combat was, he said, his main reason for writing *Under the Sun of Satan*, a title which in this context has a special meaning.

Bernanos posed questions which, now increasingly irrelevant, were once principal concerns of Christian society: What is the nature of God? What does God expect of human beings? If God is all-powerful, how does one explain the nature of evil? Donissan searches for the path which will lead him to the discovery and understanding of God. In this quest, he has to test the power of his own faith by testing the power of evil as depicted in a literal incarnation of Satan. This fictitious struggle coincides with Bernanos' determination to find answers to enable him to come to terms with his own anguish and with his desire to return the attention of his fellow humans to the purer values of the past, to make them again contemplate the central purpose for their existence.

*Critical Context*

After World War I, royalism and ultraclericalism were considered *passé*, but enough Frenchmen still believed in them that *Under the Sun of Satan* became a best-seller. Perhaps Bernanos' counterreformatory *Weltanschauung* was also appealing as a reaction against secular writers, such as André Gide, whose stories reflected situational ethics. Whatever the reason, a book with a strongly Christian theme found a surprisingly strong market.

Bernanos' later writings continued in the vein of this early success. Many of his books have priests as the protagonist; like Donissan, they struggle for a sense of religious purpose, seeking to serve God despite their limitations. As Menou-Segrais tells Donissan, "There is no way of judging your sincerity and clairvoyance except by your acts. What you do will bear witness for you."

This obligation to lead a life of example reappears in the novel generally regarded as Bernanos' masterpiece, *Journal d'un curé campagne* (1936; *Diary of a Country Priest*, 1937), which received a grand prize from the French Academy. Here the hero, a young priest dying of cancer, concludes that the real grace is to love oneself humbly "just as we might love any suffering member of the body of Jesus Christ." Upon such basic elements of traditional morality, as much as on his stylistic mastery, rests Bernanos' importance as a Catholic novelist.

For later generations, even less concerned with the religious issues that he tried to popularize, Bernanos' prose, and certainly his ponderous expository organization, might make for difficult reading. Of more relevance to a society secured in the turbulent world of actual, rather than spiritual, strife, his later account of the Spanish Civil War, *Les Grands Cimetières sous la lune* (1938; *A Diary of My Times*, 1938), might well be regarded as his real masterpiece, and his compassion for the suffering of the common man his true Christian morality.

## Sources for Further Study

Blumenthal, Gerda. *The Poetic Imagination of Georges Bernanos: An Essay in Interpretation*, 1965.

Bush, William. *Georges Bernanos*, 1969.

Guiomar, Michel. *Georges Bernanos, "Sous le soleil de Satan": Ou Les Ténèbres de Dieu*, 1984.

Hebblethwaite, Peter. *Bernanos: An Introduction*, 1965.

Speaight, Robert. *Georges Bernanos: A Study of the Man and the Writer*, 1974.

*Wm. Laird Kleine-Ahlbrandt*

# DER UNTERGEHER

*Author:* Thomas Bernhard (1931-    )
*Type of plot:* Anti-*Künstlerroman*
*Time of plot:* 1981
*Locale:* Wankham, a village in Upper Austria
*First published:* 1983

> *Principal characters:*
> THE NARRATOR, an Austrian writer and former pianist now
>     living in Madrid
> WERTHEIMER (DER UNTERGEHER), an Austrian amateur
>     philosopher and former pianist who hanged himself twelve
>     days before the beginning of the story
> GLENN GOULD, the Canadian-American piano virtuoso and
>     their friend, who recently died of a stroke

## The Novel

Returning from the funeral of his friend Wertheimer in Switzerland to his Vienna apartment, which he is trying to sell, the narrator decides on the spur of the moment to visit Wertheimer's hunting lodge in Upper Austria. Although he also owns a house in the area, he plans to stay overnight at a desolate inn in the nearby village. As he enters the inn, he begins to reflect on the lives and careers of his two closest friends, Wertheimer and Glenn Gould, whose deaths threaten to overwhelm him. The three met twenty-eight years earlier, in 1953, at a master class given by Vladimir Horowitz at the Mozarteum in Salzburg. Accomplished pianists at the time, both Wertheimer and the narrator were so overcome by Gould's virtuosity that they gave up their own careers as concert pianists, got rid of their valuable pianos, and turned to fruitless intellectual pursuits. Nevertheless, the three remained "life-friends" and visited one another in Salzburg in 1955 and in New York in 1969. It was Gould who named Wertheimer "Der Untergeher" (the founderer). The narrator finds the name appropriate, for unlike himself, who escaped the stifling cultural and political climate of Austria and had pretensions as a writer in Madrid, Wertheimer remained in Austria, a mere dabbler in philosophy.

Gould, whom the narrator calls "the most important piano virtuoso of the century," is the subject of the book on which the narrator has been working for nine years. The two first met on the Mönch mountain, also known as "suicide mountain," in Salzburg, quickly became friends, and, together with Wertheimer, rented a house in the suburban town of Leopoldskron, in order to escape Salzburg's obtuseness and animosity to art and the intellect. The house, which formerly belonged to a Nazi sculptor, was ideal for Gould's eccentricities and clowning. Gould, "the most clairvoyant of all fools," established the "total order" that he needed for his obsessive piano playing by, among other things, squirting the house's monumentally ugly sculptures with champagne, cutting down an ash tree that was blocking his window, and practicing Johann Sebastian Bach's *Goldberg Variations*, the work that was to become his trademark, without interruption until early in the morning.

According to the narrator, Wertheimer's ambitions as a piano virtuoso ended even before he met Gould, when Wertheimer first heard Gould play the *Goldberg Variations* in a classroom in the Mozarteum. In the Leopoldskron house, it became even clearer that the narrator and Wertheimer were no match for Gould's fanatical genius. He was the triumphant one, they the failures. Eventually Wertheimer auctioned off his Bösendorfer grand piano in Vienna, while the narrator gave his Steinway to a provincial teacher's nine-year-old daughter, who destroyed it in short order. While all three men over the years barricaded themselves from the world in their respective apartments and retreats (Gould in New York, Wertheimer in Vienna and in his hunting lodge, and the narrator in Madrid), only Gould's isolation led to any productive activity. After thirty-four concert appearances, Gould refused to play in public again and allowed himself to be heard only through his legendary recordings. In his forest studio, he perfected himself "to the extreme limit of his and in essence all piano-instrumental possibilities." He died of a stroke, apparently while playing the *Goldberg Variations*.

Wertheimer never recovered from Gould's death, which only intensified his insecurities, his sense of inferiority, and his suicidal tendencies. Soon after word reached him of his friend's death, his sister, whom he had tyrannized for years in their exclusive Viennese apartment, suddenly left him to marry an extremely wealthy owner of a Swiss chemical company. He took revenge on her by hanging himself from a tree outside her house in a village near Chur, Switzerland. As the narrator, who in the course of his narrative walks from the inn to the hunting lodge, discovers from Franz, one of Wertheimer's woodsmen, Wertheimer had carefully planned his final days. He invited his friends, including the narrator, and his former fellow music students, whom he despised and avoided for years, to stay at his lodge. Preoccupied with writing his book, *On Glenn Gould*, the narrator ignored Wertheimer's repeated invitations. The day before the guests arrived, Wertheimer burned the stacks of papers on which he had written his life's work in the form of thousands of aphorisms. He also ordered a worthless, badly out-of-tune piano from the Mozarteum. After not having played for more than a decade, Wertheimer proceeded to perform works by George Frideric Handel and Bach on the piano every time his guests were in the house. Driven wild by the unbearable noise, they caroused in the village and tore apart the lodge, until after two weeks he sent them packing. Shortly thereafter he left

for his sister's. Finally, alone in Wertheimer's room, the narrator listens to
Gould's recording of the *Goldberg Variations*, which had been left on Wertheimer's record player.

### The Characters

In the narrator's remembrances of his friends, it is remarkable how similar
their backgrounds were. All three of them came from wealthy families that
had no sympathy or understanding for their musical talents. They all studied
the piano as a way to get revenge on their parents, intentionally isolated
themselves from a world they saw as barbarous, and suffered from lung disease, which forced them to live in the country, which they hated. Both
Wertheimer and Gould died when they were fifty-one, the same age as the
narrator and even Thomas Bernhard when he wrote *Der Untergeher*. Despite
these similarities, the narrator repeatedly contrasts Glenn Gould's artistic
success with Wertheimer's failure—at one point he describes Wertheimer as
"the exact opposite of Glenn Gould"—while his own achievement in life
seems to consist chiefly in surviving, in not foundering on his renunciation of
a musical career.

The narrator's adulation for Gould is tempered by his awareness of
Gould's total sacrifice of himself to his art. During the summer of the Horowitz course, the narrator coined the phrase "piano radicalism" to describe
Gould's obsession with perfection, his intolerance of imprecision, and his
total self-discipline. At the time, he expected that Gould would quickly be
destroyed by the monstrosity of his task, the reckless simplicity of his life's
goal: to become an art machine. The ideal for him was to become superfluous as Glenn Gould, to be the piano, the Steinway, so that nothing, most of
all himself, stood between Bach and the Steinway: *"Glenn Steinway, Steinway Glenn only for Bach."*

As the narrator approaches Wertheimer's hunting lodge, he realizes that
when he returns to Madrid he will have to begin his Glenn Gould essay over
again, for now he is able to understand Gould's art only in contrast to
Wertheimer's non-art. Wertheimer had far too little courage and too much
anxiety to become a virtuoso pianist, which requires, according to the narrator, "a radical fearlessness toward everything and everyone." He was too
timid, for example, to tackle the *Goldberg Variations*. Plagued by self-doubt
and self-pity, Wertheimer never discovered his own uniqueness but remained
condemned to perpetual imitation, which the narrator sees as a cause of
Wertheimer's restlessness and his addiction to walking to the point of exhaustion. He blamed his misfortunes on his sister, who was for him nothing more
than his page-turner in the years when he still played the piano. In theory
and in his aphorisms, he had "mastered all the unpleasant things in life, every
despairing situation, the whole wearing evil in the world, *but practically, he
was not capable of mastering anything at all.*" The bizarre performance on the

out-of-tune piano at the hunting lodge and his suicide were the only decisive and original acts of his life.

## Themes and Meanings

The narrator longs to achieve in his writing Glenn Gould's level of perfection and virtuosity on the piano, while at the same time he fears that he, too, is no more than a founderer, a dilettante, and a candidate for suicide. He takes great pains to differentiate himself from Wertheimer and identify with Gould, yet in twenty-eight years of writing he has published nothing and is determined to destroy his "Glenn-manuscript" as soon as he returns to Madrid. Nevertheless, despite his own and Wertheimer's failure, there remains for him the enormously positive example of Glenn Gould, who prevailed over an ignominious world, whose recordings of Bach are timeless, and whose art is a monument of resistance against the decay and barbarity of modern civilization.

*Der Untergeher* is in part a poignant tribute to the historical Glenn Gould, who died in October, 1982. Yet it is also a work strongly rooted in Bernhard's own biography. A reclusive, misanthropic perfectionist, Bernhard, too, is a man obsessed with his art and as fanatic in his social and artistic habits as Gould was. In *Der Untergeher*, he displays his own formal virtuosity. The hypnotic rhythmic intensity of the novel's sentences propel the narrator's lengthy monologue. This monologue, which is delivered as he stands motionless in the inn and waits for the innkeeper, occupies two-thirds of the book and is broken suddenly by her unexpected appearance. The only other character whom the narrator encounters is Franz, Wertheimer's woodsman, whose story of Wertheimer's last days at the hunting lodge serves as a coda to the novel. Deftly repeating and varying a limited number of motifs and phrases, Bernhard establishes a fugal structure for the novel and thereby mimics in his own idiosyncratic way Bach's keyboard variations.

## Critical Context

Following in the wake of Bernhard's five-part autobiography (1975-1982; published in English under the title *Gathering Evidence*, 1986), *Der Untergeher*, like the narratives *Beton* (1982; *Concrete*, 1984) and *Wittgensteins Neffe: Eine Freundschaft* (1983; *Wittgenstein's Nephew*, 1987), strives to blur the distinctions between fiction and nonfiction, biography and autobiography, and the fictive and real worlds. Although these later prose works use the calamitous themes of Bernhard's first four novels—*Frost* (1963), *Verstörung* (1967; *Gargoyles*, 1970), *Das Kalkwerk* (1970; *The Lime Works*, 1973), and *Korrektur* (1975; *Correction*, 1979), they do so with greater detachment and humor and in a more readable and engaging style.

Common to all Bernhard's protagonists is an austere intellectual isolation, the condition for the creative fulfillment for which they long but which they never achieve. Glenn Gould's "world-virtuosity" in *Der Untergeher* is thus exceptional in Bernhard's prose works and yet is countered by Wertheimer's perversely negative example. Still, the grotesquely comic tragedy of Werthei-mer's final decline serves as a faint, parodying echo of the genuinely communal creative moments in the Leopoldskron house in 1953.

*Sources for Further Study*

Fetz, Gerhard. "The Works of Thomas Bernhard: Austrian Literature?" in *Modern Austrian Literature*. XVII, nos. 3/4 (1984), pp. 171-192.

Meyerhofer, Nicholas J. "On Biography as Autobiography: Thomas Bern-hard's *Der Untergeher* (*The Succumber*)," in *St. Andrews Review*. No. 30 (1986), pp. 15-19.

_____ . *Thomas Bernhard*, 1985.

Sharp, Francis Michael. "Literature as Self-Reflection: Thomas Bernhard and Peter Handke," in *World Literature Today*. LV (Autumn, 1981), pp. 603-607.

Wolfschütz, Hans. "Thomas Bernhard: The Mask of Death," in *Modern Austrian Writing*, 1980. Edited by A. Best and H. Wolfschütz.

*Peter West Nutting*

# THE VAGABOND

*Author:* Colette (Sidonie-Gabrielle Colette, 1873-1954)
*Type of plot:* Romance
*Time of plot:* Six months during the 1900's
*Locale:* Paris and several provincial towns
*First published: La Vagabonde*, 1911 (English translation, 1955)

> *Principal characters:*
> RENÉE NÉRÉ, the narrator, a mime and dancer
> BRAGUE, her mentor, partner, and comrade
> MAXIME DUFFEREIN-CHAUTEL, her admirer, a wealthy,
>    handsome, idle man-about-town
> HAMOND, her old friend, a painter
> MARGOT TAILLANDY, her friend and the sister of her former
>    husband, Adolphe

## The Novel

Divorced after eight years of her husband's faithlessness and cruelty, Renée Néré has been struggling to support herself as a music-hall performer for the past three years. The first of the book's three parts opens as she waits in her dressing room until it is time for her to perform. Renée meditates briefly on her solitary condition, the cold of the night, and her faith in chance and good luck; she checks her makeup in the mirror that she hates to face, then goes off to perform, no longer depressed and anxious but confident and controlled.

In this first third of the novel, Renée's life as an artiste is delineated: her work as a mime and a dancer, her friendly but casual relations with her fellow performers, the small flat that she shares with her maid, Blandine, and her dog, Fossette, and her introduction to Maxime Dufferein-Chautel. Maxime presents himself at her dressing-room door one evening, and Renée summarily dismisses him as an unwanted and awkward intruder, charming and respectful though he seems to be. She meets him again, in more formal and proper circumstances, after a private engagement arranged by his brother. Night after night, Renée's admirer watches her performance from the front row of the stalls and patiently waits for her.

With her old friend Hamond acting as a go-between, Renée and Maxime become slightly more friendly. The three have dinner together, Maxime visits her, and she acknowledges that she has an admirer, but nothing more than that. Eventually, their acquaintance deepens, but not into intimacy, despite Maxime's pleas. This situation continues until Renée signs a contract for a six-week tour with Brague and his pupil. Now she must decide between Maxime and her career, as she recognizes that she cannot allow him to accompany her and that she is not yet ready to give up the wandering life, which, for all its discomforts and difficulties, suits her. She prevaricates, promising to give herself to her patient suitor, but not until the tour is completed. She leaves Paris, troubled in mind, full of both regret and hope.

The final third of the book recounts Renée's travels from one place to another; sometimes she is in a different location each day, sometimes the group stays in one town for a few days. This part of the story is told primarily in the form of letters to Maxime, interspersed with brief accounts of performances, conversations, and thoughts about her relationship with him and what it means in terms of her view of herself and her life. The book ends with her final letter to him and the thoughts that she directs toward him as she leaves the letter unfinished.

## The Characters

The protagonist's disastrous marriage, her inability to continue her writing career after her divorce, and the vicissitudes of life as a music-hall performer have all helped to shape her outlook. Deluded in love, feeling disappointed and deprived by her perception of herself as a failed writer, struggling to attain recognition in her present profession, Renée is still an admirable rather than a pitiable woman. She faces the fact that the approach of her mid-thirties does not have the same meaning for her that Maxime's similar age has. She knows, rather than fears, that his love will decline as her beauty fades. She does fear her sensuality, however, recognizing that it may betray her into making an impulsive decision that could lead her once again into misery. Yet the factor that seems to provide the greatest tension is her independent spirit, which pervades everything that she thinks, feels, does, and says. She is candid, sometimes even brusque, impartially sympathetic with her fellow artistes, even as she holds herself aloof from them. Tough, brave, sensitive, and forthright, she is the center of the novel, and all the other characters merely help to reveal her to the reader.

Brague, an insistent taskmaster, drives and cajoles and sometimes insults Renée, but he also watches out for her and is tactfully reticent most of the time. Hamond, a gentle, affectionate, melancholy friend, who is himself disappointed in love, nevertheless hopes that Renée can once again experience it. Her closest female friend is Margot, the younger sister of Renée's former husband. Now fifty-two, Margot is cynical, eccentric, outspoken, compassionate, and devoted to the younger woman.

Maxime, Renée's putative lover, is no match for her, though he is by no means unlikable. Handsome, strongly but not aggressively sexual, patient in his love, he is appealing but not overwhelmingly so. Content to be supported and spoiled by his mother, he is something of a vagabond himself—drifting from woman to woman, taking pleasure as it comes but not actively seeking it. At first called "the Big Noodle" because of his boyish awkwardness,

Maxime soon shows his aptitude for love. He remains, however, merely another of the supporting actors in this story.

When Renée talks with her friends about her plight, they all give her good reasons to yield to Maxime's pursuit. Brague bluntly points out that her performance is being affected, Hamond reflects on how sad it would be if she were never to love again, and Margot is amused, understanding, and frank. As she responds to each of them, Renée becomes increasingly aware of her own inclinations and the direction that she will take. Thus, her three friends help to clarify the complexities of her resistance, as she struggles with her loneliness, her poverty, her love of solitude, her sensuality, and her attraction to Maxime.

### Themes and Meanings

The plot of this novel is uncomplicated, and the characters are all really supernumeraries, except for the central figure, the principal "vagabond," Renée. The epithet that gives the book its title personifies its theme: Only by wandering in pursuit of the fulfillment of her talents, by cherishing her solitude and privacy, by keeping relationships casual and temporary, can a woman attain the autonomy she seeks. The factors that militate against this achievement, as sketched above, are not as important as the nature of the woman herself, who possesses the determination and self-knowledge that enable her to work toward her goal despite its pain and cost. The book clearly indicates that the effort is worth the battle and that any other outcome would render the woman's life meaningless and servile.

The significance of her heroine's life is not expressed as a universal truth about the lives of all women, but Colette does appear to suggest that women would do well to examine closely their motivations and values, and those of men as well. In this particular book, she does not seem to think that men are as capable as women at this effort. She is somewhat contemptuous toward men, though good-humored, tender, and sympathetic.

### Critical Context

*The Vagabond* was the first novel that Colette wrote without the actual or claimed collaboration of her husband, Henri Gauthier-Villars, commonly known as Willy. Already a noted and admired writer at the time of its publication, with this novel Colette was acknowledged by French readers as one of the most prominent and talented writers of her time. The book is autobiographical in many ways—the facts of the heroine's life, the character of her first husband, and the qualities of the heroine herself.

Colette creates a world that has the authenticity of experience and the impact of shared emotions and ideas in *The Vagabond*. As one critic states, "*The Vagabond* . . . reads as a remarkably just and debonair study of a female consciousness waking to the possibility of independence—a feminist novel to shame, in its subtlety, the feminists."

The language of the book is richly sensuous, full of physical and natural images, and both sensitive and straightforward. The voice of the author is as distinctive and distinguished as was the woman who wrote the book. Although it is not one of her most popular or best-known works, it deserves a wide and attentive audience.

*Sources for Further Study*
Chauvier, Claude. *Colette*, 1931.
Cotrell, Robert D. *Colette*, 1974.
Le Hardouin, Maria. *Colette: A Biographical Study*, 1958.
Marks, Elaine. *Colette*, 1960.
Mitchell, Yvonne. *Colette: A Taste for Life*, 1975.
Stewart, Joan Hinde. *Colette*, 1983.

*Natalie Harper*

# VICTORIA

*Author:* Knut Hamsun (Knut Pedersen, 1859-1952)
*Type of plot:* Romance
*Time of plot:* The late nineteenth century
*Locale:* A small Scandinavian village
*First published:* 1898 (English translation, 1929)

> *Principal characters:*
> VICTORIA, the daughter of the Master of the Castle
> JOHANNES, a miller's son and a poet
> OTTO, a chamberlain's son
> CAMILLA, who is, as a child, rescued from drowning by
> Johannes and later becomes his fiancée

## The Novel

Once upon a time there lived a dreamy, solitary child, a miller's son named Johannes. Sometimes he was invited to play with Victoria and Ditlef, the children who lived in a nearby mansion known as the Castle. So begins this fairy-tale romance that conveys a pervasive sense of long ago and far away. As the book opens, Johannes, fourteen, has been called upon to row the children of his betters and their friends to an island. Among them is the enchanting, ten-year-old Victoria. When Johannes attempts to help Victoria ashore and to join the group in their adventure, he is brutally reminded of his place by the churlish Otto, the son of a chamberlain. The always-amiable Johannes contents himself with his favorite escape: fantasy. He is Sultan, and Victoria is begging to be one of his slaves, or he is chief pirate, with Princess Victoria his chief treasure.

Years pass. Johannes is sent away to town for school, rarely returning home because of the expense, but never does he forget Victoria. She is his inspiration; all of his poems have been written to her. Yet when he sees her again, she seems aloof, their conversation banal. When Johannes saves a child from drowning and temporarily becomes a hero, he exults in the knowledge that Victoria has seen him do it but is soon deflated when he discovers that she has taken little notice. In subsequent years, he is tormented because Victoria's social circles are closed to a miller's son, which he will always be— even though he is also beginning to be known as a poet. When he next encounters Victoria in town, where he is a student, she is staying at the Chamberlain's house, and she is wearing what appears to be an engagement ring. Shaken, Johannes pours out his heart: She is the only one whom he has ever loved, and everything he has ever written or tried to become is for her. She reveals that she has carried one of his poems next to her heart and that she loves him. Johannes' ecstasy is extreme but short-lived. Searching for her the next day, he finds her at the theater, accompanied by Otto. She at first totally ignores Johannes, then she humiliates him by her condescension. Later, she tells him that everything is impossible for them; there is too much that separates them; her father would never consent.

Johannes feels that his soul has withered, but he immerses himself in his writing and poetic reveries, which continue to revolve around Victoria. He publishes a book which becomes a success and goes abroad without telling anyone where. Two years pass. Johannes returns home and encounters Victoria gathering flowers in the woods that they once roamed as children. She invites him to a party at the Castle and, seeing his reluctance to accept, adds that she will have a surprise for him there. He notes that she wears no ring. When Victoria later sends a special invitation to him by messenger, he joyfully accepts and prepares to enter the Castle for the first time. In the drawing room, he finds many important guests, including the Chamberlain and his Lady and their son, Otto, now a lieutenant. When Victoria finally enters, she gives Johannes his surprise: She presents Camilla, whom Johannes, years before, saved from drowning, now an attractive young woman of eighteen. The party is a celebration of Victoria and Otto's engagement. Camilla is a consolation prize for Johannes. Bitterly noting that Victoria is again wearing a ring, he tells her not to take it off again. She replies that she is certain that she never will. Johannes and Victoria thus continue to wound each other throughout the remainder of the day. The truculent Otto, taking note of the strange tension between the two, blackens Johannes' eye and loudly announces that he is going to join the Laird's shooting party.

Within hours, news comes that Otto has been killed in a hunting accident. Victoria, hysterical, cries out to Johannes, "He was a hundred thousand times better than you." Later, Victoria goes to Johannes and explains that her father, a fiercely proud man, had compelled her to accept Otto because they needed Otto's money to avoid financial ruin. She had stalled, saying that in three years she would marry Otto, but as the day drew nearer, she begged her parents to insure her life instead and allow her to drown herself. She has always and only loved Johannes. To this passionate declaration, he has only one response; "I'm engaged." He and Camilla have entered into a secret understanding that one day she will marry him. Meanwhile, Victoria's father, attempting through insurance to save something for his heirs and unable to face ruin, takes advantage of everyone's absence during Otto's funeral to torch the Castle and himself.

When Johannes returns to town, he becomes so absorbed in his writing that he has little time to escort his secret fiancée to the balls and parties that she wishes to attend. By mutual agreement, Richmond, an Englishman, becomes her escort. Soon the two fall in love. Johannes is oddly unaffected by this revelation. He extends his blessing and returns to his writing, too preoccupied to attend a party at Camilla's home that he knows Victoria will attend. One night, Johannes arrives home to find an old acquaintance waiting in his doorway, the former tutor and aspiring poet from the Castle. He had not seen the tutor since the disastrous engagement party. At that time, the tutor confessed that he had not married because his first love had rejected him, but now he has married a widow and has thus instantly acquired a family, clothes, shoes, house, and home. Johannes congratulates him and patiently listens to him babble. Suddenly, the tutor asks Johannes whether he has heard about Victoria. In confusion, Johannes replies yes, and then no. The tutor tells him that she is gravely ill with tuberculosis, that she attended a party at Camilla's family home, where she danced like a mad person, and that she collapsed in a pool of blood and had to be carried home. In fact, he tells Johannes, Victoria is dead. He hands Johannes a letter which she asked him to deliver after her death and leaves, his mission ended.

Johannes, struggling to take in the fact that Victoria is dead, opens the envelope and reads: "Dear Johannes, When you read this letter I shall be dead." She is able at last to be perfectly honest. She clings to life but knows that there is no hope for her. She bitterly regrets that she has been unable to show how much she has loved him. She begs forgiveness for the many unkindnesses and injuries she has inflicted on him. She asks him not to see her in her coffin. She thanks him "for every single day and hour," and the letter and the book end.

## The Characters

Despite the novel's obvious fairy-tale and romantic qualities, Knut Hamsun has given his major characters some roundness and depth. Johannes is much more the poet than the peasant. He is sensitive, introspective, imaginative, and emotionally intense. He is at times brooding and solitary, frequently seeking solace in nature. At another time, he is capable of staying up all night, singing loudly to himself for excess of joy. Unhappily for him, he is also a romantic in his belief that first love is the only true love, that love can conquer all obstacles, and that love means perfecting oneself in order to be worthy of the beloved.

In the beginning, Victoria and Johannes enjoy the easy equality of children, but the world of money and class difference inevitably intrudes more and more. Yet even when it seems that Victoria has entirely rejected him, he still draws his inspiration from her, still struggles to become worthy of her. She is obviously something more than Victoria. She becomes an object of his idealized love, all the more necessary and desirable because she is unavailable.

In one surrealistically repellent dream, he is at the bottom of the sea "in front of a huge doorway." There he "meets a great barking fish. It has a mane on its back and it barks at him like a dog. Behind the fish stands Victoria. He stretches out his hands to her, she has no clothes on, she laughs to him and a storm blows through her hair." When he wakes from this forbidding dream, he leaves town and the country, as if in flight from the real, sexual woman. The suggestion is that Victoria, as an unattainable ideal, is in some way necessary to his psyche and to his writing. If attaining Victoria were truly his greatest wish, why does he not seek her out after he is released from his promise to Camilla? He stays away from Camilla's party although he knows Victoria will be there, and thus misses his last chance to see her.

Victoria is the Princess. She is her father's daughter in her pride, her class consciousness, and her occasional snobbery (for example, when she tells Johannes that Otto may be less handsome than he, but at least "he is a well-bred man. And that means something"). She is the cold aristocrat when she shows disdain for Johannes' father after he calls at the Castle. (He came only because she asked for news of Johannes.) She can be cruel—inviting Johannes to her engagement party and then mistreating him there. She can also be passionate and sincere; her letter has a terrifying honesty. Besides pity and fear of mortality, it reveals considerable self-knowledge. She writes, "O God, if you knew how I have loved you, Johannes. I have not been able to show it to you, so many things have come in my way, and above all my own nature." She adds, "Papa was hard on himself in the same way and I am his daughter." The father's nature is a fierce pride of position and place, which justifies the sacrifice of an only daughter to a loveless marriage and, when that fails, requires self-immolation.

Victoria's nature is somewhat more difficult to understand. She is obviously drawn to Johannes; she would rather be with him than with anyone else, and she would rather drown than marry a man she does not love. Yet she does nothing but acquiesce to her fate, at times seeming almost to revel in it. Perhaps she is the kind of woman who finds the dreadfully involuntary subjugation of love difficult to forgive. Perhaps love wounds her pride, because it destroys her proud illusions of self-sufficiency. It is possible to speculate about Victoria and about Johannes, but Otto and Camilla are one-dimensional characters who have little to do in the novel but be true to their respective types: Otto, a privileged and aggressive boor, and Camilla, a jejune debutante.

### Themes and Meanings

Into the romance of the Peasant-Poet and the Princess, Hamsun has interwoven many stories and anecdotes about love, ostensibly the writings and musings of Johannes. One story tells of two mothers, one dressed in black, the other in cheerful blue. The one wears mourning clothes because one of her three daughters died. Yet she died ten years ago, and still the mother grieves. The one in blue is having an affair. Her husband pretends not to know, stoically and considerately spending evenings at his club. One night, he comes home early to let his wife know that he knows, jealously seizes her, and proposes that they give "a pair of horns" to the man who just left. She screams and calls the maid. He recovers himself. The next morning, their farce is resumed; she is concerned for his health and the "extraordinary attack" of the previous night; he agrees, adding that "it takes it out of one to be witty at my age. I'll never do it again."

Another story tells of the rapture of a love strong enough to endure until death. A lord and his lady are growing old, having been happily married for many years. When the proud lord falls ill and loses all of his hair, he assumes that his wife's love must be diminished. She cuts off "all her yellow hair, to be like her husband whom she loved." Much later, the Lady is paralyzed; believing her helplessness and emaciation must prevent her husband from loving her any longer, she says she would gladly die. He vows that he loves her more, that she is more beautiful to him now than in her youth. He disfigures himself with acid. Such stories, of faithfulness and adultery, of altruism, grief, jealousy, and passion, expand Hamsun's theme of love.

*Critical Context*

Hamsun once said, "*Victoria* is nothing more than a little poetry. A writer may have some poetry he wishes to get rid of, particularly if for ten years he has written books that strike you like a fist." Clearly, *Victoria* is very unlike Hamsun's novels of psychological realism of the 1890's—*Sult* (1890; *Hunger*, 1899), *Mysterier* (1892; *Mysteries*, 1927), and *Pan* (1894; English translation, 1920)—and there is much that is poetic in the novel. Hamsun's setting, with its Castle and its allegorical characters known only as the Master and the Lady of the Castle, the Chamberlain and his Lady, the Tutor, and the Miller, helps create the feeling of a romance, the antithesis of realism. Yet the novel does not, for all its poetry, successfully wall out reality. The preoccupation with death and tragedy in Johannes' writings is a grim undercurrent to the romance elements of the novel. Victoria's letter to Johannes is unlike the sentimental letter written by a dying heroine in a romance. Its extreme honesty may not strike like a fist, but it sears and burns. Finally, it seems that a difference in class is not the only or even the real thing which separates the Peasant-Poet from his Princess. Their tragedy seems more a product of their somewhat neurotic selves than of implacable fate and cruel society.

*Victoria* became a great commercial success for Hamsun. In Norway, it is his best-known and best-loved book, and for a long period it was considered an appropriate confirmation present. It has become one of the most famous love stories in world literature.

*Sources for Further Study*
Ferguson, Robert. *Enigma: The Life of Knut Hamsun*, 1987.
Gustafson, Alrik. "Man in the Soil," in *Six Scandinavian Novelists*, 1940.
Larsen, Hanna Astrup. *Knut Hamsun*, 1922.

McFarlane, J. W. "The Whisper of the Blood: A Study of Knut Hamsun's Early Novels," in *PMLA*. LXXI (1956), pp. 563-594.

Næss, Harald. *Knut Hamsun*, 1984.

_____. "Who Was Hamsun's Hero?" in *The Hero in Scandinavian Literature*, 1975. Edited by John M. Weinstock and Robert T. Rovinsky.

*Karen Kildahl*

# VIPERS' TANGLE

*Author:* François Mauriac (1885-1970)
*Type of plot:* Psychological and social realism
*Time of plot:* 1930, with flashbacks from the 1870's to the end of World War I
*Locale:* Calèse (a rural estate near Bordeaux), Bordeaux, and Paris
*First published: Le Nœud de vipères,* 1932 (English translation, 1933)

> *Principal characters:*
> LOUIS, a sixty-eight-year-old retired lawyer and miser
> ISA FONDAUDÈGE, Louis' wife
> HUBERT and
> GENEVIÈVE, Louis' surviving children, who plot against him
> JANINE, Louis' granddaughter, who witnesses his last days
>     and inherits his diary

## The Novel

*Vipers' Tangle* is Louis' record of the social and psychological forces which have shaped his solitude. The first part of his account is prompted by an explosion of hatred and vengeance resulting from his wife's forty-five years of silence and separation. His need to be understood as more than merely a miser set upon disinheriting his children and to probe the sources of his feelings sets him upon a spiritual adventure of discovery and change. What Louis begins as a letter to Isa, his wife, to be read after his death, subsequently becomes a diary and, more important, a defense, a confession, and a self-revelation to be passed on as a part of the family inheritance.

Louis' rage confusingly leads him from an account of the day of his solitary sixty-eighth birthday to a report of his youth, his training as a lawyer, and his meeting and marriage with Isa. Interspersed with observations on the hypocritical religious practices of the bourgeoisie and on the power which money and property afford, Louis' thoughts gradually focus on the major incident that destroyed his faith in love and set off his fury with Isa: her confession of love for a man named Rodolphe. Louis discovers that he had been deceived into a marriage created only to save Isa's reputation. He feels not jealousy but horror at the confirmation that he was, after all, one of those whom others cannot love.

The Easter season provides Louis with an opportunity to depict his family's long-term conflicts: the contesting of his liberal, anticlerical attitude and the attempts to secure money for the family—this time for a business project of Geneviève's son-in-law. Then, Louis slowly reveals further sources of his rage against Isa: her complete focus on the children, even to the extent of ignoring works of charity; her indifference, especially to his notable success with the Villenave case; her battles with him over the religious training of the

children; her not loving him, thereby forcing him to turn to infidelity and
financial gain as the only sources of satisfaction; and her inability to believe
that the soul of their daughter, Marie, lives on after death.

To complete this indictment of Isa and her religious practices, Louis inter-
weaves depictions of those who have served as models of faith and love and
who have, consequently, contributed to his spiritual development: Marie,
who prayed sincerely and loved the poor; Abbot Ardouin, whose belief in
Louis as "very good" gave Louis sufficient strength to resist temptation with
Marinette, Isa's sister; Marinette, who elicited tender feelings of comfort
from Louis and who relinquished a fortune for love; and finally, Marinette's
son, Luc, whose piety and prayers inspired Louis with an awareness of an
"unknown substance" and his first experience of offering money out of genuine concern. The dramatic climax of this section of the book occurs during a
hailstorm, when Louis recognizes his heart as a "vipers' tangle" and turns
from a preoccupation with property and gain toward a blind force which he
senses may be Love: "I can no longer harvest anything in the world. I can
only learn to know myself better."

The second part follows a long night and day of a family conspiracy to find
Louis' wealth and to secure the patrimony, "the sacred rights of the family."
During his conversations with Isa, he experiences their first real communication and gains new faith in the possibility of love. His paranoia and fury over
the conspiracy, however, are so powerful that Louis flees to Paris to find a
new heir, his illegitimate son, Robert. His efforts only lead to despair, for
Robert betrays him by plotting with Louis' son and son-in-law; yet in the
midst of the treachery at Saint-Germain-des-Prés, Louis remembers Abbot
Ardouin and Marie and senses "an unknown world of goodness" just beyond
his reach. His consuming loneliness leads him to contemplate the existence of
God. Although Robert has become a part of "the enemy," Louis makes a
second effort to detach himself from his possessions and provides Robert
with a yearly income surpassing that which the family has offered.

Finally, after his ultimate despair at being deprived of a final communication with Isa before her death, Louis releases his fortune to his offspring.
This action is, in part, prompted by an understanding of Hubert's sincerity in
securing the family honor. When Phili, the husband of Louis' granddaughter,
Janine, runs off with a singing instructor and his wife's fortune, only Louis
and Janine perceive the role which the others have played in shaping Phili's
character; they alone acknowledge his potential for good. During his final
days, Louis urges Janine to consider faith beyond the mechanical gestures of
religion. He dies knowing that he has been understood and hoping that he
has touched another's life. The last entry in the diary indicates that Louis has
found that Love which he has so long sought.

Attached to Louis' notebook are a letter from Hubert to Geneviève, in
which Hubert casts doubt on their father's spiritual change, and a letter from

Janine to Hubert, in which she testifies that her grandfather had held three interviews with a priest and had intended to take his first communion at Christmas. Janine pleads with her uncle not to destroy the diary, for it is proof of the true object of Louis' heart.

## The Characters

Louis, the narrator-protagonist, writes his diary in an effort to escape solitude. He confesses to hatred, infidelity, and love of money in a desperate attempt to find sympathy and understanding. In the process of explaining or justifying himself, he documents those virtuous acts which have gone unnoticed and provide evidence for a more positive definition of his character. He views himself as the victim and the enemy, only to discover that other family members play the same roles. His lucidity and his courage to confront himself and others lead to a change of heart which illustrates his own dictum: "The art of living consists of sacrificing a lower passion for a higher one."

Isa is at the center of Louis' struggle. She holds the keys to understanding the absence of love that has driven him to claim money as the object of his heart. She is also the catalyst which releases years of anger, and her death precipitates his final detachment from worldly possessions. More important, as Louis attacks her silence, superficiality, and religious hypocrisy, he is better able to acknowledge her good qualities. In recognizing Isa's, Louis is later prepared to accept the underlying goodness in other family members. Her second confession, of hurt at his unfaithfulness and anticipation of his return to her bed, tempts Louis, once again, to believe in love.

Like Isa, some of the other, less well developed, characters bring Louis to understand that he has viewed himself and others too one-sidedly. With Hubert, Geneviève, and Phili, he recognizes that he is not the only one to constitute a "monster" and an "enemy." They, with Robert, rekindle Louis' dying anger and push him to the despair which prepares a contrite heart. They serve as the instruments which lead him to abandon hope in the world. As Louis reorients his life, however, he begins to see good in even the most flagrant example of sensuality and materialism, Phili. Louis learns to accept Hubert's dedication to family honor, Robert's weakness as a pawn, and Janine's stupidity. In fact, Janine's simple hope not only becomes a model to emulate; her companionship provides true communion for her grandfather. In the end, it is Janine who bears an irrefutable testimony of Louis' metamorphosis.

Louis' growing faith and gradual transformation are nurtured by the positive examples of the more one-dimensional characters in the book: Marie, Abbot Ardouin, Marinette, and Luc. Recollections of their charity and love turn Louis' attention away from the world, even in the midst of conspiracy and betrayal, and provide a realistic basis for his hope.

*Themes and Meanings*

The central theme of *Vipers' Tangle* is spiritual transformation. As Saint Teresa of Ávila's quotation at the front of the novel suggests, Louis ignorantly pursues false gods. In dealing with anger and vengeance, Louis unmasks the social values which wield such power: comeliness, inheritance (material and psychological), professional status, competition, social class, and love of money. As his hatred dies, so do these objects of the heart.

The structure of the novel reflects his struggle. Interruptions in the diary, for example, are caused not only by fatigue, illness, or poor lighting conditions, but also, more important, by his explosive emotions. As these emotions especially disorient Louis in the beginning, the past is confusingly merged with the present. In addition, Louis' fear of further rejection from Isa and his horror at facing his own monstrosity cause him to hesitate in his narration. The narrative gradually gains more order as he dispels anger and fear and moves toward change and acceptance.

François Mauriac uses many stylistic devices to convey his theme. The "vipers' tangle" is the central metaphor for Louis' avarice, paranoia, and hatred. The serpent image is specifically extended to describe the money belt that Louis offers to Luc: a "boa." The bed is an ironic symbol of "the desert" of love which characterizes his life. Dialogue provides a realistic technique for depicting conflict and conspiracy and Isa's important revelations. The seasons are associated with Louis' spiritual odyssey: spring rains and hail, with his detachment from the land; summer heat, with the eruption of the fury that, in spite of illness, compels him to flee to Paris; autumn, with Louis' spiritual harvest. His agony especially surfaces during the period of Good Friday and Easter; the events surrounding Bastille Day precipitate his personal revolution and foreshadow his freedom; and his birth into the Church is scheduled for Christmas. Additional religious motifs include memories of prayer; ringing of bells; hypocritical gestures, such as Hubert's sign of the cross; and churches, such as the one which suddenly appeared on the horizon—"like a living body"—after Isa destroyed Louis' faith in love, and also Saint-Germain-des-Prés, in which Louis experienced both betrayal and the workings of salvation.

*Critical Context*

*Vipers' Tangle* is Mauriac's masterpiece and a principal example of the Catholic novel in France. The narrator-protagonist point of view, the structure, the dualistic characterizations, and other devices all combine to produce a credible and powerful portrait of conflict and change. The depiction of grace in *Vipers' Tangle* is more successful than in any other piece of fiction by Mauriac. In addition, as is typical of his writing, many details are autobiographical. Louis' anticlerical attitude is drawn from Mauriac's father, grandfather, and Uncle Louis. His descriptions of the protagonist as sickly, frail, competitive, afraid of being mocked, and superior in intellect and writing to his peers, as well as his descriptions of early life in Bordeaux, reflect Mauriac's youth.

Many of Mauriac's other works share several important themes with *Vipers' Tangle*. The fictional character with whom Louis shares the greatest affinity is Fernand Cazenave of *Genitrix* (1923; English translation, 1960). *Vipers' Tangle* deals with the hypocritical, religious practices of the bourgeoisie that form a major theme in Mauriac's works from *Destins* (1928; *Destinies*, 1929) to *La Pharisienne* (1941; *A Woman of the Pharisees*, 1946). His success in depicting the spiritual void, a world without love, of which *Vipers' Tangle* is the best example, earned for Mauriac the Nobel Prize for Literature in 1952.

*Sources for Further Study*

Batchelor, R. "Art and Theology in Mauriac's *Le Nœud de vipères*," in *Nottingham French Studies*. XII (1973), pp. 33-43.

Flower, John E. *A Critical Commentary on Mauriac's "Le Nœud de vipères,"* 1969.

——————. *Intention and Achievement: An Essay on the Novels of François Mauriac*, 1969.

Paine, Ruth B. *Thematic Analysis of François Mauriac's "Genitrix," "Le Désert de l'amour," and "Le Nœud de vipères,"* 1976.

Tartella, Vincent. "Thematic Imagery in Mauriac's *Vipers' Tangle*," in *Renascence*. XVII (Summer, 1965), pp. 197-199.

*Wade Provo*

# THE WALL JUMPER

*Author:* Peter Schneider (1940-        )
*Type of plot:* Social criticism
*Time of plot:* The early 1980's
*Locale:* West Berlin and East Berlin
*First published: Der Mauerspringer*, 1982 (English translation, 1983)

*Principal characters:*
> THE NARRATOR, a graduate student from West Germany
> who has lived in West Berlin for the last twenty years,
> occasionally visiting East Berlin and the German
> Democratic Republic
> ROBERT, his friend, an emigrant from the German
> Democratic Republic who now lives in West Berlin
> LENA, the narrator's former girlfriend, who is also an
> emigrant from the German Democratic Republic and now
> lives in West Berlin
> POMMERER, an East German writer who lives in East Berlin
> DORA, the narrator's aunt, who lives in Dresden in the
> German Democratic Republic
> GERHARD SCHALTER, the narrator's landlord
> MR. KABE, the wall jumper
> WALTER BOLLE, a border violator
> MICHAEL GARTENSCHLÄGER, a defector from the German
> Democratic Republic

## The Novel

The Wall Jumper is a narrative essay or a collection of short stories assembled by the narrator according to a variation of the Scheherazade principle of *The Arabian Nights' Entertainments*. In *The Wall Jumper*, the narrator decides to collect and narrate stories about the divided city of Berlin, and whoever he meets is invited to tell him a new and better story. The work defies classification. It is not a novel, a novella, or a diary. It is perhaps best characterized as a narrative essay divided into five parts, mixing memoir with essay, anecdote with meditation, and narrative with political observation.

As part 1 begins, the narrator describes his approach by plane to Berlin. The plane, traveling from West Germany, must cross the city and the Berlin Wall three times in order to land against the wind at Tegel Airport in West Berlin. The narrator then describes the scene of his arrival at Schönefeld Airport in East Berlin to show the confusion of foreign tourists about the divided city. An Eastern European tourist cannot understand why he cannot share a taxi with the narrator to downtown Berlin: There are no taxis from Schönefeld Airport to West Berlin. The place the narrator calls home is not even shown on East Berlin city maps. The narrative then switches to a discussion of the Wall, built in August, 1961, by the East German government, and its depiction on city maps in East and West Berlin. The narrator moved to West Berlin immediately following construction.

The reader is introduced to Robert, the narrator's friend, whom he regularly meets for breakfast at a café. Robert, an emigrant from East Berlin, is an expert at the pinball machines at the café. When the narrator informs Robert that he is collecting stories about the divided city, he feigns a lack of interest in the topic. For Robert, the so-called German Question, the question of German reunification, which is part of the West German political agenda, does not exist, although he is deeply influenced by the effects of the partition.

The first story told is that of Gerhard Schalter, the narrator's landlord in West Berlin, who maintains his expensive West Berlin apartment by buying staple foods in East Berlin. Initially attracted to the other side of the wall by a love affair, Schalter changes his political ideology as a matter of course, coming to see the advantages of the social system in East Berlin. He appears to have moved to the other side of the Wall, as the narrator reports that a moving van took his furniture away.

The next story is about Mr. Kabe, the wall jumper of the novel's title, a West Berliner who has jumped the wall fifteen times simply because it is there. In East Germany, Kabe is arrested as a border violator but put under psychiatric observation when his interrogators cannot find a political or criminal intent. Finally, Kabe is turned over to the permanent delegation of the West German government in East Berlin, which returns Kabe to West Berlin. Three months later, Kabe promptly repeats his offense. The West Berlin authorities, however, fail to get at Kabe by legal means, because he has only crossed a state border that does not exist in the eyes of the West German government. In terms of constitutional law, Kabe has only been exercising his right to freedom of movement. When the West Berlin authorities incarcerate Kabe in a hospital because of his self-destructive tendencies, they have to release him: Kabe's repeated jumps only prove that the Wall can be crossed going east without damage to body or soul. Released from the hospital, Kabe returns directly to the Wall to perform one of his fifteen jumps. Even a change of residence to southern Germany does not prevent Kabe's return to Berlin and a repetition of his urge to overcome the Wall.

Part 2 shows the narrator going by *S-Bahn* (city railways) from West Berlin to East Berlin, arriving at Friedrichstrasse Station. He recalls a previous visit with his former girlfriend Lena to her family. Lena had left her family during the days of the Wall's construction. The narrator realized that the family, meanwhile, had become Lena's homeland. The family fulfilled a need which, in the apartment they shared in West Berlin, the narrator could not satisfy.

This time, the narrator visits Pommerer, a writer living in East Berlin, who tells him the story about the two Willys and Lutz, three filmgoers. The three boys, who live in a house directly at the East Berlin side of the Wall, jump the Wall every Friday for the sole purpose of going to see motion picture Westerns in West Berlin and then return to East Berlin after the show, until they are discovered and found guilty of repeated violation of the passport law and illegal border crossing. The narrator's visit with Pommerer introduces the reader to the special difficulties that intellectuals face in the German Democratic Republic—for example, obtaining travel permits to the West or gaining approval of publication.

Part 3 features the story of Walter Bolle and the reactions of the narrator and Robert to a violent street demonstration in West Berlin, reactions which reveal their different backgrounds. Bolle, who has spent seven years in East German prisons for various border violations after he attempted to escape across the Wall, becomes a double and triple agent when he is released to West Germany for a ransom, with the sole mission of destroying the Wall. Declaring a single-handed war on the German Democratic Republic, Bolle only endangers people in the West. When given a suspended prison sentence in West Berlin, he disappears as a confused man, having lost all identity.

A violent street demonstration on West Berlin's Kurfürstendamm Street reveals the different perspectives of the narrator and Robert, whose mentalities are determined by their backgrounds. While the narrator, with his Western perspective, views the demonstration as a spontaneous protest, Robert perceives it as a police-organized provocation to justify future crackdowns, basing this on his experience in the German Democratic Republic. Similar differences are revealed when the narrator's relationship with Lena is recorded.

At the center of part 4 is the story of Michael Gartenschläger, another defector from the German Democratic Republic, who is driven to dismantle the self-triggering explosive devices installed along the border. At his third attempt, he is killed by automatic rifle fire from East German border guards.

The rest of part 4 deals with Pommerer's public protest on behalf of a fellow writer who was fined because he had published a novel in the West without permission from the East German copyright office and with the narrator's visit with his Aunt Dora in Dresden, where he is not allowed to meet with his cousin who is doing his military service. (Soldiers in the East German army are forbidden any Western contacts.) The narrator admits, "[I]t will take us longer to tear down the Wall in our heads than any wrecking company will need for the Wall we can see." If Germans still have a common fatherland, it survives only in their language.

In part 5, the Iron Curtain comes down to put an end to the narrator's visits to East Berlin. It is as though he has challenged the border guards one time too many. They take his car apart completely, only to find nothing. The narrator is then denied permission to enter the German Democratic Republic and, in accordance with international protocols, given no reason.

## The Characters

The narrator and protagonist of *The Wall Jumper* is to some extent an autobiographical figure. Like his narrator, Peter Schneider has lived in West Berlin since 1961, was a student at the Free University, and found himself confronted with the Wall, built to shut off the flight of an ever-increasing number of citizens to West Berlin. While living in West Berlin, Schneider went very often to East Berlin and also made trips into the German Democratic Republic. Schneider's protagonist is a man caught between the "here" and the "over there" of the Wall, between two states and their political cultures. The narrator's memories of his earlier life—his childhood, World War II, the defeat of Germany, and its occupation by Soviet and American troops—explain his state of mind, which is as divided as his nation. There is, so to speak, a wall in his head which he cannot tear down. Although his trips beyond the Wall begin as a campaign to overcome the Wall and deconstruct the divisions that it has caused, the narrator realizes the futility of his attempts when he is finally denied permission to enter East Berlin. The other characters of the novel, even the narrator's friend Robert and his girlfriend Lena, are not fully developed; they serve as examples of the division between East and West Germany.

## Themes and Meanings

The schizophrenia of Berlin is the central theme of *The Wall Jumper*. As the title suggests, the division can be overcome, but, as the narrative shows, it can be done only physically, not mentally. The wall jumper's predicament exhibits a much more serious flaw than a pathological desire that he cannot control: He is unable to choose between East and West. In this fashion, the wall jumper's story figures as a symptom of the pathology of Berlin as a schizophrenic city. This schizophrenia, officially sanctioned by East and West to prevent the outbreak of a more serious disease, is shown to be causing a number of cases like that of the wall jumper. His case is symptomatic of the general condition of the city.

As the narrative develops, it becomes obvious that the narrator himself is not immune to the disease. He realizes that he cannot tear down the wall in his own head. Like the characters of his numerous anecdotes, the narrator could jump across the Wall, but he cannot overcome the mental division, established by history, in his own and in others' minds. The characters cannot speak to one another without their states speaking through them.

The Wall is the central metaphor of the novel, providing a semiotic system of disjunction and junction. The *S-Bahn* and the telephone are images of interconnection, whereas the Wall with its watchtowers and border guards represents disconnection or separation. All other images are subject to this binary system of division and flow.

The narrative shifts between three readily distinguishable locales—the modern city of West Berlin with all of its Western trappings, the city of East Berlin, which is not as modern and lags behind in terms of consumer goods, and the hinterland of the German Democratic Republic, a mysterious country associated with the past.

Finally, the novel shows the relationship between man, city, and history. The narrator realizes that, like history, the city of Berlin is a text to be read, a text which he can read but not comprehend. Like a future archaeologist, the narrator can only conclude that the Wall will probably still be standing when no one is left to move beyond it.

## Critical Context

*The Wall Jumper* is Schneider's second important work. With his first novel, *Lenz* (1973), modeled after a novella by Georg Büchner, a nineteenth century revolutionary German author, Schneider became the spokesman for a whole generation of young Germans involved in the student movement and alienated from the political culture of the government in office during the 1960's.

In *The Wall Jumper*, his first novel published in the United States, Schneider confronts the issue of the division of Germany, symbolized by the Berlin Wall. Rich in documentary references, *The Wall Jumper* is a primary example of the literature of facts of the 1980's.

Schneider has also published a novel entitled *Vati* (1987; dad), which concerns the biography of Josef Mengele, the infamous concentration camp doctor who escaped from justice to South America, as seen from the perspective of his own son. Mengele's son belongs to Schneider's own generation, which has yet to face its Nazi heritage, and Schneider's novel is an attempt to meet this obligation.

## Sources for Further Study

Demetz, Peter. *After the Fires: Recent Writings in the Germanies, Austria, and Switzerland*, 1986.

Houston, Robert. "Up Against the Wall: *The Wall Jumper* by Peter Schneider," in *The Nation*. CCXXXVIII (March 17, 1984), p. 328.

Kaes, Anton. Review in *Library Journal*. CIX (April 1, 1984), p. 734.

Rushdie, Salman. "Tales of Two Berlins: *The Wall Jumper* by Peter Schneider," in *The New York Times Book Review*. LXXXIX (January 29, 1984), p. 13.

*World Literature Today*. Review. LVII (Spring, 1983), p. 288.

*Ehrhard Bahr*

# THE WATCHMAKER OF EVERTON

*Author:* Georges Simenon (1903-     )
*Type of plot:* Psychological realism
*Time of plot:* The mid-1950's
*Locale:* Everton and other New York villages and cities, and various Eastern and Midwestern locales
*First published: L'Horloger d'Everton*, 1954 (English translation, 1955)

> *Principal characters:*
> DAVE GALLOWAY, a forty-three-year-old watchmaker
> BEN, his sixteen-year-old son
> MUSAK, Dave's friend, a cabinetmaker
> LILLIAN HAWKINS, Ben's fifteen-year-old girlfriend
> WILBUR LANE, the attorney hired by Dave for Ben

*The Novel*

*The Watchmaker of Everton* is a story about the failure of a family. Dave Galloway, the watchmaker of the title, leads an existence that is as regularized as the watches and clocks that he repairs. Every day of his life is marked by a routine that is kept so faithfully that he is hardly aware of it. For more than fifteen years, since his wife deserted him, he has cared for Ben, his son, now sixteen years old. Fulfilling the roles of both parents, Dave consciously seeks his son's respect and love.

Late one Saturday evening, after he has had his usual night out with his friend, Musak, Dave discovers that Ben has disappeared with a suitcase and Dave's car. The mother of Lillian Hawkins, Ben's girlfriend, comes to Dave's home and tells him, accusingly, that her daughter has stolen some money from home and gone away with Ben. Dave spends an anxious night, wondering what has happened. On Sunday morning, he is told by the police that Ben and Lillian have killed a salesman and stolen his Oldsmobile, having abandoned Dave's vehicle along the road. Soon the news becomes public, and Dave awaits further information. Against his will he is drawn into the events. At last, word comes that Ben and Lillian have been captured in Indiana, where they went to be married. Musak helps Dave get a flight to Indianapolis, where Ben is being kept by police before being turned over to the New York authorities, but to Dave's surprise and sorrow, Ben refuses to see him. A passenger on the same plane that returns Ben and Lillian to New York, Dave is left alone with his thoughts. Georges Simenon allows the reader to look into Dave's mind: Dave's anguished reflections are among the recurring flashbacks in the narrative. Collectively, these thoughts give information about the past, rounding out the present.

The preliminary hearing comes, and then the trial, and Dave still has not received his son's acceptance. At the trial, the verdict is guilty, and the sentence is life imprisonment for Ben and Lillian. Sing Sing, where Ben is sent, is scarcely twenty-three miles from where Dave lives. The father is entitled to visit his son once a month, but the first visit is futile and unproductive, because Ben has not come to regard his father as one of his own kind. Dave is ready to take as much time as needed, however, to make Ben understand how alike they are, if only in their revolt; through revolts of one kind or another, especially ones totally unacceptable to society, they have both tried to set themselves free. Soon, it is discovered that Lillian is pregnant by Ben, and Dave dreams happily of the time when he can talk with his grandson and "reveal to him the secret in men."

## The Characters

Dave is the only character in *The Watchmaker of Everton* who achieves any degree of roundness. Simenon gives his character life by looking into his mind. His motives are explained with each thought or action, and his past experiences are connected with those of the present, thereby unifying the psychological motifs and the parts of the story. Because Simenon is more concerned with telling a story about the modern world than with creating believable characters, however, even Dave does not receive the author's complete attention. Once he is understood to be Everyman, Dave is little more than a stereotype. Readers will identify with him, however, and sympathize with him, because Simenon treats him with understanding and humanity.

The other characters are seen only through Dave's eyes. Ben scarcely has any existence except as Dave perceives him; he is a constant presence merely because Dave is constantly thinking about him. Dave's failed relationship with his son is the reason for the story, and thus the details of the novel are often about Ben. Interestingly, although she is not a character in the present narrative, Ben's mother—Dave's wife—is more fully realized than Ben, perhaps because she exercises such a forceful influence on the lives of others, especially Dave's. She led Dave to the one significant revolt in his life. Lillian is like Dave's former wife only insofar as she is a catalyst in Ben's revolt, for Lillian, like her parents, is peripheral to the major incidents of the novel.

Indeed, all the other characters are presented either to give Dave definition or to round out the action. Musak is described rather than dramatized. He is in the story only to help account for the way in which Dave spends his time. Wilbur Lane, Ben's lawyer, through a few brush strokes of Simenon's word-painting, comes to life for a short time, only to fade back into Dave's reflections on his family.

## Themes and Meanings

Helplessness in the face of destiny is a main theme in *The Watchmaker of Everton*. Watchmaking as a symbol of creation is employed ironically in the novel, since Dave is completely removed from the processes which determine his existence. He is controlled by life rather than controlling it. That his story is essentially plotless is a mirroring of reality, for life does not move along a course determined by those people living it. Ironically, Dave believes that, somehow, he can bring order to disorder, change the unhappy past to make a happy present and future.

Guilt is a natural consequence for Dave when things do not go well. He blames himself more than he does Ben for the murder of the salesman. He is brought to this conclusion, as well, by the fact that he believes that others blame him too. Although it is not his fault that his wife deserted him, leaving him alone to bring up Ben, he is right in believing that society has censured him for the absence of a maternal influence on his son.

Unfortunately, it is impossible for Dave to explain himself, and it is equally impossible, in the world of Simenon's novel, for anyone else to comprehend him. The universe and its inhabitants are incapable of understanding or of being understood. From this truth comes a more comforting truth, that there are no absolutes for judging individuals: The person who is not entirely innocent is also not entirely guilty. After all, the universe is made up of human beings.

A person, having human limitations, has, or ought to have, little expectation of life, of lasting happiness. If Simenon's characters do not always show that they are aware of this, Simenon always leaves his readers with this inescapable conclusion. More often than not—as is the case with Dave in *The Watchmaker of Everton*—a Simenon character finds contentment in illusions and dreams. Escape is as often psychological as physical. As Dave dreams of the past events which brought about present ones, he also attempts to create a better future by imagining happy things to come. He imagines a grandson, for example, before Lillian's child is born, a grandson with whom he will talk. Although he is in prison, Ben is always with Dave in his mind. Yet Dave's imaginings are not evidence of clinical insanity but of efforts to create a semblance of sanity in a chaotic and indifferent world.

Simenon does not philosophize or preach or attempt to convey meanings in his books; neither does he interpret or explain. In the present novel, as in all of his works, he presents an individual who deals with life's conflicts in whatever way that he can. Dave looks upon what life has been, what it is, and what it can be. That he is mistaken in his reading of events past, present, or future is what, for Simenon, makes him most human. Dave's creation of a dreamworld is as valid as another person's accurate perception of reality.

In a dreamworld, the arbitrary or fanciful or insubstantial has its own solidity. Thus, Dave the dreamer makes himself believe that he, like his son, has also been capable of revolt. He married a woman who was unacceptable to society, thumbing his nose at those, including his mother, who disapproved. Dave's father similarly had once shown a measure of revolt when, after a life of kowtowing, he had stayed out all night long. Dave draws his father, his son, and himself together as kindred spirits united against the world. His grandson, too, will eventually share in this unity and will hear from him "the secret in men." What is this secret? One can only guess, and many have tried. Whatever the secret is, it cannot be communicated by Dave or through him. Simenon uses a device that is rather new to novelistic technique: He puts his character onstage and, instead of explaining him by an omniscient vision, allows the character's actions or thoughts to explain themselves. Much of the forcefulness of *The Watchmaker of Everton* lies in what its author does not say.

*Critical Context*

Having written more than two hundred novels under his own name and hundreds under various pseudonyms, Georges Simenon is best known as the creator of detective novels about Inspector Maigret. Nevertheless, the Maigrets, as they are often called, are far more than conventional mystery stories. Without discernible plots, they are more concerned with the motives and other facts behind the murder than with locating the murderer. In the attention they give to realistic human behavior, they are, essentially, psychological studies.

Simenon considers his psychological novels, of which *The Watchmaker of Everton* is one example, to be his most important work. He is indebted to Honoré de Balzac for his realism and to Fyodor Dostoevski for his psychological probing. Modern schools of thought involving psychoanalysis, scientific determinism, and existentialism also are significant influences on Simenon's fiction, which he stopped writing in 1972, when he turned to his memoirs and autobiographical reflections.

*The Watchmaker of Everton* is one of several novels that Simenon wrote with an American setting. He is at his best on familiar ground, that of France or another Western European country, but he usually succeeds in being universal, timeless, and placeless. He is considered by many great writers to be one of their number, but he is often criticized for the very thing for which he is also often praised, that is, for writing a large number of works at such a fast pace. Still, he has an unquestioned permanence among modern writers, and other writers are among the first to declare that fact.

*Sources for Further Study*

Becker, Lucille F. *Georges Simenon*, 1977.
Bresler, Fenton. *The Mystery of Georges Simenon*, 1983.
Galligan, Edward L. "Simenon's Mosaic of Small Novels," in *South Atlantic Quarterly*. LXVI (Autumn, 1967), pp. 534-543.
Mauriac, Claude. "Georges Simenon," in *The New Literature*, 1959.
Raymond, John. *Simenon in Court*, 1968.

*David Powell*

# THE WATERFALLS OF SLUNJ

*Author:* Heimito von Doderer (1896-1966)
*Type of plot:* Historical realism
*Time of plot:* The late nineteenth and early twentieth centuries
*Locale:* Vienna and environs
*First published: Die Wasserfälle von Slunj*, 1963 (English translation, 1966)

> *Principal characters:*
> ROBERT CLAYTON, a British machinery manufacturer who
> establishes a factory in Vienna
> HARRIET CLAYTON, Robert's wife
> DONALD CLAYTON, Robert and Harriet's son, who meets a
> tragic death at the waterfalls of Slunj
> MONICA BACHLER, Donald's lover and the second wife of
> Robert Clayton
> CHWOSTIK, a financial wizard who is employed by the
> Claytons
> ZDENKO, a young student

## The Novel

In *The Waterfalls of Slunj*, Heimito von Doderer traces the fortunes and misfortunes of two generations of a British manufacturing family who set up a business enterprise in pre-World War I Austria. The work is a "total novel," designed to capture the customs and manners of Europeans living during the height of the Austro-Hungarian Empire. A love song to a bygone era, this epic work describes in great detail the social fabric, landscapes, atmospheric conditions, and even the sounds and odors of antebellum Vienna and its environs. Sympathetic but not overly sentimental, the novel re-creates a panoramic view of everyday life among the rich and middling sorts who lived along the gaslit, cobbled streets of old Vienna.

The story opens in the late 1870's with the marriage of Robert and Harriet Clayton. Robert, the son of a well-to-do machinery manufacturer from southwest England, and his bride, Harriet, spend their honeymoon in the vicinity of Vienna, near the beautiful falls of the Slunjcica River. Precisely nine months later, their first and only child, Donald, is born.

Upon returning to Great Britain, Robert learns of his father's decision to establish a subsidiary firm in the southeastern provinces of the Austro-Hungarian Empire. Having been given responsibility for opening the new factory, Robert returns to Vienna, seeks personnel recommendations from Andreas Milohnic (a hotel clerk whom the Claytons met while they were on their honeymoon in Austria) and hires a man named Chwostik as the office manager. Under Chwostik's able direction, the Claytons' factory becomes an efficient and profitable business enterprise, and Robert achieves social and economic prominence. In time, Donald, who spends much of his youth in England with his grandfather, completing his education, returns to Vienna to assist his father in the family business.

The novel centers on the relationships between young Donald and his family, friends, and associates. Although remarkably similar to his father in physical appearance (acquaintances refer to the father-son pair as the "English brothers"), Donald lacks the confidence and individuality of the other Claytons. Donald's life is a series of frustrations and disappointments. A self-centered bachelor, he lacks the courage even to consummate his love for Monica Bachler, the one woman who adores him.

While on an extended business trip to England, Donald realizes that he loves Monica. Upon returning to Vienna, however, he receives a cool reception from his former admirer. Confused and exasperated, Donald leaves on another business trip. While in Budapest, he is duped into seducing Margot Putnik, the unhappily married wife of a business client. Typical of other experiences in Donald's unfulfilled life, the intended affair is foiled by the timely arrival of Margot's husband, Laszlo Putnik. Donald, embarrassed and broken by yet another rejection, determines to make a belated plea for Monica's affections. Yet, before he can reach Vienna, Donald learns the surprising news that his father, now a widower of several years, and Monica are announcing their own engagement.

Failing as a lover, a friend, and a businessman, Donald loses his will to live. He visits the waterfalls of Slunj, not knowing that he is returning to the site of his conception. There he meets his tragic end. While Donald is walking over the cataracts, the railing snaps, and he stumbles over the narrow wooden bridge. Nearby rocks halt the fall of his body, but not his fears. Donald dies of fright, even though he drops only a few feet, onto a ledge and not into the falls.

*The Characters*

In some ways, Doderer's *The Waterfalls of Slunj* resembles the three-decker novels of the late nineteenth century. His leisurely prose, his use of long, descriptive passages flooded with color and imagery, and his cast of hundreds of characters who are intricately, almost mechanically, interrelated—these are the conventions of the Victorian novel. On several occasions, Doderer also uses the Victorian novelist's habit of addressing the "gentle reader," intruding upon the narrative with personal comments of affection or denigration regarding his characters and even explicitly banishing characters from the book. For example, after a minor character serves her purpose, Doderer writes:

The moment has come when it has become possible for us to eject Frau Wewerka from our composition. . . . Grant it, O reader, to this thy entreating author! Grant him the exquisite delight of bestowing two positively whacking boxes on the ears, by means of which Frau Wewerka is catapulted out of this book and shot off to the horizon, where she bursts and scatters in disgusting spray.

On another occasion, Doderer ejects from his pages two redeemed prostitutes, Finy and Feverl, only to readmit them at a later time when the plot thickens.

A historian in his own right, Doderer purposely introduces a rich variety of characters in order to portray Vienna in its grand diversity. The range of his sympathies is wide, for most of his characters—engineers, businessmen, "nice" Viennese ladies, and prostitutes—possess admirable or at least tolerable qualities. Doderer, however, shows no compassion for Frau Wewerka and her little duplicate, Frau Wenidoppler, unredeemable servants of mammon—the one Viennese type Doderer loathes.

Doderer excels in his portrayal of characters who are neither sophisticated nor highly articulate. Several of his minor characters, such as the aforementioned prostitutes Finy and Feverl, evoke more sympathy and appear more lifelike than the principal characters. As the narrator, Doderer himself becomes bored with Donald, his protagonist, whom on several occasions he dismisses as a "paperweight," an insignificant nobody. At times, Doderer even digresses from the central plot to give sudden prominence for a few pages to the concerns of his supporting cast, only then to eject them "with a hearty kick in the behind." Other minor characters, however, such as the five Harbach girls, are hardly more than names, identified with generalized attributes (the Harbach girls are "tall") that have little to do with the time, the setting, or the plot. Keeping track of such marginal characters (who often are linked, sometimes by coincidence, with other figures later in the narrative) requires attentive reading.

Doderer's narrative voice is distant and dispassionate. The reader is like a social spectator who views the flow of events but does not participate emotionally in them. Even Donald's tragic death evokes only minimal sympathy. Some readers also find Doderer's characters too obviously manipulated and predictable. From the beginning, it is clear that Chwostik will succeed and that Donald is doomed. Doderer's principal characters in *The Waterfalls of Slunj*, like those in his other works, rarely surprise the reader; instead, they consistently follow the course their creator meticulously charted for them before he wrote the book.

## Themes and Meanings

In *The Waterfalls of Slunj*, as in Doderer's earlier novels, the imagery of water is an effective and powerful motif. More than simply a metaphor for life, water is presented as a primordial force which exerts a profound influence on the work's prominent characters. Throughout Doderer's tales, likable characters are directly equated with water (often running water), while the inept who refuse to experience life to its fullest—those confined to what Doderer calls the "second reality"—are separated and paralyzed by the "wall of water."

The differences between the leading characters, Robert and Donald, are reflected in their relationships with water. The story opens with Robert and Harriet experiencing emotional ecstasy at the sight of the waterfalls of Slunj. Here, Robert makes contacts for an adventuresome, fulfilling career, and Donald is conceived.

Unlike his father, Donald spends his entire life in that "second reality" of emotional barrenness. His inability to achieve true selfhood is metaphorically expressed through his relationship with water. As a child, Donald's nurse sings to him by a lake on his grandfather's estate. The lake, however, brings not peace but nightmares:

> The lake had reared up as though swinging on a horizontal axis: its once flat, gleaming surface became a terrifyingly towering, sheer wall of water, immeasurably high. There it was, directly outside the windows of the room where Donald slept, rearing, solid water that threatened to crash down upon him at any moment.

Later, when Monica prepares to make love with Donald, it begins to rain and Donald, paralyzed by another "wall of water," cannot go into the next room where his lover is ready to embrace him. In the end, when Donald visits the waterfalls of Slunj, he slips and dies of fright. He literally is frightened to death by the roaring currents of life.

Donald's timidity is also contrasted with the vitality of other characters who are immersed in the flowing waters of life. When Chwostik accepts, as Donald could not, the invitation of Monica for an erotic adventure, they cross a river in a ferry, even though "the water was very close, running fast." Similarly, on the very day of Donald's death, Zdenko—a student who possesses the confidence that Donald lacks—approaches the powerful waterfalls of Slunj with a sense that he is soon to experience "the greatest, the essential adventure of his life." Again, even the prostitutes Finy and Feverl are cleansed and given a second chance in life when they jump into the waters of the Danube Canal and save a small girl from drowning.

Thus water, for Doderer, is a purifying, positive force often equated with life itself. Its fluidity is the converse of the rigidity that confronts those characters who choose to abide in the "second reality." The ideal human, in Doderer's mind, approaches the waterfalls of life without hesitation or fear, knowing that he or she can swim in the waters of life. Similarly, the waterfalls, around which the very earth trembles, bring both procreation and death. To Doderer, they suggest the ultimate reality.

## Critical Context

*The Waterfalls of Slunj* was the first part of a planned tetralogy, an ambitious project intended to be as large in scope and scale as Doderer's masterpiece, *Die Dämonen* (1956; *The Demons*, 1961). Doderer's death in December, 1966, however, deprived readers of the completed work. Fortunately, *The Waterfalls of Slunj* can be read as an autonomous unit.

A soldier and captured prisoner in two world wars and a scholar with a doctorate in Austrian history, Doderer distrusted the panaceas for social ills that were offered from both the political Right and the Left. To Doderer, such ideologies simply clouded one's perception of truth, forever keeping one in an illusory and false world of "second realities." Thus, as a novelist, Doderer avoided creating characters as the embodiments of ideas. He refused to cultivate the dream at the expense of reality.

With the trained eye of a historian, Doderer instead dutifully recorded the manners of the people and the scenery of the countryside during the height of his country's glory. Convinced that "the novel is a perpetual quest for reality" and that the task of the novelist is "the reconquest of the external world," Doderer became Austria's greatest poet of the sights and sounds of old Vienna. In reading his prose, sympathetic students cannot help but become Viennese themselves.

## Sources for Further Study

Bachem, Michael. *Heimito von Doderer*, 1981.

Haberl, Franz P. "Water Imagery in Doderer's Novels," in *Books Abroad.* XLII (Summer, 1968), pp. 348-353.

Hamburger, Michael. *From Prophecy to Exorcism*, 1965.

Hatfield, Henry. "The Human Tragicomedy: Doderer's *Die Wasserfälle von Slunj*," in *Books Abroad.* XLII (Summer, 1968), pp. 354-357.

Ivask, Ivar. "Heimito von Doderer: An Introduction," in *Wisconsin Studies in Contemporary Literature.* VIII (Autumn, 1967), pp. 528-547.

Swales, M. W. "The Narrator in the Novels of Heimito von Doderer," in *The Modern Language Review.* LXI (January, 1966), pp. 85-95.

*Terry D. Bilhartz*

# WE

*Author:* Yevgeny Zamyatin (1884-1937)
*Type of plot:* Fantasy
*Time of plot:* The twenty-ninth century
*Locale:* A city-state known as the One State
*First published: My,* written, 1920-1921; corrupt text, 1927; complete text,
   1952 (English translation, 1924)

> *Principal characters:*
> D-503, the narrator and the protagonist, a mathematician
>    and builder of the spaceship *Integral*
> O-90, his girlfriend and registered sexual partner
> R-13, his friend, who shares 0-90 with him, an official poet of
>    the One State
> I-330, the woman with whom he falls in love, a leader of the
>    revolution
> THE BENEFACTOR, the authoritarian leader of the One State

*The Novel*

   *We* is a first-person narrative written as a diary by D-503, a mathematician
and builder of the *Integral*, a spaceship destined to travel to other planets to
subjugate the inhabitants who may still be living in the primitive condition of
freedom. The diary is to be carried on the space mission and is addressed to
the unknown beings of these planets in order to explain and justify their subjugation. The structure of the novel is based on forty diary entries which
describe a futuristic society of the twenty-ninth century in which all citizens
live in a single city-state called the One State, under the authoritarian rule of
the Benefactor and the watchful eye of a secret police force known as the
Guardians. The society developed as a result of the Two Hundred Years'
War, in which the city triumphed over the country, and has separated itself
from the primitive world of the ancients by the protective Green Wall.

   The inhabitants of the One State live in a rationally planned society in
which all activities are programmed according to the Table of Hours. The
only human activity which has not been completely organized is the sexual
act. Citizens are allowed free unscheduled time each day, referred to as the
Personal Hours, in which they are allowed to draw the curtains of their glass
rooms and engage in sexual or creative artistic activity. Love and marriage
have been eliminated. Any citizen may register to have sexual relations with
any other citizen by obtaining a pink coupon. Conformity of thought, dress,
and behavior is rigidly enforced. All citizens wear blue-gray uniforms and are
identified by a number. Any number who deviates from the norms of the

One State is arrested and publicly executed by the Machine of the Benefactor. Each year, the Benefactor is unanimously reelected in a mass public meeting referred to as The Day of Unanimity.

Initially a loyal supporter of the One State, D-503 gives the title "We" to his diary to emphasize that he is recording not his individual thought, but the collective wisdom of the One State. As D-503 records events, however, he begins to describe his own personal thoughts and feelings. The diary reflects D-503's gradual change in consciousness as he begins to question the rational principles imposed by the One State on its citizens and rediscovers his lost individuality represented by the emotional part of his personality, which the One State has repressed. The catalyst for D-503's change in attitude is his encounter with I-330, a temptress and secret revolutionary with whom he falls in love. D-503's passionate attraction for I-330 awakens primitive feelings of jealousy and irrational urges, causing him mental anguish as his rationally controlled existence begins to disintegrate. His developing relationship with I-330 leads to a crisis in his relationship with his sexual partner, O-90, whom he shares with his friend, the poet R-13.

As D-503 rediscovers his emotional, irrational self, he is recruited by I-330 in a plot to seize the *Integral* and revolt against the One State. The plot is discovered; the revolutionaries, led by I-330, attempt a coup, but they are arrested. The One State views the revolt as an illness which can be cured by subjecting all numbers to the Great Operation, a type of lobotomy which surgically removes the center of imagination from the brain in order to restore all citizens to a condition of childlike obedience. D-503 is summoned by the Benefactor, forced to undergo the lobotomy, and watches passively as I-330 is tortured and condemned to be exterminated by the Benefactor's Machine. D-503, once uncertain and rebellious, is now submissive and loyal. He concludes his diary, reaffirming his belief in the principle of a rationally controlled society and the ultimate victory of the One State over the revolutionaries, for "Reason must prevail." Yet the ultimate outcome of the revolution is left in doubt. Hope for the future is represented by O-90, who, having become pregnant with D-503's child, has escaped beyond the Green Wall to give birth and to rear the child among primitive creatures, the last representatives of humankind still living in a state of freedom.

## The Characters

*We* portrays the psychological development of the narrator, D-503, as he struggles to integrate reason and emotion through the assistance of I-330, whose Latin letter *I* symbolically suggests both individuality and integration. D-503 realizes the necessity for integration when I-330 takes him beyond the Green Wall, and he discovers hairy, primitive creatures representing the emotional part of the human personality which the totally rational citizens of the One State have forgotten: "Who are they? The half we have lost? $H_2$ and O?

And in order to get $H_2O$ . . . the two halves must unite." As a mathematician, D-503 lives exclusively by reason until he discovers strong, irrational forces within himself—symbolically represented by his hairy hands, which relate him to the primitives of the forest. Yevgeny Zamyatin's repeated mention of D-503's hairy hands functions as a leitmotif and represents Zamyatin's method of individualizing his characters by focusing on a single physical trait which suggests the essence of that character's personality. In his essay "Zakulizy" ("Backstage"), Zamyatin describes his characteristic technique of concentrating on "the essence, the extract, the synthesis, revealed to the eye within one-hundredth of a second."

A visual leitmotif associated with I-330 is her furrowed brow suggestive of an $X$, representing the unknown. It is the unknown which both attracts and frightens D-503 in his encounter with I-330. The $X$ on I-330's brow disturbs him, just as the discovery of the mathematical concept of the square root of minus one caused him to suffer as a schoolboy because it remained beyond his comprehension. D-503's fragile sense of self is threatened by any confrontation with the unknown which may cause him to change his mathematically ordered and controlled existence.

Although D-503 constantly praises the beauty of the straight line, which he identifies with the order of the One State, his ambivalence toward deviation from the norms of the state is reflected in his attraction to his sexual partner, O-90, who is ten centimeters shorter than the Maternal Norm. Unlike the straight line, O-90 is characterized by roundness. She complicates D-503's life by loving him and desiring to bear his child in violation of the rules of the One State, which require all childbearers to measure a certain height. O-90's desire for a child is a form of rebellion against the rules of the One State. When D-503 accedes to her request to have a child, his act is as subversive as his agreement to aid the revolutionaries led by I-330.

D-503 is intimately linked with another deviant number, R-13, a state poet who, like D-503, initially supports the One State but joins the revolutionaries and is killed during the abortive revolt. R-13 shares O-90 with D-503, but he regards his relationship with her as merely sexual and assents to the love relationship which O-90 develops with D-503. The visual leitmotif associated with R-13 is his Negroid lips. This physical characteristic, combined with the fact that R-13 is a poet who is required to write verses in the service of the One State, represents Zamyatin's deliberate association of R-13 with the fate of the nineteenth century Russian poet Alexander Pushkin. Pushkin, whose Negroid features were clearly distinguishable, became an unwilling court poet during the reign of the authoritarian Czar Nicholas I, who acted as Pushkin's personal censor. Zamyatin's association of R-13 with Pushkin is intended as an ironic commentary on the parallels between censorship in nineteenth and twentieth century Russia.

Zamyatin's main characters emerge as unique individuals clearly distinguished from the conformist numbers of the One State. They function as an affirmation of Zamyatin's humanistic belief in the value of the individual personality.

## Themes and Meanings

The symbolic title "We" suggests the main theme of the novel: the struggle to preserve the individual "I" against the pressures to conform represented by the collective "We." I-330 is the major character affirming individuality in the novel. She personifies the revolutionary principle of energy, which Zamyatin regards as a positive force, since it represents change. As I-330 explains to D-503: "There are two forces in the world—entropy, which leads to happy equilibrium, and energy, which leads to destruction of equilibrium, to tormentingly endless movement." In I-330's view, the One State personifies entropic thought and must be destroyed. She regards revolution as inevitable, since there is no final revolution (just as there is no final number). Zamyatin develops similar ideas in his essay "O literature, revolyutsii, èntropii i o prochem" ("On Literature, Revolution, Entropy, and Other Matters"), in which he affirms revolution as the major force for combating dogmatism. In Zamyatin's view, "Dogmatization in science, religion, social life, or art is the entropy of thought," which can be overcome only through heresy.

Zamyatin purposely casts I-330 in the role of a heretic who rebels against both the psychological entropy of the One State and the Christian religion of the ancients. Like the first rebel, Satan of Christian mythology, she revolts against authority. She refers to herself as anti-Christian; her sharp, pointed teeth suggest the Devil; and the revolutionaries she leads call themselves Mephi, a derivative of the name Mephistopheles from the German *Faust* legend. I-330, like Mephistopheles, represents the principle of skepticism and eternal striving in life.

*We* reflects Zamyatin's preoccupation with the interrelated problems of freedom, authority, and happiness first posed in nineteenth century Russian literature by Fyodor Dostoevski. I-330, like Dostoevski's Underground Man in *Zapiski iz podpolya* (1864; *Letters from the Underworld*, 1913; better known as *Notes from the Underground*, 1918), revolts against a social order based on scientism, determinism, and the mechanistic, mathematical laws of nature and reason represented by the formula $2 \times 2 = 4$. Like the Underground Man, I-330 rejects any social order based on a dogmatic formula.

Another Dostoevskian theme is incorporated in the portrayal of the Benefactor, who resembles the Grand Inquisitor in Dostoevski's novel *Bratya Karamazovy* (1879-1880; *The Brothers Karamazov*, 1912). The Benefactor, like the Grand Inquisitor, wishes to provide human beings with happiness at the expense of freedom, since, in his view, human beings value security more than freedom and are happy only in an obedient, childlike state. Zamyatin illustrates through I-330 that human beings will reaffirm their free will and revolt against an imposed social or political structure which denies them their individuality and freedom.

*Critical Context*

Zamyatin's *We* represents a modern, impressionistic style of writing characteristic of early twentieth century avant-garde art. In a public lecture delivered in 1918 entitled "Sovremennaya russkaya literatura" ("Contemporary Russian Literature"), Zamyatin described himself as a neorealist who viewed life through a microscope in order to discover the incredible nature of "true reality that is concealed under the surface of life." Zamyatin's concentrated, microscopic vision accounts for the exaggerated images characteristic of his style. As the postrevolutionary Soviet regime consolidated its control of the arts, modernist innovations were discouraged, and Zamyatin felt increasingly isolated. Ostracized when excerpts from *We* were first published in Prague in 1927, Zamyatin resigned from the All-Russian Writers' Union in 1929 and emigrated to France in 1931.

Although Zamyatin foresaw the trend toward thought control and censorship which characterized Joseph Stalin's totalitarian regime, *We* is more than a prophetic satire of Stalin's Russia. It is a warning against conformist trends in the West, which Zamyatin detected and satirized in his novella *Ostrovityane* (1918; *The Islanders*, 1972), a preliminary sketch for *We* written as a satire on British middle-class respectability when Zamyatin served as a naval engineer in Great Britain during World War I.

In its assertion of the value of the irrational in life and the importance of individual freedom, *We* continues a Russian literary tradition represented by Dostoevski. The elements of fantasy and scientific speculation in the novel reflect Zamyatin's interest in the works of H. G. Wells, whom Zamyatin read and admired. *We*'s antiutopian themes belong to twentieth century consciousness, anticipating Aldous Huxley's *Brave New World* (1932) and directly influencing George Orwell's *Nineteen Eighty-four* (1949).

*Sources for Further Study*

Brown, Edward J. *Brave New World: Essays in Criticism*, 1976.
Collins, Christopher. *Evgenij Zamjatin: An Interpretive Study*, 1973.
Richards, David John. *Zamyatin, a Soviet Heretic*, 1962.
Shane, Alex M. *The Life and Works of Evgenij Zamjatin*, 1968.
Struve, Gleb. "Zamyatin," in *Russian Literature Under Lenin and Stalin, 1917-1953*, 1971.

*Jerome J. Rinkus*

# WHAT A BEAUTIFUL SUNDAY!

*Author:* Jorge Semprun (1923-    )
*Type of plot:* Social criticism
*Time of plot:* World War II
*Locale:* The Buchenwald death camp near Weimar, Germany
*First published: Quel beau dimanche*, 1980 (English translation, 1982)

*Principal characters:*

THE NARRATOR (GERARD SOREL), a man who, like the author, Jorge Semprun, survives Buchenwald and who matter-of-factly recalls life there as an interned Communist

FERNAND BARIZON, the outspoken Spanish Communist inmate of Buchenwald who one winter's day exclaims, "What a beautiful Sunday," a remark which the narrator always remembers

WILLI SEIFERT, the imprisoned German advocate of the Communist Youth Movement who is given some authority over fellow prisoners

HENK SPOENAY, another Buchenwald prisoner and the friend of the narrator, who works as a liaison between the inmates and the German SS

JOHANN WOLFGANG VON GOETHE, the eighteenth century German writer who described the wooded region in which the Buchenwald camp was later established

JOSEF STALIN, the Russian dictator whose bloody villainies make the narrator reconsider his dedication to Communism

## The Novel

*What a Beautiful Sunday!* takes its name from a startling remark uttered by prisoner Fernand Barizon on a clear winter's day in the Buchenwald death camp, one of the Nazis' most infamous human slaughterhouses. Looking back on his time at Buchenwald from the perspective of several decades, the narrator, known among other names as Gerard Sorel, remains fascinated by Barizon's remark and tries to discover why he finds it so insightful. The novel is author Jorge Semprun's attempt to comprehend the incomprehensible: his youthful infatuation with Communism, his increasing involvement in international struggles to make Europe communistic, his internment in Buchenwald, and his subsequent realization that Communism is as much a sham as any other human institution. It is a novel of one man's education and coming to maturity.

Slowly, even obliquely, through anecdotes and snatches of recalled conversation, Semprun re-creates the hell of Buchenwald. It is not Semprun's intention to add another journalistic treatise about death camps to the collection of such reports. He wants to establish what it was like to be one of the better-favored camp residents whose lot was not as terrible as that of the Jews, Gypsies, Russians, and other hated races or nationalities. A secondary purpose is to superimpose the madness of mass killings upon the sylvan woodland of Buchenwald, a place made famous by the poet Johann Wolfgang von Goethe in the eighteenth century.

The story begins with the depiction of a lone oak tree. Self-contained, aloof, an emblem of God-supplied beauty, its slender branches framing the smoking crematorium, the tree, spared by the Nazi camp creators out of respect for Goethe, is both a thing whose beauty separates it from the camp and an integral part of camp life. To gaze upon it allows the prisoners to realize that a higher power is at work in the universe and can be found even in Buchenwald. The tree, which at first glance appears ordinary, takes on a supernatural glow when the narrator recalls Goethe and the lost world of his Germany which the tree symbolizes. The violence and horror of the twentieth century, so concentrated in camps such as Buchenwald, are never far from him. As he looks at the tree one day, he is nearly killed by an SS guard waving a pistol. The guard apparently is ready to shoot him when the narrator asks the guard to look at the tree and think about its connection to the revered Goethe. For a moment, even SS terror is overcome by civilized impulse as the guard puts away his gun.

Goethe's strolls through the woods, often referred to by the narrator, supply an ironic contrast to the strolling machine-gun carrying guards of Buchenwald. Nature, which Goethe saw as a companion to man, is reduced to a helpless onlooker, a mute observer of man's cruelties toward others. Yet nature is as mute in Russia, to which escapees from Buchenwald often flee only to find death in one of Josef Stalin's concentration camps. Forests and steppes which seemed to be a refuge cannot hide or sustain returning Russians from their countrymen. The power of evil is simply too strong and all-pervasive.

Gradually, the reader is introduced to the inmates of Buchenwald, several of which, by word and deed, challenge the narrator's communistic faith in man's ability to rise out of his bestial nature and become concerned with the rights and needs of others. Along with camp heroism is exhibited treachery and greed with one inmate using his fellow inmates to achieve selfish ends. At times, prisoners mirror their guards' worst traits, so much so that it is easy to imagine them treating prisoners as badly as they themselves were treated if they could trade places with their captors.

The daily indignities of life in the camp lead some prisoners to come to terms with the SS in charge of their unit. Henk Spoenay, a Dutch inmate, and Willi Seifert, a German, join with the narrator in helping the Nazis administer their section. Unlike some prisoners with responsibilities, however, they become camp assistants because they want to aid fellow prisoners. True to their Communist ideals, they believe that by cooperating with the SS guards they will be able to make life more tolerable for the prisoners under their jurisdiction by getting them more food or an occasional creature comfort. Their sector is helped principally because the internees are Communists rather than Jews. Jews, at the bottom of the camp's pecking order, are marked for early death; they are systematically slaughtered in gas chambers and then thrown into vast ovens for burning. The narrator and his fellow prisoners at least have hopes that they may last long enough to escape annihilation; the hated minority prisoners have no such hopes. As soon as they get off the trains coming from the West, they are separated into groups, gassed, and burned.

Communism is continuously examined throughout *What a Beautiful Sunday!* Its failure as a doctrine upon which people can build their lives is evident in Buchenwald where most Communists, upon accepting the lot of prisoner, turn to the selfish pursuit of power and influence rather than to activities which would ease the sufferings of their friends. Their betrayal of Communist ideals only serves to illuminate the greater betrayals of the Ukrainian camp guards who help the SS push innocent people into the gas chambers, and the still greater betrayals of Josef Stalin's henchmen against a huge number of fellow Russians condemned as enemies of the state. Semprun speaks of the camps of the gulag, which he learned about when Aleksandr Solzhenitsyn's novel *Odin den Ivana Denisovicha* (1962; *One Day in the Life of Ivan Denisovich*, 1963) was circulated in the West, and of his ensuing total disillusionment with the Communism of his youth. The pain he endured at Buchenwald is secondary to the pain he felt when confronted by his advocacy of a false cause. He recalls the brave Russian soldiers—boys for the most part—who found their way out of Buchenwald and sought refuge in their homeland, only to be killed when they arrived. Betrayed, Semprun is compelled to tell the terrible story about a failed creed in an evil century.

### The Characters

*What a Beautiful Sunday!* focuses on Jorge Semprun's personal reminiscences about his incarceration in Buchenwald, but also deals with postwar experiences in France and, to a lesser extent, in Spain. The narrator is a thinly veiled version of Semprun. Those characters who, like the narrator, not only try to survive in Buchenwald but also improve the existences of other inmates are seen in retrospect as complicated individuals, each displaying his own blend of courage and cowardice, openness and deceit, subjection to authority and defiance of that authority.

The narrator is often in awe at the everyday deportment of Henk Spoenay, his highly organized, clever, and at times brave Dutch friend, of the wit and intelligence of Willi Seifert, the wily German Communist who understands the workings of the guards' minds, and of the outspoken nature of Fernand Barizon, fellow Spaniard whose good humor and nonchalant attitude help others overcome fear.

All of the main characters are members of the Communist Party or are sympathizers with its aims and, as such, provide readers with a variety of opinions about the directions the Party takes. Some, like the narrator, will give up their belief; others, like Barizon, will cling to it despite all evidence suggesting that it has failed to live up to its ideals.

Yet all the characters share a certain cardboard cut-out appearance. One learns little about them and next to nothing about their inner life, so it is often difficult to envision them "in the round." They appear to be devices by which Semprun can discuss the effects of concentration camps upon those interned or prove points about Communism and its failure as a creed. The most memorable characters are not differentiated at all: The Russian inmates of Buchenwald have a wild, colorful attitude toward life, yet the reader does not learn about any of them individually. Their love of freedom and their disdain for mere survival is admirable; their escape from Buchenwald is miraculous.

Another admirable and memorable character is not really part of the novel's action, yet has a great effect upon the prisoner. Goethe is more spirit than mortal, his ghost stalking the novel, haunting every character who ever wanted to believe in his lofty vision of humankind. The lone oak tree serves as a repository of his spirit and asks many questions, chief among them, "How could man have done this to his fellow man?" Goethe's is a gentle voice, amid the horrifying cries of victims and tormentors. The oak tree's nobility of spirit and its silent beauty remind the reader that despite these horrors there is a supernatural presence which infuses the lives of people such as Goethe, who open themselves to beauty and wonder and spurn the debased pursuits of money, fame, and power.

*Themes and Meanings*

*What a Beautiful Sunday!* is both dirge and hymn. It is a condemnation of human callousness and brutality as well as a celebration of the human spirit which creates, loves, and sustains. It is a novel of education, in that the narrator recalls how he discovered certain truths about human nature during his time at Buchenwald.

One lesson he learns is that the worst circumstances cannot destroy his ability to appreciate life's joys and revelations. Little events take on great meaning while larger events pale into insignificance. An oak tree seen on a winter's day becomes the emblem of love and beauty. A fellow prisoner's idle jest illuminates life and enriches it, even while a crematorium belches smoke from burned human beings and the shrieks of the doomed can be heard in the distance. Love, hope, courage, and faith conquer evil in this novel. Yet human political systems, whether they be National Socialism or Communism or capitalism, cannot supply man with what he needs to live and make life meaningful. In short, Semprun warns the reader about believing in any system; heaven is not meant to be on earth, nor can it ever be here.

The narrator also learns that there are far worse things than being sent to a concentration camp by an enemy. The worst thing is to give one's life to a belief which turns out to be not only unrealistic and unattainable but also completely false. Communism is like James Joyce's Ireland: an old sow eating her farrow. Those young people who devoted their lives and hearts to the spreading of Communism throughout the world were among the first Stalin massacred. His successors, though not as cruel, were, in Semprun's estimation, just as untrue to the belief that all who labor for their comrades will create utopia on earth.

In the final estimation, *What a Beautiful Sunday!* is about the search of one man for life's meaning. If by the novel's end he has not yet found meaning, he at least realizes where it never has resided. Beware of creeds and ideologues, he warns, for pursuing their vision of paradise may lead to Treblinka, Buchenwald, and the camps of the gulag.

*Critical Context*

Because the novel functions brilliantly both as a condemnation of a false political system and as a novel of education, it has much in common with several germinal twentieth century novels, including Ernest Hemingway's *The Sun Also Rises* (1926), with its emphasis upon disillusioned youth and lost faith; James Joyce's *A Portrait of the Artist as a Young Man* (1916), with its protagonist who rejects both his native Ireland and Catholicism; F. Scott Fitzgerald's *The Great Gatsby* (1925), in which Jay Gatsby learns too late about the shallowness and destructiveness of materialism; and Günter Grass's *Die Blechtrommel* (1959; *The Tin Drum*, 1961), in which a midget learns at firsthand the horrors of nationalism run amok. Though the novel gives the reader a picture of cultural disintegration from the perspective of a victim of man's cruelty, its essentially gloomy assessment of life in the twentieth century is at odds with its praise of the courage, audacity, inventiveness, and playfulness of man under siege. In this, the author joins with a number of modern writers, including Graham Greene, John Steinbeck, Heinrich Böll, Kurt Vonnegut, Jr., and Samuel Beckett. *What a Beautiful Sunday!* is a unique and important addition to Continental fiction dealing with World War II and its aftermath.

*Sources for Further Study*

*Booklist*. Review. LXXIX (October 1, 1982), p. 190.

Boyers, Robert. "The Voyage of Jorge Semprun," in *Atrocity and Amnesia: The Political Novel Since 1945*, 1985.

*Kirkus Reviews*. Review. L (August 1, 1982), p. 898.
*Library Journal*. Review. CVII (September 15, 1982), p. 1771.
*Publishers Weekly*. Review. CCXXII (September 17, 1982), p. 104.

*John D. Raymer*

# WHEN I WHISTLE

*Author:* Shusaku Endō (1923-    )
*Type of plot:* Social realism
*Time of plot:* The 1960's
*Locale:* Tokyo, Japan
*First published: Kuchibue o fuku toki*, 1974 (English translation, 1979)

> *Principal characters:*
> OZU, an aging Japanese businessman caught in a moral gap
>     between two generations
> FLATFISH, Ozu's childhood friend, whose relationship with
>     Ozu is revealed in flashbacks.
> EIICHI, Ozu's son, whose opportunism and greed grieve his
>     father and lead to their inevitable alienation
> AIKO, the object of Ozu and Flatfish's adolescent infatuation
>     who in her later years becomes a patient of Eiichi
> DR. II, a malevolent and unscrupulous doctor

*The Novel*

*When I Whistle* explores the ethos of contemporary Japan and in particular the contrast between two generations, focusing on a father and son. In alternating chapters, Shusaku Endō shifts the focus from the protagonist, Ozu, who is preoccupied with the memories of his adolescence, to his son Eiichi and his opportunistic medical career. Here Endō provides the reader with a panoramic view of the very different moral visions animating the young men and women of the war years and their children.

The novel begins with the protagonist, Ozu, riding along on a bullet train, returning to Tokyo from a mundane business trip. Here he encounters a person who seems vaguely familiar but whom he cannot quite place. This man turns out to have been a fellow student at Nada Middle School some forty years before. Their brief conversation provokes an extended reminiscence that transports Ozu back to a simpler, more serene time in his life. Upon seeing boats on the lake, he conjures up his schoolboy friend, Flatfish, and their adventures together in an idyllic time before World War II, when the Japanese educational system sought to inculcate the virtues of pride and industriousness. While his stern teacher tried to build character, Ozu spent his school hours daydreaming about the young women he and his best friend, the unsophisticated but endearing Flatfish, would pursue, literally, once the school day had ended.

The romance and innocence of his adolescence is captured for Ozu in the enduring image of Flatfish's "tiny head being tossed about by the waves as he swam desperately for the open sea" in pursuit of a girl, Aiko, whom he had met by chance and with whom both were madly in love. While militarism gripped their nation, Ozu and Flatfish preferred the frivolous joys of childish classroom pranks and chasing girls.

At the end of his trip, Ozu is ushered back into the present and into the grim reality of his own lackluster career and the tension felt between himself and his son. Eiichi is portrayed as an up-and-coming surgeon at a metropolitan hospital, whose aggressiveness and insensitivity to his patients and colleagues is well-known but is excused as part of the new generation's tools for survival. "Times are different," Ozu's wife observes, "Young people now can't survive if they don't push others out of their way. There's really nothing else Eiichi can do." Like his dubious role model, the imperious Dr. Ii (who prescribes worthless drugs for his patients because the pharmaceutical company which produces them funds his research), Eiichi is a "natural" product of his environment, experienced in "using" people—from a nurse to a doctor's daughter to a colleague—and perfectly willing to use untested drugs on his unsuspecting terminally ill patients.

Ozu is unable to whitewash his son's behavior and again retreats into his reveries of the years just before the war and Flatfish's dogged determination to win Aiko's hand in marriage. The beautiful Aiko, "like a chrysalis transformed into butterfly," in fact becomes for Ozu the living symbol of all that is pure and authentic in Japanese culture. Ozu's flashbacks come to an end, however, when he recalls learning of Flatfish's death from a battlefield disease and his search for Aiko to tell her of his passing. The death of Flatfish confirmed for Ozu that "every source of human happiness . . . vanished" after the humiliating defeat in World War II.

The two generations are brought into sharpest relief as the story nears its end and Ozu learns accidentally that Aiko, widowed from the war, is one of Eiichi's patients, an "experiment," no more and no less important than anyone else, since "patients come and go. There's no time to get sentimentally attached to each one." The practice of medicine for Eiichi is a business more than a profession; efficiency, "progress," and profit are its hallmarks. Ozu is shocked by his son's materialism and coldness; impulsively, he sends flowers to Aiko in Flatfish's name as he mourns the past and dreads what he sees of the future.

Tormented by Aiko's eventual death, Ozu finds himself driven by overwhelming nostalgia to locate his old school, which he finds modernized and depersonalized. When he seeks out Aiko's childhood home, he finds that it has been bulldozed, and he resigns himself to the fact that "beautiful things, things from the treasured past were now disappearing all over Japan." Groping for "a meaning of life concealed somewhere," Ozu realizes that "he alone is still alive" to preserve a semblance of the proud but humane civilization that once was.

## The Characters

*When I Whistle* reveals a key aspect of Endō's talent, the ability to create contemporary characters with realism and subtlety, while avoiding excessive sentimentality. Effectively using flashbacks from prewar and postwar Japan, Endō ironically juxtaposes the "new" Japan with the old in his novel's main characters and finds modern Japan, though presumably more open to the West, in its own way even less congenial to the Christian values and simple human kindness the novelist seeks to inculcate.

Ozu, the protagonist, is a humble businessman; his contempt for the ethos of modern Japan and his general nostalgia for the older Japan is slowly revealed in his conversations with acquaintances on trains and with his family. Everywhere he turns he finds evidence of disintegrating respect for life, but especially in his enterprising son; Eiichi's professional success and worldly sophistication are vivid contrasts to his father's simple concerns for trust and commitment among his fellows. Ozu is increasingly drawn to a world of shadows and dreams, wherein he can revisit Flatfish and the lovely teenage Aiko. While these memories are vividly drawn, the characters of Flatfish and Aiko are evoked more than developed.

Eiichi, desperate to rise within his profession, identifies himself with a grim, work-oriented Japan: driven, technological, spiritually barren, the culture of Western imperialism his father had fought to defeat. Eiichi finds his father's basic humanism backward and unpleasant, a needless sentimentality that impedes his career goals. When father and son are united by the illness of Aiko, their differing values are highlighted; for Eiichi and his colleagues, Aiko is not a person with dignity, deserving of care, special attention, or love, but a convenient subject for experimental cancer treatments.

Ozu parts from his son in muffled despair, confronting a predatory Japan, conquering no longer with bayonets or aircraft but with sheer economic and technological prowess, devoid of a spiritual center.

## Themes and Meanings

In *When I Whistle*, Endō is concerned to draw a number of disturbing contrasts between wartime and present-day Japan while scrupulously avoiding, in translator Van C. Gessel's words, "painting either period in a romantic light." What, Endō asks, is the legacy of the war generation, what kind of Japan has resulted from the devastation of World War II? Part of his answer is seen in the life-style of Eiichi, the ruthless young surgeon of *When I Whistle*; unaffected by the tragedy of Hiroshima and Nagasaki, and unable to see his patients as anything but specimens for his own experiments, he extends the imperialistic impulse of prewar Japan by ignoring the past and worshipping the present. The accumulation of material possessions is the only source of meaning for the new generation.

This striking thematic element in *When I Whistle* is made more powerful by its pervasive medical and hospital imagery. Chronic heart and lung problems have plagued Endō throughout his adult life and consequently he has spent much time in hospitals; in the early 1960's, Endō underwent a series of major surgical procedures, resulting in the removal of one lung. Japan emerges in *When I Whistle* as one large cancer ward, the malignancy of rampant materialism uncurable, the placebo of success a momentary distraction in the face of a godless eternity.

As a Christian, Endō is an apologist for a set of values he believes is indigenous to the West but foreign to Japanese soil. A convert who recognizes the irony that Japan has become less spiritual as it has become more Westernized, Endō constructs themes which generally revolve around a protagonist confronted with the ruins of a native culture to which he is drawn and by which he is repulsed. Ozu is thus an exemplar of Endō's despairing vision of the postwar era—an open-hearted Japanese seeking answers and finding only the echoes of the past.

*Critical Context*

Endō wrote *When I Whistle* between his two more celebrated historical novels set in the seventeenth century, *Chimmoku* (1966; *Silence*, 1969) and *Samurai* (1980; *The Samurai*, 1982). In those novels, the conflict between Christian values and Japanese culture is explicitly examined.

Given that Endō was one of the first Japanese to study in Europe after the war, it is easy to see how his submersion in European culture intensified his appreciation for the impact of Christianity on the West. This appreciation has forced him to recognize the spiritual vacuum in Japan which *When I Whistle* explores—demonstrating that the absence of belief in a transcendent deity makes difficult if not impossible the recognition of moral absolutes.

Endō's novels often elicit comparisons with those of the British Catholic writer Graham Greene. His compelling though sinful and often stumbling characters captivate and endear themselves to the reader in the same way that Greene's faltering saints do. Yet a better comparison among contemporary Christian writers would be with the American Catholic novelist Walker Percy. Percy's serious exploration of the disintegration of authentic Christianity in the jaded West and his attempts to redeem it novelistically resemble Endō's own agenda in addressing both his Oriental and Occidental readers.

*Sources for Further Study*

Allen, Louis. "Rastignac of Tokyo," in *The Listener*. CI (April 12, 1979), pp. 530-531.

Cunningham, Valerie. "Death in the Afternoon," in *New Statesman*. XCVII (April 13, 1979), p. 527.

King, Francis. "Experiments," in *The Spectator*. CCXLII (April 14, 1979), pp. 23-24.

Mathy, Francis. "Shusaku Endō: Japanese Catholic Novelist," in *Thought*. XLII (Winter, 1967), pp. 585-614.

Rimer, J. Thomas. *Modern Japanese Fiction and Its Traditions*, 1978.

Updike, John. "From Fumie to Sony," in *The New Yorker*. LV (January 14, 1980), pp. 94-102.

*Bruce L. Edwards*

# THE WIND
## Attempted Restoration of a Baroque Altarpiece

*Author:* Claude Simon (1913-    )
*Type of plot:* Antistory
*Time of plot:* The 1950's
*Locale:* A small town in the south of France
*First published: Le Vent: Tentative de restitution d'un retable baroque*, 1957
  (English translation, 1959)

> *Principal characters:*
> ANTOINE MONTÈS, an outsider who inherits a vineyard
> ROSE, a waitress at the hotel where Montès lives
> JEP, Rose's husband, a gypsy
> MAURICE, a fertilizer salesman and would-be blackmailer
> CÉCILE, the tomboyish daughter of Montès' cousin
> HÉLÈNE, her sister
> THE NOTARY, the spokesman for the town
> THE NARRATOR, a teacher and writer who befriends Montès

### The Novel

Antoine Montès arrives in a small town in the south of France to claim the vineyard bequeathed to him by a father he has never known. Thirty-five years earlier, his mother left his father after learning of his infidelity. She did not tell her husband that she was pregnant, declined to divorce him or accept money from him, and never allowed him to see his son. Montès is expected to sell his father's property, for which he is offered a large sum of money, but shocks the town by announcing that he intends to stay.

When Montès attempts to fire the bailiff who oversees the vineyards, the man, whose daughter was his employer's mistress, refuses to leave and sues Montès. Living in a shabby hotel nearby, Montès becomes attached to Rose, a waitress, and her two young daughters. Because the town thinks that he is going to be rich, he also attracts the attention of a well-to-do cousin and his two daughters, Hélène, an aloof, pregnant wife, and Cécile, a rebellious tomboy.

Rose's husband, Jep, a gypsy, has stolen some jewelry but does not know how to get rid of it. Because Rose wants Montès' help, Jep assaults the outsider for interfering in his life. Nevertheless, Montès takes the jewels and hides them in his hotel room. Maurice, a young fertilizer salesman who lives in the hotel, attempts unsuccessfully to blackmail Montès about Rose and the stolen jewels. Finding a note from Cécile, who is strangely drawn to the slovenly Montès, Maurice offers to sell it to her father only to have Hélène trick him into giving it to her.

Maurice has told Hélène all about Montès and Rose, and she informs the police that Jep has stolen the jewelry. As the officers arrive, Jep, who thinks that his wife has betrayed him, kills Rose and is shot to death by the police. The shattered Montès wants to adopt Rose's girls, but nuns give them to someone else and will not tell him where they are. Meanwhile, he loses the suit brought against him by the bailiff, and the vineyards are damaged by a hot, dry summer. Montès is forced to sell his property for less than it was worth six months earlier. He is more devastated by the loss of Theresa, Rose's older daughter, however, and is haunted by memories of "her impassive Inca mummy's face."

## The Characters

Antoine Montès has no clear identity since all that is revealed is what the other characters think about him, and they see primarily what is on the surface: unkempt appearance, tattered raincoat, beret, camera always hanging from his neck. Montès looks older than his age and is said to resemble someone who has just escaped from a concentration camp or "one of those characters that seem to have stepped out of Daumier: dusty, heronlike and threadbare." Montès is a walking contradiction, seeming both apelike and aristocratic. His gentle nature makes him seem almost saintly, but he is also dangerously naïve. (Claude Simon has acknowledged the influence of Fyodor Dostoevski's 1868 novel *The Idiot*, English translation 1887.) Montès has a "catastrophic gift of attracting trouble the way other people attract dogs or money" and has a "fundamental inaptitude for being aware of life, things, events except by the intermediary of his senses, his heart."

Montès affects people by making them, without any effort on his part, think that he has qualities belying his appearance. He works an "incomprehensible spell" on people—especially women and children, those considered weak by his society. When Cécile asks why he pretends "to be such a fool," he is unaware of any pretense. Rose has a similarly mysterious effect on him, making him "sense the secret pulsation of her blood." The only lengthy conversation they have involves "perhaps the only words of love he had ever heard and spoken in his whole life... though the subject of love had not come up once (in words)." Montès' single avowed passion is taking pictures of everything—though he photographs Rose but once. It is almost as if he is seeking stability by capturing details on film. According to the unnamed narrator of *The Wind*, "He loves things that don't move."

Montès is frequently compared with the wind which blows throughout his stay in the town. Both display "the same willful stubbornness, as if the gale also contributed to the tacit conspiracy of men and elements that seemed to have brought him, driven him, forced him back to where he had come from." Like the wind, he is simply there, purposeless, waiting to die—death being the only possible solution to his struggle. Also like the wind, Montès cannot be understood. Both the town and the reader are conscious of him without truly knowing him.

Two other characters are important as sources of information about Montès. The notary with whom he does legal business is the spokesman for the town. Seeing profit as the primary human motive, he thinks that Rose is interested solely in Montès' money, and he cannot understand what Cécile sees in the stranger since she has a higher social position. He is considered "a sort of ancient chorus" by the narrator, to whom the notary relays accounts of his meetings with Montès. Montès' only friend, the narrator (who is a teacher and writer) understands passion as a motivation. Since Montès describes more than he explains, it is up to the narrator to decipher this enigmatic figure, finding in him much greater depth than does the notary. The narrator tries to penetrate the mind of Montès, conveying "what I sensed, what he himself must have actually known." He sees Montès as a drowning man but does not consider himself to be a lifesaver: "I had merely passed within arm's reach and he had clutched at me." The narrator views his task as uniting the seemingly unrelated fragments of Montès' story.

*Themes and Meanings*

The epigraph of *The Wind* is from Paul Valéry: "The world is incessantly threatened by two dangers: order and disorder." This dichotomy is clearly illustrated by the chaos unintentionally created by the peaceful, passive Montès. He thinks that order can exist simply through the force of his will, that he can ignore time, can arrest it in his photographs. This illusion is burst with the murder of Rose.

Nor is there any order in the natural world. When Montès arrives, "the wind, a virtually continuous tornado of undirected, unreasonable violence, threw itself upon him, assailed him, furiously encompassed him." Throughout the novel the wind remains "the indefatigable, permanent gale ceaselessly galloping down the diaphanous sky, growing wild, intoxicated with its own rage, its own useless power." It distorts the appearance of nature, covering green life with a coat of dust. The wind resembles time, moving but making no headway, emphasizing the fragility of the order that man has tried to impose.

Simon is concerned with the fragility—and superficiality—not only of people's conceptions of order but also of their view of reality, as the narrator's method of assembling the facts of the story at second, third, or fourth hand illustrates. Another narrator might make a totally different interpretation of Montès' life. Simon implies that people's senses and intelligence are inadequate to evaluate events objectively. Delving into the nature of reality, Simon wonders about the role of language, asking whether words describe an event or create it. The mystery, beauty, drama, and complexity of life are the same as those of language. *The Wind* dramatizes the ambiguousness of memory, the unreliability of evidence, the difficulty of knowing the truth about others and oneself.

Simon's themes are underscored by his method of writing: cumulative sentences which sometimes stretch for pages, unfinished statements, and parentheses within parentheses. His style, which is strongly reminiscent of the William Faulkner of *The Sound and the Fury* (1929) and *Absalom, Absalom!* (1936), illustrates the fragmented reality his characters' experience. Even the narrator is aware of the difficulty of his task:

> [N]ow that it's all over, trying to report, to reconstitute what happened is a little like trying to stick together the scattered, incomplete debris of a broken mirror, clumsily struggling to readjust the pieces, getting only an incoherent, ridiculous, idiotic result."

### Critical Context

*The Wind* began what Simon's critics have identified as the middle period of his career as a novelist. The style in his earlier fiction was inconsistent, artificial, and occasionally confused. With *The Wind*, he relied more upon descriptions, reflecting the influence of paintings and photographs. It was the first of his novels not to take a conventional approach to fiction; fewer conventional elements appeared with each succeeding novel.

After *The Wind*, Simon began to be grouped with the French New Novelists, who reject the importance of plot, character, and verisimilitude while emphasizing confusion, illusion, and the faulty way in which reality is perceived. More than any of the other New Novelists, Simon uses language unconventionally: distorted syntax, pronouns with unclear, multiple antecedents, missing punctuation. He explores the possibilities of language while asking what the novel can communicate and how it can do so.

### Sources for Further Study

Birn, Randi, and Karen Gould, eds. *Orion Blinded: Essays on Claude Simon*, 1981.

Fletcher, John. *Claude Simon and Fiction Now*, 1975.

Jiménez-Fajardo, Salvador. *Claude Simon*, 1975.

Loubère, J.A.E. *The Novels of Claude Simon*, 1975.

Sturrock, John. *The French New Novel: Claude Simon, Michel Butor, Alain Robbe-Grillet*, 1969.

*Michael Adams*

# THE WIND FROM THE PLAIN,
# IRON EARTH, COPPER SKY, and
# THE UNDYING GRASS

*Author:* Yashar Kemal (Yaşar Kemal Gökçeli, 1922-      )
*Type of plot:* Social realism/folktale
*Time of plot:* The 1950's or early 1960's
*Locale:* The Çukurova region of Turkey, in south central Anatolia
*First published: Ortadirek,* 1960 (*The Wind from the Plain,* 1963); *Yer demir, gök bakır,* 1963 (*Iron Earth, Copper Sky,* 1974); *Ölmez otu,* 1968 (*The Undying Grass,* 1977)

*Principal characters:*
> HALİL TAŞYÜREK, an elderly man, probably in his seventies
> MEMET TAŞBAŞ EFENDİ, an old and venerated man from the area
> MEMİDİK DELİBAŞ, a young man from the region
> SEFER EFENDİ, the Muhtar or local headman
> MERYEMCE, an older woman
> ZALACA, another older woman from the area
> ZELİHA, a younger woman
> ADİL EFENDİ, an official who supervises the local tax collection
> ŞEVKET BEY, an important functionary from the region
> MUTTALİP BEY, a major landowner

## The Novels

This sprawling saga of village life in the cotton-growing region of Turkey is held together largely by its sequential handling of events that affect the lives of several major characters. The series as a whole may be said to revolve about the fates of Old Halil Taşyürek and Memet Taşbaş, aged but oddly venerated vagabonds, and Memidik Delibaş, a younger, much more serious sort. Arrayed against them are various local officials. Their most persistent opponent, Sefer Efendi, the Muhtar or headman, tries to arrange matters very much in his own way. Although time and dates are not discussed specifically, changing seasons, notably the transitions from winter to spring and summer, are awaited as marking new periods in the villagers' lives. In this manner, about one year passes during the sequence of three novels, as such matters are formally reckoned. Some events are recorded alongside memories or flashbacks, and a vaguely illusory atmosphere attaches to some occurrences. All the while, situations affecting various people are carried forward from one novel to the next. In particular, acts of vengeance or defiance against arbitrary power and authority lead to prolonged complications, which unfold during the later portions of these works.

*The Wind from the Plain* begins with the cotton harvest at a village on the plains of southern Turkey; the autumn winds that blow across the region seem to herald another cycle in the local people's migratory activity. Recollections of past escapades are summoned forth; most of these involve Halil, who perennially has been regarded as the instigator of mischief and trouble in various forms. In addition, there are some squalid little arguments about whether he or Meryemce, an older local woman, should ride on an aged horse; in time, the woman's son puts in his claims as well. Before the matter is resolved, the horse falls over dead, and all of them arrive late at their destination. Rumors circulate that the Muhtar intends to benefit from the discrepancy between the villagers' low wages and the income expected from the harvest. Other odd events take place when Halil disappears for a certain period, and it is thought that he has died or been murdered. An unpleasant interlude of another sort takes place when a local woman comes before the Muhtar; she alleges that someone from another village took her away, seduced and degraded her, and then left her at the mercy of the elements. Halil, who seems to reappear as mysteriously as he has vanished, approaches the others with a scheme by which they may appropriate that part of the cotton crop which the Muhtar seemingly wants to reserve for his own enrichment. Toward the end of the novel, it ironically turns out that weeds predominate in much of the land that they are to work.

The threads of these intertwined stories are taken up again in *Iron Earth, Copper Sky*. Icy rains signal the gathering force of winter; when no one can account for Halil again, the others are inclined to take hints of his demise more seriously. Indeed, a formal memorial service is read in his name. Shortly thereafter, it turns out that he was hiding in a corncrib, biding his time until the authorities had supposedly forgotten about him. In an odd gambit to bolster the villagers' loyalties, the Muhtar announces his plan for the remission of taxes. As the winter snow begins falling, the local people spirit away their possessions. They hide livestock and other bulky items in caves to leave the impression for revenue purposes that they have few goods to declare. The whole scheme founders on the mutual suspicions and jealousies that trouble relations between the Muhtar and the older, more eccentric Memet Taşbaş. When Adil Efendi, who is to supervise tax assessments, does not appear when expected, the villagers acclaim Taşbaş as a virtual saint with his own mystical powers. In an odd response, he startles them with a stunning and thorough display of public self-vilification. Another rivalry of sorts commences during the middle segments of this novel, when Memidik Delibaş, a solemn, unsmiling young man, makes his appearance. Almost from the outset, he regards the Muhtar as insufferably condescending. After the Muhtar has one of his hirelings beat Memidik, the younger man determines to seek his revenge. Their reciprocal enmity flares up repeatedly during the remainder of the saga and is resolved only at the very end. For the time, however, the Muhtar is forced to abandon his usual domineering ways when it is revealed that he has been secretly in communication with Adil Efendi; the Muhtar's scheme for tax avoidance is exposed as a rather flimsy ruse. Angry villagers storm the headman's house; his standing among the common people has fallen precipitously, while Taşbaş is still held in open veneration. The Muhtar then plots with the police to have the other man arrested. Though the Muhtar pays them to make it appear that he resisted them, the local people quickly grasp the intent of the Muhtar's ploy. They openly disdain him even as Taşbaş is being led away by gendarmes. As the snow begins to thaw further, rumors arise that Halil has come back and is hiding out in one of his lairs.

While the Muhtar's attempts to intimidate the villagers have made many enemies, it is Memidik who actually attempts to settle old scores. During the opening chapters of *The Undying Grass*, he stalks his nemesis, knife in hand, and comes away believing that he has accomplished his purpose. Shortly thereafter, in a neighboring town, Halil turns up and is recognized by some of the people there as a semilegendary brigand. After Halil returns to his own village, everyone seems confused and perplexed: Memidik is bemused by dark thoughts about the Muhtar's fate; Zalaca, an older woman, believes that somehow Meryemce has fallen victim to foul play; fantastic stories about Taşbaş also make the rounds.

After more stories about dark deeds circulate, Halil is almost arrested for the presumed murder of Şevket Bey, a prominent official. Halil is left again at liberty, however, when it is pointed out that in the absence of a corpse such charges seem implausible. Memidik begins to wonder more and more if he has somehow mistaken one man for another and thus struck down Şevket instead of the Muhtar. These bizarre and tragicomic interludes, in which, rightly or wrongly, the missing are supposed dead and every manner of dastardly deed is hinted, seem to bring into the open underlying tensions and resentments. This web of subplots, in which odd events are presented from the standpoints of different characters in turn, also increases the level of suspense as one village mystery is followed by another. As the novel progresses, these situations are resolved, each in its own way. During this last work, the most sustained romantic-erotic encounters in the series also take place: These adventures involve Memidik in some rather curious situations, first with a slightly deranged married woman, and then much more seriously with Zeliha, a graceful young woman of about his age.

All the while, murkier problems continue to haunt the young man; Memidik's perplexity is compounded as he must deal with the Muhtar, an antagonist who is alive and doubly vengeful. For his part, the Muhtar schemes to have others implicated in the disappearance of Meryemce, but this ploy misfires once she returns nonchalantly to her home. In a vision, Memidik believes that Taşbaş has appeared before him, resplendent in saintly vestments and followed by seven balls of light. Other villagers make similar claims, but visitation of this sort seems unlikely when the real Taşbaş, who has escaped from the police and remained hidden in a cave, decides suddenly that he will return to the villagers.

As the older men come back, the aura that surrounds them fades briefly. Halil becomes involved in a scheme to pilfer cotton at night; when at last he is led away as a thief, the others turn out to spit on him. During this time, Taşbaş' preternatural powers are also called into question. Although the common people have virtually accepted him as a saint, he is unable to influence the elements; a destructive rainstorm takes place in spite of his incantations. Even worse, he is caught in a melon-stealing escapade that exposes him to ruinous ridicule; when he tries to get away, he is rather badly beaten as well. Evidently, the Muhtar hopes that once the village elders have been discredited, he will gain wider acceptance as the people's leader.

At about this same time, Muttalip Bey, a wealthy landowner, appears at the front of a procession featuring tractors and other farm equipment. The Muhtar hopes that this display of modern technology will undermine public belief in the local holy man. Possessed by a spirit of unknown provenance, Taşbaş removes himself from the others for good when he walks out into the sea and is drowned. Even Halil's transgressions are forgotten when the others come out to pay homage to their departed spiritual guide. As the cotton harvest reaches its conclusion, the Muhtar's presence, in his black coat, riding boots, and whip, becomes unbearable to Memidik. All along, the younger man has been haunted by specters of his rival's end, the more so in view of the Muhtar's intermittent threats and taunts during their various meetings. In a few brief moments, Memidik plunges his knife three times into the older man, before the others quite know what has happened. Soon thereafter, Memidik is visited by the others while he is in prison. Zeliha comes three times, bringing him cigarettes and fresh grapes. Halil is the last to see him; they both regard the eagle which circles three times overhead as a mark of hope for the future.

## The Characters

Although the reader's sympathies are probably drawn in certain specific directions, in these works the author is not necessarily partisan or heavy-handed in his treatment of any major figure. The novels are all constructed around a series of episodes, each of which allows scope for the viewpoints of various characters. Even the all-too-human hopes and fears of the seemingly loathsome Muhtar are allotted some attention. At intervals, the fates of important individuals are discussed from the points of view of other interested parties. In addition, at times, there are some interesting suggestions of mass psychology as well, in which hearsay and rumors are transmitted in rapid succession among a number of people. Nevertheless, such effects, which evoke the social atmosphere of rural Turkey, do not lessen the author's concern for the particular features of various individuals. Some characters are depicted in greater detail than others, but none is really slighted. Moreover, without descending to satire or mere caricature, the idiosyncratic, indeed eccentric qualities of many people are fully portrayed; while the villagers often seem to form groups or to take sides about significant issues, each is depicted in uniquely specific terms. They all have their foibles and peculiar penchants, which in many cases seem to give them a sort of quirky charm.

The older men occupy a special position; they are accorded tolerance or esteem, sometimes, indeed, in spite of what they may do or say. In particular, Taşbaş is regarded as a repository of mystical wisdom, and not merely because he works in obscure or mysterious ways. Because of the public veneration that has grown up around Taşbaş over the years, the Muhtar and his cohorts cannot proceed against him directly; for his part, Taşbaş gives voice more explicitly to the others' distrust of their officials. Possibly for this reason, the villagers are willing to consider his occasional misdeeds as peccadilloes, and he incurs no lasting censure. Similarly, his solemnity and outward serenity allow them to overlook his practical inability to work natural wonders. Among the others, there seems to be a need to believe in his special powers. Halil, on the other hand, is regarded more as a colorful old rogue who represents the living embodiment of historical traditions. He is not always taken seriously, and he has a tendency to ramble on about past events after the others have grown tired of such matters; nevertheless, his neighbors are bemused by his uncanny ability to survive escapades of every sort. He is also granted a certain amount of the respect that old brigands have often received in rural Turkey. He is not regarded as particularly dangerous to the common people, and there is some question as to whether he has been very successful in his exploits, but his genial defiance of established authority leads others to believe that there may be ways around the arbitrary demands of their formal leaders. Halil's efforts at self-enrichment are more pathetic than serious; the villagers seem to let such episodes pass, once they have denounced and humiliated him for the moment. He is sometimes suspected of being behind certain untoward events, but the others evince a genuine concern when Halil himself disappears for any period of time.

Among the younger generation, Memidik is portrayed in some detail, although only at intervals, whereas others are depicted largely as examples of unusual local types. Memidik is approximately twenty years old and has served as a corporal with the army engineers; whatever aspirations for personal advancement he may have would seem limited by the unvarying routine of agricultural work. Although he has not found a calling suitable to his ambitions, he does not adapt easily to the petty tyranny of village life. His flights of romantic passion, which are deeply and genuinely felt, may also contribute to his dissatisfaction with the mundane forms of degradation to which many in the area must submit. While it is not unusual, apparently, for village officials to threaten or beat the local people as a means of instilling their versions of discipline and order, Memidik considers such incidents as sufficient cause for his vendetta with the Muhtar. Memidik is a solemn, unswerving sort of young man who, for good or ill, will not bend or adapt easily to time-honored forms of injustice. He is also not particularly adept at stalking his intended victim; in this respect, he does not seem to have the instincts or outlook of a true outlaw. When the others come to his prison cell, it is evident that their sympathies lie with him.

There are a number of other characters who add color and variety to the narrative; none, however, is depicted in an implausible or farfetched manner. Some of the men have been driven to odd or eccentric behavior by lives of unremitting and monotonous work. There are also some young men who have left military service because of lack of discipline or medical problems. In general, a certain amount of respect is accorded to those who perform their share of work and do not yield lightly to the demands of the authorities. Shirkers and the overly subservient are regarded with disdain, though some admiration is conferred on those who devise ingenious schemes to avoid unnecessary labor.

The women are not quite so closely drawn as the men, though some of the stronger female characters are respected and indeed feared for their tenacity in upholding their own interests. This is particularly the case with Meryemce, who defiantly resists Halil's efforts to push her from her preferred place. Even when she seems to be hurt, she stubbornly insists on carrying out her household duties. During times when she is displeased with various men, she pointedly refuses to speak to them directly and instead addresses trees or rocks; the others think that she is mad, but this tactic proves effective. Indeed, it would seem that the women who tend households and work in the cotton fields often expend as much labor as anyone else; some of them, like Meryemce, are not as frivolous or seemingly shiftless as many of the men. In other ways, however, certain women seem prone to more submissive behavior or are willfully used by the men for their own ends. For that matter, there are also women who are susceptible to visions which impart ethereal qualities to people and places they know. In particular, Zalaca is troubled by odd apparitions in her sleep, some of which involve Taşbaş; other dreams feature strange symbolic scenes in which dark clouds, serpents, or other wild animals appear. In certain respects, the women are at least as likely as the men, if not more so, to give credence to the folk versions of quasi-religious beliefs that endow ordinary sights and occurrences with strange mystical connotations. On another front, the involvement of women in romantic-erotic interludes seems to reveal a desire that roughly matches that of male drives; for her part, Zeliha treats Memidik with a care and concern that fully uphold her side of the affair.

The major characters who are in positions of authority are not very sympathetic sorts, but their machinations are indicative of some rather interesting and idiosyncratic leanings. The Muhtar is adept at devising odd and twisted schemes of various sorts, but he is unable to hit upon any stratagem that will gain the villagers' allegiance. He seems to resent the sway that Taşbaş and other village elders have among the common people, but the Muhtar may actually make matters worse for himself by attempting to discredit his presumed rivals. Although it is recorded that the Muhtar has married three times, he tries to ingratiate himself with other local women by hearing their complaints and offering his interpretations of their dreams. Such efforts are of limited utility, however, and indeed, on other matters, he must in his turn bow to the authority of other officials in the region. In some instances, he is rather badly mishandled by police officers. Others who hold power are quite daunting and arbitrary in their actions. Adil Efendi will find one way or another to exact the taxes due him from the villagers, while it is said of Şevket Bey that once, in a fit of anger, he killed his mistress and two other people who happened to be on the spot; once he had three wives, but he divorced all of them at once. At the end, it is not clear whether the death of the Muhtar, and possibly that of Şevket, will alleviate the villagers' lot; capricious and tyrannical government seems to be the rule among those who hold power in the area. Another approach, as exemplified in the grandiose plans of Muttalip Bey, could involve the use of technical means to limit the useful employment available to many of the common people.

*Themes and Meanings*

This series of novels depicts the unvarying traditions of Turkish village life in a manner that seems broadly typical of such communities; the observation that, for generations, rural folk have migrated across the steppes of Anatolia in seasonal processions suggests cyclical historical movements. Some people seem to be aware of progress in the outside world: There is mention of military jets flying overhead, and even claims (premature for the time frame of the novel) that journeys to the moon are taking place. On the other hand, Muttalip Bey seems amused at the technical ignorance that seems to prevail in the region; tractors and other kinds of machinery seem almost alien to the villagers' way of life. Most characters appear to operate within a limited frame of reference; there is little talk of events in Ankara or Istanbul, the centers of Turkish social and commercial life. Moreover, the historical memories that are summoned forth by the reminiscences of the older men, such as Halil, deal largely with violence and upheaval in later Ottoman times or during the early years of the Turkish Republic. This oral tradition, which dwells upon acts of brigandage and defiance, is meant to conjure up heroic images from the past. Beyond the chronic struggles that arise with local officials, most people affirm in vague terms their attachment to democratic ideals, which they believe are implicitly joined to Turkish national values; apart from fleeting mentions of prominent party leaders, however, there are few real indications of continuing interest in questions of Turkish politics.

Far more vital influences on the villagers are popular religious convictions, some of which betray odd heterodox origins or are rooted in folk ways. Conceptions of Allah are frankly anthropomorphic: Many people, the women especially, believe in a black-eyed, white-bearded deity who watches directly over them. Appeals for divine assistance are uttered during times of difficulty. Some villagers believe that there is a seven-story heaven that they may reach. It is thought that the spirits of saints inhabit trees, and sometimes intercession is asked of them. Often maledictions in the name of Allah or other religious figures are used by the villagers to signify their displeasure. Elsewhere, there are some references to Shi'ite doctrine; the legend that Jesus Christ was crucified on Mount Ararat is also mentioned from time to time. Overtly religious beliefs sometimes are mingled as well with references to peris, or spirits, which are thought to inhabit caves or other remote areas. Another folk belief involves a forsaken graveyard, where brave men fear to tread; after a domestic quarrel, Meryemce approaches it with trepidation. Other odd effects come from efforts to interpret Zalaca's dreams; she takes them as portents of anticipated events, such as the coming of tax collectors. Taken together, this odd assortment of religious and folk practices is not altogether consistent, and indeed there are some variations in what different people believe. No one seems to mind, however, and this curious mixture of faith and credulity may assist many people with the toils and cares of their daily lives.

The villagers seem to hold certain moral values that may be inferred from both their dealings with public officials and with one another. Respect for authority is limited at best; the common people do not regard the government as useful even in preserving order. In certain instances, indeed, they seem to believe that disputes may be settled strictly among themselves. It is significant, for example, that they openly disapprove of police measures against Taşbaş but instead devise their own measures for signifying disapproval when his transgressions are made known. Powers of taxation are regarded as arbitrary and despotic; even the Muhtar, a government official, is willing to countenance means by which the state's impositions may be evaded. This curious coexistence of standards which encourage at least some amount of honest work but counsel a profound distrust of the state's means of enforcement seems to underscore this essential dichotomy in the values by which the villagers actually live.

## Critical Context

After Yashar Kemal had published his first novel, *İnce Memed* (1955; *Memed, My Hawk*, 1961), he embarked upon the trilogy beginning with *The*

*Wind from the Plain*. The setting is essentially similar, and there are a certain number of resemblances where peasant ways of life are concerned, but in the later sequence of works, characterization focuses more directly on the oddly individual qualities of older villagers, whose responses to the demands of authority lead neither to open resistance nor to flight. To be sure, in *Iron Earth, Copper Sky* and *The Undying Grass*, tension arises as the rivalry between Memidik and the Muhtar finally leads to outright violence. In its way, *Memed, My Hawk* presents a sharper contrast between authority and violent revolt; government officials operate more explicitly by force rather than by the oblique, grasping means that the Muhtar employs. For that matter, *The Wind from the Plain* and its sequels show a sense of broad, indulgent humor. Thus, while the earliest work is a tale of high adventure, the others retell rather curious episodes from the timeless fabric of rural lore. Both approaches depend to a great degree upon folk traditions; in a larger sense, themes of banditry are complemented by popular religious concerns that, in the later works, endow ordinary people and events with their own particular qualities.

In other works, Kemal pursued further variations of these issues while charting new courses. His recurring interest in his original protagonist, and in adventure narratives as such, was reflected in *İnce Memed II* (1969; *They Burn the Thistles*, 1973). His continuing fascination with oral traditions led him further afield in the novels *Ağrıdağsı efsanesi* (1970; *The Legend of Ararat*, 1975), *Binboğalar efsanesi* (1971; *The Legend of the Thousand Bulls*, 1976), and the two volumes of *Akçasazın Ağaları* (1973-1975; *The Lords of Akchasaz*, 1973-1975). There, as in other works, problems of crime and official brutality are explored alongside folk legends that suggest underlying patterns of social consciousness. Further elaboration of these themes may be found in subsequent works that take up such issues in narratives set along the coast of the Black Sea or in the Istanbul area. The dilemmas of power and justice do not yield ready resolutions in this realm which the author has depicted.

Although novels have been written in Turkey since the late nineteenth century, and, indeed, some interesting and distinguished examples of work in this genre have pointed to the possibilities which this form of narrative fiction offered, the movement from stylized to more realistic creations took place only slowly. Other literary efforts sought to record the oral traditions that were passed down for generations among masses of largely illiterate people. While he was by no means the first to utilize village themes, or to raise moral issues in rustic settings, Yashar Kemal's ability to fuse these various trends and to recapture the peasant ethos of rural Anatolia has won for him recognition as one of Turkey's premier novelists. In this sense, the reception accorded his works provides ample testimony to the evocative powers of these most typically Turkish forms of creative expression.

*Sources for Further Study*

Binyazar, Adnan. "The Yaşar Kemal Phenomenon," in *Edebiyat*. V, nos. 1/2 (1980), pp. 205-220.

Halman, Talat Sait. "Turkish Literature in the 1960's," in *The Literary Review*. XV, no. 4 (1971/1972), pp. 387-402.

_____ . "World Literature in Review: *The Undying Grass*," in *World Literature Today*. LI, no. 4 (1977), pp. 676-677.

_____ . "World Literature in Review: *The Wind from the Plain*," in *Books Abroad*. XLIV, no. 1 (1970), pp. 181-182.

Öztürk, M. Orhan. "Yaşar Kemal's Social Psychology," in *Edebiyat*. V, nos. 1/2 (1980), pp. 131-133.

*J. R. Broadus*

# THE WOMAN FROM SARAJEVO

*Author:* Ivo Andrić (1892-1975)
*Type of plot:* Psychological and social criticism
*Time of plot:* 1900-1936
*Locale:* Sarajevo and Belgrade
*First published: Gospodjica*, 1945 (English translation, 1965)

> *Principal character:*
> RAJKA RADAKOVIĆ, a spinster from Sarajevo

## The Novel

The beginning of *The Woman from Sarajevo* finds Rajka Radaković, a middle-aged spinster, in Belgrade, the capital city of Yugoslavia, where she moved after World War I from her native Sarajevo. She has lived alone with her mother since the age of fifteen, when her beloved father, a well-known businessman, died, bankrupt and in disgrace. In flashbacks, the story of her happy childhood and unhappy girlhood is told. The only child, withdrawn and overly serious for her age, she felt secure while her father was alive. Just before he died, he warned her to "save, save always, everywhere and in everything," and not to trust people because "all our feelings and concerns for others show our weaknesses only." He wanted to warn his child not to become a victim, as he had, of scrupulous ethics in business, which had brought him to ruin. This warning marks the beginning of an aberration in young Rajka that will eventually grow to monstrous proportions. She takes her father's advice literally and from an early age begins a life of excessive thrift and self-denial that borders on obsession. As soon as she comes of age, she takes over her father's business and, with a remarkable dexterity, rebuilds the family fortune, mainly by lending money at exorbitant rates. She denies both her mother and herself all normal pleasures, save for very basic needs. She isolates herself from her friends and, little by little, turns away all family friends and most of her relatives. Her life centers exclusively on money matters, out of a pathological fear that she will suffer the same financial ruin as her father. That insecurity, coupled with some peculiar strains in her character—excessive egotism, selfishness, miserliness, and lack of normal human drives—follows her throughout her life, until she ruins everyone with whom she associates and, finally, herself.

Not even World War I can make her change her ways. As a Serb, she escapes the pogroms, to which many of her compatriots have fallen victim, mainly by continuing her old way of life—by lending money and even supporting the enemy. Because of her activities, she is forced to flee with her mother to Belgrade, where she loses herself in a big city while finding greater opportunities for financial deals. As in Sarajevo, she shuns relatives and friends, oblivious to the world outside her narrow financial concerns. Not even her uncle, a friendly and sociable man, succeeds in drawing her out of her shell.

To be sure, she meets people and even allows herself to become friendly with some of them, but such efforts last only a short time; in the end, the old distrustful Rajka reasserts herself. There is only one occasion when she lets her guard down and allows herself to be sidetracked from her single-minded direction. An attractive and pleasant young man, a war hero, needs money to obtain a Ford dealership and asks Rajka for it. Because he resembles so much her younger uncle, whom she loved and who died young and penniless because of his irresponsibility, Rajka lends the young man a sizable amount of money, against her better judgment. When, after patiently waiting for him to return the money, she discovers that he has been squandering it on women and an easy life, she is almost crushed, but she recovers. She is also reaffirmed in her belief that no one is to be trusted and that one must think of oneself exclusively. The most disturbing aspect of this affair is her realization that she has let her emotions guide her even after so many years of conditioning herself to do the opposite.

This experience makes Rajka even more suspicious of everything, so much so that she develops a persecution mania. She is frightened to death by the apparition of an intruder who, she thinks, has come to rob her, and she dies of a heart attack, all alone. Her body is discovered two days later by a mailman.

### The Characters

The main character of *The Woman from Sarajevo* is Rajka. All other characters are only props in Ivo Andrić's efforts to draw the unusual character of this woman. Rajka is the quintessential miser, recalling the classic examples of the type portrayed in works such as Plautus' *Aulularia* (*The Pot of Gold*), Molière's *L'Avare* (1668; *The Miser*, 1672), and Jovan Sterija Popović's *Tvrdica: Ili, Kir Janja* (1837; the miser). She leaves little to the reader's imagination as far as her avarice is concerned. She saves on firewood, for example, while her hands are purple, her lips are gray, and her nose is red from the cold. She dresses poorly, without attention to fashion and to the normal woman's need to adorn and beautify herself. To Rajka, beauty is insanely expensive, a worthless and fickle thing. One can always save and shortchange time, warmth, light, food, rest—even when it seems to be impossible. She refuses to make a donation to any charitable cause, which earns for her the nickname "Shylock in a Skirt." She carries her stinginess into the nonmaterial world, such as in her relationships with other people; unless necessary, she does not say even "hello."

Andrić describes her succinctly at a later stage in her life:

Her ties even with the deceased relatives are weaker and weaker. . . . In town she doesn't see anybody. She doesn't need people; they pass her by, are born, grow and die, yet they are only one of the harmful or useful, good or dangerous factors in her savings. Otherwise she is not aware of their presence and has nothing in common with them. Even time does not exist for her—only the deposit and pay-off deadlines. There is no future, and the past is buried.

At that late stage in her life, she finds the greatest pleasure in watching with glee her gold pieces, "the basis, meaning and goal of life." Her only goal is to add to the principal and watch it grow. In addition, she refuses to marry throughout her life, even though she had suitors in the beginning. For this reason, she is called "Miss" and is better known by the nickname than by her own name.

Rajka seems to be a pathological miser and seems to have no redeeming qualities. Andrić provides two explanations for her affliction. One is a desire to avenge and redeem her father, who was ruined financially and who eventually died from grief because of his trust in others and his desire to help rather than to amass wealth. Rajka's justification for her behavior, stemming from the experience of her father as she understood it, is rather simple: The world is basically evil, selfish, insensitive, even cruel; it kills soft and honest people like her father, but is subservient before the hard and unscrupulous ones, like herself. She has therefore become avaricious, insensitive, and even cruel only to protect herself from the evil world, and if she avenges her father's untimely death in the process, it will give her an added satisfaction.

This kind of thinking reveals the second reason for her behavior—her insecurity and her inability to lead a life without fear. Left fatherless early in life, with a good-hearted but weak mother, she finds security and solace in wealth, which will protect her from all evil. For a long time this proves to be true, as far as her financial independence is concerned. Her insecurity is best expressed by her refusal during the war to identify with fellow Serbs, especially students and revolutionaries: "My life does not depend on those people but on my work. When I suffer a loss or damage, no one will come and ask me how I am and whether I can manage." This rather naïve rationalization explains why she feels happy at the time, "like a mole which burrows blindly in the darkness and silence of the soft earth, in which there is plenty of food and there are no barriers and dangers." Security provided by money becomes a god to which Rajka is willing to sacrifice everything.

Thus, an inborn trait in her character, her desire for revenge, and her insecurity complex have combined to create a monster of a human being. Still, Andrić does not leave her without some redeeming qualities. Her desire to avenge her father and her insecurity are all too understandably human. Moreover, when she for once shows understanding and compassion with the young war hero, she is bitterly deceived, which confirms her distrust and forces her to shun people for the rest of her life.

Other characters are much less developed, so that Rajka's strong character is constantly in the limelight. Her mother is present only in body. Unable to stand up to her daughter's will, she leads the life of a meek, powerless person. Rajka's business partners are also constantly overshadowed by her iron will, and her uncles do not seem to be able to bridle her selfishness either. Perhaps the strongest of the secondary characters is Rajka's father, but he quickly disappears from the scene, looming over the rest of the novel as the driving force in Rajka's relentless quest for wealth, revenge, and security.

## Themes and Meanings

Just as Rajka is the primary character of the novel, so her avarice is its primary theme. Greed is one of the basic elements of human character, and as such it is a timeless subject. Although milder variations can be found in many other works, avarice is the exclusive focus of only a few works of literature. Andrić approaches his theme from a purely psychological angle, as a character trait of only one person and not of a social class, race, or nationality. Indeed, while she is in many ways a typical miser, Rajka is not an easily recognizable cliché, as is Molière's miser or William Shakespeare's Shylock. Hers is an individual aberration and, as such, is all the more convincing. It is also interesting that she is the only woman among the group of prototypical misers. Finally, Rajka has a few more redeeming qualities than do other archetypal misers; thus she is developed more fully as an individual. The use of a novel for this purpose allows Andrić more room for a direct psychological illumination.

This is not to say that there are no other themes or subthemes in the novel. There is, for example, the concern with the father-daughter relationship, with all the psychological implications worthy of Freudian analysis; also of interest is the novel's depiction of social conditions in the Balkans in the first third of the twentieth century, especially the relationship between business partners and the way in which business was conducted at this time and place. Yet these subthemes are left in an embryonic stage, confirming the fact that the author's primary intention was to create an unforgettable character, subjecting everything else to that intent. As a result, the reader sees a somewhat single-minded work, with the satisfying compensation of having a fully developed and richly layered character study.

## Critical Context

*The Woman from Sarajevo* was the third novel by Ivo Andrić written in Belgrade in a relatively short span of time, during his enforced retirement in World War II. After writing *Na Drini ćuprija* (1945; *The Bridge on the Drina*, 1959) and *Travnička hronika* (1945; *Bosnian Story*, 1958; better known as *Bosnian Chronicle*, 1963), which are artistically superior and much more expansive works, it is understandable that in *The Woman from Sarajevo* Andrić shows signs of narrowing the scope and moving inward. One would be tempted to think that Andrić wrote this novel as a form of relaxation after his previous lengthy novels, but the intense concentration on one character and on a single theme requires as much energy. While the two other novels in many ways surpass *The Woman from Sarajevo*, there are some qualities that make this work a worthy companion to its predecessors: the concentration on one character and the resulting depth; the brilliant penetration into the psyche of a woman unusual in many ways; the strange attachment to this character, an attitude that Andrić has shown in few other works; and the attention to the more modern era, whereas most of Andrić's work dwells in the distant past. For these reasons, this novel, though less acclaimed critically than most of Andrić's other works, has a significance and charm of its own. It is indeed a worthy detail in the panoramic mural of Andrić's world that continues to intrigue and enchant his readers.

## Sources for Further Study

Džadžić, Petar. *Ivo Andrić*, 1960.

Goy, Edward D. "The Work of Ivo Andrić," in *The Slavonic and East European Review*. XLI (1963), pp. 301-326.

Hawkesworth, Celia. *Ivo Andrić: Bridge Between East and West*, 1984.

Mihailovich, Vasa D. "The Reception of the Works of Ivo Andrić in the English-speaking World," in *Southeastern Europe*. IX (1982), pp. 41-52.

Rosslyn, Felicity. "Ivo Andrić and *The Woman from Sarajevo*," in *Serbian Studies*. II (1984), pp. 21-40.

Zuckerman, A. Review in *The New York Times Book Review*. LXX (April 11, 1965), p. 4.

*Vasa D. Mihailovich*

# THE WOMAN IN THE DUNES

*Author:* Kōbō Abe (1924-      )
*Type of plot:* Existential realism
*Time of plot:* 1955
*Locale:* A small village which is nearly buried in the dunes of a Japanese
   seaside
*First published: Suna no onna*, 1962 (English translation, 1964)

> *Principal characters:*
>    NIKI JUMPEI, a teacher and insect collector
>    THE WOMAN, the woman who lives in the dunes
>    THE VILLAGERS, similar to a Greek chorus representing the
>       community, an old man and the younger men who haul
>       the sand

## The Novel

*The Woman in the Dunes* is about Niki Jumpei, a Japanese schoolteacher in his thirties who is thoroughly entrenched in the bureaucracy of postwar Japan. He is a team player—a company man who harbors a small cache of rebellious, or rather independent, thoughts. For recreation one holiday, he leaves his wife or lover, the reader is never sure which, in the city while he takes a train to the seaside for a weekend of insect collecting in the dunes, hoping to find a new form of beetle so that he may name it after himself and have a fleeting moment of fame.

The book opens with speculations about Jumpei's disappearance. A co-worker/amateur psychologist suggests that Jumpei has committed suicide and points to insect collecting as a sign of his unresolved Oedipus complex, his deep-seated behavioral disorder. As no one has heard from him for seven years, he is pronounced dead at the end of the first chapter.

The narrative then recounts what has actually happened to him. Wandering on the dunes looking for a beetle with frail, hairy legs, he misses the last train home. All the while he does this, he speculates upon the nature of sand, its mobility, its flexibility, its inability to take shape on its own. He decides to stay in the nearby village, so small that he must room with one of the inhabitants. An old man he meets along the road takes his request for room and board to the community center. The town elders decide to board him with a woman who lives alone after having lost her husband and child in a sand slide. The inhabitants live in homes pitted deep within the dunes. After being lowered by a rope into her home, Jumpei soon discovers that he is to be her mate/prisoner—the choice is up to him—and that he has been indentured into the village's service as a sand shoveler. The villagers must shovel sand throughout the night to ensure the existence of their homes. If one house is abandoned to the sand, each house in the tiny village strand is threatened; thus the motto of the village: Love Your Home.

Jumpei is horrified at this futile situation, and the plot revolves around his plans for escape and his relationship with the woman in the dunes. She is never named; she is merely the woman. Jumpei and the woman gradually come to have a relationship, both sexual and emotional, though he is scornful of her dogged existence, her blind loyalty to the village and to her home.

Jumpei makes three attempts to escape the sand pit which is his home; the third one is successful, but he ends up being trapped in a larger, natural sand pit on the outskirts of town, and his recapture becomes his rescue, as he would surely have died if left to his own devices. After this episode, he seems to settle into his existence with the woman; the work is difficult but time moves quickly. Their relationship is genuine and natural, whereas his relationship with the "town woman" was cerebral and defensive. The woman in the dunes does beadwork during the day in her spare time to earn enough money for a radio and a mirror. Jumpei, however, chooses to make a crow trap, "Hope," in the hope that a crow will be lured by the fish bait and become buried alive in his box. Seeing his trap sprung, he plans to release the crow after having first taped a call for help on its leg.

Instead of luring a crow, the bait attracts nothing but bacteria. Miraculously enough, however, the box accumulates precious water by way of one of the properties of sand, capillary action—water much purer than the water they are accustomed to using. He is overjoyed at his discovery. Meanwhile, the woman becomes pregnant, though the pregnancy is obviously ectopic, destined to be aborted and perhaps even threatening the life of the woman, who begins to hemorrhage. Because of the severe nature of her plight, the woman is taken out of her pit to a nearby veterinarian for professional help. The rope ladder is left and Jumpei is free to escape. He chooses to stay, rationalizing that now he has a "two way ticket" and that he can choose to escape at a later date. Besides, he is excited about the water trap and wants to talk about it with the villagers, the only ones who could truly share in his enthusiasm. He does not openly acknowledge his tie to the woman or to their "elemental" way of life. The book ends with two official documents, a notification of missing persons filed by his mother and, years later, the declaration of his death upon being missing seven years. The reader never learns what happens to the woman.

### The Characters

Niki Jumpei is the insect under the magnifying glass. Told from the third-person-limited point of view, *The Woman in the Dunes* hovers over his actions and his conscious thoughts, revealing a less than sympathetic Everyman, a man who relies too much upon his rational mind and too little on his instincts and emotions. As his "city woman" terms it, he has psychological venereal disease.

Though at times he displays some insight into the existential plight of man, and though he assumes that his understanding is deeper than that of the people around him, either in the city or the village, he is ignorant of his attraction to the woman in the dunes except in the physical sense. He can only acknowledge that there is something more than sexual in their relationship, but beyond that he is not equipped to probe. At one time he muses about who is indebted to whom—the woman to the man for his labor, or the man to the woman for her care. At the end of the novel, he is still as much in the dark as to his own psychological underpinnings as he was when the book began, only now he seems content, free from his urge to escape now that he knows he can.

The woman is both the archetypal woman—the shifting sand pit, the Freudian hole, the earth mother—and a real woman—a sensuous, living, breathing human being tied to the earth, comfortable with her body, at one with her existence and those around her. Though she is not cerebral, she is logical and resourceful, and though tender, she can also be violent. Nameless—and at one point while sleeping she is nearly obliterated by sand, becoming like a sculpture—she is more realized as a character than Jumpei, the man with an official identity.

The villagers represent the social mind-set of the provincial community. They are individuated only in the fact that one is old, the one who discovered Jumpei and lured him into the communal trap, while the others are young and vigorous. Both young and old are dedicated to the survival of the community, sharing common values and goals, placing the group before the individual.

## Themes and Meanings

Kōbō Abe's *The Woman in the Dunes* is like a glass box of sand that can be shaken and shifted into one form and then another, so clear yet so plastic are its possible interpretations. On one level, the novel is an existential parable of man's plight: the trap in which all people live, the futility of all human efforts, the folly of individuality, the narrowness of group perception, the meaningless ritual of everyday existence. It can also be read as a Marxist critique of bourgeois life—the meaningless attempts to get ahead, to escape human destiny, which is a group destiny and not an individual one. Jumpei's pretentions are as empty and futile as shoveling sand from the bottom of a sand pit. He represents the middle class; the woman represents nature and the natural "man," one who cooperates and lives within a social context. *The Woman in the Dunes* also has its Freudian overtones: the watchtower or phallus representing male authority, the patriarchy hovering over both the man and the woman in the pit, keeping them in line; the ceaseless, mechanical action of the shovel in the sand (the penis in the vagina); the pit enclosing the man, threatening to suffocate him (the threat of woman to man, enclosing and suffocating him in the womb/vagina), his individuality smothered in the family and in society.

On a literary level, the novel can also be thought of as a satirical takeoff on the traditional Japanese confessional "I novel." Written in the third person, it reveals, though not so sympathetically, the plight of the hero, his struggle for survival and identity in a hostile and foreign land. It can also be construed as lightly autobiographical (Kōbō Abe lived in the Manchurian desert as a boy), an artist's coming-of-age novel. Abe also addresses the theme of deracination or rootlessness in twentieth century man: the man without a village, the man without an identity, wandering lost in the shifting, morally amorphous universe.

*The Woman in the Dunes* deals with all these themes and more. Like the sand, it is both solid in its meaning and fluid in its paradoxes. Like Franz Kafka, Abe demonstrates with satiric humor the futility of man's plight in a hostile universe. He also reveals man's own blundering inability to see his existence for what it really is: either a series of shared moments that can be filled with kindness and passion or routine menial servitude made bitter by mutual distrust. In the end, Jumpei is not foolish because he chooses to embrace the pit; he is foolish because he cannot admit his decision. He pretends that he does not choose the pit when in actuality he does. With a touch of Zen Buddhism, Abe shows that the only way to transcend the pit is to embrace it, the pit being life and all of its limitations, the pit being death, with all of its implications, the pit being sex and the instinctive animal in man, with all of its complications.

### Critical Context

*The Woman in the Dunes* was one of the first internationally acclaimed Japanese novels. Though Japanese in detail, it is certainly universal in its implications and was and still is one of the most famous Japanese novels in English. In 1962, it was awarded the Yomiuri Literature Prize in Japan and was made into an internationally acclaimed film in 1963 by Hiroshi Teshigahara, winning the Jury Prize at the Cannes Film Festival that same year. In 1964, it was translated into English.

Known as the least Japanese of the Japanese postwar writers, Kōbō Abe is closer to Franz Kafka, Jean-Paul Sartre, Albert Camus, and Fyodor Dostoevski than he is to his Japanese contemporaries Yukio Mishima and Yasunari Kawabata. In 1948, after having received a medical degree that would never be used, he wrote his first novel, *Owarishi michino shirubeni* (as a signpost for the road I have come). In 1951, he won the Akutagawa Prize for his story "S. Karuma-shi no hanzai" (the crime of Mr. S. Karuma). *Tanin no kao* (1964; *The Face of Another,* 1966) was also made into a film by

Teshigahara. Among Abe's other works are the novel *Moetsukita chizu* (1967; *The Ruined Map*, 1969), the play *Tomodachi* (1967; *Friends*, 1969), the novel *Hakootoko* (1973; *The Box Man*, 1974), and the radio play *Bō ni natta otoko* (1957, 1969; *The Man Who Turned into a Stick*, 1975).

## Sources for Further Study

Harvat, Andrew. "The International Style in Japanese Literature," in *An Introduction to Japanese Literature*, 1974.

Kimbal, Arthur G. "Identity Found: *Woman in the Dunes*," in *Crisis in Identity and Contemporary Japanese Novels*, 1973.

Kokusai Bunka Shinkokai. "Abe Kōbō," in *Introduction to Contemporary Japanese Literature: 1956-1970*, 1972.

Nakamura, Mitsuo. "Development of Postwar Literature," in *Contemporary Japanese Fiction: 1926-1968*, 1969.

Yamanouchi, Hisaaki. "In Search of Identity: Abe Kōbō and Ōe Kenzaburō," in *The Search for Authenticity in Modern Japanese Literature*, 1978.

*Sandra Christenson*

# A WOMAN OF THE PHARISEES

*Author:* François Mauriac (1885-1970)
*Type of plot:* Social and psychological realism
*Time of plot:* From the early 1900's to World War I
*Locale:* Bordeaux
*First published: La Pharisienne*, 1941 (English translation, 1946)

> *Principal characters:*
> LOUIS PIAN, the elderly narrator of the story, which begins
>     when he is thirteen years old
> JEAN DE MIRBEL, his school friend
> ABBÉ CALOU, a parish priest who lives a few miles from the
>     Pian country estate
> BRIGITTE PIAN, Louis' stepmother

## The Novel

*A Woman of the Pharisees* is a complex weave of troubled and fallible characters, of suffering and redemption, both secular and spiritual. Above all, Louis Pian's story is a study of his self-righteously religious stepmother, Brigitte Pian, and those whom she victimizes and destroys before she finally faces the truth of her loveless, vindictive "piety."

The story opens at Louis' school, at the end of the term and the beginning of his friendship with Jean de Mirbel. Jean's brutal uncle has decreed that Jean, because of his poor performance at school, may not spend the summer holiday with his mother. Instead, he is to be sent to live and study with the Abbé Calou at Baluzac, a few miles from the Pian country estate at Larjuzon. Louis is excited that his friend will be so near, though when Jean and Louis' sister, Michèle, meet and fall in love, Louis becomes angry and jealous, inadvertently causing disastrous repercussions later for the young lovers.

Also staying at Larjuzon during the summer is M. Puybaraud, a teacher at Louis' school. He has been invited by Louis' stepmother supposedly to tutor Louis during the holiday; in fact, Brigitte wishes to break up an attachment Puybaraud has formed with Octavia Tronche, a delicate young woman who teaches at a Free School sponsored by Brigitte. She has learned of the love between Octavia and Puybaraud because of Louis' betrayal of his teacher's trust: He has told his stepmother of a letter to Octavia that Puybaraud asked him to post privately.

Brigitte fails to persuade either Octavia or Puybaraud to give each other up for what she sees as a higher calling to God in the convent and priesthood. When they marry, Brigitte punishes them by using her influence to deny them any employment, thus forcing them to live in poverty on her charity. Octavia later dies in childbirth, lacking even the basic comforts and the help that might have saved her child.

Meanwhile, Jean, living with the Abbé Calou, falls into difficulties of his own. His mother, the Comtesse de Mirbel, whom he adores, comes to visit him at Baluzac but firmly refuses to allow her son to spend the night with her at her hotel in Vallandraut. Undaunted, Jean slips out at night, borrows the priest's bicycle, and rides to the hotel, only to discover eventually that his mother is really at a different hotel in Balauze, a few miles away, and that she is with a lover. After Jean catches a glimpse of the two of them at their hotel window, he turns back in despair to Baluzac, falls ill along the way, and loses consciousness. He is later found by the Abbé Calou, returned to the kindly priest's house, and nursed back to health.

Brigitte, however, has learned about Jean and Michèle's love and their secret meetings—she has been led to the discovery by Louis' indiscretion during a jealous outburst—and, in a rage, she forbids Louis and Michèle to visit Jean while he recovers. For good measure, she gets her husband to agree to send Michèle to a girls' school, away from any contact with Jean. The Abbé Calou, attempting to help Jean, has the girl secretly send him news of herself which is to be passed on to Jean. The correspondence is discovered and cut off, however, and Brigitte moves to destroy the priest by complaining of him to the archbishop. When Jean, in desperation, briefly elopes with the local chemist's wife (a woman who has deliberately seduced the boy in order to settle a grudge against the priest), Jean's mother also complains, ultimately causing the Abbé to lose his parish.

When the school term begins, Brigitte separates from her husband, taking Louis to live with her in town. It is at this point that the disasters begin to accumulate which force Brigitte to see herself for what she is. The first to occur is the death of her husband, Louis' father. Left alone at Larjuzon, he discovers a letter that Brigitte had found and "accidentally" left behind proving his first wife's unfaithfulness, and he drinks himself to death. Octavia's death during childbirth and Jean's elopement, two incidents which arouse both Louis' and Michèle's hostility toward their stepmother, follow. Brigitte begins to suffer intensely, as her conscience condemns her for her heartless actions in the name of piety. In an effort to atone, she encourages Jean and Michèle's engagement and begins visiting the Abbé Calou, who is living in disgrace with relatives. It is the priest who gives to Brigitte the absolution that she craves, and when he dies, it is in her arms.

Brigitte's new spiritual awakening culminates in an intense, loving relationship with her Protestant doctor, over the objections of his family. Though he is killed in an accident, Brigitte's love transcends his death, leaving her quietly serene. In contrast, Jean and Michèle, who have married, live troubled lives marked by bickering and reconciliations. Louis, the observer-narrator, never marries.

*The Characters*

Initially, Louis is not a very attractive character, shallow and self-centered as he is. At times, his behavior with his stepmother is annoyingly close to toadyism, at least until Octavia's death; yet he lacks any real feeling for Brigitte, or indeed for anyone except his sister and his friend. Since Michèle and Jean's love for each other relegates Louis to the background of their lives, the dominant emotions of his youth become jealousy and loneliness. His main role is that of observer and analyzer, rather than participant, in the dramas and heartbreaks around him. He is the character to whom secrets are confided, even though he cannot really empathize. He is the reader of diaries and letters, the onlooker at others' actions. Louis grows up to be a rather bloodless figure, never really touched by the passions which move the characters about him.

Brigitte, on the other hand, is a truly formidable creation. Secure and sincere in her belief in her own moral perfection, she manages to clothe every vindictive act she commits with the robe of pious concern for her victim's salvation. She is the cousin of her husband's first wife, and she cannot suppress her jealousy of the dead woman. She attempts to efface her predecessor from M. Pian's memory by looking for, and finding, evidence of the first Mme Pian's adultery. Though Brigitte manages to resist revealing her knowledge for some time, as soon as she senses that her control over her husband has weakened, she apparently arranges for him to make the discovery that kills him. Her treatment of the other two couples in the story reveals her puritanical distaste for sexual love; her destruction of the Abbé Calou is the act of a woman determined to violate that which she cannot dominate, as she has done with her husband. At times, she is uneasily aware of the sterility of her faith, but it takes several tragedies—all directly or indirectly her fault—to turn her toward that love and humility which are the basis of true spirituality. Even then, she retains a vestige of her Pharisaical nature: She is quite proud of her ability to recognize the error of her ways so late in life.

Jean and Michèle are two characters whom Brigitte does not manage to harm permanently. Jean, brutalized by his uncle and ignored by his mother, first finds love and then acceptance with the kindly Abbé Calou, but an older priest's fatherly affection is not enough to turn Jean away from the recklessness and immorality for which he seems destined. Only Michèle's love genuinely moves him—but even that has its limitations, since Jean confesses to Louis later in life that he hates being loved. Jean is also the focus of Louis' adolescent admiration and then of his jealousy when Jean falls in love. Jean is a cautionary example of impulses allowed to run unchecked; as the object of the Abbé Calou's unconditional love, he serves as a foil for the priest, whose kindness rarely fails him, even though his love is not returned.

The Abbé Calou, indeed, is arguably the most loving and lovable character in the novel. He is the embodiment of the highest form of love, which gives endlessly, asking and expecting nothing in return. His genuine spiritual perfection contrasts dramatically with Brigitte's arrogant religiosity. Ironically, the priest suffers for his love, sacrificed as he finally is, like a modern Christ figure, to others' petty vengeance. Also Christ-like, he forgives his greatest tormentor, bringing her to an understanding of true Christian love.

### Themes and Meanings

François Mauriac is a Catholic writer exploring the Catholic themes of sin, grace, and redemption. Certainly these themes are exemplified in Brigitte's false spiritual progress, contrasted as it is with the genuine grace and piety of the priest. Moreover, in the troubles of Jean, Mauriac creates a wandering soul who turns away from the love and prayers of the priest and is subsequently battered by temptation and despair. Though he does marry Michèle, the marriage is depicted as a rather shaky one, punctuated by quarrels and reconciliations. Such physical love, Mauriac seems to say, is frail and finite.

The novel is also an examination of the bourgeoisie, which Mauriac knew well: Brigitte is a social snob as well as a religious one. She is happy, for example, to welcome the Comtesse de Mirbel in her home, despite that lady's faintly unsavory reputation, because of the Comtesse's social position. It is this same snobbery which impels Brigitte to dominate the lives of those whom she considers to be her inferiors, such as the Puybarauds. It is revealing of her attitude to social class that the Puybarauds' love is treated much like a moral abomination.

Finally, Mauriac dramatizes, through Louis, the awakening of an adolescent to the knowledge and suffering of adulthood. Presented as a sexual innocent, Louis is slow to appreciate and understand the intensity of the love between Jean and his sister. Yet from the moment at which the relationship commences, Louis' view of human relations seems permanently shadowed with melancholy. As he informs the reader, the only time that he has ever known that he felt deeply is when he was suffering. To be an adult, Mauriac seems to say, is to be forever emotionally dissatisfied. Only spiritual love brings peace.

### Critical Context

*A Woman of the Pharisees* is considered to be the last of François Mauriac's great novels. Set in Bordeaux, Mauriac's birthplace (and the setting for his other novels), it concentrates on Mauriac's own social class—the bourgeoisie—as indeed all of his novels do. Wallace Fowlie has written that Mauriac's world is one "of three major characteristics: provincial, bourgeois and Christian." Within this confined world, Mauriac, deeply influenced by the philosopher Blaise Pascal, explored themes of personal anguish and social corruption from a Christian perspective. In *A Woman of the Pharisees*, Mauriac also focused on the spiritual corruption of hypocrisy.

In addition to his many novels, Mauriac also wrote poetry, plays, biographies, and literary criticism. He was also a journalist during the Spanish Civil War and World War II. In 1933, Mauriac was elected to the French Academy, and in 1952, he was received as a member of the Academy of Sciences, Belles Lettres, and Arts of Bordeaux. It was also in 1952 that he was awarded the Nobel Prize for Literature.

*Sources for Further Study*
Fowlie, Wallace. "The Art of François Mauriac," in *A Mauriac Reader*, 1968.
Iyengar, K. R. Sprinivasa. *François Mauriac*, 1963.
Smith, Maxwell. *François Mauriac*, 1970.
Speaight, Robert. *François Mauriac: A Study of the Writer and the Man*, 1976.

*Lynn McDonie*

# THE WOMEN AT THE PUMP

*Author:* Knut Hamsun (Knut Pedersen, 1859-1952)
*Type of plot:* Satire
*Time of plot:* The late nineteenth century
*Locale:* A small coastal town in northern Norway
*First published: Konerne ved vandposten*, 1920 (English translation, 1928)

*Principal characters:*
OLIVER ANDERSON, an emasculated cripple
PETRA, his wife, a woman of loose morals
FRANK, a son of Petra and a student of philology
ABEL, a son of Petra and a blacksmith

## The Novel

Knut Hamsun's title indicates his novel's subject: The town pump is the center of life in a small town, because it is notoriously a gathering place for gossips. Few of Hamsun's characters of either gender seem to have much more to do than to participate in the gossip, raillery, and persiflage which in such a town flow like water from the pump. The novel's pervasive ironic tone arises from the distance between characters' views of themselves and their importance and the omniscient narrator's view of these little people and their little lives:

> Oh, that little anthill! All its inhabitants are occupied with their own affairs, they cross each other's paths, push each other aside, sometimes they trample each other under foot. It cannot be otherwise, sometimes they trample each other under foot. . . .

This peculiarly misanthropic novel is lacking in plot. Incidents take place, sometimes repercussions are reported (as in the mail robbery) but other times not. Hamsun's interest is in the daily lives of the people on whom he reports.

The book opens with a dramatic moment in the town's life: The town's only steamer, the *Fia*, owned by Counsel Johnsen of the Wharfside, sets sail on its maiden voyage. Aboard as a deckhand is young Oliver Anderson, son of a widow. After an accident at sea which left him maimed and impotent, he returns home with a wooden leg. Petra, to whom he was engaged, returns his ring, and Oliver and his mother sink into a destitute state. Some days, he rows out to fish, but he realizes little profit from that. One day his luck changes; he discovers an abandoned ship and for a time lives well on money from salvage. When Petra comes back willing to marry him, he thinks it is more good luck. Petra soon has a son whom they name Frank and, later, another son named Abel. Oliver is eventually lucky enough to have a family of five children.

Oliver and Petra's marriage consists (as it must) of mutual deception and self-deception, lies, and evasions. Still, it is not an unhappy life, judged according to the standards of these characters, who ask nothing of themselves and very little from anyone else. Oliver is not a jealous man and does not have much dignity. He uses his knowledge of his sons' paternity to blackmail the wealthy Counsel Johnsen into giving him a job as warehouseman. He evades his chief creditor by offering him his wife's sexual services. As a cripple, he plays on the townspeople's sympathies to get what advantage he can. He is pathetically content with little: some sweets, a new hat, a colorful tie. When he finds some stolen bank notes, he is ecstatic and becomes, in his own eyes, a great man so long as the money lasts. Any sympathy which can be elicited for Oliver, so deformed in body and spirit, must come as a consequence of his attitudes toward his children. Despite the fact that none of them is his and that this fact has gradually leaked out at the town pump over the years, he is a devoted and proud father. Still, his altruism should not be overstated. He benefits from his children, both socially and economically, and he looks to them for support in his old age.

Frank, the eldest, is to Oliver a brilliant scholar, but Hamsun makes it clear that Frank is actually a dull grind, and, in his pursuit of philology, the very embodiment of sterile academic learning. When Frank eventually reaches his full potential for priggishness by becoming Headmaster of the local school, Oliver is extremely proud:

> at that moment no one came and told Oliver that he was a childless man. His children were nothing but pure invention on his part, granted, but he had them, during the whole of their childhood and growing-up . . . he and they knew each other, they called him father, . . . and now Frank was returning to his native town, a great and learned man.

Abel, his other son, seems to be one of the few sympathetically portrayed characters in the book. Apprenticed early to Carlsen the Blacksmith, he becomes almost a son to him, almost compensating Carlsen for his bitter disappointment in his own son. Intelligent, sensitive, industrious, and a generous contributor to the family's support, Abel soon takes over the shop. He frequently finds ways to give Oliver extra spending money. In Oliver's eyes, however, Abel can never compare with Frank. Abel also fails to find favor with the young woman on whom he has set his heart, Little Lydia. As so often is the case in Hamsun's novels, first love is impossible, but Abel, a realist, is content with another. The remaining children, two daughters, known only as Blue Eyes and Brunette, exist only to be married off to their respective swains, one improbably named Drawing-pin, the other, Edevart, son of Jörgen the Fisherman. (The use of demeaning names is common in the novel.)

## The Characters

Besides Oliver Anderson and his family, Hamsun has included representatives from all social strata of the town, from Double Counsel Johnsen (tradesman, shipowner, and recipient of the Cross of Danish Order of Knighthood) to Olaus the Glazier (foul-mouthed town drunk, blue and disfigured from a blasting charge which exploded in his face, and lacking one hand). Yet Hamsun's omniscient editorial narrative technique allows readers to see that there is little real difference between the "high" and the "low," except that the "high" have more money. It seems that both Johnsen and his son, Scheldrup, have had sexual relationships with Petra Anderson, as has another town luminary, Frederickson the Lawyer, member of the Storthing. Frederickson can be persuaded not to foreclose the mortgage that he holds on Oliver's house if he receives frequent visits from Petra. Supposedly, he would like to marry Fia, daughter of Counsel Johnson. Yet when it appears that Johnsen's ship, the *Fia*, has sunk uninsured and that Johnsen's financial ruin is imminent, Frederickson finds it easy to shift his attentions to Fröken Olsen, whose father's financial prospects are improving. The Doctor is yet another particularly repellent character—bitter, arrogant, and cruel. Hamsun reserves his purest scorn for such white-collar types, showing them to be calculating, ruthless, corrupt little men.

Yet even when Hamsun presumably wishes to present a more positive character, as in the Postmaster, for example, the result is at best a shift from the repulsive to the merely exasperating. The Postmaster, a failed architect become full-time philosophical bore, tires everyone with his interminable babbling on such subjects as the transmigration of souls. After his son is implicated in a mail robbery, he loses his wits and seems to have been struck dumb.

Olaus the Glazier also comes to a bad end. As the town's other notable cripple, he has had a relationship of complex hatred with Oliver. When Oliver's pedant son, Frank, arrives home from his studies in order to assume the position of Headmaster, the drunken Olaus makes loud, taunting remarks about Oliver's impotence, Petra's prodigious fertility, and Frank's paternity. Oliver decides such insolence is not to be borne; it may even threaten Frank's position. In the middle of the night, Oliver arranges for some oil barrels to tumble down and crush Olaus as he lies sleeping under a tarp on the wharf.

## Themes and Meanings

It would be difficult to enumerate all Hamsun's satirical targets in *The Women at the Pump*, but clearly two of the larger ones are education and democracy. Hamsun holds out little hope for those who are educated in the pedantic manner of Oliver's son Frank and even less for those whom Frank will instruct. Frank's headmaster is himself a philologist:

[N]obody could make less boast of his philology. He never mentioned the leaders, the men of original research; probably he knew nothing about them, scarcely their names even, what had he to do with genius! His vocation was not to make discoveries, he had only to teach, just teach. Teach so as just to make a living, teach so as just to be able to conduct his pupils through their lessons to the examination.

On this philosophy of education as the transmission of truly dead knowledge, the narrator comments: "A meagre and melancholy existence, poverty and intellectual darkness, decline, wear and tear, blindness. If only it were madness, that would be decreed by fate, a folly sent from Heaven; but this was human, ape-like."

At the same time, there is no Rousseauistic correlation between the simple and the good. The philogists and educators have no corner on apelike behavior, as the novel demonstrates. There is room to doubt what kind of society can be made from the Olivers of the world:

There he goes, limping home. He is something of a wreck, a little imperfect in himself; but what is perfection! The life of the town realizes its image in him, it is a crawling life, but it is just as busy for all of that. It begins in the morning and lasts till night, then the people lie down to rest. And some of them lie down under a tarpaulin.

In a passage such as this (with which the novel concludes), Hamsun's sardonic, antidemocratic side is unmistakable.

*Critical Context*

*The Women at the Pump* shocked Hamsun's readers, particularly since it was published in 1920, the same year in which he was awarded the Nobel Prize for Literature for his great paean to the common man, *Markens grøde* (1917; *Growth of the Soil*, 1920). One commentator wittily remarked that if there had been an award for the least idealistic work of literature—in addition to the Nobel Prize's award for the most idealistic and uplifting—then Hamsun might have won both for that year.

Critics have attempted to explain the novel's misanthropy, citing Hamsun's disillusionment because the Germans, with whom he had sympathized, lost World War I, the war the Postmaster calls "the Englishman's war." Hamsun's lifelong Anglophobia is evident in the Postmaster's denunciation:

your Englishman has a religion of his own in this world and justifies it in an entirely English manner. He reduces one people after another to subjection, takes away their independence, castrates them and makes them fat and quiet. Then one day the Englishman says: Let us now be just according to the Scriptures! And so he gives the eunuchs something which he calls Self-government.

Some critics associate Hamsun's increasingly elitist and antidemocratic views with the years he spent in the United States (1882-1884 and 1886-1888). His book *Fra det moderne Amerikas aandsliv* (1889; *The Spiritual Life of Modern America*, 1969) is a satirical record of his experiences and expresses his views that cultural advance and refinement is not likely to take place in a democracy.

Like Strindberg, Hamsun was drawn toward German virility, masculinity, and militarism. Unlike Strindberg, he lived long enough to have to reexamine the implications of his antidemocratic views. He did so in *Påa glengrodde stier* (1949; *On Overgrown Paths*, 1967), a book of reflections written while he was awaiting trial for his pro-Nazi views during World War II. The book belies the court's conclusions about Hamsun's "permanently impaired mental faculties," but its author remains an enigma.

Traditionally, satire has the instruction and improvement of its audience in view. In *The Women at the Pump*, Hamsun's excessive and vitriolic misanthropy is more likely to repel than reform.

*Sources for Further Study*
Ferguson, Robert. *Enigma: The Life of Knut Hamsun*, 1987.
Gustavson, Alrik. *Six Scandinavian Novelists*, 1940.
Larsen, Hanna Astrup. *Knut Hamsun*, 1922.
Næss, Harald. *Knut Hamsun*, 1984.
—————————. "Who Was Hamsun's Hero?" in *The Hero in Scandinavian Literature*, 1975. Edited by John M. Weinstock and Robert T. Rovinsky.

*Karen Kildahl*

# WOMEN OF MESSINA

*Author:* Elio Vittorini (1908-1966)
*Type of plot:* Social realism
*Time of plot:* 1945-1946; epilogue, 1949
*Locale:* An unnamed village in the center of Italy, at the base of the Apennine Mountains, not far from Bologna; various railroad cars as they travel throughout Italy
*First published: Le donne di Messina,* 1949; revised, 1964 (English translation, 1973)

> *Principal characters:*
> THE NARRATOR, an unnamed Italian whose father worked for the railroad
> UNCLE AGRIPPA, the narrator's uncle, an elderly man retired from the railroad
> SIRACUSA, Uncle Agrippa's daughter who ran away from home during the war
> VENTURA (also known as UGLY MUG), a former Fascist officer and Siracusa's lover
> CARLO THE BALD, a former Fascist working as a domestic spy for the Italian government

*The Novel*

*Women of Messina* focuses on the social and moral aspects of life in Italy immediately after World War II. Elio Vittorini explores how his physically ravaged and spiritually defeated homeland recovers from the horrible experiences of war. An anonymous village becomes the focal point of the narrative, with a sizable subplot involving the train travels of Uncle Agrippa.

The commune-like village of war refugees and their families creates itself quite by accident. When a truck carrying a large group of refugees stalls and cannot be restarted, a member of the group disembarks and decides to settle in a destroyed village which he can see in the distance. Weary of traveling without a set destination, several other refugees join the first man, called Thorn. Among the first to leave the truck is Thorn's best friend, Whistle. Whistle will eventually be considered the unofficial mayor of the small village because of his ability to see all sides of an argument and to sum up matters well.

While the village is gradually being made inhabitable, the narrative switches focus to Uncle Agrippa's travels. Agrippa converses with everyone who appears friendly on the trains and tells them the story of his lost daughter, his only child. This daughter, Siracusa, left home during the war, supposedly to seek adventure, or at least a sense of community that her home lacked. Agrippa, a widower, carries pictures of his daughter to aid in finding her, but they are mostly from her childhood and she is now a grown woman. The narrator emphasizes that Agrippa searches in a haphazard and often useless manner for Siracusa; the elderly man is actually enjoying his travels through Italy and the sense of purpose his search gives him.

Also on a search is Carlo the Bald, whom Uncle Agrippa knows from the train routes. Carlo, a former Fascist, works for the new Italian republican government, reporting unlawful activities. His interest focuses on the un-named village and its inhabitants, who sell scrap metal for money. These scraps are from ruined war machinery scattered across the land and are tech-nically the property of the Italian government. Carlo hopes to dissolve the village by arresting or scaring away Ventura, who seems to be at its spiritual center. Carlo the Bald had served as a minor officer for the Fascist republic with Ventura; he hopes that some form of blackmail will cause Ventura to leave the village.

The narrative shifts to the early stages of growth in the small village, em-phasizing the unplanned nature of its development. The former peasants and partisans (for they are a mixed group, representing all Italy) first clear the land. They build primitive housing, often using the bases of partially erect buildings from the original settlement. The people, numbering seventy-nine in the early months of the community, sleep in a half-destroyed church.

In September of 1945, one of the original villagers comes back to survey her homeland. Her name is Antonia, and her small horsecart quickly be-comes the prized possession of the commune. Since everyone possesses the land and tools in common, the villagers use the cart for the good of all. Eventually, parts for an abandoned truck are brought to the village on the cart from the nearest city; soon, the community enjoys the luxury of a motor vehicle to bring larger supplies from the city. Meanwhile, Antonia has brought back to the village many peasant refugees who were its inhabitants when it was destroyed. With these additions, the population of the commu-nity swells to 150. All the inhabitants work hard during the summer and fall to rebuild the area and to plant a crop of wheat. When the winter sets in, however, the farmers among the group try to rest, as was their former pat-tern in life. Disputes arise when the former city men and factory workers in the village, notably Whistle, try to make the farmers work all winter long. An informal register which the narrator has found records the psychological repercussions of these events in the community. A small number of people leave during the first winter, some for a brief time and others permanently. Even Thorn takes the horsecart and is gone for five months.

The community survives these upheavals, and the wheat crop is a good one. A generator is completed in April, bringing electricity to the village. During the summer of 1946, an unofficial but large posse of men comes look-ing for Ventura because of some unspoken war crimes on his part. They are unable to capture him, and Carlo the Bald's plan to crush the village by removing Ventura from it fails. In an epilogue to the novel, set in 1949, the narrator describes Ventura, a less vital and spirited man than he was a few years earlier, at home in the village with Siracusa. She remains unfound by her father Agrippa, who still travels the train lines in 1949.

## The Characters

Vittorini leaves his major characters only partially defined. His main concern is with their psychological states, but these are often related by a narrator who is a vague, unnamed person. This narrator, who knows some things about village life as well as about Uncle Agrippa's life, is an Everyman character. He seems to represent all of Italian life after World War II. He evaluates how daily living has changed from prewar times to 1945 and 1946. He feels nostalgia for the innocence and beauty of the simple way of life, close to the earth, that his nation lost during the war. He also misses his relatives who have died during the harsh war years; in this way, he resembles Vittorini himself.

Several interesting minor characters make appearances in the village and on the trains. One outstanding minor figure is Barberino, an old woman who is a visionary or seer. She can view scenes in detail at great distances that no one else in the commune can discern; she may represent the best of old Italy looking forward to a new age. Among the villagers she befriends is Siracusa.

Siracusa is a strong woman who manages to live with the often remote and sometimes disturbed Ventura. Ventura keeps his past a secret from his lover, yet he is a powerful and quiet force in bolstering the morale of the villagers. He was an officer during the war on the side of the defeated Fascists, and he still commands respect among men by his bearing.

Two young partisans, known as Red Kerchief and Toma, are among the more active members of the commune. When the posse of young men comes searching for Ventura, Toma and Red Kerchief find old friends among them. Persuaded by talk of good jobs and modern luxuries in the cities, Red and Toma leave the village with these friends during its second summer.

A portion of the narrative is given over to a dialogue of voices of the villagers themselves. Several of the peasants—the Widow Biliotti, Elvira La Farina, Cataldo Chrisa, and Pompeo Manera—explain the differences that arose between them and the leadership of the village during the harsh first winter. The farmers tell of the lack of food, in large part brought about by a lack of planning. Whistle and other former city men, such as Ventura, Thorn, and Toma, explain how their psychology differs from that of the farmers. The voices Vittorini employs in this section are various and distinguishable; one person often picks up the thread of a tale after another has left off, providing a chain of events relating the community's long, difficult winter.

The women of Messina, for whom this book is named, are the hard-working, sometimes unkempt peasant women who form the backbone of the village in its early days. They stand in sharp contrast to Carlo the Bald, a sneaking, conniving character who wishes to ruin the village. Carlo's one good quality seems to be his tolerance of and friendship for Uncle Agrippa, which is shown in the epilogue. Carlo and Agrippa talk often of the village in its beginning days, although Agrippa has never seen it, and Carlo gains his information only by spying. In this epilogue, especially, Agrippa comes to represent the Italy of the past: a friendly, innocent, and warmhearted man, out of place among a newer, somewhat colder generation. Carlo fits in better with the new Italy, as he continues to inspect land for the Italian government; his kindliness in talking to Agrippa, who now often bores the other passengers, shows that he has some capacity for sympathy.

## Themes and Meanings

Vittorini is an author very much concerned with the human condition, especially in its social aspects. His story of the postwar, reconstructed village reflects the story of all human development. The group of refugees forms a commune, not purposefully but naturally, since it is the only step they can take given their circumstances. Vittorini shows that as building progresses, these refugees begin to reclaim more of their individual rights and freedoms. While all slept in partitioned spaces in a half-erect church in the first days, they come to desire privacy and construct separate, distanced houses when the extra supplies are available to them. These individual houses also reinforce the concept of private ownership of goods that gradually reenters village life. During the first winter, farm animals are held in common, but later, when everyone is more prosperous, animals are privately owned. Another of the author's concerns is the amount of freedom and individuality necessary in communal living. Did individuals break away from the group because the community failed to sustain them spiritually, or did such individualism occur as a healthy, natural outgrowth that would further strengthen the community? Vittorini leaves such questions unanswered in *Women of Messina*. When the novel closes in 1949, the village remains, but it has lost much of its rural charm. It now has many of the conveniences of the city, which Vittorini seems to consider unnecessary encumbrances. These luxuries weaken the moral and even the physical strength of the villagers. Even the women of Messina have grown soft and fat. Vittorini reinforces the idea that a somewhat harsh life builds moral character and a sense of community in his epilogue aboard the trains in 1949. Only Uncle Agrippa is a friendly, outgoing person; the younger people around him ignore his talk and even snub him. They are caught up in their own world of material goods, especially the students.

Vittorini's artful writing in *Women of Messina* exhibits a satisfying range of style. This novel contains his fine lyric intensity in descriptions of landscapes and the movement of the sun. In the section of the book devoted to the dialogues of the villagers, the style becomes crisp and laconic, accurately depicting the peasants' speech.

*Critical Context*

*Women of Messina*, in its revised form, was Vittorini's last novel. He wrote it at the end of World War II and published it in Italy in 1949 but was disappointed with that version. He rewrote the book fourteen times, drastically changing its structure and plot. In 1964, he published what he thought was the final version of *Women of Messina*.

This novel is Vittorini's longest, a large undertaking that he hoped would reflect all of Italian life in the postwar years. He wanted to capture the diversity, the charms, and the strengths of the Italian people as they heroically reclaimed their land from the horrors of Fascism and the ravages of war. *Women of Messina* includes several themes that the author analyzed in his earlier works, *Il garofano rosso* (1948, written 1933; *The Red Carnation*, 1952) and *Conversazione in Sicilia* (1941; *In Sicily*, 1948). Whereas these ideas received separate treatments earlier, they converge in *Women of Messina* in one all-encompassing setting. Vittorini handles his various materials well, but critics consider *Women of Messina* a flawed work that does not fully resolve conflicting ideologies or even its various artistic styles. Perhaps Vittorini wanted *Women of Messina* to be that way—a novel of diversity and some conflict, reflecting his view of Italian life in the late 1940's.

*Sources for Further Study*

Cambon, Glauco. "Elio Vittorini: Between Poverty and Wealth," in *Wisconsin Studies in Contemporary Literature*. III, no. 1 (1962), pp. 20-24.

Heiney, Donald. *Three Italian Novelists: Moravia, Pavese, Vittorini*, 1968.

Lewis, R. W. B. "Elio Vittorini," in *Italian Quarterly*. IV (Fall, 1960), pp. 55-61.

Pacifici, Sergio. *A Guide to Contemporary Italian Literature: From Futurism to Neorealism*, 1962.

Schott, Webster. "Elio Vittorini's Hoping and Nonhoping," introduction to *Women of Messina*, 1973.

*Patricia E. Sweeney*

# WONDERFUL FOOL

*Author:* Shusaku Endō (1923-    )
*Type of plot:* Comic drama
*Time of plot:* The 1950's
*Locale:* Tokyo, Japan
*First published: Obaka san*, 1959 (English translation, 1974)

*Principal characters:*
GASTON (GAS) BONAPARTE, a bumbling French seminary
    student who comes to Japan as a missionary
TAKAMORI, Gaston's Japanese pen pal, who becomes his
    befuddled host upon Gaston's surprise arrival in Tokyo
TOMOE, Takamori's sister and bemused companion of Gaston
    during his misadventures in Tokyo society
ENDŌ, a gangster in the Tokyo underworld who kidnaps
    Gaston in order to force his compliance in a murder

*The Novel*

   Set twelve years after the end of World War II, *Wonderful Fool* tells the
story of Gaston (Gas) Bonaparte, a failed French seminary student and a
bona fide descendant of Napoleon himself who decides to forgo formal
church endorsement and travel to Japan as a missionary. Having met a native
Japanese through correspondence, he embarks upon a spiritual adventure,
hoping to use the home of Takamori, a clerk, and his sister, Tomoe, as his
"base."

   While reading one of Gas's poorly written letters in broken Japanese,
Takamori realizes with some horror that Gas is coming to visit them.
Unimaginative and unsentimental, they harbor no suspicions about his plans
to spread, independent of his church, the news of faith and love to the long-
neglected Orient. Instead they conjure images of a French nobleman or film
star who will honor them with his visit. When Gas arrives in Japan on a
third-rate steamer, they find it unusual and unsettling. Upon first acquaintance, both Takamori and Tomoe feel betrayed; a descendant of Napoleon
should not be a bumbling, clumsy oaf, "a tramp with the body of a horse."
However well-intentioned, he clearly is utterly ineffectual, unable to speak or
understand Japanese except in the most primitive way, and thus completely
ill-prepared for cross-cultural communication.

   Their trip to a sushi bar on the way home from the shipyard becomes emblematic of the way in which the gangly, uncoordinated Frenchman consistently scandalizes his hosts. Brandishing a Japanese loincloth—given to him
by a malevolent sailor on the steamship—as a table napkin, Gas humiliates
his hosts. In his simple, trusting manner, Gas later mistakes the advances of a

prostitute for the simple congeniality of the Japanese people, marking himself as clearly a stranger in a strange land, a wayfarer whose language and thought processes set him apart from everyone. In a telling moment, Endō has Takamori observe, "All he's done since he arrived is walk around and make friends with dogs and children," moving Gas toward the Christ figure he is clearly intended to become. Tomoe is equally mystified at Gas's presence, wondering if Gas could be a smuggler or a spy.

After a series of embarrassing episodes, Gas begins to sense that he is imposing on his gracious hosts and announces that he is leaving behind their polite but restrained hospitality, ostensibly "to meet more Japanese people," but intending privately to embark upon a personal crusade to bring the love of God to the streets of Tokyo. Accompanied only by the mongrel of a dog that has befriended him, Gas moves through the squalor of Tokyo's underworld as he steadily gropes toward his own destiny—toward his own Gethsemane and eventually his own Golgotha.

The key relationship in the novel emerges in an encounter between Gas and the gangster Endō soon after he has left the home of Takamori and Tomoe. Having taken up with the lowlifes of urban Tokyo, Gas finds himself in the company of the tubercular Endō, a professional killer who has in process a plot to murder the man he believes is responsible for his brother's death. Kidnapping Gas, Endō tries to compel him to help him get revenge, but Gas repeatedly manifests an innocence and love uncommon in the streets of Tokyo and endears himself to the hardened and morally drained underworld figure. As the story moves to its swift conclusion, Gas thwarts Endō twice and eventually dies in saving both men from killing each other. His climactic and heroic acts on behalf of two criminals beyond redemption earn for him the reverence from Takamori and Tomoe which his tenderness and tolerance so clearly warranted. In a final scene, Gas, apparently drowned in his mission of mercy, is remembered as a "lone egret, flapping snow-white wings," a traditional Japanese figure of peace and transfiguration.

## The Characters

*Wonderful Fool* features as protagonist the bumbling Gaston "Gas" Bonaparte, who is far from the debonair, suave Frenchman Tomoe had imagined him to be while reading his correspondence. Physically awkward and culturally naïve, he quickly becomes a burden for the sophisticated Japanese. As the story progresses, however, he evolves into a classic "fool for Christ's sake," whose selflessness and genuine love for his fellowman—and even for a mongrel pet—reflect the Christian attributes Shusaku Endō wants his reader to recognize and embrace. Like Christ, Gas has "no place to stay" and finds his greatest joy in the company of children and the "unrighteous," those who recognize their unredeemed state and lack a smug pretense of goodness. Gaston Bonaparte is thus a "fool" in a Shakespearean sense, one who may unexpectedly speak as well as dramatize the truth in a most poignant way with his own life.

Takamori and Tomoe emerge as "typical Japanese" in Endō's view, oblivious to the "good news" of the self-giving love which Gas wishes to impart. It is only after Gas disappears that his redemptive personality and mission are revealed to Takamori and Tomoe and they are enabled to act in humanitarian compassion toward their fellows within their own land. Takamori, a young office worker with no particular ambition, comes to see his rejection of Gas as "abandoning the best part of myself." Tomoe is herself a pragmatic career woman, lacking in personal commitment or sentiment and unable to recognize until the very end that while Gas may have been a fool, "he is a wonderful fool."

In the long run, neither Takamori nor Tomoe is as well developed or as personalized as Gas; by contrast, Endō, the hardened criminal whom Gas lovingly confronts, is precisely drawn, an underworld character worthy of any Dickens novel. Endō becomes symbolic of the despondency and regret, deep-seated in Japanese society, that only a transcendent, divine love can penetrate and transform. That the novelist named this gangster after himself seems too much of a coincidence not to reflect the extent to which he himself has struggled with his identity as a Christian in a society whose Christian population numbers less than 2 percent.

*Themes and Meanings*

In *Wonderful Fool*, Endō has made it his mission to explore and explain the chasm between the nontheistic East and the Christian West, especially the spiritual abyss that separates them. Specifically, he has chosen to draw attention to the person of Christ in His native culture by creating an unforgettable and endearing but ultimately ironic Christ figure in Gaston Bonaparte. Gas arrives in a Japan pervaded by moral apathy and a desperate need to find an ethical center rooted in eternal values—something which, in Endō's view, can only be provided in the Divine Incarnation.

The Japan represented in Takamori, Tomoe, and the criminal Endō "sucks up all sorts of ideologies, transforming them into itself and distorting them in the process." Rather than merely mirroring this moral and social malaise about him, however, the novelist has sought to foster and exemplify such religious concepts as sin, redemption, and resurrection in the confrontation between Gas, Endō, and Kobayashi, the target for Endō's revenge. *Wonderful Fool* dramatizes, in the novelist's words, the Japanese "numbness to sin and guilt," juxtaposing it with Gas's tender conscience when he refuses to stand aside and allow "nature to take its course" and chooses to interpose himself between Endō and his wicked plans.

*Wonderful Fool* is thus a parable about faith, the inevitable fate of a trusting soul who determinedly opens up his life and his heart to all he encounters. His naïveté leads him to offend every significant social norm of Japanese society and even most patterns of everyday common sense. The final scenes of the novel powerfully capture Endō's vision of contemporary Japan: a social mudswamp in which a wise fool battles with all of his strength to redeem two hoodlums who want neither redemption nor life, but whom he redeems all the same.

*Critical Context*

*Wonderful Fool* may be seen as a transitional work between Endō's earlier, lighter works set in contemporary Japan but untranslated into English, and his better-known and more serious historical fiction represented in *Chimmoku* (1966; *Silence*, 1969) and *Samurai* (1980; *The Samurai*, 1982). *Wonderful Fool* bridges these two periods of Endō's work by demonstrating his versatility as a novelist with a penchant for combining humor and pathos in the pursuit of serious themes. In *Wonderful Fool*, Endō's comic narrative style complements a maturing grasp of plot structure to elucidate Endō's central themes. Its backdrop and, indeed, the backdrop of all Endō's works, is the congenital failure of Japanese culture to nurture a transcendent faith and to recognize its eternal relevance for its people. In his oeuvre Endō attempts to craft an authentically Eastern vision of Christian faith obstinate enough to endure even in soils which have never been fertile for its growth.

The Christian vision of Shusaku Endō revealed in *Wonderful Fool* thus has at its center a dramatically Eastern Jesus, the humble but single-minded "fool" who abandons all to reach those who are not so much hostile as they are indifferent, not so much faithless as they are cynical. This "foolish" Jesus—distinguished from the often bombastic and authoritarian Jesus imported from the West—drives his readers beyond the shallow, impotent Christianity lurking behind much of modern faith. To reach them, Endō is challenged to defamiliarize Christ in His conventionally distant and supernaturally holy character, portraying Him instead as a profoundly tender, self-sacrificing, and moral human being—an elder brother, not an omnipotent Lord.

*Sources for Further Study*

Gallagher, Michael. "Shusaku Endō: Japanese Catholic Intellectual," in *The Critic*. XXXVI (Summer, 1979), pp. 58-63.

Mathy, Francis. "Shusaku Endō: Japanese Catholic Novelist," in *Thought*. XLII (Winter, 1967), pp. 585-614.

Ribeiro, Jorge. "Shusaku Endō: Japanese Catholic Novelist," in *America*. CLII (February 2, 1985), pp. 87-89.

Rimer, J. Thomas. *Modern Japanese Fiction and Its Traditions*, 1978.

*Bruce L. Edwards*

# XALA

*Author:* Ousmane Sembène (1923-      )
*Type of plot:* Satire
*Time of plot:* The early 1970's
*Locale:* Dakar, the capital city of Senegal
*First published:* 1973 (English translation, 1976)

> *Principal characters:*
> ABDOU KADER BEYE (EL HADJI), an African businessman
> who has prospered since Senegal's independence
> ADJA AWA ASTOU, his first wife, a devout Muslim
> OUMI N'DOYE, his second wife, a youngish woman with
> Westernized and extravagant tastes
> N'GONE, his third wife, an attractive young woman
> YAY BINETA, the *badyen* or paternal aunt of N'Gone
> RAMA, eldest daughter of El Hadji and his first wife

## The Novel

*Xala* narrates several weeks in the life of an African businessman, Abdou Kader Beye, called "El Hadji." The brief novel traces his rapid decline from affluence to total humiliation and ruin.

As the novel begins, El Hadji is at the peak of his career, a rich man respected and even envied by his fellow businessmen. He is about to be married to his third wife, N'Gone, a pretty young woman who has flattered him with her attentions. Taking a third wife marks him as a "captain," a leader in West African culture, in which a man's success is measured by the number of wives he can support. Each of El Hadji's wives has her own villa and well-appointed household, complete with cars, a chauffeur, and many money-hungry children.

El Hadji collects his two wives and takes them (as custom dictates) to his wedding party, where they are to meet the new wife and welcome her without jealousy. The first two wives—Adja Awa Astou and Oumi N'Doye, respectively—leave, and as the party descends into raucous ribaldry, El Hadji is taken away by Yay Bineta, his new wife's officious aunt, who has functioned as the matchmaker. It is Yay Bineta's responsibility to prepare the husband and wife for their wedding night, and she therefore encourages El Hadji to perform certain tribal rituals to ensure his potency. He refuses, dismissing the acts as foolish superstition.

Alone with his new bride, El Hadji is filled with desire, but the unthinkable happens: He is impotent. Never before has such a thing happened to him. When he admits his failure to Yay Bineta, she tells him that someone must have put a curse of impotence, a *xala* (pronounced "hala"), upon him.

For days El Hadji agonizes over his problem, consulting countless *mara-*

*bouts* (healers) and paying exorbitant fees to them, with no result. He neglects his business, and his financial affairs, already under pressure as a result of his lavish life-style, begin to crumble. Worse, all of his colleagues have heard of his *xala*, and El Hadji alternately seeks their advice and runs from them, humiliated.

Finally, El Hadji's faithful chauffeur takes him far into the countryside, to a healer famous for his success with the *xala*. In an area so remote that El Hadji's Mercedes must be abandoned in favor of a cart, the two men finally locate the healer, who promises to cure El Hadji for a very high fee. El Hadji writes a check and the treatment begins. Suddenly, El Hadji realizes that the curse has indeed been lifted.

He rushes back to the city, to his new bride, only to discover that she is having her menstrual period. Yay Bineta advises him to take comfort with another wife and return to N'Gone in a few days. Yet after a night of love with his second wife, El Hadji realizes that his troubles are not over. Preoccupation with the *xala* has taken his attention away from his financial affairs, which require constant supervision; El Hadji discovers that his business is about to fail. His colleagues, envious of his previous success, now see an opening for themselves in his misfortune, and they vote to cast him out of their powerful association. His banker refuses to lend him money. The next day, movers repossess his cars and furniture. Worst of all, the check that El Hadji gave to the *marabout* bounces, and the *marabout*, in spite, restores the *xala*. Yay Bineta decides that her niece can do better than remain married to an impotent, now-impoverished fifty-year-old man, so she has the unconsummated marriage annulled. El Hadji's second wife returns to her parents.

Only his first wife stands by him. On the day of his ruin, El Hadji goes to her house to seek refuge from creditors. The next morning, he is shocked to find a beggar outside, the same beggar who has haunted his office building for years. Other infirm and diseased beggars slowly fill the house as El Hadji listens in amazement to the beggar, who tells him that El Hadji ruined his family and reduced him to beggary many years before. The *xala* was the beggar's curse, his long-planned vengeance.

The only cure, the beggar continues, will come if El Hadji stands naked while all the beggars, who are pillaging the house, cover him with spittle. Desperate, El Hadji agrees. Meanwhile, police, expecting a riot, have surrounded the house. As the novel ends, the beggars are abusing El Hadji and spitting on him, but outside the police wait with loaded guns.

## The Characters

The central character, El Hadji, is an object of satire, not a tragic hero. Through him, Ousmane Sembène attacks the Senegalese elite, who prosper while others starve. El Hadji lives in a world of contradictions, believing that he has control over them. The title by which he is known, "El Hadji," refers to the fact that he has made a pilgrimage to Mecca. To a devout Muslim, this pilgrimage should be the culmination of a devout life, but for El Hadji it was merely a vacation: He lives a completely secular life.

El Hadji's experience as a businessman is part of the satire. He believes that he is in control, when in fact his business is failing. He believes that he is liked and admired by his colleagues, yet they turn against him as soon as the opportunity arises. He believes that having three wives gives him three homes, when in fact he is an unwelcome guest in each of the three. He believes that tribal rituals are merely hocus-pocus, but when the *xala* descends upon him, it is a *marabout*, not a Western doctor, whom he seeks.

The *xala* reveals El Hadji's nature most fully. To him, sexual prowess is the essence of life. One night of sexual failure throws him into a profound depression, and as word of the *xala* spreads, El Hadji becomes more and more comical in his inability to deal with any other part of his life. His wealth, his families, and his business are ignored in his obsession with restoring his sexual powers. By making the *xala* the center of the novel, the author satirizes the "new African" and his shallowness.

Other characters in this brief novel serve mostly to show some aspect of El Hadji's life. Exceptions to this limited role are two women, Yay Bineta and Rama, El Hadji's daughter; the two represent opposite roles available to women. Yay Bineta is the traditional woman, whose power is expressed in the home. Her concern revolves around getting her niece married properly and prosperously, with all customary rituals observed. She hectors El Hadji unmercifully about his *xala*, and the difference in their social rank renders her sudden power over him more comical.

Rama exemplifies the modern African woman. She believes in nationalism, education, and sexual freedom for women; she despises her father for being a polygamist but is not reluctant to take his money. She is not treated as a heroine, because even her more admirable beliefs are based solely upon her self-interest and a desire to distinguish herself from the older generation. Indeed, in the crucial last episode of the book, Rama fails to understand the anger of the beggars; thus, she is clearly identified with the corruption exemplified by her father.

*Themes and Meanings*

Ousmane Sembène's social background is different from that of many of his Francophone African contemporaries: He was not educated in French-speaking schools in order to be integrated into the African-French power structure. He was reared in a fisherman's family, serving in the French army during World War II and working as a stevedore. His partly self-imposed distance from the corridors of power is reflected in his writings. *Xala* shows his anger at the mindless voraciousness, the simple consumerism of the "new African." What is the meaning of freedom, Sembène seems to ask, if its fulfillment is a life of further oppression by one's own countrymen?

El Hadji is the primary target of Sembène's satiric attack. Self-involved and foolish, he is willing to cheat his fellows, bleed the lower classes, and call such behavior good business. The whole narrative builds toward the final confrontation between El Hadji, once all-powerful, and the miserable beggar, whom he cheated years before.

This ending shows Sembène's pessimism. The beggar and his troop of victims amply avenge themselves on El Hadji, covering his naked body with spittle as he stands helpless. El Hadji finds this humiliation less great than the continuance of the *xala*: Masculinity is the only one of his possessions that he can now hope to regain. Yet this defeat of El Hadji does not result in a lasting gain for the beggars: The last sentence of the book indicates that they will be shot as they emerge from El Hadji's house. The vision of *Xala* is indeed a grim one.

*Critical Context*

Sembène's output is as untraditional as his background. He is best known for an earlier novel, *Les Bouts de bois de Dieu* (1960; *God's Bits of Wood*, 1962), which describes the effects of a 1940's labor dispute upon the striking Africans and the resident Europeans. The novel pays tribute to the spirit of the strikers, many of whom were shot by police or starved to death.

As a result of his antiestablishment attitude, in some literary circles Sembène is less respected than other Francophone Africans. Author Camara Laye, for example, depicts the French-African background as nearly idyllic; some critics see Laye as too accommodating to colonialism and believe that Sembène has the more valuable insights, while others think that Laye attains a larger, more integrated vision and that Sembène is too partisan.

In recent years Sembène's focus has been on filmmaking instead of fiction: He believes that film reaches the working classes, with whom he wants to communicate, more successfully than fiction can. Written in 1974, his screenplay of *Xala* caused one critic to hail him as Africa's finest independent filmmaker.

*Sources for Further Study*

Blair, Dorothy S. *African Literature in French*, 1976.

Chinweizu, Onwuchekwa Jemie, and Ihechukwu Madubuike. *Towards the Decolonization of African Literature*, 1983.

Erickson, John D. *Nommo: African Fiction in French South of the Sahara*, 1979.

Gakwandi, Shatto Arthur. *The Novel and Contemporary Experience in Africa*, 1980.

Palmer, Eustace. *The Growth of the African Novel*, 1979.

*Deborah Core*

# YOUNG TÖRLESS

*Author:* Robert Musil (1880-1942)
*Type of plot:* Philosophical realism
*Time of plot:* The mid- or late nineteenth century
*Locale:* A celebrated boarding school in a small town in the eastern territories of the Austrian empire
*First published: Die Verwirrungen des Zöglings Törless*, 1906 (English translation, 1955)

*Principal characters:*
TÖRLESS, a boy on the verge of adolescence in his first year at boarding school
BASINI, a weak and unintelligent classmate
REITING, one of Törless' friends
BEINEBERG, another friend

## The Novel

One afternoon, young Törless, a boarding school student, and some friends accompany Hofrat and Frau Törless to the railway station. The Törlesses are returning home after a visit to their son's boarding school. The prestigious reputation of the school has been the determining factor in sending Törless there, in spite of the considerable distance involved. Indeed, Törless readily adapts to his new surroundings: An early case of what seems to be homesickness soon disappears, and he finds friends such as Prince H., a sensitive and delicate boy, and, later, the more rough and masculine Reiting and Beineberg. Acknowledging the other boys' superiority of size and age, Hofrat Törless commends his son to their vigilance before he boards the train with his wife.

On the way back to school, Törless and Beineberg, the only two of the group who have permission to stay out longer, stop off at a cake shop and then visit Bozena, a prostitute at a tavern of ill repute. When they arrive at school, Reiting calls a meeting of himself, Törless, and Beineberg; he has discovered who has been stealing from the lockers. In their secret lair in the attic, they learn the details from Reiting: Basini, another classmate, is in debt to everyone and claims to have only borrowed the money. He must be punished. Törless, who believes the thief should be reported, is taken aback at Reiting's suggestion that he not be. The boys finally agree simply to keep Basini under close surveillance, at least for the present. Törless is further confused by his parents' response to the situation; not only do they not express shock and surprise but they also recommend giving Basini a chance to reform. He does not understand and tears up their letter in despair.

One night very late, Beineberg wakes Törless from his sleep and leads him to the attic to talk. Previously, Beineberg had observed Reiting and Basini having sex and explains that now he holds Basini in the palm of his hand, a power he fully intends to use: He will torment Basini in the name of spiritual training. On one hand, Törless does not fully comprehend Beineberg's meaning. On the other hand, he senses that Basini is destined to play an important part in his own life, and he feels a need to make sure that Basini stays for a while.

The next day, Reiting and Beineberg approach Törless. They have been conspiring and have fixed the time and place of Basini's moment of reckoning: eleven o'clock that night in the attic. They meet at the appointed time and, as the other two beat the naked, groaning Basini, Törless observes his own reactions. He is dizzy with excitement which turns sexual, making him feel disconcerted and ashamed. They hold an interrogation during which Basini is forced to agree to comply with all of their terms and orders from that point forward.

During the mathematics period the following day, Törless decides that since the subject matter of this class forms part of his so-called preparation for life, it might yield some answers to the strange riddle which has been vexing him ever since entering the school. He makes an appointment with the mathematics master, but to his dissatisfaction, he is discouraged by the master, who determines that the answers to Törless' questions would be beyond his ability to comprehend. Later, Beineberg confirms the ineptitude of the masters to deal with anything outside the systems that they have studied (although Beineberg himself relies on Eastern models to perceive existence). Some strange dreams about Immanuel Kant conjure Törless' childhood memories of wanting to be a little girl, and he takes solace in his sensuality, which sets him apart from such clever persons as Kant. Yet the link with Basini (who had referred to himself as a sensualist in a conversation with the prostitute) is reinforced.

There is a four-day holiday from classes, and while most of the other boys visit family or friends, Törless and a few others, including Basini, remain. Almost at once, Törless is possessed by the thought of being alone with Basini. The lust which has been awakened in him grows until it consumes him, and when Basini comes to his bed in the middle of the night, Törless allows himself to be seduced. He enters into a new relationship with Basini, feeling sympathy for this despicable creature and even jealousy toward Reiting and Beineberg. Nevertheless, this tenderness soon develops into disgust as Törless' former desire seems increasingly senseless and repulsive to him. While Reiting and Beineberg plan more punishment for Basini, Törless becomes altogether indifferent.

Several days after the boys return from their holiday, the three friends convene in the attic. Reiting and Beineberg contrive how they might best humiliate Basini and force him to knuckle under completely. Reiting envisions handing him over to the class, instigating a mass movement that will tear him to pieces. Beineberg plans to carry out a spiritual experiment: He will hypnotize Basini in an effort to reestablish lost contact with the soul. (The experiment ends with the furious lashing of Basini, who has tricked the other into believing he has been under hypnosis all along.) Conditions become intolerable for Basini, and, when the first opportunity arises, he approaches Törless, pleading for his protection. Törless refuses. Just at that moment, Reiting finds them together talking, and he tries to intimidate Törless (who has insulted him in front of Basini) but to no avail: Törless has withdrawn from the entire affair. Even when Reiting and Beineberg both threaten to expose him as Basini's accomplice, Törless remains uncooperative.

Now Reiting's plot regarding Basini is set in motion as he and Beineberg start spreading rumors among the other boys at school. Törless had left a note warning Basini that he was to be handed over to the class but apparently not in time to spare him from a preliminary, brutal bullying by a crowd of boys. Basini then turns himself in to the headmaster, and a very strict investigation ensues. Panic-stricken by the thought of having to explain himself to his teachers, Törless runs away from school, only to be picked up shortly thereafter in the next town. He is still in a state of agitation and near exhaustion when he is called before the masters and the chaplain. In one critical instant, Törless is suddenly able to see the solution to the riddle and can articulate it to the menacing assembly of masters. He tells them that things are just things, but sometimes they are seen with the eyes of reason and sometimes with the eyes of the soul.

Basini is expelled, and Törless decides to leave the school. Silence and skepticism have replaced his feelings of despair, and his mother is slightly surprised to find a composed, not overwrought, son waiting for her to take him home. Törless is now able to understand the life that his parents lead.

*The Characters*

The duality of existence that is postulated in *Young Törless* is expressed, among other ways, through the characters. They symbolize certain concepts and, like the protagonist himself, who exists only as an inner man, they are somewhat less than human. There are at least two groups—Reiting and Beineberg on one hand and Basini, Bozena, and Prince H. on the other hand—that form dichotomies through their inclusion in the novel. First, Reiting and Beineberg represent two great tendencies in the history of civilization: Western thought versus Eastern thought. Reiting admires Napoleon Bonaparte and dreams of *coups d'état* and high politics. He knows no greater pleasure than setting people against one another through complicated intrigues and reveling in his victims' hate. In this way and by boxing almost daily, he claims to be practicing for life. Beineberg, however, feels an affinity with the philosophers and holy men of India. His interest is the legacy of his father, who was a general in the British Service there and brought home with him a feeling for esoteric Buddhism. The general dreamed that he might achieve dominion over others through the exercise of certain spiritual powers. Whereas Reiting sacrifices other human beings to be able to observe the process, Beineberg's object is the furtherance of a profound inner knowledge. Nevertheless, both subordinate humanity to an abstract conceptualizing which, if originally beneficial to humanity, ultimately enlists humankind in its own service.

Reiting and Beineberg operate within guidelines established by society. Törless' class is like a small state, complete with laws, mass movements, and wars, and his two friends have assumed the role of leaders, each in his unique way. Yet there is another world, dark and mysterious, which exists apart from the solid everyday world of respectable citizens. Törless intuits it, mainly in the form of an ineffable longing that torments him and which will find an object in Prince H. (who has an idyllic aura), Bozena (who provides a refuge from incomprehensible social order), and Basini (who cultivates Törless' desire which then grows into some new and aimless craving). It is these dark, inner forces which Törless associates most closely with life itself. That association is made clear when he notes that all seemed dead at the school after the expulsion of Basini. Törless' final discovery is the necessity of the coexistence of these worlds.

## Themes and Meanings

The theme of *Young Törless* is self-development. The main character, after a number of wanderings, false starts, and mistakes, chooses the right path and becomes a mature member of society and a well-balanced human being. Törless' experiences while at the boarding school represent intermediate stages within the larger process of growth. Away at school, he becomes aware of a yearning that takes a variety of shapes. He feels homesick at first, but when this subsides, it leaves a void rather than contentment: He is still unformed. He attempts to fill the emptiness through friendship with Prince H., but this relationship is artificial and superficial, so he devises a pretext to end the association. He then becomes the disciple or assistant to Reiting and Beineberg, who give him protection and advice since they are better versed in the political machinations of the school. He joins them so as not to lag behind, but he must finally outgrow them too, because he has the subtler mind. In contrast, they are incapable of understanding his search for something natural, something within himself, because it is so unlike their own quests for power over others. He must look for his answers in the company of Bozena, who partially liberates his inner being through degradation, or Basini, who, through another sort of debasement, makes possible the growth of desire.

While his relationships and experiences contribute to his self-development,

Törless is tried in one basic episode which helps him achieve passage from one level of life into another. Törless feels drawn to Basini, but once that desire subsides, he becomes indifferent toward him and exasperated with the intrigues of Reiting and Basini. He knows not only that something is over but also that one more step lies between him and the termination of this phase of his mental development. When Basini's wrongs are discovered by the other boys at school and the headmaster, Törless must act. His escape attempt reveals his despair at making himself intelligible in the impending accounting for his behavior, as he still does not quite know what he senses. Finally, the pressure of the confrontation between him and his peers and teachers culminates in a moment of crisis. Törless is able to explain with clarity and coherence the compatibility of reason with insight, intellect with soul, and the conscious mind with the innermost being. The tension between objective reality and the subjective world is resolved as he comes to understand the necessity of both within the structure of society. He emerges victorious from his trial, his own person at a new age.

*Critical Context*

Robert Musil's novella displays many features of the *Bildungsroman* (novel of self-development), Germany's greatest contribution to world literature. An American counterpart of this late eighteenth or early nineteenth century literary form can be found in the works of Mark Twain, several of which deal with the process of maturity and integration of the individual into society. Generally, the protagonist makes the transition from child to young adult as he wanders along a path of adventure and misadventure, which finally brings out his best qualities. He is on his way toward fulfillment of his calling or potential within society, although first he rebels against it in order to gain a sense of his inner mission.

That society is a stable and controllable entity is a discovery that Törless will eventually make. By the close of the novel, Törless is on the threshold of a new life. Having gained confidence in his innate abilities, he is now free to grow, like a plant unfolding. Overall, there is optimism stemming from the belief in the inherent ability of man to better himself and improve his world.

In *Young Törless*, two events prove to be critical to Törless' development: the separation from his parents and his sexual adventures with Basini (an unusual choice of episode, putting Musil ahead of his time as a writer). Törless' growth is triggered by the one and completed as a result of the other. His rebellion is less an act of defiance than a disassociation from Reiting and Beineberg and from the school. As his confidence builds to the point at which he can talk above the heads of his teachers, he also achieves a certain type of independence; while he will return to his family, he is self-reliant in the sense that his experience—problem and solution—is his own rather than anything borrowed. On the way home, he sees things differently.

He recalls his former bewildered self in contrast to his new attitude of quiet contemplation, secure in the knowledge that he has taken a step forward in his personhood. There is a hint of promise as he prepares to enter the adult world.

*Sources for Further Study*

Luft, David S. *Robert Musil and the Crisis of European Culture, 1880-1942*, 1980.

Lukács, Georg. "The World of the Novel of Education and the Romanticism of Reality," in *The Theory of the Novel*, 1971.

Pascal, Roy. "Johann Wolfgang von Goethe—*Wilhelm Meister's Apprenticeship*," in *The German Novel*, 1956.

Peters, Frederick G. *Robert Musil, Master of the Hovering Life: A Study of the Major Fiction*, 1978.

Sanford, Nevitt. "Action to Promote Personality Development: Some Basic Concepts," in *Self and Society: Social Change and Individual Development*, 1966.

                                                                    *Krista Ratkowski Carmona*

# ZAZIE IN THE METRO

*Author:* Raymond Queneau (1903-1976)
*Type of plot:* Farce
*Time of plot:* Thirty-six hours in the years following World War II
*Locale:* Paris
*First published: Zazie dans le métro*, 1959 (English translation, 1960)

*Principal characters:*
> ZAZIE, a young girl, barely pubescent
> GABRIEL, her uncle, who earns his living dancing as a
> ballerina in a nightclub
> TROUSCAILLON, a man of many names: PEDRO-SURPLUS,
> TROUSCAILLON, BERTIN POIRÉE, HAROUN AL RATIONS

## The Novel

In *Zazie in the Metro*, Raymond Queneau presents a world of apparent meaninglessness, a world opposed to authority of any variety, where death is devoid of meaning and where one value is as fine as another. His characters are not constructed of many facets, but simply there. They are given substance by the incongruous but dominant traits manifested in the here and now of the novel. These traits can be neither disputed nor discussed in terms of cause and effect. Much of the humor of the novel derives from the words themselves: puns, allusions of all sorts, Parisian street language, sexual insults with myriad implications. Queneau attacks both the rigidity of written French and the narrow-minded prudery of bourgeois society.

The action of the novel is circular: Zazie arrives in Paris by train, stays with her uncle, Gabriel, and departs from Paris thirty-six hours later. Zazie's one goal before her arrival has been to ride the metro, but the metro is shut down because of a strike.

The world of this novel unites the Paris that tourists see, such as the Eiffel Tower, with the underground Paris of street-smart denizens who take over the city after dark. Queneau's vital linguistic world serves to create a mood or atmosphere in which the characters and their actions are less significant than the manner in which they are described. Hence, *Zazie in the Metro* is a farcical comedy, using constant reversals of language, of situation, and of identity—usually sexual identity—as sources of humor. Finally, it is clear that Queneau's farce demonstrates the idiocy of assigning personality traits to individuals on the basis of gender.

The plot, such as it is, focuses on a young girl, Zazie, who has been left with her uncle so that her mother can pursue her Parisian lover. Because Gabriel works at night, Zazie is left alone in the morning while he sleeps. Gabriel's landlord, Turandot, sees her in the street and tries to stop her from exploring Paris alone. Zazie, however, manipulates the assembled crowd, telling them that he is trying to make her do unspeakable things. Turandot is nearly lynched and only with difficulty sneaks back to his own turf.

Zazie is soon approached by a man who feeds her and speaks of blue jeans; while she does not trust him, she desperately wants "blewgenes," which the man buys for her. When Zazie takes the package of jeans and tries to elude the man, he beats her at her own game. Before she can tell a new crowd that he is trying to molest her, the man tells them that Zazie is a thief, and everyone carries on about the sanctity of property.

Believing that the man is a policeman, Zazie lets him take her back to Gabriel's apartment. When the man, Pedro-surplus (also known as Trouscaillon, among other names), accuses Gabriel of being a "hormosessual" and is rude to Gabriel's wife, Marceline, Gabriel throws him into the trash. Zazie's aroused curiosity continues through the remainder of the book: Is Gabriel a homosexual? What is a homosexual?

Wanting to show Paris to Zazie, Gabriel—by means of his brother-in-law, Charles, and Charles's taxi—takes her to the Eiffel Tower. While Zazie and Charles are above, Gabriel becomes the admired idol of a group of tourists below. Eventually, Gabriel has the tourists change their itinerary to eat at the Spheroid Brasserie, a tourist trap, and to come to the Mount of Venus to see him perform the "dying swan" as Gabriella. Fyodor Balanovitch, the official guide who is supposed to have his tourists in Gibraltar by the next day, is also aware of the profit to be made from the tourists who have been beguiled by Gabriel. The tourists, who have an incredible command of esoteric languages but few wits, are happily treated to all the horrors of which tourists in France have complained: being cheated, lied to, and insulted.

Around uncle and niece, other characters inexplicably collect, such as the Widow Mouaque, who, with a private income, has no occupation and who becomes obsessed with Trouscaillon. Trouscaillon, who knows that he can have the Widow on his terms, goes back to Gabriel's apartment as Bertin Poirée and attempts gracelessly to rape Marceline. A transvestite Pied Piper, Gabriel brings not only the tourists but also his friends—including Turandot's parrot—to the Mount of Venus. Gabriel's only disappointment with his performance is that Marceline is not there to admire him.

From the nightclub, Gabriel and his entourage go to the Queen of Night for onion soup. An all-out brawl develops between Gabriel's company and the waiters. Gabriel's side is victorious, but armed agents (authorities of order are never good in this novel) descend on the restaurant. The Widow is fatally shot—in spite of her private income. Gabriel and his friends are miraculously lowered on a lift to the basement of the Queen of Night and directed through the sewers to the just reopened metro, where they separate to take different lines. Although Zazie is finally on the metro, she is unconscious, asleep in Gabriel's arms.

Marceline, the lowerer of the lift, has brought Zazie's suitcase and takes Zazie from Gabriel to deliver her to her mother at the train station. Only at this moment does the reader learn that Marceline is actually Marcel. This reversal of the sexual identity of Gabriel's spouse exemplifies Queneau's determination to keep the reader—or viewer, in this cinematic novel—from believing that appearance is reality or that there is an explanation for reality. The attempted rape of Marceline and the death of the Widow in the riot shock the reader, but, in Queneau's world, violence and death are facts without meaning.

## The Characters

In this novel, Queneau parodically categorizes character by gender. The female characters are stereotypically one-dimensional: They are motivated by their sexual drive. Zazie's mother, Jeanne Lalochère, lusts for her male lover; the Widow lusts after Trouscaillon, and Zazie lusts for her jeans. The good Marceline, who does not seem to lust even for Gabriel, proves to be a man, not a woman. The male characters, on the other hand, are not lustful, but caring and responsible. They are better women than the women; they do not conform to any of the male stereotypes.

Zazie's command of street lingo and sexual innuendo denotes a worldly experience not usually associated with an eleven-year-old child. Yet she is also a child who was attacked by her drunken father. She was saved by her mother's intervention, ax in hand; her mother was carrying on with the pork butcher at the time. Zazie has saved all the newspaper clippings from her mother's trial which mention her own name (her mother was acquitted of her husband's murder and lauded in the tabloids), and she seems to see herself as starring in a film of her own. Her one basis for judging people is whether they move and talk as they do in the movies. At this age, Zazie's extraordinary sexual curiosity can be satisfied by a pair of tight-fitting jeans. When she is older, she will be a Circean threat to men, like every other woman.

Gabriel—an allusion to the archangel—at age thirty-two has yet to be crucified. He is a colossus of a man who enjoys making people laugh and who is satisfied to think of himself, with childlike satisfaction, as an artist. Because he is so large, smaller men harass him, but he is against violence— even when Zazie continues to pinch him viciously to get him to answer her questions. He enjoys wearing men's perfume from the House of Fior, and he believes that understanding is the basis for education. Gabriel has many friends who return his trust with loyalty: Turandot tries to protect Zazie because she is Gabriel's niece; Charles's taxi is usually at Gabriel's disposal; Gridoux stoutly defends Gabriel to Trouscaillon. Marceline-Marcel is completely devoted to Gabriel, without any apparent sexual motive.

Trouscaillon, the apparent villain, a man of many names, does not always know who he is. When confronted by others, he maintains that he has other and better identities. He immediately decides that Gabriel is an "Aunt Nancy," or homosexual, because he earns his living as a ballet-dancing drag queen, wears perfume, and manicures his own nails. Trouscaillon, a man of appearances, can only judge others by their appearances. He lusts after Marceline, never knowing that she is a he. Since he is most often seen as a member of the forces of order, as a policeman, Trouscaillon emerges as incompetently diabolic, successful only in causing confusion and consternation.

Laverdure, Turandot's parrot, provides choral commentary on all the characters in the novel. His constant reminder, "talk, talk, talk—that's all you ever do," is an accurate assessment of the people around him. As Gabriel's band separates in the metro, Turandot speaks the parrot's line, while Laverdure bids the others goodbye. In *Zazie in the Metro*, Laverdure—a resurrected Loulou, borrowed from Gustave Flaubert—speaks truth.

### Themes and Meanings

*Zazie in the Metro* is a novel in which there is constant confusion about sexual roles. For example, when Zazie wants to know what a homosexual is, Marceline tells her that a homosexual is a man who wears blue jeans. When Zazie is recognized, because of her language, by a driver from her hometown, the driver says that he did not know her dressed as a boy, that is, clad in jeans. One must keep in mind that Marceline, a substitute mother to Zazie, wears dresses and is in fact Marcel.

Of all the characters, Gabriel is indisputably the most admirable: He does not take life or himself too seriously; he is essentially at ease and enjoys making others laugh. Gabriel is not concerned with any traditional image of masculinity. In spite of his size and gender, he is a superior woman in terms of all the stereotypical female virtues—for example, with his patience and forbearance with his niece. He is the only heroic figure in the novel, an amalgam of the best male and female personality traits. He is the friend, provider, and daily companion to Marceline-Marcel; the protector of those who are weaker; the trusted leader of the other male characters. Gabriel consistently reminds Zazie that she must accept the world as it is.

This novel opposes order in general: the order of any traditional concept of character, any adherence to a structured plot, any authority which attempts to impose meaning on experience but only adds to the confusion. Reality may have no metaphysical value, but by the end of the novel, the metro is running again. In Queneau's world, what more could one ask?

### Critical Context

*Zazie in the Metro*, the most popular of Queneau's novels (Louis Malle made it into a film), was his seventeenth book. It was preceded by *Le Dimanche de la vie* (1952; *The Sunday of Life*, 1976) and followed by *Les Fleurs bleues* (1965; *The Blue Flowers* , 1967) and *Le Vol d'Icare* (1968; *The*

*Flight of Icarus*, 1973). Before *Zazie in the Metro*, Queneau was best-known for his *Exercices de style* (1947; *Exercises in Style*, 1958). A poet and a novelist, Queneau also wrote on science, philosophy, history, and mathematics. He was an editor for Gallimard, the publishing house, and the director of the *Encyclopédie de la Pléiade*. He also wrote a number of screenplays.

Queneau was a great admirer of James Joyce, as well as of William Faulkner and Joseph Conrad. A member, along with Engène Ionesco, of the Collège de Pataphysique, a strange organization devoted to the bizarre tradition of Alfred Jarry, and with more than a passing acquaintance with Dadaism and Surrealism, Queneau was an eclectic. A student of Plato and Hegel, he was interested in ordinary people and in the philosophical implications of everyday life, but his surpassing love was of language itself. His writing frequently attempts to reproduce spoken language, with its neologisms, street slang, and allusions turned upside down. For Queneau, the banal repetition of spoken words becomes exciting and comical, revealing both the sense and the nonsense of the human condition.

*Sources for Further Study*

Brée, Germaine, and Margaret Guiton. *An Age of Fiction: The French Novel from Gide to Camus*, 1957.

Cobb, Richard. *Raymond Queneau*, 1976.

Le Sage, Laurent. Review in *Saturday Review*. XLIII (October 15, 1960), p. 25.

Redfern, W. D. *Queneau: "Zazie dans le métro,"* 1980.

Rexroth, Kenneth. Review in *The Nation*. CXCI (December 24, 1960), p. 507.

*Carol Bishop*

# THE ZONE
## A Prison Camp Guard's Story

*Author:* Sergei Dovlatov (1941-    )
*Type of plot:* Critical realism
*Time of plot:* 1963-1965 and 1982
*Locale:* A strict regime labor camp for criminals in Komi, in the northern
    Soviet Union
*First published: Zona: Zapiski nadziratelia*, 1982 (English translation, 1985)

> *Principal characters:*
>     SERGEI DOVLATOV, the author of "Letters to the Publisher"
>         (sections of the novel which alternate with untitled
>         chapters)
>     BORIS ALIKHANOV, a guard in the penal isolator cells and an
>         intellectual, who evidently represents Dovlatov in the
>         novel
>     BORIS KUPTSOV, a prisoner fascinating to Alikhanov, who
>         refuses to work, regardless of the punishment
>     Lance Corporal "FIDEL" PETROV, an ignorant, occasionally
>         cruel but, in the end, likable guard

*The Novel*

It is difficult to assign a clear-cut genre to *The Zone*. First, it is only barely
fictional, based as it is on the author's experiences as a prison guard while
serving in the Soviet army in the early 1960's. Sergei Dovlatov states, while
leaving room for some "accidental" fictionalizing, that all essential names,
events, and dates are real and therefore "any resemblance between the characters in this book and living people is intentional and malicious." The book
proper consists of fourteen untitled chapters; some are mere sketches and
others are well-developed "short stories." They are not connected by plot so
much as by characters, some of which are merely names, who appear and
reappear, and by the grimly exotic setting. The title identifies the part of the
settlement reserved for the prisoners.

These chapters are all presented within a "frame story" consisting of fifteen letters written by the author to his publisher, Igor Markovich Yefimov.
(Yefimov brought out the original Russian edition in the United States in
1982, four years after Dovlatov had emigrated to that country.) The letters,
usually sent from New York City, but also from Minneapolis, Boston, Dart-
mouth, and Princeton, cover the period between February 4 and June 21,
1982. Arranged in chronological order and in strict alternation with the
"chapters," the letters frequently remark on the author's problems in organizing the smuggling of microfilmed sections of the book out of the Soviet

Union. (Thus Dovlatov plays a witty variation on the device of the "found manuscript.") Dovlatov also makes a number of remarks on the aims and intentions of the fictional or literary material alternating with the letters. In this way, the two parts of the book are unified to some extent in their content but differ considerably in tone, the letters at times being uncomfortably self-conscious. Undoubtedly, too, many of these are not real letters but inventions, though based on a real correspondence. The letters serve, however, as a continuing reminder of the great distance in time and place between Siberia in the 1960's and New York in the 1980's. Furthermore, the literary material is so interesting and powerful that it tends to render the letters unobtrusive.

There is a further unusual problem in classifying this work. Although the book must finally be termed an autobiographical novel, the character associated with the author is by no means clearly identified. Only long after his first appearance does the character Boris Alikhanov appear to "be" Dovlatov. Alikhanov is introduced by an omniscient author, not a narrator, and is perceivable as similar to Dovlatov only by those readers who are familiar with the author's childhood years. Shortly after Alikhanov's first appearance, the novel is presented not by the author alone, but by the author alternating with an unnamed narrator, who seems nearly the same as the author. Finally, in a crucial chapter, this narrator is identified as Alikhanov. There is further confusion in the last chapter of the novel, which is otherwise a major literary achievement, where this same narrator, who seems as though he must certainly be Boris Alikhanov, is called "Bob" by one of the other characters and is not otherwise named. To the reader of this novel in translation, the culminating adventure of the book seems to be happening to an entirely new character named "Robert"; a Russian reader would understand that "Bob" (more usually "Boba") is a shortened form of "Boris." Thus, there is a minimal unity in the novel achieved through the mutual identity of the omniscient author, the writer of the letters, and the character Boris Alikhanov.

Because even Alikhanov appears in only a few chapters, it is difficult to speak of a true plot. Alikhanov does develop, over the course of the book, a deep sympathy for the prisoners he is assigned to guard, even while realizing that any of them might kill for a package of tea. Once, against all the rules, he takes part in one of the prisoners' drinking sessions, gets extremely drunk, and wakes up under arrest. The guard has become a prisoner.

This minimal action dramatizes the central thesis of the novel as stated by Dovlatov the "letter writer": The prisoners are not superior to the guards— as is often maintained in such prison literature as that by Fyodor Dostoevski and Aleksandr Solzhenitsyn—nor are the guards superior to the prisoners— as implied in "police" literature from G. K. Chesterton to Agatha Christie. Rather, guards and prisoners are the same. In the camps, observes Dovlatov, the two groups speak the same slang, sing the same songs, have the same crew cuts, endure the same cold, eat the same bluish oatmeal, and even wear similar uniforms. Each deserves the role of the other. Dovlatov insists that "all of my stories are written about this [theme]."

## The Characters

Boris Alikhanov, as a stand-in for Dovlatov, is an interesting figure. His name, for one thing, is strange. It is described as "foreign," and the character is regarded as foreign by all: zeks (prisoners), guards, officers, and civilian workers. "Even the guard dogs considered him foreign." The name emphasizes a remarkable existential alienation that the author, perhaps somewhat romantically, assigns to himself. It should be noted, however, that Dovlatov himself, whose surname is only accidentally Russian, is a giant of a man who is half Jewish and half Armenian and is also looked upon as "foreign" wherever he goes in the Soviet Union—a country that counts in its population 130 different nationalities, practically all of which are represented in *The Zone*.

A random selection of surnames belonging to guards and zeks alike yields the following list: Pakhapil, Balodis, Tkhapsayev, Gafiatulin, Chichashvili, Shakhmametiev, Kemoklidze, Ovsepyan, Dzavashvili, Dastyan, Tskhovsebashvili, Prishchepa, Tvauri, Belota, Agoshin, Galimulin, Mamai, Chaly, Topchil, Beluga, Shumanya, Tsurikov, Agayev, Butirin. This clever mix of names, including Russian ones, dramatizes the role of the camp as a microcosm of the Soviet Union and Alikhanov-Dovlatov as a Soviet rather than only a Russian.

"Alikhanov" is a vaguely Asian or Caucasian name, not necessarily Jewish. Alikhanov is never identified as Jewish, but he clearly speaks for the author in his ironic response to the anti-Semitic remarks of one of the guards: "[Those kikes] are everywhere... from Raikin to Karl Marx. Take the venereal disease clinic at Chebyu. The doctors are Jewish, the patients are Russian. Is that the Communist way?"

Alikhanov's individualism makes it easy for him to respond to the individualism of Boris Kuptsov, one of the prisoners who continually refuses to work. Alikhanov himself is forced to assign the malingerer to long stretches in the "isolator," where he then also has to guard him. One day, Kuptsov, in front of Alikhanov, chops off his own hand with an axe to ensure that no one ever again will force him to work against his will. He calls himself a "soloist" and insists that one, as opposed to the mass, is always right. It is partly in response to Kuptsov's Dostoevskian self-mutilation that Alikhanov eventually "goes over" to the prisoners. Alikhanov's rebellion is inarticulate, confused by alcohol, and undoubtedly a mistake. Dovlatov takes pains not to romanticize it.

One of Alikhanov's best friends among the guards is "Fidel" Petrov, who acquired his nickname at a political class for guards: When asked to name the members of the Politburo, he started off with Castro. At first Petrov, a notorious boozer, is irresponsible in relationship to Alikhanov, but in the closing chapter he is forced by circumstances to be the responsible one and is obliged to escort his friend into the "zone" as a prisoner.

Both reversals and parallels in the roles of the characters provide a satisfactory literary structure for Dovlatov's narrative. An important element in the novel's general approach to characterization is humor. For example, Gustav Pakhapil, an Estonian guard who drinks only chartreuse, wants to know, upon his arrival at the camp, if there are any "dames" in the vicinity. "Even many," he is told. "[There's] Solokha, Raya, [and] eight Dunyas. . . ." Gustav is overwhelmed with joy, but it turns out that Solokha is a mare, the "Dunyas" are the camp homosexuals, and only Raya is real—the camp nurse, who has thick ankles, tiny discolored teeth, and "damp skin."

Another source of humor is the captain who worries about the guards drinking too much on New Year's Eve but cannot bring himself to forbid their doing so, because no drinking at all would be "anti-Marxist utopia." Discovering and inventing humor in the most hellish of settings is one of Dovlatov's special achievements in this novel and as a writer generally.

*Themes and Meanings*

A theme already touched upon is the transformation of the model guard Alikhanov into a drunken prisoner, symbolizing the fundamental similarity between soldiers and zeks. Dovlatov underscores this similarity by giving the individualistic Alikhanov and the anarchistic Kuptsov the same given name: Boris. As the first names are seldom used, the discovery of this "coincidence" by the reader almost has the character of an epiphany. In like manner, critics have noted that an exchange of gestures between a zek and a woman he sees only once in fourteen years appears as an epiphany of love. Makeyev is marched in a convoy to an exterior construction site; Isolda approaches, her overshoes sinking down into the mud of the tundra, her steel teeth flashing. He tosses a handmade plastic cigarette holder toward her. She passes a knitted scarf to him across the rows of men. Such transparent moments, which touch guards and prisoners alike, occur several times in the novel.

Dovlatov insists in a letter to his publisher that although the world of the camps was horrible, "Nevertheless, I smiled no less frequently than I do now, and was not sad more often." He is capable of true poetic nostalgia for that world when, in the final episode, he is being escorted through the settlement by Fidel, "past the dilapidated stone gates of the shipping section, past the huts buried in snow, past the mess hall with white steam pouring from its open doors, past the garage where automobiles all faced one way like cows in a meadow. . . ." Yet he also realizes "with fear how unaccustomed I had grown to the things that make life worth living" and "how much happiness had swept by me on those nights full of hatred and fear, when the floorboards crack from the frost and dogs bay in the kennel and you sit in the isolator and listen to Anagi-Zadye clinking his manacles behind the wall and the miserable, frozen, unchanging days drag on. . . ."

Dovlatov's terse yet poetic style found unexpected reception, for a Russian émigré, in *The New Yorker*, which published not only the last chapter of *The Zone*, as a short story titled "Straight Ahead," but six other short works as well, between 1980 and 1987. The stories reflect one basic idea, without sentimentality: that people everywhere—prisoners and free men, females and males, Russians and Americans—are fundamentally the same.

## Critical Context

Parts of *The Zone* were first written when the author was very young. Not publishable in the Soviet Union, Dovlatov's account of prison life had to wait two decades for its first appearance in English, in the United States. Reviewers tended to be critical of the book for its formal problems, which possibly resulted from misdirected avant-gardism, while admiring it greatly for its unique point of view in the genre of prison literature: that of the guard rather than the prisoner. *The Zone* has an automatic polemical relationship with the works of Solzhenitsyn and Dostoevski. Dovlatov observes: "Solzhenitsyn describes political prison camps. I—criminal ones. Solzhenitsyn was a prisoner. I—a prison guard. According to Solzhenitsyn, camp is hell. Whereas I think that hell is in us ourselves." There is further conflict with both Solzhenitsyn and Dostoevski in that Dovlatov is not religious. "More than that," he avers, "I'm a nonbeliever. And I'm not even superstitious." One senses animosity toward Solzhenitsyn, despite Dovlatov's denials of it, but genuine respect for Dostoevski. The possible influence of Dostoevski on Dovlatov may be seen in this work in such characters as Kuptsov and in the "regular Noah's ark" of prisoners so similar to Dostoevski's Tartars, Circassians, and Mohammadans in *Zapiski iz myortvogo domo* (1861-1862; *The House of the Dead*, 1915). A further parallel between Dovlatov and Dostoevski is the Christmas theatricals that are staged by the prisoners in both *The Zone* and *The House of the Dead*. Dovlatov makes a concession to Dostoevski in choosing a religious holiday for his play to be performed, but he speaks irreverently from his own time by casting his zeks in the roles of Vladimir Ilich Lenin, Feliks Dzerzhinski, and other Communist heroes.

## Sources for Further Study

Clark, Katerina. "Souls in the Gulag," in *The New York Times Book Review*. XC (October 27, 1985), p. 45.

Fiene, Donald M. "Sergei Dovlatov, *Zona: Zapiski nadziratelia*," in *Slavic and East European Journal*. XXVII (Summer, 1983), pp. 272-273.

Grimes, William. "A Novel of Crime and Freezing Punishment in Russia," in *Christian Science Monitor*. LXXVIII (January 21, 1986), p. 26.

Karriker, Alexandra H. "Sergei Dovlatov: *Zona*," in *World Literature Today*. LVII (Autumn, 1983), p. 654.

Serman, Ilia. "Teatr Sergeia Dovlatova," in *Grani*. L, no. 136 (1985), pp. 138-162.

*Donald M. Fiene*

# ZOO
## Or, Letters Not About Love

*Author:* Viktor Shklovsky (1893-1984)
*Type of plot:* Epistolary autobiography
*Time of plot:* The 1920's
*Locale:* A Russian émigré colony in Berlin
*First published:* Zoo: Ili, Pisma ne o lyubvi, 1923 (English translation, 1971)

> *Principal characters:*
> VIKTOR SHKLOVSKY, the narrator, a Russian novelist, literary critic, and political émigré living in Berlin in 1922
> ELSA TRIOLET (also called ALYA), the estranged Russian wife of the Frenchman André Triolet

*The Novel*

In 1924, Yuriy Tynyanov, a Formalist critic, said of Viktor Shklovsky's *Zoo: Or, Letters Not About Love*: "The book is interesting in that a single emotional core provides the basis for a novel, and a feuilleton, and a scholarly paper." The comment covers the contents of this unusual mix of a novel. Shklovsky, an unwilling Russian émigré in Berlin in 1922, uses his own painful experience of unrequited love for Elsa Triolet, the estranged Russian wife of a Frenchman, as the core of a novel expressing his sense of dislocation in the West and his views on literature and his literary comrades.

The novel is arranged as a series of letters to Elsa (Alya is her Russian nickname.) A second subtitle Shklovsky uses, "The Third Héloïse," refers to the stories of the love of Héloïse and Abélard in the Middle Ages and of the lovers in Jean-Jacques Rousseau's *La Nouvelle Héloïse* (1761). In both these stories, the lovers are devoted to each other; they are frustrated by outside forces. The third Héloïse is not so satisfactory a beloved; Shklovsky's love is frustrated by the woman herself. She cannot love him in return. While she grants him the opportunity to write to her (and occasionally to telephone), she makes the stipulation that he must not write or speak about love.

This prohibition motivates the actual content of most of the letters: Shklovsky's ideas about literature and his sketches of Russians in the Berlin literary scene. The result is a tale of a barely suppressed but strong love for a woman of whom the lover himself rather disapproves. The story serves as a structural line for matters that engage him perhaps even more seriously: the world of literature and literary theory. Yet each of these topics somehow returns to the topic of love.

The first edition of the novel includes twenty-nine letters. (Five letters were added in later editions, while other letters were subsequently omitted.) Seven of the twenty-nine are from Elsa. (She actually wrote them, later expanding the one on Tahiti into a book of her own.) The rest are by Shklovsky, and they are autobiographical, representing his feelings and thoughts during this painful but productive year in Germany. They include an elegy for Velimir Khlebnikov, a highly experimental poet friend of his; letters to his literary friends at home, urging them to work; scenes of Berlin life, especially in contrast to the war, revolution, and civil war he has just lived through at home; his own literary ideas; responses to Elsa's letters; and occasional violations of her prohibition. Other letters describe Aleksei Remizov, the publisher Zinovyi Grzhebin, Andrey Bely, Aleksandr Blok, Leo Tolstoy, Boris Pasternak, Stendhal, Fyodor Dostoevski, Ilya Ehrenburg, and others. He is always interested in their ideas on literary technique as well as in catching, in words, their images as human beings.

The letters are highly metaphorical. It is as if he compares everything and everyone he sees to the inner compulsion of his love. The metaphors are part of his new theory and are thus fresh and full of new insight.

For example, in letter 4, the elegy for Khlebnikov, Shklovsky writes about the weather, linking it first to politics and then to love. He says that he hates cold weather, that Peter betrayed Christ because he wanted to warm himself at a fire and got caught up in the public opinion around the fire. Russia, he says, is cold; it (and he) betrayed Khlebnikov, who was generous and idealistic, like Christ himself. He remembers that Khlebnikov, too, loved a woman who did not respond to him. He says, ironically, that the soldiers who killed Christ and the state which let Khlebnikov go without a place to lay his head were not responsible; they "did not understand Aramaic." In short, ordinary people do not understand poets or what poets understand. They are cold, and their desire to warm themselves makes them lack compassion. The soldiers who killed Christ were like the nails, not responsible for the death. Love is like the nails, he says, but love has made men write books, bringing civilization. This network of interrelated metaphors expresses Shklovsky's anger against the conditions that let Khlebnikov perish, his ironic attitude toward Elsa's failure to love, and his own transformation of his pain into the novel.

The zoo metaphor in the book seems to have begun as a theme for a group of hostile character sketches of émigré types that he abhorred, but it changed as the novel took shape. Since the Russians in Berlin lived near the zoological garden, the animal figures occur naturally in the setting. He prints Khlebnikov's poem "Menagerie" as an epigraph to the whole novel, a vivid poem in which all the animals remind the poet of human beings. Shklovsky says that he doubts that people have the right to hold their distant relative, the ape, in prison without a trial. Again, the metaphor is political, but he moves it to the personal realm as well: Shklovsky is himself caged by Elsa's prohibition.

Shklovsky applies the animal imagery to literature: "As a cow devours grass, so literary themes are devoured; devices fray and crumble." Hence, the constant task of writers is to renew traditional forms, and that task leads them to new material in art. Free artists, he says, are like monkeys. It is hard for monkeys and artists to live in the world. ("Walking on sidewalks is hard for monkeys—a way of life foreign to them.") It follows, then, that human women are incomprehensible to these creatures.

Elsa, the incomprehensible woman here, becomes a metaphor for all that Shklovsky hates in Berlin as an exile. Her European manners and bourgeois tastes demand that he eat with a fork and keep his trousers pressed. He, in a long-standing Russian literary tradition, contrasts East and West, Russia and Europe. Recent Russian experience of war and revolution makes such fastidiousness seem mad. Yet he worries that as exiles, Russian men will lose their talent as surely as they lose their women. They need to be at home; the local is the vital in art. The consumerism of Europe that Elsa represents is vulgar in the context of Soviet Russia's deprivations.

Letter 22 is one of the most serious discussions of literary theory. Art is a world of "independently existing things," not a "window on the world." Words and their relationship to one another, "thoughts and the irony of thoughts, their divergence"—such are the content of art. Shklovsky says that complex works of art grow out of simpler forms, and shifts to new forms come when all the contrasts in older forms are exhausted. As a result of the exhaustion of psychological motivation in the novel, emphasis has shifted to individual components, as in a variety show, and "the master of ceremonies emerges as the hero." A self-conscious exposing of the devices takes place, like a Czech clown whom he saw in a circus, who parodied and exposed all the other acts. In this way, the narrator in *Zoo* becomes the most important figure, the letters exist as separate individual components, and the writer makes explicit remarks on the devices that he is using to achieve his effects. Thus, to emphasize the importance of letter 19 (a letter from Elsa), Shklovsky employs a witty device: He crosses it out with a big red cross and tells the reader not to read it.

The last letter is addressed to the All-Russian Central Executive Committee; it is a request to return to Russia. "I cannot live in Berlin," Shklovsky says. He feels bound to the new Russia. The book has been about "misunderstanding." The unresponsive, Europeanized woman is set against the vivid images of the literary life in the Soviet Union and the narrator's passion for his own language. His loneliness in the book can be relieved only by a return to his native land.

*The Characters*

Elsa appears directly only in her own seven letters. She presents herself as a self-indulgent, intensely feminine, and creative woman. She never promises Shklovsky what she cannot give him; in fact, in one letter she says that she knows she is "good for nothing" in that she can, but does not, use her books, her piano, the telephone, or his love.

Shklovsky presents her in his letters (though rarely, because of the prohibition against mentioning love) as having first let him think that she could love him and then having withdrawn—but not so far as to drive him away. He comes to see her love of comfort as part of the bourgeois world of the West that seems so hostile to him with his war experiences. Nevertheless, he makes her sound bewitchingly attractive, and he admires her letter about Tahiti (though he plays with her metaphors in such a way as to instruct her in how to write fresh ones).

Shklovsky, as the main narrator and letter-writer, receives fuller characterization. The nature of the qualities that he values in the Russian writers whom he depicts—their magnanimity, their talent, their devotion to art, their wisdom—makes clear his own value system. His imaginative play with metaphors of his own and others shows his feverishly agile and creative mind. The seriousness and brilliance of his letters about art show the depth and value of his commitment to his profession. The range of his interests and the freshness of his metaphors suggest the scale of the man. The resolution to ask for the right to return to Russia in terms sure to limit his creative freedom argues the deep connection that he feels with his country.

## Themes and Meanings

This story of unrequited love becomes much more than an intimate exploration of an imaginative man's feelings when caught in such a situation, though that exploration, freshly worked out, does account for the slender structural line of the novel. As Shklovsky makes clear in the second (first Moscow) edition of the book, the frustrating love affair becomes a metaphor for his life in exile, while the frustration, at the same time, motivates him to write the story: Love and frustration have often inspired cultural artifacts.

The original idea for the book—a series of vignettes about Russian writers and émigré figures—still accounts for much of the content of the work. Yet that content is not simply a miscellany; it takes focus from the woman's prohibition that the man may write, but not about love. In fact, all the vignettes subvert the prohibition, saying something about love at the same time that vivid pictures of the subjects emerge. That the main love affair is unrequited makes appropriate the theme of longing, separation, and misunderstanding that these Russians sense in their European exile. The contrast between East and West gets poignant treatment here: The pain and deprivation of war and revolution have given the Russians values which materialistic (though inflation-riddled) Berlin cannot share. The woman becomes an image standing for that contrast; her rejection of the writer becomes his rejection of the West. The form of the novel, he says at one point, will determine the outcome of the love affair.

The passion of the man for the woman is not, moreover, as strong as his passion for literature, and new ideas about literature emerge as a major theme of the novel. At the same time, the novel demonstrates some of these new ideas: the intimacy of detail; the emphasis on the separate part rather than the grand design; the irony, by which alone the writer can bear his absurd position; fresh metaphors; and the nature of the impingement of literary tradition on new forms.

The novel is, in short, a new form whose main subject is new form; the theme is the pain of exile and irrelevance in a foreign land for a writer whose deepest commitment is to new forms in literature, to the play of words. They must be the words of his own language. Those forms have emerged from the exhaustion of old forms, just as new forms of life have emerged through war and revolution in his own land.

## Critical Context

Shklovsky remained attached to this novel, as his prefaces to successive editions show: He continually reinterprets that time in his life which the love affair represents. Exile gave him time for, and unrequited love made necessary the torrent of, his creative activity in Berlin. The theoretical excitement among members of Opoyaz (the Society for the Study of Poetic Language), the group of Formalists in Petrograd during the civil war, could here be translated into experimental creative work. Since so many avant-garde Russian writers were in Berlin at the time, the importance of the work could receive immediate appreciation as breaking new ground.

Both Boris Eikhenbaum and Yuriy Tynyanov saw the work as a new form of documentary novel. The autobiographical material is used for interpretation of experience in new terms—in new forms to match. One critic has noted that Shklovsky uses letters the way some writers of early nineteenth century Russia used them to renew and colloquialize diction and to discuss theory. The work also demonstrates fascination with the ambiguity of words and new principles of structure that the Formalists were exploring. It repeatedly "bares the device," making the reader aware of the artifice in what has become a major twentieth century literary practice.

The underlying pattern of previous epistolary novels of tragic love affairs casts an ironic light on this modern example. The highly colloquial and metaphorical language in which the book is written continues the Formalist challenge of the symbolist and realist literature of Russia's immediate past. Richard Sheldon, the English translator of the novel, sees the protagonist's constantly talking about love while not talking about love as paradigmatic of Shklovsky's whole contradictory, ironic mode of writing.

Shklovsky's theoretical work and practice have had pervasive influence on Russian twentieth century writers. *Zoo* had five Russian editions, and it has been translated into French, German, Italian, and English. Only the English edition includes all the letters of the various Russian editions. As Shklovsky's reputation continues to grow outside the Soviet Union, the novel's experiments continue to receive attention.

*Sources for Further Study*
Erlich, Victor. *Twentieth Century Russian Literary Criticism*, 1975.
*Library Journal*. Review. XCVI (December 1, 1971), p. 4031.
*Listener*. Review. LXXXVII (February 24, 1972), p. 249.
Sheldon, Richard. Introduction to *Zoo: Or, Letters Not About Love*, 1971.
Simmons, Charles. "But Let's Not Talk About Love," in *The New York Times*. CXXI (January 24, 1972), p. 31.

*Martha Manheim*

# MASTERPLOTS II

## WORLD FICTION
## SERIES

# TITLE INDEX

I

# TITLE INDEX

# TITLE INDEX

# AUTHOR INDEX

ABE, KŌBŌ
  Inter Ice Age 4, II-711
  Ruined Map, The, III-1315
  Woman in the Dunes, The, IV-1769
AGNON, SHMUEL YOSEF
  Bridal Canopy, The; In the Heart of the
    Seas, *and* A Guest for the Night, I-194
  Simple Story, A, IV-1448
AKSYONOV, VASSILY
  Burn, The, I-200
  Island of Crimea, The, II-737
  Ticket to the Stars, A, IV-1600
ALAS, LEOPOLDO
  Regenta, La, III-1267
ALESHKOVSKY, YUZ
  Kangaroo, II-790
ANDRIĆ, IVO
  Bosnian Chronicle, I-182
  Woman from Sarajevo, The, IV-1764
ANDRZEJEWSKI, JERZY
  Ashes and Diamonds, I-80
APPELFELD, AHARON
  Age of Wonders, The, I-29
  Badenheim 1939, I-101
  To the Land of the Cattails, IV-1616
  Tzili, IV-1682
ASCH, SHOLEM
  Nazarene, The, III-1085

BALZAC, HONORÉ DE
  Louis Lambert, II-896
  Quest of the Absolute, The, III-1236
  Sarrasine, III-1351
  Splendors and Miseries of Courtesans, The ,
    IV-1516
BAROJA, PÍO
  Tree of Knowledge, The, IV-1650
BASSANI, GIORGIO
  Garden of the Finzi-Continis, The, II-511
  Gold-Rimmed Eyeglasses, The, II-557
BECKER, JUREK
  Sleepless Days, IV-1458
BECKETT, SAMUEL
  Company, I-291
  How It Is, II-644
  Ill Seen Ill Said, II-664
  Trilogy, The, IV-1661
BELY, ANDREY
  Silver Dove, The, *and* Petersburg, IV-1442
BENET, JUAN
  Meditation, A, III-988
  Return to Región, III-1272

BERNANOS, GEORGES
  Mouchette, III-1045
  Under the Sun of Satan, IV-1694
BERNHARD, THOMAS
  Concrete, I-300
  Correction, I-323
  Gargoyles, II-516
  Holzfällen, II-603
  Lime Works, The, II-866
  Untergeher, Der, IV-1700
BETI, MONGO
  Poor Christ of Bomba, The, IV-1214
BIENEK, HORST
  Silesian Tetralogy, The, III-1436
BIYIDI, ALEXANDRE. *See* BETI,
    MONGO
BÖLL, HEINRICH
  Billiards at Half-Past Nine, I-152
  Clown, The, I-281
  Group Portrait with Lady, II-562
  Lost Honor of Katharina Blum, The, II-870
  Safety Net, The, III-1326
BROCH, HERMANN
  Spell, The, IV-1506
BUGAYEV, BORIS. *See* BELY, ANDREY
BULGAKOV, MIKHAIL
  Heart of a Dog, The, II-583
  Master and Margarita, The, III-976
BUTOR, MICHEL
  Change of Heart, A, I-239
  Mobile, III-1021
  Niagara, III-1093
  Passing Time, III-1173
BUZZATI, DINO
  Bàrnabo of the Mountains, I-116
  Tartar Steppe, The, IV-1548

CALVINO, ITALO
  Baron in the Trees, The, I-121
  Castle of Crossed Destinies, The, I-216
  Cloven Viscount, The, I-277
  If on a Winter's Night a Traveler, II-659
  Invisible Cities, II-727
  Mr. Palomar, III-1015
  Non-existent Knight, The, III-1113
  Path to the Nest of Spiders, The, III-1178
CANETTI, ELIAS
  Auto-da-Fé, I-95
CÉLINE, LOUIS-FERDINAND
  Castle to Castle, North, *and* Rigadoon, I-
    221
  Death on the Installment Plan, I-353

# AUTHOR INDEX